ALL
TOGETHER
NOW

Other books by Richard D. Kahlenberg

*A Notion at Risk: Preserving Public Education
as an Engine for Social Mobility* (ed.)

The Remedy: Class, Race, and Affirmative Action

Broken Contract: A Memoir of Harvard Law School

A Century Foundation Book

ALL TOGETHER NOW

Creating Middle-Class Schools through Public School Choice

RICHARD D. KAHLENBERG

BROOKINGS INSTITUTION PRESS
Washington, D.C.

Copyright © 2001
Paperback edition copyright © 2003
THE CENTURY FOUNDATION
All rights reserved. No part of this publication may be reproduced or transmitted in any form or by any means without permission in writing from the Brookings Institution Press, 1775 Massachusetts Avenue, N.W., Washington, D.C. 20036 (fax 202/797-6195 or email: permissions@brookings.edu).

Library of Congress Cataloging-in-Publication data
Kahlenberg, Richard D.
    All together now : creating middle-class schools through public school choice / Richard D. Kahlenberg.
        p.   cm.
    Includes bibliographical references (p.   ) and index.
    ISBN 0-8157-4810-8 (cloth : alk. paper)
    ISBN 0-8157-4811-6 (pbk. : alk. paper)
    1. Educational equalization—United States. 2. Education—Economic aspects—United States. 3. Public schools—United States. I. Title.
    LC213.2 . K35 2000   00-010567
    379.2'6'0973—dc21   CIP

9 8 7 6 5 4 3 2 1

Typeset in Minion

Composition by
Betsy Kulamer, Washington, D.C.

Contents

Foreword

THE AMERICAN POLITICAL SYSTEM is an amalgam of tradition and innovation. Our idea of self-governance is rooted in medieval milestones in English history, such as the Magna Carta and the Oxford Principles, and our Constitution clearly reflects centuries of evolution in Western thought concerning justice, representation, and governance. The essentially home-grown aspects of the American system include such notions as shared governmental jurisdiction (federalism) and universal public education. Probably the best way to study these innovations in operation is to look closely at the area of elementary and secondary education. Federal, state, and local governments, including special school district jurisdictions, all play a role in education. Moreover, education is accepted as the key to an informed electorate that is necessary if democracy is to work.

So perhaps it should not be a surprise that education is among the top concerns of the American public. Despite the centrality of education, however, the actual public policy debate is decidedly thin. Conservatives, perhaps, win the prize for boldness, but many scholars argue that their principal proposal—publicly funded private school vouchers—is likely to do more harm than good for low-income children (the ostensible beneficiaries) and could undermine America's historic commitment to public education as an engine for both social mobility and cohesion. Progressives, meanwhile, have backed a number of smaller ideas—reducing class size, better teacher training, beefing up Head Start, raising standards—but even taken together these ideas are simply not ambitious enough to meet the task at hand. In the pages that follow, Century Foundation senior fellow Richard D. Kahlenberg adds much-needed substance to the debate by offering a bold and provocative idea: giving every American child the right to attend a school in which the majority of students come from middle-class homes.

The great challenge, of course, is to find creative ways to bring socioeconomic integration about, keeping in mind that the current economically based segregation of schools did not develop by accident but reflects, in some part, the distribution of political power. Kahlenberg believes that the ideas outlined in the book, which provide a blueprint for change, are well timed to ride the wave of two great changes that are under way: the decline of racial desegregation and the explosion in public school choice. Racial integration is a dying legal strategy, and civil rights groups have supported socioeconomic integration in San Francisco and elsewhere as a way to indirectly salvage some racial integration without running afoul of court decisions prohibiting the use of race. And in all areas of life, Americans are seeking greater choice. Today, roughly one-quarter of all students attend private schools or public schools of choice, and support for greater public school choice has risen dramatically, from 12 percent two decades ago to more than 70 percent today. Although many elites still like the idea of being able to purchase the right to attend a particular public school, parents who cannot afford to live in the very best neighborhoods object to mandatory residential assignment. And parents across class lines are looking for particular schools that meet their children's individual needs, for example, a smaller school for a shy child or an arts school for a budding artist.

In keeping with our long-standing commitment to American education, which includes the publication of *Making the Grade* (the report of a 1983 task force on federal elementary and secondary education policy) and *Facing the Challenge* (the report of a 1992 task force on school governance), The Century Foundation has supported such analyses of America's educational system as *Hard Lessons: Public Schools and Privatization*, by Carol Ascher, Norm Fruchter, and Robert Berne; *The Way We Were? The Myths and Realities of America's Student Achievement*, by Richard

Rothstein; Gordon MacInnes's paper, "Kids Who Pick the Wrong Parents and Other Victims of Voucher Schemes"; and *A Notion at Risk: Preserving Public Education as an Engine for Social Mobility*, edited by Richard Kahlenberg.

In recognition of the continuing importance of this issue, The Century Foundation will soon be sponsoring a task force on the common school and a task force on low-income students in higher education. Over the coming months, we will be publishing two volumes edited by Gary Orfield: *Raising Standards or Raising Barriers? Inequality and High Stakes Testing in Public Education* and *Hard Work for Good Schools: Facts, Not Fads, in Title I Reform*. In addition, we are supporting books by Richard Rothstein and James Guthrie on school financing and by Joan Lombardi on child care policy and educational opportunities.

In *All Together Now*, Kahlenberg combines an old and very American idea—the common school—with a new and very American idea—choice among public schools—in order to better pursue the goal of equal educational opportunity. On behalf of the trustees of The Century Foundation, I thank him for his contribution.

RICHARD C. LEONE
President
The Century Foundation
September 2000

Preface to the

Paperback Edition

IN THE TWO AND A HALF YEARS since the initial publication of *All Together Now*, the practice of economic school integration has seen some dramatic developments. In May 2003, a front page *New York Times* article noted the "growing movement" toward integration of schools by income to raise student achievement and avoid legal complications associated with racial integration.[1] First carried out in the early 1990s in a small Wisconsin town, conscious efforts to reduce school poverty concentrations are now a part of the plan to improve education in places as diverse as San Francisco, California; Raleigh, North Carolina; St. Lucie County, Florida, and Cambridge, Massachusetts. The number of students attending public schools in districts that factor economic status into student assignment has jumped from roughly 20,000 in 1999 to 500,000 today. By comparison, the number of students attending private schools with publicly funded vouchers stands at about 15,000.[2]

1. Sara Rimer, "Schools Try Integration by Income, Not Race," *New York Times*, May 8, 2003, p. A1.
2. William G. Howell and Paul E. Peterson, *The Education Gap: Vouchers and Urban Schools* (Brookings, 2002), table 2-1, p. 29. The recent adoption of a voucher plan in Colorado will increase this number modestly in the near future.

The passage of the landmark No Child Left Behind Act of 2001 is having important ramifications for economic school integration in a couple of respects. Under the federal act, all school districts nationwide are required to allow students in underperforming high-poverty schools to transfer to better-performing public schools within the district. A priority is given to low-income and low-achieving students, so the policy serves, in effect, as a modest but national program of economic and academic desegregation. There are limitations to the law, and some communities have tried to talk families out of transferring, but at its best, the law puts the federal government on the side of allowing poor families trapped in failing schools to transfer to better-performing schools within the public system.[3]

At a broader level, the act requires states to raise achievement levels for students of all racial, ethnic, and economic backgrounds. Over the long haul, this should put pressure on schools to integrate economically, for educators know full well that significantly raising achievement will prove impossible under current conditions, because no one has figured out how to make high-poverty schools work on a systematic basis. *All Together Now* outlines the long-standing evidence on how economic segregation undercuts achievement, and research published since then confirms this finding.

According to the U.S. Department of Education's *Condition of Education 2002*, all children, poor and middle class, perform substantially worse in schools with concentrations of poverty. Indeed, middle-class children attending high-poverty schools (those with more than 75 percent low-income students) perform worse, on average, than low-income children attending middle-class schools. On the fourth grade National Assessment of Educational Progress (NAEP) math test, for example, low-income students attending schools with a majority middle-class student body score higher on average (219) than middle-class children attending high-poverty schools (212).[4]

Of course, some high-poverty schools have managed to be successful, but they are very rare. In December 2001, the Education Trust published a study that purported to find some 3,592 high-poverty schools that achieve at high levels, but a reanalysis of the data by Economic Policy Institute

---

3. See, for example, Richard D. Kahlenberg, "A County's Failing Policy," *Washington Post*, June 24, 2002, p. A19 (describing the efforts of Montgomery County, Maryland, to dissuade families from transferring under the law).

4. National Center for Education Statistics, *The Condition of Education 2002* (U.S. Department of Education, 2002), p. 58.

researcher Douglas Harris found that in fact students in high-poverty schools perform much less well than students in more affluent schools, particularly when one looks at performance over a period of years. Using the Education Trust definition of a high-performing school (scoring in the top third of the state in either reading or math), Harris noted that there are more than 21,000 low-performing high-poverty schools. Whereas 18 percent of high-poverty schools are high performing, 55 percent of low-poverty schools are—three times the rate of success. Because test scores fluctuate from year to year, so that any individual year can represent a large number of "flukes," Harris sought to find out which schools have achieved sustained success—for two years, in two grade levels, in two subjects. Under that definition, he found that just 1 percent of high-poverty schools are consistently high performing, compared to 24 percent of low-poverty schools; that is, high-poverty schools are twenty-four times less likely to be consistently successful than low-poverty schools.[5]

None of this means that "poor kids can't learn." In the past couple of years, a number of new local and national studies have found that low-income students (as well as middle-class students) do better in majority middle-class schools than they do in high-poverty schools. Among the examples:

—In a study of fourth-grade students in Madison-Dane County, Wisconsin, schools published in July 2002, researcher David Rusk found that for every 1 percent increase in their middle-class classmates, low-income students improved 0.64 percentage point in reading and 0.72 percentage point in math. Thus for a given low-income student, the difference between attending a school with a 45 percent middle-class student body and one with 85 percent middle-class students on average meant "a 20 to 32 percentage point improvement in that low-income pupil's test scores." Rusk found that middle-class children saw a decline in test scores as the percentage of low-income classmates increased, but that the rate of decline "was less than half the rate of improvement for low-income pupils." Moreover, using census data, he found that this decline in majority middle-class

5. See Craig D. Jerald, *Dispelling the Myth Revisited: Preliminary Findings from a Nationwide Analysis of "High-Flying" Schools* (Washington: Education Trust, 2001); Richard Rothstein, "An Accountability Push and Fuzzy Math," *New York Times*, March 29, 2002, p. A21; Doug Harris, "Beating the Odds or Losing the War? A National Portrait of Student Achievement in High-Poverty Schools" (Washington: Economic Policy Institute, forthcoming).

schools may very well have been a result not of classmate influences but of the fact that "middle-class" students in economically mixed schools were not as well off as "middle-class" students in affluent schools. (The category "middle class" included all those above the 30th percentile in income.) By contrast, low-income students were more uniformly low income across schools. Once schools passed a 60 percent low income threshold, both low-income and middle-class scores declined significantly.[6]

—In a study of third-, fourth-, and fifth-grade students in Denver, Colorado, schools published in May 2002 by the Piton Foundation, Dianne Lefly, research manager of the Denver Public Schools Assessment and Testing Department, found that low-income students perform at much higher levels in majority middle-class schools than in majority poor schools. Some 53–54 percent of low-income students attending schools where less than 50 percent of their classmates were low income had proficient or advanced reading scores on the Colorado Student Assessment Program, while only 33 percent had such scores in high-poverty schools (those with 75 percent or more students eligible for free or reduced-price lunch). Middle-class children in such high-poverty schools had lower passing rates (49 percent) than low-income children in middle-class schools (53–54 percent).[7]

—In a study of 50,000 students in third through eighth grades in Montgomery County, Maryland, schools published in September 2001, the *Washington Post* found that "the overall performance of individual students differed dramatically depending upon the overall level of poverty in the school they attended. Lower-income students performed their worst at schools where the student population was overwhelmingly poor. But when lower-income students attended schools where most of the students were more affluent, they achieved higher scores—matching or exceeding the county average."[8]

Unfortunately, new research also finds that economic school segregation is growing. According to a study conducted by David Rusk for The

6. David Rusk, "Classmates Count: A Study of the Interrelationship between Socioeconomic Background and Standardized Test Scores of 4th Grade Pupils in the Madison-Dane County Public Schools," mimeo, July 5, 2002.

7. Alan Gottlieb, "Economically Segregated Schools Hurt Poor Kids, Study Shows," *Term Paper* (May 2002), pp. 1–2.

8. Brigid Schultz and Dan Keating, "Pupils' Poverty Drives Achievement Gap," *Washington Post*, September 2, 2001, p. A1.

Century Foundation, economic school segregation increased in the 1990s in fifty-five of the largest 100 metropolitan areas, was stable in fourteen, and declined in twelve (data were unavailable for nineteen).[9] While some studies have found heartening progress on reducing economic segregation by *neighborhood*, Rusk's findings are consistent with Harvard professor Gary Orfield's research finding that American *schools* are resegregating by race.[10] The problem is likely to get worse in the future. In coming years, many school desegregation orders are likely to expire, with districts returning to a system of "neighborhood schools" that reflect economic and racial segregation. Rusk's study projects that economic school segregation will increase in all but six states between now and 2025.

Recognizing the research, a growing number of cities have acted to establish economic integration programs. *All Together Now* profiles programs in La Crosse, Wisconsin (7,600 students); Wake County (Raleigh), North Carolina (101,000 students); and Manchester, Connecticut (7,800 students); and mentions programs in Maplewood, New Jersey (6,400 students), and Coweta County, Georgia (18,000 students). The early results in these communities have been promising. In La Crosse, which has the longest-running plan, test scores have risen and the district has a very low dropout rate, despite having a relatively high poverty rate.[11] In Wake County, nearly 90 percent of students performed at or above grade level on recent state tests.[12] In part because of these successes, economic school integration has spread to several additional jurisdictions:

9. David Rusk, "Trends in School Segregation," in The Century Foundation Task Force on the Common School, *Divided We Fail: Coming Together through Public School Choice* (New York: Century Foundation Press, 2002), p. 65.

10. For discussion of Paul Jargowsky's study finding that residential poverty concentrations declined in the 1990s, see Robert Pear, "Smaller Percentage of Poor Living in High-Poverty Areas," *New York Times*, May 18, 2003, sec. 1, p. 26. For evidence of rising racial segregation of schools, see Erica Frankenberg, Chungmei Lee, and Gary Orfield, *A Multiracial Society with Segregated Schools: Are We Losing the Dream?* (Cambridge, Mass.: The Civil Rights Project, Harvard University, January 2003).

11. Richard Mial, "La Crosse: One School District's Drive to Create Socioeconomic Balance," in Task Force on the Common School, *Divided We Fail*, pp. 133–34.

12. Walter Sherlin, "N.C. Integration Story Saw Tree, Not Forest," *Education Week*, June 19, 2002, p. 14.

—*St. Lucie County, Florida.* In January 2001, the St. Lucie School Board modified its controlled choice plan of student assignment to emphasize socioeconomic diversity over diversity by race. Under the new system, parents are asked whether the family qualifies for food stamps and whether the children qualify for free or reduced-price lunch. The district has 31,000 students.[13]

—*San Francisco, California.* In April 2001, the San Francisco School Board adopted a new student assignment plan that replaced a racial desegregation scheme with one that seeks socioeconomic diversity. The district now uses a seven-part definition, including socioeconomic status (has the student participated in free or reduced-price lunch, Calworks, or public housing programs?); academic achievement (has the student scored below 30th percentile on the Stanford 9?); mother's educational background (has she had post-high-school education?); student's language status (limited English or not proficient?); quality of student's prior school (lowest ranking in California's Academic Performance Index?); student's home language (other than English?); and residence in different geographic area. The system has 60,000 students.[14]

—*Charlotte-Mecklenburg, North Carolina.* In August 2001, the Charlotte Board of Education, under legal pressure, voted to drop a long-standing racial desegregation plan and implemented a controlled choice plan that allows parents to rank their preferences among schools, and gives special consideration to students who are eligible for free or reduced-price lunch and currently attend schools whose free and reduced-price lunch numbers are 30 percentage points above the district average. Priority is also given to low-income students "where their choice would enhance the free and reduced lunch status but not create a concentration of free-reduced lunch status above 50 percent in the receiving school." Beginning in 2004–05, priority is also given when the student reads below grade level

13. Suzanne Robinson, "Schools Adopt Economic Policy," *Vero Beach Press Journal,* January 25, 2001, p. A12; Paula Holzman, "Growing Schools Seek More Space," *Stuart News/Port St. Lucie News,* August 4, 2002, p. A1.

14. See Michael Fletcher, "Diversity's Future? Socioeconomic Criteria, Not Race, Used to Desegregate San Francisco Schools," *Washington Post,* March 18, 2002, p. A1; and San Francisco Unified School District, "Excellence for All: A Five-Year Comprehensive Plan to Achieve Educational Equity in The San Francisco Unified School District for School Years 2001–02 through 2005–06," April 4, 2001 (rev. January 24, 2002).

and the home school performs 10 percentage points below the district average for reading. The goal is to ensure that "schools don't have a concentration of low-income students or students who perform below grade level." Charlotte-Mecklenburg has 108,000 students.[15]

—*Greenville, South Carolina.* In late 2001, the Greenville Board of Trustees voted to adopt a new student assignment scheme that eliminated the use of race but sought to reduce the "concentration of low-income students" and the "concentration of low-achieving students." The board rejected, however, a more aggressive plan to ensure that no school has more than 50 percent of its students eligible for free or reduced-price lunch. Greenville has 61,000 students.[16]

—*Brandywine, Delaware.* In November 2001, the school district backed a flexible student assignment plan that would keep all schools between 16 and 47 percent low income, as opposed to a neighborhood assignment plan that would have allowed schools to range from 6 percent to 73 percent low income. The district cited extensive research showing that students would have suffered under the neighborhood school plan, which would have elevated levels of concentrated poverty. In March 2002, the Delaware State Board of Education approved Brandywine's flexible student assignment plan as a justified exception to a state law generally favoring neighborhood schools. Brandywine has 10,000 students.[17]

—*Cambridge, Massachusetts.* In December 2001, the Cambridge School Committee voted to amend its public school choice program to require that all public schools fall within a ±15 percentage point range of the dis-

15. See Charlotte-Mecklenburg Schools, "Adopted Student Assignment Plan, 2002–03," www.cms.k12.nc.us/k12/assign/choice_priorities_0203.htm; Charlotte-Mecklenburg Schools, "Applying for Choice," www.cms.k12.nc.us/k12/choice/brochure/priorities.asp; Karla Scoon Reid, "Charlotte District, Still in Limbo, Presses Ahead with Choice Plan," *Education Week,* September 5, 2001, p. 10; and Karla Scoon Reid, "Charlotte Schools Desegregated, Court Rules," *Education Week,* October 3, 2001, p. 3.

16. Paul Alongi, "Hearings on Students' Schools Set," *Greenville News,* January 27, 2002, p. 1B; Paul Alongi, "Meek Offers Proposal on Student Dispersal," *Greenville News,* March 27, 2002, p. 1B.

17. See Brandywine School District, "The Brandywine Plan," submitted to the Delaware State Board of Education, November 15, 2001; Delaware State Board of Education, "Decision In re: Neighborhood School Plans of Delmar, Seaford, Appoquinimink, Colonial, Christina, Red Clay Consolidated and Brandywine School Districts," March 28, 2002.

xx | PREFACE TO THE PAPERBACK EDITION

trictwide percentage of students eligible for free or reduced-price lunch (40 percent). In the second year of the plan, the range will be reduced to ±10 percentage points, and in the third year, to ±5 percentage points. Cambridge has 7,300 students.[18]

—*Rochester, New York.* In October 2002, the Rochester Board of Education unanimously adopted a controlled choice plan that gives parents a chance to choose any public school within the district and includes "socioeconomic fairness guidelines" measured by free and reduced-price lunch ratios at the school level.[19] Rochester has 37,000 students.

—*San Jose, California.* In June 2003, the San Jose Unified School Districts' board of trustees voted to adopt a plan to allow public school choice, using eligibility for free or reduced-price lunch as the main factor in approving or disapproving choice transfers.[20] The district has more than 32,000 students.

A number of other communities are actively discussing the possibility of socioeconomic school integration, including Lee County (Ft. Myers), Florida; Nashville, Tennessee; and Palm Beach County, Florida.[21]

All of the existing socioeconomic programs have been adopted voluntarily rather than by court order, although a number of communities faced legal pressure to find race-neutral ways to accomplish student integration. Some districts turned to economic criteria as a way to preserve successful racial integration programs, because whereas any use of race in student assignment is subject to strict scrutiny by courts, the use of economic criteria is subject to very little scrutiny. At the same time, economic integration plans generally produce a fair amount of racial integration as a by-product. According to an analysis by the Urban Institute's Duncan

18. Mary Hurley, "Income Level Eyed on School Selection; Cambridge Enacts Cutting-Edge Plan," *Boston Globe*, December 19, 2001, p. B1; Edward Fiske, "Controlled Choice in Cambridge, Massachusetts," in Task Force on the Common School, *Divided We Fail*, pp. 170, 196.

19. See "Resolutions Voted on by the Rochester Board of Education, Business Meeting," October 17, 2002, p. 48 (Resolution 2002-03: 342).

20. Larry Sloanker, "S.J. Unified May Look at Income for Diversity," *San Jose Mercury News*, June 20, 2003, p. A1.

21. See Jennifer Booth Reed, "School Choice," *Fort Myers News-Press*, June 11, 2002, p.1A; Jay Hamburg, "Schools' Focus May Shift to Economic Diversity," *Nashville Tennessean*, July 15, 2003; Kimberly Miller, "Board Considers Income-Balanced School Choice," *Palm Beach Post*, July 8, 2003, p. 1B.

Chaplin, income integration will produce between 56 and 80 percent as much black-white integration as will race-conscious integration, depending on how wide a geographic area is covered by the plan.[22]

The U.S. Supreme Court's decision in June 2003 sustaining the use of race to promote diversity at the University of Michigan Law School may partially remove the legal cloud hanging over race-conscious integration plans in the K–12 context, though the implications are not entirely clear. In that case, *Grutter v. Bollinger,* and a companion case involving the undergraduate program, *Gratz v. Bollinger,* the Court approved the use of race, but said schools must evaluate candidates as individuals, rather than using race mechanically; must limit the duration of programs using race; and must "periodically review" whether race-neutral alternatives could also work.[23] Since K–12 integration plans are fairly mechanical in nature and do not normally consider assigning students on the basis of "individual" qualities in the same way as selective colleges do, it is hard to see how schools will meet this requirement. Moreover, while the Supreme Court held that existing race-neutral alternatives to affirmative action are inadequate at highly selective colleges, the situation may be different for K–12 institutions. Because most primary and secondary public schools do not select students by test scores, the racial achievement gap does not present the same challenges to race-neutral alternatives as in higher education.

Many researchers, educators, and public officials now believe that the economic school integration movement should be taken to the national level. In 2001 The Century Foundation assembled a twenty-five-member blue-ribbon Task Force on the Common School, chaired by former Connecticut governor and U.S. Senator Lowell P. Weicker Jr., to review the evidence and make recommendations. (I served as its executive director.) The panel of teachers, superintendents, union representatives, business leaders, scholars, civil rights activists, and former government officials issued its report, *Divided We Fail: Coming Together through Public School Choice,* in September 2002. The report recommended, among other things, that "federal, state, and local governments adopt a policy goal of giving every child in America the opportunity to attend an economically and racially inte-

22. Duncan Chaplin, "Estimating the Impact of Economic Integration of Schools on Racial Integration," in Task Force on the Common School, *Divided We Fail,* p. 98.

23. *Grutter v. Bollinger,* 2003 U.S. LEXIS 4800 *61–*62 (2003); *Gratz v. Bollinger,* 2003 U.S. LEXIS 4801 (2003).

grated school."[24] The subject of the lead story in *Education Week*, the report was denounced by some, like former assistant education secretary Chester Finn, and cheered by many others, including Sandra Feldman, president of the American Federation of Teachers, who pledged to find an AFT district that supported the task force's recommendations and seek to experiment with the best ways to make them work.[25]

Inexorably, momentum appears to be building for districts to address, after years of neglect, the fountainhead of educational inequality: the separation of poor and middle-class families in American schools.

24. Task Force on the Common School, *Divided We Fail*, p. 5.
25. Linda Jacobsen, "Report Relates Better Schools and Diversity: Economic Desegregation Is Priority, Panel Says," *Education Week*, September 18, 2002, p. 1.

Acknowledgments

THIS BOOK HAS BEEN four years in the writing, and I've accumulated a number of debts. Thanks, first, to John J. DiIulio Jr., who suggested that I contact The Century Foundation (then the Twentieth Century Fund) about my next project. John wrote a letter in support of my application with the Fund, as did Chip Lupu, Chuck Robb, and Stephen Joel Trachtenberg. Thanks to all of them.

William Julius Wilson, who serves on the Foundation board, has been very supportive of this project throughout, and suggested that I seek supplemental funding from the Spencer Foundation of Chicago. The support from John Barcroft of the Spencer Foundation proved instrumental. It allowed me to travel to conduct research in Massachusetts, Wisconsin, New York, Minnesota, and Maryland, and to hire a series of research assistants.

Throughout the first half of this project, I was a fellow at the Center for National Policy in Washington, D.C. Many thanks to Mo Steinbruner, Mike Petro, Mike Calabrese, Marc Weiss, and Richard McGahey for their support and counsel. During that period, I greatly appreciated having access to the excellent library facilities at George Washington University and thank Stephen Joel Trachtenberg and Scott Pagel for arranging that.

Thanks to those who took the time to talk with me about my project in a number of localities. In Cambridge, Massachusetts, thanks to Michael Alves, Barbara Black, Bobbie D'Allesandro, Mary Lou McGrath, Gary Orfield, Roger O'Sullivan, Leonard Solo, Alice Turkel, Charles Willie, and Alice Wolf. In La Crosse, Wisconsin, thanks to James Birnbaum, Neil Duresky, Ken French, Cathy Fuchs, Joe Heim, David Johnston, Joan Kent, Robert Keuchmann, Fred Kusch, Margaret Larson, Roger LeGrande, John Medinger, Sue Mormann, Rob Percy, Mary Stanek, Betsy Stannard, Richard Swantz, Julie Vollmer, Thai Vue, and Terry Witzke. In Wausau, Wisconsin, thanks to Richard Allen, Richard Ament, Byron Barrington, Tom Berger, Deborah Hadley, Mark Hadley, Bryan Hendricks, John Ihde, Jeffrey Lamont, Fred Prehn, Larry Tranberg, Scott Williams, and Ya Yang. In Louisville, Kentucky, thanks to Ron Crouch, Steven Daeschner, Holly Holland, and Beverly Moore. In Montgomery County, Maryland, thanks to Helen Chasset, Alan Cheung, Reginald Felton, Leslie Grimmel, Ross Mills, Holly Searl, Paul Vance, and Chuck Williams. In Minneapolis, thanks to john powell and Joe Nathan. In Boston, thanks to Evans Clinchy, Robert Gittens, Charles Glenn, Elizabeth Lermann, and Deborah Meier. In New York, thanks to Robert Crain and Marianne Lado. And in Washington, D.C., thanks to Marshall Smith and David Tatel. In addition, I had helpful conversations with Patricia Barker (Maplewood, New Jersey), Duncan Chaplin (Washington, D.C.), Justin Cummins (Minneapolis), Julian Guthrie (San Francisco), David Levine (San Francisco), Ruth Teichroeb (Seattle), Ruy Teixeira (Montgomery County), and Doug Tuthill (St. Petersburg, Florida).

I have had a number of extremely helpful research assistants, without whom this book could not have been written. Thanks to David Liu, Christine Nemacheck, Janet Kim, Jason Peckenpaugh, Mike Shumsky, Christina Jordan, Rob Wiygul, Kate Bloniarz, Sarah Meltzer, Chris Wilcox, Joe Doctor, and John Falcicchio.

During the course of the writing of this book, I had the opportunity to present my work-in-progress in a number of settings, an exercise that was very helpful to my thinking. Thanks are due to those institutions, and the people who arranged my talks, including George Washington University Law School (Richard Pierce), Howard University Law School (Frank Wu and Lisa Crooms), the Economic Policy Institute (Ruy Teixeira), the Singapore Club (Robert Embry and David Rusk), and the Social Democrats (David Jessup, Rita Freedman, and Penn Kemble).

At The Century Foundation, my deepest thanks to Dick Leone and Greg Anrig Jr., as well as Beverly Goldberg, Bernard Wasow, Ruy Teixeira (who suggested the book's title), Ken Emerson, David Smith, Jason Renker, Christy Hicks, Thad Hall, Janne Nolan, Carol Starmack, Laurie Ahlrich, and Lisa-Joy Zgorski. At the Brookings Institution Press, thanks to Bob Faherty, Chris Kelaher, Becky Clark, and Colin Johnson. And for excellent copyediting, thanks to Katherine Kimball.

A number of friends and family were helpful as always. Those who read an early draft of my arguments include Ken Dameron, my parents Jeanette and Richard Kahlenberg, Janet Kim, Ross Mills, Dinah Moche, Richard Parker, Jason Peckenpaugh, Richard Pierce, David Rusk, Mark Sherman, Mike Shumsky, Maureen Steinbruner, Don Stewart, William Julius Wilson, and the late Adam Yarmolinksy .

Thanks above all to my wife, Rebecca, and daughters Cindy, Jessica, and Caroline, who never cease to amaze me.

1

Introduction

IN A SOCIETY marked by some of the highest rates of income and wealth inequality in the industrialized world, we in the United States put enormous stock in the idea that strong public schools serve, in the words of Horace Mann, as "the great equalizer."[1] However, Mann, the noted nineteenth-century educator, believed that to give all students a chance to achieve and do well in life, public schools had to be "common schools," educating disadvantaged and advantaged children under one roof. Separate schools for the children of the poor and the working class, on the one hand, and those of the wealthy and the middle class, on the other, are inherently unequal, he believed.

The animating vision of this book is that all schoolchildren in America have a right to attend a solidly middle-class public "common school." They may not have a right to middle-class parents, or a right to live in a middle-class neighborhood, or a right to a middle-class income and life-style. But every child in the United States—whether rich or poor, white or black, Latino or Asian—should have access to the good education that is best guaranteed by the presence of a majority middle-class student body.

Today, in about 75 percent of American public schools, a majority of students are from middle-class households. (This

1

book uses a standard definition of middle-class income as more than $32,000 for a family of four, the eligibility threshold for the subsidized school lunch program.) Those schools tend to work pretty well at educating children, whatever their individual family circumstances. In the other 25 percent of schools, the majority of students are from low-income households, and those schools overwhelmingly fail to educate children to high levels of achievement. When parents describe certain schools as "bad" they are usually talking about schools dominated by poor children. This parental attitude is not fundamentally racist or classist. It is based on the historically validated social reality that when public schools educate poor students separately from other students, the high-poverty schools do not normally provide an equal, or even adequate, education to their students. In an overwhelmingly middle-class country such as ours—where the parents of almost two-thirds of students are solidly in the middle class—we should be able to find creative ways to ensure everyone access to a good middle-class education.

It is important to note that the right to attend middle-class schools should apply to middle-class children, too. Small numbers of middle-class children should not be assigned to schools in which a majority of children are poor, just to achieve some greater degree of economic mixing. Middle-class children also perform less well, on average, in majority-poor schools, and they should not have to attend them, just as poor children should not be compelled to do so. This book strives to hold the proposal to a standard rarely met in the era of racial desegregation: that supporters of integration should be willing to send their own children to the integrated schools they advocate. The evidence suggests that middle-class children are not hurt by economic integration as long as schools remain predominantly middle class; that poor students are able to raise their levels of achievement and attainment and success as adults by attending middle-class schools; and that the lives of all students, and of the nation, are enriched by exposure to diversity, even as students are bound together in a common enterprise.

Time to Create More Middle-Class Schools

Revolutionizing school assignment policies to ensure that the student bodies of all schools are predominantly middle-class schools is an ambitious goal. But it is time to take this significant step for two important reasons.

First, existing efforts to realize the ideal of equal educational opportunity have fallen short. For the past half century, we have tried to promote equal opportunity— to tap into the potential of all American children and thereby to raise the overall level of achievement—by pursuing a twin strategy of racial integration and compensatory educational spending. We now know that neither strategy has achieved what we had hoped. Racial integration was cut off at the knees in 1974, when the Supreme Court effectively exempted most suburban jurisdictions from desegregation plans. As a result, city-centered busing plans helped promote white flight and, in many cases, integrated only those poor white and poor black students left behind. These racially integrated but predominantly poor schools failed to raise achievement or improve life chances for their students because the academic benefits of integration to blacks stem not from the whiteness of classmates but from higher achievement and aspirations found among the children of the middle class.

The other strategy, pouring greater and greater amounts of money into high-poverty schools, has also proved disappointing. Money does matter to educational achievement, but research—and common sense—tells us that the people who make up a school, the students, parents, and teachers, matter more. Financial investment alone cannot significantly improve schools in which large numbers of classmates misbehave and ridicule achievement, parents are inactive, and the best teachers transfer out as quickly as possible.

In short, although the two principal strategies of the past forty years have been positive and necessary, they are ultimately limited and flawed tools for attaining the goal of equal opportunity. Our schools remain highly segregated by economic status. Today, low-income twelfth-grade students read on average at the level of middle-class eighth-graders.[2] Children whose families are in the bottom income quintile are twice as likely to drop out of high school as those from families in the top quintile.[3] In the end, some 76 percent of high-income students complete bachelor's degrees, compared with a mere 4 percent of low-income students.[4]

Abraham Lincoln noted that education is "the most important subject we as a people can be engaged in."[5] In *Brown* v. *Board of Education*, the Supreme Court reiterated the importance of education: "In these days, it is doubtful that any child may reasonably be expected to succeed in life if he is denied the opportunity of an education"—a statement far more true now than it was in 1954.[6] Today, education spending constitutes the single largest budget item in nearly every state budget;[7] and yet we fail, miserably, to educate large segments of our population.

Second, this backdrop of failure has opened the way for a dramatic new assault on public schools by conservative advocates of private school vouchers. This movement, which has gained a greater hearing than at any time in recent memory, capitalizes not only on the popularity of "choice" but also, ironically, on the importance of equity. In 1998, five Republican governors joined to make the following declaration: "We believe every child, regardless of social or economic status, should have the same variety of educational opportunities, wonderful teachers, and safe schools as the most privileged children enjoy."[8] Implicit in the conservative argument that it is unfair to trap poor children in bad local schools is the profound truth that neighborhood assignment can be a source of great unfairness to poor people.

In reality, the call for equity through a voucher system is usually misguided: privatization under most circumstances will only further segregate the schools by race and class because the "choice" that advocates talk about ultimately resides with private schools rather than with students. Yet conservatives are right—and politically adroit, as well—to call for dramatic change. In a 1997 NBC News–*Wall Street Journal* survey, 58 percent of Americans agreed that "we need to make fundamental changes" in public education, compared with 35 percent advocating "some changes," 4 percent favoring "minor changes," and just 1 percent arguing for "no changes at all."[9]

Instead of advocating dramatic change, Brown University's Michael Alves notes, "education reform is out there trying to make *Plessy* v. *Ferguson* work."[10] Progressives have embraced a variety of modest steps: reducing class size, encouraging the voluntary adoption of national standards, ending promotion based on social development rather than academic achievement, promoting charter schools, and ensuring better teacher training. These good ideas are positive steps in the right direction; but even if all those changes were enacted (which they will not be) they would not accomplish half as much as embracing Mann's one big idea of economically integrated common schools. Economically separate schools are the fountainhead of countless discrete inequalities, and the best guarantee that a school will have what various individual reforms seek to achieve—high standards, qualified teachers, less crowded classes, and so on—is the presence of a critical mass of middle-class families who will ensure that these things happen. The social class of a student body is so significant that poor children attending middle-class schools perform on average better than middle-class children attending high-poverty schools.[11]

If Mann's old idea is to work today, it must be married to a new one: public school choice. Because neighborhoods are increasingly separated by class, advocates of common schools should latch on to the revolution in public school choice (charter schools, magnet schools, alternative schools, and the like) to ensure that these movements promote, rather than undercut, integration. In so doing, the common school approach can build on the best elements of the existing big education ideas—vouchers, racial integration, and compensatory spending—while avoiding the drawbacks of each.

Like advocates of a voucher system, proponents of the common school approach believe in choice of schools rather than compulsory assignment based on where one can afford to live. Both groups seek to shake up the system, to provide competition between schools, and to close down failing schools. But unlike voucher advocates, backers of common schools consciously seek integration of students as a way of promoting social mobility and social cohesion. Common school advocates also fundamentally believe in public education as more accountable than private education and as more likely to instill democratic values and unify a diverse nation.

Like advocates of racial integration of public schools, proponents of the common school approach acknowledge that in determining school quality, the people in the school community are more important than the average expenditure for each pupil or the physical facilities; that all benefit from exposure to diversity; and that separation breeds distrust and disunity. But in place of busing to achieve racial balance, the common school approach employs legal tools to ensure suburban participation in integration efforts, uses choice rather than compulsory assignment, avoids the constitutional problems now associated with using race in student assignment, and avoids as well the insulting assumption that predominantly black schools are inferior by emphasizing that economic status, rather than race, drives school quality. Common school advocates note that *Brown* v. *Board of Education* addresses only the most glaring shortcoming of a much larger failure to give all students access to good schools.

Like advocates of equal and compensatory spending, advocates of common schools believe in genuine equal opportunity for all students; and like backers of programs from Head Start to Title I, they believe that policy remedies should be geared to economic status more than race. Unlike advocates of equal spending, however, common school supporters believe separate schools for middle-class and poor students—even if they are equally funded—are inherently unequal. They openly acknowledge that existing compensatory programs like Title I have been hugely disappointing and believe that spending will be much more effective in raising achievement in integrated schools.

In sum, while avoiding the pitfalls of each approach, the common school strategy builds on the insight of voucher advocates about the importance of choice over local school assignment, the insight of *Brown* on the importance of student body over per capita spending, and the insight of Title I and compensatory programs on the primacy of class before color. By synthesizing the best elements of each strategy and making common schools common (rather than the exception), economic integration can help fulfill the promise of public education as a powerful engine for social mobility.

An American Idea

Although the idea of reviving common schools is not currently part of the mainstream political discussion among cautious politicians, it is profoundly American, and by tapping into three central American values—fairness, unity, and choice—it should resonate deeply with the public. Americans want schools to be fair, to serve as a basis and training ground for meritocracy rather than aristocracy. Even as Americans are disappointed with public schools in practice, they overwhelmingly support the idea of open and democratic public education as an institution.[12] (When is the last time a politician said he was a "proud product" of a private school?) Americans are fairly judgmental of the poor, but they have a more generous attitude toward poor children and view bad schools as a source of poverty that needs to be addressed.

Americans also want their schools to be a source of unity and cohesion, particularly as our society grows more ethnically and racially diverse. Public schools are a place in which people of different backgrounds come together to learn, among other things, what it is to be an American. Most people realize that segregation of public schools, whether by law or in fact, precludes that type of assimilation and the process of Americanization.

Finally, in more recent years, Americans have become increasingly enamored of school choice. Liberty, of course, is a deeply American notion, and part of the reason the busing of the 1970s and 1980s aroused so much anger is that parents whose students were shipped to schools outside of their neighborhoods had no say in the matter. Today, Americans are increasingly realizing that poor children, trapped in bad neighborhood schools, lack choice just as surely as those who were bused, and we have seen an astonishing rise in support for public school choice.

None of the three predominant educational strategies reconciles all three of these values. Vouchers provide choice without fairness or unity: they are unfair because they allow schools, rather than students and their parents, to decide who enjoys the best education, and they promote disunity because they tend to segregate schools by class and religion. Busing seeks unity but sacrifices choice, and, to a certain degree, fairness: remedying historic wrongs with reference to children born after the laws were changed did not strike people as fair, nor did the double standard under which primarily poor whites were involved in integration efforts; in addition, the heavy hammer of busing left little room for choice. Compensatory spending programs provide fairness but without unity or choice: the Title I program is premised on the idea of extra money for separate poor schools, so it is not designed to promote unity; and because the poor cannot take Title I funds with them under current law, the program is not premised on choice. Only the common schools strategy, achieved through public school choice, simultaneously holds out the promise of fairness and social mobility, the yearning for national unity and assimilation through the spread of middle-class values, and, for the first time, genuine choice in education for all American families. By melding new and old, common school choice honors the trio of values that other plans must trade off against one another.

La Crosse, Wisconsin, was the first town to explicitly endorse economic school integration in the early 1990s. The plan, school board member and local attorney Roger LeGrand recalls, was seen neither as radical nor as liberal; the issue was one of "fairness." The school board consisted of some progressives and some "very conservative" members, all of whom liked the idea "of giving everybody from whatever background . . . the same shot." The plan was not dreamed up by "crazy liberal professors," LeGrand says; "I always thought this whole thing was just about America . . . where the sun comes up in the morning, and kids, no matter where they are, all go to the same school."[13]

Chapter Outline

Chapter 2 begins the discussion by outlining three goals of American public education: to prepare workers in a global economy, to prepare citizens in a democracy, and to forge national unity among diverse Americans. The chapter then evaluates the sobering evidence that America's public schools today are not promoting equal opportunity or social mobility but tend to replicate and freeze a student's economic position at the level of his or her parents' and that racially and economically separate schools undercut the goals of promoting citizenship and American unity.

Chapter 3 begins to build the affirmative case for economic school integration, drawing its inspiration from the comment of one educator that "there is no need to add to the criticism of our public schools. . . . The question now is what to do."[14] The chapter reviews the sociological evidence on integration, the vast majority of which suggests that allowing poor students to attend middle-class schools will increase their academic achievement and attainment, provide them access to better social connections, and improve their chances of long-run success without reducing the achievement of middle-class children. It reviews the evidence that directly bears on economic integration of schools as well as evidence from related fields (the effects of economic neighborhood integration and the effects of racial school desegregation). It then turns to evidence that suggests the common schools approach will also promote the other goals of education, bringing about a better realization of unity in a diverse democracy.

Chapter 4 explains why socioeconomic integration of schools matters. Classmates provide a "hidden curriculum" in all schools. In high-poverty schools, peers are likely to have smaller vocabularies and less knowledge to share; they tend to have lower aspirations and negative attitudes toward achievement and to engage in anti-achievement behavior (cutting classes, failing to do homework). Similarly, levels of student disruption are higher, and student mobility and absences are greater, all of which interferes with teaching. Among parents, the poor are less likely to be involved in school affairs, to ensure high standards, and to put pressure on administrators to fire or transfer bad teachers. These parents are less likely than parents in middle-class schools to volunteer in class, to have the ability to apply political pressure to ensure adequate funding, or to provide private financial support. The evidence shows that because of these aggregate differences between students and parents in high-poverty and middle-class schools, teachers in poor schools are on the whole of lower quality: they are more likely to be unlicensed or inexperienced, to teach out of their field of concentration, to have less formal education, and to score lower on teacher tests. Teachers in high-poverty schools are also likely to have lower expectations and to teach a watered-down curriculum.

The discussion in chapter 5 follows from that in chapter 4, detailing why attempts to improve separate but equal schools through piecemeal efforts at reform (trying to improve standards, encourage parental involvement, and equalize public spending, for instance) tend to fail. The chapter then reviews the various disappointing efforts to make high-poverty schools "effective" and explains why universal reforms, such as reduction of class size, can create their own inequality when background differences between poor and rich schools are not addressed.

The chapter then explains why two large-scale reforms—racial desegregation and school vouchers—fail to bring the full benefits of the common school. Racial desegregation has suffered from four sets of problems. First, whereas race once offered the legal rationale to order desegregation, the legal posture has recently changed 180 degrees so that some districts seeking to integrate voluntarily are now being forbidden from doing so. Second, demographic shifts, particularly the growth of the black middle-class population, have made racial integration a less reliable proxy for the more important educational issue of economic integration. Third, as a matter of psychology, some blacks have criticized integration efforts, challenging the assumption that majority black institutions are inherently inferior. Fourth, politically, racial desegregation court orders have served to divide the New Deal progressive coalition of working-class whites and blacks, a development that has had broad consequences in the larger push for equal opportunity.

Vouchers have failed because they generally produce greater socioeconomic concentration, not less; divert funds to the wealthy; and will further divide Americans by race and religion. Chapter 5 closes by noting that on closer examination the apparent success of some Catholic schools with significant poor populations in fact underlines the importance of common schools. Because these schools are populated in great part with self-selected striving poor families, who are more like middle-class families in values and aspirations, Catholic schools are very different from public high-poverty schools and are replicable only with middle-class public school populations.

Chapter 6 explains how socioeconomic desegregation might be achieved in concrete and practical terms. It makes recommendations on how socioeconomic status should be measured and suggests that those students ineligible for the federal free and reduced-price lunch program (those students whose families are living at no more than 185 percent above the poverty line) be defined as middle class. The chapter also examines the optimal mix of poor and middle-class children and sets a middle-class minimum of 50 percent. It then spends a fair amount of time exploring a promising mechanism for achieving integration—namely, "controlled choice," a system under which families choose from a number of public schools and choices are honored with an eye to integration. Controlled choice offers several advantages over three other leading models: forced busing, uncontrolled choice, and magnet schools. The vast majority of the nation's districts can achieve majority-middle-class schools within existing boundaries, but for those districts in which economic balancing with majority-middle-class schools is a numerical impossibility, the chapter explores the use of metropolitan-wide choice. The chapter also addresses the important issue of life inside newly integrated schools: the role of transitional programs, ability grouping and tracking, and discipline codes.

Chapter 7 examines the various political and legal strategies that could be employed to encourage or require states to adopt an economic integration plan. It reviews the political evidence that the popularity of school choice is reducing America's once-strong attachment to the neighborhood school; that district lines are more malleable than they once were; protections that can be put in place to ensure that the middle class will buy into socioeconomic integration; how the interests and values of the middle-class are served by efforts to assimilate the poor; and the reasons why important interest groups—business, teachers unions, and civil rights groups, among them—are likely to back economic school integration. It also looks at promising case law, building on a significant breakthrough in Connecticut, that suggests economic integration may be constitutionally required by a number of states. Finally, it discusses the federal sticks and carrots that can be used to encourage economic integration.

Chapter 8 rebuts various arguments made against economic desegregation. It explains why economic integration need not be stigmatizing or patronizing to poor children in the way some racial integration schemes were sometimes seen as insulting to blacks. It takes on the issue of whether parents who have paid a premium for houses in certain school districts should be able to "buy" the right to have their children attend a given public school and to exclude others from attending. The chapter looks at what sort of impact moving away from "neighborhood schools" will have and reviews the evidence suggesting that the benefits of integration far outweigh the benefits of local assignment. It explores the philosophical and political reasons to focus reform efforts on schools rather than on inequalities rooted in family and neighborhood residence.

Finally, and most significant of all, chapter 8 explains how economic integration through controlled choice differs from the forced racial busing of the 1970s. It examines, through the example of busing in Boston, Massachusetts, precisely why economic integration today is less likely to promote middle-class or white flight: the importance of using choice rather than busing; the importance of guaranteeing a middle-class majority; the way in which new legal tools should allow economic integration efforts to include suburban jurisdictions, and the importance of that inclusion to issues of flight and issues of equity.

Chapter 9 examines in depth a few jurisdictions that are on the cutting edge of the new socioeconomic integration. La Crosse, Wisconsin, voluntarily implemented an economic balancing plan; Wake County, North Carolina, recently moved from a system of racial integration to one emphasizing economic status; and Manchester, Connecticut, uses a modified system of controlled choice to integrate its students economically.

| 2

American Schools Today:

Falling Short of Our Goals

IN A NATION founded on free enterprise, capitalism, and private property, why is the notion of public education—paid for and run by the state—so deeply rooted that 90 percent of American schoolchildren attend public schools? Why did Thomas Jefferson, a great proponent of limited government, also propose free and universal education? Why did the United States, which generally stands to the right of Europe on so many issues of social welfare—from public housing to income support—lead the way on universally accessible public education, paid for by all members of society whether or not they have children who use public schools? In a society that balks at constraints on liberty, freedom, and autonomy, why have all states made elementary and secondary education compulsory since 1918? Why, today, do even proponents of private school vouchers concede the public role in funding those vouchers?[1]

The central argument made in favor of free, universal, and compulsory education is, of course, that the public has a strong interest in ensuring that all of society's children are educated. Virtually every state constitution provides for public education to create productive workers, self-governing citizens, and loyal Americans. First, employers need educated workers, and some of the brightest scientists and most creative entrepreneurs may come from poor and working-class families who could not otherwise afford education. Central to the notion of publicly supported education is Jefferson's idea of America as a "natural aristocracy," which he viewed as more just and efficient than an "aristocracy of wealth." Jefferson proposed universal education to promote "the selection of the youths of genius from among the classes of the poor" and declared, "We hope to avail the State of those talents which nature has sown so liberally among the poor as the rich, but which perish without use, if not sought for and cultivated." Today, John Coons argues, there is great untapped potential among the poor, and there is "no graver threat to the capitalist system than the present cyclical replacement of the 'fittest' of one generation by their artificially advantaged offspring."[2]

Two factors have increased the importance of education to economic competitiveness. The rise of the global economy has made the United States a direct competitor with international trading partners as at no other time; and increasing reliance on technology puts a higher premium on brains over brawn in the work force. According to a 1994 conference of leading industrial nations, the pace of technological change has left those with only a high school diploma inadequately trained. The key to creating more high-wage jobs is to upgrade education, "particularly for those who are least skilled."[3]

Related to this idea is the notion that poor children who are not properly educated are more likely to engage in various social pathologies, including crime, bad parenting, and drug abuse.[4] This economic argument can also be couched in moral terms: we should provide equal opportunity to students born into poor as well as wealthy families not only because it is good for the economy, and good as a means of preventing crime, but also because it is fair and right to allow all individuals to develop their natural talents to the fullest. In American society, the philosophical justification for tolerating large degrees of inequality of result among adults is that we provide equal opportunity at the beginning of the race—and public education is understood to be central to that aspiration.

Second, democracy requires a thinking people who are not easily swayed by demagoguery; and it requires that elites perceive a commitment to democratic equality (respect for the concept of one person, one vote). Jefferson argued that schools were necessary "to ensure that citizens would know how to protect their liberty." All nations, Paul Gagnon notes, provide an excellent education to "those who are expected to run the country," and the quality of that education "cannot be far from what everyone in a democracy needs to know." John Dewey knew that education and democracy were inexorably intertwined: citizens need education to responsibly choose political leaders and hold them accountable; and education helps citizens interact with one another and learn from one another between the elections every two or four years. At an even more basic level, all states (whether democratic or not) require an educated citizenry for their political survival, in order to attract a qualified fighting force during times of war.[5]

A democracy requires not only that citizens be intelligent and well informed but also that they hold to a set of common values. In the case of the United States, Jennifer Hochschild and Nathan Scovronick note, those values "include loyalty to the nation, acceptance of the Declaration of Independence and the Constitution as venerable founding documents, appreciation that in American constitutionalism rights sometimes trump majority rule and majority rule is supposed to trump intense desire, belief in the rule of law as the proper grounding for a legal system, belief in equal opportunity as the proper grounding for a social system, [and a] willingness to adhere to the discipline implied by rotation in office through an electoral system."[6] Groups that are successful, economically and socially, may not naturally come to tolerance and to the idea of democracy, in which all citizens have equal political rights. Public schools can help nip budding feelings of superiority that certain privileged races or economic groups might feel.

Third, American public schools serve the important function in a nation of immigrants of promoting social cohesion and instilling in marginalized groups—people of color, the poor—hope for their future, a commitment to country, and a respect for American ideals. The idea, Neil Postman writes, is not to teach a "psychopathic nationalism" about American superiority but to inspire "a common attachment to America's history and future, to America's sacred symbols, for its promise of freedom. The schools are, as such, the affirmative answer to the question, Can a coherent, stable, unified culture be created out of people of diverse traditions, languages, and religions?" Public education, wrote Felix Frankfurter in 1948, is "the most powerful agency for promoting cohesion among heterogeneous democratic people . . . at once the symbol of our democracy and the most pervasive means for promoting our common destiny."[7]

How well are American schools doing in achieving this trio of goals? Not nearly as well as they could be.

Academic Achievement and Worker Preparation

It is well established that Americans lag educationally. In math and science, U.S. fourth-graders do fairly well, but our eighth-graders do less well and our twelfth-graders score below the international average. In the Third International Math and Science Study, released in 1998, of twenty-one industrialized countries, American twelfth-graders ranked nineteenth in math and sixteenth in science. In other subjects, even our fourth-grade performance is dismal: on National Assessment of Educational Progress (NAEP) tests conducted in 1997, half of American fourth-graders could not identify the Atlantic or Pacific Oceans on a map. A 1992 study estimated that roughly 42 million American adults are functionally illiterate.[8]

Moreover, much of our problem is concentrated in the bottom tiers.[9] As Gerald Bracey notes, among the best students (the top 50 percent), American and Japanese test scores in mathematics are comparable. It is those American students in the bottom half who lag far behind their Japanese counterparts. Bracey concludes that "the top third of our students are world class . . . [and] the second third are not in any serious academic trouble; the bottom third are in terrible shape."[10] A recent Organization for Economic Cooperation and Development (OECD) Adult Literacy Survey found that among employed people between the ages of sixteen and twenty-four, 20 percent of Americans can barely add two numbers together, compared with 8 percent of Canadians, 5 percent of Swedes, and 2 percent of Germans.[11] A 1988 Ford Foundation Report found that "raising the scores of those at the bottom is the surest and most cost-effective way of raising the average." The Japanese, the Ford Foundation report notes, take great pride in having "the best bottom 50 percent in the world." As James Fallows writes, "The most important fact about Japan's educational success is that the average performance is so good not because the best scores are so high but because the worst ones are. . . . Japan has the most fortunate lower class."[12]

America's disadvantaged children do not fare nearly as well. All the evidence suggests that instead of transforming inherited positions, our education system tends to perpetuate them and exacerbate inequality.[13] The gap between rich and poor grows over time. In first grade, the reading achievement gap between average students in high-poverty and low-poverty schools is 27 percentage points; by eighth grade, the gap is 43 points. Conservatives like Milton Friedman note that the public schools, dedicated to the idea of equal educational opportunity, "in practice exacer-

Defining Equal Opportunity

In saying that we have not achieved equal educational opportunity, it is fair to ask a few questions: What would be considered success? What is a reasonable goal for our public schools? Obviously, some students will always perform better than others, given variations in natural talent and effort. But shouldn't equal educational opportunity mean that children from different racial and economic groups should be equally represented among the high and low achievers?

This was the radical idea at the center of the 1966 Coleman Report—that equal opportunity should not be defined merely as equal inputs (spending, teachers, facilities, and the like) but also that results should be independent of family background. That is, it should not be possible to walk into a hospital maternity ward and predict, with some degree of certainty, that the poor and minority children will be the low achievers ten or twenty or thirty years hence. In Martin Luther King Jr.'s words, "the job of the school is to teach so well that family background is no longer an issue."[1]

However, is this goal, to make achievement independent of social origins—to help facilitate, in the words of George Smith—"a convergence in the average outcomes for different groups, even though they began from different starting points"—attainable? The overwhelming evidence suggests that although genetic differences account for much of the difference in individual achievement, they do not explain gaps between blacks and whites or between poor and rich.[2] On the other hand, even though environment explains the differences in group achievement, equal schools can hardly equalize group results because

1. James S. Coleman, "Toward Open Schools," *Public Interest*, vol. 9 (Fall 1967), p. 21; James Fishkin, *Justice, Equal Opportunity, and the Family* (Yale University Press, 1983), p. 4; King, quoted in Alan B. Krueger, "Reassessing the View That American Schools Are Broken," *FRBNY Economic Policy Review*, March 1998, p. 37.

2. George Smith, "Positive Discrimination by Area in Education: The EPA Idea Re-examined," *Oxford Review of Education*, vol. 3, no. 3 (1977), p. 271. The Murray-Herrnstein thesis that racial and economic gaps represent innate genetic facts has been roundly demolished; see, for example, Christopher Jencks and Meredith Phillips, introduction to *The Black-White Test Score Gap* (Brookings, 1998), p. 3; Richard Nesbit, "Race, Genetics, and IQ," in Jencks and Phillips, *The Black-White Test Score Gap*, pp. 86–102.

much education takes place outside the school—before school, after school, on weekends, and during summers. "No matter how much schools improve," notes Richard Rothstein, "it is fantasy to expect classrooms whose students have parents that did not graduate from high school to achieve the same fourth-grade reading scores as those classrooms where parents are college graduates."[3]

Although persistent differences in home environment make it unlikely that the gap in achievement between rich and poor will ever completely close, the logic of "learning curves" suggests that schools should be able to reduce the gap. A person first learning to type makes faster gains in speed with additional practice than a more experienced typist; by the same logic, if a poor student starts off with ten units of knowledge on average and a middle-class child has twenty, each additional gain for the middle-class child is more difficult to achieve. Although it is true that gaps in individual student achievement grow as students increasingly "fan out" between first and twelfth grade, the link between those high on the fan and those from higher-income families is not inevitable, for in other countries, as E. D. Hirsch notes, the performance gap between rich and poor narrows over time.[4]

In addition to making the academic bell curve less dependent on family origins, public policy could seek to raise the overall level of achievement—so that, for example, the percentage of students reading at a predetermined absolute level increases. As Leon Botstein notes, if we cannot change the fact that some will always do better than others, we can try to push the bell curve to the right, just as Olympic runners have, over time, increased the average speed at which they run the hundred-yard dash.[5]

3. Richard Rothstein, *The Way We Were: Debunking the Myths of America's Declining Schools* (New York: Century Foundation Press, 1998), p. 4.

4. See L. L. Thurstone, "The Learning Curve Equation," *Psychological Review Monograph Supplement*, vol. 26, no. 3 (1919), cited in Frank Restle and James G. Greeno, *Introduction to Mathematical Psychology* (Reading, Mass.: Addison-Wesley, 1970), pp. 8–22. See also James S. Coleman and Thomas Hoffer, *Public and Private High Schools: The Impact of Communities* (Basic Books, 1987), p. 64 (it is harder for students who begin with high scores to achieve the same level of gain as students who begin with lower scores). E. D. Hirsch, *The Schools We Need and Why We Don't Have Them* (Doubleday, 1996), pp. 43–44.

5. Leon Botstein, *Jefferson's Children: Education and the Promise of American Culture* (Doubleday, 1997), pp. 34–35.

bate the stratification of society and provide highly unequal educational opportunity."[14]

The lower levels of achievement among the poor translate into lower levels of attainment (length of schooling), including high school graduation. Among high school students graduating in 1992, 86 percent of high-income children were academically qualified for admission to a four-year college compared with just 53 percent of low-income high school graduates. In part because of this lack of educational preparation (and in part because of tuition barriers), poor and working-class students are one-half as likely to attend four-year colleges as those from the top income quartile (28 versus 66 percent) and four times as likely to end their education with high school (40 versus 10 percent).[15] At elite colleges, the poor and the lower middle class are severely underrepresented: those at the bottom 28 percent of the socioeconomic scale make up only 3 percent of the student population.[16]

The large gap between rich and poor in student achievement and attainment translates into large differences in income and wealth among adults, which will, in turn, affect the life chances of their children.[17] About 70 percent of Americans stay in the same socioeconomic class into which they were born; the children of poorly educated parents make up just 2 percent of the professional and managerial class. Although the United States prides itself on having less class rigidity than that found in Europe, study after study has found that, in fact, our rates of social mobility are no better.[18]

Moreover, social mobility may be further reduced in future years. Economists have noted that inequality of result has been growing in the last quarter century.[19] In 1979, the median income of Americans in the ninety-fifth percentile was thirteen times that of those in the fifth percentile; by 1996, the multiple was twenty-three.[20] This growing inequality in result in the current generation is likely to reduce social mobility in the next, because the rich can give yet greater advantages to their offspring, and the poor yet fewer. This state of affairs is not only unfair, it is also bad for our economy. Some might cynically say that what matters is the top (we will always need some people to sweep the floor), but this is not the view taken by business, or by Ronald Reagan's National Commission on Excellence in Education, which recognized that the United States cannot have quality without equal opportunity.[21]

Though short-term trends suggest that the U.S. economy can thrive despite low test scores, our mediocre educational performance has until recently been made up for by our edge in the number of years that students attend school. Erik Hanushek noted in 1998 that "the United States [has] substituted quantity for quality." This is now changing, however; "many countries that have had higher student achievement are beginning to rival the United States on quantity grounds. This suggests that the U.S. economy faces new and different levels of competition in the years ahead."[22]

The failure to educate our poor children adequately also means increased crime and welfare dependency and reduced future earnings.[23] According to 1995 congressional testimony, 82 percent of juvenile delinquents are inadequate readers, and 75 percent of prison inmates are functionally illiterate.[24] Another study has found that more than 80 percent of prison inmates are high school dropouts. Many argue that the balance has been lost, as many American cities spend more on law enforcement than on education. Others appeal to the fiscal rationale: the cost of imprisoning a juvenile in a secure facility in New York City is $93,000 a year, about eleven times the cost of educating him as a child.[25]

Democracy and Unity

The other two key goals of public schools—to promote the workings of democracy and to build a unified nation—are also being severely undermined by growing economic and racial isolation in the schools.

It cannot be good for society when many white students grow up seeing black people primarily as criminals on the nightly television news broadcast; or when black ghetto residents fear leaving their neighborhoods in the belief that if they do so they are likely to be lynched by the Ku Klux Klan.[26] It cannot be good when poor black schools are filled with children who believe the Central Intelligence Agency has planted drugs in the ghetto or that acquired immunodeficiency syndrome (AIDS) is a white conspiracy while in other all-white middle-class schools children are terrified of black people. It cannot be good when an all-white jury acquits Rodney King's assailants or a nearly all-black jury acquits Nicole Brown-Simpson's assailant. Even conservatives like Lawrence Mead acknowledge that "the solution for the disadvantaged must mean integration, that is, an end to the separation so that the disadvantaged can publicly interact with others and be accepted by them as equals."[27]

For one thing, the prevalence of separate schools for rich and poor undercuts the primary lesson of democracy—that we are all social equals—whereas the creation of common access to common schools will underline it. Deborah Meier writes that "in school, kids sit down next to their classmates, whoever they are. Parents proudly come together at school concerts, weep together at graduations, and congregate in times of crisis at public hearings and PTA meetings. Public schools therefore offer opportunity for a sense of community otherwise sorely missing, for putting faces and names to people we might otherwise see as mere statistics or categories."[28]

The common school—attended by children from all backgrounds—reinforces democracy and is, indeed, "a manifestation of the social contract," in the words of Kern Alexander. The journalist Charles Peters recalls that the public school he attended while growing up in Charleston, West Virginia, though horribly segregated by race, was economically integrated: "Rich and poor were brought together so that we could get to know one another and acquire a faith in democracy that was not theoretical but grounded in real life." This economic integration, Peters says, helped prevent the middle class from making "the error of the liberal who assumes that the poor are all deserving [or] that of the conservative who thinks they are all lazy or dumb." If we in America prize tolerance of others, we must realize that separation impedes that goal. Most educators believe, similarly, that economic and racial diversity in schooling is part of a good education.[29]

In addition, separation naturally undermines loyalty and patriotism among those left out and left behind.[30] Segregated schools undercut loyalty indirectly and sometimes even explicitly. An Afrocentric charter school in Michigan observes African Independence Day and Malcolm X Remembrance Day rather than Labor Day, Memorial Day, or Presidents' Day. The school newsletter states that "the traditional concept of Thanksgiving, like the Fourth of July, really has nothing to do with us," and students begin the school day with a pledge "to my African nation." Another Michigan charter school has an almost entirely Armenian student body and faculty, and the principal keeps a small Armenian flag next to the American flag on her desk.[31] If entire groups are educated in separate schools, this isolated population may grow disaffected and alienated and be more open to demagogues, from Louis Farrakhan and Al Sharpton to David Duke and Pat Buchanan.

Conservatives sometimes criticize the public schools for failing to promote assimilation and for fostering tribalism through multiculturalism, but they rarely pause to ask whether the de facto economic and racial segregation of students might be a contributor to this balkanization. Only common schools can make the rhetorical lessons—we are all in this together, we must rely on each other—ring true to rich and poor alike.

As our nation grows increasingly diverse, racially, ethnically, and religiously—with immigration surging to rates unknown since the late nineteenth century—there is now, as never before, the need for cohesion. "What happens when people of different ethnic origins, speaking different languages and professing different religions, settle in the same geographic locality and live under the same political sovereignty?" asks Arthur Schlesinger Jr. in *The Disuniting of America*. "Unless a common purpose binds them together, tribal hostilities will drive them apart." The public schools are meant to "Americanize" immigrants, with the hope of "forging common cultural bonds that transcend demographic and economic differences."[32]

It is therefore very bad news indeed that our nation's schools are becoming more segregated by race and income. Before the invention of the automobile and the suburbanization of America, most people lived within walking distance from their place of work, and the spatial division of classes was not nearly so great as it is today. Before World War II, John Goodlad notes, "the sons and daughters of mill owners, shop proprietors, professional men, and day laborers attended [school] side by side. School boundaries, reaching out into fields and hills to embrace the pupil population, transcended such socioeconomic clusterings as existed."[33]

Then came white suburbanization, followed by black middle-class suburbanization, and, finally, stratification between suburbs, all of which resulted in large increases in poverty concentrations among both black and white populations left behind. In 1950, almost 70 percent of metropolitan-area residents lived in central cities; by 1990, the balance had shifted, with 60 percent of metro-area residents residing in suburbs. Paul Jargowsky's 1997 study, *Poverty and Place*, concludes that "high-poverty neighborhoods, be they black ghettos, Hispanic barrios, or even poor white neighborhoods, have been growing at an alarming rate. Between 1970 and 1990, the number of persons living in ghettos, barrios, and slums in the U.S. grew by 92 percent, and the number of poor people living in them grew by 98 percent." These findings are confirmed by an array of other studies.[34] Meanwhile, the affluent became more concentrated: in 1970, according to Douglas Massey, the typical affluent person lived in a neighborhood in which 39 percent of residents were affluent, but in 1990, that figure was 52 percent.[35] (The reader of this book may have few neighbors who lack a four-year college degree, even though 75 percent of Americans fall into that category.) Taken together, overall economic segregation is increasing and is currently greater in the United States than in any other leading industrial democracy.[36]

Concentrations of residential poverty naturally translate into greater concentrations in school poverty. The shift from the nineteenth-century nomenclature, "common school," to the more modest modern term, "public school," is symbolic of the change.[37] Although we are an overwhelmingly middle-class nation, about one-quarter of schools are majority low income.[38]

The good news in all of this is that racial concentration by residence is on a slow downward slope. The index of residential racial concentration averaged 84.5 in 1979, 80.1 in 1980, and 77.8 in 1990. Even so, these gains are offset by a drastic cutback in school desegregation efforts. In the early 1990s, for the first time since *Brown* v. *Board of Education*, racial segregation in southern schools began to increase. Nationally, the percentage of black students attending predominantly minority schools, according to a 1999 report of Harvard University's desegregation project, fell from 76.6 percent in 1968–69 to 62.9 percent in 1980–81, but by 1996–97, the figure had moved back up to 68.8 percent. In twenty-five of the nation's largest inner-city school districts, schools are more racially segregated today than they were in 1954.[39] These cutbacks in racial school desegregation efforts have indirectly resulted in further economic school segregation as well.[40]

The overall picture, then, is that of a scissors, says Richard Morin: "If satellites could use their time-lapsed photography to map economic and racial segregation in the United States, they would have recorded during recent years two trends: a sharp rise in economic segregation, and a slow decline in racial segregation." David Rusk argues that "we are substituting Jim Crow by race with Jim Crow by income."[41] It is clearly time for new strategies to supplement existing efforts. We need something bigger than school uniforms or reduced class size to address the magnitude of the problem. It is time to implement, at long last, the common school ideal, schools integrated by class as well as race, a new strategy to which we now turn.

| 3

The Case for Economic

School Desegregation

THE NINETEENTH-CENTURY Massachusetts educator Horace Mann believed that if American public schools were to serve their function of creating productive workers, informed citizens, and loyal Americans, those schools had to be common schools in which "the children of all classes, rich and poor, should partake as equally as possible in the privileges" of the enterprise. The presence of high-achieving students raises the standard of achievement, he argued, and "the mass will rise again and reach it. Hence the removal of the most forward scholars from a school is not a small misfortune." In addition, Mann worried, if the advantaged families were to withdraw from the common schools, they would be less active in ensuring the quality of the schools and less willing to support annual public appropriations.[1]

To inculcate a belief in democracy, Mann argued, what better way to teach privileged children that they share a common humanity than to teach them in the same school with the poor. "One of the objectives of the common school," Leon Botstein reminds us today, "is to teach Americans that as citizens and before God, everyone is equal."[2] Separate schools insidiously undermine the democratic message, no matter how vigorously the teacher preaches the tenets of equality under the law.

Mann firmly believed that education in the common school was necessary to bind a people from diverse backgrounds and religions—an issue
more pressing in America than in homogeneous European nations. Mann
had observed religious riots in Boston in 1837 and thought it essential that
Americans of diverse religious persuasions should be taught to peaceably
coexist. The nation's economic and ethnic diversity, Mann believed, could
split it asunder unless a common school education for all instilled shared
values.[3] Mann's vision offered something for everyone. For liberals, there
was the promise of upward mobility by exposing poor children to higher
aspirations and new possibilities. For conservatives, there was the promise
of economic assimilation and stability and the inculcation of American
values. For both, there was the promise of a better functioning democracy.

One hundred and thirty years later, as the nation struggled to purge
itself of the most egregious violation of the common school ideal—segregation by race—a well-known sociologist from the University of Chicago,
James Coleman, sought to revive the idea of school integration based not
only on race but on social class as well. In the introduction to a 1970 book
devoted to the question of equalizing school spending, Coleman had the
bad manners to point out that the book's subject, "financial resources," left
unaddressed "a second kind of educational resource, in the form of other
children in a school. . . . Beyond the provision of equal financial resources
for education, toward which this book provides a path, the larger question
must be raised." In testimony that year before the U.S. Senate Select Committee on Equal Educational Opportunity, Coleman again pointed out
that disadvantaged students attending segregated schools are "deprived of
the most effective educational resources contained in the schools: those
brought by other children as the result of their home environment."[4]

In the years since, however, no one has taken up Coleman's concern
about social class integration. In the last half century, progressives have
properly tackled a number of important educational issues having to do
with race (desegregation), religion (compulsory school prayer), ethnicity
(bilingual education), gender (discrimination in athletics), and disability
(mainstreaming). When progressives do talk about economic class in education, they are usually addressing equal and compensatory funding
through programs like Title I of the Elementary and Secondary Education
Act and Head Start.

When parents say they want to live in areas with good public schools,
however, they do not normally mean institutions with the highest rate of
expenditure for each pupil as much as places with solidly middle-class

environments. Given a choice between a high-poverty school that spends more, on average, for each pupil and a middle-class school that spends somewhat less, most parents would not have a hard time choosing the middle-class school.[5] Parents know what Coleman knew and what fifty years of sociological data have made clear: being born into a poor family places students at risk, but to be assigned then to a school with a high concentration of poverty poses a second, independent disadvantage that poor children attending middle-class schools do not face. Taken together, being poor and attending schools with classmates who are poor constitutes a clear "double handicap." Yet in the United States, David Rusk notes, "we surround children from the weakest families with the weakest neighborhoods and the weakest schools." America's problem, Rusk continues, is not third-world-style poverty in the sense of large-scale malnutrition; America's problem is concentrations of poverty.[6]

Taking steps to integrate schools by economic status will significantly promote the three goals of education: to prepare workers, citizens, and Americans. Economically integrated schools will raise the achievement and improve the life chances of the poor without reducing the achievement of the middle class, and it will further the secondary goal of promoting a vibrant democracy and unity amid diversity.

Economic Desegregation Prepares Workers

The socioeconomic composition of schools has a significant impact on individual students' life chances, mostly because of its effects on academic performance but also because schools provide networks for employment later in life. To begin with, a great deal of data provides direct evidence regarding the importance of a school's socioeconomic status on life chances, in terms of both academic achievement in school and subsequent accomplishments as adults.

The notion that the socioeconomic status of classmates has a powerful effect on academic achievement is, as Gary Orfield and Susan Eaton note, "one of the most consistent findings in research on education." The seminal study is James Coleman's exhaustive 1966 report, *Equality of Educational Opportunity* (popularly known as the Coleman Report), which finds that "a pupil's achievement [appears to be] strongly related to the educational backgrounds and aspirations of the other students in the school. . . . Children from a given family background, when put in schools of different social compositions, will achieve at quite different levels." Summarizing the report's findings in the *Public Interest,* Coleman noted that "the educational resources provided by a child's fellow students are more important for his achievement than are the resources provided by the school board." So important are fellow students, the Coleman Report found, that "the social composition of the student body is more highly related to achievement, independent of the student's own social background, than is any school factor." Frederick Mosteller and Daniel Moynihan, reviewing Coleman's findings, conclude that "students [matter]. The higher the social class of the other students the higher any given student's achievement."[7] Similarly, Christopher Jencks, reanalyzing Coleman's data, has found that poor black sixth-graders in middle-class schools were twenty months ahead of poor black sixth-graders in schools with high levels of student poverty; his findings for poor whites were similar. To put these figures in perspective, Jencks estimates that no other school characteristic makes more than one month's difference in sixth-grade reading, math, or verbal achievement.[8]

Conservatives like Chester Finn, who are generally pessimistic about the role of resources in raising achievement, acknowledge that "the principal exception" in Coleman's study is that "disadvantaged children were found to learn more when they attended school with middle-class youngsters." Thirty-three years later, *Education Week* noted that the Coleman Report was still "widely regarded as the most important education study of the twentieth century" and that Coleman's finding "that a school's socioeconomic background is a strong determinant of its students' achievement" continues to be validated in education studies. Dozens of studies conducted before and after the Coleman Report have come to similar conclusions.[9] Almost all of these studies (unlike Coleman's) control for self-selection bias (that is, the possibility that poor students in middle-class schools may come from particularly motivated families) by tracking students over time.[10] "One of the most effective ways to improve children's cognitive skills," concludes Harvard's Richard Murnane, "is to put them in an environment with other children who want to acquire cognitive skills and whose families support such learning."[11] A list of some of the leading studies follows:

—In 1986, a national assessment of the Chapter 1 program found that the chances that a disadvantaged student would fall into the bottom quartile of achievement were twice as high for a student attending a high-poverty school as for a student from a low-poverty school (59 versus 28 percent). Moreover, the study found, middle-class students attending high-poverty schools were more likely to be underachievers than poor students in middle-class schools (37 versus 28 percent).[12]

—Also in 1986, J. Douglas Willms, looking at students in Scottish schools (which had sought to desegregate by socioeconomic status), found large achievement effects traceable to a school's socioeconomic status. Willms found that a student with average characteristics attending a school with a mean socioeconomic status half a standard deviation above the national mean scored 40 percent of a standard deviation higher than a similar student at a school with a mean socioeconomic status half a standard deviation below the national mean.[13] In a 1992 study of segregation in California, Russell Rumberger and Willms found that "average achievement levels are higher in schools with students of higher socioeconomic status, independent of the effects of individual socioeconomic status on individual achievement." In 1996, Willms and Esther Ho Sui-Chu, looking at data from the National Education Longitudinal Study (NELS) involving 24,599 eighth-grade American students, found that "student achievement is higher in high SES [socioeconomic-status] schools, even after student background at the individual level is taken into account." In math and reading scores, in particular, the researchers found, "the SES of a school had an effect on achievement that was comparable to the effects associated with the SES of a family."[14]

—In a 1990 longitudinal study looking at factors that influence gains in achievement among high school students, John Chubb and Terry Moe emphasized the importance of school organization but also found school socioeconomic status to be "strongly associated" with achievement gains between sophomore and senior years. In addition, they found that "through their peers, students are influenced by the families of other students in a school." By contrast, spending was "unrelated to student achievement," and racial composition was "not related (in a statistically significant way)."[15]

—A 1994 study, published by the Urban Institute, of more than one thousand public-housing students in Albuquerque, New Mexico, found that after controlling for home environment a poor child attending a school in a neighborhood with 20 percent poverty is likely to score thirteen percentile points higher than a similar child in a neighborhood school with 80 percent poverty. A 1998 Urban Institute study similarly found that the social context of a school, as measured by peer family income and parental education, was "strongly associated with individual student test scores [on the Scholastic Aptitude Test] even after controlling for individual student background characteristics."[16]

—In 1997, a congressionally authorized longitudinal study of forty thousand students concluded that "the poverty level of the school (over and above the economic status of an individual student) is negatively related to standardized achievement scores." The study supported the general findings of an earlier national study reporting that "the poverty level of certain schools places disadvantaged children in double jeopardy. School poverty depresses the scores of all students in a school where at least half of the students are eligible for subsidized lunch, and seriously depresses the scores when over 75 percent of students live in low income households."[17]

—David Rusk's 1998 study of the effect of poverty concentrations on school districts in Texas in the 1995–96 school year found that a middle-class school environment "significantly improves poor children's academic achievement." Controlling for income, Rusk compared the Texas Assessment of Academic Skills (TAAS) passage rates of low-income children in two districts: Alamo Heights, with a 17 percent low-income population, and San Antonio, with an 88 percent low-income population. Although San Antonio spent slightly more than wealthier Alamo Heights on each pupil ($5,333 versus $5,284), 61 percent of the low-income students in Alamo Heights passed the exam, compared with only 39 percent of San Antonio's low-income students. Classmates trumped expenditure. The lesson of the study, Rusk concludes, is that to improve public education we should "stop moving money" and, instead, "move families."[18]

—Stephen Schellenberg concludes in his 1999 study of some sixty thousand students in four school districts in Minnesota over three years that "the degree to which poor children are surrounded by other poor children, both in their neighborhood and at school, has as strong an effect on their achievement as their own poverty." Although neighborhood poverty effects are strong, Schellenberg finds that poor students who continue to live in poor neighborhoods but attend much more affluent schools of choice show "markedly higher scores."[19]

In addition to the effect on academic achievement, school socioeconomic status has been found to have an important influence on educational attainment—the total number of years of schooling. As far back as 1961, John Michael found that when controlling for ability and family socioeconomic status, the chances of attending college rose substantially for children attending schools with higher socioeconomic status. For example, among lower-middle-class children who scored in the top 25 percent on the Scholastic Aptitude Test (SAT), the chances of attending college were 38 percent for students attending low-status schools but 57 percent for those who attended high-status schools.[20]

Porter Sexton's 1985 study in Portland, Oregon, similarly found that individual dropout rates were closely tied to school dropout rates and that when students were reassigned to new schools, their dropout rates more closely resembled that of the new school than that of the previous school. More recent studies find that students in high-poverty neighborhoods and schools "are far more likely to drop out of school than poor students who live in economically mixed neighborhoods." Others have found that peers have a stronger effect on attainment than parents or teachers.[21]

Academic achievement today appears to play a significant role in determining lifetime economic success. This was not always so clearly the case. In 1972, Mosteller and Moynihan noted that most studies "do not find adult social achievement well predicted by academic achievement." Because luck plays such a large role in determining economic success, Jencks concluded in 1972, egalitarians should not focus on "marginal institutions" like schools but rather should seek to equalize resources among adults. The economy has changed significantly, however, over the past thirty years. Recent studies by June O'Neill and Ronald Ferguson have found that "reading and math test scores are important predictors of earnings for young men." Similarly, Eric Hanushek notes, numerous studies conducted in the 1990s have found that "the earnings advantages to higher achievement on standardized tests are substantial."[22]

Although for certain positions, employers may not care whether an employee can do nuclear physics, achievement serves as a rough proxy for responsibility: students who show up at school on time, and do their homework, are likely to pass; and this is relevant to those seeking to hire punctual and conscientious workers. For those hoping to find more than dead-end jobs, a college degree is more important than ever, Marc Tucker explains, because employers know that watered-down standards and social promotion make a high school diploma less meaningful than it once was. Jencks and Meredith Phillips note that the world has changed significantly since the 1970s and that "eliminating the test score gap" between blacks and whites would "reduce racial disparities in men's earnings and would probably eliminate the racial disparities in women's earnings."[23]

Achievement is also closely linked to attainment: those who do not do well academically are most likely to drop out, and those who achieve high levels of academic success are most likely to pursue college and graduate degrees.[24] According to a study of thirty thousand high school students, the typical dropout has grades at the sixteenth percentile of those who do not drop out. In addition, educational attainment is a more significant factor today in determining economic success than it was in the early 1970s; indeed, attainment now leads the list of "the strongest immediate determinants" of economic fortune.[25] Whereas in the late 1960s and 1970s, the wage premium for a college degree over a high school diploma was a mere 15 percent (prompting Richard Freeman's book, *The Overeducated American*), today it is 76 percent.[26] The gap between the earnings of high school graduates and those without a high school diploma has also increased, from 19 percent in 1979 to 40 percent in 1996. By another estimate, high school graduates earn one-third more than high school dropouts, and college graduates earn 235 percent as much. The chances of being in adult poverty are more than ten times as great for high school dropouts as for college graduates (36.3 versus 3.2 percent). Indeed, students who complete the last two years of high school reduce by 60 percent their chances of living in poverty as adults. Of course, it is possible to make a good living without a college degree, Richard Harwood notes; a longshoreman, for instance, can make $80,000. The median income in 1994 for men with less than a ninth-grade education, however, was $11,000 for men, and for similarly educated women, $6,200.[27]

High school graduates can be admitted to some colleges whatever their level of academic achievement; but attendance at selective colleges that examine high school achievement brings significant economic rewards.[28] William Bowen and Derek Bok's 1998 study of twenty-eight selective colleges found, for example, that on average, male graduates of the entering class of 1976 earned $101,900 a year compared with $63,100 for other college graduates. Among black males, the comparable figures were $85,000 and $46,800. Folk myth to the contrary, those who achieve higher grades in college also earn higher pay as adults.[29]

Schools also contribute to economic success in ways not strictly linked to academic achievement or attainment. Extensive research confirms the commonsense notion that connections and social networks are crucial to finding employment.[30] In the racial context, Gary Orfield has noted, research finds that "the networking effects of desegregation may be far more important than the cognitive effects."[31]

Similarly, school peers influence the chance of teen pregnancy for girls. Out-of-wedlock birth to teenagers is almost twice as common among low-income girls of all races as among other girls; a girl born into the bottom 20 percent by income is eight times more likely to have a baby before reaching the age of twenty than is a girl born into the top 20 percent (40 versus 4.9 percent). Moreover, high rates of pregnancy among peers influence the behavior of individual students. In 1985, Dennis Hogan and Evelyn Kitagawa found that, controlling for family, moving from a medium- to a low-socioeconomic-status neighborhood increased the chances of black girls between the ages of thirteen and nineteen becoming pregnant by one-third. Jonathan Crane has found that after controlling for family, blacks living in the worst neighborhoods were more than twice as likely to be teenage mothers as similar blacks living in the best neighborhoods; for whites, the multiple was three times.[32] These findings are confirmed in many other studies. Ethnographic studies find that in high-poverty ghettoes, having a baby is often taken as proof that a woman is seen as desirable to men. Citing the work of Leon Dash, Mickey Kaus notes that in the ghetto girls "are often ridiculed by other girls if they remain virgins too long in their teens."[33]

Teenage pregnancy can have a large impact on intergenerational poverty. William Galston notes that to reduce dramatically the chances of living in poverty, individual Americans have to do three things: finish high school, marry before having children, and postpone having children until after they have reached the age of twenty. Children born to families who do these three things have just an 8 percent chance of living in poverty, whereas the likelihood for children from families who do not is 79 percent.[34]

For academic and nonacademic reasons, then, the effects of the socioeconomic status of classmates last long into adulthood.[35] Research by Claude Fischer and colleagues reports that attending a disadvantaged school has a significant impact on the likelihood that a student will live in poverty as an adult. Controlling for individual ability and family home environment, attending a school with high concentrations of poverty increases the chances of adult poverty by a factor of between three and four compared with attending a low-poverty school (14 versus 4 percent). Another study, which followed students for nine years, starting in the ninth grade, found that high school social composition had an impact on earnings independent of achievement. Controlling for a student's family social class and test scores, those attending schools with students of higher socioeconomic backgrounds had higher incomes as adults than those who attended school with classmates who were less advantaged. The gain in income was twice as large from this effect for low-status as high-status students.[36]

Data from Neighborhoods

The second set of data providing support for economic desegregation of the schools is drawn from the wealth of studies finding that the socioeconomic status of neighborhoods influences the life chances of individuals in the neighborhood. Because desegregation of schools does not remove children from the neighborhoods in which they reside, we must take some caution in drawing inferences. It is probably true that the combined influence of neighborhood and school is somewhat greater than the influence of school. Many of those who study neighborhood effects believe, however, that the greatest portion of the effect lies in schools, as opposed to neighborhoods, because social networks are "denser" in schools than in neighborhoods.[37] Families may try to insulate themselves from neighborhood effects by keeping to themselves; but at school, constant contact with others is unavoidable. In any event, studies indicating that neighborhood environment and peers exert important influences provide at least indirect confirmation of the studies cited above indicating the strong influence of a school's social environment.

The thesis that neighborhoods exert strong influences on both children and adults, brought to public attention most prominently by William Julius Wilson, is now, note Fischer and his colleagues, a "standard finding in sociological and economic research."[38] If neighborhoods did not matter, they note, Americans would not "try so hard to find and afford 'good neighborhoods.'" Douglas Massey and Nancy Denton, surveying the research in 1993, found that "where one lives—especially, where one grows up—exerts a profound effect on one's life chances. Identical individuals with similar family backgrounds and personal characteristics will lead very different lives and achieve different rates of socioeconomic success depending on where they reside."[39] Whereas sociologists used to find neighborhood effects more readily than economists, today many economists also argue that neighborhood effects are strong.[40]

—Linda Datcher's 1982 study of the effects of family and community background on the education and earnings of black and white men aged twenty-three to thirty-two found that "neighborhood differences are at least as important as family characteristics in explaining the gaps between black and white achievement."[41]

—Mary Corcoran and colleagues have found that after controlling for home environment, the percentage of families on welfare in a given neighborhood strongly influences educational attainment. In her 1987 study, every increase of 10 percentage points in welfare recipients translates into a decline in educational attainment of a half year. In her analysis, two years later, of data from the Panel Study of Income Dynamics, Corcoran and colleagues found that parental income explains much of an individual's income, but after controlling for family income, living in a neighborhood with large numbers of welfare-dependent families was a "substantial" disadvantage.[42]

—In 1991, James Rosenbaum and colleagues found in their study of Chicago's Gautreaux program that inner-city students whose families moved to publicly subsidized housing in the affluent suburbs as part of a court-ordered housing discrimination remedy were much more likely to succeed than similar students whose families moved instead to other parts of Chicago. The students who moved to the suburbs were four times less likely to drop out (5 versus 20 percent), almost twice as likely to take college preparatory courses (40 versus 24 percent), twice as likely to attend college (54 versus 21 percent), and almost eight times as likely to attend a four-year college (27 versus 4 percent).[43] Because 95 percent of movers chose the first available placement, whether in the city or in the suburb, the greater success of suburban movers is unlikely to be related to self-selection. Indeed, researchers have lauded the Gautreaux findings as particularly reliable because the study involves a "natural experiment" of random placement.[44]

—In 1991, Jonathan Crane found that after controlling for family, the probability of dropping out and giving birth out of wedlock is closely related to the socioeconomic status of the neighborhood. The chances that black male teens would drop out increased from 8 percent in neighborhoods in which 75 percent of households were of low socioeconomic status to 35 percent in neighborhoods that were 97 percent low status.[45]

—In 1996, Nancy Gonzales and colleagues found that peer and neighborhood influences were powerful determinants of school performance for African American adolescents and indeed had a stronger effect than family influences.[46]

—In 1998, Jens Ludwig and colleagues studied the Moving to Opportunity program, comparing 358 Baltimore children between the ages of twelve and eighteen. They found that children randomly assigned to Section 8 housing in low-poverty neighborhoods showed "a sizeable and significant reduction in the percentage of boys arrested for violent and other crimes."[47]

The evidence on the effects of neighborhood environment is so commonplace that public policy advocates now almost uniformly recommend the deconcentration of public housing, and many advocate the literal demolition of existing high-rise public housing buildings. The 1974 Housing and Community Development Act, which introduced Section 8 housing vouchers, explicitly calls for the "spatial deconcentration of the poor." In the 1980s and 1990s, there was agreement across party lines that public housing policy should seek to avoid what one senator has called entire "zip codes of pathology."[48] Public housing projects, said Henry Cisneros, President William J. Clinton's first housing secretary, "have become traps for the poorest of the poor rather than a launching pad for families trying to improve their lives." In 1998, federal legislation with bipartisan support sought to restore the original idea behind low-income housing—to encourage a mixture of lower-middle-class and working-poor families in subsidized housing programs. Republican representative Rick Lazio argued that "the best environment to address poverty is a mixed-income environment, where poor people have role models and hope. If you do not have an environment that successfully addresses poverty, you are condemning an entire population to live in despair."[49]

Data from Racial Desegregation

The third set of data that bears on the question of whether economic school desegregation will improve the academic achievement and life chances of disadvantaged students concerns the effects of racial school desegregation. Race and class are not identical—sometimes racial integration does not involve socioeconomic integration—but an obvious overlap exists, and evidence from racial desegregation studies provides some indirect confirmation of studies involving economic school integration.

Most (though not all) relevant studies find that following racial desegregation, test scores of black students increased and the scores of whites did not decline.[50] For example, in 1977, Robert Crain and Rita Mahard found the number of studies with positive findings on black achievement outnumbered those finding negative results by a ratio of three to one (forty positive, twelve negative). Desegregation appears to have closed the gap between black and white test scores by one-fifth within the first two years, making it "the most effective tool for raising black achievement located by researchers." In a 1982 review of ninety-three studies, Crain and Mahard found that desegregation, when begun early, can result in a gain in black achievement equivalent to one grade level. In 1983, Mahard and Crain concluded that desegregation erases "nearly half the gap" between average IQ scores and those of blacks. Those studies that suggest mixed outcomes, Amy Stuart Wells points out, often looked at achievement results following a single year of desegregation—such a short period of time that results are unlikely to be evident.[51] A 1990 study of Dallas schools finds that between 1980 and 1989, following integration, the achievement gap between black and white students narrowed from 35 percentage points to 16, and an exhaustive review conducted by Janet Schofield for the state of Connecticut published in 1995 found positive effects on reading (but not on math) and on college attendance. Writing in 1997, Wells and Crain conclude that "there is mounting evidence that African Americans who attend desegregated schools are more likely to achieve at higher rates and have higher aspirations than those in segregated schools [and] are more likely to go on to college and secure high-status jobs."[52]

In addition to individual studies of student performance in particular cities before and after desegregation, the national trends provide strong circumstantial evidence that desegregation has positively influenced black scores. The desegregation of American public schools between 1970 and 1990 coincided with an "extraordinary" rise in black test scores, including a 50 percent reduction in the gap between the reading scores of black and white seventeen-year-olds. Desegregation also coincided with a dramatic rise in black high school graduation rates, from 55 percent in 1970 to 83 percent in 1986.[53] Moreover, researchers note, the largest gains occurred in the South and in rural areas, where the greatest extent of desegregation took place. Finally, researchers also note that the recent reversal in desegregation trends in the early 1990s has been accompanied by a reversal in black test scores; black test scores have declined precisely as resegregation has occurred.[54] (By contrast, there has been no comparable decline in Title I funding to link to the recent reversal in black scores.) In 1996, Debora Sullivan and Robert Crain found that the gap between black and white fourth-grade reading scores was narrowest in the states where blacks were least isolated from whites (West Virginia and Iowa) and the largest in states where blacks were most racially isolated (New York and Michigan).[55]

Metropolitan Gains Tie Race to Socioeconomic Status

The indirect support these racial desegregation findings provide for economic desegregation is strengthened by the fact that greater achievement gains were found when racial integration went beyond city boundaries to involve entire metropolitan areas.[56] Strong achievement gains were found in metropolitan desegregation efforts in Wilmington, Delaware; Hartford, Connecticut; Charlotte-Mecklenburg, North Carolina; St. Louis, Missouri; Louisville, Kentucky; and Nashville, Tennessee. As Crain and Mahard note, metropolitan plans are presumably more successful because they involve white suburban students of higher socioeconomic status.[57] Researchers have found that when looking at achievement, "significant benefits of school desegregation arise only when socioeconomic, as well as racial, integration occurs." In addition, the connections made by black students are particularly helpful in integrated schools in which the white students are better off.[58]

Indeed, for many years sociologists have concluded, almost unanimously, that the reason racial desegregation improves the academic achievement of blacks derives not from the whiteness of classmates but rather from their economic status. Coleman's 1966 study, for example, finds that the "beneficial effect of a student body with a high proportion of white students comes not from racial composition per se but from the better educational background and higher educational aspirations that are, on the average, found among whites." Accordingly, Coleman notes, poor blacks or whites would benefit from attending a middle-class black school, but poor blacks would not benefit academically from attending schools with poor whites.[59] Coleman's study, conceived in the spirit of the 1964 Civil Rights Act's concern for racial equality, concludes that social class matters more than racial composition.[60]

Numerous studies conducted before and after Coleman's report have reached a similar conclusion: from an achievement standpoint, the social class of a student's classmates matters more than their race.[61] Even Gary Orfield, a leading proponent of racial desegregation, notes that "educational research suggests that the basic damage inflicted by segregated education comes not from racial concentration but from the concentration of children from poor families." Classmate behaviors, from cutting class to watching television to dropping out, are all more closely correlated with class than with race.[62]

Studies have also found that racial desegregation is far more effective than compensatory spending in raising student achievement, after controlling for family social class. Controlled studies in St. Louis, San Francisco, and Norfolk, Virginia, conducted in the 1990s all find that an integration strategy yielded much greater academic gain for similarly situated students than compensatory programs in racially and economically segregated schools. In the San Francisco study, researchers tracked three groups:

black children in high-poverty schools receiving "large infusions of new money," black children in high-poverty schools with new faculty and educational programs, and black children in integrated schools. "The most significant gains were made by children who went to desegregated schools," Peter Edelman notes, "even though those schools did not receive any additional resources." Edelman, who observes that the integration effect "seems to have occurred not for reasons of race but of class," concludes that "the policy implications of these results are momentous."[63]

The state of Missouri vividly demonstrates the advantages of integration over compensatory spending. In St. Louis, an interdistrict integration plan allowing twelve thousand inner-city black children to attend suburban schools has produced tangible improvements in life chances, according to researchers. In Kansas City, by contrast, a court order to spend twice as much for each pupil than surrounding suburban districts produced few results. Spending on reduced class size, full-day kindergarten, expanded summer school, after-school programs, effective schooling techniques, and increased teacher salaries yielded only "modest incremental improvements" in test scores, according to the court-appointed monitor.[64]

Even strong advocates of equal spending acknowledge that classmates matter more than spending. Jonathan Kozol, who has spent a lifetime writing about spending inequities, asserts that "money is not the only issue that determines inequality. A more important factor, I am convinced, is the makeup of the student enrollment, who is sitting next to you in class. When virtually every child in the class is poor, a mood of desperation develops, a sense of hopelessness. . . . When poor kids share the class with rich children and upper-middle-class kids, kids who grow up with infinite dreams, those dreams become contagious and every child benefits." Similarly, Vanderbilt University's James Guthrie, who has written extensively about ways to equalize spending, insists that "if there is one thing that is more related to a child's academic achievement than coming from a poor household, it is going to school with children from other poor households."[65]

Net Increase in Achievement

If high poverty concentrations are not conducive to learning, might not economic integration simply serve to increase the number of pathological environments, hurting middle-class children and resulting in a net decline in achievement? Are current concentrations of poverty and wealth educationally optimal?

Critics worry that, with integration, problems of violence, drugs, and low achievement, now confined to a limited number of schools, will spread to other schools, bringing down the children who now have a chance to succeed in predominantly middle-class schools. If part of the theory of economic integration is that the positive influence of middle-class children will rub off on the poor, is it not reasonable to suspect also that the negative influence of some of the poor children will rub off on those from the middle class? Others argue it is one thing to support the old one-room schoolhouse with the laborer and factory owner's children sitting side by side, but something quite different to try to integrate the underclass.[66]

These concerns cannot simply be written off as racist: whereas some white parents opposed racial integration because they incorrectly equated black skin with crime, drugs, and low achievement, it might be considered more rational to oppose economic integration on the ground that low-income students of all races are statistically more likely to cause trouble, exhibit antisocial behavior, and learn slowly, thus siphoning off teacher attention to the rest of the class. Given the wider range of school readiness in an economically mixed school, might it not be harder for teachers to teach than in a more homogeneous environment? Might not the lower-ability middle-class children who now benefit from exposure to high-ability middle-class children be brought down by poor low-ability children?[67]

If the contention were true, if socioeconomic integration were to meaningfully reduce the achievement of middle-class children, it would drive a stake in the heart of the effort, both practically and, for some, philosophically. As a practical matter, if integration affirmatively hurts middle-class children, parents will resist it or flee the public schools. No parents want to sacrifice their children as part of a risky social experiment. As a philosophical matter, there is a Kantian concern about using middle-class students as martyrs to the cause of other children, when doing so would hurt their own chances of success.[68]

Fortunately, a wealth of data suggest that middle-class children are not, in fact, hurt by the presence of disadvantaged classmates, even as disadvantaged classmates benefit from such an environment, so long as the schools remain predominantly middle class and so long as some ability grouping is employed. Several sources of data bear on this question.

Fundamentally, we know that as a result of racial integration, test scores of black students increased and white scores did not decline.[69] Although much of the research on desegregation is hotly contested, this is one fact that even opponents of busing concede is well established. According to

Crain and Mahard, "Virtually every writer on the subject has agreed that white test performance is unaffected by desegregation. We think it is safe to assume that this issue is settled." David Armor, a fierce busing opponent, wrote in 1995 that "virtually all studies of desegregation and achievement have found little or no change in achievement or other educational outcomes for white students."[70]

This seems too good to be true. How is it possible that the poor benefit from integration and the middle class are not hurt? There are three basic reasons: the majority culture of a school holds disproportionate influence; the poor are more sensitive to school environment, and the advantaged disproportionately influence it; and sensitive ability grouping allows the quick to progress but also exposes the poor to the middle class.

Numbers and Nonlinearity

Most research finds that the effects of classmate poverty are nonlinear: there appears to be a "tipping point," a "threshold" or "critical level" at which the cumulative impact of classmate poverty becomes much worse.[71] Writing about neighborhood poverty, Crane finds that in bad neighborhoods, "the whole was greater than the sum of the parts": change in neighborhood status at the bottom had fifty times the effect on black dropout rates as changes in neighborhood status in the middle. Hogan and Kitagawa similarly find no effect on teen pregnancy of living in a high- versus middle-status neighborhood but a significant negative effect in moving from a middle- to a low-status neighborhood. Crane concludes that "the nonlinear pattern of the model's results implies that desegregation [by class] would have large net benefits. It would greatly reduce dropping out and childbearing among teenagers from the worst neighborhoods yet would increase these problems among those from other communities very little."[72]

Researchers find that schools tend to establish cultures and that the successful schools are those in which a majority of the students are middle class. In terms of academic achievement, a number of researchers have put the dividing line at 50 percent black or low income.[73] Some place the critical point slightly lower. On the other hand, some recent studies define the threshold as the point at which 75 percent of households are eligible for the free and reduced-price meals (FARM) program (that is, 25 percent middle class).[74]

Most researchers, however, have converged around the 50 percent mark. A study conducted by the U.S. Department of Education of twenty thousand eighth-grade students found that 50 percent FARM-eligible presents a clear threshold. This study finds that test scores gradually decline as one moves from schools with fewer low-income children to those with more—as one would expect, given the aggregation of individual at-risk students. A separate school-related effect appears to kick in at the 50 percent low-income rate, as well. The authors find that "while there was a steady decrease in average test score as the school [low-income] level increased, the greatest decrements are found as one moves into the two most poor categories. Students in these schools—those with 51–75 percent and 76–100 percent of their students eligible for free or reduced-price lunch—have substantially lower scores than their counterparts in other schools on all four subject area tests."[75] Similarly, David Rusk, in his study of 186 Texas school districts in the 1995–96 school year, finds that middle-class students do fine in schools in which a majority of students are from middle-class households. Rusk notes that low-income students can be a drag on middle-class achievement "but only, it appears, when [they] begin to form a majority of the school population." Because numbers matter, integration of underclass children should be feasible, because they represent an estimated 5 percent of the poor—or about 1 percent of the American population.[76]

The notion that low-income students benefit from attendance at majority-middle-class schools while middle-class students are not hurt may be difficult for some people to accept. Many may assume that if poor children are disruptive, spreading them between schools will simply more evenly distribute the troublemakers. However, as Malcolm Gladwell points out in his book, *The Tipping Point*, much of human behavior is contagious, even acts that would not ordinarily be thought of as such, like criminal activity or suicide. In addition, change is often nonlinear—as when rain suddenly turns to snow—so we should "abandon this expectation about proportionality." Taken together, these two ideas mean that an individual child, placed in a high-poverty school environment, may misbehave and show little concern for achievement, but if put instead in an environment in which there is a "critical mass" of students who value achievement, he or she may well act quite differently.[77] In this way, socioeconomic integration does not merely spread more evenly those students who are bad influences; it reduces their overall numbers.

Differential Sensitivity and Influence

It is also important to note that poor children appear to be more heavily influenced by their school environment than children from wealthy or middle-class households. This "differential sensitivity" to school environment, one of the central findings of the 1966 Coleman Report, has been dubbed "Coleman's Law." Coleman finds that blacks are twice as affected by school social environment as whites and that integration is "asymmetric in its effects," having "its greatest effect on those from educationally deficient backgrounds."[78] The reason, Coleman explains, is straightforward: for those with strong family backgrounds, aspirations and achievement are more firmly rooted; those with weaker family backgrounds, who spend less time under adult supervision, are more open to the influence of peers—a finding consistently reached by researchers.[79] This conclusion comports with findings that the disadvantage of growing up in a single-parent household is twofold: in addition to the effect of reduced income, there is an independent effect having to do with reduced parental attention. (Today, poverty is a particularly good marker for single parenthood: in 1960, 24 percent of poor families were headed by unwed mothers; by 1993, that figure had risen to 53 percent.)[80]

The disproportionate effect of school environment on the poor also derives from the "larger reservoirs of undeveloped talent" of disadvantaged children, in Alan Wilson's words. Middle-class children learn a great deal at home, Jencks and Mayer note, whereas "poor children must learn such skills at school if they are to learn them at all." For example, one of the benefits to poor students from integration is that they are able to pick up tips on how to apply to college. Orfield has found, in a study of five thousand students in Indiana, that "kids whose parents aren't educated have no idea how to negotiate high school and get ready for college and if they don't get that from their school and from the peer group that's in their school, they're just not going to get it."[81] Obviously, middle-class children who are educated with poorer peers will not be "pulled down" in the sense of losing knowledge about how to apply to college.

Subsequent studies have almost universally confirmed Coleman's findings regarding relative sensitivity.[82] The flip side of this is that advantaged children are often looked to as leaders and have disproportionate influence, according to numerous studies.[83]

In addition, the sensible use of ability grouping and discipline policies can guarantee that the benefits of economic integration to poor children will not occur at the expense of middle-class students. A new influx of poor children into a middle-class school will mean, on average, an increase in the number of slower students, though the change in ability range will not be enormous, given that 80 percent of the variance in achievement is already within schools rather than between them.[84] Fair ability grouping and discipline policies should allow the top students to progress at their own speed while exposing poor children to middle-class values and habits and should also provide a safe and productive environment for all students (see chapter 6).

Setting aside the issue of achievement, will middle-class children be physically endangered by socioeconomic integration? Here it is important to distinguish between general disruption (which is a serious problem) and actual violence, which is exceedingly rare. Students are generally safer in classrooms than walking down the street; indeed, more than 99 percent of children murdered in 1992–93 were killed outside of school. The chance of suffering a school-associated violent death in 1998 was less than one in a million, according to the Departments of Justice and Education. In 1997, twice as many people were killed by lightning as were killed in American schools.[85] Serious violent crimes committed by children between the ages of eleven and nineteen are almost three times as likely to occur away from school as at school or going to or from school. Although stories about schools with metal detectors abound, a 1996–97 Department of Education survey found that only 1 percent of schools routinely use them.[86]

It is also important to recall the power of tipping points. Integrating disadvantaged children into predominantly middle-class schools does not just evenly distribute difficult students, it also reduces bad behavior overall. For one thing, breaking up concentrations of disorder is likely to make the problem more manageable for individual principals and teachers to handle because isolated incidents do not present the overwhelming challenge of daily disorder. Gangs are less likely to form, and students are less likely to carry weapons for "self-protection," when concentrations of poverty are broken up.[87] For another, several studies document a peer effect on crime and on student misbehavior and suggest that delinquency rises disproportionately when poverty is concentrated.[88]

Community Benefits

In addition to improving the educational achievement of the poor, school integration by class (as well as by race) has important social benefits. There is, after all, much more to education than boosting test scores. John Dewey believed, as Thomas Geoghegan notes, that "the purpose of education wasn't to skill kids up for the New World Economy [or] to get ahead of the other kids, but for all the kids to act together . . . to teach kids to live in a democracy." If achievement is the exclusive benchmark, Leon Botstein notes, then the Nazi officer who rounded up children to be exterminated and then "sat down to play Mozart, Beethoven, and Chopin beautifully" must be considered a "success."[89] Apart from achievement effects, socioeconomic integration, and the racial integration it entails, is likely to produce a more cohesive and humane society, one in which people are less likely to view one another as "others"—with the added benefit of taking the direct focus off race per se.

Given the strong overlap between race and class generally in the United States—and particularly between race and concentrated poverty—economic integration is likely to bring about a good deal of racial integration, as well. Indeed, if the Supreme Court applies its reasoning in affirmative action cases to school desegregation and declares voluntary integration efforts by race unconstitutional, socioeconomic status may become the best means of achieving racial integration.[90]

In 1999, 33 percent of African Americans, 30 percent of Hispanics, and 14 percent of whites under the age of eighteen were poor. Furthermore, poor blacks are much more likely to live in concentrated poverty than poor whites, in large part owing to housing discrimination. In 1990, in 320 metropolitan areas, three-quarters of poor blacks and two-thirds of poor Hispanics, but only one-quarter of poor whites, lived in census tracts with poverty levels higher than 20 percent. One in three poor blacks, but only one in twenty poor whites, lived in extremely poor neighborhoods (40 percent or more living in poverty). Of poor and nonpoor Americans, 1.4 percent of whites, 10.5 percent of Hispanics, and 17.7 percent of blacks lived in districts with poverty levels of 40 percent or higher.[91]

Accordingly, heavily minority schools are much more likely to be high-poverty schools than heavily white schools. Only one in twenty predominantly white schools is poverty concentrated compared with more than 80 percent of predominantly black and Latino schools. Schools that are 90–100 percent black and Hispanic are fourteen times more likely to be majority poor than schools that are 90 percent or more white. Students of color are much more likely to attend high-poverty schools: in 1988, 39.5 percent of Native Americans, 38.5 percent of Hispanics, 36.1 percent of blacks, 14.9 percent of Asians, and 6.9 percent of whites attended schools in which more than 50 percent of the population were eligible for free or reduced-price lunch.[92]

There is a good deal of evidence that integrated schools can succeed in promoting democratic values and national unity. In 1974, Justice Thur-

Educational vs. Social Engineering

It is worth emphasizing that the social as opposed to educational achievement benefits of socioeconomic integration are not the central rationale for the policy. The primary argument for economic integration is that there is an individual right to enjoy equal educational opportunity to improve student achievement, and the argument that communities will benefit from integration (whether or not educational achievement and life chances of the poor improve) is secondary. Standing alone, the argument from social benefits is more vulnerable to the attack of social engineering and to the charge of unfairness to individual students.

The social engineering attack says school reform should be focused not on creating a utopian society but rather on educating children and raising their achievement. Busing schoolchildren to accomplish racial integration can and has been attacked for "using children to achieve social reforms that adults to date have been unwilling to accomplish" and for treating children as "pawns on a chessboard." Critics of racial busing continually employed this dichotomy—between adult goals and the educational achievement of children—to great effect. Stokely Carmichael and Charles Hamilton, for example, have argued that "the real need at the present is not integration but quality education."[1] The

1. Carl F. Hansen, *Danger in Washington: The Story of My Twenty Years in the Public Schools in the Nation's Capital* (West Nyack, N.Y.: Parker Publishing, 1968), p. 105 ("using children"); Robert Coles, "The Desegregation of Southern Schools," in Hubert H. Humphrey, ed., *Integration vs. Segregation* (New York:

good Marshall declared, "Unless our children begin to learn together, then there is little hope that our people will ever learn to live together." Studies dating back many years confirm that students who attend racially integrated schools are more likely to have interracial friendships as adults.[93] In the 1970s and 1980s, ten separate studies unanimously found that black students attending integrated schools were also more likely to attend integregated colleges, live in integrated neighborhoods as adults, and send their children to integrated schools.[94] In the 1990s, new studies continued to find that interracial contact has benefits for both blacks and whites. Studies find black and white children who attend desegregated schools are related fairness critique asks why an individual child's right to get a good education should be trumped by the larger societal goal of promoting integration.

Socioeconomic integration directly answers both the social engineering and fairness critiques. The primary rationale for integration of schools is that it is essential to raising educational achievement; the individual child's education is first and foremost in importance, and the key argument is made directly on conservative turf. By extension, the reason it is fair to integrate students is that a middle-class child's desire to attend a particular school for the quality of the education provided there is not pitted against the abstract societal good of integration but rather against another child's equally worthy desire to attend the same school. The central rationale for economic integration is tied to equal opportunity rather than to diversity, to justice rather than to social utility. In the words of an attorney in Wake County, North Carolina, which adopted an income integration program in 2000, economic integration of public schools is "educational engineering," not social engineering.[2]

Thomas Crowell, 1964), p. 208 (citing James Kilpatrick, "pawns"). Steve Farkas and Jean Johnson, *Time to Move On: African-American and White Parents Set an Agenda for Public Schools—A Report from Public Agenda* (New York: Public Agenda, 1998), p. 10. Stokely Carmichael and Charles V. Hamilton, *Black Power* (Random House, 1967), p. 157.

2. Ann Majestic, quoted in Ben Wildavsky, "A Question of Black and White: Wrestling with Ways to Maintain Diversity," *U.S. News and World Report*, April 10, 2000, pp. 26–27.

"less likely to express negative views about members of the other race" and that black graduates of desegregated schools are "less likely than graduates of segregated schools to believe that antiblack discrimination is widespread." We know that the limited integration society has achieved has resulted in rising intermarriage rates.[95]

Moreover, socioeconomic integration is uniquely positioned to promote unity because it is capable of achieving a good measure of racial integration without the balkanizing effect that the use of race itself can entail. In recent years, race-conscious policies have sometimes promoted an insidious racialism on both the left and the right.

On the left, an abiding focus on race has replaced class, and many intellectuals have come to view the white working class not as people deserving of greater opportunity but as bigots who are no longer part of a progressive coalition. On the right, too many conservatives equate poor with black, not realizing, as the late Bayard Rustin has noted, that many of the pathologies associated with the ghetto are really matters of class, which afflict the white poor as well. Television, too, presents poverty with a black face 65 percent of the time, even though only 29 percent of American poor people are black.[96] Both sides have conspired to use race as a proxy for class, which robs poor whites of the solicitude they deserve from our public policies and stereotypes middle-class blacks as subscribing to a set of attitudes and behaviors more closely associated with poverty.

| 4

The Significance of the Socioeconomic

Makeup of Schools

The adults have created this system.

WHY IS IT SO MUCH more difficult to educate children in high-poverty schools, and how does socioeconomic integration remedy these problems? What makes a school good or bad is not so much the physical plant and facilities as the people involved in it—the students, the parents, and the teachers. The portrait of the nation's high-poverty schools is not just a racist or classist stereotype: high-poverty schools are marked by students who have less motivation and are often subject to negative peer influences; parents who are generally less active, exert less clout in school affairs, and garner fewer financial resources for the school; and teachers who tend to be less qualified, to have lower expectations, and to teach a watered-down curriculum. Giving all students access to schools with a core of middle-class students and parents will significantly raise the overall quality of schooling in America.

The Influence of Fellow Students

At the center of any school are the students, and students' life chances are influenced by their classmates in two major ways. First, students learn from one another, as well as from their teachers; thus, the presence of motivated and high-achieving classmates contributes to, while the presence of unmotivated and low-achieving classmates detracts from, an individual student's likelihood of success. Second, even if individual students are not themselves influenced by peers, the behavior of fellow students—such as cooperation or disruption in the classroom—can create an environment that is either conducive or hostile to learning and success, both in school and in life.

Peer Influences

Classmates provide students with what the psychiatrist Charles Pinder-hughes calls "a hidden curriculum." He explains, "What the pupils are learning from one another is probably just as important as what they are learning from the teachers." Coleman went further, suggesting that "a child's learning is a function more of the characteristics of his classmates than those of the teacher." Because fellow students outnumber the teacher often by twenty-five or thirty to one, this finding is not entirely surprising, especially given the fact that an individual student stays with fellow students year after year, whereas a particular teacher normally has only two semesters in which to make an impact on any student. In addition, students care more about the impressions of their peers than those of their teachers. Coleman found in a study of ten schools that students were fourteen times as likely to say it was harder to accept disapproval from peers (43 percent) than from teachers (3 percent).[1]

Numerous academic studies have established the power of peer influence, which is particularly strong among school students, who are still finding their way in the world. Laurence Steinberg's study of twenty thousand students over three years finds that although family is the central influence over early-elementary schoolchildren, "for a large number of adolescents, peers—not parents—are the chief determinants of how intensely they are invested in school and how much effort they devote to education." This is increasingly true as the strength of the American family has declined.[2]

The Boston College psychologist Peter Gray asks, "Whom do [children] want to please? Are they wearing the kind of clothing that other kids are wearing or the kind that their parents are wearing? . . . from an evolutionary perspective, whom should they be paying attention to? Their parents—the members of the previous generation—or their peers, who will be their future mates and future collaborators?" Others observe that upper-class British children, largely cut off from their parents, raised by nannies, and sent early to boarding schools, end up more like their parents than their nannies or teachers primarily through the influence of affluent peers, not parents; and that although parents are likely to pass down cooking habits (because children do not learn to cook in the presence of peers), many other activities—such as studying and engaging in delinquency—are highly influenced by peers, in whose presence these activities do take place. (Teenage smoking, for example, is predicted more accurately by whether a teenager's friends smoke than by whether his or her parents smoke.)[3]

Setting aside values and motivation for the moment, we know that students teach academic content to one another. Because students study together and learn from one another, any given student is likely to learn more when his or her fellow students have a greater mastery of knowledge and information. It is important to acknowledge, therefore, that on the whole, students from middle-class homes achieve at higher levels than students from poor homes, so on average, students attending middle-class schools benefit.

The tie between social class and achievement has been found in society after society and between rich and poor societies throughout time. The 1966 Coleman report exhaustively established that in the United States, social class is the single most important determinant of academic achievement.[4] These lower levels of achievement among disadvantaged students are not surprising given the tremendous obstacles they face—including inadequate nutrition, medical care, and housing.[5] In addition, studies find that poor children are exposed to about one-third as much language as children of professionals, receive about one-fiftieth the amount of one-on-one reading as middle-class children, and are half as likely to be taken to museums and one-third as likely to visit the library. During summer vacations, middle-class children continue to make educational gains while many lower-income children virtually cease to learn.[6] So deprived are many children from poor homes that watching television—which depresses achievement of middle-class children—has been found to sometimes raise achievement for some poor children because even the worst TV is more enriching than their home environments.[7]

A fourth-grade child of any background who attends an urban school is likely to be surrounded by peers who "can't read [or] understand a simple children's book," according to a 1998 *Education Week* analysis. In high-poverty urban schools, "two-thirds or more of students perform below the basic level on national tests." A 1993 study of Title I found that students in low-poverty schools score, on average, 50–75 percent higher in reading and math than students in high-poverty schools. Overall, students in high-poverty schools are four times as likely as peers in low-poverty schools to fall into the bottom quartile of achievement (47.5 versus 11.9 percent).[8] In math, students are seven times as likely to score in the top quartile in low-poverty as high-poverty schools (35 versus 5 percent).[9]

Significantly, for our purposes, the achievement level of classmates appears to influence the achievement of a given student, in part because high-achieving classmates can help teach fellow students content.[10] One three-year study of Philadelphia students, for example, found that "in elementary schools, students who test at grade level or lower are distinctly helped by being in a school with more high-achieving students"—a finding confirmed by other studies.[11] Students with low-achieving classmates may figure out an answer to a particular exercise from the textbook or the teacher; but students in the high-achieving environment have a third source of correct answers—their peers. Poor children in integrated schools can tap into other knowledge that middle-class children take for granted: knowledge gained from visits to the library, to the museum, or from travel. (Similarly, classmate achievement influences any given student's achievement because it influences the teacher's expectations for the class and the pace of instruction.)

One informal way in which a classmate's achievement rubs off is through the development of vocabulary. Although the media have paid most attention to the question of Ebonics and the difference between "black English" and "standard English," there is a deeper and more long-standing gap between the language and vocabulary skills of the haves and the have-nots. "The differences in language and number competence between lower- and middle-class children are significant by the time the child is four years old," notes Jerome Kagan, "and are awesome by the time he enters the first grade." On the whole, poor children come to school with about half the vocabulary of middle-class children of the same age.[12]

Students' vocabularies are influenced by those of their classmates. James Coleman has observed that "going to school with other children whose vocabulary is larger than one's own demands and creates a larger vocabulary." By analogy, an English-speaking child "will learn French more quickly in a classroom of French children than from the best French teacher." Why, asks Malcolm Gladwell, "do the children of recent immigrants almost never retain the accents of their parents? How is it that the children of deaf parents manage to learn how to speak as well as children whose parents speak to them from the day they were born? The answer has always been that language is a skill acquired laterally—that what children pick up from other children is at least as important as what they pick up at home."[13]

Vocabulary has always been important to intellectual development, because language is essential to the conceptualization of new ideas. Today, however, language skill has an added, more pressing practical significance. Whereas language differences were of little concern to employers in the industrial economy, in the growing service economy workers relate directly with customers and clients, and businesses are therefore more concerned about vocabulary and language skills.[14]

Peer influence also affects students' motivation to learn. A student attending a middle-class school is more likely to be exposed to highly motivated peers than one attending a high-poverty school. Student motivation can be measured by looking directly at student attitudes (concerning academic performance and educational and occupational aspirations) and at student behavior (class attendance and completion of homework assignments).

A variety of studies have found that middle-class children on the whole place greater value on working hard and doing well academically than low-income children. According to polls of school officials, students in advantaged schools are more likely to place a priority on learning (64 versus 49 percent), and teachers in advantaged schools are much less likely to have difficulty motivating students to learn (50 percent, versus 23 percent who report no such difficulty) than in disadvantaged schools. A 1999 Urban Institute report found that among nearly forty-five thousand Americans surveyed in 1997, children in advantaged families were more engaged in their schoolwork than children in disadvantaged families. In a study of the Gautreaux project, in which low-income African American families were given access to subsidized housing in Chicago suburbs, mothers said that their children's new suburban peers were more than twice as likely to be "good influences" as their former inner-city peers (69.3 versus 27.4 percent).[15]

Ethnographic studies have long documented a distressing tendency among some low-income black students to denigrate academic success, hard work, standard English, routine jobs, being on time, and within-wedlock birth as "acting white" and to develop an "'oppositional culture' that inverts the values of middle-class society."[16] In 1997, Jay Osborne, a professor at the State University of New York at Buffalo, reported that the self-esteem of black boys depended less and less on academic achievement as they moved on from eighth grade until, in twelfth grade, there is no discernible link at all. One black teacher in the Bronx told columnist Bob Herbert that she has "male students who would rather be paraded in handcuffs before television cameras than be caught reading a book."[17]

Significantly, Philip Cook and Jens Ludwig, looking at national data, have found that the issue of "acting white" has more to do with class than race. Controlling for class, they find that blacks do not cut classes, miss school, or complete fewer homework assignments than whites; rather, poor people of all races are more likely to cut classes, miss school, and do less homework.[18] This finding is consistent with a tendency sociologists have long documented among members of lower social classes: a devaluation of education and a "resistance" toward middle-class achievement norms.[19] In Corpus Christi, Texas, for example, a researcher found that white working-class students, known as "Kickers," and working-class Mexican American students shared similar attitudes toward education—"Both Kickers and Chicanos make the statement: We have no need to conform to the norms of middle-class Anglo society"—and show little aspiration for college or professional occupations. A 1996 study found that across racial lines, schoolchildren living in poverty exhibited "maladaptive motivational orientations toward scholastic tasks." Paul Willis's study of working-class youth in England finds the prevalence of a culture that discourages achievement.[20]

In many affluent high schools, those who excel academically are held up to the larger community as models; but in some low-income schools, academic achievement is widely denigrated. The *Wall Street Journal* reporter Ron Suskind provides a particularly poignant portrait of the negative pressure faced by a studious black teenager, Cedric Jennings, who attended a high-poverty high school in Washington, D.C. In the opening scene of Suskind's book, *A Hope in the Unseen*, Jennings is avoiding the awards assembly because he does not wish to be subjected to a barrage of taunts: "'Nerd!' 'Geek!' 'Egghead!' And the harshest, 'Whitey.'" Jennings recalls having attended an earlier ceremony, at which he received a hundred-dollar check for high grades, only to be confronted by a menacing classmate with a gun.[21]

Disadvantaged students do not, of course, have a monopoly on norms that denigrate academic achievement. American culture worships athletes and movie stars, not scholars. However, the data clearly show that high-poverty schools are more likely to breed a culture of anti-achievement and that an anti-achievement culture is not at all monolithic across schools.[22] Some studies find that many students pressure their peers against the use of drugs, others that peers generally "encouraged achievement." In fact,

Signithia Fordham and John Ogbu found that when the inner-city youth who had been chastised for "acting white" were placed in an environment of high achievers, peer derision for achievement disappeared. Among students whose friends are likely to continue education after high school, for example, a higher percentage have a positive attitude toward grades than among those whose friends are unlikely to continue after high school.[23]

Why are poor children more likely to cast aspersions on achievement? On the whole, poor parents are less likely to communicate the importance of education to their children. A study of sixteen hundred Canadian high school students found that parents with high socioeconomic status were twice as likely as parents with low socioeconomic status to take an interest in their children's education, more likely to encourage their children to do their homework, less willing to accept below-average performance, and less likely to say education is not very important. In some circles, rising beyond one's origins can be seen as rejection of the group, even traitorous, studies find.[24]

Conservatives, such as the late Edward Banfield, tend to see the devaluation of education among the poor as rooted in personal failings: an inability to be appropriately future oriented and a failure to defer gratification. Liberals argue, by contrast, that for poor people, particularly minorities, the very real obstacles of deprivation and discrimination result in a sense of hopelessness that renders education of little value. Liberals also note that the shorter time horizon is natural in a life that is unpredictable, one in which food and shelter cannot be taken for granted. More than thirty years ago, the British Plowden commission noted that in low-income and working-class neighborhoods "the jobs people do and the status they hold owe little to their education [and thus] it is natural for children as they grow older to regard school as a brief prelude to work rather than an avenue to future opportunities." Whatever the causes, the tendency of the poor to emphasize short-run goals and to devalue education and hard work means that high-poverty schools will, on the whole, devalue those traits.[25] Whether caused by a poverty of values (according to conservatives), a poverty of income (in the liberal view), or some combination of the two, the correlation exists: attending a high-poverty school is detrimental to students' life chances.

By contrast, part of the greater motivation to achieve in middle-class schools may derive from the higher initial levels of achievement students bring with them to school. Coleman found that valuing academic achievement is contagious: if a certain number of students come from high-achieving homes, competition will naturally ensue; and the fact that some competition exists makes it harder to succeed, which only makes the prize of academic achievement all the more valuable.[26]

Just as studies consistently find that poor children place less value on academic achievement, so many studies find that the poor have lower educational and occupational aspirations than middle-class students. As demonstrated in chapter 3, student attainment rises in wealthier schools, in part because students in these schools have higher educational and occupational aspirations—which rub off on other students. An array of studies going back forty years has found that low-income children have lower educational and occupational aspirations, even when controlling for intelligence. That is to say, high-achieving poor students have lower aspirations than high-achieving upper-middle-class students. The daily life of students growing up in poverty does not often include lofty dreams. The journalist Alex Kotlowitz tells the story of two young boys growing up in a Chicago housing project. Surviving into adulthood is not a given for these boys; the two "knew more funerals than weddings." LaFayette, a ten-year-old, tells Kotlowitz, "If I grow up, I'd like to be a bus driver." "If," Kotlowitz notes, "not when."[27]

In low-income schools, students ask one another, "Are you going to college?"; in wealthier schools, the question is, "What college are you going to?" A 1997 congressionally authorized study of Title I found that parents in high-poverty schools were much less likely to expect their children to graduate from college than parents in low-poverty schools (52 versus 74 percent).[28]

In some high-poverty schools, the dropout rate—which nationally has plummeted—may still exceed two-thirds. One study found that in 1992 the dropout rate for the lowest 20 percent by family income is more than twelve times the rate for the highest 20 percent by income (25 versus 2 percent). Few students graduating from high-poverty high schools are likely to be going on to college: just 15 percent of inner-city graduates do. Nationally, among high school graduates in 1996, 78 percent of high-income students, but only 49 percent of their low-income cohort, enrolled in college the following fall. Studies have found that although low-socioeconomic-status students desire to do better economically than their parents, their absolute level of aspirations tends to be lower than those of high-status students because the baseline is low. The view of what level of education is required "to get along well in the world" varies depending on parental socioeconomic status.[29]

Significantly, for our purposes, the effect of peer aspirations has independent effects on a given student's aspirations. James Coleman explains that "particular individuals who might never consider dropping out if they were in a different high school might decide to drop out if they attended a school where many boys and girls did so." As far back as 1959, Alan Wilson found that 59 percent of the sons of manual workers in predominantly white-collar schools aspired to college compared with 33 percent of manual workers' sons in predominantly blue-collar schools. In measuring occupational aspirations, Wilson found that the effect of school composition was even greater than the effect of family: boys from white-collar homes attending blue-collar schools were less likely to aspire to professional occupations than boys from blue-collar homes attending white-collar schools (35 versus 44 percent).[30] Dozens of subsequent studies in more recent years have generally confirmed that, controlling for family background and academic record, attending a high-socioeconomic-status school raises educational aspirations—and attainment.[31]

There is also evidence that in high-poverty schools, students are less likely to attend class and complete homework—behaviors that speak volumes about their peers' motivation. The evidence on cutting classes is stark. In 1988, eighth-grade students from low-socioeconomic-status families were twice as likely to cut classes as those from high-socioeconomic-status families. Seventh-graders in high-poverty schools are four times as likely to have been excessively tardy as students in low-poverty schools. Teachers in high-poverty schools are more likely to say that student absenteeism is a moderate or serious problem than teachers in low-poverty schools. At Cedric Jennings's high school, student attendance in classes varied by the weather; on sunny days, classrooms were often half empty.[32]

Similarly, some, though not all, studies find that students in high-poverty schools spend less time on homework. In 1990, tenth-graders in high-poverty schools averaged 6.5 hours of homework a week compared with almost 8 hours a week in low-poverty schools. This statistic is consistent with findings that, on the whole, those ethnic groups with lower average socioeconomic status do less homework each week than ethnic groups with higher socioeconomic statuses. At his Washington, D.C., high school, Jennings was often the only student to complete his homework; and teachers lavishly praised him for doing merely what was assigned. As a result, class time was often spent doing "the previous day's homework."[33]

Part of the reason low-income children spend less time on homework may be that they are busy watching television instead. A 1993 congression-

Is Peer Influence Overblown?

The discussion of the importance of fellow students and peer influence raises two other questions that need to be addressed. First, might not values, norms, and achievement influence the choice of peers, rather than the other way around? That is, might the direction of causation be reversed so that high-achieving students choose peers like themselves rather than being influenced by their peers in a meaningful sense? Second, does the discussion of peer influence let students off the hook too easily? Dropping out of high school or joining a gang or engaging in sex or drug use are acts of independent will for which individual students—not "peer pressure"—are ultimately responsible. Can't kids "just say no"?

With respect to the first objection, researchers have tried to control for the causal direction by conducting longitudinal studies that follow a student's values over time, and these studies continue to find a strong peer influence.[1] Controlling for initial ability, Joyce Epstein finds that "high-scoring friends positively influence affective and academic outcomes." Students with initially low scores who chose high-achieving friends generally had "significantly higher scores one year later than similar students with low-scoring friends." Similarly, Epstein's longitudinal study measuring aspirations finds that "having some or all friends with college plans makes a dramatic difference in the change toward college plans for students in grades six, nine, and twelve." In 1996, Stein-

1. Joyce Levy Epstein, "The Influence of Friends on Achievement and Affective Outcomes," in Joyce Levy Epstein and Nancy Karweit, eds., *Friends in School: Patterns of Selection and Influence in Secondary Schools* (Academic Press, 1983), p. 198. Nina S. Mounts and Laurence Steinberg, "An Ecological Analysis of Peer Influence on Adolescent Grade Point Average and Drug Use," *Developmental Psychology*, vol. 31 (1995), p. 918.

ally mandated study of Title I found that seventh-graders in high-poverty schools were twice as likely as seventh-graders in low-poverty schools (44 versus 21 percent) to watch more than four hours of television on school days. Similarly, a 1996 National Center for Education Statistics (NCES) study found that in a 1994 survey of fourth-graders, nearly 40 percent in poor school districts watched television six hours or more a day, compared with 22 percent of fourth-graders nationally. Using 1996 NAEP data, the berg reported that a study of students tracked over three years found that a B student whose friends are A students is likely to see his or her grades rise over time, whereas a B student whose friends are C students is likely to see his or her grades decline; peers have an independent effect on a student's performance.[2]

With respect to the second objection, it is of course true that peer pressure can excuse only so much. However, the sociological studies that suggest a powerful peer influence support what most people know to be true of the human condition: that we all model our behavior after that of our peers and come to believe that what is common to our experience is also legitimate. This is true across socioeconomic lines, from public high schools to elite law schools. It is particularly true of those in adolescence—a period of "heightened vulnerability," scholars note—because it is "a time when individuals often have questions about their identity and their ability to function independently." Individuals of strong will can ultimately resist peers, but we know many will not, and so it is appropriate, as a matter of public policy, to maximize the number of students who have positive rather than negative peer environments. No less a conservative than U.S. Supreme Court Justice Warren Burger, writing for a unanimous Court, has noted that "children who have . . . been educationally and culturally set apart from the larger community will inevitably acquire habits of speech, conduct, and attitudes reflecting their cultural isolation."[3]

2. Epstein, "The Influence of Friends," pp. 179, 196. Laurence Steinberg, *Beyond the Classroom: Why School Reform Has Failed and What Parents Need to Do* (Simon and Schuster, 1996), pp. 143, 147–48.
3. Richard D. Kahlenberg, *Broken Contract: A Memoir of Harvard Law School* (New York: Hill and Wang, 1992). Steinberg, *Beyond the Classroom*, p. 141. *Milliken v. Bradley (II)* 433 U.S. 267, 287 (1977)

NCES calculates that students eligible for free or reduced-price lunch are roughly twice as likely to watch five or more hours of TV per day in the fourth, eighth, and twelfth grades.[34]

There is a peer effect, as well: "neighborhood social milieu influences a student's work habits," a 1990 study concludes. Thomas Kindermann's 1993 study found that individual fifth-graders, when they moved from a clique that valued schoolwork to one that did not (or vice versa), saw their own attitudes toward schoolwork shift over time. Not surprisingly, the number of hours of homework assigned correlates directly with average NAEP reading scores of seventeen-year-olds, and excessive television viewing is associated with low academic success.[35]

Classroom Environment

Whether or not students are actually influenced by peers to change their own behavior, going to a high-poverty school on average depresses their achievement and long-run life chances because the environment is generally less conducive to success. In high-poverty schools, teachers have a harder time educating students for four reasons: their attention is often diverted from teaching by high levels of disorder; the large numbers of slow learners and students for whom English is a second language require extra teacher attention; large amounts of student mobility and turnover make teaching more difficult; and large numbers of student absences are disruptive and can breed apathy. In addition, over the longer haul, high-poverty schools are less likely to have classmates whose families can help individuals get jobs through networks of connections.

Studies going back fifty years find that low-income students present, on average, more behavioral problems.[36] One national study has found that principals in high-poverty elementary schools are twice as likely as principals in low-poverty schools to report problems with vandalism or theft (36 versus 17 percent), talking back (42 versus 18 percent) and physical fights (63 versus 40 percent)—a finding confirmed by other studies.[37] Eighth-grade teachers in high-poverty schools are almost twice as likely as those in low-poverty schools to report spending at least an hour a week on discipline (21 versus 12 percent), and principals in high-poverty elementary schools are three times as likely as principals in low-poverty schools to report that "physical conflict" is a problem. Among seventh-graders, suspension rates were three times as high in high-poverty schools as in low-poverty schools (20 versus 6 percent). In high-poverty schools, students are twice as likely to report feeling unsafe as students in low-poverty schools (12 versus 6 percent), and their teachers are more than three times as likely as teachers in low-poverty schools to report that weapons are a problem (21 versus 6 percent). There is one exception to the rule: secondary teachers in low-poverty schools are more likely to view student alcohol use as a problem than their colleagues in high-poverty schools (67 versus 54 percent).[38]

These links between poverty and behavioral problems may in part be explained by the absence of father figures. According to Sara McLanahan, children of single parents are more likely to cause trouble than those with two parents. Moreover, income poverty can cause stress and hostility in families that exacerbate behavioral problems in school. A 1994 study found that "among four- to eleven-year-old children, the odds of a poor child having one or more psychiatric disorders such as an attention deficit hyperactivity disorder, a conduct disorder, or an emotional disorder was more than three times that of nonpoor children."[39]

Not surprisingly, studies find that a safe, disciplined school environment is critical to the promotion of learning. Researchers from the Educational Testing Service have observed that disorder "erodes the learning environment for all students" and that "a sound disciplinary policy is a prerequisite for a sound academic policy." Indeed, a key reason that reduction in class size increases achievement among eighth-graders is that it improves the teacher's ability to "reduce problem behavior." Lower levels of delinquency are credited with much of the Catholic school success. Likewise, a 1997 congressionally authorized study of Title I found that a hallmark of high-poverty schools' doing better than expected was a "more orderly school environment." Teachers who are threatened by students may have trouble concentrating, and students who feel endangered may stay away from school altogether. According to one study, one in nine students stay away from school out of fear—one in three in violent areas. The late Albert Shanker has observed that "you deprive children of an opportunity to learn if you do not first provide an orderly environment in the classroom and in the school."[40]

High-poverty schools are also likely to have large numbers of students who are slower learners and need special individualized attention. We know, for example, that because of untreated health problems, poor children are disproportionately learning disabled and in need of special education—but because their parents are less aggressive, they are less likely to get the special tutoring they need and deserve. In Rochester, where high concentrations of poverty have led to a lawsuit, the local columnist Mark Hare notes that "teachers can provide extra help and attention to a few children in every class, but when nearly the whole class is needy, teachers can be quickly overwhelmed." High-poverty schools are also likely to have large numbers of non-English-speaking students. In Wausau, Wisconsin, one advocate of economic desegregation explained, "I went into the kindergarten class and I watched this teacher, and I watched the frustration and the boredom of the white children because she was teaching 'bathroom,' 'light switch,' basic English to these kids who had no conception of English." Teachers in Wausau advocated integration of poor and middle-class students because they knew the basic truth, one parent explained, that "if you have a challenge, the more you divide the work, the easier the work is." Studies find that concentrations of low-ability students make the teaching of reading particularly difficult; "schools need a core of motivated and academically able students to provide a stable base for instruction."[41]

In addition to the stress on teachers caused by physical disruption and an overwhelming number of high-needs children, teachers in high-poverty schools must grapple with the pressures presented by student mobility. Numerous studies have found that poor people (across racial lines) move much more often than middle-class people.[42] The poor are more mobile because they are much more likely to be renters than home owners, they have higher rates of eviction, and they are sometimes engaged in migrant agricultural work. One national study has found that about 34 percent of students in high-poverty schools transfer each year, compared with 14 percent of students in low-poverty schools.[43]

Moving can be disruptive to the education of those who leave, but it is also disruptive to those who remain behind, according to studies of students in Alabama and elsewhere.[44] Teachers in highly mobile schools have to spend much of their time getting to know the new students and bringing them up to speed.[45] A teacher in a stable classroom may have to get to know thirty students in a year, but the teacher of a class of highly mobile students may need to know fifty students over the year. Because new students do not know their classmates or teachers, educators find that "many transfer students act out." In addition, while educators say it is important that teachers establish rules, expectations, and routines in classrooms in the first few weeks of school, transfer students must be taught them anew. In like fashion, researchers have found, new students lack the "shared knowledge base acquired from previous instruction and required for subsequent learning." (An early reader may be used to phonics, while the new school uses the whole-language approach.) Teachers complain that the influx of new students often requires them to backtrack, devoting "valuable class time to review material." The shock to a teacher in receiving a new student, often with no advance warning, adds stress; and teachers complain that additional paperwork takes time away from preparation and lesson planning—all of which also reduce teacher morale. Socioeconomic integration will ameliorate the concentration of mobility problems; and if public school choice is used to achieve integration, it will reduce overall levels of mobility because a family that moves from one neighborhood to another will not need to switch schools as under a neighborhood school system.[46]

Student absences, like student mobility, are disruptive and more likely to occur in high-poverty schools. Low-income students are almost twice as likely to miss at least three days a month, for reasons both voluntary (cutting class) and involuntary (higher rates of untreated health problems).[47] Among seventh-graders, one study has found that students in high-poverty schools are four times as likely as those in low-poverty schools to miss more than twenty school days a year. In the city of Baltimore, 35 percent of public school students were absent more than twenty days in 1996, a rate three times that of suburban Baltimore County schools. Absenteeism, like mobility, is a problem not only for the students who miss class but also for fellow students whose teachers are diverted while helping absent students catch up. Empty desks can also send a message to those who show up for class that they are wasting their time and that attending school is not to be valued.[48]

In the long term, attending a school with few middle-class peers is likely to reduce the life chances of poor children by cutting them off from important networks capable of opening up employment opportunities. One study finds that 57 percent of job seekers use personal contacts to get their first job and 50 percent have done so finding their most recent job. These networks include not only family and good friends but acquaintances, as well. For the poor, studies find, acquaintances are particularly important because friends and relatives are unlikely to be in a position to help.[49]

Amy Stuart Wells and Robert Crain have found empirical evidence to support the old adage that who you know is more important than what you know. Reviewing twenty-one studies, they suggest that the long-term effects of school desegregation are even more impressive than the short-term achievement gains. They find that blacks who attended desegregated schools are more likely to work in white-collar and professional jobs in the private sector and white employers are more likely to hire blacks who attended suburban high schools, in part because they are more likely to be familiar with the student references.[50]

The Influence of Parents

The second major reason that middle-class schools provide a better learning environment on average has to do with the parents, who are directly responsible for the school's higher economic status. Educated middle-class parents are more likely to be involved in their children's schools, to insist on high standards, to rid the school of bad teachers, to ensure adequate resources (both public and private)—in effect, to promote effective schools for their children.

Parental involvement in schools varies dramatically. Some parents volunteer in the classroom every week; others are hard pressed to remember the name of their children's teachers. Moreover, socioeconomic status has been found to be the "primary predictor" of parental involvement.[51] The 1988 National Education Longitudinal Study found that parents of high socioeconomic status are more than four times as likely to belong to the PTA and almost twice as likely to have contacted the school about the academic program as low-socioeconomic-status parents. A 1993 study of Title I found that parents in low-poverty schools were more than twice as likely to volunteer in the classroom as parents in high-poverty schools. A 1998 Department of Education study found teachers in high-poverty schools were about half as likely as teachers in low-poverty schools to say that parents supported their efforts (23 versus 41 percent).[52] Numerous other studies have linked socioeconomic status and parental involvement in schools over many years.[53]

In low-income schools, the Carnegie Foundation for the Advancement of Teaching reports, parental involvement is often abysmally low: in one Los Angeles junior high school with an enrollment of eleven hundred, only a dozen parents showed up for a parent-teacher meeting; in New Orleans, where parents are required to pick up report cards, 70 percent remained unclaimed two months after parents were notified. In Montgomery County, Maryland, parents in wealthier schools demand additional conferences with teachers, whereas parents in poorer areas are often unwilling to attend conferences, so teachers must go to the children's homes if they wish to meet with the parents. At Philadelphia's inner-city Fairhill Elementary School, reports the *Washington Post*, the school "is so desperate to get parents of children there more interested in education that it pays the women $250 for every 100 hours of help they give teachers and students. . . . Small bribes are another tool: Parents who visit classes are rewarded with free product samples—detergent, soap—that the school collects." At inner-city West Side High in New York City, only one in ten parents shows up for an open house, Christina Rathbone notes, and as a result, the teachers outnumbered the parents at conferences. The quality of parental involvement can also differ by economic status.[54]

The lack of parental involvement in high-poverty schools matters, because studies have long found that such involvement raises student achievement in three ways. Most obvious, parental involvement at home, such as helping with homework, raises achievement. Some studies find that having a parent volunteer in the school raises a student's achievement by signaling to the child that school is important and signaling to the teacher that the family values education (thereby raising teacher expectations for the child).[55] The most significant finding, however, is that when parents volunteer in the classroom and participate in school activities, they raise the average achievement level of all children in the school. For example, a 1996 study using NELS data of 24,599 eighth-graders reports that "a child's academic achievement did not depend so much on whether his or her own parents participated, but on the average level of participation of all parents at the school."[56] Other studies find that "when parents volunteer in school they enrich the overall learning environment, strengthen social networks, and affect the norms and expectations for all children in the school."[57]

John Chubb and Terry Moe identify parental involvement as one of the defining characteristics of an "effective school" and find that middle-class schools are much more likely to be effective—a finding confirmed by other studies. The bipartisan Goals 2000 legislation has as a key tenet the belief that increasing "parental involvement and participation" will build stronger schools. Higher levels of achievement in Catholic and private schools are also attributed in part to higher levels of parental involvement. The benefit of attending a school in which parents are active has been found to be particularly pronounced for low-income students.[58]

Of course, in the extreme, overly intrusive parental involvement in the school can impede education if large numbers of aggressive parents create a hostile environment for teachers.[59] Today, however, most teachers see parental involvement as crucial and would be pleased to see more parents volunteer in the classroom. A 1998 survey of teachers, conducted by Louis Harris and Associates, has found that "teachers are far more receptive today than they were a decade ago to having parents more involved in the schools." The study reports that more than 80 percent of teachers said they want parents more involved in education, and 70 percent want parents to volunteer at the school.[60] Overall, socioeconomic integration would ensure the presence of large numbers of active middle-class parents in all schools, thus equalizing this important resource.

Active parents insist on high standards and high-quality teachers and ensure adequate resources in a way that teachers and administrators do not always do on their own.[61] Parent volunteers can help teachers individualize instruction, freeing up the teacher's time and effectively reducing the student-to-teacher ratio. In addition, parents who are active in their children's schools, and particularly parents who have been in the classroom to volunteer, are in a better position to put pressure on the school to improve the curriculum than are parents who are less aware of what is going on. Studies find that low-income parents are less likely than middle-class parents to complain about their children's schools—even though we know, from an objective standpoint, that high-poverty schools are more in need of improvement.[62] Middle-class parents insist on a challenging curriculum and set of expectations, pushing teachers to expect more when homework assignments appear too elementary.

Involved parents know which classrooms are not functioning well enough and can raise issues of teacher quality with the principal. One study has found that in low-income schools, because parents are on the whole less attentive, teachers unions are better able to protect unqualified teachers. Chubb and Moe have found that in schools in which it is relatively easy to transfer or fire teachers, 68 percent of parents are above average in socioeconomic status, but in schools in which it is difficult to transfer or fire teachers, only 35 percent of parents are above average in socioeconomic status.[63]

Finally, middle-class parents are likely to ensure that their child's education is backed up with adequate financial resources in four distinct ways. First, middle-class parents are likely to use their political clout to ensure that enormous disparities in spending will not be tolerated. Despite various equalization efforts, wealthy districts spend about twice as much for each student as poor districts, even after deviant high and low districts are excluded.[64] Important steps have been taken to close the racial gap in spending.[65] The class gap, however, is enormous: the wealthiest 10 percent of districts in the United States spend almost ten times the amount spent for each pupil in the poorest 10 percent. Funding in U.S. schools remains wildly uneven compared with schools in Europe.[66]

There is nothing foreordained about using property taxes to fund schools, and some states do not. The main reason inequities survive is that politically powerful middle-class constituencies benefit; integration across district lines would reverse this dynamic, giving some middle-class parents a stake in reducing spending inequities.[67]

So too, socioeconomic desegregation would help ensure the reduction of within-district disparities in funding, also linked to political pull.[68] It is well established that wealthier and better-educated Americans are more likely to vote and to make political contributions.[69] The old argument that money follows whites to desegregated schools within the same district (that "green follows white") has, to a degree, been borne out. In Tampa, Florida, for example, following desegregation, ill-equipped formerly black schools were transformed overnight. "Sod was trucked in to green up the schoolyards. Libraries were added. Air conditioners were bought and plugged in. Fences were erected, science labs installed, vocational facilities expanded," according to the *Washington Post*. If green follows white, it is most likely to follow those whites with green.[70]

Second, middle-class parents are increasingly supplementing school budgets through private fund-raising efforts, so that even if public funds were equalized, the amounts spent for each pupil at different schools would never be equal. According to one national survey, parents in low-poverty schools are twice as likely as parents in high-poverty schools to be "very involved" in fund-raising (80 versus 37 percent). In the suburbs, these foundations rely not only on individual donations but also on connections that parents have with businesses to support local schools.[71]

Particularly in places like California, where spending equalization is a state constitutional mandate, private foundations have sprung up as a way of maintaining advantages. A study of tax records by two California economics professors found that the state's spending equalization decision, *Serrano* v. *Priest*, helped trigger a rise in the number of educational foundations in the state from 6 in 1971 to 537 in 1995. Studies find that between 4 and 15 percent of public school revenues now come from private sources—a figure that rivals federal spending on education.[72] In some jurisdictions, there are limits to what private fundraisers may spend their money on. In a concern for equity, for example, many school districts forbid payment of teachers' salaries by parents; in other jurisdictions, rules are more relaxed. Affluent parents in northwestern Washington, D.C., for example, routinely chip in money to hire public school teachers.[73]

Third, highly engaged middle-class parents are more likely to ensure that school spending is used efficiently to educate students rather than line the pockets of administrators. Some evidence suggests that although students in some inner-city districts receive as much funding as their suburban counterparts, much of the spending is wasted, in part because parental involvement is geared not toward ensuring efficient spending but rather toward getting jobs.[74] In poor areas of New York City, Sara Mosle notes, "schools are often the only decent employer," and school boards bend to pressure to overhire and to employ political cronies rather than the best educators. In 1997, the Washington, D.C., Control Board found that the administrative staffs in district schools were three to four times larger, per capita, as those in neighboring suburban school districts. In Baltimore, the number of staff (administrators, principals, teachers, and other staff) nearly doubled, from 5,463 to 10,622, between 1950 and 1995, despite a drop in student enrollment of 7 percent. In New York City's Community School District 9 in the Bronx, Nicholas Lemann has found, "public schools are still where the money and jobs are: the driving force of this school district has long been political patronage, not education"; some English-speaking students were incorrectly placed in bilingual classes to protect the jobs of bilingual teachers. Nationally, high-poverty schools receiving large amounts of Title I money see employment of Title I aides as "a jobs program for members of the community," says the Department of Education's Mary Jean LeTendre. Heavy reliance on Title I aides has come under criticism as an inefficient use of money, but there are strong adult constituencies for the continuation of current spending patterns.[75]

The fact that poor people are more likely to see schools as opportunities for employment in the bureaucracy does not suggest that the poor are more corrupt than the middle class or care less about children. However, when large numbers of parents in the community are struggling, it is harder for school boards and administrators to make necessary cuts or to fire underperforming teachers because these teachers are neighbors and friends, not just employees—and they know the children of those parents will surely be hurt when the parents are fired. The same principle does not apply in middle-class communities, where people already have well-paying jobs and do not need to turn to the public school system for employment.

Fourth, socioeconomic integration helps address a spending inequity that is ignored by mere equalization—that is, the greater "educational load" that certain high-poverty schools face. All agree that it is more expensive to educate poor children than middle-class children; estimates of the differential range from 20 to 300 percent more.[76] Children in high-poverty schools are more costly to educate in part because of the greater home difficulties they bring and in part because high-poverty schools have extra expenses: addressing vandalism, replacing textbooks taken by transient students, and paying for security guards. In addition, to attract a teaching staff of comparable quality (experience, education, and talent), high-poverty schools must pay teachers a premium to teach in what are deemed undesirable surroundings.[77] The fact that "equity" requires more than "equality" in spending (in the sense of fiscal neutrality) is one of the major reasons that progressive litigators have shifted their focus in recent years from "equality" to "adequacy" lawsuits.[78]

Without integration, it is highly unlikely that all these spending inequities can be addressed. As Orfield and Eaton note, "To provide equal opportunity within segregated schools and districts, school officials would have to set up mechanisms to provide the most resources to the most disadvantaged, who happen to be the most powerless."[79]

In the next chapter, it is argued that money alone is insufficient to ensure equal opportunity, and that economic integration is important because it brings not only an equalization of spending but also advantages stemming from middle-class students and parents and teachers unrelated to spending in itself. That is not to say, however, that money is unimportant. Obviously, the money that middle-class parents ensure helps the education of their children—to repair schools, reduce class size, purchase new equipment, and the like. When a New Jersey court asked the superintendent of wealthy South Brunswick what he would do if he were limited to Trenton's meager average expenditure for each pupil, he replied that the cuts would be an "absolute disaster" and that he "would quit" if he had to stop buying new computers, was unable to paint the high school, and was required to drop courses.[80]

The Influence of Teachers

The socioeconomic status of students and their parents exerts a profound impact on the quality of a school (its emphasis on achievement, its level of orderliness, its resources, and so on). These advantages and disadvantages are compounded by the third group, teachers. If life were fair, the best-qualified teachers would be found in the disadvantaged schools, where they are most needed. In fact, as a general rule, the best teachers are drawn to the schools with the highest socioeconomic levels, exacerbating existing inequalities. Moreover, teachers generally have higher expectations, and offer a more enriched curriculum, at high-socioeconomic-status schools—all factors that produce higher levels of achievement by students.

Teacher Quality

Studies find that in high-poverty schools, teacher vacancies are harder to fill. In addition, teachers are less likely to be licensed, less likely to be experienced, more likely to teach "out of field" (not in their subject area), less likely to have master's degrees, and less likely to score well on teacher exams.[81]

Studies dating back forty years find that low-income schools have a difficult time finding and keeping good teachers and must rely disproportionately on emergency substitutes.[82] These studies have found that because most teachers do not seek vertical mobility (that is, to become an administrator or principal), job progress is marked by horizontal mobility (that is, moving from poor schools to wealthier ones). Most teachers consider it a promotion to get out of a poor school.[83]

National surveys find that schools in central-city districts have three times as many unfilled teaching positions as schools in other districts. Principals are much more concerned about science vacancies in inner-city schools than their counterparts in better-off schools (97 versus 67 percent). High-poverty schools are also twice as likely as low-poverty schools to report difficulty in hiring teachers (24 versus 11.4 percent).[84]

Teachers in high-poverty schools are sometimes so desperate to leave that they switch jobs in the middle of the school year. Teacher mobility during the school year is four times higher in high-poverty than in low-poverty schools (8 versus 2 percent). Eighth-graders in urban schools are twice as likely as those in nonurban schools to report that at least one teacher has left in the middle of the school year (58 versus 27 percent). A single urban class may have as many as fourteen teachers in a single year.[85] Nationally, more than 30 percent of beginning teachers leave the profession in the first five years, and attrition rates are higher in high-poverty than in low-poverty schools. Moreover, those teachers leaving the profession from high-poverty schools are more than twice as likely to say they left because of dissatisfaction with the teaching profession (as opposed to personal reasons or retirement) as those in low-poverty schools.[86]

Facing vacancies that are hard to fill, administrators must choose between a number of bad alternatives. "If no qualified new hire can be immediately found, principals usually fill the opening with an unqualified teacher, use a substitute teacher, increase other teachers' class sizes, or course loads, or cancel the course altogether," writes Jeannie Oakes. As a result, urban teachers are twice as likely as nonurban teachers to have no license or only an emergency or temporary license (14 versus 7 percent). Hiring at the last minute, principals must make do with these "Labor Day specials," with their emergency credentials, says Sandra Feldman, the president of the American Federation of Teachers (AFT). Even when they are credentialed, teachers in high-poverty schools are more likely than their colleagues in low-poverty schools to have less than three years' experience (12 versus 7 percent).[87]

Teachers in high-poverty schools are much more likely to be teaching "out of field," that is, outside their major or minor in college.[88] According to a 1997 Department of Education study, the rate of out-of-field teaching in middle and high schools was one in three nationally and almost one in two in high-poverty schools. In high schools, the National Commission on Teaching and America's Future has found, teachers were much more likely to teach out of field in high-poverty than in low-poverty schools in math (40 versus 28 percent), science (20 versus 14 percent), English (31 versus 19 percent), and social studies (18 versus 16 percent).[89]

Teachers in high-poverty schools also tend to have less formal education. Among newly hired teachers in 1994, according to the National Commission on Teaching and America's Future, teachers in high-poverty schools are considerably less likely than those in low-poverty schools to have master's degrees (14.7 versus 24.3 percent). Among math and science teachers in high-poverty schools, the percentage with a master's in their teaching field is also lower (16 versus 34 percent). At the extreme, Title I teachers are often "teaching aides," 90 percent of whom do not have a college degree. Title I director Mary Jean LeTendre comments, "If we had our gifted and talented children [rather than the disadvantaged] being taught by someone with less than a college degree, we would have an uprising on our hands."[90]

There is also new direct evidence that teachers in poor and minority schools have lower test scores than teachers in middle-class and white schools. To put this in context, it is important to remember that the entire nationwide pool of teaching talent is not as strong as it could be. Scholastic Assessment Test scores of those intending to be educators have long been below the national average. In 1998, nearly 60 percent of prospective teachers in Massachusetts flunked a new teacher exam—scoring below the equivalent of a D.[91]

Among the weak pool of educators, students in high-poverty schools get the weakest. In an exhaustive study covering nine hundred school districts in Texas, Harvard's Ronald Ferguson reported in 1991 that teacher quality and student socioeconomic status "are highly correlated." Higher-socioeconomic-status districts "find it easier, with any given salary scale, to attract teachers with strong skills and experience." The percentage of college-educated parents in a district has "a highly significant influence" on the supply of the best qualified teachers. John Kain and Kraig Singleton, in a Texas study of three times the number of students as surveyed in the

Coleman Report, find that where teacher ability is measured by verbal scores on the Texas Examination of Current Administrators and Teachers (TECAT), there is "a clear sorting of teacher ability by schools of differing racial/ethnic and income composition."[92]

Inner-city principals are much less likely to rate the science teachers in their schools as highly competent (48 versus 73 percent), and fellow teachers in high-poverty schools are almost three times as likely to say their colleagues lack sufficient interest and background for math and science (26 versus 9 percent). Even Sandra Feldman, president of the AFT, which represents primarily urban teachers, notes that when it comes to schools in poor areas, "if you can breathe, you can teach in most of these schools." The National Commission on Teaching and America's Future notes that we now have "a bimodal teaching force in which some teachers are increasingly expert and others are wholly unprepared."[93]

High-poverty schools will have an even harder time recruiting given the looming shortage of teachers. In 1998, the U.S. Department of Education projected that 2.2 million public school teachers must be hired in the next decade; and Secretary of Education Richard Riley has noted that "this need for more teachers will put pressure on school districts to lower their standards and hire unqualified individuals." Many of those being replaced are high-quality female teachers who entered the profession in an era when gender discrimination funneled bright women into teaching rather than law, medicine, or business.[94]

Several factors lead the best teachers to middle-class schools. The most obvious is that high-poverty schools have lower teacher salaries, on average, than low-poverty schools. In 1993–94, the best-paid public school teachers earned $49,100 in low-poverty districts and only $36,100 in high-poverty districts, a difference of more than 35 percent.[95] A number of other issues, however, also come into play. Teachers in high-poverty schools are likely to spend much more of their time disciplining students, and they face a greater likelihood of being in physical danger themselves. Teachers in high-poverty schools are less likely to report having adequate resources and supplies for teaching. One of the biggest complaints of inner-city school teachers is that they have "significant voids" in the basic materials necessary to teach—a complaint lodged by 59 percent of teachers in high-poverty schools compared with 16 percent of teachers in more affluent schools.[96]

Teachers in high-poverty schools are also less likely to report having a great deal of influence over the curriculum (28 versus 41 percent). This phenomenon is likely to become more prevalent with the spread of programs like Success for All, which require teachers to follow minute-by-minute "scripts" when they teach in high-poverty schools. Similarly, as additional states adopt high standards for students, teachers have a new incentive to avoid low-performing high-poverty schools that are slated to close if improvements are not made.[97]

Teacher tenure rules may also contribute to the flow of bad teachers to high-poverty schools. Underqualified teachers who are mistakenly hired in a middle-class school are unlikely to be fired outright because union rules make their removal difficult. But middle-class parents are unlikely to tolerate their presence year after year. The solution? Bad teachers are usually transferred—often to a high-poverty-school dumping ground. Once there, they have nowhere to be demoted to; Milwaukee mayor John Norquist notes that "in most big cities, the only time a teacher is fired is if they commit a felony."[98]

The problem is self-perpetuating. Because high-poverty schools are difficult places to work, morale is low. (Teacher absenteeism is twice as likely to be a problem in urban as in nonurban schools.) Talented instructors who teach in high-poverty schools because of an idealistic commitment may grow discouraged as they watch their brightest colleagues leave. The quality of faculty colleagues is important to teachers for moral and professional support and because they can learn lessons from colleagues and, increasingly, must collaborate with them.[99]

The National Commission on Teaching and America's Future came to a disturbing conclusion in 1996: "In the nation's poorest schools, where hiring is most lax and teacher turnover is constant, the results are disastrous. Thousands of children are taught throughout their school careers by a parade of teachers without preparation in the fields they teach, inexperienced beginners with little training and no mentoring, and short-term substitutes trying to cope with constant staff disruptions. It is more surprising that some of these children manage to learn than that so many fail to do so."[100]

Not surprisingly, studies find that teacher quality is significant to the educational achievement of students.[101] Ferguson's 1991 Texas study of 2.4 million students finds that school quality accounts for between one-third and one-fourth of the variation in test scores and that most of the differences in school quality arise from differences in teacher quality. Ferguson also has found that "teachers' experience and test scores are important predictors of test scores for students." Controlling for family and community background, Ferguson looks at the influence of four variables on student test scores: teacher test scores, the student-to-teacher ratio, teacher experience, and teachers' postgraduate training (master's degrees). According to the report, after the first grade, teacher test scores "account for about one-fifth to one-quarter of all variation across districts in students' average scores" on tests. Teacher experience accounts for "a bit more than 10 percent of the interdistrict variation in student test scores." The percentage of teachers with master's degrees accounts "for about 5 percent of the variation in student scores across districts" but only for grades one through seven. Ferguson's study confirms the findings of others that teacher quality (as measured by the college attended) helps predict student performance.[102] The significance of teacher quality to academic achievement is confirmed in numerous other studies, including ones in Tennessee, Massachusetts, and Alabama.[103]

Teacher Expectations and Curricular Offerings

An array of studies also demonstrate that teachers are more likely to have higher expectations and principals are more likely to offer high-level courses in schools with a higher socioeconomic status. "Whether schools are public or private, the social class of the students has been and continues to be the single most significant factor in determining how a school works and the intellectual values it promotes," writes Deborah Meier. "The higher the student body's economic status, the meatier the curriculum, the more open-ended the discussion, the less rote and rigid the pedagogy, the more respectful the tone, the more rigorous the expectation, the greater the staff autonomy."[104]

With respect to expectations, studies have found that "the level and pace of group instruction, the standards of excellence and adequacy, the expectations for role-performance . . . all systematically vary by the class composition of the schools."[105] The Commission on Chapter 1 (now Title I) noted in 1993 that "the *low* expectations in our suburban schools are *high* in comparison to expectations in urban schools and rural schools with concentrations of children in poverty." Indeed, a 1997 congressionally authorized study of Title I reports that when measured against standardized test scores, "a grade of 'A' in a high-poverty school is equivalent to a grade of about 'C' in a low-poverty school." Nicholas Lemann, writing about Orr High School in Chicago's ghetto, reports that to get an A in a sophomore English class required only "the ability to write one's name at the top of the page and anything—anything—somewhere else on the page." Tellingly, a 1993 study finds that although students in low-poverty schools are more likely to be publicly praised for their academic work, students in high-poverty schools are twice as likely to receive awards for mere attendance. When low-income children are concentrated in a single school, William Yancey and Salvatore Saporito note, a discouraged, and discouraging, climate can develop among teachers who begin to feel that "these kids can't learn."[106]

The difference in the curricula of middle-class and poor elementary schools can be dramatic. Studies find that instruction in low-income schools is "more likely to rely on workbooks, dittos, and prefabricated kits, and to emphasize memorization and recitation over problem solving and independent thinking." As a result, researchers note that whereas students in more-advantaged schools "develop advanced skills and conceptual understanding [and] explore challenging content," students in high-poverty schools are "subject to 'transmission' styles of instruction, the teaching of discrete 'basic skills' and algorithms unrelated to concepts, and more repetition of less challenging content." Stephen Raudenbusch's 1997 study using NAEP data, for example, finds that students with more highly educated parents are more likely to have a math teacher who emphasizes mathematical reasoning as part of the instruction. In effect, the difference in elementary curriculum can be thought of as a form of "tracking" that is patently unfair and unmeritocratic because it is based not on ability but on residence.[107]

At the high school level, the expectations of counselors are also important, and these vary by a school's socioeconomic status. Researchers at Johns Hopkins University have found high-scoring but low-income students to be much less likely to go to college, not for lack of financial aid but because counselors are overwhelmed by the need to keep low-achieving children from dropping out and do not encourage the high achievers to carry a college-prep course load, take the SAT, or apply for financial aid. By contrast, Wells finds that inner-city St. Louis students who were given the opportunity to attend middle-class suburban high schools benefited from the higher expectations of the school counselors. "In their suburban schools they attend college fairs, are constantly reminded by their counselors and peers about college opportunities and deadlines, have access to a wealth of information on the college application process, and are assigned to college counselors with strong ties to college admissions offices across the country."[108]

With respect to course offerings and content, a number of studies have found that curriculum is closely tied to a school's socioeconomic composition.[109] At the elementary school level, one study of fifth-grade social studies classes finds a watered-down curriculum in working-class schools. At the middle school level, algebra and foreign languages are more than twice as likely to be offered in suburban as poor inner-city schools. At the high school level, advantaged schools offered at least twelve advanced-placement (AP) courses in 1994, whereas disadvantaged schools offered between zero and four.[110] The discrepancy in AP offerings in California was brought into the public spotlight in 1999 when civil rights groups challenged admissions policies at the University of California, noting that admissions officers gave extra points for AP courses taken when half the state's public high schools—many with large minority and poor populations—offered no AP courses in the 1997–98 school year. By comparison, a select group of high schools—4 percent—offered twenty-one or more advanced-placement courses.[111]

Gifted and talented classes are also less likely to be offered in high-poverty than low-poverty schools (70 versus 83 percent). High-poverty schools are much less likely to offer calculus than other schools (54 versus 82 percent). A 1995 federal report finds that high-poverty schools are also less likely to offer other important math and science courses than middle-class schools.[112]

Paul Gagnon notes that the historical idea that Europe educates only an elite, whereas in the United States we educate all, "has been turned on its head; they now educate the masses and we the much smaller 'elite.'" By 1991, Gagnon observes, the French and Japanese had graduated more than three times the U.S. proportion of high school students with rigorous academic programs. This unequal content necessarily yields unequal results, he says, noting the question of a Parisian school teacher to an American: "How can you say your schools are democratic, when they do not require all students to study history, literature, the arts and language, philosophy, and different ideas of politics and economics—are you trying to disarm your lower classes?" Educational experts and courts now agree that equality of opportunity requires not only equal spending but also equal program and curriculum.[113]

It could be argued that the lower expectations of teachers and the limited course offerings in high-poverty schools are not entirely unfounded; after all, poor children, on average, achieve at lower levels than middle-class children. Rather than being malevolent, racist, or classist, might not teachers in lower-class schools simply be reacting to social reality?[114] To a certain degree, this is surely true. In many U.S. schools, teachers do not assign rigorous homework because they know from experience that parents are not likely to ensure that their children complete the work. Expectations are not all-determining, and raising expectations will not entirely erase the gaps in academic performance between the rich and poor. Christopher Jencks notes, for example, that the low expectations of teachers cannot explain the entire black-white academic gap because some differences already exist when children enter school. There are, however, three reasons to think that the higher expectations and curriculum prevalent in middle-class schools could improve achievement of low-income students in socioeconomically integrated classes.[115]

First, there is some evidence to suggest that the lower performance of lower-socioeconomic-status children stems in part from the expectations themselves; that low expectations partly contribute to lower performance, becoming a self-fulfilling prophecy.[116] The percentage of children who cannot master a basic curriculum is fairly small—on the order of 2–4 percent. Just as the expectation of a bank failure can cause a run on a bank, precipitating a failure, so a ten-year-old student whose teacher expects him to read at a first-grade level is unlikely to read at a fifth-grade plane. It has long been known that when teachers are tricked into believing that certain randomly chosen students are gifted, those students see large achievement gains. Recent literature reviews have confirmed that effects of expectations can themselves be quite large.[117]

In some cities and in some states (though not all) the standards movement to raise expectations and toughen curriculum has been credited with raising achievement, and some say high expectations account for part of the success of students in Catholic schools and Japanese schools.[118] High expectations have been a staple of the "effective schools" movement since the 1970s. So widely is it believed that expectations matter that it has been written into our public policy: the 1994 reauthorization of Title I requires that Title I students be held to the same high standards as other students.[119]

Second, in high-poverty schools, bright students suffer because the instruction is pitched not to them but to the group, whose overall level of achievement is low. To a certain extent, teachers must aim their lessons at the middle of their classes. One 1983 study, for example, finds that teachers' "instructional activity, in particular how much they cover, is geared to groups and not to individuals." The problem, as Christopher Jencks notes, is that a high-achieving low-income student is unlikely to be pushed to his potential because the "instruction to his classroom will be aimed not at him but at the laggard majority."[120] In socioeconomically integrated schools, it is more likely that there will be a critical mass of students at all ability levels, and poor children will be more appropriately placed because students will be grouped by ability, not residential wealth.

Third, bright students obviously suffer in high-poverty schools in which parents do not successfully demand the offering of high-level courses, and having a substantial number of high-achieving middle-class classmates will improve the chances of bright low-income students. If there is not a critical mass of students who wish to take a calculus class, for example, the principal of a cash-strapped school will find it hard to justify offering the course, and we know that many do not. Just as small high schools often do not have enough students to create demand for high-level courses, so large high schools with small numbers of high-achieving students also have insufficient demand. "It is one thing to take as given that approximately 70 percent of an entering high school freshman class will not attend college," Coleman writes, "but to assign a particular child to a curriculum designed for that 70 percent closes off for that child the opportunity to attend college." Not surprisingly, studies find that students who take more demanding courses make more academic progress, independent of prior achievement.[121]

Socioeconomic integration of schools takes on the systemwide inequalities that derive from a school's students, parents, and teachers. It attempts to give all students a chance to attend middle-class schools, in which a majority of students set the tone that academic achievement is to be valued and that aspirations should be set high, students learn from one another's differences, misbehavior is kept under control and does not become contagious, and teachers are not overwhelmed by large numbers of high-need students. In these economically integrated schools, a critical mass of parents will be active in the school, which should raise the overall level of involvement. These active parents will help teachers in class and ensure high standards, adequate resources, and efficient spending in a way that also promotes equality rather than widening the existing gap. In these integrated schools, teachers will come to institutions based on their educational philosophies, not the student makeup, and with strong parent involvement in every school, no school will become a dumping ground for teachers rejected by the better schools. We know that separate schools for better-off and poor children are unequal, but if we provide incentives for economically integrated schools, the spread of middle-class environments can benefit all students.

| 5

The Difficulty with Alternatives

to Socioeconomic Integration

SOCIOECONOMIC INTEGRATION requires a great deal of planning, restructuring, and political will, and policymakers will look to alternative ways to achieve the goals advanced. The alternatives on offer thus far fall into two categories: piecemeal reforms (improvement of standards, teacher enhancements, reduction in class size, and the like) to address discrete inequalities and global responses (racial desegregation and vouchers) to address those that are more universal.

The Piecemeal Alternatives

Policymakers have argued that the inequality in teacher ability can be corrected by paying premium salaries in high-poverty schools; that the inequality in curriculum can be corrected through tough state or national standards; that the inequality in discipline problems can be corrected through tougher discipline codes and zero-tolerance plans; that inequality in spending can be corrected through state lawsuits; and on and on. Most of these piecemeal efforts to address individual elements of inequality are worthy of support, but they have proved insufficient to combat inequality because the people in a school—the teachers, parents, and fellow students—are more important than structural reforms and because the structural reforms are unlikely to take place unless the people are changed.

Teachers

In theory, the inequities in curriculum and expectations found in high-poverty and middle-class schools could be eliminated by establishing a common core of standards and expectations for all schools. This approach makes sense and is beginning to make important inroads in certain locations. On the whole, however, the standards movement is unlikely to address the enduring differences in curriculum and expectations, and in a couple of senses, standards without integration could exacerbate inequality.

Exhorting teachers from above to push pupils in high-poverty schools to reach higher standards is inadequate because it asks teachers to disregard their daily experience with their pupils. Deborah Meier notes that teachers are reacting to "centuries of realities. . . . Kids from poverty have, the world over, always done worse than kids of better means." James Liebman similarly notes that studies find that when black students attend all-black schools, teachers tend to have low expectations and that "simply ordering teachers to raise expectations for low-achieving children does not work" without desegregation.[1]

In 1999, researchers Jane David and Patrick Shields reported that standards-based reform in seven poor urban districts sponsored by the Pew Charitable Trusts had proved difficult to implement, in part because "teachers and administrators struggle with their own beliefs about standards and the children they teach. For some, the notion of all children reaching [similar] standards flies in the face of their day-to-day experiences." Julia Smith and Valerie Lee note in a study involving expectations and high school restructuring that past reform efforts "have commonly been met with strong resistance." In Kentucky, similar reforms proved far better at equalizing spending than at raising standards, given teacher skepticism about whether all children could meet high standards. By contrast, integrating poor children into predominantly middle-class schools shakes up the system in such a dramatic way that teachers have little choice but to adjust expectations to the new mix of students.[2]

It is also difficult to raise standards in high-poverty schools because high standards require good teachers—something we know high-poverty schools lack. Linda Darling-Hammond explains that "teacher expertise and curriculum quality are interrelated because a challenging curriculum requires an expert teacher." Adam Gamoran has found that without improved teacher preparation, "the impact of curriculum reform will undoubtedly be modest at best." In a 1999 report, Heather Hill, David Cohen, and Susan Moffitt of the University of Michigan, looking at efforts to raise standards and toughen the curriculum in the state of California, find that only a "small fraction" of math teachers offer the richer curriculum; those most likely to adopt the new curriculum are math teachers in the most affluent schools. Teachers in high-poverty schools are only half as likely as teachers in affluent schools even to understand the new approaches urged by reformers.[3]

The standards movement has not only been fairly ineffective for students in poor schools, when applied to economically segregated schools, it can even create new inequalities. In some states, such as Maryland and Kentucky, schools with good principals who work hard to improve test scores are given monetary rewards.[4] The logic, of course, is to provide incentives for improvement. The result, however, is that the schools that are already doing well and making the biggest improvements get more money to make further improvements, while the students unlucky enough to be stuck in schools that have leveled out or are in decline lose out.

As well, the standards movement can be used as a tool by the right wing to undercut public education as an enterprise. One reason the bar was set so high in Virginia, critics charge, is that headlines about widespread failure rates would help feed the movement for vouchers. In Virginia, 97 percent of the state's schools failed to reach the benchmarks established in the first round of testing in 1998.[5]

Finally, the risk of the standards movement is that it will spawn high-stakes assessments—tests required before promotion to another grade, or for graduation from high school—without providing the poor with the means to pass, in which case large numbers of poor and minority children will simply fail. Although high-stakes exams should have the effect of giving poor children a better cause of action to enforce a legal right to the opportunity to learn (OTL), this has not always worked in practice. Federal OTL standards, contained in the Goals 2000 legislation, for example, are fairly weak.[6]

If inequality in curriculum and expectations is difficult to address short of integration, perhaps inequality in teacher quality could be dealt with by paying teachers in high-poverty schools a premium—what is sometimes called teacher "combat pay." President Clinton, for example, has proposed providing college scholarships to students who agree to teach for at least three years in high-poverty schools.[7] These efforts have had a hard time succeeding, however, for three reasons.

First, getting the best teachers into the worst schools requires that the most cash-strapped districts, with the least powerful parents, use an expensive weapon to lure the best teachers away from middle-class schools. Given the undesirability of teaching in high-poverty schools—concerns about safety, discipline, supplies, and lack of parent support—salaries would have to be perhaps $20,000 higher to offset negative working conditions.[8] By comparison, economic integration ensures some good teachers at all schools.

Second, smaller efforts, like President Clinton's scholarship plan, are unlikely to do the trick. As noted in chapter 4, attrition rates in urban schools after three years of teaching approach 50 percent. The problem is not so much getting bright young teachers into high-poverty schools but, rather, keeping them there. Clinton's requirement of a three-year commitment falls far short of what is needed. Third, unions are resistant to combat-pay schemes. A *Washington Post* report notes that "teacher union representatives generally have resisted such proposals, saying all teachers should be compensated equally and should 'have the right to say yes or no' to where they work."[9]

Parents

Although equality of teaching is hard to achieve amid economic segregation, equality of parental input is harder yet. In theory, we could try to equalize parental influence by promoting parental involvement classes in poor areas and ensuring equal, or greater, spending in poor schools. Both, however, are uphill battles. Ideally, steps could be taken to reach out to poor parents and to assure them that they are welcome in the school. Such programs are well-intentioned, but attempts to raise parental involvement in Chicago, in Title I schools, and elsewhere have not been as effective as hoped.[10] Significantly raising parental involvement among the poor has proved difficult, for a couple of reasons.

Fundamentally, parental involvement programs rest, in part, on a false assumption: if poor parents could only be educated and motivated, they would participate just as fully in schools as middle-class parents. The lack of participation, however, may not stem from laziness or indifference; in low-income families, the primary concern may be daily existence, not education.[11] Lower-income parents may also have less-flexible working hours; and in areas with large numbers of single-parent families, there is simply a smaller pool of parents to draw upon for help.[12] Moreover, those disadvantaged parents who are able to volunteer may be discouraged by the absence of a critical mass of other parents in high-poverty schools, reluctant to pull all the weight by themselves.

By contrast, there is some evidence that if middle-class parents were more evenly distributed across schools and if lower-income parents were to observe middle-class parents demanding—and effecting—change, they would become more engaged themselves, thereby raising the overall national level of parental involvement in schools. Examining NELS data, Ho Sui-Chu and Willms's 1996 study finds that "irrespective of their own SES, parents were more likely to volunteer or attend PTO meetings if their children attended high SES schools than low SES schools." "It is likely," the authors conclude, "that when there is a strong concentration of high SES parents in a school community, an ethos of greater school participation is more easily established." (Although some might worry that middle-class parents in integrated schools would look out only for the other middle-class children, Ho Sui-Chu and Willms find that increased volunteering among parents apparently "reduces inequality between social-class groups.")[13]

The other great parental equalization scheme, of course, is an unthinkable one: reducing parental involvement so that middle-class parents do not provide such an advantage. In economically segregated schools, the issue of parental involvement presents a difficult dilemma. On the one hand, parents who volunteer in class or provide donations to the PTA are acting on noble and wholesome impulses, which public policy should generally encourage. On the other hand, the involvement of parents in wealthy areas provides enormous advantages over poorer schools, advantages that undermine the equality of opportunity for which public schools are meant to stand.

In 1997, this issue came to a head in New York City, when parents in Greenwich Village raised $46,000 in private funds to keep a fourth-grade teacher from being cut from their local public school. The parents at P.S. 41 argued they should be able to chip in to reduce overcrowding, to make the jobs of teachers less stressful, and to improve education for their children. "Our fundraising does not take one penny away from any other student in New York City," one parent noted. Superintendent Rudy Crew nixed the private fundraising, however, saying that if wealthier schools could buy extra teachers, the whole premise of equal education would be undercut. One parent who did not contribute to the fund explained her view: "Increasingly, public education has become a two-tiered system of schools that have and schools that have not. If we pay teachers' salaries out of our own pockets, the divide will only become greater."[14]

In economically stratified schools, there is no good answer to this dilemma—a choice between greater inequality or a leveling down of parental involvement.[15] Economic integration, by contrast, cuts the Gordian knot presented by the Greenwich Village case: it will harness positive impulses to improve education to promote the welfare of all students rather than to perpetuate the advantages of the fortunate.[16] Middle-class parents who wish to give money or time will be encouraged to do so, but they will end up helping everyone rather than only an elite.

The Greenwich Village case also raises the larger issue of school spending. The obvious alternative solution to the inequality of spending that flows from economic segregation is to mandate equal and compensatory spending directly. This has been attempted in several states, and it is an effort worthy of support. Poor children deserve just as much spending on education as middle-class children. Having said that, the evidence on the effectiveness of compensatory spending by itself is sobering.

Compensatory approaches have run into the stubborn reality, grounded in the 1966 Coleman Report, that in determining an individual student's achievement, family influence is most significant, followed by the economic status of classmates; spending matters least. Coleman found that average expenditure for each pupil accounts for less than 1 percent of the variance in educational achievement, "nothing approaching the assumed relationship," as Mosteller and Moynihan note. Coleman wrote that "the results clearly suggest that school integration across socioeconomic lines (and hence across racial lines) will increase Negro achievement, and they throw serious doubt upon the effectiveness of policies designed to increase non-personal resources in the school." Subsequent studies have generally confirmed that fellow students are more significant in student achievement than per pupil expenditure.[17]

Similarly, so-called *Milliken II* remedies—court-ordered compensatory spending in segregated schools—have been of limited success. In city after city, extra cash in place of desegregation has produced little or no achievement gains for disadvantaged children. In Detroit, for example, after the expenditure of $238 million over twelve years, students still were seven times as likely to fail the math standard as other students in the state. Given an educators' wish list—remedial reading and communication, parental involvement programs, a multiethnic curriculum, better teacher training, nonbiased testing, and so forth—segregated schools have failed.[18]

Milliken II spending in Little Rock, Arkansas, Austin, Texas, and Prince George's County, Maryland, has failed to produce substantial gains for minority students.[19]

Similarly, the disappointing results of Title I appear linked to the program's emphasis on spending over desegregation. In 1997, a congressionally authorized three-year longitudinal study of Title I involving forty thousand students found that students receiving Title I services performed no better than similar students who were not receiving such services. Gary Natriello and Edward McDill, reviewing the evidence in 1999, note that between the mid-1960s and the mid-1990s, funding for Title I increased 652 percent; $117 billion had been appropriated, but after numerous reforms, several studies have found, the program has produced only "small, short-term, achievement effects," and Title I is "still failing to meet the expectations of policymakers."[20] A 1999 Department of Education study, finding "promising results" from Title I reforms, was largely dismissed as political and as having failed to prove its case.[21] Gary Orfield notes that enormous expenditure over more than thirty years has produced no "evidence of significant educational gain." Even in cities that spend "substantially more per student than their surrounding suburbs," he finds, performance is poor under conditions of racial and economic segregation.[22] Worse yet, on the margin, Title I can actually provide a perverse incentive to encourage concentrations of poverty because the program gives flexibility in spending only to those schools with more than a 50 percent low-income population.[23]

Other spending programs, like those aimed at remedial summer schooling, have also proved disappointing. Some researchers, noting that poor children often fall behind during summers off, have said that we should increase spending to extend the school year or provide remedial summer school programs—a movement likely to accelerate as schools move to curb social promotion; but the evidence to date on summer schooling is not encouraging.[24] To the extent that summer programs are as economically segregated as the regular schools, their limited impact should not be surprising.

The argument made here, that integration is more effective in raising achievement than compensatory spending, could be seen, James Traub notes, as "a strikingly conservative conclusion" that "it is values and culture, not resources, that determine academic outcomes." Values are important, but the argument outlined here is more complicated than "values, not resources" and far different from those that claim money does not matter.[25] Indeed, one of the advantages of socioeconomic integration is that middle-class parents will use their political weight to bring greater equality of resources. The more modest point is that funding is insufficient, by itself, to provide genuine equal opportunity because money is only one part of what determines an educational environment; that integration is more effective than compensatory spending; and that compensatory funding appears particularly ineffective in socioeconomically isolated environments. Money clearly does matter, but breaking up concentrations of poverty—which will also tend to equalize funding—matters much more.

In theory, spending very large amounts of money on high-poverty schools might improve the life chances of the poor as much as socioeconomic integration, but to bring poor children up to adequate levels of achievement (one element of improving life chances) is extraordinarily expensive. The estimates vary widely, running as high as 300 percent more, depending on how the goal is defined, and make the project, Christopher Jencks and Meredith Phillips note, "politically inconceivable."[26] "The typical American voter," they write, "might accept a system of educational finance that gave schools with unusually disadvantaged students 10 or 20 percent more money per pupil than the average school. But few Americans would accept a system that gave disadvantaged schools 50 or 100 percent more money than the average school." Merely equalizing funding has proved difficult enough.[27]

In any event, the equal and compensatory spending approach has fallen short for two fundamental reasons. First, it ignores peer effects, failing to address, as Gary Orfield and David Thronson note, "the most important ingredient of a good school—classmates prepared to learn and connected to real opportunity in society."[28] Second, it ignores the other resources that middle-class parents bring to their schools. Equal public spending does not equalize volunteered hours, private fundraising efforts, or the vigilant role active parents play in making sure that the money is spent well and does not merely fund a local jobs program. Nor does equalization reflect the differing educational loads of middle-class and poor students, which can be considerable.

In the end, spending equalization without integration is a trap. Because spending without integration has had disappointing results, it may fuel a backlash against further spending efforts. As Maryland state superintendent Nancy S. Grasmick has said, "I don't think there's any appetite in the state or the nation to contribute dollars with no measurable outcomes."[29] Integration, by contrast, is likely to restore the good name of education spending by producing tangible results.

Fellow Students

Even if ambitious programs were enacted to address spending, curriculum, teacher quality, teacher expectations, and parental involvement, all of these would leave unaddressed the question of the third set of actors—fellow students—and their powerful effect on education through peer influence and environment. Student discipline strategies are possible, but they are much harder to implement in the context of concentrated poverty, in which officials are rowing against a strong tide of negative peer pressure, and the problem is overwhelming in nature. In theory, unequal peer motivation and achievement might be addressed by reducing class size so that the middle-class teacher would have a fighting chance.[30] Unequal access to networks might be addressed through an elaborate mentoring program. Extra personnel could help teachers adjust to the extreme student mobility found in high-poverty schools. The list goes on.

Taken together, insisting on the notion of neighborhood schools and, at the same time, insisting on something like equality of educational opportunity would require that a mind-boggling amount of money be spent on children from society's least powerful families: hefty premiums to good teachers to entice them to teach in high-poverty schools; classes of only three or four students, allowing middle-class teachers to exert as much influence on children as do their peers; salaries for a bevy of professional child advocates to play the role that a strong PTA plays in middle-class schools, ensuring that money is spent on children, not administration; a public fund to match all privately raised funds that middle-class parents donate; a special "exchange" program between middle-class and poor schools to expose students to diversity; special counselors to help poor children develop contacts with potential employers, contacts they would have made through other students in an economically integrated school; another set of counselors to help students and teachers adjust to the constant mobility of poor families; an elaborate security force to maintain order and discipline against the odds; all this on top of special educational, bilingual, and Title I funds (doubled or tripled in amount) to begin to compensate for home environment. All this is the beginning only of an endlessly tangled web.

The Poor Track Record of Fixing High-Poverty Schools

For all these reasons, it is not surprising that those who have tried to "fix" high-poverty schools have had a difficult time. Although it might be simpler to achieve integration by fixing inner-city schools first, so that the middle-class families would return automatically, the problem, as Myron Orfield notes, is that nobody knows "how to fix monolithically poor schools."[31] The dichotomy between economic integration and quality schools presents a false choice; the two are, in fact, almost always inseparable.

Just as the equal and compensatory spending strategies have been disappointing, so too the school reform models have been largely unsuccessful in high-poverty schools. Individual "effective" high-poverty schools exist, but none has proved replicable. Efforts to improve schools generally—through initiatives like class-size reduction and an emphasis on technology—tend to produce new inequalities among segregated schools.

The effective-schools movement, begun in the 1970s, centers around the idea that through the employment of small schools, cooperative learning, an integrated curriculum, and longer academic periods, students in high-poverty and high-minority schools can do quite well. Piggybacking on this idea, in 1991, President George Bush proposed the creation of 535 New American Schools programs, which would serve as models of innovation to the nation's 110,000 schools. In 1997, Congress passed the Comprehensive School Reform Demonstration Program—better known as Porter-Obey, after the authors of the legislation—to fund research-based schoolwide reform.[32] However, those who have sought to identify "effective schools"—those that do very well with high-poverty populations—have been hard pressed to produce significant numbers of examples, and the literature has been roundly criticized for methodological flaws.[33]

Of course, particularly gifted teachers and principals do sometimes produce phenomenal results in highly segregated schools, results that often gain widespread media attention.[34] Upon closer examination, however, the startling successes usually have holes or are hard to replicate, and it would be unwise to base social policy on the expectation that such extraordinary teachers and principals will be the norm.[35] Following is a list of a few leading examples:

—Math teacher Jaime Escalante made tremendous strides with Hispanic students in Los Angeles and was the subject of a book, as well as a movie, "Stand and Deliver." In 1991, 143 of Escalante's students at East Los Angeles's heavily poor James Garfield High School took the AP calculus test, with a phenomenal 61 percent passage rate. Many of Escalante's students, however, were middle class, bused in from surrounding areas. His success required extra money and especially dedicated teachers willing to work evenings and weekends. Most important, after Escalante left Garfield, the number of students taking the AP calculus test dropped from 143 to

37, and the percentage passing dropped from 61 percent to 19 percent. When Escalante tried to replicate his program in his new school, Johnson High in Sacramento, he discovered that "building a calculus program here is much more difficult."[36]

—Robert Slavin's Success for All (SFA) whole-school reform has been widely implemented and by 1998 had been adopted in eleven hundred schools. Studies have found that by the end of first grade, SFA students were three months ahead of control groups and, by the end of fifth grade, a year ahead of the control group in reading ability.[37] Critics point out, however, that most positive SFA evaluations have been done by Slavin himself and that independent evaluations have been much less sanguine.[38] Success for All may well make the best of the difficult situation found in high-poverty schools, but the evidence of effectiveness is much less clear than that for socioeconomic integration. Most comparable programs fare worse than Success for All and do not even keep comparative statistics.[39]

—Many news accounts point to success in El Paso, Texas, where two-thirds of residents are low income and where the percentage of students passing state exams rose from 35 percent in 1993 to 61 percent in 1996.[40] But El Paso's success has also been questioned by some. Northwestern University's G. Alfred Hess, for example, notes that the Texas TAAS test is "a relatively low-level, minimum competency test," which 84 percent of students pass. The success of low-income students, therefore, is "of considerably less significance" than it would be if the exams in question were more rigorous, high-proficiency tests that measure skills important in the new economy. Daniel O'Brien points out that the closing of the gap between 1994 and 1997 in the percentage of students passing the TAAS reading test by ethnic group and economic group "may [have been] due to the ceiling effect, as Anglo passing rates for 1997 reached 92.4 percent."[41]

—In 2000, the Heritage Foundation published a report, entitled *No Excuses*, meant to show that high-poverty schools can work well. Heritage was proud of finding as many successful schools as they did—the author "found not one or two [but] twenty-one high-poverty high performing schools," but these schools were dwarfed by the seven thousand schools nationally that the Department of Education identifies as high poverty and low performing. The Heritage report highlights the degree to which individual principals were responsible for each school's success. The problem, Johns Hopkins University's Sam Stringfield noted in 1997, is that success that is associated with "a wonderful principal who has worked hard and developed a wonderful faculty" is "not replicable."[42]

Although the techniques of the effective-schools program have been incorporated into Title I and have been adopted by more than half the nation's school districts, the high-achieving low-income school is still extremely rare.[43] The list of cities that employ the effective schools strategy—Chicago, Milwaukee, Minneapolis, New York, San Diego, St. Louis, and Washington, D.C.—does not inspire confidence. Overall, a 1997 congressionally authorized study of Title I has found only "a small number" of high-poverty schools that perform better than expected—and these schools are marked by higher parental support and lower student and teacher mobility (factors that are hard to control). A 1998 study produced by *Education Week* and the Pew Charitable Trusts sought to identify "a solidly successful urban district, in which even extremely poor and minority children achieve at high levels," but concluded, "there are none." The report quotes the University of Wisconsin professor Martin Haberman, who states that "there are no model urban school systems." David Rusk, writing in 1998, concludes that "despite several decades of trying, there are no examples of high-poverty, big city school systems that have produced high student achievement levels." Jencks and Phillips note that though some formulas seem to work well, the problem is that "schools seldom implement these programs in exactly the way their designers expected or intended. A program may work well initially, when it is closely supervised by a dedicated innovator, but may have no detectable effect when the innovator tries to bottle it and sell it off the shelf."[44]

Of course, high-poverty schools should be encouraged to use research-based best practices; but best practices may be impossible to implement when they are expensive and require high expectations, skilled teachers, and active parents. Finding creative mechanisms so that the majority of students in all schools are middle class is the surest way to bring about the very elements identified by advocates of the effective schools program as essential to a school's success—"high expectations . . . an orderly, relatively quiet, and pleasant atmosphere . . . [and] a large number of adult volunteers."[45]

In recent years, as the country has emphasized quality over equality in education, progressive politicians have searched for new broad-based education-spending programs that will benefit all students, on the theory that a rising tide will lift all boats. The Clinton administration has, in particular, emphasized universal programs like reducing class size and wiring all schools to the Internet. These programs have positive elements and will do some good, but both point to the truth that as long as separate schools serve rich and poor, systemwide programs will tend to reflect and even reinforce the existing inequality of the schools themselves.

One bright exception to the rule that spending approaches are disappointing is the growing body of research showing that reducing class size in the early grades can raise student achievement, including important evidence from the Tennessee Student-Teacher Achievement Ratio (STAR) experiment.[46] In smaller classes, teachers can get to know students better and can better attend to individual needs. Some critics, however, say the evidence on class size is less clear than portrayed.[47] Others note that class sizes are already roughly equal for schools with high and with low percentages of black students and students receiving free lunch.[48] From an equality viewpoint, the biggest concern with the reduction of class size involves the question of who will be teaching the new smaller classes. The drive to reduce class size requires an expansion in the number of new teachers, which may involve a lowering of standards; and we know where the worst teachers are likely to end up. As a result, reducing class size may produce a fair amount of shifting around, with the few good teachers now in high-poverty schools moving to middle-class schools.[49]

When California reduced class size, the need to hire 12,500 teachers resulted in a 100 percent increase in the number of teachers in elementary schools granted emergency licenses. Not surprisingly, those least qualified often ended up in the high-poverty schools, as middle-class schools raided the few good teachers from high-poverty schools. Officials questioned whether it was better to have an inadequate teacher with few students or a solid teacher with more students. Although reducing class size appears to be a worthwhile initiative, if implemented in the context of economically segregated schools, the measure will not necessarily yield a net gain in equal opportunity.[50]

In addition to the plan to reduce class size, the Clinton administration has pushed technology as a way of promoting greater equality of opportunity for poor children. In particular, Clinton and his vice president, Albert Gore, have encouraged an effort to link up all schools to the Internet, believing that with access, disparities in resources like school libraries will make much less difference than in the past. Historically, however, technology has, to the contrary, often reinforced the divide between the haves and the have-nots. A 1997 Educational Testing Service report finds that nationally, schools have one computer for every ten students, but in high-poverty schools the ratio is one computer for every thirty-five students.[51] Although Clinton and Gore are right to argue for equality in technology, it is doubtful that technology by itself will prove to be the great equalizer, because students in high-poverty schools are unlikely ever to catch up; the "digital divide" simply reflects the underlying economic inequality.

Global Solutions

If the piecemeal strategies are of limited effectiveness, what about global school reforms that seek to shake up the education system in more fundamental ways? Over the past half century, there have been two major efforts to completely overhaul K–12 education. Progressives have pushed school desegregation to promote equity, and conservatives have pushed private school vouchers as a way to spur competition and also, they say, to provide greater opportunity for low-income and minority children.

Limitations of the Racial Desegregation Strategy

In 1954, in *Brown* v. *Board of Education*, the Supreme Court sought to overturn the most significant subset of America's failure to live up to the common school ideal. The primary purpose of *Brown* was, of course, to dismantle an egregious and insulting system of legalized racial apartheid in the nation's schools. Given the overlap between race and class in this country, however, racial desegregation had the potential to achieve a fair amount of economic integration, and for a long time, emphasizing race had legal advantages, as well, because the Constitution forbids purposeful segregation by race but not by class.

Racial school desegregation as an equal opportunity strategy, however, is now severely limited in four major respects: as a legal matter, relying on race is quickly becoming more of a liability than an advantage; educationally, the focus on integration by race, as opposed to class, has missed the key element of what makes schools good or bad; psychologically, racial desegregation begs the question, "Why are predominantly black schools assumed to be bad?"; and politically, racial desegregation has created difficulties in keeping together the progressive coalition of working-class whites and blacks that might push for greater educational opportunity.

In 1999, forty-five years after the *Brown* decision, Elaine Jones, the director-counsel of the National Association for the Advancement of Colored People (NAACP) Legal Defense Fund, declared that "there has been a massive retreat from the educational promise of *Brown*." The "paradox of *Brown*," the *Nation* has noted, is that on the one hand the case "changed everything"—laying the foundation for the Montgomery, Alabama, bus boycott and the Civil Rights Act—but in the realm of school desegregation it has ultimately "changed little." As Brown University's Michael Alves notes, "Segregation is alive and well, but desegregation is dead."[52] Beginning in the early 1970s, four waves of court decisions undercut the radical potential of *Brown* to transform American education.

First, the Supreme Court made the decision that northern de facto segregation did not present a constitutional violation. Rather, findings of intentional discrimination by the school board (in the North) or the state legislature (in the South) were required to trigger a desegregation remedy. If a school board purposefully gerrymandered boundaries to separate white and black students, this de jure discrimination required a remedy; but if a school board drew a boundary that, based on residential patterns, it could reasonably foresee would result in racial concentrations, no violation would necessarily be found.[53]

Second, the Court found that desegregation remedies would normally be limited to individual school districts, so that separate suburban jurisdictions would generally not be incorporated into desegregation orders. In the 1974 case of *Milliken* v. *Bradley,* the Court declared that because the Constitution speaks only to de jure segregation, suburban school districts not directly responsible for segregation must be excluded from desegregation orders.[54] As a practical matter, those white families who could afford to leave were given an easy way to avoid desegregation by moving beyond the reach of court orders.

Studies began to show that the *Milliken* loophole helped produce desegregation orders that were sometimes counterproductive and actually resulted in increased segregation. James Coleman, whose 1966 study provides empirical support for integration, published a report in 1975 finding that a desegregation order within a given district often had the effect of creating segregation between districts. Looking at nineteen cities between 1969 and 1973, eight of which had desegregation plans and eleven of which did not, Coleman found that all districts saw white flight, but those experiencing school desegregation saw white flight at four times the rate expected. By 1994–95, the nation's ten largest big-city school districts all had minority populations ranging from roughly 70 to 90 percent.[55]

Third, in more recent years the Court has been increasingly willing to release formerly segregated districts from desegregation orders, making clear their judgment that judicial enforcement of *Brown* is a temporary endeavor. In a series of cases—*Board of Education of Oklahoma City* v. *Dowell* (1991), *Freeman* v. *Pitts* (1992), and *Missouri* v. *Jenkins* (1995)—the

Court spelled out just how easy it was for a district to achieve unitary or desegregated status and how difficult it would then be, once unitary status had been declared, to have a judge reassert jurisdiction to combat the segregative effects of new school plans.[56]

As a legal matter, to be considered "unitary" a district need not be integrated in a layman's sense.[57] Districts in which students are racially isolated can be declared "unitary" if "good faith" efforts have been made to eliminate segregation "to the extent practicable" and the remaining concentrations are linked to de facto segregation, not vestiges of de jure segregation. In the *Freeman* case, DeKalb County, Georgia, was released from student assignment oversight—even though the district was 47 percent black and twenty-eight of its seventy-four elementary schools were either more than 90 percent black or more than 90 percent white—because the concentrations were deemed to be consistent with residential patterns and not a vestige of de jure segregation. In the *Dowell* case, the Court gave the eventual go-ahead to release Oklahoma City even though the new student assignment plan resulted in thirty-three of its sixty-four elementary schools having black populations above 90 percent or below 10 percent.[58]

Taken together, Gary Orfield and Susan Eaton note, these cases "view racial integration not as a goal that segregated districts should strive to attain, but as merely a temporary punishment for historic violations, an imposition to be lifted after a few years. After the sentence of desegregation has been served, the normal, 'natural' pattern of segregated schools can be restored." In the 1980s and 1990s, Savannah, Fort Worth, Houston, Norfolk, Dallas, Denver, Buffalo, Little Rock, Oklahoma City, Pittsburgh, Austin, Cincinnati, Cleveland, Wilmington, Broward County (Fort Lauderdale), Mobile, Kansas City, DeKalb County, Nashville, St. Louis, Kansas City, San Diego, Prince George's County, and Los Angeles were released by federal courts from desegregation orders.[59] Although some desegregation orders remain on the books, the future trajectory is clear: with almost no new cases and the demise of old court orders, racial desegregation is simply moving off the radar screen. In 1995, many legal experts predicted that within ten years, few districts will still be under court order.[60]

Fourth, some courts are now finding that voluntary race-conscious efforts to combat de facto segregation are themselves unconstitutional. Whereas in the past most conservative firepower has been aimed at ending voluntary affirmative action programs at universities, today many white families are challenging voluntary integration policies in kindergarten through twelfth grade, as well. In the leading case, *Eisenberg* v. *Montgomery*

County School District, the U.S. Supreme Court let stand a Fourth Circuit Court decision barring the use of race in a student transfer policy designed to maintain racial integration. Similar challenges to race-conscious student assignment have prevailed in San Francisco, Boston, Houston, Buffalo, Charlotte-Mecklenburg, North Carolina, and Akron, Ohio.[61] The logic in these rulings is consistent with a string of affirmative action cases involving education and contracting that require findings of discrimination to justify racial classifications—but the issue is not entirely settled.[62]

The new line of cases involving kindergarten through twelfth grade, if affirmed by the Supreme Court, would turn traditional civil rights strategy on its head. For years, the conventional wisdom has held that even if the goal is socioeconomic integration, racial integration should be emphasized because—as Gary Orfield notes—"the Fourteenth Amendment and the civil rights laws prohibit unequal treatment of racial minorities in public institutions, but they provide little, if any, protection against unequal treatment of the poor." Efforts to make economic class a "suspect category" like race, triggering strict judicial scrutiny, have failed, so litigators have generally led with the racial focus.[63]

Ironically, the opposite logic may soon apply. Racial desegregation cases are rarely filed, because it is hard to tie present-day racial concentration to past segregative acts or laws. Instead, it is the opponents of racial desegregation who are more likely to get a hearing in court and to have voluntary racial desegregation programs struck down. In a complete turning of the wheel, officials in Arlington, Virginia, Wake County, North Carolina, San Francisco, Broward County, Florida, and elsewhere are adopting policies that emphasize class over race as a way to try to achieve some racial integration in a constitutional manner.[64]

The second major problem with the racial desegregation strategy is that from an equal opportunity vantage point, as noted earlier, what matters most is not racial integration but economic integration. An exclusive focus on race ignores the possibility and significance of intraracial class-based integration (between poor and middle-class blacks and between poor and middle-class whites), and it sometimes produces racial integration that does not result in class integration (poor whites with poor blacks or middle-class whites with middle-class blacks) and therefore does little to improve the life chances of students that comes with economic integration.

From the standpoint of achievement, it has always made sense theoretically to integrate some poor blacks into middle-class black schools because black schools in which a majority are middle class can and have achieved at high levels. On a practical level, as late as 1975, the majority-black majority-middle-class school was an oxymoron. Nancy St. John argued at the time that "middle-class black families . . . do not yet exist in sufficient concentrations to create genuinely middle-class, majority-black schools."[65] Twenty-five years later, however, the possibility of class integration within the black community has increased, as a result of both the growth of the black middle class and the flight of middle-class blacks from cities to the suburbs. Whereas extreme discrimination used to keep blacks as a group largely poor—as late as 1940, approximately 90 percent of blacks lived in poverty—today the black poverty rate has fallen below 30 percent, the lowest rate in U.S. history, and there is a substantial middle-class black population, constituting an estimated 33–40 percent of the black population.[66] In fact, the economic gap between poor and rich blacks is even greater than it is between poor and rich whites and is also, Orlando Patterson notes, greater than the economic inequality between blacks and whites. As the middle-class black population grew, its members followed other middle-class groups to the suburbs in dramatic numbers. Between 1970 and 1995, the black suburban population grew by 7 million, a far greater number than the population that moved to the North in the great black migration between 1940 and 1970 (4.4 million). In the 1980s, the black suburban population rose 34 percent, four times the growth rate of suburban whites.[67]

As a result, a growing number of majority-minority schools are also majority middle class. In suburban DeKalb County, Georgia, for example, three high schools are more than 90 percent black but have fewer than 20 percent of their students receiving free lunches. Even among extremely segregated schools—with 90–100 percent minority populations—in some 43 percent a majority of students are not receiving free lunch.[68] Racial integration strategies miss the opportunity to integrate poor blacks into middle-class black schools.

Similarly, there is some potential for integrating poor whites into middle-class white schools, which a strict racial focus completely bypasses. Nationally, the number of poor whites is more than double the number of poor blacks. Depending on how the term *high poverty* is defined, as many as half the nation's high-poverty schools are majority white and as many as 50 percent of students attending high-poverty elementary schools are non-Hispanic whites.[69] In schools with more than 40 percent FARM participation, the average total student population is 51 percent white, 29 percent black, 15 percent Hispanic, and 6 percent other.[70]

In the early 1970s, researchers found that although only one school in Duluth, Minnesota, was racially concentrated, six were concentrated with low-income students. In the early 1980s, scholars looking at Cambridge, Massachusetts, began advocating integration by class as well as race after finding that of thirteen elementary schools, the two with the lowest level of performance were low income and largely white.[71] Since then, the number and size of white ghettos nationally has grown substantially, and in the 1980s, the largest increase in concentrated poverty was among non-Hispanic whites. According to the Urban Institute, the number of Americans living in underclass white neighborhoods rose 85 percent between 1980 and 1994. There are significant white ghettos in Columbus, Philadelphia, and Memphis. Nationwide, by one estimate, there are slightly more white-slum census tracts than Hispanic-barrio census tracts. The white underclass, writes Orlando Patterson, "remains one of the best-kept secrets among American journalists and social scientists."[72]

Finally, many racial integration plans have done little good in terms of academic achievement and opportunity because they have not also involved class integration. "One of the leading reasons for skepticism about central city school desegregation plans," says Gary Orfield, "is that they don't produce any class advantage" and instead involve mostly blacks "with a few poor whites mixed in." This happens quite often under *Milliken,* for if the decision gave whites a way out of integration, studies find, it was the affluent whites who were most likely to flee.[73] Desegregation plans in Cincinnati, Minneapolis, Little Rock, Boston, and Lowell, Massachusetts, all fell most heavily on low-income whites. Today, civil rights advocates put new emphasis on the fact that racial desegregation, to bring academic gains, must also involve socioeconomic integration.[74]

Third, the distinction between racial segregation and that based on class has taken on psychological importance as the nature of racial segregation has changed. When blacks were segregated by law and could not choose to attend integrated schools even if they wished to, there could be little question of its insulting character. Justice John Harlan noted in his dissent in *Plessy* v. *Ferguson* that the obnoxious theory behind forced separation was that blacks are "so inferior and degraded that they can not be allowed to sit in public coaches occupied by whites."[75]

As the question moved from what to do about de jure segregation to what to do about de facto segregation, however, the issue took on a different cast. As Randall Kennedy argues, there is an obvious "racial insult" when the state enforces segregation, but there may be no racial insult when a black child attends a neighborhood school "if the child's parents genuinely prefer that the child attend an all-black institution." One could argue that the issue of stigma actually reversed itself: that efforts to demolish de facto racial segregation assumed that blacks could not possibly choose to aggregate and that they needed to sit next to whites to improve their ways. Isn't it "psychologically damaging," William Raspberry asks, to tell black children "that what is wrong with their predominantly black school is that it has too many kids who look like them?" Blacks across the political spectrum have noted that the attempt to disperse blacks whenever they become a majority in a school has condescending undertones. On the left, Stokely Carmichael and Charles Hamilton have said that the notion implicit in school integration is that "the closer you get to whiteness, the better you are."[76] On the right, Clarence Thomas declared in *Missouri* v. *Jenkins*, "It never ceases to amaze me that the courts are so willing to assume that anything that is predominantly black must be inferior."[77]

The best answer to Thomas, as Gary Orfield notes, is that separate is unequal not because "something magic happens to minority students when they sit next to whites" but because minority schools are often "isolated high-poverty schools that almost always have low levels of academic competition, performance, and preparation for college or jobs." If that is true, isn't the continued focus on race as a proxy for poverty just as insulting and stigmatizing as the news media's practice of showing pictures of blacks in stories about poverty?[78]

Fourth, racial desegregation has had an unintended political effect that cannot be ignored. For progressives and for African Americans, racial desegregation efforts have often alienated potential allies—white working-class voters—and helped turn them against government and progressive solutions generally. Racial desegregation was a necessary and justified step in cases in which there was evidence of prior discriminatory acts, but the fact that busing plans tended not to address issues of economic inequality had the political effect of driving a stake into the heart of the old New Deal coalition of working-class whites and blacks. The Boston busing crisis, discussed in more detail in chapter 8, illustrates these problems as well as any, as the issue pitted working-class whites and blacks against each other for many years in a state of war from which they are only now recovering. Whereas racial busing put these groups at each other's throats, economic desegregation would bring these groups together in common cause.

Limitations of the Private School Voucher Strategy

If the left's global solution, racial desegregation, looks increasingly out-dated, what about the right's big idea—private school vouchers? On the surface, publicly funded private school vouchers could provide the sort of systemwide solution that would raise achievement and provide greater equity and social unity. For one thing, because vouchers move us beyond neighborhood school assignment, they might in theory promote integration. For another, a pure voucher system, which would provide each family with a set number of dollars to be spent on public or private school, may be the surest method for bringing about equal spending.[79] Upon closer examination, however, it appears clear that vouchers will provide less equity, lower overall achievement, and less unity than even our currently flawed system of economically segregated public schools.

Research suggests that most choice schemes that include private schools will exacerbate socioeconomic concentrations, rather than alleviate them, by skimming off the best and most motivated students. In Sweden, a voucher experiment instituted in 1992 promoted ethnic and economic segregation as Swedish-origin children and well-off immigrant children abandoned low-income immigrant schools. Likewise, in Chile, according to a study by the Stanford professor Martin Carnoy, a voucher program adopted in 1980 resulted in the flight of middle- and upper-class families to private schools. As a result of this increased segregation, the test scores of lower-income students dropped sharply between 1982 and 1988. Recent research in New Zealand confirms these earlier findings.[80] Increased segregation is likely to be the result in the United States, as well, for three primary reasons.

First, because we are a nation that today sends almost 90 percent of students to public schools, any voucher scheme is likely to supplement, rather than supplant, the public school system, and the children of the least motivated families are most likely to be left behind. Voucher advocates who rightly wish to liberate poor children from failing schools must concede that the total number of children attending private schools is going to be relatively small in the foreseeable future. Today, only about 12,000 of the nation's 52 million students participate in publicly funded voucher programs.[81] Even if the number of students attending private schools doubles through a voucher scheme, nearly 80 percent of students will still attend public schools, so vouchers are unlikely ever to replace public schools.[82]

Even if vouchers raise the achievement of the students who participate—and the evidence is mixed—the larger question is what happens to the vast majority of students left behind. All the evidence suggests that those who would prefer to choose their elementary and secondary schools tend to be the most motivated and ambitious, and those who attend their neighborhood schools without considering alternatives are the least, so greater segregation is likely to result.[83] Voucher proponents claim all schools will benefit from competition, but all the evidence in this book suggests that increased segregation will markedly reduce the life chances of the remaining public school students.

Second, most voucher schemes provide only small amounts of money for use by families, so as a practical matter, vouchers are likely to be used mostly as subsidies to middle-class families who can afford to pay part of private school tuition. Under a system of universal vouchers, the price of private education would presumably rise with the government subsidy—just as college tuition has risen with the expansion of student loans. As a result, limited vouchers would provide a way out for the middle class, leaving the public schools increasingly concentrated with poor and working-class students.[84]

Third, because private schools can be selective—and because achievement and behavior correlate with socioeconomic status—unregulated private choice is likely to cream off the wealthiest public school students. Under voucher schemes, Senator Edward Kennedy has noted, "the real choice is given to the private schools, not parents or students." This is the weakness in the argument that poor children should have a chance to go to Sidwell Friends School just as Chelsea Clinton did. As Al Shanker remarked, "That would happen if they could pass Sidwell's stiff entry requirements and if their parents could come up with $12,000 to $14,000 over and above the amount of the voucher." Students who do not stack up academically, or who misbehave, can and are expelled from private schools. Conversely, if legislation were to require that private schools receiving public vouchers use a lottery admissions system, the number of schools willing to participate would most likely be very small. In Florida, for example, only 23 of 1,603 private schools signed up to take part in the state's voucher scheme, which requires participating schools to admit students by lottery.[85]

Setting aside the question of economic integration, most voucher plans are regressive because they would divert public resources to wealthy families whose children already attend private schools but now pay their own way. According to a 1987 General Accounting Office report, the wealthy are eight times as likely as the poor to use private schools (31 versus 4 percent).[86] A 1993 National Household Education Survey found low-income families were five times less likely than high-income families to choose private school (3 versus 15 percent) and those whose parents' education had ended with high school were eight times less likely than those with graduate school education (2 versus 16 percent). Even Catholic schools—supposedly the working class's private alternative—have student populations with median family incomes at 121.5 percent of the public school median and parental education levels that are twice as high as those of the public schools (24 percent of mothers having four-year degrees compared with 12 percent in public schools).[87] Providing a subsidy to these relatively well-off families who today pay out of their own pockets is a hard decision to justify on equity grounds.

In addition, private school vouchers are likely to undercut the citizenship- and democracy-promoting function of the public schools. The U.S. Supreme Court has recognized the public schools as "the most vital civic institution for the preservation of a democratic system of government."[88] Private schools cannot play the same role for three sets of reasons.

First, because vouchers are likely to promote economic segregation, they will make elite students less likely to genuinely believe in the philosophy of one person, one vote and will make the downtrodden more likely to feel alienated from the mainstream. Second, across class lines, vouchers are likely to underline and harden religious and racial differences, making a unified democracy in a diverse nation that much more difficult to maintain. In the Netherlands, for example, one study found that the use of vouchers to attend separate religiously affiliated schools has "reinforced the religious segmentation within society." The late Al Shanker argued that whereas traditionally public schools "take all comers," with vouchers "you'll end up with kids of different religions, nationalities, and languages going off to different schools to maintain their separateness, and I think we'd have a terrible social price to pay for it. You'll end up with creationist schools, Louis Farrakhan schools." Shanker argued that "now, when the ties that bind us seem especially fragile, shouldn't we be working to strengthen [the common school] ideal instead of abandoning it?" As Michael Kelly argues, "Public money is shared money, and it is to be used for the furtherance of shared values, in the interest of *e pluribus unum*." The problem with vouchers (and some charter schools) is that "they take from the *pluribus* to destroy the *unum*."[89]

Third, because private schools are not accountable in the way public schools are, there is no guarantee that they will promote the democratic values that are a central part of the public school curriculum. The Supreme Court wrote in *Ambach* v. *Norwick* that public schools are responsible for "inculcating [the] fundamental values necessary to the maintenance of a democratic political system" and in *Plyler* v. *Doe* that public schools "are an important socializing institution, imparting those shared values through which social order and stability are maintained."[90] Unregulated private schools, by contrast, can be segregated academies that promote racial supremacy or black separatism—or Marxism or Nazism—all with public funds. The conservative activist Ron Unz notes that Polly Williams, the chief backer of vouchers in Milwaukee, served as "a 'colonel' in a local black militia that around the time of the Gulf War threatened to become a violent fifth column on behalf of Saddam Hussein."[91]

Although public schools can be required by democratically elected bodies to teach respect for the rule of law, toleration of racial and religious minorities, and belief in democracy and equal opportunity, private schools cannot be required to teach these things to the same extent. So too, private schools are not bound to respect constitutional rights as are public schools: in Milwaukee, a student who, in a speech in her English class on black separatism, criticized her private school for racism was suspended; when she sued, her case was thrown out of federal court because the Constitution does not apply to private schools. A central problem with vouchers, as Michael Kelly notes, is that "a pluralistic society cannot sustain a scheme in which the citizenry pays for a school but has no influence over how the school is run."[92]

If universal vouchers are problematic, what about voucher schemes that are limited to poor students stuck in troubled schools? Today's most hotly debated voucher plans call for vouchers for the poor only. Voucher programs are means-tested in Milwaukee and Cleveland, as are congressionally proposed vouchers for the District of Columbia. On the surface, means-tested vouchers would appear to increase economic integration because they give poor students a chance to escape high-poverty schools, an apparently progressive idea. "To require poor people to go to dangerous, dysfunctional schools that better-off people fled years ago, and that better-off people would never tolerate for their own children—all the while intoning pieties about 'saving' public education is worse than unsound public policy," comments Jonathan Rauch. "It is repugnant public policy."[93]

One can agree with Rauch that poor children trapped in bad schools do deserve to be free to choose better schools, however, and still believe the choice should be limited to publicly accountable, democracy-promoting, nation-unifying public schools. The conservative argument for allowing poor children to escape bad schools is potent; their secondary premise, that escape must occur to private schools, is the weak link in their argument.

There is also a prudential concern with means-tested vouchers. Even if private school vouchers for the poor are defensible, they provide a foot in the door for voucher proponents who may wish to expand the program quickly. In Milwaukee, for example, Mayor John Norquist has proposed universalizing access to vouchers by bumping up the income cap from $23,328 for a family of three to $100,000 and then eliminating the cap entirely.[94] The Republican concern for poor children trapped in bad schools is welcome; but the historic constituency of conservatives is not the downtrodden, and over time the wealthy are likely to demand the same subsidy.

Note that the argument outlined here against vouchers is like the Supreme Court's not-never-but-almost-never notion of "strict scrutiny" under the equal protection clause: there should be a very strong presumption against vouchers that can be rebutted with a compelling justification. Chapter 7 outlines one carefully circumscribed exception: vouchers are justified when and only when, for political or logistical reasons, they would achieve more socioeconomic integration than public school choice.

One final note on this issue. Some point to the relative success of disadvantaged children in private Catholic schools as evidence that high-poverty schools can work, if we only could replicate what Catholic schools do—promote high standards, parental involvement, and strict discipline policies. It is true that poor children generally do better in Catholic schools than in public schools. Far from demonstrating that high-poverty public schools can work, however, the Catholic school example underlines the importance of attending a school with a predominantly middle-class culture. Poor children do well in Catholic schools in large part because such schools are today's best approximation of the common school.

Obviously, much of the reason Catholic schools perform better on the whole is that the student body is better off economically and schools select students rather than taking all comers. The further finding that individual students from disadvantaged backgrounds (controlling for motivation) do better in Catholic schools than in public schools is also not surprising, given that their classmates are better off and the schools are generally more integrated by class and race than the public schools.[95] The "common school effect" found by Coleman and others studying Catholic schools—a closing of the gap between the achievement of rich and poor—is to be expected, because most Catholic schools better approximate a common school mix than do public schools.[96]

What about cases of individual Catholic schools that have high concentrations of poverty—exceptions to the Catholic rule—and still manage to perform very well? Doesn't that disprove the common school thesis? Not at all. First, the general aura of success among Catholic schools derives mostly from middle-class parochial schools; high-poverty Catholic schools do not perform particularly well.[97] Second, those that do better than expected are attracting the most motivated poor, those who are closer to middle-class families in values, norms, and aspirations. The voucher experiment in Milwaukee underlines this fact: even though families participating in the program were just as poor as other Milwaukee parents (60 percent on public assistance), the parents were more educated, had higher educational aspirations for their children, were more likely to help their children at home, and were, even before the program, more likely to volunteer in the school. In some 70 percent of Catholic schools, testing is a requirement for admission, and some 12 percent of students are rejected after applying.[98] (In addition, the children who do not conform to middle-class values can, of course, be quickly expelled from Catholic schools.) The features that do make the schools better—parental involvement, high standards, and strict discipline—are much easier to implement among the special population of poor attracted to Catholic schools and are difficult to replicate in the public schools, unless those public schools are predominantly middle class.

The evidence in this chapter suggests that the importance of a school's socioeconomic status is inescapable. Because students, parents, and teachers matter so much to school quality, piecemeal efforts at reform fall short. The left's global reform, racial desegregation, is of limited effectiveness, and the right's global reform, vouchers, is likely to be counterproductive. By contrast, efforts to make all schools predominantly middle class are likely to have a significant impact on the life chances of poor children. The next chapter takes on the difficult question of how we can move closer to this goal.

| 6

How Socioeconomic Integration

Can Be Achieved in Practice

IN A COUNTRY with fifteen thousand semiautonomous school districts, varying vastly in population and acreage, implementation of a policy of socioeconomic integration will obviously require adaptation to different realities.[1] Integration in central cities, urban areas, and suburbs presents different challenges, and political and legal landscapes differ from state to state. Nevertheless, broad goals can and should be defined, and general themes can be articulated, on which individual districts will pursue variations. The ultimate goal, simply stated, is that public policy should make predominantly middle-class schools available to all students.

This aim may not be fully realizable in every school district in the near future. The more modest goal of this book is to suggest a paradigm shift such that socioeconomic integration becomes an explicit and overriding public policy goal, to be implemented to the greatest degree possible. Incremental changes in numerous diverse jurisdictions can have a significant positive impact on the lives of individual students and should themselves be considered signs of progress and success.

In devising plans for economic desegregation, we are not starting from scratch. Over the past thirty years, a number of individual school districts have implemented the idea, including: La Crosse, Wisconsin; Wake County (Raleigh), North Carolina; Manchester, Connecticut; Maplewood, New Jersey; San Diego, California; and Coweta County, Georgia.[2] As of this writing, a number of other communities are actively exploring, or have explored, the notion, including Montgomery County, Maryland; San Francisco, California; Seattle, Washington; Cambridge, Massachusetts; Pinellas County (St. Petersburg), Florida; Murfreesboro, Tennessee; Jefferson County (Louisville), Kentucky; Mecklenburg County (Charlotte), North Carolina; Charleston, South Carolina; Fayetteville, Arkansas; Howard County, Maryland; Charles County, Maryland; Palm Beach County, Florida; St. Lucie County, Florida; Wausau, Wisconsin; Rochester, New York; Harrisburg, Pennsylvania; Duluth, Minnesota; and Dayton, Ohio.[3] (Chapter 9 examines a few of these jurisdictions in some detail.) Many other districts pursue socioeconomic integration quietly, without announcing the goal. Internationally, Scotland's secondary schools were reorganized in 1965 as part of a "deliberate policy to 'desegregate' SES groups."[4]

Defining Policy

What criteria should be used to promote the goal of achieving majority-middle-class schools? The goal is to employ a measurable and objectively definable proxy for a certain set of behaviors and attitudes so that a critical mass of students in every school will have high aspirations and value achievement and not act out or move too often; and a critical mass of parents will be active in the school, insist on high standards and good teachers, participate in fund-raising, and know how to wield power—all of which will help attract a fair number of teachers who are educated, enthusiastic, and unafraid.

Of course, economic class is only a proxy for these behaviors and attitudes, so in theory, one might seek to more evenly distribute children by achievement, aspiration, discipline record, and the level of involvement of their parents. In this way, each school would have a core group of good influences. Today, for example, in New York City, certain magnet schools have quotas for slow readers to ensure that all reading levels are represented, and Wake County, North Carolina, tries to balance both the student population reading below grade level and the population of low-income students.[5] However, student economic status is a better tool for a number of reasons.

For one thing, information is much more readily available on family income (for example, eligibility to receive free or reduced-price lunches) than on such questions as how many hours a week a student spends on homework versus watching television, whether a girl is having sex and is likely to become pregnant and drop out, or how many hours a year a student's parents spend volunteering in the classroom. Calculating data on the relative positive and negative influences a given student and parent bring to the school is intrusive and highly complicated.

For another, economic status is much less manipulable than the host of behaviors and attitudes we are interested in measuring. Suppose a popular school were oversubscribed with high-achieving children, advantaging low-achieving applicants. In order to get in, some students might claim to have low aspirations, or do poorly on a diagnostic achievement test, if these were the direct measures upon which admissions were based. By contrast, families are unlikely to choose to live in poverty in order to get their children into certain programs.[6]

It has been noted throughout this book that socioeconomic status is the most accurate predictor of the various behaviors and attitudes that interest us—far more predictive than race. How, then, should socioeconomic status be defined? In other contexts (like affirmative action in college admissions), several factors are considered, because university financial aid officers have access to a wealth of data and a meritocratic judgment includes consideration of a number of obstacles overcome; but here it makes more sense to choose among the three standard indicators of socioeconomic status: parental income, parental occupation, and parental education.[7] Occupation probably should not be the key indicator because it is harder to quantify than parental education or income. Parental education is highly correlated with the relevant student factors—such as educational aspirations and achievement—and disclosure of the number of years of schooling may be seen as less confidential than disclosure of income, as one Cambridge, Massachusetts, school official found. Nonetheless, there are two reasons to favor an income measure over parental education. First, family income has been demonstrated to be at least as good a predictor (or "marker") as parental education for a variety of factors determined to be relevant.[8] Second, although districts do not now have access to parental education levels, they do have information on whose parents are low income, so using income does not require new intrusions into the privacy of families.

Ideally, a perfect mix of students from high-, middle-, and low-income families might be sought: differences in achievement, aspirations, parental involvement, and the like do occur at all gradations; so that affluent children are likely to have higher aspirations than middle-class children, just as middle-class children generally have higher aspirations than the poor. For practical reasons, however, most plans contemplating socioeconomic integration have been limited to two categories—poor and nonpoor (or middle-class)—though a three-tier system is also possible.[9] To ascertain each student's socioeconomic background, and then seek a perfect mix of students at each school from various gradations, raises serious questions of privacy and administrative feasibility. Moreover, most sociological studies have emphasized that school atmosphere is determined by the percentage of low-income students rather than the percentage of high-income versus middle-income students. The key policy goal is to break up harmful concentrations of poverty.[10]

Determining Income Cutoff Points

If a bifurcated income-based definition is used, several options are available. Administrators can piggyback off a number of existing federal programs that have income cutoffs, including eligibility for the Free and Reduced-Price Meals (FARM) program, Medicaid, Temporary Assistance to Needy Families (TANF, the successor to Aid to Families with Dependent Children [AFDC]), food stamps, and public housing. Another more informal (and cruder) proxy for income is whether students live in low-income neighborhoods, an approach San Diego and San Francisco employ.[11] School districts already have access to much of the federal data; indeed, under the 1994 reauthorization of Title I, every year school districts are required to collect data to rank school attendance zones by concentration of low-income students, using federal aid programs as a basis for determining which schools have the highest concentrations of low-income children.[12]

Which of the measures is most appropriate to use? The most generous alternative is the FARM program, under which students are eligible for free meals if their families live at or below 130 percent of the poverty line and for reduced-price meals at 185 percent of the poverty line. In the 2000–01 school year, for a family of four, the poverty line is $17,050, the free-meal cutoff is $22,165, and the reduced-price-meal cutoff is $31,543. Public housing assistance is available to families whose incomes fall below 80 percent of the median area income. Medicaid varies from state to state but has a federal floor at 133 percent of the poverty level, and the food stamp program uses a cutoff at 128 percent of the poverty level.[13]

The argument for the highest cutoff—reduced-price lunch—is that it helps identify the lower-middle-class population as well as those in actual poverty, which is probably a good approach because both groups are normally economically and educationally disadvantaged. Indeed, sociologists often define disadvantaged schools not as those in which 50 percent of students live in poverty but as those in which 50 percent of students are eligible to receive free or reduced-price meals.[14] In addition, using FARM data rather than poverty data makes it less likely that integration will occur mostly between poor and working-class children, as was often the case under racial desegregation. Inclusion of children who are eligible for reduced-price meals could also minimize stigma, because middle-income families would not be able to identify new children as impoverished or working class.

On the other hand, there are two arguments for using a lower cutoff, such as the poverty line. On the merits, although FARM-recipient students above the poverty line may be struggling, it is very likely that their parents are employed, and many sociologists have argued that values diverge most sharply between the working and the nonworking. Work, William Julius Wilson argues, "is a regulating force" in people's lives. It "imposes disciplines and regularities. . . . In the absence of regular employment, life, including family life, becomes less coherent." Hardworking families who are above the poverty line but qualify for reduced-price lunch may provide an environment quite different from that of families dependent on public assistance.[15] Particularly in less expensive areas of the country, FARM eligibility may reach too high. In addition, to the extent the system relies on such snapshots of a child's economic status, the poor are less likely to jump into the middle class, whereas a FARM-eligible student might over time.

Politically, there may be an argument for using the narrower category to determine which students live in poverty because it makes the issue more manageable. The FARM population is about double the poverty population—33 versus 17 percent.[16] Middle-class parents may be more receptive toward socioeconomic integration resulting in a classroom in which less than one-fifth of students are poor than one in which nearly two-fifths of the students receive subsidized lunch.

Ultimately, districts in different parts of the country may use different cutoffs depending on the cost of living. A family that qualifies for FARM in New York City is likely to be much worse off than a FARM-eligible Wyoming family. In La Crosse, Wisconsin, residents implementing a socioeconomic integration plan balked at the higher reduced-meal figure and chose free-lunch eligibility instead because reduced-lunch-eligible children were not considered disadvantaged by the community. If a consistent

Answering Concerns about Data on Free Lunch Eligibility

The data on eligibility for free and reduced-priced meals have been criticized as both overinclusive and underinclusive. Some critics note that the statistics undercount low-income children, particularly at the middle school and high school levels, where some students who are eligible for participation do not apply because they are embarrassed to acknowledge publicly that their families are poor. Others worry about the opposite problem—ineligible students who fraudulently apply, a problem that might grow if school placement is determined by subsidized-meal eligibility.[1] There are three answers to these problems.

First, several procedures are in place to guard against fraud. Application forms require participants to provide a social security number or food stamp or welfare case number and inform applicants that school officials may verify information provided. A parental signature is also required, in which parents certify that statements are true, and parents are notified that deliberate misrepresentation "may subject the applicant to prosecution under State and Federal Statutes." Under current law, authorities must verify randomly selected applications, requiring those audited to provide evidence of income from pay stubs or from welfare agencies.[2]

Second, to address the problem of underinclusion, particularly at the high school level, better enforcement is needed of regulations that have been on the books for two decades prohibiting public dissemination of the identity of students receiving free and reduced lunch. Increasing automation will likely reduce the problem as many school districts move to using a bar-coded swipe card system, which ensures privacy for students receiving FARM.[3]

1. Michael J. Puma and others, *Prospects: The Congressionally Mandated Study of Educational Growth and Opportunity—Interim Report* (Bethesda, Md.: Abt Associates, July 1993), p. xxx. Geoff Gould, *School Lunch Breakthrough: Politics, Technology Spur Expansion of Food Programs* (Arlington, Va.: National School Public Relations Association, 1972), p. 25.

2. Department of Agriculture, "Eligibility Guidance for School Meals Manual" (Washington, August 1991), pp. 10, 42, 50. The minimum percentage to be randomly audited is 3 percent, which tracks with IRS auditing procedures.

3. These regulations provide that FARM-recipient students not be required to stand in separate lines and are not to receive tickets of a different color and

A third solution is to base high school and middle school data on elementary school FARM participation. This practice is already used both nationally and locally to estimate middle school and high school poverty levels. In 1996, the U.S. Department of Education authorized school districts to use a "feeder pattern concept" in ranking middle and high schools for Title I purposes; districts may "project the number of low-income children in a middle school or high school based on the average poverty rate of the elementary school attendance areas that feed into that school." In Montgomery County, Maryland, the district distributes money to schools based on "educational load," which it defines as "the percentage of students in the school who *ever* received free or reduced meal service." This practice is sound from a sociological standpoint because economic deprivation in a child's early years is known to be a good proxy for certain achievement and behavior of children in later years of life—whether or not the child stays poor.[4]

that tickets are to be mailed to students to ensure anonymity; Gould, *School Lunch Breakthrough,* pp. 27–28; Joan Drummond, "School Electronically Monitors Kids' Lunch," CNN (www3.cnn.com/CNN/bureaus/chicago/stories/9705/bigbro/detail/index.htm [May 12, 1997]). Note also that the issue of stigma may be overplayed; part of the reason high schools have lower FARM rates than elementary schools is that many poor high school students drop out before graduating; James M. McPartland and Will J. Jordan, "Older Students Also Need Major Federal Compensatory Education Resources," in Gary Orfield and Elizabeth DeBray, eds., *Hard Work for Good Schools: Facts Not Fads in Title I Reform* (Cambridge, Mass.: Harvard Civil Rights Project, 1999), p. 103. The subsidized lunch program saw a jump in participation in 1991 when school districts nationally began to automatically certify students whose families received public assistance; see Robert A. Harrow Jr., "Lunch Program Reflects Surge in Suburban Poor," *Washington Post,* October 2, 1996, pp. A1, A11.

4. Department of Education, *Policy Guidance for Title I, Part A: Improving Basic Programs Operated by Local Educational Agencies* (1996), p. 30. Montgomery County (Maryland) Public Schools, *Schools at a Glance, 1998–1999* (Rockville, Md.: Dept. of Educational Accountability, 1998), p. 225. Robert M. Hauser and Megan M. Sweeney, "Does Poverty in Adolescence Affect the Life Chances of High School Graduates?" and Greg J. Duncan and Jeanne Brooks-Gunn, "Income Effects across the Life Span: Integration and Interpretation," in Duncan and Brooks-Gunn, eds., *Consequences of Growing Up Poor* (New York:

continued on next page

Answering Concerns about Data on Free Lunch Eligibility, *continued*

Russell Sage Foundation, 1997), pp. 575, 597, 604; Duane F. Alwin and Arland Thornton, "Family Origins and the Schooling Process: Early versus Late Influence of Parental Characteristics," *American Sociological Review,* vol. 49 (1984), pp. 786–87, 798; Rima Shore, *Rethinking the Brain* (New York: Families and Work Institute, 1997), p. 13.

Note that a district using the "ever received" standard will have a larger total number of students in the FARM category since the total ever receiving subsidized meals is higher than the total receiving them at any one time. To the extent that federal provisions against "disclosure" of FARM eligibility are interpreted as interfering with a district's use of the data for integration purposes, the law can be amended, or a district can simply ask parents directly whether or not they meet a certain income criterion.

---

national policy is desired, local cost-of-living differences can be readily accommodated.[17]

Finding the Proper Mix

What is the ideal socioeconomic balance of students toward which school districts should strive? Three factors enter into the equation: Academically, what proportion of middle-class children are required to ensure that middle-class values predominate? Politically, what is a stable mix of poor and middle-class children that will be tolerable to middle-class parents and will not prompt substantial middle-class flight? Logistically, what is the existing mix of poor and middle-class children in defined geographic areas?

The goal of socioeconomic integration is not mixing for its own sake but, rather, promoting a good educational opportunity for all children. It appears that as one moves on the continuum from poverty-concentrated to middle-class schools the poor begin to benefit sooner than the middle class avoids being hurt.[18] As a practical matter, the point at which middle-class children are hurt is the more important question because policies that will hurt middle-class children in a meaningful way (even if those policies help poor children marginally more, yielding a net plus for society) will never be enacted.

As discussed at length in chapter 3, middle-class children are not hurt by socioeconomic integration so long as schools remain at least 50 percent middle class. In the racial desegregation context, even fierce opponents of busing concede that the achievement of white students did not decline in integrated schools with substantial minorities of black students that remained majority white. White scores did decline when whites attended schools that were predominantly black (and, presumably, predominantly poor).[19]

Our public policy also defines 50 percent low income as a significant cutoff point. In determining which schools should receive funding for schoolwide Title I programs (as opposed to Title I programs for particular students within a school), the Congress in 1994 lowered the level from 75 percent low income to 50 percent low income beginning in the 1996–97 school year. This change was advocated, Joseph Fernandez notes, because "research indicates that overall student performance declines when over half of the students in a school are poor." Likewise, a new program designed to help disadvantaged students go to college, called GEAR UP (Gaining Early Awareness and Readiness for Undergraduate Programs), provides aid for students in middle schools in which at least 50 percent of students are eligible for free or reduced-price lunch.[20]

The goal of socioeconomic integration, establishing schools in which at least 50 percent of students are not FARM eligible, is much different from the goal of integration in the racial context. *Brown* was primarily concerned with dismantling segregation, not creating an optimal educational environment, so it was not surprising that plaintiffs sought a roughly proportional mix, whether the district was majority black or majority white. In Detroit, for example, the NAACP sought to bring each school to within a 15-point range of the 70 percent black, 30 percent white aggregate breakdown. In Clarendon County, South Carolina, federal officials sought racially proportionate schools that would be 5–17 percent white. In Prince George's County, Maryland, as the black student population grew to 72 percent, the court set maximum black enrollment requirements for magnet schools at 86.6 percent for elementary schools, 90.8 percent for middle schools, and 90.3 percent for high schools.[21]

The primary goal of socioeconomic integration, in contrast, is improved educational achievement; economic balance is merely the means to that end. Therefore, in a high-poverty district, a precise balancing resulting in a ratio of 25 percent middle class to 75 percent poor in all schools should not be sought. In rare cases in which a district is not majority middle class (about 14 percent nationally), the appropriate remedy would be a cross-district integration program to ensure majority-middle-class schools.[22]

The second important tipping point is political. Although sociologists may find that the educational quality of a school starts to decline once it becomes more than 50 percent low income, parents may believe there is an earlier tipping point—perhaps at 40 percent low income—and begin to flee the school, quickly bringing the school to the 50 percent mark and beyond. What is the socioeconomic tipping point?

Because most of the focus in the past has been on racial, rather than socioeconomic, integration, the best evidence of popular response to integration comes from the racial context. There is fairly widespread agreement that whites do not respond at all to changes in black enrollment below 25 percent but that dramatic flight occurs when the composition of the student body surpasses 50 percent black.[23] Some racism is obviously at work here, but something else as well: given the argument made by liberals, year in and year out, that schools must be integrated because majority-black schools are inferior, it is no surprise that white parents refuse to send their children to majority-black schools. Others note that the 50 percent mark may represent a desire by whites, who are accustomed to majority status, to avoid situations in which their children would be in a minority.[24]

One widely agreed upon tipping point for schools—cited by courts and others—is 40 percent black.[25] In a study of one hundred southern cities experiencing desegregation, one researcher found that there was on average no white flight when blacks constituted less than 35 percent of the school population but that majority-black districts saw significant white flight. Desegregation plans have been highly stable with white-to-minority ratios of 67 to 33 percent (Wilmington), 63 to 33 percent (Jefferson County–Louisville), and 60 to 40 percent (Charlotte-Mecklenburg). In Cambridge, Massachusetts, desegregation has been stable in a district that is only 42 percent white; and the Montclair, New Jersey, district is stable with a 1998 enrollment of 45 percent white and 55 percent minority.[26] The tipping point, of course, depends in part on the way in which integration is pursued, with tipping less likely to occur, for example, when ability grouping is kept in place.

As will be explained more fully in chapter 8, there are good reasons to think the tipping point for socioeconomic integration through public school choice in the early twenty-first century may be closer to 50 percent low income as opposed to the 40 percent figure found for racial desegregation through mandatory busing in the 1970s. Briefly, socioeconomic tipping points may be somewhat higher than racial tipping points because part of the racial tipping process is driven by the desire of blacks to aggregate to the 50 percent point, whereas the poor do not have a similar desire to aggregate. In addition, achieving integration through public school choice rather than mandatory busing is likely to reduce the anger over loss of control that spurred much flight. Finally, to the extent that socioeconomic integration also involves racial integration, opposition has declined as racial tolerance has grown over the past thirty years.

It is also important to note that setting a goal for all schools of 50 percent or more middle-class populations not only reduces the chances that the policy will produce middle-class flight; it also should reduce the silent middle-class flight that occurs every year under a system of neighborhood schools. Today, some middle-class families who are assigned to local schools that are majority poor opt for private school. Making all schools predominantly middle class should draw back into the public school system some of those families, thereby increasing the overall presence of middle-class families in the public school system.[27]

The third factor in determining the ideal socioeconomic balance is the demographic reality of the existing student socioeconomic mix. What kind of economic balance is feasible? Nationally, the good news is that today, the vast majority of school age children are not poor. Whereas in 1949, the numbers of poor and nonpoor children were roughly equal (52 percent nonpoor, 48 percent poor), in 1999, nonpoor children outnumbered poor children by 83 percent to 17 percent. Even using data on FARM eligibility (which is too generous a measure in many parts of the country), the public school population nationally is about 67 percent middle class and 33 percent working class and poor.[28]

Of course, the national figures represent the average numbers, which vary widely from state to state. As a constitutional matter, because states are ultimately responsible for education, the state-by-state low-income breakdowns are more relevant than national (or school district) data. Nationally, forty-eight states have a majority of students above the FARM-eligibility income level. Only Mississippi, Louisiana, and the District of Columbia have FARM-eligible majorities, and in Mississippi and Louisiana the cost of living is low, meaning not all families eligible for FARM are necessarily disadvantaged. (The average teacher supporting a family of four in those two states would qualify for FARM benefits.) If actual poverty data are used, all states have a majority of nonpoor students, ranging from 93 percent nonpoor in New Hampshire to 62 percent nonpoor in the District of Columbia.[29] Within states, therefore, it should be possible, using creative strategies, to achieve majority-middle-class schools most of the time.

Within existing school district lines, in the vast majority of districts— 86 percent—FARM-eligible students are in the minority; economic integration could readily be implemented within the district. If poverty is the measure, 95 percent of all students live in districts in which fewer than 40 percent of students live in poverty. Even among large urban districts, the mean percentage of students in poverty is below 20 percent.[30]

The reason such a high percentage of districts are majority middle class is threefold: in the South, most districts are county based and so encompass both city and suburb within a single school district; in the past few decades, much poverty has moved from cities to inner-ring suburbs; and historically, much poverty has been dispersed in large rural school districts.[31] In absolute numbers, nonurban schools enroll almost two-thirds of the nation's poor students. Nevertheless, many of the 14 percent of districts that have FARM-eligible majorities are inner-city districts. Fortuitously, they are surrounded by wealthier suburban areas in close proximity, making interdistrict plans logistically feasible. In all, the economic desegregation of the public schools will involve integrating the roughly 25 percent of schools nationally that now have majority FARM-eligible populations with the 75 percent that do not, so that all of America's schools will have majority-middle-class populations.[32]

Elementary versus Secondary Schools

The evidence suggests that socioeconomic integration of schools will be helpful at both the elementary and secondary levels. Integration is important at the secondary school level because most studies find that peer influence and social class composition have their greatest effect as children grow older and become more independent from their families.[33] Adolescents care more about peer acceptance, and spend more time unsupervised, than younger children; in addition, a single teacher does not oversee the student, and classes are generally larger, so the relative influence of teacher and peer shifts toward peers. Other differences between low- and high-socioeconomic-status schools become more crucial in secondary school, as well: differences in course offerings and in student behavior such as class cutting and sexual activity. Politically, socioeconomic integration of high schools is likely to be implemented somewhat more easily because parents have fewer reservations about their children's riding buses to high schools, which already cover broader geographic areas.[34]

The integration of elementary schools, however, is also important. Socioeconomic integration in the early grades has a profound effect because its impact is cumulative. In the racial desegregation context, study after study has found the largest achievement gains coming when desegregation begins early. The transition to middle school is much more difficult for students who must make a switch from a high-poverty elementary school to a mixed middle school than for those who have been in a mixed environment from an early age. Studies find that fifth-grade test scores "effectively determine course-taking patterns in middle school, and the middle school patterns in turn determine high school placement."[35] High school may also be too late to integrate some children because many low-income children drop out of school entirely after completing the eighth grade.

The benefits of early integration are also important socially. Experience with racial desegregation suggests that students are more likely to form strong peer relations across lines when they are exposed early in life to individuals different from themselves, before prejudices of various sorts set in. Young children are more open to friendships across socioeconomic lines, as well. The role of classroom volunteering by parents—which varies by socioeconomic status—is also greater in the elementary years. Finally, socioeconomic integration has a greater capacity to make a significant difference in elementary school because the existing imbalances there tend to be larger than in secondary schools. By secondary school, various elementary populations are aggregated and less economically segregated.[36]

Implementing Socioeconomic Integration

Many tools are available to maximize the number of schools with more than 50 percent middle-class students. When certain schools become overcrowded, school boundaries can be adjusted with an eye to socioeconomic integration. When new schools are built, they can be placed on the boundary lines of economically distinct neighborhoods to draw a student body from both. Transfer policies can condition approval on a contribution to, rather than a subtraction from, the goal of socioeconomic integration.

In the end, however, it is hard to achieve socioeconomic integration merely by fiddling around the edges of a system that uses mandatory school assignment based on residence. So, too, the experience of the past thirty years suggests the old alternatives to neighborhood schools—"free choice," mandatory busing, and the creation of magnet schools—are all flawed. Instead, communities are turning to a hybrid approach that achieves integration through regulated choice, effectively "magnetizing" all schools.

Controlled Choice

The controlled choice, or conditional choice, strategy was formulated by Professors Charles Willie, of Harvard University, and Michael Alves, of Brown.[37] Under existing controlled choice plans, rather than assigning students to neighborhood schools, which tend to reflect stratified residential patterns, school districts allow parents and students to choose the public school they would like to attend within a given geographical region; no guarantees are made; districts then honor these choices in a way that promotes racial integration. Although controlled choice has traditionally been designed to promote racial balance, it can easily be modified to achieve economic balancing, through what might be called common school choice.

Under most controlled choice plans, families provide a first, second, and third choice of schools at the levels of kindergarten, sixth, and ninth grades. Information and outreach programs attempt to ensure that parents are well informed. A central officer makes the decisions, so that individual schools cannot pick those promising students they believe will be easiest to teach. The process of assignment must be objective and shielded from political influence.[38]

Sensible accommodations are made to give preference to students who live within a short walk to the school; in the Cambridge, Massachusetts, controlled choice plan, for example, students within one-eighth of a mile are given preference. Similarly, once a child is admitted to a school, a younger sibling should be given preference so that families are not divided. Plans can be phased in gradually, grandfathering existing student placements to minimize disruption. Variations on the controlled choice plan are possible (for example, preferred choice, under which parents are guaranteed the neighborhood school as a fallback), though they offer less promise for integration.[39]

Controlled choice is designed to maximize parental satisfaction. Before plans are implemented, families are surveyed to see what kinds of choices they would like for their children.[40] If the survey finds that 40 percent of parents want a highly disciplined environment with uniforms, and only 10 percent want a French immersion school, then the makeup of the choices should reflect that general preference. For parents who say they believe it is too early for their children to specialize, options for "regular" schools should be made available. Respect for parent choice and preference continues after the initial decisions are made in the "signatures" that attach to various schools. Schools that are undersubscribed year after year will be closed down or reconstituted. Schools that are continually oversubscribed and deemed successful will be replicated.

Controlled choice has been used in about one in twenty districts nationwide, including several cities in Massachusetts (Boston, Brockton, Cambridge, Chelsea, Fall River, Holyoke, Lawrence, Lowell, Northampton, Salem, Somerville, and Springfield) as well as Seattle, Washington; Milwaukee, Wisconsin; Little Rock, Arkansas; San Jose, California; Indianapolis, Indiana; Montclair, New Jersey; White Plains, New York; Yonkers, New York; Buffalo, New York; East Harlem, New York; Glendale, California; St. Lucie County, Florida; Fort Meyers, Florida; LaGrange, Georgia; Rockford, Illinois; Troup County, Georgia; Pawtucket, Rhode Island; and Mobile, Alabama.[41] In the 1990s, 18 percent of Massachusetts students attended school in districts with controlled choice, and if other school systems with active public choice are included the figure rises to 25 percent. Controlled choice has bipartisan support, and the Cambridge controlled choice plan was lauded by President George Bush, his secretary of education, William Bennett, and the conservative Manhattan Institute. In only a few cities has the controlled choice mechanism run into serious political trouble. Controlled choice based on race has come under legal attack recently, but the economic version advocated here currently faces no such legal difficulty.[42]

Studies find that in public schools of choice, attendance rates are generally higher and dropout rates are lower. Achievement gains have followed the adoption of controlled public school choice—or a modified version of controlled choice—in a number of cities, including Cambridge, Montclair, Buffalo, and Lowell.[43] Controlled choice combines the best elements of—and improves upon—three alternative models of school assignment: compulsory assignment (through busing or by residence), uncontrolled choice, and magnet schools.

CONTROLLED CHOICE VERSUS COMPULSORY ASSIGNMENT. Controlled choice offers several advantages over traditional compulsory assignment schemes that either assign students based on residence or bus them based on a combination of residence and race. Whereas in the early days of desegregation, resistance was so obdurate that "choice" was usually an excuse for avoiding integration, today there is something of a policy consensus that choice should be part of the desegregation effort, and since 1981 most desegregation plans have used some element of choice.[44]

Choice fundamentally adds a right rather than taking one away. Whereas desegregation by forced busing made parents feel impotent— pawns in a system run by others—controlled choice gives them a new voice. We already have choice for those who can afford to buy into good neighborhoods or to choose private schools, but a system of public school choice greatly enlarges the circle of people who can exercise that choice. "The debate is not whether we'll have education choice," says Joe Nathan; it is, rather, "whether state and local governments will expand educational choice to low- and moderate-income people." In this way, public school choice plans combine greater freedom with greater equity. Public school choice, the AFT's Bella Rosenberg writes, attempts to create a system in which "no child [will] be trapped in a bad or poor neighborhood school simply because of the economic or social circumstances of his parents."

Unlike busing for racial balance, public choice has intrinsic educational merit in that it allows different schools to emphasize different pedagogical approaches or curricular themes among which parents can choose, based on the individual needs of their children. Students who will languish in a regular school might flourish in a Comer school, a small school, a Montessori school, an international-baccalaureate school, a Dewey-inspired progressive school, a back-to-basics school, a classical-studies school (Mortimer Adler), a multiple-intelligence school (Howard Gardner), a gifted and talented school, a future-studies school, an international-studies school, a whole-language school, a bilingual school, or a school specializing in the arts, science, business, or computers.[45] Parents can choose between an E. D. Hirsch–style "core-knowledge" school, which emphasizes coverage of broad swaths of academic material, or a Theodore Sizer–style "essential school," which emphasizes in-depth knowledge about a much smaller number of topics. Indeed, choice has such independent educational merit that it is often advocated in school districts in which desegregation is not an issue. Some evidence suggests that public school choice raises student achievement.[46]

So too, choice allows for a better correspondence between teachers and school philosophies of education. Many educators believe it is important for teachers to agree with a principal on their school's educational philosophy in order to be part of an effective team. As Evan Clinchy and Frances Kolb note, however, teachers are often assigned to "neighborhood schools on the basis of existing vacancies and seniority, whether or not they agree with the particular school's philosophy and educational practices."[47] A system of controlled choice allows both students and teachers to be matched individually with educational beliefs. Everyone benefits when that matching occurs.

Choice also spurs competition and puts pressure on administrators to improve bad schools. Under busing or neighborhood assignment, bad schools are assured a steady stream of students. Under choice, a school that fails, year after year, to provide a hospitable learning environment—even with a new economic mix of students—may be shut down by the school board. Studies find that public school choice results in greater performance by both the choice schools and the remaining neighborhood schools because bureaucracies become more responsive to the need for change.[48]

Of course, for the market analogy to work there must be consequences for schools that perform poorly. Severely underchosen schools should be closed and the buildings used to house "franchises" of the overchosen schools. Willie and Alves recommend that undersubscribed schools be given three years to improve, and in several cities that use controlled choice, failing schools have been closed.[49] Under normal circumstances, districts are hesitant to close failing schools because principals can blame high poverty rates for poor performance. Controlled choice takes away this excuse. Because properly implemented controlled choice plans will put large numbers of middle-class parents in all schools, where they will exert pressure to ensure that all schools are serving children, remaining differences in quality will truly be the fault of the school. Unlike busing or residential assignment, choice provides tangible evidence of a school's success: parents who are displeased with a school's performance can "vote" the school out of existence.

Controlled choice has also been found to spur parental involvement. It has long been known that parents who choose private schools are more active, though some have discounted this greater involvement because private school parents are a self-selected motivated group who, having plunked down their own money, are likely to want to monitor their investments. Public school choice is also associated with greater parental involvement. The process of choosing a school, writes Deborah Meier, "creates bonds between parents, teachers, and students that are in themselves important."[50] In addition, parents may feel a greater incentive to be involved because they believe that choice gives them greater leverage with school authorities. Some parents may feel "greater affiliation" with a chosen school because they "approve" of its focus. Empirical studies in Minneapolis, Alum Rock (California), Boston, Milwaukee, New York, and New Jersey have found that parental involvement increased after the adoption of school choice.[51] Parents feel especially empowered when school officials, in setting up a controlled choice plan, survey parents in advance about the kinds of pedagogy and subject specialties the parents want.[52]

Under controlled choice parents cannot avoid desegregation by moving to a different neighborhood within the school district. When school desegregation is accomplished by redrawing boundary lines, parents have the option of moving—sometimes only across the street—so that their children can attend less integrated schools. Under Supreme Court decisions, courts are powerless to address changing demographic patterns, and schools are unlikely to voluntarily redraw boundaries on an annual basis to maintain racially balanced schools.[53] When an entire district is under controlled choice, residential location within the district makes no difference. This advantage holds even outside the desegregation arena: choice is more responsive to general shifts in population that leave a neighborhood school system with some schools overcrowded and others underutilized. Similarly, controlled choice allows a student who moves within the district to remain in his or her school, reducing disruption to the child's education as well as to the school.[54]

While the "control" in controlled choice means that some families' choices may be constrained in order to implement the integration goal, the evidence suggests that in practice, only rarely are children assigned to schools they do not want to attend in order to satisfy integration requirements. In any event, in comparison with the prevailing system of neighborhood assignment, controlled choice represents a large net increase in parental choice.

The degree to which parental choice and socioeconomic integration conflict depends on the prevalence of three phenomena. First, to what degree do parents, even when given a choice, prefer the neighborhood school for reasons of convenience? Because neighborhood schools tend to reflect economic and racial residential segregation, the preference for neighborhood schools will mean that poor children may trend toward schools in poor neighborhoods and rich children to schools in rich neighborhoods. Second, to what degree, in the aggregate, do whites and blacks and rich and poor tend to prefer different types of schools? If parents' choices of pedagogical approaches sort out roughly by class—with rich parents preferring progressive education and language immersion and poor parents preferring back-to-basics schools and schools stressing obedience—then choice may result in economic stratification independent of neighborhood. Third, to what degree will the desire of families to aggregate by race undercut the effort to integrate by class, given the overlap between the two? If these three phenomena are potent, then the goal of economic balance will strongly conflict with choice. The evidence suggests, however, that a well-run system of controlled choice can normally honor both choice and integration.

For one thing, there is substantial evidence that sufficient numbers of parents will choose a school other than the neighborhood school. Many parents are willing to send their children to distant magnet schools with the promise of a better educational fit for their children—indeed, many magnets have long waiting lists; similarly, more than 70 percent of charter schools have more applicants than they can accommodate.[55] Increasingly, in some school districts, parents are so desperate to move their children out of inferior neighborhood schools that they will commit fraud and lie about residency to get their children into better suburban schools. In Boston, many minority students are willing to take long bus rides to attend suburban schools; under the voluntary Metropolitan Council for Educational Opportunity (Metco) program, which has a waiting list of seven thousand students (twice the size of the current program), some 25 percent of Metco parents register their children before the child's first birthday. The same is true of similar programs in Hartford, Rochester, Chicago, and Louisville.[56]

The popularity of vouchers among low-income and African American communities in particular suggests that where better education is available, families will be willing to travel beyond the neighborhood school. When a philanthropist contributed money for a thousand scholarships for Washington, D.C., students to attend private schools, more than seventy-five hundred students—about 10 percent of the public school enrollment—applied. When Cleveland began its publicly funded voucher program for two thousand students, some six thousand families signed up. In 1999, philanthropists Theodore Forstmann and John Walton offered forty thousand private scholarships for poor students in kindergarten through eighth grade; more than a million students applied, including 44 percent of all eligible students in Baltimore.[57]

In 1998, a Public Agenda poll found that 60 percent of black parents would "switch their kids from public to private school if money were not an obstacle," suggesting that they are not wedded to neighborhood public schools when superior offerings are realistically available. Most significantly, a 1996 Gallup/*Phi Delta Kappan* poll found that 45 percent of all parents would choose schools outside of their neighborhoods for their children if given the chance.[58]

In areas in which controlled choice has been implemented and parents are accustomed to the concept, the numbers choosing nonneighborhood schools can be even higher. Alves has found that under Cambridge's controlled choice plan, 60–65 percent choose a school other than the neighborhood school; in Boston, 45 percent initially chose nonneighborhood schools, and the percentage later climbed to 57 percent. According to Boston school committee chair Bob Gittens, a recent study has found that "people are choosing schools that may not be the closest in terms of distance . . . [based on the school's] perceived quality."[59] In Montclair, New Jersey, another controlled choice district, the majority of families choose nonneighborhood schools. Even if small numbers of parents—as low as 15 percent—choose nonneighborhood schools, the schools could be significantly more integrated than under a system of residential assignment.[60]

For another, the evidence suggests that parental tastes in pedagogy do not neatly break down along economic and racial lines. Although some early studies found that the poor trended toward structured programs and the wealthy toward unstructured programs, more recent hard evidence suggests broad similarities.[61] In Cambridge's controlled choice plan, racial groups did not vary in their choices. Alves and Willie have found that "the pattern of school choice is remarkably similar for both majority and minority parents, thereby minimizing mandatory assignments due to race"; the same was true in Boston and in Lowell, Massachusetts. Charles Glenn notes that desegregation succeeded in Springfield and Worcester, Massachusetts, because "black and Hispanic and white parents were roughly the same" in their pedagogical preferences.[62]

Finally, evidence suggests that today most Americans put a higher premium on the quality of education than on the racial makeup of the student body. Although African Americans may have legitimate reasons to aggregate, polls suggest that most blacks support residential integration; only one-fifth wish to live in all-black areas. Whereas in 1964, 62 percent of blacks wanted to live in "mostly black" neighborhoods and only 4 percent in "mostly white" neighborhoods, today, large majorities of blacks wish to live in integrated neighborhoods. In a survey of ghetto residents in Chicago in the late 1980s, only 23 percent said that if given the option to move they would prefer to stay in their own neighborhood. Massey and Denton have found that the majority of blacks want to live in neighborhoods that are roughly half white and half black, and 95 percent are willing to live with a 15 percent black population. In a Detroit study, parents ranked "safety" and supportive "values" as most important considerations in their children's schools; the lowest rank was given to schooling with children whose parents have "educational and occupational backgrounds similar to me." Meanwhile, among whites, the percentage who said they would move if a black moved into the neighborhood dropped from 44 percent in 1958 to 1 percent in 1998.[63]

If only limited numbers of blacks and whites value aggregation over education, it is even less likely that the poor will want to aggregate. For one thing, from an academic standpoint, economic integration is in the self-interest of the poor who will do better; racial integration does not in itself benefit blacks academically. For another, although there are legitimate reasons that an ethnic group may wish to aggregate (to promote an ethnic culture, for example), the poor do not have a specific culture they wish to preserve.

Two additional steps can be taken to reconcile choice and integration. First, to the extent that preimplementation parent surveys reveal any socioeconomic leanings toward certain programs (for example, wealthier parents trending toward progressive or alternative schooling), the district can place those progressive programs in formerly blue-collar neighborhood schools so that the tendency of some to prefer neighborhood schools counteracts the pedagogical preference. In this way, middle-class and working-class parents are more likely to divide their choices between schools, with some favoring neighborhood and others opting for a preferred pedagogy. This strategy has proven highly successful in Montclair, where 95 percent of students receive their first choice and schools are nicely balanced by race and by socioeconomic status.[64]

Similarly, because part of the reason certain schools may be underchosen will have to do with the school's past reputation, officials can place the most popular pedagogical approaches or subject areas (as revealed in the parent survey) in the previously stigmatized school. Under controlled choice, a new influx of middle-class families will put pressure on schools to improve. If this does not work, severely underchosen schools should be closed and reopened with a clean slate of faculty and leadership.

A second mechanism, which maximizes choice but maintains basic integration, allows schools to employ a band or range of socioeconomic makeup rather than a rigid number. Although the goal might be 33 percent FARM-eligible students in every school, schools might be permitted to fall within a range of, for example, 15–45 percent FARM eligible, to accommodate choice. Court orders involving racial desegregation have typically used a guideline of plus or minus 15 percent.[65]

Taking these facts together, the number of students in controlled choice districts who are assigned to schools not of their choice is very small. Boston and Cambridge boast placement in first-, second-, or third-choice schools at around the 90 percent level—a rate replicated in other jurisdictions using controlled choice, like St. Lucie County, Florida; Lowell, Massachusetts; Montclair, New Jersey; and White Plains, New York.[66] Moreover, most of those who do not receive their first choice are turned down because of overall space limitations having nothing to do with racial balance. Glenn notes that in 1990, only 1.7 percent of students assigned to Boston schools (238 of 14,041 first-, sixth-, and ninth-graders) "were either denied a place or assigned involuntarily to a place that another student was denied in order to meet the requirements of desegregation." In a 1995 Bain and Company survey, 80 percent of parents said they were satisfied with controlled choice, and 72 percent said they preferred having a choice to assignment based on neighborhood schools.[67]

Although some critics fixate on the 1.7 percent whose choice is constrained by integration goals, the movement from neighborhood schools to controlled choice represents an enormous expansion of choice, particularly for the poor. Today, private school choice is still largely the province of the well-to-do; families making less than $15,000 a year are five times less likely to choose private schools as those making more than $50,000; and those with no education beyond high school are eight times less likely to choose private schools as those with graduate degrees.[68] Among those assigned to public schools, the poor are almost twice as likely to be assigned to schools they did not choose even indirectly, through residential choice. By contrast, those with little education and income are twice as likely as the wealthy to use public school choice.[69]

Researchers estimate that roughly 36 percent of all elementary and secondary schoolchildren attend neighborhood schools consciously chosen by their parents in deciding where to reside—and that wealthier families are much more likely to have done so. For many families, choosing a residence based on school district is a luxury; as Alves expresses it, "The priority of the family is they've got to find a decent place to live that they can afford." For the poor, assignment to unpopular neighborhood schools is a fact of life. As a practical matter, Glenn notes, poor and working-class people are effectively denied what is considered by the Universal Declaration of Human Rights (1948) a "right to choose the kind of education that shall be given to their children."[70]

It is ironic, Glenn notes elsewhere, that in moving from assigned schools to controlled choice, critics focus on the small amount of control rather than the enormous flowering of freedom. "An inevitable cost of freedom is to experience remaining constraint as galling," he writes. "So long as children are simply assigned to school involuntarily on the basis of where they live, of course, the issue of disappointment does not arise."[71] Moving to controlled choice means that 90 percent get one of their top choices—as opposed to the 36 percent who today choose a neighborhood school—and it is unreasonable to focus on the 10 percent who fail to have their choice honored rather than the majority who realize a net gain in choice.

Because choice redistributes opportunity, the chance of each child is equal to that of every other and is not contingent upon a parent's ability to pay. Whereas affluent families today can purchase a 100 percent lock on a particular school, and many poor families effectively have no choice, under controlled choice everyone has a 90 percent chance for basic satisfaction. Controlled choice provides an overall net increase in choice and a fairer distribution of choice, as well. Choice uses equality to increase freedom for the poor, while continuing to allow the middle class a variety of common school choices; in this way, equality becomes a source of freedom, not its enemy.[72]

CONTROLLED VERSUS UNCONTROLLED CHOICE. If it is true that choice and integration do not normally conflict in controlled choice plans, then why not just use uncontrolled choice? Why the need for "control"? The problem is that uncontrolled choice can actually produce more, not less, segregation. Like electricity, Joe Nathan notes, public school choice is "a powerful tool capable of producing helpful or harmful effects, depending on its use."[73] Four elements of controlled choice plans are crucial to ensuring that plans promote, rather than undercut, socioeconomic integration.

First, choice must be controlled to avoid the "prisoner's dilemma" issue—that people act based in part on how they think others will act. If race and economic status are not considered, patterns of racial and economic segregation may be hard to break. Traditionally, middle-class parents, when considering neighborhoods and visiting schools, ask about test scores, which are given in absolute terms, rather than as the value added by a school.[74] Because socioeconomic status is linked to test scores, those schools that had middle-class populations in the past are likely under uncontrolled choice to draw disproportionate numbers of highly informed middle-class parents, while low-income schools will attract few middle-class families, and the cycle will continue.[75] If affluent parents have no guarantee that the new computer-centered school located in a tough neighborhood will have a predominantly middle-class student body, they may choose conservatively, based on what schools middle-class children have attended in the past, rather than based on the school theme.

This has been the experience in places like Kansas City and Prince George's County, where magnet schools, despite the expenditure of extra money, were unable to attract middle-class white students. These districts face a chicken-and-egg problem: in order to attract middle-class students, the key prerequisite is not so much the expenditure of money—many central cities already outspend suburban areas—as it is a critical mass of other middle-class children.[76] But who will go first? Similarly, a poor black family may like the back-to-basics emphasis in a school found in an affluent white neighborhood but hesitate to apply because the parents do not want their child to be isolated as the only student of color in his or her class.

In either case, parents do not have true choice in pedagogy. With controlled choice, on the other hand, the fear of being an economic or racial "pioneer" is eliminated from the equation. Christopher Jencks notes that "if the traditions and distinctive identity of a school depend not on the character of the student body but on the special objectives and methods of the staff, middle-class parents who approve of these objectives and methods will often send their children despite the presence of poorer classmates." Because schools will develop distinct themes or pedagogical strategies and all schools will have a similar economic makeup, families will choose schools based on an emphasis on French, or a back-to-basics approach, or the fact that the school provides an after-school program, rather than the anticipated social class of the students.[77]

The second crucial feature of controlled choice plans is that they require every family to choose a school, even if their choice is the neighborhood school. There is mounting evidence that when parents must take the initiative to choose, unregulated and poorly designed public school choice plans can actually exacerbate rather than alleviate concentrations of race and class.[78] The key problem, studies show, is that the least educated parents are least likely to avail themselves of choice, and the most aggressive parents, predominantly middle class and highly educated, dominate the system. This is particularly true when parents gain an edge by camping out all night to be first in line. Richard Elmore and Bruce Fuller conclude that "a large part of the stratification problem seems to result from parents and students who simply do not choose, rather than from differing preferences among those who do choose. That is, once parents and students make the decision to choose and actively exploit the opportunities that decision presents, they seem to have preferences that are remarkably similar across race and social class."[79]

Controlled choice protects against that possibility by requiring people to make a choice of schools. Because no family is guaranteed its neighborhood school, everyone has incentive to choose. Business recognizes that for the competitive aspects of choice to be fully realized, all parents must be required to choose, and the National Alliance of Business has endorsed "mandatory choice." Well-designed controlled choice plans also provide for mail-in registration so that there is no advantage to being first in line.[80]

Third, controlled choice plans strictly limit the number of schools that can handpick students, whereas uncontrolled choice plans—including voucher schemes—generally do not. In principle, there is a place for a small number of selective public high schools—such as Thomas Jefferson in Virginia, Stuyvesant in New York, or Boston Latin—and these schools should not be required to admit a certain percentage of students from disadvantaged backgrounds.[81] Poor children can earn their way into these elite public schools through hard work; and indeed, such schools can provide an escape from poverty for hardworking poor students. Many elite public schools—Scarsdale, or New Trier—tend to be based on the wealth of parents, but a school such as Bronx High School of Science is quite different.

That having been said, controlled choice plans should strictly limit the number of public schools that use admissions tests. If the number of such public academies were to proliferate, they could be used as a way to avoid the economic desegregation plan of a district. The competitive-school loophole to the general economic integration plan must remain small, or it will swallow the rule.

Particularly as schools become more publicly accountable, those schools with a choice of students will have a powerful incentive to pick the brightest ones. As Natriello and colleagues note, "There are only two ways to get high-achieving students: recruit them, or transform low achievers into high achievers. Currently it is easier to recruit high achievers than to create them." If schools choose students, those schools that begin as popular will grow even more so; schools that begin as less desirable will grow more so, as well. Even where schools are not permitted to choose students, schools that are not subject to controlled choice can find ways to subtly discourage students who are likely to drag down scores from applying or to encourage low-scoring students to drop out.[82]

Fourth, controlled choice plans pay transportation costs and offer information outreach; uncontrolled choice plans often do not and can thereby effectively exclude participation of the poor. In Richmond, California, for example, a plan allowing students to choose from forty-five schools saw only forty-one hundred of thirty-one thousand students choose a nonneighborhood school and actually exacerbated racial segregation, in part because the plan required parents of elementary schoolchildren to pay their own transportation costs. In the case of city-to-suburb choice plans, experience shows low levels of participation among poor minorities in districts that required parents to pay part of their transportation costs (Minneapolis and St. Paul) but much greater participation where the state paid for transportation (St. Louis and Milwaukee). The transportation costs are not unmanageable: according to a 1994 Department of Education study, 72 percent of school systems offering elementary transfer choice provide free transportation, as do 57 percent for middle schools and 48 percent for high schools.[83]

Well-informed choice can be encouraged by giving notice on television, mailing out letters clearly explaining the choice system, and making the choice forms easy to return. Outreach to poor parents was critical to the success of New York City's District Four program.[84]

CONTROLLED CHOICE VERSUS MAGNET SCHOOLS. Controlled choice also offers a better approach than magnetization of a few schools within a district. Magnets aspire to contribute to integration by admitting students from many neighborhoods and using a distinctive curriculum or form of instruction to draw in a racially balanced population. Magnets also create new forms of unfairness, however, and are inherently limited in their reach.

First, magnet schools create new inequities because they typically receive more funding than the regular schools (to provide, for example, better scientific equipment). On average, magnet schools spend 10–12 percent more for each pupil than other schools, and some magnets spend as much as double the average amount. Nicholas Lemann asks, "Is it fair for school districts to operate two classes of schools, one plainly better than the other?" In 1998, Public Agenda's focus groups found some dissatisfaction with magnets. "'In order to get the higher-income white kids into the projects, they have a magnet school,' began an African American parent in Raleigh. 'I'm ticked because my son wasn't allowed to go to that school.

This school has everything; I have to drive past it everyday. It makes my blood boil.'" Another black parent commented, "Why not make all the schools like that?"[85]

Second, not only do magnet schools receive more money, they also often cream off the best students, teachers, and parents. Because magnets normally rely on the motivation of parents to apply—and because balancing is based on race, not class—they tend to attract middle-class whites and the most advantaged blacks. Many disadvantaged families simply will not apply at all. One study of magnet programs in Philadelphia and Houston found that the policies "have reduced racial segregation but have increased the economic segregation of students" by drawing high-status students away from low-income schools. A recent study of magnet schools in St. Louis and Cincinnati has similarly found that "social class creaming" was prevalent. Nationally, low-income students are underrepresented in magnet schools, according to the Department of Education. "Magnet schools have neatly substituted class for race or neighborhood," notes Lemann, "as the governing principle of a segregated school system."[86]

In the case of selective magnet schools, this problem is especially acute: schools admit the students who are the easiest to teach, who also tend to be the most affluent. According to studies, two-thirds of magnet schools are selective "by some admissions criteria," and 15 percent are highly selective, using test scores. In the case of secondary magnet schools, more than half use admissions tests. Some selective magnets reject as many as 95 percent of applicants. In addition, some magnet schools are free to expel students who do not perform at prescribed levels, a power conventional public schools lack. Extra funding goes to the most advantaged students—a reversal of the principle of funding by need. As a result, Charles Glenn notes, "there is a widening gap between students who grab the brass ring—who get into selective magnets—and those who don't." Magnets also often attract the very best teachers, and they can siphon off the most active parents, those who would otherwise push for needed change in less successful schools.[87]

Third, in certain districts, while the magnet schools themselves might be racially integrated, they often leave other schools more racially segregated. Particularly in high-minority districts, packing the few whites into magnets (to create an even racial mix in schools) can leave the rest of the schools all black.[88] This creates dissatisfaction among those in nonmagnet schools and severely limits the reach of integration efforts.

Fourth, because magnets are more expensive, their number is by necessity limited, and large numbers of students are rejected and are consigned to traditional public schools with inferior resources. One study finds that magnet schools serve an average of 5.2 percent of students. For desegregation purposes, Jennifer Hochschild writes, "magnets are better characterized as a drop in the bucket than a cure for what ails us." Even in large urban districts, where magnet schools have taken greatest hold, only 20 percent of students attend magnets, the remaining 80 percent attending the other nonmagnet schools.[89]

Controlled choice, by contrast, requires everyone to choose, "magnetizes" all schools, eliminates the double standard, and maximizes the chances that families will receive their top choice of education. Whereas magnet schools reject large numbers of applicants, in school districts that use controlled choice, as noted, as many as 90 percent of families receive one of their first choices. Controlled choice has proved more popular in some communities because it maintains the benefits of choice inherent in the magnet approach without creating a two-tier system. Similarly, whereas magnet schools cream off the best parents, under controlled choice, middle-class parents may be assigned to any school, placing pressure on inferior schools to improve or die.[90]

Controlled choice does adopt the insights of the magnet school approach—that the reputation of a school is an enduring thing and that middle-class parents will need incentives to send their children to schools in poor neighborhoods that were, under the old regime, educationally inferior. Instead of creating new inequities through extreme variations in spending, however, controlled choice attracts middle-class parents with the promise of a middle-class environment and other carrots—for example, placing the most popular curriculum in a previously inferior school. In addition, the most creative and well-respected principals can be placed in the former high-poverty schools as a way of attracting good teachers and middle-class families.[91] (The additional incentives required to lure middle-class children across district lines are discussed momentarily.) All this is meant to provide equality: the idea is that underchosen and unpopular schools should get extra help, not as a way of creating a new school that is twice as good as all the others but as a way of creating equality—much as losing athletic teams get the first pick of new talent in the next year's draft.

Metropolitan Choice

As noted earlier, in most school districts nationwide, majority-middle-class schools can be achieved within district lines. In the 14 percent of districts with majority-low-income populations, however, metropolitan solutions make more sense. Two basic approaches are possible: district consolidation and interdistrict choice.

DISTRICT CONSOLIDATION. District consolidation is the ideal solution when existing district lines demarcate economic divides. Court cases have clearly established that because states are constitutionally responsible for education, they have the authority to create, alter, or dissolve school districts as they wish. Indeed, through consolidation, the number of school districts in the United States has declined from 130,000 in the 1930s to about 15,000 today. An astounding eight of every nine districts have been absorbed.[92] City boundaries themselves are not rigid; between 1950 and 1990, more than 80 percent of central cities expanded their boundaries by 10 percent or more. In the 1990s, school districts in Chattanooga and Knoxville, Tennessee, and Durham and Greensboro, North Carolina, merged to make metropolitan districts.[93]

District consolidation is preferable to interdistrict transfers because consolidation makes all students feel welcome. Gordon Bruno, a former school superintendent who proposes merging the Hartford, Connecticut, school district with twenty-one surrounding suburban districts, told the New York Times that "municipal boundaries stand in the way of the profound message that these are all our students. As long as we try to accomplish integration by transporting across district lines . . . students will always be viewed as visitors."[94]

District mergers are also often independently justified as a way to trim costs and streamline bureaucracies. The superintendent of schools in Guilford County, North Carolina, cited cost savings as a major rationale for the consolidation of three districts to create the new Guilford County school district, with fifty-nine thousand students, the third largest in North Carolina. Governor Christine Todd Whitman cited cost savings and the prospect of property tax reductions in backing a referendum in 1998 to consolidate New Jersey school districts. Sometimes the consolidation of city and suburbs is driven by Republicans wanting to incorporate more conservative voters into the fold. There is a great deal of potential for further district consolidation, particularly in the North. New Jersey, for example, has about half as many students as Florida but ten times as many districts.[95]

INTERDISTRICT CHOICE. In areas where district mergers are not politically feasible, the other option for districts serving more than 50 percent low-income populations is interdistrict choice—a system of controlled choice that takes place across existing district lines. Logistically, interdistrict programs hold great potential for socioeconomic integration because the nation's poorest regions (the cities) are located right next to the wealthiest regions (the suburbs), and the inaccessible regions (rural areas) are often economically mixed. Today, almost 80 percent of the American public lives in metropolitan areas.[96]

Rather than creating enormous zones with intolerably long bus routes, most metropolitan areas can be carved up into compact "zones" containing a portion of the city and a portion of an adjoining suburb, within which choice is made available. In Detroit, a court-ordered plan to create a new consolidated district made up of the city and fifty-three suburban jurisdictions, involving 750,000 students, sounded highly unwieldy on its face. The plan (which was struck down by the Supreme Court for constitutional, not logistical, reasons) was made manageable through the creation of fifteen clusters, each containing a portion of Detroit and two or more suburbs. Because black Detroit neighborhoods tended to abut white suburban areas but were often separated from white urban areas, the dissenters on the Supreme Court noted that the metropolitan plan "would be physically easier and more practical and feasible than a Detroit-only plan" and entailed the purchase of 350 new buses rather than the 900 buses required for the city plan. The same observation has been made of the Boston public schools. Some of Boston's wealthy suburbs were closer to black areas of Boston than the white working-class Boston neighborhoods to which black children were being bused. In Detroit, because many students in the area already rode buses, the metropolitan plan would not have involved busing "substantially more students," and no student's ride would have been longer than forty minutes. The dissent cited other working metropolitan school jurisdictions covering large areas of land, including Charlotte-Mecklenburg, North Carolina (550 square miles), and Mobile County, Alabama (1,248 square miles). The zone or cluster approach has made controlled choice more manageable in numerous jurisdictions, including Boston, Fall River, and Lowell, Massachusetts, and St. Lucie, Florida, where districts are broken into three or four zones, reducing maximum travel times to no more than forty minutes.[97]

VOUCHER EXCEPTION. In a few cities, like New York, interdistrict choice may not always be geographically possible, in which case the limited use of vouchers should be considered. Despite the general opposition articulated in chapter 5, vouchers might be used as a last resort in those cases in which interdistrict choice will not work for reasons of politics, capacity, or distance, as long as protections are built into the voucher scheme to ensure that it promotes rather than undercuts socioeconomic integration. Politically, because private vouchers can be used anywhere, they circumvent the argument that district lines are sacred. In some circumstances, private schools may address the practical difficulty of inter-district choice if middle-class schools are already overcrowded or are geographically located far enough from the city to make transportation prohibitively burdensome.[98]

ATTRACTING MIDDLE-CLASS STUDENTS INTO CITIES. Urban schools located in low-income areas will obviously have a more difficult time attracting suburban children than suburban schools will have in attracting low-income children, in part because urban schools have not historically been very good and because parents may not be willing to gamble that the presence of other middle-class families will over time improve the schools. But it is important to remember that to achieve the goal of making all schools predominantly middle class requires only that a certain subset of students cross district lines. For example, in a predominantly poor city (30 percent middle class, 70 percent poor) surrounded by more affluent suburbs of total comparable size (90 percent middle class, 10 percent poor), all schools in the area can achieve a solid mix of 60 percent middle class and 40 percent disadvantaged if just 30 percent of the urban and suburban students agree to cross lines. Complete success could be achieved while allowing more than two-thirds of students to stay put. Moreover, the experience with racial integration suggests that if an even smaller number of middle-class families can be convinced to try a new program, and if their experience is positive, word will spread quickly (see discussion on page 227).

The question is how to get the first set of suburban families to make the choice to transfer. Some suburban students may be drawn by the inherent excitement of attending a diverse city school rather than a sterile and homogeneous suburban school. One affluent student from Hopewell, New Jersey, who voluntarily transferred to Trenton High School, explained that "Hopewell is understimulating, suffocating, a suburban void where teenagers are expected to hang out at the WaWa, do a few do-gooder things, or be mildly depressed." Other students might seek a competitive advantage in college admissions. One suburban student who transferred to a New Haven school said that his move would help him write a more interesting college essay and that because the urban student body was less academically competitive, his class rank had improved.[99] Most suburban families will require something more, however, and several steps should be taken to address this issue in advance of the adoption of economic integration plans.

First, efforts should be made to improve the physical plant of urban schools. Part of parents' concern about urban schools has to do with run-down facilities, so parents must be assured, as a threshold matter, that the schools their children attend are structurally sound and modernized. Fortunately, polls show strong support for greater funding for school construction and modernization, even if it involves the expenditure of billions of dollars. A 1998 Gallup/*Phi Delta Kappan* poll finds 86 percent support for "providing funds to help repair and replace older school buildings."[100] Second, just as, at the district level, popular educational themes should be placed in less desirable schools, so too those programs that are found to be popular with suburban parents (according to local parent surveys) should be placed in urban schools to make cross-district transfer more attractive. Third, those suburban parents who agree to send their children to economically mixed schools should be assured of a reduced class size compared with economically homogeneous schools. The greater student heterogeneity found in economically integrated schools provides an educational justification for reducing class size and does not create a new inequality.[101]

Fourth, urban schools should capitalize on the advantages they hold over most suburban schools deriving from their proximity to urban attractions. Many major universities are located in urban areas, and urban public schools can form associations with them. Several universities are already setting up public charter schools that offer a chance to try new pedagogical approaches. Some colleges allow high school students to take classes; Yale, for example, has opened some classes to students attending New Haven public schools.[102] Alternatively, suburban students might be lured to urban public schools that become affiliated with urban sports arenas or athletic teams. Schools specializing in the arts can affiliate with urban museums. At the high school level, schools can build relationships with urban employers to offer internships and work experiences at those kinds of institutions not generally located in the suburbs. These types of carrots can work: in St. Louis, some fifteen hundred suburban students attend urban schools as part of a voluntary interdistrict choice program.[103]

Of course, in the very worst urban neighborhoods, attempts to lure suburban children with various goodies will probably prove unsuccessful. Those dangerous schools should be shut down and new schools built, either in a safer section of the city or in the suburbs. This approach will place an increased burden for construction on other areas, but when suburban districts experience a spike upward in enrollment within their districts, they make accommodations and do not tell their own residents there is not enough room for them to attend public school. Federal support will be necessary to offset the increased costs to suburban communities. Support should also be given to poor neighborhoods to do what suburban communities do when schools are closed (usually owing to declining enrollment): convert them into day care centers, health clinics, libraries, or twenty-four-hour community centers.

These measures toward urban-suburban integration will cost a fair amount of money. The good news is that the public, and political leaders, are willing to spend more resources on improving public education. In 1998, by a margin of 73 to 7 percent, Americans said government is spending too little, not too much, on public education. According to a 1997 NBC/*Wall Street Journal* poll, Americans said—by a 70 to 23 percent margin—that they would be willing to pay more in taxes if the money goes to education.[104] The education research says spending on programs that improve economic integration is likely to raise overall achievement, which should further bolster future support for education spending.

Other Issues

Four final sets of questions deserve consideration. In integrating schools by socioeconomic status, should schools also consider such factors as race and language? What transitional programs are necessary to implement socioeconomic integration? What should be done about ability grouping? What sort of discipline policies should be put into place?

Integration by Race and Language

Socioeconomic integration will produce a fair amount of racial integration, not only because people of color are disproportionately poor but also because the concentration of poverty is closely linked to racial discrimination in housing and is particularly shouldered by black Americans.[105] Using race in addition to income in student assignment may well prove unconstitutional, in which case the policy arguments become moot. Until the Supreme Court so rules, however, the argument against using race as a supplementary consideration is much less powerful than in the affirmative action context, because there is no merit principle at stake when assigning children to nonselective elementary and secondary schools and because the "burden" on nonbeneficiaries is much smaller.[106] The issue of whether to count language as well as income is intertwined closely with the issue of bilingual education, and attempts to integrate students explicitly by language make less sense in districts in which bilingual programs provide an educational rationale for clustering language-minority students.

Transitional Programs

Our forty-year experience with racial integration suggests that it is important to provide emotional and academic support to students placed in an environment starkly different from the one to which they are accustomed. Part of the reason certain integration programs have been particularly successful is that they use support personnel to ease the transition to desegregated environments for all students. As Robert Crain notes, "the notion that you can just toss kids of different races and class backgrounds in a classroom together and everything will work out fine was discarded 20 or more years ago."[107] The importance of transition programs is reduced (though not eliminated) when integration plans "grandfather" students in kindergarten through twelfth grade in their current schools and are phased in beginning with kindergartners.

Ability Grouping and Tracking

Ability grouping presents a difficult dilemma for proponents of socioeconomic integration and deserves some extended discussion. On the one hand, middle-class parents (and many teachers) will need assurance that poor children, who often come to school less prepared, do not slow down the faster children. Ability grouping is a time-honored practice that allows teachers to gear lesson plans to students of different levels of ability. It is difficult for one math teacher to instruct a class that simultaneously includes gifted students who can handle advanced math and slower students who have not yet mastered the multiplication tables. Slower students are likely to feel swamped and frustrated, and faster students bored and unchallenged, by a pacing aimed at the middle of the class.

On the other hand, extreme forms of tracking may serve simply to resegregate the classrooms within a school building by economic status and race, thus undercutting the very benefits socioeconomic integration seeks to achieve.[108] The 1988 National Education Longitudinal Study survey found that low-income and minority eighth-graders are twice as likely as white and upper-income eighth-graders to be placed in a remedial math class. Some take the view that there is little difference between de facto seg-regation of schools and tracking in classrooms, labeling these within-school effects "second-generation discrimination." Derrick Bell, for exam-ple, argues that "tracking is no different than any other educational policy which causes racial separation—like system-wide segregation—and deserves no greater solicitude."[109] Might not tracking leave poor children all in the same classroom, with negative peer influences, the worst teach-ers, and the least active parents?

The best compromise to this difficult issue is to employ some ability grouping combined with significant protections for poor and minority students. Most practicing educators believe some form of ability grouping is essential. A 1990 study has found that two-thirds of middle school stu-dents are subject to ability grouping, while another study conducted in the same year reports that 89 percent of eighth-graders are grouped by ability. In the early grades, ability grouping for reading is "nearly universal."[110]

For years, a debate has raged among educators on the question of whether tracking and ability grouping help or hurt students overall, but recent research suggests the terms of the debate have narrowed to whether grouping is positive or simply neutral.[111] A 1997 congressionally author-ized study of Title I finds that a key characteristic of high-poverty schools that perform better than expected is "greater use of tracking by student ability." Ronald Ferguson's review of the "highest quality" studies finds that tracking classes has no negative impact on slow children and a small posi-tive overall impact and that ability grouping within a class increases math achievement for all. At the secondary level, if putting an end to tracking means the elimination of more demanding courses, such a move "seems ridiculous," as Jencks and Phillips note.[112]

Because parents, teachers, and students strongly support tracking, attempts to detrack schools have faced severe political response. As Mickey Kaus argues, the purists who insist on no ability grouping are likely to get completely segregated schools. He sensibly proposes a compromise: "A mild form of tracking might reassure the affluent and ambitious while keeping kids of all types in the same public school."[113]

If some ability grouping is both necessary and inevitable, eight steps can and should be taken to ensure that the poor are protected. Many of these protections are already in place at many schools today. Tom Loveless of the Brookings Institution notes that today's ability grouping is "not your mother's tracking system." First, properly structured ability grouping differs from general tracking in that it provides all students with an academic (as opposed to vocational) curriculum and teaches much of the same material, if at a different pace.[114]

Second, well-implemented ability grouping aggregates students on the basis of different strengths in different classes, so that a student might be in the fastest group for one subject (math, for example) but the middle group for another subject (say, English). Some teachers refine the practice even further, grouping by unit within subject: a math teacher may give a pretest for graphs and form groups accordingly; a month later new groups may be formed based on performance on a pretest for probability. Ability grouping by individual classes or units reduces the chances of mistaken placements and also reduces the stigma associated with lower groupings.[115]

Third, fluidity between groups must be ensured so that a student who accelerates is not kept in a slow group. According to Loveless, studies of transcripts find that today "most students may independently move up or down in each subject's hierarchy." For example, Loveless notes, a transcripts study analyzing five Maryland high schools found that during high school 59.9 percent of students changed math levels and 65.4 percent changed science levels.[116]

Fourth, properly structured ability grouping applies only to certain subjects. If two-thirds of middle schools group by ability for some subjects, it is also true that nearly 80 percent of schools have some ungrouped classes. This is a sensible compromise: traditionally, schools group by ability for math, reading, and English but not for social studies, civics, and homeroom (or schoolwide activities like field trips and assemblies), allowing the gifted to excel in academic subjects but not completely isolating them into separate tracks.[117]

Fifth, at the earlier grades, ability grouping usually occurs within classes, so that students of various abilities share the same classroom but break out into different reading groups or math clusters. As a matter of values, this arrangement makes sense. In kindergarten or first grade, it is hard to talk about children "earning" higher tracks because ability is likely to reflect parental influence much more than a child's own ability. As a practical matter, differences in ability are likely to be larger and more pronounced at the later grades. This is the Japanese model: virtually no ability grouping in the elementary schools and rigid test-based ability grouping thereafter.[118]

In these mixed-ability classes—in certain subjects in middle school and high school, on certain topics in elementary school—new teaching styles that emphasize group and cooperative learning make it possible for children of all abilities to learn together. Cooperative learning, one advocate explains, "substitutes the incentives of the athletic team for the anomie of the individualist classroom." In a report published in 1987, Robert Stevens and colleagues note that fifteen years of research involving more than fifty field experiments strongly suggests that cooperative learning in small heterogeneous groups—in which students work in four-member clusters and are graded as a group—allows students to "achieve consistently more than do students who are in traditionally taught classes." In David Johnson and Roger Johnson's 1989 review of 375 studies, students engaged in cooperative learning achieved at a level two-thirds of a standard deviation above those taught in a competitive or individualistic situation. The authors also find that cooperative learning resulted "in more higher-level reasoning" and "more frequent generation of new ideas and solutions." Finally, cooperative learning keeps students in school longer, reducing attrition rates.[119]

Why does cooperative learning boost academic achievement? In group learning, students are required to provide one another with "elaborated explanations of concepts." The notion, Jean Piaget argued, is that discussion of ideas is needed to create the cognitive disequilibrium from which learning springs. Everyone—from teachers to law students who form study groups—knows that the best way to learn is to teach: to explain a concept to others requires a higher level of understanding and clarification. Indeed, Uri Treisman has found that the greater reliance of Chinese-American students on study groups at Berkeley helps explain the group's relative academic success in math.[120]

Whereas lecturing by a teacher does not work particularly well in mixed socioeconomic status and ability groups, because it assumes all students are learning at the same pace, cooperative learning actually works best with heterogeneous groups. Johnson and Johnson have found that "in heterogeneous groups there is more elaborative thinking, more frequent giving and receiving of explanations, and greater perspective taking in discussion material, all of which increase the depth of understanding, the quality of reasoning, and the accuracy of long-term retention."[121]

Although it might be tempting to ridicule "cooperative learning" as the pipe dream of egalitarian leftists, in fact business is one of the practice's biggest proponents. Studies find that employees are much more likely to be fired for inability to get along with others than for incompetence and that cooperative learning promotes social skills. In the work force itself, business giants like Ford, AT&T, and Motorola are now using cooperative teams to promote productivity. Kentucky's education reform stresses cooperative learning, and the statewide test, one observer notes, includes "performance-based questions that asked students to solve problems in groups as they might later do in a business setting."[122] The principal of Virginia's elite science-based Jefferson High School, which in 1995 topped the country with 112 National Merit semifinalists, expressed his philosophy thus: "Einstein is dead. It's not the lone genius but the laboratory team that has produced most of the new thoughts and inventions of the last half century." In Japanese schools, the New York Times notes, "the entire program aims to teach children to work together and to cooperate in solving problems. And by and large it works." The Japanese are able to raise up their bottom without pulling down their top, and Japanese students place at the top in international academic rankings.[123]

Sixth, it is absolutely essential that steps be taken to ensure that racial or class bias does not enter into decisions on ability-group placement. The presence of disproportionate numbers of minority children in slow tracks presents a red flag for possible bias, and in some instances, ability grouping has been found to be purposefully discriminatory. In Little Rock, Arkansas, for example, the Eighth Circuit Court found that blacks were placed in low tracks nine times as often as whites, compared with the national ratio of 2.5 to 1. In 1996, testers found that white parents visiting schools in New York City were much more likely than black parents to be told about classes for the gifted and talented.[124]

Today, most studies find that the bias in tracking is based on class rather than race. After controlling for achievement, Adam Gamoran and Robert Mare found that high-socioeconomic-status students were 17 percent more likely to be in the college track than low-socioeconomic-status students. Claude Fischer and colleagues observe that even among students with identical math scores, 42 percent of lower-class students were in the college track, compared with 57 percent of higher-class students. Indeed, the authors note, "students who miss one-quarter of the mathematics questions but come from advantaged backgrounds had as much chance of being in the college track as the impoverished student who answered every question correctly."[125]

Our civil rights laws strike the right pose on these questions: statistical racial imbalances create a presumption of discrimination, but administrators are given the opportunity to rebut the presumption with reference to legitimate ability and behavior issues that are race neutral in character. In cases in which the imbalances cannot be justified and discrimination appears to have played a role, courts have appropriately struck down tracking procedures and required that new procedural safeguards be put into place. Where discrimination has not played a role, courts have appropriately upheld ability grouping.[126] All parents—including powerful middle-class parents—have an interest in eliminating bias because where it festers, the whole ability-grouping apparatus is jeopardized.

To protect against bias, whether racial or economic, the Catholic school model—in which students are assigned to academic tracks rather than choosing them—may make more sense. The more ability grouping is based on demonstrable merit—as opposed to the discretion of administrators, who may be influenced by aggressive parents or hidden prejudices against poor or minority students—the more likely are the poor to be fairly placed in higher groups. (In some jurisdictions, as many as a third of students designated as gifted and talented did not actually test into the program but were included at the insistence of aggressive parents.)[127]

Seventh, ability group placements should take into consideration both test scores and economic disadvantage as a better approximation of true merit. Grouping students by achievement scores alone is, as Richard Allington of the State University of New York at Albany notes, really "achievement grouping" rather than "ability grouping" because achievement is imperfectly aligned with innate ability. Students who have done well despite significant obstacles should be given particular consideration in tracking assignments.[128] The preference must be small, however, or it will undercut the entire academic justification for ability grouping, which is to put children of like manifest ability together.

Eighth, conscious efforts should be made by principals to assign strong teachers to all tracks within a school. If schools are judged by the performance of all economic and ethnic groups—a practice employed in Texas and elsewhere—principals will have incentives to avoid the concentration of all the best teachers in the highest tracks.

When these eight protections are in place, Derrick Bell's charge that ability grouping is no different from school segregation rings hollow. For one thing, the values that underlie ability grouping are obviously quite different from the values that underlie neighborhood school assignments. Academic success, particularly in the later grades, is a trait for which children themselves are at least in part responsible, whereas school assignments based on residence are completely beyond a student's control and say nothing about his or her behavior or diligence. Although a student might be thought to have "earned" a position in a high-ability class through hard work and self-discipline, no student can be said to have earned assignment to a fancy neighborhood school. The goal of socioeconomic integration is not to level students (*pace* Kurt Vonnegut's satirical story in which the intelligent people are required to wear electronic devices on their heads that emit shocks to prevent deep thoughts). Instead, the idea is to give all children a shot at good schools, in which they will then compete to be placed in the fastest ability group. When opponents of desegregation raised the issue of ability grouping in the 1950s, Thurgood Marshall remarked that the answer was "simple. Put the dumb colored children in with the dumb white children, and put the smart colored children in with the smart white children—that is not a problem."[129]

The effects of ability grouping are also quite different from those of economic separation based on residence because ability grouping is much less absolute. In Montclair High School, for example, ability grouping has been attacked because minorities make up 20 percent of the honors track but 51 percent of the student body.[130] Twenty percent representation, however, is not the kind of complete separation often found between schools.

In addition, even those low-income students who end up in the lower tracks of integrated schools are likely to be better off than they were in high-poverty schools. For one thing, even the less able teachers in charge of lower tracks in middle-class schools are, on average, of higher quality than the highest-tracked teachers in low-income schools. For another, studies find that the low expectations of middle-class schools are higher than the expectations in high-poverty schools.[131] Finally, the poor children stuck in low tracks in mixed-income schools will benefit from the advocacy of middle-class parents whose children are slow and share the low track with them.

More important, as already noted, ability grouping does not occur in all classes or at all grade levels. Some studies do find that students choose most of their friends from the same curricular track, but a substantial minority of friends (25 percent) come from other tracks.[132] Similarly, students will mix in extracurricular activities, particularly in middle school and high school years. In later grades, extracurricular activities provide an important forum for socializing across socioeconomic and racial lines. Moreover, as Nancy Karweit points out, because extracurricular activities are chosen on a voluntary basis, they hold the basic ingredients for strong friendships: "mutual interest, shared values, and common activities." One study of twenty high schools finds that friends are likely to be involved in the same extracurricular activities. Other studies find that students who participate in extracurricular activities are more likely to have best friends of a different racial or ethnic group than those who do not.[133]

Critics will note that some degree of self-segregation may occur between races and classes, even when they meet on common ground. These divisions are less likely to occur at the elementary level than in secondary schools, however, and school policies can make a big difference in this regard. Including diverse readings in the curriculum and assemblies with multicultural themes has been found to increase intergroup interaction during recess. Cooperative learning techniques, which are widely employed as a way to enhance achievement, also have the effect of increasing and improving intergroup relations.[134]

Moreover, adolescence is a time when students rebel against societal attitudes—including attitudes about race and class—and researchers find that youth culture often cuts "across class boundaries." Studies also find that peer groups are more likely to cut across class lines in schools than in neighborhoods.[135] Researchers looking at poor black students who were moved to the Chicago suburbs under the Gautreaux plan feared that children might not mix well in the new environment. They found, however, that children who moved to the suburbs had the same mean number of friends—six—as children who moved to other parts of the city; and they did not spend a statistically significant different amount of time playing alone.

In school, popularity is often based on good looks and athletic prowess, which also spans race and class lines. Some studies find that lower-status students seek out higher-status classmates as a way to raise their own status. As we know from the racial desegregation history, despite the widespread complaint about balkanization, students attending integrated schools still have more friends of another race than those who do not. As Malcolm Gladwell notes, people tend to be friends "with the people we do things with as much as we are with people we resemble." Studies find people do choose friends of similar gender and race, but proximity is the more powerful factor.[136]

It is also important to recall the evidence cited in chapter 4 that even "weak ties"—as opposed to close friendships—can have an important impact on people's life chances, including employment opportunities down the road. A majority of adults get their jobs through connections, and those connections are usually acquaintances rather than close friends. The attitudes of acquaintances and campus leaders, not friends, have been found to significantly influence students' attitudes toward grades and their political philosophies. "The close friends of a young person, while significant influences in a young person's life, are only a small part of the total complex of peer influence," says Laurence Steinberg.[137]

Discipline

Like well-implemented ability grouping, fair but strict disciplinary codes are essential to successful socioeconomic integration, as progressive integrationists have noted. It was probably a "tragic misstep" in the 1960s and 1970s that "we allowed public schools to back away from rigorous standards and discipline at the very moment we attempted for the first time" to integrate the public schools, as Wendy Puriefoy and Deborah Wadsworth observe. Today, the pendulum has swung on school discipline issues, both in the courts and in the legislatures, with schools adopting strict "zero tolerance" policies across the board.[138]

Strict discipline will disproportionately affect poor and minority students, for as noted earlier, there is a strong association between income and disciplinary problems. Middle-class parents will need assurances, however, that inappropriate behavior will not be tolerated and that school environments will be safe and productive. Polls find that the public views "lack of discipline" as the largest problem of the public schools, and if not addressed, it will drive away middle-class parents (who can afford alternatives). As Al Shanker has argued, "Does it make sense to destroy the education of twenty-five or more students because we are trying to 'rehabilitate' one?"[139]

Preliminary evidence suggests that strict codes of discipline can have an important effect on reducing problems and are more likely to be insisted upon by active middle-class parents. In October 1998, the Departments of Education and Justice issued the first "Annual Report on School Safety," which noted reductions in crime and weapons in the nation's schools. Individual studies in Texas, West Virginia, California, Connecticut, and New Jersey and a new national study all suggest that tough new discipline policies are bearing fruit.[140]

As with ability grouping, steps must be taken to ensure that bias does not affect discipline decisions.[141] So long as there is no evidence of bias, students who create discipline problems are committing acts of free will that disrupt the education process, and as a matter of policy they should be held accountable. Parents across racial lines support strict discipline. A 1998 poll by Public Agenda found that 97 percent of whites and 93 percent of blacks say it is absolutely essential that schools be free of weapons, drugs, and gangs, and 87 percent of white parents and 82 percent of black parents say it is absolutely essential for schools to "make sure students behave themselves in class and on the school grounds." Similarly, 81 percent of black and 86 percent of white parents say "taking persistent troublemakers out of class so that teachers can concentrate on the kids who want to learn" is an excellent or good idea; and 86 percent of white and 78 percent of black parents strongly approve of "permanently" removing children caught with weapons or drugs.[142]

The effects of separation by residential school assignment, on the one hand, and separation by discipline codes, on the other, are quite different. Although disciplinary codes may have a racially and economically disproportionate impact, only a small percentage of students will be suspended or expelled, and the vast majority of newly integrated students will benefit from the new middle-class environment. Under the desegregation plan in St. Louis, for example, suburban schools may turn a child away based on his or her past disciplinary record, but there are nevertheless long waiting lists of applicants for suburban schools under the plan. After prescreening, some 15 percent of transfer students from St. Louis are subsequently suspended, usually for fighting, but the vast majority—85 percent—have no disciplinary problems in the new setting. Nationally, it is estimated that only 3 percent of American schoolchildren are chronically aggressive.[143]

Our current system of economic segregation is supported in part by middle-class parents who take the undeniable association between poverty and misbehavior as an excuse to exclude all poor children. As Paul Jargowsky notes, however, "most ghetto and barrio residents do not engage in the behaviors considered typical of the underclass."[144] Rather than refusing to send children to a school with poor children, isn't it much more fair to have strict discipline codes that weed out the bad apples based on actual behavior rather than their parents' wealth?

7

Political and

Legal Strategies

EVEN IF ECONOMIC school integration is desirable and logistically possible, the proposal faces obvious political obstacles. In some measure, economic school segregation may reflect the current distribution of political power in the United States. It would be a mistake, however, to assume that these political realities are fixed. A case can be made for the voluntary adoption of integration plans on the local level, particularly if advocates tap into the self-interest of influential groups such as teachers, civil rights groups, and business. In addition, advocates can draw on language in state constitutions to provide a legal nudge for integration, and they can push federal incentives that may provide a powerful impetus for promoting the American Common School.

Local Voluntary Programs

Voluntarily adopted programs face an uphill political battle, but today there is good reason to believe that innovative economic integration programs within and between districts can capitalize on the growing movement toward public school choice. Three obstacles stand in the way of voluntary acceptance of economic integration: the existing attachment to neighborhood schools, the apparent rigidity of existing school district lines, and middle-class resistance to economic and racial integration. Each of these hurdles is surmountable.

The American Attachment to the Neighborhood School

Any school superintendent knows that the smallest change in student assignment (down to a one-block change in a school boundary) will be met with some resistance. Even leaving aside, for the moment, the issue of integration, the transition from neighborhood school assignment to public school choice will be controversial; some families will be outraged, others delighted. There will be opposition from those who feel that by buying into a particular neighborhood they have "bought" into a neighborhood school, only to see their property values fall, and also from those who see their neighborhood school as a source of community and do not want it to be changed. However, there are four reasons to expect that the public will support school choice over residential assignment: The shift will result in at least as many winners as losers; the concept of choice has inherent philosophical appeal to Americans; according to the polls, the public wants choice; and legislatures are already moving toward choice.

The shift to choice results in a net increase in options, as noted in chapter 6. The wealthy will no longer enjoy a guarantee that their children will attend the neighborhood school; but they can still choose it and, under most controlled choice plans, have up to a 90 percent chance of success—good odds, considering that even under a neighborhood school system there are no guarantees that boundaries will not be redrawn. Meanwhile, poor and working-class families, who effectively had no choice under residential assignment systems and are often stuck in schools not to their liking, will see a big jump in choices. As a result, some affluent neighborhoods may see a decrease in property values, but for everyone whose values go down, someone else's will go up, because the value of a house formerly assigned to a "bad" school will appreciate under choice.[1] (The separate issue of whether this is fair is taken up in chapter 8.)

Choice also has a great deal of philosophical appeal for Americans. Choice means competition, which Americans like because it gives them more leverage with school officials; and it allows Americans, who have grown accustomed to choice in other areas, to match the school to their children's needs. As Richard Lamm notes, "We can choose among a hundred breakfast cereals [and] two hundred makes of automobiles"; parents want real choice in areas as important as education, as well. A middle-class family with a shy child who is more likely to prosper in a smaller school is likely to welcome that option. There is support across the ideological spectrum for public school choice, from feminists who want single-sex education to conservatives who want back-to-basics schools, from egalitarians who see the possibility of improving schools for the poor to libertarians who instinctively prefer the free market choice model.[2]

In addition, public school choice appeals to the American value of fairness in education. Conservatives, ironically, have laid much of the intellectual groundwork regarding the social justice of greater choice by exposing the fact that neighborhood schools can be a source of great injustice for the poor. In their advocacy of private school choice, conservatives argue, passionately, that the poor should not be stuck in bad schools. Clint Bolick comments that "we'd like to see other parents, particularly low-income parents, have the same choice as Bill Clinton." William Bennett suggests that "poor parents ought to be able to make the same kinds of choices that middle-class parents can make for their children." Conservatives argue, fervently, that bad inner-city schools should be subject to competition or even shut down; that extra money will do little to save inner-city schools; that what poor children need is good models of middle-class virtue: hard work, hard study, and so forth. Of course, all these arguments support public school choice as well as vouchers. Amy Stuart Wells and Robert Crain have remarked that "if their goal really is to help low-income black and Latino students 'escape' from bad urban schools, perhaps they should advocate a [public school choice] program like the one in St. Louis." Some do.[3]

Public opinion data show that support for public school choice has exploded. Between 1980 and 1990, the percentage of Americans who agreed that parents should have public school choice shot up from 12 to 62 percent. Throughout the 1990s, support has remained in the 60–70 percent range.[4] Support cuts across class and racial lines, though it is somewhat higher among minorities and the poor, and it is likely to rise in coming years because younger people, who are more familiar with school choice, are the most supportive of all.[5] Younger Americans do not accept the old model of mandatory assignment; they want and expect options.

The support for public school choice is bipartisan. Among conservatives and business leaders, Republican presidents Ronald Reagan and George Bush, Michigan governor John Engler, former Xerox chairman David P. Kearns, busing opponent David Armor, and the business-backed Committee for Economic Development have all supported public school choice.[6]

POLITICAL AND LEGAL STRATEGIES | 149

Among progressives, Bill Clinton and Al Gore are strong supporters of public school choice, and liberal academic supporters include Deborah Meier, Theodore Sizer, William Julius Wilson, John Coons, and Stephen Sugarman. People for the American Way supports public school choice as part of a five-step plan to strengthen public schools, and the bipartisan National Governors' Association has long endorsed public school choice. In the 2000 presidential election, both candidates backed greater public school choice.[7] Whereas private school vouchers sharply divide the American electorate, public school choice is a compromise that individuals on both sides of the voucher debate can agree upon. One researcher has found that "the American people share more extensive agreement over the desirability of [public school] choice than on any other educational matter."[8]

Finally, legislation enacting public school choice has already passed in state legislatures across the country. The change has come in three waves: during the 1970s, alternative schools of choice proliferated; in the 1980s, magnet schools took hold nationally; and in the 1990s, open enrollment and charter schools sprang up.[9]

Liberal transfer policies have long existed in a majority of school districts, but in recent years, the transfer concept has changed not just in degree but in kind. The number of magnet schools has exploded from about a thousand in the early 1980s to more than four thousand today. The supply has not kept up with demand: half of the magnet schools have waiting lists. The 1990s began with no charter schools at all; today there are sixteen hundred in thirty-six states. In major cities such as New York, students choose from more than two hundred schools listed in a three-hundred-page catalogue.[10] Meanwhile, nonmagnet schools of choice—those offering choice for purposes other than desegregation—have multiplied: a 1994 report commissioned by the U.S. Department of Education concludes that an absolute majority of students living in districts with more than one school now have choice as an option. Today, nearly 25 percent of American students attend public or private schools of choice, up from 20 percent in 1993.[11]

All in all, the evidence suggests a new educational model in which the knot between residence and school is loosening. "The American tradition of the neighborhood school," predicts Edward Fiske in the *New York Times*, "may be going the way of the McGuffey's Reader and the one-room schoolhouse."[12] The question is not whether choice is in our future: public school choice already exists in many communities, and it is coming to many more. The real remaining question is whether the progressive possibilities inherent in the choice movement can be harnessed to bring about greater equality of opportunity.

District Lines More Malleable?

In most cases, socioeconomic integration can occur within districts, but in 14 percent of cases, integration will require choice across existing district lines in order to maintain majority-middle-class schools. What are the prospects that suburban jurisdictions will agree to take in children who live outside the district? Setting aside for the moment opposition based on the fact that interdistrict choice will mean socioeconomic integration, the primary opposition to interdistrict programs will likely be that district residents, who pay high taxes for local education, should not have to pay for the education of outsiders.[13]

In reality, however, taxpayers are already paying for the education of "outsider" children, those who are not residents of the district. Today, combined federal and state support outweighs local support for education, in most instances, so that taxpayers are already helping fund all the schools in the state. Whereas local taxes provided 83 percent of school funding early in the century and 64 percent in the 1940s, today local funding has dropped to less than 50 percent. Three states—Hawaii, New Mexico, and Michigan—do not even rely on local property taxes as a basis for funding. Minnesota and Alabama both provide about 70 percent of funding for kindergarten through twelfth grade education at the state level.[14] In North Carolina, the state pays the base salary for all teachers. Today, there is support across the political spectrum to eliminate reliance on the property tax for education in the belief that real estate taxes are an outdated and inappropriate way of taxing because they use an eighteenth-century model for measuring wealth.[15]

In addition, states are reasserting their constitutional obligation holding them ultimately responsible for education. In the 1990s, states acted to change the governance, or completely take over, the school districts in Baltimore, Chicago, Cleveland, Compton, East St. Louis, Hartford, and Jersey City, Newark, and Paterson, New Jersey. (The New Jersey takeovers placed 10 percent of New Jersey schoolchildren in schools under direct state control.) States, which have always had a hand in accrediting schools to ensure basic minimums of health and safety, minimum classroom size, and teacher certification, are today setting curriculum standards that all localities must meet, a movement often led by conservatives. By 1999, forty-nine states (Iowa being the exception) had implemented or were developing standards, and forty-seven states had some form of statewide assessment.[16] We have long since passed the time in which districts educated students autonomously, without regard to what state they were located in.

The conventional wisdom may hold that the suburbs will never allow an influx of students from outside the district, but a surprising number of schools already do. Today, eighteen states have public school choice laws that "give children rights to enroll in public schools outside their district of residence," in many cases bringing funds with them. (A much larger number of states authorize intradistrict choice.) According to one estimate, some three hundred thousand students now participate in interdistrict choice programs.[17] The standards movement may also mean more choice; in Missouri, Kansas City schools were recently decertified, which had the effect of giving city students a right to transfer to schools outside the district. Business strongly backs interdistrict choice, and the National Alliance of Business has called for removing state provisions that give districts veto power to exclude transfer students. Interdistrict plans, notes Charles Glenn, have the potential to "break down not only racial barriers but also barriers between the affluent and the nonaffluent, city and town."[18]

Moreover, many cities have interdistrict transfer programs specifically designed to promote racial integration.[19] Some of the programs are purely voluntary; others began under court order but now survive in large measure because of community support. These programs have continued to thrive, sometimes for several decades, for three reasons. First, there is strong demand: despite the disadvantages that come with a long bus ride, interdistrict programs have had no difficulty recruiting inner-city residents to participate, and there are frequently long waiting lists. Second, interdistrict programs work: they raise overall achievement levels, boosting the scores of poor minorities without pulling down the middle-class children. (Indeed, middle-class parents say they like the diversity.) Third, states have often provided "double funding" of transferring students, sending state aid to the new receiving suburban district but causing no reduction in state aid to the city district left behind.[20]

Among the leading purely voluntary programs are ones found in Hartford, Boston, and Rochester. Project Concern, Hartford's voluntary interdistrict plan, started in 1966, with 265 inner-city Hartford students attending thirty-five schools in five Hartford suburbs, and by the 1980s had grown to include more than a thousand students attending seventy-two schools in thirteen suburbs. The program, renamed Project Choice in 1998, is slated to expand to between five thousand and six thousand students, in response to a state court decision.[21] The program has survived since its birth in the idealistic 1960s in large part because of its success. A number of studies conducted over three decades have consistently found that compared with control groups, Project Concern participants (who were randomly chosen) made more academic progress, had higher career aspirations, were much more likely to attend college, had fewer incidents with the police, and were less likely to become teenage parents.[22]

In Boston, since the 1960s, inner-city children have been voluntarily bused to suburban schools under the Metco (Metropolitan Council for Educational Opportunity) program. The plan originally involved 220 black students and seven suburban communities; by the mid-1990s, the number of Metco students had risen fifteenfold to 3,200 students in thirty-seven suburban schools. Certain individual suburban districts now take in more students than were enrolled under the entire original program: in the 1997–98 school year, Newton alone enrolled 401 students, Brookline 289, and Lexington 278. Suburban communities receive supplemental state funding in return for accepting Metco students, funds that benefit suburban and Metco students alike. The program has strong political support, and in December 1997, John Silber, chair of the state Board of Education, proposed expanding the program.[23] Metco students do exceedingly well compared with their inner-city peers. According to a 1996 survey, conducted by Harvard's Gary Orfield, of Metco juniors and seniors, a full 96 percent plan to attend four-year colleges—an extremely high rate, even discounting for the self-selection of students (students must apply to participate). Socially, students report positive interracial contact. Some 91 percent of students said they had a good or excellent experience "learning to get along with people from different backgrounds," and very few reported serious discrimination. In interviews with Metco alumni, more than 90 percent said they would participate in Metco if they had it to do over again or would send their children through the Metco program.[24]

In 1965, Rochester began the voluntary Urban-Suburban Interdistrict Transfer Program, which, funded by the State of New York, grew to include more and more districts and today serves some six hundred city students attending six suburban districts in Monroe County. Approximately three thousand students are on the waiting list. (In 1999, a lawsuit prompted a federal judge to order that the program admit a white student, but in 2000, the Second Circuit Court of Appeals upheld the program.)[25]

In addition, several cities have interdistrict programs that were originally court-ordered but now continue on a voluntary basis. In these cases, courts have found that the suburbs did have a role in promoting de jure segregation and could not be let off the hook from desegregation efforts, as were most schools under *Milliken*. Even after courts have ruled that districts need not continue desegregation efforts, a number of communities have decided to continue modified integration efforts voluntarily, including St. Louis, Wilmington, and Indianapolis.

In 1983, faced with evidence of interdistrict de jure racial segregation, the state of Missouri, the city of St. Louis, and the surrounding suburbs entered into an agreement that provided an interdistrict remedy, in which black inner-city children could transfer to white suburban schools and in which St. Louis's magnet schools would seek to attract white suburban students. The agreement between the city and twenty-three suburban school districts stipulated that inner-city children would be bused to some 122 suburban schools in the sixteen suburban districts that had the smallest percentage of black residents (less than 25 percent). These districts were required to increase black enrollment to levels between 15 and 25 percent. At the time the settlement was reached, in eleven of those sixteen suburban districts virtually all students were white; by the 1996–97 school year, the thirteenth year of the program, the student populations of all suburbs were at least 13 percent black.[26] In 1995–96, 12,700 black city students and 1,500 white suburban students crossed district lines to attend school, out of a total St. Louis schools enrollment of 42,000 pupils. With nearly a quarter of city students participating, the St. Louis plan is the largest interdistrict transfer program nationwide.[27]

Under the scheme, the state gives the participating suburban districts "incentive payments" to take inner-city children, carries the transportation costs, and pays St. Louis one-half the state aid for students who transfer to suburban schools as well as extra money for magnet schools to attract white students. Inner-city students are permitted to choose the suburban school they wish to attend or to stay in St. Louis. Schools may screen out students based on past disciplinary record but not based on academic skills.[28]

Because the program is a remedy to de jure segregation, it was not meant to be permanent, and in 1996, the State of Missouri, seeking to cut costs, asked a federal judge to call hearings to determine when the program should end. Business leaders strongly supported a continuation of the program, arguing that the metropolitan area as a whole cannot survive unless the city core functions well. Supporters pointed to research indicating that inner-city children attending St. Louis suburban schools had higher levels of achievement, were nearly twice as likely as their peers in city schools to complete high school, and were more likely to attend two- and four-year colleges.[29] Moreover, one study found that although African American students attending city magnets had higher pretest scores than transfer students, transfer students consistently outperformed their peers at magnet schools in growth in test scores. There was no evidence that white achievement declined; and discipline problems were relatively minor.[30]

In 1999 the parties agreed to a settlement under which court supervision would end but some integration efforts would continue. Much of the extensive city-to-suburb transfer program would remain in place, with state funding to continue for at least ten years. As Amy Stuart Wells observes, "Given what's happened in other cities with court orders that have ended, this is positive in terms of keeping desegregation alive."[31]

In Delaware a federal district court ordered cross-district busing in 1978 between Wilmington and suburban New Castle County schools. The "9-3" plan provided for children to be bused to suburban schools for nine of their twelve school years and for suburban children to attend city schools for three years. Four new districts were created—Brandywine, Christina, Colonial, and Red Clay—each with some suburban and some urban students.[32]

At first, the Wilmington plan was strongly opposed, and public support for the schools declined. In 1979, one year after desegregation, only 44 percent of parents rated the schools as good or excellent. Within a few years, however, support rose, and by 1983, fully 62 percent of the public rated the schools as excellent or good. Citizens with children actually in the schools were more satisfied than citizens without children or those whose children attended private schools. Even ardent busing critics conceded that desegregation of Wilmington and suburban New Castle County resulted in significant black achievement gains on the California Achievement Test. In 1995, a federal judge declared the jurisdiction unified and released the Wilmington area from federal court supervision, a ruling that was upheld on appeal. In 1998, *Education Week* reported that "even with the end of the desegregation order, the four city-suburban districts have agreed to maintain their present structure—at least for now." In the spring of 2000, five years after the district was declared unified, the basic integration mechanism was still in place.[33]

In Indiana a federal district court ordered busing in 1979 between primarily black areas of Indianapolis and primarily white suburban areas of

Marion County. Although Indianapolis had merged with Marion County in 1969, the legislature purposely limited the school district to the original city boundaries in order to prevent school integration. By 1997, fifty-five hundred black students were being bused to six predominantly white suburban districts. Today, Indianapolis enjoys the highest level of school desegregation in the Midwest. An effort to gradually end the interdistrict program over a thirteen-year period was opposed by suburban districts that wanted the program to continue.[34]

Middle-Class Acceptance of Socioeconomic Integration

Even if Americans accept choice within districts and some cross-district choice, that does not necessarily mean that they will tolerate choice mechanisms that foster economic integration. Why would middle-class parents, many of whom are happy with homogeneous schools as they are, agree to a change that would bring greater diversity to their children's schools, particularly when there appear at first glance to be other progressive, and less threatening, ways to improve the scores of all—decreasing class size, increasing teacher competency, and increasing teacher expectations?[35]

Given the history of race-based compulsory busing, political support for economic integration will obviously not come easily. Strong political leaders have a fighting chance, however, if they adequately address the issues that concern the middle class: why properly designed socioeconomic integration will not hurt the middle class; why the middle class has a positive interest in integration; and why choice programs will work better for all concerned if they include socioeconomic controls.

As was noted in chapter 3, the empirical evidence indicates that middle-class children will not be hurt by socioeconomic integration so long as schools are majority middle class. Political opinion is not based on the findings of sociological studies, however, and prointegration leaders will need to emphasize three easily understood points. First, because middle-class parents are very concerned about numbers, it should be emphasized that under the program, no child will be assigned to a majority-low-income school; all schools will be predominantly middle class. Second, leaders should emphasize that appropriate ability grouping will be maintained, a key consideration for middle-class parents. In Montclair, New Jersey, middle-class parents were generally supportive of a controlled choice system that balanced schools racially, but there was an enormous uproar from middle-class parents in 1993 over a proposal to end ability grouping in ninth-grade literature classes. One observer, who is critical of tracking, nevertheless concluded that "to keep white students in the schools, [the system] must maintain ability grouping."[36]

Finally, leaders should emphasize that strong discipline codes will be enforced, another key middle-class concern. Polls find that "overall, school safety and student conduct worry people more than mediocre or poor academic achievement."[37] Today's parents, however, do not see integration as inevitably linked to school disorder. Although many white parents (61 percent) fear that an influx of African American students might bring more social problems, discipline problems, or academic problems, 71 percent of white parents also said an increase in these problems was not unavoidable and that schools could prevent these problems if they were to act effectively.[38]

The second political argument for socioeconomic integration is that it helps the poor—which is the right thing to do, as a matter of morality, and is also in the long-run self-interest of the middle class. The idealistic part of the argument will appeal to a certain subset of the middle class on the basis of values. These parents take the view articulated by John Dewey—"what the best and wisest parent wants for his own child, that must the community want for all of its children." This moral argument should not be dismissed politically, particularly given that the subject is children.[39] If people were always guided strictly by narrow self-interest, a majority-white country probably would not have passed the 1964 Civil Rights Act, because it was in the narrow interest of white workers to continue to reap a (blatantly unfair) discrimination advantage over blacks. Figures like Martin Luther King Jr., appealing to a higher moral sentiment, were able to convince Americans that fairness and justice (and enlightened self-interest) should prevail over narrow self-interest.[40]

Of course, appeals to morality alone are often insufficient (otherwise, it would be hard to explain enormous gaps in the average expenditures for each student that endure year after year). The political fate of socioeconomic integration will most likely be decided on the question of interests as much as values. Is it in the interests of middle-class children for the poor to do well? The answer is contested.

Some argue that even if a policy does not hurt middle-class children in the sense of affirmatively reducing their achievement, nevertheless, for the poor to do better will mean that middle-class students will lose their existing competitive advantage. Dinesh D'Souza tells of speaking at prep schools and asking students, "Who believes in equal opportunity?" All the hands go up. He then replies, "Well, none of your parents do, otherwise they wouldn't have sent you here." Mickey Kaus points out that education is a "competitive good" whose acquisition is qualitatively different from the acquisition of material goods. "I can enjoy listening to an expensive stereo system even though all my neighbors also have one. But a big part of the reason I would pay to send my kid to Exeter is precisely that my neighbors' kids won't get that advantage."[41] Self-interest may be particularly strong in the schools arena, because parental self-interest is mustered on behalf of their children and cannot be dismissed as crass selfishness. Because children are powerless, parents feel an awesome duty and responsibility to be their advocates and may go even further in protecting the interests of their children than they would in protecting their own.

Even conceding the competitive nature of education, however, most observers believe it is in the enlightened self-interest of the middle class for poor children to be well educated. If it were true that parents were concerned only about maximizing their own children's competitive edge, then they would try to ensure that everyone else's children were wholly uneducated; parents would want not only the very best education for their own children but the very worst (or no education at all) for the competition. Of course, this vision is absurd. Economies are dynamic, and new jobs are created in response to a more-educated work force. We have developed a system of free and universal education in this country that is not only publicly funded but is also compulsory, because it is in everyone's interest that all of the children in the society are educated. The reason we do not leave it up to each parent to decide whether to send his or her child to school, and do not require each family to pay its own way, is that we all benefit from an educated citizenry. Even the most radical individualist supporters of private school vouchers believe they should be publicly rather than privately funded. Education, it has been noted, is "one of the few American institutions that tries to take the notion of equality very seriously."[42]

In particular, the middle class knows that it benefits when public education promotes the nation's economic competitiveness and reduces social pathology, and these are potent political arguments to make. The sociologist Alan Wolfe has found that Americans very much want to assimilate disadvantaged groups.[43] Political leaders should appeal strongly to the arguments laid out in chapter 3, that the economic stability of the middle class is dependent on the overall competitiveness of the U.S. economy, which requires a well-educated work force, and that education is crucial to the reduction of social pathologies like crime and drug abuse. We all benefit when the poor are economically assimilated because those joining the working or middle class gain a stake in society and are much less likely to engage in antisocial behavior. No one benefits when certain segments of society, trapped in a perpetual cycle of poverty, are alienated and without hope and feel they have nothing to lose.

Into the final calculus as to whether it is in the interest of middle-class people for the poor to be well educated, add one additional factor: poor children, even in socioeconomically integrated environments, are not as a group going to be fully competitive with middle-class children. The advantage of being raised in a middle-class home is estimated at one-half a year's achievement for every year of a mother's educational attainment.[44] Though much better off with the penalty of a high-poverty school removed, children from poor families will still labor under the burden of being raised in poor homes. The school can do only so much; and middle-class children will continue to have advantages outside the school—trips to museums, parents who carefully check their homework, a safe and quiet environment in which to study.[45]

Moreover, the schools themselves will not be fully equal under socioeconomic integration. As noted in chapter 6, although a perfect socioeconomic school mix might be desirable from an equal opportunity standpoint, as a practical matter most districts will simply use FARM eligibility as the measure of family income. Even in a district in which 28 percent of the population of all schools are FARM eligible, in some schools the balance will be mostly upper middle class, in others mostly upper blue collar (just above the FARM level), and in yet others a mix thereof.[46] In addition, controlled choice cannot eliminate all of the school advantages garnered by vigilant middle-class parents. In practice, the highest rates of acceptance into first-choice schools are for those who register on time—as high as 95 percent. Those parents who miss registration deadlines apply at a time when many of the most desirable schools are already fully subscribed. Because poor parents may be less educated about deadlines, and because they are more likely to move into a school district midyear, studies find that the poor are most likely to be assigned.[47]

The fact that genuine equal opportunity will never be attainable—that it can be approached more closely but never realized—is, of course, a frustrating reality. On the other hand, this very limitation may be a political saving grace for middle-class parents looking for the competitive edge. On balance, then, a system of socioeconomic integration will help some children of the poor achieve at high levels and avoid lives of crime and drug addiction and illiteracy, without, in many cases, directly threatening the life chances of middle-class children, who continue to enjoy out of school advantages that public policy can do little to correct.

There are several other reasons that it is in the direct political interest of the middle class to promote socioeconomic integration. First, the middle class knows that political stability requires a unified country and that separation by race and class breeds disunity. Polls find that Americans of all ethnic groups want schools to teach commonality: a 1998 Public Agenda survey found that 80 percent of Americans in each racial category said it is "absolutely essential" for schools to teach students that "whatever their ethnic or racial background, they are all part of one nation." Americans also want students to learn "the common history and ideas that tie all Americans together." Bill Clinton, who has mastered the art of tapping middle-class sentiment, based his 1997 racial reconciliation effort on this fairly conservative idea of America as one nation. This notion of a united country is deeply American, which is why Abraham Lincoln's citation of Biblical wisdom—"a house divided against itself cannot stand"—resonates so strongly.[48]

Second, many in the middle class realize that their children will not be fully educated unless exposed to some racial and economic diversity. According to a 1998 poll by Public Agenda, 77 percent of black parents and 66 percent of white parents say it is very important or somewhat important that their "own child's school be racially integrated." This finding mirrors other polling data, including a 1996 *Phi Delta Kappan* poll finding 83 percent of the public view interracial schools as desirable.[49] This desire for what might be called a "manageable" amount of diversity may help explain why some integration plans are voluntarily kept in place long after the court order stipulating them has expired.

Third, the argument for socioeconomic integration will appeal to the middle class's desire to save taxpayer money by emphasizing that integration yields more bang for the buck. Under economic integration, rather than pouring money into failing schools, schools in which learning does not take place will be closed down, and students from these schools (large numbers of whom are likely to be low income) will need to be integrated into new schools that work (and have larger numbers of middle-class students). This tough medicine has popular bipartisan support. In 1999, President Clinton declared, "I don't think any child should be trapped in a failing school. . . . From now on, we must say to states and school districts: Identify your worst-performing, least-improving schools, and turn them around or shut them down." Among conservatives, Florida legislators in

1999 passed legislation backed by Governor Jeb Bush stating that the worst public schools should not be defended and providing vouchers to children who attend them so they can leave.[50]

Fourth, socioeconomic integration insists that poor children deserve access to equal schools, which is surely a more conservative notion than the one underlying other progressive reforms, like Title I and Head Start—that the poor deserve extra funding above and beyond what others get. Polls show that since 1990, between 70 and 90 percent of Americans support equality of spending in public education, even when this requires shifting tax money from rich to poor communities.[51] Going the next step, however, to unequal spending in favor of the poor is a difficult one. Although twenty-eight states do have "compensatory" programs that theoretically provide extra funding to poor students, these programs, when totaled up, usually make up only a part of the deficits in local spending, and in the aggregate, wealthy students still receive more spending than the poor.[52] So too, Title I appears to survive largely because its preferential philosophy has in practice been undercut, so that 90 percent of districts actually benefit.

Economic integration reverses the preferential dynamic. The large hidden subsidy for the middle class is reversed, but so is the highly visible spending preference for the poor. Indeed, chapter 6 advocated extra funding for middle-class schools that accept disadvantaged students—enough of a premium to cover transportation, educational load, and something on top that can be used to benefit all students. This extra funding helps explain why interdistrict programs like Boston's Metco have survived.

Finally, as the country moves toward public school choice—sometimes for reasons completely unrelated to integration—promotion of both racial and socioeconomic integration should naturally follow because they help make choice programs work better. Where neighborhood schools are the norm, attempts at demographic balance appear disruptive; but where public school choice becomes the norm, the implicit baseline assumption that homogeneity is natural disappears, and the burden shifts to opponents of integration to explain why new schools of choice should not be integrated. Today, even conservative politicians are quick to say they oppose choice in situations in which it tends to increase racial imbalance.[53]

Adding socioeconomic balance will, in some instances, reduce the chances of middle-class children to get into particular schools that may have been heavily oversubscribed by other middle-class families, which will lead to the middle-class complaint that "my kid didn't get in just because we make too much money." In chapter 6 it was noted, however, that this will not occur often (because pedagogical preferences do not neatly divide along class lines).[54] Moreover, controlled choice removes much of the risk for middle-class families inherent in a system of uncontrolled choice: if choice is not controlled, middle-class parents choosing among a variety of schools may worry that if the school they wish their child to attend is oversubscribed, he or she will be assigned to a school with a large majority of children who are living in poverty. Under controlled choice, by contrast, which seeks to create middle-class majorities in all schools, there is an assurance that even when a family does not receive its first choice, the child will attend a solidly middle-class school.

In this sense, controlled choice builds on the success of magnet schools. One of the reasons that some magnets have been more successful than others in attracting middle-class white students is that some guarantee a racial makeup with which whites feel comfortable. Under such highly managed circumstances, middle-class parents are attracted by the specialty programs on offer. When that assurance is withdrawn—and magnets present a racial environment of unknown shape—middle-class parents have been less willing to send their children to specialty magnets. It is the combination of attractive pedagogy or academic specialty and stable racial and ethnic makeup that makes magnets work—and which controlled choice seeks to replicate.

Socioeconomic integration also encourages school competition by making schools more genuinely accountable and by helping to separate those pedagogical theories that actually work from those that are merely fads. Today, the causes of academic success are not always easily determined: a high-achieving class may have benefited from both an effective principal and superior teaching techniques, or it may be that the school is using mediocre techniques and has mediocre leadership but has large numbers of high-socioeconomic-status students who are, on the whole, easy to motivate and eager to learn. To judge schools with widely varying socioeconomic statuses by the same measure is absurd; as one principal of a high-poverty school points out, "the Sloan-Kettering cancer hospital would change its specialty if its mortality rates were compared to those of a general hospital."[55]

When all schools in a district have roughly the same economic distribution of students, the schools that shine will demonstrably indicate superior pedagogical approaches. The good principals and teachers will be noticed and the bad ones will be exposed; no school will receive a false subsidy of highly motivated students or be able to hide behind the claim that they could not be expected to achieve given the home life of their typical student.[56] Having socioeconomic balance in the schools helps isolate each school's independent qualities—the value added. Attempts to measure added value by controlling for a student body's socioeconomic status are problematic for a variety of reasons.[57]

Socioeconomic desegregation also taps into a popular theme that it is time for the United States to move beyond race. Michael Alves notes that a proposal to use socioeconomic status in student assignment in Cambridge, Massachusetts, was "trying to come up with a way to do what many conservatives have asked for, which was can we have income integration in this country and not just always focus on race." Even staunch advocates of racial desegregation like Columbia University's Robert Crain are attracted to socioeconomic desegregation—both on the merits and as a way of reframing the issue for political purposes.[58] Whereas racial desegregation is a predictable political loser, economic integration offers the chance for a new discussion. Socioeconomic integration also appeals to those who want forward-looking policies. Rather than seeking racial integration as a "punishment" for past sins, socioeconomic integration requires no admission of past guilt and instead focuses on what is right for the future.[59]

Interest Group Support

Political scientists and politicians know that it takes more than aggregate public support to move an idea. Significantly, socioeconomic integration is also likely to be supported by important interest groups, including business, teachers unions, and civil rights groups—and, in contrast with the racial desegregation experience, can also expect the support of ordinary white working-class voters.

Business interests have three reasons to support economic integration. First, business has been highly involved in education reform because it is cheaper for government to properly educate future workers while they are children than for business to educate workers on the job. Today, notes William Galston, "more than 20 percent of all businesses provide remedial training for high-school graduates, at an annual cost of billions."[60] Business leaders want reform that will work and that is cheaper than large-scale spending programs. Socioeconomic integration fits the bill on both counts.

Second, business has a strong interest in strengthening the weakest link in our school system—education of the poor. Increasingly, American business is realizing that metropolitan areas represent a relevant economic unit and that "cities and suburbs rise and fall together."[61] Today, as Bruce Katz and Scott Bernstein note, "businesses now depend on metropolitan-wide markets for workers, suppliers, and customers." Employers must draw on all segments of society for their work force, and efforts to lure good employees from elsewhere may depend on the quality of education available in the area for the children of prospective employees. Not surprisingly, business leaders have emerged as strong proponents of school integration as a way of strengthening education for the entire community in places like St. Louis and in Greenville and Charleston, South Carolina.[62]

Third, businesses look for employees who will be able to get along with colleagues of all different backgrounds. The 1996 National Employers Survey found that business is increasingly interested in entry-level employees who are capable of "working in teams or participating in problem-solving groups." In La Crosse, Wisconsin, for example, businesses backed socioeconomic integration in part because they wanted workers who could get along with all kinds of people.[63]

Teachers unions constitute a second key constituency that has a strong self-interest in public school choice and socioeconomic integration. This support is crucial because teachers exert inordinate power in the Democratic Party (typically, more Democratic national convention delegates are teachers than are citizens of California).[64] In ordinary times, teachers might prefer increased spending to integration strategies because spending means higher salaries or easier working conditions (reduced class size). But these are not normal times. In 1993, public opposition to vouchers stood at 74 percent, according to a Gallup poll. By 1996, the margin had shrunk to 54 percent in favor and 43 percent opposed, and in 1998, vouchers had majority support—51 percent, as against 45 percent opposed. In the Congress, voucher proposals and variations on voucher proposals have passed both houses by substantial margins and, but for presidential vetoes, would now be the law.[65] At the state and local level, Milwaukee's unprecedented voucher experiment has now been adopted in Cleveland and by the entire state of Florida.

Vouchers are also becoming particularly popular among a key Democratic constituency—black voters—putting new pressure on the left.[66] Urban League president Hugh Price, in a widely cited speech, warns public school administrators that "if urban schools as we know them continue to fail in the face of all we know about how to improve them, then your customers will be obliged to shop elsewhere for quality education." Former

New York City chancellor Rudy Crew predicted in 1997, "I think we have ten years, tops, to turn the system around before the public gets fed up and begins to replace it with something else."[67]

As vouchers have grown more threatening—and some of the constitutional obstacles begin to fall away—union leaders have come to view public school choice as a vital substitute for vouchers rather than a prelude to them. Union leaders know that support for vouchers on the part of African Americans and others is rooted not in a love of private schools but in a desire for radical change. In a 1999 Gallup poll, 66 percent of voters gave the public schools a grade of C, D, or worse. The recent rise in home schooling—a tripling in five years—may also serve as a barometer of increasing dissatisfaction with public schools.[68] The progressive alternative must be fundamental.

Moreover, any proposal to preserve public schools must address the most disadvantaged children in the worst schools. Solutions to head off a voucher system must restore confidence in the public system, and that requires finding ways to address schools that turn out illiterates. Much of the decline in public support for public schools stems from the notion that—in the words of Baltimore mayor Kurt Schmoke—public schools "used to be a poor child's ticket out of the slums; now it is part of the system that traps people in the underclass."[69]

Although there is some evidence that public schools are doing as good a job as ever—and indeed that the gaps between black and white and rich and poor have narrowed in some respects—Americans know that the gains in achievement are not keeping up with the requirements of the new economy, which has ratcheted up the need for academic success in order to escape poverty.[70] The two fates—those of teachers and those of the poor—are inextricably linked as never before; the push for vouchers, now real, may light a fire under the teaching profession to get behind dramatic reform. If, as the data suggest, socioeconomic integration is the most effective way to improve the education of inner-city children, then teachers who want to block vouchers have a strong interest in pushing such integration. That is why public school choice, to head off a voucher system, must also involve socioeconomic integration to help the poor.

The existing system of separate schools for rich and poor also undercuts one of the strongest arguments for the public schools. We have seen that historically, public schools have been supported by the theory that they help forge a common culture and provide the glue that holds together a diverse society. Public education is supposed to be the engine for democracy and for social mobility. If the ideal of public schools as common schools is dead, however, the argument against privatization loses much of its force. Some have argued cogently that Catholic schools are the new common schools—better at integrating different economic groups and better at making achievement less dependent on family background.[71]

So too, today's segregated public schools also seem to verify the conservative bromide that "spending does not work," undercutting the case for higher teacher salaries. If schools were integrated, the expenditure of additional money would yield greater results, and teachers who want more spending to boost salaries would be in a better position to argue for it.

Apart from the voucher threat, some teachers advocate public school choice because with a system of specialized schools, teachers can better match their individual interests and special talents, either in certain pedagogical styles or in subject area. In Minnesota, public school teachers supported public school choice by a margin of 61 to 35 percent because it made them feel more professional. Teachers unions are also open to public school choice because it sometimes draws private school students back into the public school system.[72]

With respect to socioeconomic integration, teachers, being on the front lines, know firsthand the difficulty of educating students in high-poverty environments. In a number of cities that have pushed for socioeconomic integration, including La Crosse and Wausau, Wisconsin, Murfreesboro, Tennessee, and Jefferson County, Kentucky, the impetus has come directly from the grass roots: teachers approached principals, who wrote to superintendents, who went to school boards. In Jefferson County, for example, 87 percent of teachers polled agreed that "a high concentration of at-risk students affects all students' achievement."[73] Teachers know that problems can be made more manageable by dividing the labor.

Finally, the movement toward standards and accountability gives teachers a strong self-interest in socioeconomic integration. In Jefferson County, for example, teachers in high-poverty schools were motivated in part by their difficult position under the Kentucky standards and accountability movement. Judith K. Sikes, a third-grade teacher at Roosevelt Perry Elementary (where 99 percent of the student body receives subsidized lunch), told *Education Week* that schools like hers were penalized for their student body: "It reflects unfairly on the staff. They give you a benchmark [on the statewide test] over two years. If you don't make it, if you slip, they think you're in crisis." This phenomenon is likely to grow nationally, now that fully thirty-six of the fifty states have requirements that school report cards contain material such as standardized test scores and attendance and graduation rates. President Clinton, in his 1999 State of the Union address, proposed that in order to receive federal education funds, "every school district should issue report cards on every school."[74]

Support for socioeconomic integration is also likely to come from civil rights groups, which realize that under today's Supreme Court rulings, the best way to achieve racial integration may be through socioeconomic measures. In San Francisco, for example, the NAACP agreed to a settlement in 1999 to base integration primarily on socioeconomic status rather than race, and officials in the organization expressed disappointment when the school board postponed implementation of the new plan. Because of the close ties between race and class, socioeconomic integration promotes racial diversity in schools without running afoul of the general constitutional provision against using race in assignment except to remedy discrimination.[75] Assignment based on economic status has satisfied plaintiffs seeking the elimination of race, defendants seeking to maintain racial diversity, and judges seeking constitutional solutions.

Advocates of racial integration in Arlington, Virginia, turned to socioeconomic factors after racial criteria were struck down by a federal court. Progressives involved in lawsuits in Rochester, New York, St. Petersburg, Florida, Minneapolis, Minnesota, and Hartford, Connecticut, are all examining class status as a way of avoiding constitutional problems associated with race-based assignment.[76] For liberals primarily concerned with racial integration, socioeconomic integration may soon become the only game in town.

Finally, the support of working-class white voters, so-called Reagan Democrats, can also be anticipated. Whereas under racial desegregation working-class whites focused on keeping poor black children out of their schools, economic desegregation may shift their focus to getting their own children into middle-class schools. The first signs of this alliance in the racial desegregation context could be seen when Reagan Democrats joined blacks to push for metropolitan remedies in places like Boston, Detroit, and Richmond. In Baltimore, Jennifer Hochschild notes, working-class whites endorsed metropolitan desegregation on the theory that "their children too would benefit from access to the suburbs." In Dayton, a group representing Appalachian whites declared that "busing economically disadvantaged children around urban ghettos, both white and black, is the inevitable result when busing is limited to center cities. . . . Ideal desegregation would be the economic integration of all children and educational resources" and a "mixture of economic levels."[77]

In Minnesota, the state legislator Myron Orfield has sought an alliance between black inner-city residents and blue-collar whites in inner-ring suburbs that, writes David Rusk, "has split the suburbs politically." Whereas integration in the 1970s essentially involved "rich elites pushing poor blacks on working-to-middle-class whites," Myron Orfield's approach, notes Paul Glastris, integrates everyone with "the rich—to the benefit of working- to middle-class whites and blacks."[78] The new focus on expanding educational opportunities for poor and working-class children of all races and ethnic groups is likely to turn the political tables, uniting the very groups that were antagonists in the battles over racial desegregation.

All in all, the political battle for socioeconomic integration will be hard fought. Nevertheless, systems have been created in other countries, from the Netherlands to Israel to Scotland, that encourage socioeconomic integration. In the United States, none of the great victories for equal opportunity has come easily. Federal aid to education was opposed as a dire threat to "the neighborhood school" and for literally a hundred years was beaten back each time it was introduced in Congress.[79] Then, in 1965, it passed. Today, it is an essential part of our system of education.

Legal Strategies

In many jurisdictions, voluntary political strategies for achieving socioeconomic school integration may need to be supplemented by legal strategies to nudge communities in the right direction. Ideally, the legal argument would be made at the federal level—merging the theories of *San Antonio* v. *Rodriguez* (with its focus on economic class) and *Brown* v. *Board of Education* (with its focus on integration). In the 1960s, there was some reason to believe that de facto economic concentrations might be found unconstitutional, and one federal court, in the case of *Hobson* v. *Hansen*, did so hold.[80] The problem, of course, is that the U.S. Supreme Court ruled against the plaintiffs in *Rodriguez* and has curtailed the radical promise of *Brown* by limiting its reach to de jure segregation. Legal efforts to spur socioeconomic integration must, consequently, be focused at the state level.

State Education Law

In 1977, Justice William Brennan suggested that because a conservative U.S. Supreme Court had given a cramped reading to equal protection guarantees, state courts should take up the slack. "State constitutions, too," he wrote, "are a font of individual liberties, their protections often expanding beyond those required by the Supreme Court's interpretation of federal law." Litigators have taken up Justice Brennan's suggestion with particular gusto in the field of education, for whereas the U.S. Constitution makes no mention whatsoever of education, forty-eight of the fifty state constitutions make provisions guaranteeing education to the citizens of the state.[81]

A number of state supreme courts have already held that all students deserve access to equal educational opportunity and have used the finding to strike down unequal spending across district lines. The same argument could easily be used to find that de facto concentrations of poverty are unconstitutional. As James Coleman has argued, "the educational resources available to each child in a school include as an important component the educational backgrounds of the other children in the school— and any state which dictates the school or school district to which each child goes is unequally distributing those educational resources, however equally it is distributing financing."[82] At the state level, three major cases bear on this important question: *Sheff* v. *O'Neill* (Hartford); *Paynter* v. *New York* (Rochester); and *NAACP* v. *Minnesota* (Minneapolis).

Although no state court has yet squarely held that de facto economic concentrations pose a state constitutional violation, one major court has come tantalizingly close. In 1989, plaintiffs in Hartford, Connecticut, filed a complaint in *Sheff* v. *O'Neill*, arguing that de facto racial and economic segregation of students in Hartford and its suburbs violated the Connecticut constitution. Although the argument clearly departs from federal law, in 1996 the plaintiffs prevailed in a state supreme court decision that, if replicated, will have a revolutionary impact on school desegregation and education generally. The Connecticut Supreme Court itself declared that *Sheff* was "the most significant ruling by this court in this century."[83]

At the heart of the case was a simple fact: "Hartford's children attend schools that are the most racially, ethnically, and economically isolated in the state." In Hartford, fully 63 percent of students were eligible for free and reduced-price meals, while the FARM rate for fifteen of the twenty-one surrounding suburbs was less than 10 percent. Racially, Hartford public schools were 95 percent minority, while the suburbs are heavily white.[84]

In a typical Hartford fifth-grade class of twenty-three students, Columbia University's Gary Natriello testified, a teacher would have "three [children] who were born with low birth weights, three born to mothers using drugs, and five born to teen-age mothers; fifteen living below the poverty line, fifteen living with single parents, and eight living in inadequate hous-ing; twenty-one members of minority groups; up to twelve from homes in which English is not spoken, and nine whose parents do not work." The contrast with the suburbs could not be more striking. As James Traub notes, Hartford, one of the ten poorest cities in America, sits in the middle of the wealthiest state in the country. Achievement in the city was abysmal. Over the years, Hartford had tried everything, including contracting the Hartford schools out to a private company—but all efforts had failed.[85]

The plaintiffs' case was different from traditional state cases focusing on spending because it noted that although Hartford already outspent the surrounding suburbs, money was not enough to produce equal opportu-nity. The case was also different from traditional desegregation cases in two respects: it focused on economic as well as racial segregation, and it went after de facto segregation. The University of Connecticut Law School professor John Brittain has noted that *Sheff* involved "a new theory of unequal educational opportunity due to a high concentration of poor chil-dren in an urban school district."[86]

In addition to making a traditional racial claim, plaintiffs argued that concentrations of poverty had a harmful effect on students. Brittain declared that "the most signal fact about Hartford is not that it's 92 percent nonwhite but that it's 63 percent poor." Teachers and administrators in Hartford told the *New York Times* that though "the most obvious differ-ence" between Hartford and suburban schools "is race," in fact "a greater chasm . . . is poverty." Civil rights groups have focused on race, these teach-ers said, but "economic isolation is the real root that has made segregated schools a problem."[87]

The plaintiffs cited testimony of experts—including Dr. Mary Kennedy, the author of several congressionally sponsored studies of Chapter 1, Dr. William Trent of the University of Illinois, and Gary Orfield of Harvard—on the harms associated with concentrations of poverty in a school. Kennedy noted that the achievement of all students is lower in high-poverty schools; that they fall increasingly behind as they proceed in their education; and that reductions in poverty concentrations have had posi-tive effects. Trent commented that, after controlling for family socioeco-nomic status and race, concentrations of poverty in a school reduce educa-tional attainment, occupational attainment, and future income.[88]

Plaintiffs also noted that even David Armor, who testified for the state in defense, "conceded the harmful effect of the concentration of poverty in the schools." The state conceded that "by eliminating concentrations of poverty we should see improved student achievement." The lower court, which was generally hostile to the plaintiffs' case, had also acknowledged that "the concentration of poverty and at-risk students lead to adverse educational outcomes."[89]

Plaintiffs cited testimony of teachers that "the concentration of at-risk children in Hartford's classrooms overwhelms the normal teaching process." One principal remarked to the journalist James Traub that "it's not like they don't have these problems in the suburbs too, but you can deal with it if it's isolated." High-poverty majority-minority schools offered fewer advanced course offerings, and their teachers had less experience and were less educated. Hartford had twice as many first-year teachers as the state average and a lower proportion of teachers with master's degrees than any of the surrounding twenty-one communities. Student expectations were low; one teacher told Traub, "If you talk about college, they'll say, 'What's college? I don't know anyone who's been to college.'" One minority parent told the attorney Marianne Lado that she was hesitant to send her child to Project Concern's suburban transfer program because she did not want her exposed to white racism, but when she found that her daughter's fourth-grade class was using the same text used in the suburbs in first and second grade, she signed her daughter up for Project Concern immediately.[90]

The state of Connecticut, pointing to federal precedents for guidance, argued that the state should be held responsible only for de jure racial segregation, an argument that prevailed in the lower court. But the Connecticut Supreme Court, in its pathbreaking 1996 decision, held that de facto racial segregation of the public schools violates the Connecticut constitution. The court chose not to decide the more novel question of whether economic segregation is unconstitutional—but explicitly left open that possibility.[91]

The racial rather than economic focus of the court's decision was unfortunate for psychological, legal, sociological, and political reasons. First, the racial focus left the decision open to attack from both the left and the right on grounds that it was condescending to say blacks need integration to achieve. Second, the emphasis on racial de facto segregation left the decision vulnerable to legal attack under the federal constitution because some courts have held that basing student assignment decisions on race in an effort to combat de facto racial segregation is itself unconstitutional and impermissible.[92] Third, the racial emphasis left the majority open to the dissent's pointed criticism that the lower court had found that academic achievement is linked not to the racial composition of the student body but rather to the effects of poverty, both in the family and in the school. An emphasis on class segregation, by contrast, would have been consistent with the findings of the dissent—and with the thrust of the plaintiffs' argument, as the *New York Times* noted, "that the heart of the problem" was economic segregation. Fourth, given the unfortunate realities of racial politics, a decision based on socioeconomic status might not have been burdened with the political baggage associated with race that the *Sheff* case now carries.[93]

Although not directly on point, *Sheff*'s ruling that de facto segregation by race is unconstitutional is a highly relevant precedent for the economic segregation argument because it represents a crucial departure from the federal decision that segregation presents a violation only if it is intentional. The *Sheff* court found that in allowing de facto segregation of the schools, the state failed to meet its affirmative obligation to provide "a substantially equal educational opportunity."[94] The Connecticut Supreme Court cited two reasons that the de facto–de jure distinction from federal constitutional law does not apply under state constitutional law—reasons that parallel the way in which state courts have distinguished state spending decisions from the *Rodriguez* holding.

First, whereas the federal constitution imposes only a negative obligation—thou shalt not segregate by law—and contains no fundamental right to education, the state constitution in Connecticut imposes an affirmative obligation to provide schoolchildren with "substantially equal educational opportunity," holding the state responsible for "omissions" as well as affirmative acts. Second, whereas the federal courts were constrained by concerns about "federalism," the Connecticut court noted that this principle does "not restrict our constitutional authority to enforce" the state constitution.[95]

The step from *Sheff*'s central holding (that de facto racial segregation is unconstitutional) to a holding that the state must also remedy de facto economic segregation is a very small one. Indeed, if equal educational opportunity is the key principle, the economic composition of a school is, in fact, more important than its racial composition, according to a mountain of sociological evidence—evidence even the *Sheff* dissenters explicitly acknowledged.

The breakthrough in *Sheff*, the ruling that de facto segregation presents a constitutional violation, is significant not only on the violation side but also in terms of the remedy. Inherent in the U.S. Supreme Court's decision to limit *Brown* to de jure segregation was the *Milliken* court's limitation of remedies to existing school district boundaries. Because the scope of the remedy is limited to the extent of the violation, desegregation normally will be limited to a given school district's boundary. When the violation involves de facto segregation, however, the *Milliken* boundary limitation no longer applies.[96] Herein lies the truly revolutionary impact of *Sheff*: because the violation involved de facto segregation, Hartford could reach out to the suburbs in crafting a meaningful remedy. Marianne Lado, then an attorney with the NAACP's Legal Defense Fund, observed that *Sheff* "sends a message that you have to conceive of the people of a metropolitan area as being in the same boat, and you can't draw a line around an inner city and say, 'Survive or die on your own.'" The case applied not only to the Hartford area but also to the entire state of Connecticut.[97]

In addition, the *Sheff* decision is not subject to the time constraint that hangs over *Brown*. The remedy of de facto segregation by race or class is not tied to an act of wrongdoing that can be cured through a process of achieving "unitary" status. Because the violation involves de facto rather than de jure segregation, the remedy is required as long as de facto segregation exists, and so it will not "expire" in the way *Brown* remedies have. The *Sheff* remedy is permanent.

In practice, implementing an adequate remedy in *Sheff* continues to be a struggle. The plaintiffs informally suggested an interdistrict remedy in which 25 percent of Hartford students would attend suburban schools and ten magnet schools would be built in Hartford to attract middle-class white students. Plaintiffs noted that 70 percent of Connecticut schoolchildren already rode buses to school. Instead, Republican governor John G. Rowland appointed a twenty-two-member Education Improvement Panel to make recommendations. In January 1997, the panel proposed a series of reforms, including public school choice across district lines and expanded charters and magnet schools.[98]

In 1997, the state legislature enacted a more modest plan, incorporating some but not all of the panel's ideas: interdistrict choice, magnets, and financial incentives for integration. In all, according to Education Commissioner Theodore S. Sergi, 100,000 of the state's 540,000 public school students in the 1998–99 school year participated in public school choice and interdistrict educational programs. The Project Concern program, renamed Project Choice, was serving more than 800 students in Hartford, New Haven, and Bridgeport, Sergi noted, with a goal of eventually serving 5,000–6,000 students.[99]

Plaintiffs called the remedy inadequate and returned to court. In March 1999, Superior Court judge Julia L. Aurigemma ruled that the state had done much to alleviate segregation—pointing to the state's new charter schools (required to reduce racial and economic isolation), interdistrict magnets, and the statewide public school choice programs paying districts to accept students from other districts—and that these remedies should be given time to be implemented.[100] Interestingly, although the Connecticut Supreme Court's decision spoke to race alone, the plaintiffs argued that racial integration must also involve socioeconomic integration; that the percentages of students whose families are on AFDC or participating in the FARM program "need to be part of the plan" in addition to the percentage of minority students. More important, the legislation adopted by the state of Connecticut spoke to "racial, ethnic, and economic isolation," as did Judge Aurigemma's decision.[101] This development is intriguing, because a federal challenge to the use of race in assignment would leave the economic provisions standing.[102]

Plaintiffs preferred a plan put together by the Connecticut Center for Social Change, a nonprofit group, which proposed consolidating Hartford and twenty-one surrounding districts into one district. The plan, known as the Unexamined Remedy, was floated in the summer of 1998. Whereas Hartford's 24,500 students are overwhelmingly poor and 95 percent minority, the new unified district would consist of 100,000 students, 66 percent white, 18 percent black, and 13 percent Hispanic, with FARM-participation rates ranging from 35 percent in the elementary schools to 17 percent in the high schools. The backers argued for using "controlled choice" within the new district, pointing to Cambridge as an example, setting a goal that all schools would fall within a range of 15 percent above or below the new district's ethnic balance. The Center for Social Change noted that the twenty-two communities were already part of a recognized Hartford Region under legislation passed by the state's General Assembly and that several districts in the South were already operating countywide districts of the size contemplated by the merger.[103]

Although there have been sharp disagreements about the shape of the remedy, all sides support some sort of interdistrict choice, made feasible by the fact that many white middle-class schools live within a mile or two of the urban schools. The decision did not lead to widespread panic, and in fact, a poll found that Connecticut residents actually supported the *Sheff* ruling (47 percent in favor, 41 percent opposed).[104]

In 1998, plaintiffs filed a *Sheff*-like case in Rochester, New York, directly challenging poverty concentrations in the city's schools as a denial of the established right to a "sound basic education."[105] Attorneys in *Paynter* v. *New York* sued the state for drawing boundaries that resulted in high concentrations of school poverty. The suit proposes that the state education commissioner "be required to develop a plan to ameliorate the effects of the concentration of poverty." Noting the association between race and poverty, the complaint also includes a charge that student assignments violated the disparate impact provisions of Title VI of the Civil Rights Act of 1964. The primary, and more novel, thrust of the lawsuit, however, is socioeconomic. As a local columnist, Mark Hare, has noted, "Is easing the racial isolation the right goal? Not any more. The real issue today is poverty."[106]

In their complaint, the plaintiffs built their case around two central arguments. First, they argue, the Rochester schools have not provided a "sound basic education," pointing to wide disparities in outcomes between Rochester and its suburban neighbors in Monroe County on a number of variables. The dropout rate is five times higher than in surrounding suburbs (7.0 versus 1.4 percent); the percentage of the freshman class that graduates in four years is more than three times higher in suburban schools than in Rochester (84 versus 27 percent), and the percentage of ninth-graders who enroll in college four years later is five times higher in the suburbs. Rochester passage rates on the New York Regents examination are typically four times lower than in the suburbs, and the percentage of Regents diplomas conferred in suburban schools surrounding Rochester is ten times greater than in the city itself. These results are, they suggested, "by any standard, inadequate."[107]

Second, they argued, the inadequate outcomes are "due, in large part, to the widely disparate concentration of poverty." Noting that poverty concentrations are extreme in Rochester—the district has a 90 percent FARM rate compared with a 16 percent rate in surrounding suburbs, a fivefold difference—they argued that poverty concentrations are harmful to academic achievement. They cited, among other things, the 1993 congressionally mandated study of Chapter 1, which found that "school poverty depresses the scores of all students in schools where at least half of the students are eligible for subsidized lunch, and seriously depresses the scores when more than 75 percent of students live in low-income households." Plaintiffs noted that the same study found poor students in low-poverty schools "performed significantly better."[108]

High-poverty schools provide negative learning environments for a number of reasons, they argued; in particular, "the concentration of at-risk children in schools and classrooms overwhelms the normal teaching process." To receive a sound basic education, plaintiffs contended, requires "a core group of middle-class students and parents in the schools." They also cited a 1998 study by the New York State Department of Education noting that high-poverty schools tend to have less funding, and teachers with less impressive credentials. By identifying the class as "all children in the Rochester City School District who must attend" high-poverty schools, they emphasized that whether a student is from a middle-class or poor family, attending a high-poverty school is a disadvantage.[109]

Plaintiffs noted that the assignment of students is not based on laws of nature and that the state's "system of school residency requirements" results in the concentrations. Finally, they argued for a remedy that addresses these concentrations directly. Plaintiffs called not for extra funding but for an injunction under which Rochester students would be afforded an education in an environment "not marked by high concentrations of poverty." As of this writing, the litigation is pending.[110]

In 1995, lawyers in Minneapolis filed suit challenging de facto economic and racial segregation of Minneapolis schools and the surrounding suburbs. Although Minnesota courts have upheld unequal spending, the state supreme court did recognize in *Skeen* v. *Minnesota* a fundamental right to an adequate education.[111] Plaintiffs argued that de facto "racial and economic" segregation violates the state's equal protection and education clauses and sought a remedy integrating Minneapolis schools with those in surrounding suburbs. Minneapolis schools have been under desegregation orders since 1972, but the federal decision did not reach suburban schools. Although Minnesota has one of the nation's most liberal interdistrict transfer laws, jurisdictions are permitted to exclude students who live outside the district for reasons of space, and out-of-district students are required to pay their own transportation costs.[112]

As a result, Minneapolis schools are increasingly populated by students of color and students who are poor. By 1997–98, plaintiffs noted, 68 percent of Minneapolis students were students of color and 66 percent were eligible for free or reduced-price lunch, compared with a statewide population that is 14 percent minority and 26 percent FARM eligible. In the suburbs of Edina and Minnetonka during the same year, the minority population was 5 percent and the FARM rate 3 percent.[113]

Plaintiffs argued that a "racially and socioeconomically integrated environment" is one component of a "constitutionally adequate education." In support of this notion, the NAACP pointed to state data showing that in 1998, "low-income students who attend[ed] suburban schools [were] . . . twice as likely to have high achievement levels as low-income students attending school in Minneapolis." The plaintiffs also cited extensive national data suggesting that in desegregated schools, the performance of students of color improves, the achievement gap decreases, graduation rates improve, chances of life success improve, and participation in social and economic life improves.[114]

Plaintiffs further argued that race and class have independent effects, with class being the primary of the two. In the companion case of *Xiong* v. *State of Minnesota,* plaintiffs stated in their complaint that "concentrated poverty, as exists in parts of the City of Minneapolis, when carried into the public schools, directly results in lower student achievement, wholly without regard to consideration of race. Racial segregation, on top of socioeconomic segregation, further exacerbates these problems and worsens educational outcomes." In April 1998, plaintiffs publicized a document indicating that school officials knew that a plan for "community schools"—which would have given more resources for segregated schools—would not work, citing a San Francisco study finding that disadvantaged students do better in schools with higher socioeconomic status levels than in high-poverty schools with extra resources.[115]

In March 2000, the parties settled the suit, reaching an agreement on a four-year experiment, to begin in the fall of 2001, to encourage greater socioeconomic integration of schools in a number of ways. Building on the state's interdistrict transfer law, the state agreed to make transportation available for low-income students (up to five hundred dollars a year) to attend suburban schools. Eight suburbs agreed to set aside a total of at least five hundred seats for low-income city students each year. Within Minneapolis, magnet schools with student populations that are wealthier than the city average will be required to set aside up to 20 percent of kindergarten seats for low-income students and up to 50 percent of seats that open up in grades one through five. Students attending schools that have demonstrated low performance for two continuous years will be given a right to transfer to other public schools. The agreement comes on top of an earlier commitment from the state legislature to build a kindergarten-through-eighth-grade Minneapolis magnet school to draw from eight surrounding suburban districts and an interdistrict school in suburban Roseville, open to students from North St. Paul and St. Paul.[116]

Beyond New York and Minnesota, the ruling in *Sheff* holds great potential for replication in other states. *Sheff* relies primarily on the equal educational opportunity principle first used by the Connecticut supreme court in finding a constitutional right to more equitable spending (*Horton v. Meskill*). A similar right has been found in eighteen other states in which spending inequities have been held to violate state constitutions, and litigation is pending in another twelve.[117] Those states that are particularly ripe for a *Sheff*-type ruling (in addition to Minnesota and New York) include Alabama, Arizona, Arkansas, California, Kansas, Kentucky, Maryland, Massachusetts, Missouri, Montana, New Hampshire, New Jersey, New Mexico, North Carolina, Ohio, Pennsylvania, Tennessee, Texas, Vermont, Washington, West Virginia, and Wyoming. The *Sheff* argument of "improving the education of poor children by breaking up their concentration in urban districts," says the *New York Times*, "is widely seen as the next step for school-finance cases" because existing spending litigation has "won more money for city schools without improving results."

Sheff's holding, that equal spending is a necessary but not a sufficient condition for equal educational opportunity, has been replicated in several other states. In all of these cases, courts have been willing to set aside the arguments that spending patterns are a form of de facto discrimination (because the economic inequity is not of the state's making); and they were able to set aside "local autonomy" arguments, placing responsibility for providing equal or adequate education on the state itself.[118]

On the remedy side, ordering a degree of economic integration is, of course, more complicated than ordering a shifting of finances, so it cannot be assumed that courts will follow a natural progression from equal spending to economically balanced schools. One of the major limiting principles of judicial power requires that the remedy involve clearly administrable judicial standards. It is important to note, however, that many states have already moved beyond equity in finance in recent years to require "adequacy" in education—providing the education necessary to assure that students will achieve a minimum passing level of competency. The new adequacy cases already involve more judicial intervention than equity for three reasons.

First, as William Clune notes, whereas the old equity cases looked at inputs, mostly in terms of financial resources, the adequacy theory seeks a minimally adequate output, in terms of academic achievement. Whereas equity was indifferent to how money is spent, adequacy requires that it be spent in a way that is reasonably likely to produce achievement. In a leading case from Kentucky, *Rose* v. *Council for a Better Education,* the state supreme court held in specific and substantive terms that the constitution required that each child must be provided with "at least the seven following capacities: (i) sufficient oral and written communication skills to enable students to function in a complex and rapidly changing civilization; (ii) sufficient knowledge of economic, social, and political systems to enable the student to make informed choices; (iii) sufficient understanding of governmental processes to enable the student to understand the issues that affect his or her community, state, and nation; (iv) sufficient self-knowledge and knowledge of his or her mental and physical wellness; (v) sufficient grounding in the arts to enable each student to appreciate his or her cultural and historical heritage; (vi) sufficient training or preparation for advanced training in either academic or vocational fields so as to enable each child to choose and pursue life work intelligently; and (vii) sufficient levels of academic or vocational skills to enable public school students to compete favorably with their counterparts in surrounding states, in academics or in the job market." In the *Abbott* case, the New Jersey Supreme Court held that the legal requirement was not "a constitutional mandate governing expenditure per pupil, equal or otherwise, but a requirement of a specific substantive level of education."[119]

Second, whereas equity required a symmetry of spending, adequacy may often recognize that poorer districts require more resources, and so judges must enter the complicated educational debate over how much more must be spent on the poor to bring them to an adequate level of education. Third, adequacy cases set a minimum threshold, preventing states from leveling down to an equality that leaves all districts with inadequate levels of spending. This requires, once again, that courts make determinations about the amount of expenditure necessary to produce a substantive level of education. Adequacy cases have been brought—and won—in Kentucky, Alabama, New Jersey, Ohio, West Virginia, Massachusetts, and Wyoming.[120]

Because adequacy looks at the substance of education—not mere spending—it has paved the way nicely for the socioeconomic integration argument. The fact that courts have been willing to get into the nitty-gritty of what is required for an adequate education—beyond simple rules about equity in spending—suggests that socioeconomic integration does not represent a new remedial frontier.

In at least one important respect, socioeconomic integration is more modest than what some state supreme courts have already required in adequacy cases. In *Abbott II*, the New Jersey court held that provision of a thorough and efficient education requires that schools "account for and attempt to remedy the problems students bring with them to school . . . problems created not by the schools but by society."[121] Socioeconomic integration does not compensate for poverty in itself; it simply ensures that in assigning students to schools, the state does not compound the problems of the poor by concentrating them in certain schools, the effect of which is to make education more difficult.

Replication of Sheff through Housing Law

In addition to education-spending cases, a number of state courts have interpreted state constitutions to require affirmative remedies of de facto economic segregation in the related field of housing. States have struck down zoning laws that have the effect of excluding the poor and have required municipalities to provide their fair share of low- and moderate-income housing. Because courts are generally more reluctant to interfere with housing than with education, the housing decisions provide important precedents in the drive for economic school integration.

The leading case in this area is the New Jersey Supreme Court's 1975 decision in *Southern Burlington County NAACP v. Mount Laurel*. The court unanimously held that zoning laws that have the effect of excluding poor people violate the New Jersey Constitution and that localities have an affirmative obligation to provide their "fair share" of moderate- and low-income housing. A municipality can, of course, zone areas for residential, commercial, and single-family and multifamily units within its boundaries, but it cannot exclude housing for low- and moderate-income people altogether. Communities are not required to take in an enormous number of low-income families—the purpose was "to create pleasant, well-balanced communities, not to create slums in new localities"—but communities are required to take their fair share. Significantly, *Mount Laurel*, which has been called "the *Roe* v. *Wade* of fair housing, the *Brown* v. *Board of Education* of exclusionary zoning," surmounted the two obstacles faced by federal constitutional claims.[122]

First, the case reached beyond race to class. Though the plaintiffs originally brought the case against the town of Mount Laurel for excluding "black and Hispanic" poor people, the New Jersey Supreme Court chose to take on the larger issue of economic class and framed the case "from the

Responding to Objections to Legal Approaches

Some will philosophically object to using a legal strategy to promote socioeconomic school desegregation—no matter how laudable the goal—on grounds that education policy is an issue for the legislatures, not the courts.[1] Judicial action is especially inappropriate under this view when it requires not a finding of neutral principles (such as "racial segregation is wrong") but an evaluation of sociological evidence (such as "socioeconomic integration is a prerequisite to equal educational opportunity").[2] Had the courts gotten into the nitty-gritty of educational policy in a case like *Brown*, it is argued, the prevailing sociological evidence could have gone the other way and shown that segregation, on average, raised achievement levels of blacks and whites. Would then the court have ordered integrated schools to be segregated?[3]

Others may have the opposite complaint about using state constitutions to achieve socioeconomic integration: state supreme courts are democratically accountable, and therefore unpopular decisions seeking integration will, in the end, not stick. Unlike the federal judiciary, which has lifetime tenure, state court judges almost always serve limited terms and must be reappointed by governors or may even be elected directly by the people.[4] State court interpretations of state constitutions can similarly be overturned by state constitutional amendment—an end that is much easier to achieve than amendment of the federal constitution.[5]

1. See, for example, Paul Craig Roberts and Lawrence Stratton, *The New Color Line* (Washington: Regnery, 1995), p. 7.

2. See, for example, James S. Coleman, "The Role of Incentives," in Adam Yarmolinsky, Lance Liebman, and Corrinne S. Schelling, *Race and Schooling in the City* (Harvard University Press, 1981), pp. 186–87.

3. James Coleman, "A Scholar Who Inspired It Says Busing Backfired," interview, *National Observer*, June 7, 1975, p. 18.

4. Carol R. Flango and David B. Rottman, *Appellate Court Procedures* (Williamsburg, Va.: National Center for State Courts, 1998), tables 5.4 (on state-by-state method of selection and retention) and 5.5 (on state-by-state terms of appellate court judges, showing that only three states have terms not limited in length (New Hampshire, Massachusetts, and Rhode Island).

5. For example, when the California Supreme Court ruled that de facto racial segregation was unconstitutional, California voters soon thereafter amended

Therefore, any state court decision that bucks public opinion is likely to be watered down.

Both objections have some merit, but the two also tend to cancel one another out. Court decisions are less democratic than legislative decisions, but when important principles are at stake—like equal educational opportunity—it is appropriate that judges serve as a prod to legislatures to do what is right.[6] In a system of representative democracy, in which powerful interests often hold disproportionate sway through the financing of elections, the judiciary should promote certain important principles, like equal educational opportunity. In the age-old question posed in the debate between Abraham Lincoln and Stephen Douglas, principle must sometimes trump popular sovereignty.[7] In 1954, the holding in *Brown* would not have passed southern legislatures, but today most people believe *Brown* was necessary and right. The decision helped educate Americans: whereas 81 percent of southerners opposed *Brown* in 1954, forty years later that number had dropped to 15 percent.[8] State courts must, as a matter of necessity, become cognizant of major social findings involving education, given the inclusion in state constitutions of substantive educational guarantees. Because the equal educational opportunity standard has nothing to do with neutral principles of law barring race segregation, it invites a "Brandeis brief"—an appeal to social reality backed up by empirical data—regarding the necessary conditions for equal educational opportunity. Courts have no choice but to follow Justice Oliver Wendell Holmes's admonition that the life of the law is experience.

The second objection—that state judges are not insulated from politics—also has some truth, but even state judges can play an important

continued on next page

the state constitution to overturn the decision; see George Judson, "Hartford Court Bars Imbalance in the Schools," *New York Times*, July 10, 1996, p. A1.

6. For the classic defense of judicial involvement in the reform of public institutions, see Abraham Chayes, "The Role of the Judge in Public Law Litigation," *Harvard Law Review*, vol. 89 (1976), pp. 1281–316.

7. Jennifer L. Hochschild, *The New American Dilemma: Liberal Democracy and School Desegregation* (Yale University Press, 1984), p. 145.

8. Gary Orfield and Susan Eaton, *Dismantling Desegregation: The Quiet Reversal of* Brown *v.* Board of Education (New York: New Press, 1996), p. 108.

Responding to Objections to Legal Approaches, *continued*

role in prodding legislatures to move in the right direction. Some state legislatures resisted court decisions requiring spending equalization, but studies confirm that these cases did produce more equality of spending in those states.[9] Similarly, while the New Jersey *Mount Laurel* decision has not reached its full potential, by the mid-1990s it had provided an estimated 250,000 low-income people with access to suburban jobs, schools, and an improved quality of life.[10] A state constitutional decision is neither wholly undemocratic nor wholly subject to political whims: it can serve as a key impetus to democratically elected legislatures to secure important rights that are in the short term politically difficult, providing political cover to legislatures to do the right thing.

9. David Card and Abigail Payne, *School Finance Reform: The Distribution of School Spending and the Distribution of SAT Scores.* Working Paper 6766 (Cambridge, Mass.: National Bureau of Economic Research, October 1998), p. 1.

10. See Charles Haar, interview, *Harvard Law Bulletin* (Summer 1996), pp. 31, 32. Between 1975 and 1986, twenty-two Mount Laurel suits were settled; Charles M. Haar, *Suburbs under Siege: Race, Space, and Audacious Judges.* (Princeton University Press, 1996), p. 89. Haar notes that 15,400 units were built in New Jersey suburbs that would not have been built but for the court decision; and between 1987 and 1992, 54,000 additional low- and moderate-income units were permissible under zoning revisions compelled by Mount Laurel; ibid., p. 131. See also Brian W. Blaesser and others, "Advocating Affordable Housing in New Hampshire: The Amicus Curiae Brief of the American Planning Association in *Wayne Britton* v. *Town of Chester,*" *Washington University Journal of Urban and Contemporary Law,* vol. 40 (1991), p. 24 (citing a 1989 *Rutgers Law Review* study reporting that the Mount Laurel project has been a success and that between 1983 and 1988, 22,000 affordable housing unites were built or planned as a result of the decision).

wider viewpoint," ruling that the zoning policies banning trailer homes and limiting the number of multibedroom apartments excluded families of all races who had modest "income and resources." Second, the *Mount Laurel* court held that there was no requirement that the zoning policies intentionally exclude poor people; if the effect was exclusion, that was sufficient to trigger higher judicial scrutiny. The remedy—like the remedy in *Sheff*—obliterates district lines and implies that there are wider commu-

The University of Minnesota Law School's john powell also makes an intriguing argument that federal constitutional law may provide an avenue for insulating state court opinions involving education from political interference. Under *San Antonio* v. *Rodriguez* and *Plyler* v. *Doe,* powell notes, the Supreme Court rejected a fundamental right to equal opportunity in education, but it did establish a federal constitutional right to a minimally adequate education. If a state supreme court were to find that a state constitution requires socioeconomic integration to guarantee adequacy, that finding could be bootstrapped to the level of federal constitutional right under the minimal adequacy definition in *Rodriguez* and *Plyler*.[11]

11. See john powell, interview with author, Minneapolis, December 19, 1997, pp. 6–7; see also john powell, "Segregation and Educational Inadequacy in Twin Cities Public Schools," *Hamline Journal of Public Law and Policy,* vol. 17 (Spring 1996), p. 357; Julius Chambers, "Adequate Education for All: A Right, an Achievable Goal," *Harvard Civil Rights–Civil Liberties Law Review,* vol. 22 (1987), pp. 68–70; *San Antonio* v. *Rodriguez,* 411 U.S. 1, 37 (1973) ("basic minimal skills necessary for enjoyment of the rights of speech and full participation in the political process"); *Kadrmas* v. *Dickinson Public Schools,* 487 U.S. 450, 467 n.1 (Marshall, J., dissenting) ("the Court does not address the question whether a State constitutionally could deny a child access to a minimally adequate education. In our prior cases, this Court explicitly left open the question of whether such a deprivation of access would violate a fundamental constitutional right"; citing *Papsan* v. *Allain,* 478 U.S. 265, 284 [1986]; *San Antonio Independent School District* v. *Rodriguez,* 411 U.S. 1, 25 n.60 [1973]). Today, 30 percent of American children in the lower grades fall below minimum competency, compared with about 2.5 percent of children in northern European nations; E. D. Hirsch, *The Schools We Need and Why We Don't Have Them* (Doubleday, 1996), p. 231.

nity obligations that transcend narrow political jurisdictions. In addition, the implications of the decision are permanent, not temporary.[123]

If New Jersey has been willing to find a constitutional violation involving de facto economic segregation in housing, it is surely ripe for an argument involving de facto economic segregation of schools. Courts have generally subjected state action involving schools to closer scrutiny than state action involving such interests as housing and nutrition. *Mount Lau-*

rel, as Charles Haar notes, is "more ambitious" than *Brown* in that it "regulates the use of the very space where humans must live not just where they may go to school." Applying *Mount Laurel* to economic school integration is in some senses a more modest application of the far-reaching precedent. Indeed, the *Mount Laurel* court took some pains to tie housing to education, noting that one reason municipalities use exclusive zoning is to keep out poor families who would raise the cost of education but contribute little to the tax base. On the education spending side, New Jersey's *Abbott* case is among the leading decisions holding that a state constitution's provision for education requires more equitable average expenditures for each child.[124] A plaintiff merging the theories of *Mount Laurel* and *Abbott* to argue for economic desegregation of schools might well prevail in New Jersey. A number of other states have followed *Mount Laurel* in looking at economic desegregation of housing, including New Hampshire, Pennsylvania, New York, California, Washington, Massachusetts, and Michigan.[125]

Opportunity to Learn in States with High-Stakes Exams

Even in states in which the constitution has not been read to require the provision of an adequate or equal education, the enactment of standards requiring that all students pass certain standardized tests in order to graduate may provide a powerful new legal basis for socioeconomic integration. Already, some courts have found that if a state is going to predicate receipt of a high school diploma on meeting certain standards, it must provide students with an "opportunity to learn."[126] If economically segregated schools effectively deny students the tools necessary to pass statewide tests, those state tests may be struck down unless the state takes affirmative steps to integrate the schools.

Federal Incentives for Controlled Choice and Metropolitan Choice

Though there is some tension between supporting policies that are in the narrow self-interest of one's own children and policies that help the disadvantaged, Americans appear to support both goals, if through different means: the local government is supposed to help their children; and the federal government should help other children. If that is true, then there should be a clear federal role in promoting economic desegregation

In the past, the federal government has played a crucial role in efforts to equalize opportunity through racial desegregation and the funding of compensatory education through Title I. Federal aid provided an extremely successful lever to help the federal courts promote school desegregation in the South. In the decade between *Brown* and passage of the 1964 Civil Rights Act, only 2 percent of southern blacks attended school with whites; by 1972, the figure had rocketed to 91 percent. "The results were phenomenal," notes Gary Orfield. Federal aid has also been essential in promoting magnet school programs and bilingual education.[127]

Although federal funding constitutes just 7 percent of school spending, the federal role in compensatory education is also crucial. A 1998 General Accounting Office study found that federal funding was particularly targeted toward the poor, providing an average of $4.73 in additional funding for each poor student for every $1 provided for every student (compared with state targeting of an additional $0.62 for each student).[128]

Federal Sticks

Over time, schools have grown accustomed to receiving federal aid, and for local school districts, the aid "turned out not to be marginal but essential." Today, federal funds help promote public school choice, charter schools, and other educational experiments.[129] Federal educational aid is no longer eschewed by conservatives on federalism grounds; today, for example, Republicans push for federal funding of private school vouchers.

This dependence gives the federal government a potent tool to use in leveraging education reform. Realizing this, President Clinton's 1999 Education Accountability Act sought to cut off funds to school districts that do not take steps to establish standards, hire better teachers, end social promotion, and adopt sensible discipline codes. Whereas federal laws have historically threatened to deny funds when districts discriminated on the basis of race, gender, and disability, New York University's Jonathan Zimmerman points out, Clinton's proposal would, for the first time, make a "decent public education a civil right." Zimmerman applauds this major departure from the existing law, arguing that "if we agree that race and sex shouldn't bar a child from learning, neither should poor teachers and weak standards."[130] This precise idea—expanding civil rights to include access to good schools—lays the groundwork for this book's proposal for a strong federal role in ensuring a civil right to attend a majority-middle-class school. Given what we know about the importance of socioeconomic integration, federal aid should be made contingent upon a district's demonstrated progress in promoting that goal.

Federal Carrots

On the flip side, federal incentives can promote integration, particularly across existing district lines. As noted earlier, to make interdistrict choice a success, middle-class school districts must have a financial incentive for economic integration. In the United States, because schools are funded locally, wealthy municipalities have a strong self-interest to exclude poor families: the presence of poor children adds to the district's educational expenses while the parents contribute little in tax revenue. The U.S. reliance on a local system of school funding, quite different from European funding mechanisms, surely plays some role in our greater concentrations of poverty, particularly for children.[131] Because schools are locally funded, Americans resist interdistrict schemes and complain, "Why should my tax dollars go to some other kid coming into our district?"

Providing extra federal funding to districts that take in low-income children from a neighboring school district would reverse the existing incentive. The federal government has an interest in this program, not only to promote equity but also to remind us, as Jonathan Kozol notes, that students do not pledge allegiance to a given city but to the United States; they are American citizens, not citizens of Cincinnati or Great Neck.[132]

One way to accomplish this goal is to reform Title I so that poor students take federal, state, and local funding with them to the new public school.[133] Just as today we "magnetize" schools in disadvantaged areas to attract middle-class students, we could also magnetize disadvantaged students to make them attractive to middle-class school districts. Theodore Sizer argues that if money followed the child, we could achieve a great deal of "class and racial integration" and do "an end run around the *Milliken* decision." For the bonus to work, experience suggests, it must be large enough to make poor children truly attractive as students—and be expendable on all students in the school.[134] Although this policy is in tension with the idea that high-poverty schools deserve extra funds, there is an independent educational rationale for providing more dollars to economically integrated schools (apart from the desire to create an integration incentive). Newly integrated schools will have a wider range in ability than heterogeneous schools, and to make the diversity manageable, these schools should be given extra resources to reduce class size.[135] (All these schemes should be distinguished from proposals like that advocated by Senator Judd Gregg, who would allow Title I funds to flow with students to public or private schools.)

Other, less dramatic incentives are possible. Federal funds could be used to offset transportation costs to districts attempting socioeconomic integration. Because these costs are often used as an argument against integration, the federal government could pick up the tab, thereby defusing a major symbolic issue used by integration opponents. Today, we spend $8 billion on Title I and virtually nothing for racial (much less socioeconomic) desegregation; given the relative effectiveness of integration over compensation, the federal government should certainly invest in this approach.[136]

Charter Schools

The federal government could also play an important role in ensuring that the charter school movement is harnessed to promote rather than undercut economic school integration. Since 1992, there has been an explosion in the number of these publicly funded schools, which are released from many bureaucratic rules and are set up with limited (typically, five-year) renewable charters. At the beginning of the 1990s, there were no charter schools; today thirty-six states have authorized charter schools, and more than sixteen hundred such schools are educating some 350,000 students. In Washington, D.C., legislation permits the chartering of twenty schools a year, a pace that, if implemented, would replace the entire existing system of schools in just seven years. Federal funding for charter schools routinely passes in the Congress by overwhelming margins, and some prominent politicians have proposed making every public school a charter school.[137]

Advocates argue that charter schools bring the benefits of vouchers without the drawbacks of privatization—a genuinely different choice without the loss of accountability. "While vouchers are an incentive to abandon the public schools," advocates say, "charters are an incentive to embrace them." Because no tuition is charged, charter schools are completely open to people of all income levels; and unlike private schools, charter schools are generally not permitted to screen students based on academics or discipline, so they cannot simply choose the pupils who are easiest to educate. Because charter schools are fully publicly funded and run on limited leases, they are much more accountable than private schools. Finally, charter schools have no religious orientation, so they do not raise questions about the separation of church and state in the way vouchers do.[138]

Charter schools have the potential either to increase or decrease socio-economic integration, depending on how they are structured. There is disturbing new evidence that some charter schools skim off the most motivated families by requiring parental "contracts," while other charters concentrate on at-risk children. Charter schools are still in their infancy, however, enrolling less than 1 percent of students nationally, and their future is still up for grabs.[139] Given the right incentives, charter schools could be a strong force for socioeconomic integration. First, as a form of public school choice, they free up students to move beyond economically homogeneous neighborhood schools. Individuals choosing charter schools by definition believe that educational program is more important than a school's proximity to home. In addition, because state boards of education are often involved in the chartering of schools, charters have great potential to promote economic integration across existing district lines—and many already do.[140]

Second, the charter mechanism provides a lever to ensure socioeconomic diversity. A public school board may write into the charter a condition that the school's student body represents a mix of economic backgrounds, with a range of, for example, 25–45 percent students from disadvantaged backgrounds. Although the general spirit of charter schools is to reduce government "regulation," charters are already required to comply with "civil rights, desegregation, and special education laws." California, Nevada, South Carolina, and North Carolina's charter laws all require schools to reflect the racial and ethnic composition of the district, and Kansas's charter law requires that schools reflect the district's "socioeconomic composition." Third, as a practical matter, because most charter schools, like magnet schools, are oversubscribed, there is some latitude for administrators to choose among students in a way that promotes integration. In a 1998 Department of Education study, more than 70 percent of charter schools had more applicants than they could accommodate.[141]

Amy Stuart Wells, of the University of California at Los Angeles, has proposed that a certain portion of federal funding for charter schools be earmarked for transportation costs for low-income children "to cross school district lines and attend a charter school in a more affluent area." She also recommends that federal funds be targeted "specifically to charter schools that are racially and socioeconomically diverse—that help lessen the vast chasm between the ethnic groups and social classes that our housing patterns reinforce." Currently, federal charter funds already have strings attached. (In 1998, the Department of Education withheld funds from Virginia charter schools because the state's law gave local boards too much control.)[142] Similar strings could be attached, too, for socioeconomic integration—furthering the long-standing federal commitment to poor children and to integration.

Vouchers

Moreover, federal carrots can also ensure that voucher programs that are enacted promote rather than undercut socioeconomic integration. The reasons vouchers will usually harm more than they will help are discussed in chapter 5, but if policymakers at the state and federal level do decide to embrace voucher programs, it is imperative that the federal government harnesses this development to try to promote socioeconomic integration. As Mickey Kaus notes, "private" does not necessarily mean more segregated; if structured properly, vouchers could promote class-mixing (even if in practice they usually do not).[143]

The federal government might use its funding of vouchers to promote integration in one of two ways. First, the government could support weighted vouchers for students from poor families to offset the larger "educational load" they present and to make the poor more attractive to middle-class private and public schools. A generation ago, Theodore Sizer and Phillip Whitten proposed a voucher system for the poor funded at three times the national average spending for each pupil, under which parents with incomes below the national median would receive some voucher on a sliding scale. President Johnson's 1966 Task Force on the Cities, chaired by Paul Ylvisaker, promoted the idea of placing a "bounty" on the heads of low-income children, both black and white, as did Christopher Jencks, and Robert Reich revived the idea in September 2000.[144] If the bounty were large enough, vouchers, if widely available, will in theory promote integration.

The other, more direct, way to ensure integration is to require that private schools wanting to avail themselves of publicly supported vouchers agree to a goal of, say, 30–50 percent low-income students. John Coons, for example, envisions a requirement that private schools receiving vouchers set aside 25 percent of a class's seats for the bottom 25 percent by income.[145] These provisions may, if put into practice, make many voucher proponents think twice about their support. Private schools, for example, may be unwilling to give up their unfettered prerogative to decide whom to admit. On the other hand, some advocates favor vouchers as a way to promote integration.[146]

State Incentives

States can also take steps to provide incentives for integration. Some states, such as Massachusetts, already provide funding carrots to schools to integrate by race. Since the 1940s, New York has had a program, funded in part by the state, encouraging regional cooperation between school districts that form Boards of Cooperative Educational Services (BOCES), a model that could be used to promote interdistrict integration by economic status.[147]

Other state policies may inadvertently magnetize poor schools or entire districts for middle-class families. Under a new Texas law, any student graduating in the top 10 percent of his or her high school class is automatically admitted to the University of Texas. Similar plans are slated for California and Florida. Some critics have noted that middle-class parents might manipulate the system by sending their children to low-achieving schools from which it would be easier to qualify for the top 10 percent guarantee.[148] From an income integration standpoint, however, such incentives are clearly positive.

8

Rebutting the Case against

Socioeconomic Integration

A NUMBER OF OBJECTIONS can be made to plans for integrating the public schools by economic status. Will socioeconomic integration overwhelm poor children? Is the notion of economic integration insulting to poor people in the same way that racial integration can be insulting to African Americans? Does socioeconomic integration undercut the noble impulse of parents to work hard and achieve so that their children might benefit from a superior suburban education? If public school choice within and between districts is adopted, will the decline of neighborhood schools destroy important community institutions? Does a focus on schools divert attention from the real sources of unequal opportunity, families and neighborhoods? Will attempts to promote socioeconomic integration entail the political difficulty of racial "busing" and inevitably lead to the flight of middle-class families to private schools? All of these objections involve legitimate concerns, but in each case, either the concern can be addressed through careful implementation of socioeconomic integration or the advantages of integration outweigh the disadvantages.

Will Socioeconomic Integration Overwhelm Poor Children?

Some critics argue that integrating poor children into upper-middle-class environments will hurt the poor. It is one thing to integrate middle-class blacks into middle-class white schools, but integrating poor blacks (and whites) into middle-class schools may involve too great a mismatch in backgrounds. Poor children, when placed in highly competitive environments, might become discouraged and be more prone to drop out of school. If poor children are picked on and ridiculed for their lower social status, their self-esteem may be undercut at a fragile age. Mixing the poor and the more well-to-do might simply make the poor resentful and envious and might actually make them more prone to criminal behavior.[1]

Some note that Gordon Allport's "contact theory" of integration—the notion that familiarity reduces prejudice—requires that there be an equality of status between the two groups, which does not hold when poor and educationally disadvantaged blacks are bused into wealthy and educationally advantaged white schools. Accordingly, the exposure of middle-class children to poor and minority children may have the undesirable effect of confirming negative stereotypes about behavior and deficient intellectual skills. Others have argued that, because the poor come to school with different sets of values from those of the middle class, they should be taught differently and that the special needs of poor children will be addressed with greater sensitivity by teachers who are used to dealing with large numbers of poor children. Some contend, similarly, that young black males also have special needs and should be taught separately from other students.[2]

This argument—that the poor will do better if they are educated apart from the rich—runs against all the evidence presented earlier that demonstrates the very opposite: the poor do much better in middle-class environments. The empirical data are clear: the data presented in chapter 3 indicate that the poor benefit from attending middle-class schools, and the data in chapter 4 demonstrate that in middle-class schools, peers are more motivated, parents more powerful, and teachers more qualified.

Although some might think that setting lower expectations for the poor is kind, compassionate, and appropriate, in fact it is debilitating. Disadvantaged students eventually need to compete in a heterogeneous world, and it does little good to shelter them. Kenneth Clark notes that "any theory that a child shouldn't be pressured, that he shouldn't be 'frustrated,' imposes on the child the most horrible form of self-depreciation. The essential ingredient in teaching children is to respect the child by insisting that he does learn." In their 1994 review of desegregation studies, Wells and Crain conclude that the evidence does not support the fear that higher academic standards will reduce the self-confidence and aspirations of black students. Paul Gagnon notes that when *A Nation at Risk* (1983) triggered curriculum reform in the 1980s and the percentage of African Americans taking prescribed academic courses rose from 10.1 percent to 41.1 percent, their dropout rate did not increase—it actually declined.[3] Researchers looking at the Gautreaux housing desegregation plan in Chicago have found that higher standards in the new suburban schools did not damage the expectations and aspirations of poor black children, and they contend that the Gautreaux experiment is a powerful refutation of the equal-status hypothesis. Coleman found that though integration into more academically challenging environments can cause a certain amount of "trauma," the "psychological discomforts are not lasting"; in fact, blacks in integrated environments gain a "greater sense of their efficacy," probably because "they see that they can do some things better than whites." Studies of low-income students in Catholic schools find they benefit from higher expectations—they drop out at a lower, not a higher, rate. Julia Smith and Valerie Lee's study using National Education Longitudinal Study data concludes that "academic press" (pushing students to do tough coursework) does not "disadvantage less able students."[4]

In Boston's Metco program, under which minority students attend suburban schools, both parents and students surveyed in the mid-1990s reported very little discrimination from teachers and peers. Asked about whether their children were faced with discrimination by administrators and staff, 2 percent of parents reported serious discrimination, and 61 percent reported none; among students, only 1 percent reported serious discrimination on the part of teachers, and 48 percent reported none; 0 percent reported serious discrimination at the hands of counselors, and 85 percent reported none. In interviews with Metco alumni, 90 percent stated they would repeat the Metco experience or send their child through Metco.[5]

Some poor children may be teased by middle-class peers, about their clothes, for instance, but schools can take steps to forestall this possibility. Requirements for school uniforms—adopted by a growing number of schools—can reduce the visible material differences between students of different socioeconomic backgrounds.[6] Fashion trends, in fact, often mimic the clothes of marginalized communities: low-slung baggy pants, currently popular among all economic groups, are meant to model prison garb.

The notion that people feel more at ease with others who are like them—an idea popular today on the left as well as the right—can constitute the height of condescension. The *New York Times* reporter Rick Bragg, in his memoir about growing up poor and white in the South, recalls that his teacher separated the class into the well-to-do Cardinals and the poor Jaybirds. "The teacher—and I will always remember this—told me I would be much more comfortable with my own kind. I was six, but even at six you understand what it means to be told you are not good enough to sit with the well scrubbed."[7]

Finally, studies have disproved the notion that certain schools are good for the poor and different schools for the rich. Willms's study in Scotland, for example, found that "there are no schools that are particularly effective for high-ability or high-SES pupils and not for low-ability or low-SES pupils, and vice versa." Some might hypothesize that poor students will feel more "comfortable" in schools with other students like themselves, but Victor Battistich and colleagues have found that there is little feeling of "community" in high-poverty schools.[8]

None of this is to say that socioeconomic integration will always run smoothly or that poor children should be plunked down into high-achieving suburban schools without benefit of support. The lesson of racial integration, however, is that well-designed transition programs, combined with careful follow-up, can make integration a success for all parties involved.

Will Socioeconomic Integration Stigmatize the Poor?

Some fear that socioeconomic desegregation might be seen to stereotype and stigmatize poor people as undesirable classmates and parents. Those children who receive free and reduced-price meals represent a diverse set of individuals and ethnic groups, with a variety of value systems and norms. Can we really say there is a "culture of poverty" distinct from "middle-class" or "suburban" culture? What about the many disadvantaged families that are poor in resources but rich in values? Even if poor parents are more likely to have certain values that are deemed undesirable by the middle class, why assume the children share these values? What of the fabulously wealthy movie stars who engage in the kind of behaviors, such as illegitimacy and drug addiction, that are usually associated with the underclass?[9] The middle class can be uptight, boring, uncaring, materialistic, and hypercompetitive. If part of the concern about racial desegregation is the condescending notion that blacks need to sit next to whites in order to learn, why isn't socioeconomic integration similarly insulting to the poor? These are serious and legitimate questions, to which there are four major responses.

First, as chapter 4 demonstrates, there are, in the aggregate, certain sets of behavior and attitudes associated with concentrated poverty that are distinct from the broadly defined middle-class sets of behavior and attitudes. These behaviors and attitudes are much more closely linked to class than America's erroneous proxy, which distinguishes between "black" and "white" culture. Student attitudes and behaviors toward cutting classes, missing school, and doing homework—and parent attitudes toward school involvement—all track by class much more than by race.[10] So too, studies find that class matters more than race in predicting excessive television viewing, high school dropout rates, academic achievement, child-rearing patterns, the size of summer learning setbacks, violence, and computer use.[11]

Chapter 4 also shows that high-poverty schools are statistically associated with more violence, earlier sexual relations, a de-emphasis on academic success, lower achievement, lower aspirations, less active parental participation, and so on. These characteristics are not unique to "ghetto poverty." William Julius Wilson calls this behavior "ghetto related" rather than "ghetto specific," to underline the fact that they occur in the larger society, although with less frequency.[12] Taken to an extreme, some of the middle-class virtues can turn into vices (materialism, workaholism), but on the whole, there are practical reasons that society values work over idleness, lawful restraint over unlawful violence, and academic achievement over academic failure.

To deny that behavior patterns differ between middle-class and high-poverty communities is not only factually wrong, Wilson notes, it also underestimates the very real obstacles that the poor living in concentrated poverty now face. As Wilson writes, "The tendency of some liberals to deny the very existence of culturally destructive behavior and attitudes in the inner-city is once again to diminish the importance of the environment in determining the outcomes and life chances of individuals." One of the key differences between black poverty and white poverty in the aggregate is that poor whites are much less likely to live in concentrated poverty. To deny the extra burden of living in concentrated poverty, therefore, misrepresents a problem disproportionately faced by poor blacks.[13]

Recognizing a culture of concentrated poverty is very different from positing genetic inferiority or a culture of poverty, which is self-perpetuating and takes on a life of its own. The premise behind socioeconomic integration is, in fact, the opposite: changing a child's environment changes the child's life chances. If one truly believed in the traditional culture of poverty, one would place little hope in socioeconomic integration, for ingrained and immutable characteristics cannot be cured by a mere change of environment.[14]

Second, though it would be wrong for an employer or university to assume that individual children living in poverty are more likely to cut classes or to be a negative influence on peers, it is something quite different to assume when assigning large numbers of students to schools that in the aggregate, those behaviors and attitudes are relevant. Sociologists know that the link between a school's socioeconomic status and its level of achievement is much tighter than the link between an individual's socioeconomic status and his or her level of achievement.[15] The commonly used term *at risk* captures this notion: statistically, children of poverty are more likely to fail, though it is of course not inevitable that they will do so. The structure of Title I, which gives extra funding to schools with high concentrations of poverty, is not seen as stigmatizing perhaps in part because it addresses groups rather than individuals.

Third, as also noted in chapter 4, to advocate socioeconomic integration one need not subscribe to Edward Banfield's view of the poor, which links poverty to an absence of wholesome values. Indeed, much of the reason attendance at a high-poverty school is a disadvantage has nothing to do with behavior that could remotely be thought of as blameworthy. For example, one of the reasons it is advantageous to be in a predominantly middle-class school is that higher levels of achievement spur greater levels of competition and raise the overall expectations of teachers. Many poor children come to school hungry and tired after a night in a crowded and noisy apartment; they may have trouble concentrating because of untreated medical conditions; they may perform less well because they are constantly switching schools following evictions; and perhaps they cannot see the blackboard because they cannot afford glasses. Similarly, a parent who is managing to live at 135 percent of the poverty line by working two jobs and does not have the flexibility from his or her employer to volunteer in the classroom, or the resources to make large contributions to the PTA, surely cannot be considered personally blameworthy. If teachers and administrators routinely are patronizing to poor parents while treating wealthier parents with respect, it is not surprising that parents of the poor withdraw and become less active.[16]

Fourth, there is a crucial distinction between the potentially stigmatizing message of racial integration and the message of economic integration. Race in this country is a rough proxy for ethnic culture, and there are legitimate reasons groups might wish to aggregate to preserve the culture. Members of minority groups might appropriately wish to aggregate precisely because it is uncomfortable to be an isolated minority. In the case of economic status, by contrast, the poor generally do not wish to preserve a culture of poverty. Poverty, unlike ethnicity, is a condition most people would like to escape. As john powell notes, while some middle-class minorities choose to cluster, the segregation of the poor "is imposed by the dominant society."[17]

In the end, the recognition that concentrations of poverty make learning difficult does not rest on the stereotype that all poor children are troublemakers or subscribe to anti-achievement values. Indeed, the theory hypothesizes the opposite: hardworking poor children, given a chance to grow up in a better environment, will do quite well and deserve the chance to prove it.

Will Socioeconomic Integration Undercut Parental Incentives?

A third objection to socioeconomic integration is that it undercuts the noble efforts of middle-class parents to provide their children with an education superior to the ones they themselves enjoyed. Under this vision, life is not so much a competitive race run by each generation but, instead, a relay race, with generations working together to further the family as a whole.[18]

There is, of course, something very appealing about this selfless notion, that parents sacrifice to increase opportunity for their children. Calvin Trillin writes eloquently of his father's dedication to his children as part of the American theme: "We have worked hard so that you can have the opportunities we didn't have." Trillin continues, "It's a grand theme partly because in its purest form it requires a suppression of ego: it requires people to think of their lives as taking meaning largely from being a transition to other people's lives—their children's."[19]

Stephan and Abigail Thernstrom argue against socioeconomic integration because it undercuts the rewards provided to those who "scrimp and save" and move out of bad neighborhoods.[20] Others argue that fiddling with school boundaries undercuts property values: individuals buy residences in neighborhoods with the expectation that their children will attend a particular neighborhood school. The right to attend a certain school is "capitalized" into the price of the house, and it is unfair, so the argument goes, to upset that expectation without compensation.

Aristocracy versus Meritocracy

A second line of thought, however, points out that viewing life as a generational relay race penalizes those children who are not lucky enough to be blessed with self-sacrificing parents. A major rationale for the imposition of an inheritance tax was Theodore Roosevelt's strong sense that in America, unlike in Europe, each generation should run its own race. Leon Botstein notes that the "absence of a perpetually stable multigenerational aristocracy constitutes the essence of democracy." When wealthy parents claim a right to purchase a superior level of public education, they pursue precisely that which Jefferson rebelled against when he argued for replacing the European "aristocracy of wealth" with an "aristocracy of virtue and talent." So too, Lincoln remarked that government's "leading object" is "to elevate the condition of men; to lift artificial weights from all shoulders; to clear the paths of laudable pursuit for all; to afford all an unfettered start and a fair chance in the race of life." The idea that the state should not penalize children for their parents' decisions is the fundamental precept underlying the Supreme Court's decision to strike down legislation seeking to deny education to the children of illegal aliens—children blameless for their parents' illegal status. Public education is meant to provide equal opportunity for children who, in Gordon MacInnes's sardonic phrase, "pick the wrong parents."[21]

Private Advantages, Public Equality

We should seek a balanced arrangement under which, *pace* Trillin, parents are allowed, indeed encouraged, to privately provide their children with advantages, but *public* policy does not conspire with families to exacerbate unfair advantages. Parents should and always will be able to provide their children with enormous head starts, by providing a warm, loving, and nurturing home environment; by taking their children to museums, by reading to them. But the public school system should not be part of the process of exacerbating unfair competitive advantages for some citizens over others.

The assumption that there is a private property right to superior public schools, which underlies some of the opposition to socioeconomic integration, cuts against the whole notion of the American public school.

Although the Constitution does protect the right of parents to purchase a private education for their children, the notion that the public school system will be used to provide the equivalent to a semiprivate education in high-status neighborhoods flies in the face of the democratic ideal. "Public schools rightfully belong to all the people," say Charles Willie and Michael Alves, and should "not be reserved exclusively for those who live in selected neighborhoods."[22]

John Dewey has argued that schools are not meant to ratify and reproduce hierarchy; rather, the purpose of public education is to fundamentally transform society. Progressive education is intended "to take part in correcting unfair privilege, and unfair deprivation, not to perpetuate them." Judge J. Harvie Wilkinson, no flaming liberal, has written, "In the end it is hard to defend neighborhood schools as part of a parent's right to pass along class advantage. The historic mission of public education has been to counter, not reinforce, social encrustation."[23]

The Effect on Property Values

Moving from a system of residentially based school assignment to one of controlled choice will, in many cases, result in a shifting of property values—a decline in neighborhoods that once had a lock on the best schools and an increase in neighborhoods in which students had previously been assigned to bad schools. One economist, for example, has calculated that if, under a choice system, a family living in Boston were guaranteed a seat at a school in suburban Belmont, the value of the Boston house would rise.[24]

The overall effect in either direction, however, is likely to be small. Controlling for other neighborhood variables, a large change in school test scores—from the twenty-fifth to the seventy-fifth percentile—results in a 2.9 percent increase in housing prices. As Gary Orfield notes, surveys identifying the factors people consider in choosing where they will live show that "schools are a relatively unimportant feature compared to price, location, physical attributes, and other factors." This would be particularly true for the 75 percent of American households that do not have children in the public schools because they do not have children, their children have grown, or their children attend private school.[25]

Regulations requiring that new housing developments include low- and moderate-income households have been opposed on the basis that the presence of such families will reduce property values. One such effort, however, a 1973 Montgomery County, Maryland, ordinance requiring that

15 percent of new housing developments be set aside for moderate- and low-income households, resulted in no reduction of property values. A 1998 study of resale prices of 1,012 dwellings located near subsidized housing found that when compared with similar units without the set-aside, "the presence or proximity of subsidized housing made no difference in housing values."[26]

In any event, a new school assignment policy would not be the first instance in which a public policy decision affected private property values. Property values can change dramatically when a subway line opens on one street rather than another. They may also be affected when school district lines are redrawn for reasons completely independent of integration (to relieve overcrowding, for example). There is no guarantee that a given house will "buy" its owners a given public school: If a school burns down, for instance, property owners have no right to demand that the school be rebuilt in the same spot. "You can't buy a public school," says Charles Glenn. "Public schools belong to the public, and they ought to be open to every member of the public. You shouldn't be able as a matter of economic privilege to be able to buy a space in a particular public school." People pay taxes to support the entire district's school system, and to a considerable degree, all the schools in a state, not just the local neighborhood school. Why should people in a certain corner of the district, who pay taxes to support the entire system, be denied access to a school in another neighborhood that they are helping to support?[27]

Will Socioeconomic Integration Destroy Neighborhood Communities?

A fourth objection to socioeconomic integration of the schools is that it will destroy a cherished American icon: the neighborhood school. Because residential areas in the United States tend to be segregated in fact by economic status and race, any effort to promote economic integration necessarily means that some children will go to schools outside their immediate neighborhoods.

The loss of the neighborhood school is troublesome, critics say, for several reasons. For one thing, neighborhood schools can serve as focal points, and when neighborhood children go off to several different schools, cohesion is lost. In the inner city in particular, choice and integration undercut the "community schools" movement, which seeks to establish schools as community centers that provide services like health care and community education in what supporters call "a marriage between

John Dewey and Jane Addams." The public schools can be one of the few positive institutions left in ghetto neighborhoods otherwise dominated by liquor stores and adult theaters. Schools can, indeed, be one of the few sources of stable employment, and one must think hard before closing them down.[28]

Associated with the decline in community, critics charge, is a decline in democracy; the larger the jurisdiction for schools, the more likely the rule of elite bureaucracies.[29] Philosophers since Aristotle have hypothesized that democracy works best in small communities. The Princeton philosopher Michael Walzer argues that local and neighborhood control over schools is the essence of democracy: "Politics is always territorially based; and the neighborhood . . . is historically the first, and still the most immediate and obvious, base for democratic politics. People are most likely to be knowledgeable and concerned, active and effective, when they are close to home, among friends and familiar enemies."[30]

In addition, critics say, because parents are more likely to be involved in schools close to their homes, parental involvement may decline with distance. Justice Lewis Powell has noted that neighborhood schools "reflect the deeply felt desire of citizens for a sense of community in their public education. . . . Community support, interest, and dedication to public schools may well run higher with a neighborhood attendance pattern; distance may encourage disinterest."[31]

Others stress practical concerns about transporting children to non-neighborhood schools: what about the cost, the time wasted, and the physical hazards? Is it right to subject students, particularly younger children in the early elementary grades, to extended bus rides? Wouldn't it be better to spend resources on improving neighborhood schools, critics ask? Distance also may discourage participation in after-school activities, putting more students back on the streets, where they are likely to get into trouble.[32]

Still others worry that a movement of children away from the neighborhood will encourage assimilation into the broader society, thus lending support to the fear that school integration is being used to "impose middle-class values" and "civilize the natives." In certain instances, members of the black community have resisted integration in favor of "community control" of institutions. Some white ethnic groups have seen schools as sources of tight-knit community, not as entrees into the broader world.[33]

These concerns are not without merit. There is a certain trade-off between integrating and fostering neighborhood communities. The costs of perpetuating economic school segregation, however, are much higher than the benefits of neighborhood schools, for a number of reasons.

Alternative Communities of Values, Not Wealth

Public school choice can itself create new communities that are in many ways preferable to geographically based ones. At their best, schools of choice can become communities of ideas, transcending class, race, and geography. Common values—stressing back-to-basics at one school, multiculturalism and cooperative learning at another—might bind together people from different backgrounds. In a highly mobile society, in which many neighbors do not know one another anyway, a community committed to an idea may be particularly valuable, filling a void left by the lack of traditional community in residential areas. This notion, of a community based on ideas and values rather than race and ethnicity, is at the heart of the American experiment.

Although some commentators wax romantic about neighborhood communities of the 1950s, residents have always been more likely to identify themselves as Bostonians than Newtonians—and public policy should encourage this broader, more inclusive notion of community.[34] Religion provides the central source of community for many Americans, and these communities clearly are not limited to those who live within walking distance of one another or who share the same income tax bracket.[35] Indeed, 86 percent of Catholic school students do not walk to school.[36]

Distressed neighborhoods have a special need for community, but the role that schools play in providing jobs for adults (and a mainstream institution for all to see) must be balanced against the essential purpose of schools, that is, to provide the best possible education for children. Studies find ghetto children do better in suburban schools in part because of the school's mix but also because of "the change in scene," Christine Rossell notes. One compromise is to turn closed-down former high-poverty schools into after-school and evening learning centers that serve as a haven for both students and adults seeking to avoid gangs and to pursue study.[37]

Choice as Highly Democratic

With respect to the concern that neighborhood schools are special forums for democracy, there are two responses. First, public school choice does nothing to change the state's constitutional responsibility for education. Parents in Alabama may have different requirements of schools from those of New York parents, and that principle of federalism and local control remains in place, even when choice takes children across school district boundaries that were created by states in the first place. Second, the use of choice has been called the ultimate democratic instrument, more democratic than school board control. Good choice plans are established only after parents are polled to see what types of schools they would like for their children. At the point of choice, families vote directly—with their feet. Bad schools are much more likely to be closed down and bad teachers fired by this kind of "voting" than by democratically elected school boards. Choice gives the poor a vote that they do not effectively exercise when school assignments are based on the incomes of neighborhood families.

Parental Involvement

With respect to parental involvement, Justice Powell's hypothesis that involvement declines with distance may have had merit in the era of forced busing, when parents felt disempowered and disconnected from new schools. However, the key to parental involvement is not geography but psychology. A 1995–96 survey of Boston's Metco program, for example, found that 80 percent of city-based minority parents had been to parent meetings in the suburbs and 70 percent had helped in fundraising, levels far in excess of inner-city participation rates.[38] As noted previously, parents who choose nonneighborhood schools tend to feel more invested and are more active, despite the added distance. Even researchers who are otherwise critical of choice schemes concur that increased parental involvement is among the results. The geographic distance to a nonneighborhood school is not normally insurmountable; schools will still be only a bus ride away, so it seems unlikely that distance itself will tip the balance in a parent's decision as to whether to attend a child's concert or a parent-teacher conference.[39]

Transportation Safety and Cost

Economic integration will require transportation of students beyond existing levels. But just how much of a burden is this? Although some concerns about transportation are legitimate, it is important to note that historically, these concerns have often been exaggerated by anti-integrationists. In the South, there was little complaint about bus rides when they were used to transport white and black children away from neighborhood schools to separate black and white schools. Even today, whites in places like Des Moines are willing to ride buses long distances to avoid integration. "All these white parents once passionately opposed to busing for integration, because it was unfair to keep children on a bus for an hour," Kozol observes, "are now putting their children on two-hour bus rides to get away from black and Hispanic children. The bus ride was never the issue. The destination was the issue." Theodore Shaw, of the NAACP's Legal Defense Fund, declares that "white people will put their children on buses to send them to West Hell if at the end of the ride there is an all-white, quality education. So busing is not the issue."[40]

Transportation expenses are modest when compared with the demonstrated benefits of socioeconomic integration in raising achievement—an investment that yields a much greater return than pouring money into high-poverty schools. Today, more than half the nation's elementary school students and about 75 percent of high school students live more than a mile from their "neighborhood" schools. The median distance traveled is about two miles.[41]

Desegregation has not meant much more transportation beyond what was previously required. While roughly 60 percent of the nation's public schoolchildren are transported to school by bus, even at the height of desegregation in the early 1980s fewer than 5 percent rode buses for desegregation purposes.[42] Bus transportation increased at a faster rate between the 1930s and 1940s than it did during the desegregation years between the 1950s and 1970s. In the 1980s, only a fraction of 1 percent of the national education budget was spent on busing for desegregation. On average, district transportation budgets rose only 2 percent to pay for more busing for racial integration.[43] (Probably in response to the political rhetoric about the cost of busing, a 1972 poll found that six in seven Americans believed that busing cost at least 25 percent of the school's budget—more than ten times the actual average cost.) More public money is spent on parochial school busing than on busing for integration.[44]

Arguments about the safety of bus rides are similarly misinformed. According to the National Highway Traffic Safety Administration, school buses are the safest form of ground vehicle transportation: on average, only 51 of 42,000 annual traffic fatalities in the United States involve children riding in or waiting for buses. Children who walk to school are two to three times as likely to be in accidents as children who ride buses.[45] School bus rides are usually short. The median bus trip for elementary schoolchildren being bused for racial desegregation purposes is less than fifteen minutes—less than half the average travel time for all school bus rides.[46]

Extracurricular Activities

In some cases, the distance involved in busing may make participation in extracurricular activities burdensome. For every poor child who does not participate because he or she faces a long bus ride, however, there may be another who is persuaded to participate because of greater peer involvement in extracurriculars found in middle-class schools. For a variety of reasons, tenth-grade students in high-poverty schools are less likely to participate in sports than students in low-poverty schools (44 versus 56 percent).[47] Surely school administrators can find creative ways, through after-school programs, to ensure that children are kept off the street during the dangerous hours after school.

Assimilation

With respect to the charge of "assimilation," it is important to distinguish between three kinds: political assimilation, economic assimilation, and cultural assimilation. The whole point of integrating social classes is to assimilate the poor economically, to teach them the values and behaviors necessary to economic success (hard work, proper grammar, access to networks), and to assimilate the various social classes politically (to understand constitutional democracy, respect for minorities, and equal opportunity). Socioeconomic integration does not seek to assimilate students culturally, however—to inculcate values, customs, or behaviors that might be loosely associated with a particular race, ethnicity, or religion (listening to country music, eating pasta, believing in the teachings of the Koran).

The public schools have long sought to achieve political assimilation, and they play an important role in making students full American citizens. It is possible to emphasize "Americanization," as the late Barbara Jordan noted in 1995, without the negative intolerance once associated with that phrase. "That word," Jordan notes, "earned a bad reputation when it was stolen by racists and xenophobes in the 1920s. But it is our word, and we are taking it back." The 1997 Immigration Commission defined the term *Americanization* as "the cultivation of a shared commitment to the American values of liberty, democracy, and equal opportunity."[48]

It is also defensible, indeed essential, that schools assimilate poor students economically. Standardized tests are demonstrably "culturally biased" in favor of middle-class culture, but as James Coleman noted many years ago, "what they measure are the skills which are among the most important in our society for getting a good job and moving up to a better one."[49] Knowledge of basic math and verbal skills are not all that is needed to succeed, but failure to teach these bodies of knowledge handicaps students who wish to do well in America.

On the right, the late conservative commentator Edward Banfield has written that "to say that the school cannot change the class culture is to deny that it can serve what many believe to be its principal purpose. The schools, many people think, exist to liberate the child from the confines—moral and emotional as well as intellectual—of his earliest environment to open higher horizons for him." On the left, the Communist intellectual Antonio Gramsci has argued, in the words of E. D. Hirsch Jr., that "the oppressed class should be taught to master the tools of power and authority—the ability to read, write, and communicate—and to gain enough traditional knowledge to understand the worlds of nature and culture surrounding them. . . . They should learn the value of hard work, gain the knowledge that leads to understanding, and master the traditional culture in order to command its rhetoric."[50] Some poor and working-class students may achieve academic success and nevertheless reject social mobility, in line with their parents' wishes. Public schools, however, should give children the option to move beyond their parents' world if they so wish.

Cultural assimilation is something quite different, and here again, the importance of socioeconomic as opposed to racial integration becomes clear. john powell argues that racial desegregation has too often been driven by the idea that there is "something wrong or deficient with black children that would be alleviated by placing them in the company of white children"; this assimilation model, he says "is one of racial supremacy."[51] Socioeconomic integration, by contrast, is designed not to break up black communities to eradicate a black culture, or Hispanic communities to break up Latino culture, but to break up poor communities to eradicate the culture of poverty. Economic and political assimilation may inevitably bleed into some cultural assimilation. However, as powell notes, there is a difference between old-style racist assimilation, which "envisions the absorption of minorities," and integration, which "envisions the transformation of the mainstream."[52] Under economic integration, some cultural assimilation will take place in all directions.

The Neighborhood School

Finally, under a system of controlled choice, those people who place the highest value on the proximity of their children's schools to their homes will still be able to "choose" the neighborhood school, along with some other neighborhood families. They will normally have a good chance of getting in—in part because many families of similar socioeconomic status in the neighborhood will choose other schools and in part because most choice programs give a preference for walkers living quite close to the school. What those wishing to walk will no longer enjoy is the right to exclude children whose families cannot afford to live in the neighborhood.

Does Socioeconomic Integration Miss the Real Point?

Another major objection to socioeconomic integration is one leveled at all school reform efforts: schools are ultimately unable to address inequalities and root problems stemming from families and neighborhoods. Rather than focusing on fairly impotent institutions like schools, the argument runs, we should redouble efforts to strengthen families and improve neighborhoods, where the real problems lie. (Alternatively, a darker argument says the differences in group results are genetically based in families, and there is little that can be done to change them.)[53]

The Coleman Report, which provides justification for socioeconomic integration, also found that in the end, the family is more important than any school factor in determining achievement. Subsequent research confirms the preeminent role of family: it is no accident, for example, that North Dakota, first among the states in percentage of intact families, scored second highest in the nation in math, while the District of Columbia, last in the proportion of intact families, scored second lowest in math. Some argue that if we do not first solve family problems, no one will want to integrate; Mickey Kaus, discussing the La Crosse, Wisconsin, socioeconomic integration plan, remarked, "I think you solve the underclass problem first, then you have a shot at mixing all the other classes together."[54] A related argument says that the elementary and secondary school years (kindergarten through twelfth grade) are "too late" in a child's development to address inequality. This contention appears to receive support not only from conservatives but also from some liberals who put increasing emphasis on brain development prenatally and in the first few years of life.[55]

A similar strain of this argument notes that children spend just 9 percent of their time in school. The positive effects of even an integrated school may be limited by the child's return to a neighborhood of concentrated poverty. Rather than simply integrating schools, this argument runs, the "ultimate solution" should focus on housing integration. Housing desegregation also reconciles integration and neighborhood schools, and it answers the charge that school desegregation is a "copout"—requiring children to do what their parents will not—by involving the entire family. Finally, the residential strategy addresses the mismatch between employment needs among city residents and employment opportunities in the suburbs—and when parents do better, children do better.[56]

Family Focus?

There is no gainsaying that the family is central to a child's success. Nevertheless, there are four major reasons to target schools over families: the behavior of children is easier to change than the behavior of adults; the influence of the American family is declining; families are protected by privacy, whereas public schools are compulsory; and poor children are, from a political standpoint, more sympathetic than poor adults.

First, children are more malleable than adults. Attempts to improve a child's home environment by changing the parents have proved difficult, just as efforts to raise parent involvement in children's education have proved disappointing. In 1988, Congress established the Comprehensive Child Development Program (CCDP) to provide social services, including drug counseling and parenting classes, to poor mothers with young children. A 1998 evaluation of the program by Abt Associates found that over a five-year period, the "CCDP did not produce any important positive effects on participating families": scores on the Peabody Picture Vocabulary test averaged 81.1 for five-year-old children in the CCDP versus 81.0 for five-year-olds not participating in the program. Other studies have come to similar conclusions.[57]

So too, trying to improve the home environment by giving poor families more money—to relieve some of the stress on parents and to provide their children with better medical care, nutrition, housing, even books—does not do much to change a child's life chances, according to two new studies. Susan Mayer's *What Money Can't Buy* finds that doubling the income of the poorest 20 percent of families would reduce teenage childbearing by only two percentile points and high school dropout rates by one percentile point, and the mean number of schooling years would rise from 12.80 to 12.83. According to Greg Duncan and Jeanne Brooks-Gunn, there is no evidence that "income transfers alone would produce a dramatic improvement in the physical health, mental health, or . . . behavioral development of [low-income] children."[58]

The problem, Mayer argues, is that home environment is not just a matter of cash flow; it is wrong to say that "the poor are just like everyone else except that they have less money." The statement might have been true after the Civil War, when many fathers had been killed, or during the Great Depression, when unemployment in some cities rose to 50 percent. Today, however, poverty is likely to be a proxy for a lack of skills, diligence, honesty, reliability, enthusiasm, dependability, or hard work, she finds.[59] Cash transfers may improve life chances for some poor children, but Mayer's research suggests it is unlikely to make poor parents read more to their children or encourage them to do their homework.

By contrast, because children are more easily influenced, schools can make a significant difference. Most Americans know that it is wrong, empirically and morally, to simply declare that because of an unenriching home environment, poor children are "uneducable" or that the reason poor children do poorly is that they are genetically inferior. Most parents know that family is not all-determining, which is why affluent parents often shop for the best school available. Correlations between family social class and achievement are lower in many nations; Belgium, Italy, Sweden, Finland, and Japan have all managed to disentangle family socioeconomic status and achievement more effectively than the United States. The German education system, researchers note, "produces a much more compressed distribution of human capital than the U.S. system."[60]

It is also empirically incorrect to argue that all is lost after a child reaches school age. Claude Fischer and colleagues note that "children's ranks on IQ tests change so much that their scores at age six account for less than half of the variation in those scores at age fifteen." James McPartland, in arguing that Title I services should be used in high school as well as elementary school, notes that there is "growing evidence that extra help for low-performing high school students can produce significant learning gains."[61] Compared with changing the behavior of parents, it is clearly easier to change the behavior of children, of any age.

Second, the relative influence of schools and peers versus family appears to have shifted since the 1966 Coleman Report, as the American family has weakened. Indeed, by 1981, James Coleman had retreated from the economic fatalism of his earlier report, finding that schools can make a significant difference. The new finding, one commentator notes, represents "a dramatic departure from the social determinism" of the first report.[62] While Coleman remained a skeptic about the degree to which spending can raise achievement, his research, and that of others, confirms the popular belief that schools obviously matter a great deal.

Coleman's shift is explained in part by dramatic changes in the American family. When the Coleman Report was published, many women with young children were home, exerting a constant influence. Over time this has changed: the number of working mothers and single parents has skyrocketed, both of which factors tend to reduce the important link between a parent's position and that of a child. In 1960, 26 percent of American children had mothers in the labor force; by 1990, that figure had risen to 59 percent. The percentage of children with no father in the household tripled from a range of 6–8 percent between 1940 and 1960 to 23 percent in 1993.[63] Whereas in 1960, 12 percent of children lived apart from one of their parents, by 1995 almost 40 percent did, and for children born in the 1980s, it is projected that more than 50 percent will live apart from one parent. According to a 1994 Carnegie Commission report, in 1960 fewer than 1 percent of American children under the age of eighteen experienced the divorce of their parents each year; in 1990, almost half experienced divorce during childhood. With the breakdown of the American family, Leon Botstein notes, "schools and institutions are becoming more, not less, crucial." Recent studies confirm that peer influence is on the rise relative to the influence of the family.[64]

Third, whereas family weakness may be at the core of much inequality, as a practical matter there are limits to what we can do in a free society to rectify that problem. In the 1820s, the Workingman's Party took equal opportunity to its logical extreme in advocating the removal of infants from the home, but most Americans would properly view such proposals today with horror. Most would also balk at conservative Edward Banfield's suggestion in the 1960s that "problem families" should be paid to send their infants and children to preschool to keep them from their family's harmful influences. In the 1990s, Newt Gingrich's call to bring back orphanages gained little traction.[65]

As a matter of liberty, and as a right of privacy, the state can interfere with family decisions only in extreme circumstances, when parents inflict harm on their children through abuse or severe neglect. "Getting parents to change their habits is even harder than getting teachers to change," note Jencks and Phillips. "Like teachers, parents are usually suspicious of unsolicited suggestions."[66] By contrast, schools already compromise the family prerogative, requiring compulsory attendance based on the public interest in ensuring that all children are educated.

Fourth, as a practical political matter, Americans will not stand for major efforts to create greater opportunity for children through help to poor parents, even if that method were a surer guarantee of equality than equal educational opportunity. Writing checks to parents—even for the ostensible benefit of poor children—is seen as enriching "unworthy" adults. (Nationally, 62 percent of household income is spent on adults and 38 percent on children.)[67] Education, by contrast, provides egalitarians with their primary opening in the United States. Whereas poor adults are seen as blameworthy, children are seen as "the deserving poor."

Public education, Jennifer Hochschild and Nathan Scovronick note, "is America's answer to the European social welfare state." Only 29 percent of Americans believe "it is the responsibility of government to reduce differences in income between people," compared with 81 percent of Italians, 64 percent of Britons, and 61 percent of West Germans, and European governments outspend the United States on welfare. By contrast, in 1993, the United States spent $5,944 for each student in elementary and secondary school, compared with the United Kingdom's expenditure of $3,914.[68]

Similarly, in 1990, Tom Smith found that only 20 percent of Americans supported provision of a basic income to all people (compared with 59 percent in the United Kingdom, 51 percent in Germany, and 48 percent in the Netherlands), but in the United States, support for helping the poor attend college was roughly the same as in Europe (75 percent in the United States, 74 percent in the Netherlands, 83 percent in the United Kingdom, and 84 percent in Germany).[69] Asked to name the top five causes of poverty, Americans cite personal failings for four causes but also cite "the failure of society to provide good schools for many Americans." Self-help programs aimed at children, such as Head Start, are "remarkably noncontroversial," Peter Skerry notes; although Head Start's effectiveness has been questioned by social scientists, it comports with American values in a way that welfare and quotas do not.[70]

This is not to say that redistribution among adults is impossible or that it should not be tried—the minimum wage and progressive tax structure are popular and important mechanisms for bringing about greater equality. The American penchant for education over welfare, however, is deeply rooted in our history. The United States, Derek Bok notes, "was the first country to proclaim the ideal of universal public education," beginning with Massachusetts in 1852 and ending with Mississippi in 1918. James Conant has observed that the Homestead Act of 1862 was meant to reward self-reliance—providing a gift to those who would better themselves through hard work—but when the frontier closed, education became America's new way of providing social mobility for the hardworking. Education spending, Gary Orfield notes, has increased during times when other social welfare programs were being cut; it has increased when liberals were in power and when conservatives were in power; and it has generally increased even during times of tax revolt. As a nation, our government spends more of our national income on education than any other activity, substantially more than on national defense or social security.[71] Polls consistently show that large majorities support yet greater spending on education, even if it means raising taxes.[72]

Neighborhoods and Housing versus Schools

It is probably true that integration of housing and neighborhoods will bring even more social benefits to poor children than merely integrating schools, and David Rusk's eloquent plea for housing integration efforts deserves strong support. That having been said, in the short run there are several reasons to believe the schooling alternative is more politically feasible and should be pursued independent of housing integration.

First, as a philosophical matter, education represents opportunity, whereas housing (along with occupation, wealth, and income) represents result; and Americans are much more willing to equalize the former than the latter. Indeed, whereas results-oriented redistributions are seen as interfering with liberty interests, education is itself a prerequisite to exercising liberty.[73] Philosophically, many more Americans believe that all children have the right to attend public schools of equal quality than believe that all adults have a right to equal neighborhoods.

Second, for these philosophical reasons, government in the United States has always had a much stronger hand in assigning schools than assigning housing. The numbers are stark: almost 90 percent of American schoolchildren attend public schools, whereas just 4.3 percent of Americans live in public housing, an "exceptionally small" number compared with other nations. (In Britain, for example, the balance between public housing and public schools is quite different: a much higher percentage attend private schools—29 percent—but many more live in public housing.) "Public education," writes James Liebman, "is about the only area of political concern in which the government (by means of long-accepted compulsory attendance laws and publicly funded schools) already has its distributive hands on a sufficient proportion of the citizenry so that the courts may rearrange them without substantially undermining their pre-existing liberties."[74] In the end, the government's role in drawing school boundary lines and making school assignments to promote social goals is historically greater than its role in zoning to create integrated communities.

Third, as a practical matter, housing integration is more difficult, and appears to have a lower tipping point, than school integration. For if people feel strongly about where their children go to school, they feel even more strongly about who their neighbors are. In Yonkers, New York, for example, residents were more willing to go along with school integration than with housing integration. As William Clune has written, "Geographical isolation of wealth is apparently an essential precondition of enjoying wealth. . . . Social scientists tell us that 'social distance' is the most prized of all goods."[75]

In addition, residents may fear that the government has fewer tools to prevent tipping in housing than in schools. Whereas school boards can to a limited degree stabilize racial balances by taking certain steps (for example, redrawing boundaries, creating magnet schools with demographic targets), once a neighborhood begins to change, there is often little that government can do.[76]

Fourth, on the other side of the coin, efforts to integrate housing threaten urban political leaders in a way that school desegregation does not. It is one thing to transport children to middle-class schools, another to move reliable voters—and potential community leaders—out of distressed neighborhoods. Indeed, President Clinton's efforts to push socioeconomic housing integration ran up against some opposition from black urban politicians for these reasons.[77]

In sum, then, although housing integration might offer additional benefits, it is more politically challenging than school integration.[78] With a few exceptions, the nation has not taken up the Kerner Commission's call for deconcentration of high-poverty ghettos. Section 8 housing was supposed to lead to dispersal of the poor from low-income areas; but studies find that "most recipients move within their own communities because of race and class barriers." Housing integration efforts have often come under attack, even from liberal Democrats. In 1994, Democratic senator Bob Kerrey blasted a Gautreaux-like housing discrimination settlement in Omaha, Nebraska, as "social engineering." In 1995, an expansion of the Clinton administration's modest Moving to Opportunity program, designed to relocate sixty-two hundred poor families into middle-class neighborhoods in six cities, was killed by none other than the liberal Maryland senator Barbara Mikulski.[79]

Moreover, though it seems logical to believe that children benefit more when both their schools and neighborhoods are integrated, some studies indicate that the additional benefit of neighborhood change is small.[80] A recent study finds that while the cumulative impact of poverty concentrations by neighborhood and school are greater than that of school alone, poor students who remain in high-poverty neighborhoods but attend affluent schools achieve "markedly higher scores." Schools apparently play a significant role compared with neighborhood (net of school) because the "density" of peers is greater in school, where students must interact and cannot withdraw behind closed doors.[81]

It is also important to note that school desegregation will help promote the ultimate goal of housing integration. The Minnesota state legislator Myron Orfield finds that typically, "local schools become socioeconomically distressed before neighborhoods become poor" because bad, high-poverty schools promote residential flight.[82] Once a school integration plan is put into effect, allowing people in urban areas to attend a majority-middle-class school in the suburbs or a city magnet, the incentive to flee to the suburbs is reduced. Cities are attractive—they often house the best universities, theaters, museums, restaurants, and sports facilities—and once middle-class families feel comfortable with kindergarten through twelfth-grade education, many will move back in.

Empirical studies confirm that racial school desegregation has often been followed by residential integration. In a study of seven metropolitan-wide desegregation plans, Diana Pearce has found that "schools tend to stamp their identity on the neighborhood, and school boundaries often actually define neighborhood boundaries." In Boston, for example, the busing of students gave residents less reason to segregate by neighborhood, and in 1999, as the city moved to end busing, it was noted that "if busing ended tomorrow, the classroom demographics would change little." East Boston, which was 1 percent minority when busing began, is now 25 percent minority.[83]

By contrast, housing integration does not always lead to school integration. Government efforts to draw working- and middle-class people into mixed housing has produced a degree of economic integration, but the middle-income people who move in tend not to have children. In West Garfield Park, Chicago, for example, middle-income empty nesters moved in, and the percentage of students receiving free and reduced-price lunch rose from 95 to 99 percent.[84]

Will Socioeconomic Integration Cause Middle-Class Flight?

The final objection to socioeconomic integration is that it sounds an awful lot like "busing," a social experiment widely viewed as a self-defeating disaster. To the extent plans are imposed by state court orders, the middle class will resist by fleeing the public schools. The top 20 percent of Americans (by income and education) are already in the process of seceding from public institutions.[85] Might not socioeconomic integration push them over the edge? Why won't socioeconomic integration result in middle-class flight, just as racial integration resulted in white flight? The plan to desegregate Boston schools epitomizes the failure of busing, but six major factors distinguish the proposal for socioeconomic integration today from what happened in Boston in the 1970s.[86] In many important respects, the plan this book puts forth is a reaction to Boston's failure—an attempt to cull the benefits of that effort while avoiding its obvious pitfalls.

In the early 1970s, a federal district court judge in Boston found that the Boston school board had discriminated against black students by gerrymandering school lines, covertly establishing a system of de jure segregation that paralleled the formal de jure segregation commonly found in the South. In 1973, 62 of Boston's 150 elementary schools were more than 96 percent white, and 32 were more than 85 percent black.[87] The judge, Arthur Garrity, ordered massive busing of white and black students in Boston to remedy years of discrimination. In keeping with the Supreme Court's decision in *Milliken* v. *Bradley*, Garrity's order limited busing to the central city and did not involve the nearby suburban areas.

When the busing began in the fall of 1974, Boston exploded. A nation that had been battered in previous summers by numerous black riots witnessed a very ugly white riot. White students, particularly in South Boston, pelted black students with rocks and beer bottles, shouting "Niggers, go home!" In a web of violence, in October 1974, writer Jack Beatty recalls, "a Haitian-born maintenance man, on his way to pick up his wife from her job at a South Boston laundry, was hauled from his car by neighborhood whites and beaten with a hammer and a sawed-off hockey stick. Apparently in retaliation, the next day mobs of black teenagers stoned white motorists passing through Roxbury, pulled several from their cars, and beat them." The violence continued on and off. In 1976, a black attorney, Ted Landsmark, hurrying to a meeting at City Hall, was attacked by white youths demonstrating against busing. One of the youths yelled, "There's a nigger! Get him!" After being kicked and hit, he was struck in the face by a white youth carrying an American flag. A stunning picture of the flag holder, poised to attack, appeared on the front page of newspapers across the country, symbolizing the ugly resistance.[88]

White flight accelerated. During the two years of implementation of busing, one-third of white students fled the Boston public schools. At the end of 1976, blacks and Hispanics constituted a majority, a crucial tipping point. In the first decade of busing, the number of white students in Boston public schools plummeted from fifty-four thousand to fifteen thousand. Between 1974 and 1989 (when a new plan was implemented), the white representation in Boston public schools declined from 60 to 25 percent.[89] As Beatty notes, "A plan designed to desegregate the schools . . . helped to resegregate them." Those students who remained, white and black, were mostly poor and working class. The middle class left, and many of the poor whites in South Boston simply dropped out of school in protest. The dropouts were known locally as "Garrity's children." By 1998, the Boston public schools were 48 percent black, 25 percent Hispanic, 17 percent white, and 9 percent Asian; in all, 74 percent of students were eligible for free or reduced-price lunch.[90]

Over time, in light of these clearly disastrous results, a conventional wisdom developed about the Boston busing crisis. Among liberals, it was clear that racism drove opposition to busing and that white northerners could be just as racist as white southerners. Among conservatives (as well as a fair number of liberals), the lesson was that forced integration was counterproductive and that busing does not work because families want neighborhood schools and do not like having their children ride buses to schools far from home. In 1992, the state senator William Bulger concluded that "if the purpose was to integrate, it failed. The schools are nearly all black now. If the purpose was to enhance education, that failed too, and the miserable test scores of the students prove that." Given the results, even some liberals now lament the Boston busing effort.[91]

There is some truth to both of these conclusions. Busing in Boston did expose a fair amount of racism and ugliness on the part of white northerners; and the compulsory assignment used by Judge Garrity, with no independent educational rationale, did help feed white flight. The story was more complicated than this, however, and over time, observers began to note that the failure of Boston was not inevitable and may have had much to do with the way in which busing was implemented. Garth Taylor's 1986 study found that majorities of white Bostonians were nonracist and were opposed to busing—suggesting the liberals' explanation for the failure was incomplete.[92] Others note that the mere transportation of students away from neighborhood schools did not drive the opposition to busing in Boston: it was the destination at the end of the ride, not the busing itself, that so angered white Bostonians.

As researchers and journalists began to explore the lessons of the Boston busing crisis, it became clear that the Boston experience had not proved that integration is impossible or that failure was inevitable; rather, the case showed that for integration to work, it must be done fairly, thoughtfully, and respectfully. Several major lessons emerge from Boston's experience—lessons that inform this book's argument for economic desegregation.[93] Whereas the purpose of busing in Boston was to remedy a wrongdoing, irrespective of its impact on educational achievement, socioeconomic integration is designed to enhance educational opportunity. Whereas Boston's plan relied on compulsory assignment, economic integration will use controlled parental choice. Whereas Boston's plan was constrained to the city limits, economic integration will often be metrowide. Whereas the Boston plan was temporary and was eventually dismantled, economic integration is permanent in nature. In addition, changing times and evolutions in attitudes (concerning the important issues of race and discipline) are likely to make integration efforts easier today than they were a generation ago. Finally, differences in the dynamics of racial and economic self-segregation should also improve the success of socioeconomic efforts.

Remedy versus Education

The first central limitation to the Boston desegregation order is that the Supreme Court over time decided that *Brown* was about remedying a historic wrong (in this case, segregation by the schools committee) rather than promoting better education of students. At its base, as the plaintiffs' attorney, J. Harold Flannery, noted, *Brown* was "a race case," not an "education case," so the remedy had to be geared toward racial balancing irrespective of the effect on education, a view endorsed by Judge Garrity. This focus was disturbing to many black parents, as Derrick Bell has noted.[94]

By contrast, the purpose of socioeconomic integration is to improve educational opportunity. Judge Garrity was correct to address the de jure racial violation (though he could have done it more skillfully), but we are now at a new stage in the fight for equal opportunity, where we must turn our attention forward from addressing past wrongs to promoting educational opportunity itself. The black activist Noel Day realized this back in the mid-1970s when he commented that both working-class whites and blacks need better schools; "if quality education has any meaning a busing program would be set up to move the [poor] white children out of South Boston, too."[95]

The different purpose has two manifestations. First, because the key to raising achievement among poor students is not breaking up black schools or white schools or Latino schools but allowing all students to attend middle-class schools, the primary focus of integration should be class, not race. Second, because the goal is higher educational achievement, socioeconomic integration is built around a guarantee of majority-middle-class schools, not proportional representation. This is a sound policy educationally, and because most studies find the "tipping point" to be around the 40–50 percent mark, the guarantee that middle-class children will not be sent to majority-poor schools is also likely to dramatically reduce flight.[96]

Compulsion and Impotence versus Choice and Empowerment

The second major problem with the Boston busing desegregation plan was its heavy-handed and compulsory nature. Parental choice was not in the picture in 1974. Each child was assigned to a particular school, possibly across town from his or her neighborhood, and parents had no real say in the matter. Busing not only involved integrating students into schools that parents believed were likely to be inferior, it also stripped parents of the power to decide their children's future. In a poll of Boston parents, some 80 percent of whites opposed the government's plan because it told parents where to send their children.[97]

This feeling of powerlessness was particularly poignant for the working-class Irish of Boston, says Robert Coles, for they "remember how they were treated for so long by the Yankees who ran the state and ran the city. They are very conscious of who is running things." "These people sense they have no control over the destiny of their lives," Coles continues. "If they show up one minute late for work, from South Boston, they're docked." The busing critic Louise Day Hicks "tapped a much broader sense of grievance, rooted less in race than in class," writes J. Anthony Lukas, "the feeling of many working-class whites that they had been abandoned." In his book *Common Ground*, Lukas describes the powerlessness felt by Alice McGoff, a working-class Irish mother: the judge had wrested "from her the one thing in the world over which she still exercised some control: her family. If they could move her children around the city like pawns on a black-and-white chessboard, then what could Alice call her own anymore?"[98]

Charles Glenn, one of the principal authors of the Boston busing plan, now says it was mishandled: "We were arrogant and we were wrong." If he had to do it over again, he says, "I would seek to base school assignments so far as possible upon well-informed parent choice," conditioned by racial balance. Fifteen years later, in 1989, Boston did move toward a controlled choice desegregation plan. Unfortunately, by this time, Boston's school population was already three-quarters minority and largely disadvantaged.[99]

Today's socioeconomic plans would begin with controlled choice, empowering working-class parents to choose any school in the metropolitan area. White middle-class flight has been shown to be reduced when choice is part of the plan—a fact courts now recognize.[100] Building choice into the desegregation effort in places like Montclair, New Jersey, has helped keep the schools from "tipping." Although the overall racial composition of the schools is majority minority, the Montclair schools are highly integrated, and the numbers have remained stable, with overall enrollment in 1998 of 45 percent white, 46 percent black, 5 percent Hispanic, and 4 percent Asian.[101]

In a 1998 poll, Public Agenda found strong opposition to "busing children to achieve a better racial balance in the schools." Seventy-six percent of white parents were opposed (22 percent in favor), and black parents were only slightly in favor (55 percent, 42 percent opposed). When choice was a part of the plan, however, support rose significantly for both groups. Asked whether they favored or opposed "letting parents choose their top three schools, while the district makes the final choice, with an eye to racial balance," white parents favored the approach (61 percent in favor, 35 percent opposed), as did black parents (65 percent in favor, 34 percent opposed).[102]

Citywide Integration versus Integration of the Metropolitan Area

The third major flaw of the Boston plan, also inherent in *Brown* (as interpreted in *Milliken*), is that busing to achieve racial balance was limited to the city itself and did not draw upon surrounding suburban jurisdictions, which were deemed innocent of the promotion of de jure segregation. In Boston, the limitation of busing to the city was a key factor in promoting white flight, reducing the academic benefit of integration, raising charges of double standards, and increasing the chance of violence.

MORE FLIGHT. The *Milliken* limitation to Boston's busing plan promoted white flight in two major ways. First, it provided an easy escape hatch for white families with means. By moving to a close-in suburban jurisdiction, wealthier families could exempt themselves from the busing order they may have opposed. Second, by exempting the suburbs, Garrity's order dramatically changed the ratio of black and white students involved in busing, a key factor in the success or failure of integration plans. Only one in eleven students in the Boston area lived in the city itself, and the vast majority of whites living in the suburbs were not included as part of the racial balancing scheme. In 1992, the Boston metropolitan area schools were 87 percent white, but the schools in the city of Boston were by then just 21 percent white.[103]

By contrast, under the logic of *Sheff*, socioeconomic integration plans will often involve entire metropolitan regions. If the experience from the racial context holds, these metropolitan-wide orders will be much less subject to white flight.[104] Studies find countywide plans experience about half the white enrollment decline found in urban desegregation plans. Those districts where busing is generally agreed to have been a success tend to be those in which suburbs and city were consolidated into one school district, places like Charlotte and Mecklenburg County, North Carolina; Louisville and Jefferson County, Kentucky; and Nashville and Davidson County, Tennessee.[105]

According to a 1998 *Education Week* report, Jefferson County schools are "thriving" compared with other urban districts nationally. In a "rare twist," the report notes, Kentucky's "largest, most diverse district is better known for its successes than its failures." Similarly, the report found that Charlotte-Mecklenburg schools, educating some ninety-three thousand students, had held on to their middle-class population; only 16 percent of the district's children were in poverty, about half the 30 percent rate for seventy-five of the nation's largest cities. Raleigh, North Carolina, which merged its school district into a single Wake County Public School system a generation ago, is experiencing "reverse white flight": the percentage of minority students declined from 30 percent in 1987 to 26 percent in 1993, as white enrollment increases outpaced minority enrollment increases.[106] Indeed, the fact that southern states are more likely to have countywide school systems is one partial explanation for why southern schools are now more desegregated than northern schools. Courts have cited the smaller likelihood of white flight as a justification for metropolitan remedies.[107]

Metropolitan plans avoid both of the issues that drove flight in Boston. First, there is the issue of numbers. Most middle-class whites do not wish to avoid all forms of integration; they merely wish to avoid high-poverty and majority-minority schools. Where suburban participation is included in a metropolitan plan, those conditions are much easier to meet. The downward spiral of white flight to the suburbs, and with it the aggravating reduction in the tax base (which causes yet more families to leave an inadequately funded system), is avoided.[108] If this pattern holds—and only small numbers of middle-class families opt out of common schools—those middle-class families who are on the fence are likely to feel comfortable with the concept of majority-middle-class schools, and the situation will stabilize.

Second, metropolitan plans are successful because it is harder to flee when one of the two major escape routes—moving to the suburbs—is effectively closed off. The other route—enrollment in private school—remains open; indeed, all citizens have a constitutional right to send their children to private schools, assuming the family can afford it. Experience shows, however, that only small numbers of families used private schools to avoid integration, and many of those did so only temporarily. During the years since implementation of *Brown,* the public schools have become more heavily populated with students of color; but that reflects a dramatic diversification of the U.S. population, not the flight of white students to private schools.[109]

In the early 1960s, before vigorous implementation of *Brown,* about 15 percent of elementary and secondary school students were enrolled in private schools; today the figure is 12 percent. During the key desegregation years, the number of students attending Catholic schools declined from 5.5 million in 1965 to 2.5 million in 1990, a drop from 12 percent of all students to 5.4 percent. In 1975, at the peak of desegregation in the South, 90 percent of southern white children attended public schools; today, more than 90 percent attend public schools in every southern state except Louisiana. Even in big cities, where schools are suffering most, only 15.8 percent of children currently attend private schools. Prince Edward County, Virginia, which for years epitomized the idea that desegregation meant white flight to private schools (after *Brown,* the public schools were literally shut down for five years), has seen whites return to the public schools so that by 1999, the district's schools were "among the most integrated in the nation," *Education Week* notes, and considered "to be among the best in this rural corner of the Old Dominion."[110]

Many readers of this book may know several people who send their children to elite private schools, but nationally, only 1 percent of Americans "attended non-sectarian private schools or send their children to them or both." Nicholas Lemann, writing in November 1998, noted that 45 million students attended public schools, compared with only four hundred thousand attending private, nonsectarian schools with annual tuition in excess of five thousand dollars—"less than 1 percent of the public school enrollment." Even if the capacity of private schools were to double, the public schools would still enroll 76 percent of students. Alan Wolfe's polling data show the upper middle class does not wish to secede—indeed, most agree that the present inequality is extreme.[111]

NO ACADEMIC BENEFIT. The second drawback under *Milliken* is that because the whites most likely to stay in Boston public schools were those least able to escape (students from poor and working-class families), racial integration did not produce much class integration, so the benefits for blacks were minimal. James Coleman noted that because the Boston desegregation plan "involved primarily lower-class communities . . . with most of the higher-achieving middle-class schools in the suburbs," it was unlikely to yield "beneficial effects on achievement."[112]

In some respects, poor whites in Boston were even worse off educationally than blacks. Noel Day notes that the percentage of students going on to college was higher in the predominantly black schools than at white South Boston High School. Indeed, after busing, the percentage of students admitted to college at South Boston High increased to the highest point in the school's eighty-year history. One poor white man told Lillian Rubin that he opposed desegregation because black children do not "talk proper English." "We haven't went to forced busing," he continued, "and we've made great strides." Jonathan Kozol describes busing as a "Pyrrhic victory," noting that under desegregation, "poor whites, poor blacks, and poor Hispanics now become illiterate together." As J. Anthony Lukas has observed, "More and more, Boston's busing program consisted of mixing the black poor and the white poor, the deprived with the deprived." "Cruelly," Jack Beatty remarks, "the newly integrated schools were no better." In 1999, the head of the Boston NAACP noted that "the Boston educational system is worse now that it was twenty-five years ago. . . . They are giving a bad education to all students."[113]

UNFAIRNESS. Restricting desegregation to the city also reduced the political acceptability of busing because white working-class Boston residents were well aware of the double standard being imposed on them by self-righteous white liberals living in the suburban areas beyond the order's reach. The Massachusetts state senator William Bulger complained, "We are being asked to do something that the rest of the world confides they won't do themselves." The forces favoring busing (and criticizing white Bostonians for racism)—the editors of the *Boston Globe*,

Harvard professors, and Judge Garrity himself—almost uniformly resided in comfortable white suburbs. "Poor whites griped and sometimes even sabotaged," Judge Wilkinson has written, "but in the end they rode."[114]

In mid-October 1974, the *Boston Globe* devoted nearly the entire op-ed page to an interview with Robert Coles, a racial integrationist and Harvard professor, in which he blasted the double standard. "I think the busing is a scandal," Coles contends. "I do not think busing should be imposed like this on working-class people exclusively. It should cross these lines, and people in the suburbs should share in it. . . . I don't think that all these experts . . . these various social scientists and those in favor of integration like myself should be in the position of delivering sermons to the people of Boston . . . of any kind . . . until we have been made part of all of this." Of people living in the suburbs, Coles remarks, "their lives are clean and their minds are clean. And they can afford this long, charitable, calm view. And if people don't know that this is a class privilege then, by golly, they don't know anything."[115]

The basic unfairness of the scheme was a major source of resistance, according to Lukas, who says that Alice McGoff, the working-class Irish-American mother he profiles, "knew full well which whites would pay the price" for racial discrimination. "It wouldn't be those who worked in the big corporate and law offices downtown, the ones who dined in those Back Bay clubs and lived in the comfortable, all-white suburbs. No, as usual, it would be the working-class whites who shared the inner city with blacks, competed with them for schools and jobs and housing, and jostled with them on the street corner." Lukas notes that "many of the angriest letters" against busing emphasized that Judge Garrity lived in Wellesley, "where his family and friends were exempt from his court orders." McGoff, Lukas continues, "had come to understand it was easy to be a liberal about other people's problems. Maybe that was why all the problems were in the city and all the liberals in the suburbs."[116]

Increasingly, South Boston residents moved toward George Wallace and later became Reagan Democrats. In May 1975, the labor movement refused to join a demonstration in support of Boston's busing program.[117] The anger at blacks, and the even greater hatred of limousine liberals, congealed into anger toward the Democratic Party, from which Democrats are still recovering. The two groups that might have allied to bring about social change—working-class whites and blacks—were, instead, placed at each other's throats.

Noel Day wrote that "instead of pushing for better schools, black people and white people [in Boston] are fighting over who will sit next to whom in some of the worst schools in the nation . . . fighting over the leavings. Racism has been used to obscure common class interests ever since it was used to defeat populism. That is the tragedy of South Boston—they think they have something worth defending." At one point, there was discussion of expanding Boston's voluntary interdistrict Metco program to include poor whites, but that effort was shot down.[118]

By contrast, metropolitan-wide socioeconomic integration addresses the legitimate equity concerns raised by working-class whites about racial desegregation: why should poor and working-class whites desegregate the public schools while wealthier whites—some of whom wrote the plans— sit on the sidelines? To the extent that opposition and flight from schools was connected to anger about equity, metropolitan plans remove that objection. Moreover, the new integration gives poor whites and blacks a chance to attend good suburban schools, which in Boston were often a short distance away.[119]

Twenty-odd years after the Boston busing crisis, the *Boston Globe* reacted to the *Sheff* metropolitan-wide desegregation suit, in the neighboring state of Connecticut, with strong approval: "The urban pathologies that plague many inner cities have roots in the kind of racial and economic isolation that pervades Hartford. Sooner or later those problems will spill over Connecticut's suburban borders. Better to open them up in the spirit of cooperation and come up with a plan that ensures justice for all."[120]

The political spinoff of socioeconomic integration would be precisely the reverse of that which flowed from Boston's racial desegregation scheme. To some observers, like the normally perceptive J. Harvie Wilkinson, the Boston experience shows "that race divides, more than class unites, the American proletariat."[121] This was true, of course, only because the dynamic of racial busing drove that particular wedge between blacks and poor whites. If the goal were readjusted, so that economic integration meant poor whites in South Boston and poor blacks in Roxbury had a shot at attending the better schools in the close-by suburbs, Wilkinson might have drawn a very different lesson. J. Anthony Lukas thought that much of the anger of the white working class could have been productively redirected. "What kind of alliance could be cobbled together from people who feel equally excluded by class, or by some combination of class and race?" Lukas asked, noting that the working-class Irish and blacks he interviewed had "far more in common than either of them" did with upper-middle-class liberals. In fact, the interests of citizens in Boston did converge—briefly—as they argued for a metropolitan remedy in a Supreme Court brief in the Milliken case and, later, for fair-share housing legislation in the suburbs.[122]

Robert Coles notes that "there are a lot of people in South Boston capable of making racial slurs. But they have other ideals too. They have contradictory and conflicting emotions. There is an identification with people who suffer, and there is a sense of fear, too." Bayard Rustin notes that the white working class is not conservative or liberal, "it is both, and how it acts will depend upon the way the issues are defined."[123]

MORE VIOLENCE. The restriction of busing to city residents and working-class and poor whites also appears to have increased the likelihood of violent resistance in Boston. Polling data make clear that poor and less educated whites are more likely to express racist sentiments.[124] Whether these sentiments reflect a lack of education or an insecurity brought about by competition with blacks, imposing busing only on the most angry group of whites was problematic, a fact of which blacks were well aware. "Unless the privileged and the comfortable are willing to become part of the process of working out the great ideals of American life," Lukas has observed, "we're going to see disasters of social policy. You put the burden on the vulnerable and the angry, and you're going to reap a whirlwind." The chaos and turmoil that ensued may itself have fed white flight. By contrast, metropolitan socioeconomic integration is not focused on those whites most likely to resist with force.[125]

In sum, metropolitan plans mean more favorable ratios of middle class to poor, a unified approach in which the suburbs are not held to a lower standard and integration not focused solely on those most likely to resist violently. Polls find strong support for this approach. Public Agenda's 1998 survey found that although whites were opposed to "busing children to achieve a better racial balance in the schools" by 76 percent (22 percent in favor), 60 percent of whites supported (33 percent opposed) "redrawing district lines to combine mostly black and mostly white districts into one school district."[126]

Different Times

The fourth major difference between the Boston busing plan of the 1970s and socioeconomic integration in the new century is that public opinion has evolved significantly on two crucial issues—race and discipline. By moving left on race and right on discipline, we have a climate much more conducive to successful integration today.

Racists will oppose socioeconomic integration because lower-income children are disproportionately black and Hispanic, but researchers note that "the last forty years have seen a dramatic change in white attitudes toward school desegregation." Recent polling data also suggest greater tolerance of diversity than was found in "tipping point" studies of southern whites thirty years ago.[127] Although polls probably underestimate the degree of white intolerance—respondents may lie in order not to sound bigoted—the general trends are nevertheless hopeful. Today's white parents, who grew up during and after the civil rights revolution, are much more tolerant than previous generations. Whereas in 1963, 47 percent of polled whites said they would not send their children to a school that was 50 percent black, by 1994 the number had dropped to 7 percent.[128]

Today, indeed, large numbers of whites do not want their children going to all-white schools in which most children come from well-to-do families; they find it stifling, and they genuinely appreciate the importance of diversity to meaningful education in America as it enters the twenty-first century. Polls find that 56 percent of Americans say more should be done to integrate schools and only 8 percent of black parents and 17 percent of white parents say less should be done. These progressive attitudes are most present among middle-class whites, who will be more involved in socioeconomic integration than they were in racial integration. The idea, as expressed by Jennifer Hochschild, is that all sides benefit from combining "the resources and expectations of the suburbs with the culture and excitement of the city."[129]

Simultaneously, and fortuitously, the nation has grown more conservative on discipline questions. Whereas racial integration occurred at a time when discipline codes were coming under attack, socioeconomic integration will occur at a time when tough discipline approaches are ascendant. Indeed, in 1999, Clinton made the adoption of "sensible discipline policies" one of the requirements for continued federal funding of schools. This evolution is critical to the success of integration efforts.[130]

Integration by Class versus Self-Segregation by Race

Whereas flight in Boston and elsewhere was driven in part by the fear that schools would quickly tip toward minority students, economic desegregation is likely to have a higher tipping point because there is no desire for solidarity among the poor the way there is on the part of racial groups. Part of the psychology of tipping is that some whites, who might accept a 50 percent black population, move when blacks constitute 40 percent of the population because they know that historically a 40 percent black neighborhood soon becomes 50 percent and then all-black. Part of the reason that 40 percent black neighborhoods become 50 percent black is not sinister: 50 percent black communities are what most blacks want.[131] In the context of socioeconomic integration (which has a racial component but is not tied strictly to racial numbers), the poor have no similar desire to aggregate, so there is not a natural push upward as there has been for blacks.

The key is to prevent the middle class from panicking. Studies find that once parents make the decision to send their children to integrated schools, they are usually satisfied. In a 1983 Harris poll, for example, 64 percent of white parents whose children were bused were very satisfied versus 11 percent not satisfied (among blacks the ratio was 66 to 6 percent).[132] Those who flee usually do so in the first year of integration, without giving integrated education a chance.[133]

Permanent Change versus Temporary Remedy

In the long run, the last flaw of the Boston busing plan—and of the *Brown* approach—is that desegregation plans were always meant to be temporary. Busing in Boston was phased out in the 1980s, and in early 1999, when Boston's Democratic mayor, Thomas M. Menino, proposed abolishing the controlled choice racial balance plan, there was no legal recourse for those who wanted desegregation to continue.[134] Indeed, later in 1999, under pressure from a lawsuit brought by white parents, Boston was forced to drop the use of race in student assignment earlier than it had previously planned.

In the 1970s, J. Harvie Wilkinson dismissed the suggestion that both poor whites and blacks could benefit from integrating with suburban students with the admonishment, "the Constitution [speaks] to race, not to class."[135] Today, those words have new meaning as a conservative Supreme Court is using the heightened scrutiny of race to strike down voluntary integration schemes. The socioeconomic plan, by contrast, would be both legal and permanent; there would be no time clock ticking as it has for racial desegregation across the country.

| 9

Practical Experience with
Socioeconomic Integration

TO EXPLORE THE WAY in which various theoretical issues have played out in practice, it is useful to examine a few of the jurisdictions that have been in the vanguard of socioeconomic integration. The most established program is that in La Crosse, Wisconsin, where school boundaries were redrawn to better balance student populations eligible for free lunch. In Wake County, North Carolina, which includes the city of Raleigh, the district recently replaced a long-standing racial desegregation plan with one that emphasizes income. Meanwhile, Manchester, Connecticut, has adopted an intriguing socioeconomic integration plan that relies heavily on public school choice.

La Crosse, Wisconsin: Redrawing Boundaries for Socioeconomic Integration

For the leading example of public school integration by socioeconomic status, we turn not to left-wing hotspots like Greenwich Village in New York, or Berkeley, California, but to La Crosse, Wisconsin, in the nation's heartland. With fifty thousand residents, La Crosse is small by national standards, but its nearly eight thousand students make it a fairly large city by Wisconsin standards.[1]

Until the early 1980s, the population of La Crosse was virtually all white but sharply divided by class. The school district, which includes some surrounding suburban towns (bringing the district population to sixty thousand), is narrow and extends vertically, bounded by the Mississippi River on one side and a line of bluffs on the other. It covers about a hundred square miles, being fifteen miles in length and seven miles wide. In the middle of this vertical strip, the town is divided by a marsh. The population of the northern side of the marsh is heavily blue collar, mostly brewery workers and other laborers. The southern side trends toward professionals, including white-collar employees of the University of Wisconsin, a small private college, and two major medical facilities (see figure 9-1).[2]

During the 1980s, La Crosse became somewhat more ethnically diverse as the town experienced an influx of Hmong refugees from Laos, many of whom had been sponsored by local churches. By 1992, Hmong refugees made up 12 percent of the population, and the schools were 15 percent minority—12 percent Asian American and 3 percent black, Hispanic, or Native American. The Hmong population is poor: in 1994, 72 percent of Asian children in La Crosse were living in poverty. But the white student population is hardly affluent. In 1992, when La Crosse implemented a program to integrate the elementary schools by income, two-thirds of the thirteen hundred elementary students eligible for free lunch were white.[3]

The city has two high schools: Logan, on the north side, and Central, on the south side. Today, there are also three middle schools and eleven elementary schools. In 1992, there were thirty-six hundred elementary school students and about seventy-seven hundred students at all grade levels. The city's socioeconomic integration occurred in two phases: first among the high schools and then, more than a decade later, and more explicitly, among the elementary schools.[4]

High School Integration

When the school superintendent Richard Swantz arrived in La Crosse in the late 1970s, Logan High School was considered the vocational school, and Central the college preparatory school. "The first thing that really hit me between the eyeballs," recalls Swantz, was that "the northside high school had a completely different set of graduation standards. They were credits below the other high school. They didn't offer the same curriculum." Logan, says education reporter Joan Kent, was "considered the other

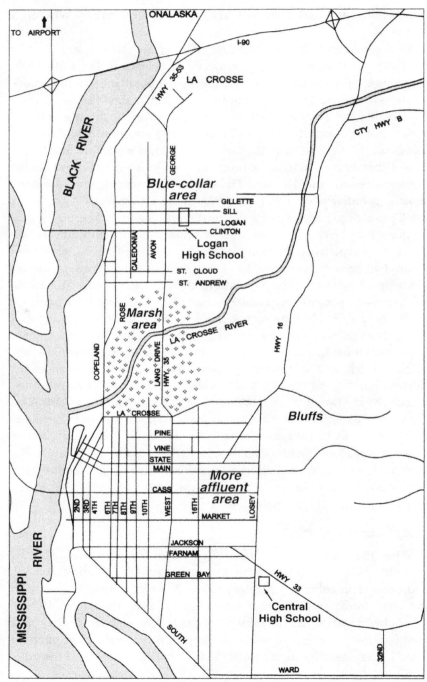

Figure 9-1. La Crosse, Wisconsin

side of the tracks. It was the place with the lowest scores. It was the place where you took more shop classes as opposed to college prep." Logan did not even offer the ACT or the SAT. The attorney James Birnbaum recalls that the two high schools split the town: "The northsiders did not associate with the southsiders. . . . Intracity athletic events were . . . emotional blood baths that mirrored the Civil War and the Crusades."[5]

Around the time of Swantz's arrival, Logan was rebuilt to accommodate more students, and because Central was overcrowded, Swantz proposed moving the boundary line, both to relieve overcrowding and to create more economic balance between the schools. His plan was to move some of the affluent children living just below the marsh to Logan High. The move was hugely controversial. "That marsh was like a Mason-Dixon line," Swantz recalls. After much debate, the board, by a vote of five to four, decided to go along with Swantz's plan. "For the first time," says the *Los Angeles Times*, "the sons and daughters of the affluent south side sat in the classrooms with blue-collar kids from across the tracks." The board president at the time, Dr. Charles Miller, remembers that his son, who was redistricted to Logan, "was one of the first doctor's sons ever to go to that high school."[6]

The University of Wisconsin's professor Joseph Heim recalls that "a lot of older people in La Crosse had a fit about this." Some moved to avoid being in the new district; others rented houses to stay in the Central district. Over time, however, the shifting of high school boundaries was considered, in the words of Mayor John Medinger, "a huge success." "By any measure," notes Heim, the "redrawing of the boundaries on that issue has had a very positive effect." The economic makeup of the two schools is now very similar: In 1997–98, the free-lunch participation rate was 18 percent at Central and 19 percent at Logan. "The schools are completely equal now," Swantz says. Whereas before the boundary change, the test scores were "significantly different" at the two schools, since then they have been "similar year in and year out." In 1995–96, the suspension and dropout rates were actually slightly higher at Central.[7]

More important, the equalization did not come about through leveling down. "Logan came up. Central did not go down," Swantz notes. In 1979–80, before the boundary change, eleventh-graders at Logan scored in the forty-ninth percentile on standardized tests, while Central eleventh-graders scored in the sixty-fifth percentile. By 1991, Logan students had risen to the sixty-second percentile, and Central students had moved up too, to the sixty-seventh percentile. Ken French, a board member who had attended blue-collar Logan, says that in his day, "one in one hundred would make something of themselves," but today Logan is "equal" to Central. The SAT results remain high. In 1995–96, average combined SAT scores were 1261, compared with 1163 in Wisconsin and 1013 nationally.[8]

Today, La Crosse has a relatively high rate of poverty statewide but a very low high school dropout rate. In 1995, when Wisconsin's larger school districts were ranked by the percentage of students on AFDC, there was a strong correlation between the AFDC rate and the high school dropout rate—as there is nationally. La Crosse was an exception to the rule. Among eighteen large Wisconsin school districts, La Crosse was the third poorest, but its low dropout rate—1.54 percent—placed it fifteenth. The number of high school dropouts districtwide went from 122 in 1981–82, just after the merger, to 23 in 1990–91. Mayor Medinger observes that "a lot of parents today would rather have their kids go to Logan for college prep than Central." Moving the boundary "took this community, which was divided between North and South, and made it a blended community for high school purposes."[9]

Elementary School Integration

The second phase of economic integration began in the early 1990s, when the district decided to build two new elementary schools to relieve overcrowding. The location of the schools required that boundary lines be withdrawn and that a certain number of students be bused. One school built in the northeast corner of town had only 60 students living nearby, requiring that another 380 students be transported. The location of these two schools was itself controversial, in that it was selected over the recommendation of a citizens' commission that the two schools be located in the middle of La Crosse, not on its edges.[10]

Seizing on this opportunity for change, teachers approached their principals, who in turn approached the superintendent, arguing that the education of children in La Crosse could be improved by breaking up concentrations of poverty. On May 17, 1991, all nine elementary school principals wrote to the Board of Education urging that new boundaries be set in a way that would balance socioeconomic groups. The board agreed and, on May 21, 1991, set ten guidelines for redistricting, one of which stated the following goal: "Redistricting shall attain a balance in each school which as nearly as possible reflects the socio-economic student profile in the total district."[11]

Under the old boundary lines, the percentage of students participating in the free lunch program ranged from 4–5 percent in some schools to

65–67 percent in others.[12] In certain high-poverty schools, the difficulty of teaching large numbers of poor children was compounded by the language difficulties of the Hmong population, which was deemed by some parents and teachers to hold back all children in those classes.

The Rationale

The drive for socioeconomic balance was based "on a variety of goals," according to Joseph Heim, "including improving the test scores and skills of all children in the district, attitudinal changes such as acceptance, tolerance, and increased self-esteem, and improved educational outcomes which would result in higher incomes after graduation." Noting low achievement levels in high-poverty schools, the principals, says Swantz, outlined the four-point rationale; better balance would "allow teachers to spend more time on lessons rather than constantly addressing the youngsters' problems; better reflect the experience youngsters would have in a multi-cultural society; allow higher-income youngsters to think beyond designer jeans and sneakers; and provide struggling students with more positive role models."[13]

The teachers union strongly supported the plan, individual teachers were instrumental in the Coalition for Children that supported the plan, and the union's attorney, James Birnbaum, was a leading proponent of socioeconomic integration. Teachers at poor schools were "concerned with classes dominated by poor children," Joseph Heim and Pamela Rodgers note. Meanwhile, teachers at one wealthy school were concerned "about the treatment that the very few poor students at that school were receiving from their more affluent peers." Teachers said students in high-poverty schools suffered because the "pool of experiences" in such schools was sharply limited. An ABC News *Nightline* reporter noted that "teachers complained too much time [at two high-poverty schools] went to personal problems less affluent kids bring, instead of to teaching." A fifteen-year veteran teacher at predominantly low-income Hamilton Elementary School said the children in high-poverty schools had "few role models."[14]

The principals noted that low-income parents tended to be less involved in the schools, and integration would mean the involvement of some middle-class parents in all schools.[15] There was also a hope that economic mixing would raise the aspirations of poor children. In an interview with district officials, *Nightline* reported that they expect that "lower-income students . . . will not only improve language skills but begin to improve their own dreams about what they might strive for." When the boundary change was approved in January 1992, board member Marianne Loeffler noted that "we can become another slum-laden Detroit or Chicago, or we can become something better. We can bring hope to our poor children."[16]

Part of the impetus also came from teachers and principals in high-poverty schools who knew that despite their best efforts, their schools would come off poorly when ranked by standardized test scores in the local papers. "It always kind of irritated me," reports principal Terry Witzke, that his school, Franklin Elementary, generally "scored at the bottom" not because of the competence of its staff but because of the socioeconomic status of the students.[17]

Swantz also believed that high-poverty schools tend to have lower expectations. "These schools that have a lot of poor children in them, I think the teachers with all the best intentions did set a lower standard." One could try to exhort teachers to raise expectations, he said, but socioeconomic mixing "is the way to do it." At the time of the move, Joyce Shanks, a professor at the University of Wisconsin at La Crosse, told the *La Crosse Tribune* that studies found working-class students are more likely to be taught by rote while middle-class children are more likely to have teachers emphasizing analytical and investigative skills.[18]

Proponents of socioeconomic balance also pointed to the success in the high schools. Swantz noted that once the high school boundary was moved to better balance the schools economically, the test score gap narrowed from 20 to 5 percent.[19] The attorney James Birnbaum reports that Logan had been "remarkably inferior" to Central and "was in danger of losing its accreditation," but with the boundary change, "La Crosse has two equally superior high schools by all measurable criteria. It is hard to argue with success." Proponents also noted that Emerson Elementary, which already had a mix of economic groups, had traditionally scored first or second among the district's elementary schools.[20]

"The main argument for what La Crosse is doing, to put it crassly," declared Professor Christopher Jencks at the time, "is that advantaged kids are a resource for any kid in a school. . . . Kids who read books, who have values we want others to acquire . . . are a scarce commodity, and it's not easy to argue that because some families have money they should have a monopoly on all those nice kids." According to Swantz, growing up in a poor family presents one disadvantage in itself, and "when you get a lot of them going to the same school, it's like a double whammy." In sum, Birnbaum has argued, "regardless of efforts to equalize staff, curriculum, and physical facilities, children segregated by socioeconomic class were inherently denied equal educational opportunities." A prodesegregation group calling itself the Community Attitudes Task Force declared, "Perhaps the most important equalizer, one of the most important factors in determining academic success, the diverse composition of the educational peer group, is currently being denied our disadvantaged population. . . . Peer role models and peer groups are learning opportunities for which there is no substitute. No matter how equal the trappings, there will be no equal educational opportunity as long as we have schools segregated by economic class, culture, and race."[21]

La Crosse officials also emphasized that everyone would benefit from ethnic and economic diversity. The assistant superintendent, David Johnston, observed that for "too long" diversity had been looked at only in terms of race. "There is another piece" to diversity, he continued, "that is simply as large. And that is the socioeconomics."[22]

The principals were also hearing from other business community leaders and the Rotary Club that business wanted employees who could "work with other people cooperatively" and that they hoped integration might promote those social skills. Teachers Betsy Stannard and Kathy Fuch reported that "business is telling us" that "people have to be able to work together. The number one problem in the workplace is not not knowing your job or not knowing the skills for your job. It's getting along with other people. And that's the number one reason for people being terminated. . . . It is people with skills not being able to get along with coworkers."[23]

Liberals like attorney Birnbaum felt it was important for wealthier children "to see what the world is really like" and to "develop some compassion"—which was unlikely to happen in a school in which "you've got 98 percent high socioeconomic groups." Another parent explained, "I don't think children should be taught that because you have money you can live in a separate world."[24]

Similarly, poor children would be exposed to worlds that they did not know existed. For example, Johnston says, in the fall when children recount what they did over the summer, in the low-socioeconomic-status schools "there would be silence. Nobody went any place." In a mixed class, there are a diversity of summer experiences, "some neat, intellectual, experiential stuff for youngsters and teachers to chew on."[25]

Board member Roger LeGrand says he was animated by the idea of the common school: "This idea of the public school as a place where everybody gets a great opportunity, whether you are rich or poor, black or white, Hmong, or anybody. And there is this wonderful situation where you all go to the same school and you get to mix." The idea, he continues, is "the old melting pot idea. I thought that was great. That was one of the great things of America that we put everybody together. And when you do tend to isolate, especially poor kids, I think they tend to feed off the poverty." Heim and Rodgers, interviewing people on both sides of the issue in La Crosse, found that several participants believed socioeconomic integration "went to the very basis of what public education is all about, and its very role in a democratic society"—a view that "the citizens in the district appear to agree with."

La Crosse officials could have framed integration in more traditional racial terms, but they chose to emphasize socioeconomic status instead for a number of reasons. "We were very careful to never look at it as a racial issue," recalls Swantz. "It was from the standpoint of poverty."[26]

First, on the merits, supporters of the La Crosse plan, like Birnbaum, said that in education, color was not the key determinant to opportunity, it was class: "It makes no difference in my view what color you are. . . . Generally, poor kids have a tough time." "I really didn't believe that race is a factor," Swantz says; "it has to do with people's wherewithal to be ready for school." "Teachers had been telling me for years," he continues, "that when you get a high concentration of children like that [poor] it really makes for some very, very special challenges." Jefferson Elementary School principal Harvey Witzenberg says that "it's not a matter of race but economics that divides our country."[27]

Second, in La Crosse, to treat the issue as racial was to marginalize the larger economic issue. Two-thirds of those on the free lunch program were white. Of thirteen hundred children receiving free lunch in 1992, only four hundred were Asian. Mayor John Medinger notes that "there is a lot of white poverty . . . a lot of people working in this community [are making] six dollars, seven dollars, eight dollars" an hour.[28] Long before the influx of Hmong children, the high school divide in La Crosse had illustrated to all the importance of class.

Third, supporters did not want to inflame racial passions. "The last thing we wanted to do," says Birnbaum, "was to create some sort of racial issue." By emphasizing socioeconomic status, proponents sought "to avoid making it into some real polarizing racial issue that would have not served anything." If race were allowed to be the focus, Johnston says, "you're going to have people playing the race card. . . . And it's an almost impossible game to play once people start playing those cards." So determined was the district to deracialize the issue, says Johnston, that administrators did not run the racial numbers on various schools under the socioeconomic plan so that if anyone asked, administrators could honestly say they did not know, that race "was not the issue."[29]

At the same time, proponents knew that racial desegregation would flow from socioeconomic desegregation. David S. Tatel, then a Washington civil rights attorney, said the La Crosse plan "sounds intriguing to me because it is a way of accomplishing racial and ethnic integration without using race and ethnicity as a factor." Thai Vue, a leader in La Crosse's Hmong community, noted that 80 percent of Hmong pupils received lunch subsidies.[30]

The Plan

In January 1992, the school board voted eight to one to redraw boundaries in pursuit of its May 1991 objective, to distribute students on the free lunch program more evenly throughout the district's elementary schools. Under the new proposal, of the thirty-five hundred elementary school students in La Crosse, nineteen hundred (54 percent) would remain in their old schools, eight hundred (23 percent) would go to different schools in order to fill the two new schools, and eight hundred (23 percent) would attend different schools to create better socioeconomic balance. The total cost of the new busing—much of it necessary whether or not socioeconomic balance was required—was $150,000 for fourteen more buses. In a budget of $45.2 million, this represented about one-third of 1 percent of spending.[31]

The district chose free lunch status (130 percent of the poverty line) rather than free and reduced-price lunch status (185 percent of the poverty line) as the income cutoff, Johnston says, because in central Wisconsin, someone making almost double the poverty line was not generally considered poor. No attempt was made to distiguish between upper-middle-class and middle-class students. Witzke says the free lunch data were available, and "there wasn't a real controversy about using that in particular." The free lunch criterion, Johnston says, was "simple. It's straightforward. It's accepted by everybody and everybody understands that. And you don't have to explain it for a month." Across the district, 30 percent of students were eligible for free lunch, and the board set its goal accordingly: socioeconomic integration will have been reached when 15–45 percent of the student body in every school consists of free lunch recipients.[32]

In general, the new boundary lines required busing of poor students to new or previously middle-class schools. A University of Wisconsin study found that children receiving free lunch were twice as likely to be bused under the plan as those who were not. Children living in the middle-class area known as Jefferson Island were the one exception: previously assigned to Emerson Elementary, under the new plan they were reassigned to poorer Jefferson. The Jefferson provision proved the most controversial element of the plan.[33]

Success of the Program

The success of the program can be judged on four criteria. Was the plan politically viable and able to withstand attack? To what degree did the plan effectively integrate students by economic status? To the extent schools were integrated, did social mixing occur between students across class lines? Finally, to what extent did socioeconomic integration raise academic achievement and improve the life chances of disadvantaged students?

POLITICAL SUCCESS? The board's January 1992 vote sent shock waves through La Crosse. Opponents of the new plan attacked incumbent board members and superintendent Richard Swantz as "big spenders." The Chamber of Commerce initially opposed the plan, and the mayor at the time, Patrick Zielke, argued that busing would hurt home sales.[34] In a regularly scheduled April 1992 election, three challengers replaced three incumbents who had supported the integration plan. In a special recall election held in July 1992, four more incumbents were replaced by opponents of the integration plan, giving antibusing forces a seven-to-two majority on the board. Recall proponents noted that they did especially well in low-income wards, suggesting there might have been a backlash among the supposed beneficiaries of the program.[35]

The newly elected board invited the nationally recognized busing opponent David Armor to speak about alternatives to the plan; and three weeks before the plan was to go into effect, the board voted to allow students to opt out of the new boundary guidelines, creating a "safety valve" for disgruntled parents. The recall leaders had publicly sought Swantz's resignation, and it was widely believed that the recall success might "cost Swantz his job."[36]

Up to this point, La Crosse's experiment looked like the classic story of a wild-eyed liberal idea rejected by sensible midwestern voters. A July 1992 *Washington Post* story was headlined, "The School Board Just Lost Touch."[37] The *Economist* declared the same month that the La Crosse experiment "looks doomed." Mickey Kaus wrote that "La Crosse is encountering the same sort of resistance that accompanied busing for racial integration."[38]

But the story does not end there. What the national media missed—the developments over the subsequent ten months—is far more significant. On July 28, 1992, the *La Crosse Tribune* published results of an informal reader survey, which found that 69 percent wanted the board to leave the boundaries alone for the time being, compared with 16 percent who wished the old boundaries to be restored. A local television poll found 70 percent of parents had "made their peace with the new boundaries."[39] When the new recall board met to consider whether to repeal the socioeconomic integration plan, twenty-three residents spoke, all of them in favor of the integration plan. Thai Vue, a Hmong immigrant, among those speaking in favor of busing, received a standing ovation from two hundred people attending the meeting. The new board voted to repeal the official socioeconomic policy but also voted five to four to keep the existing boundary lines on which the 15–45 percent goals were based and to go ahead with busing aimed at socioeconomic balance.[40]

Just nine months later, in April 1993, a group of school board candidates supportive of integration, running under the banner of Coalition for Children, managed to win back three seats, "clobbering" candidates who had been elected the previous July under the anti-integration theme. The researcher Stephen Plank notes that "the challengers ousted the incumbents by fairly large margins of victory. The top vote-getter among the newly elected challengers was a Hmong man who strongly supported the balance plan." The three recall members got the lowest vote totals. The recall board members, says Birnbaum, "were scrubbed out and scrubbed out dramatically." Joseph Heim and Pamela Rodgers pointed out that "the School Board had come full circle in one year's time." An editorial in the *Milwaukee Journal* lauded La Crosse voters for their "counter-counterrevolution." Comparing La Crosse's experience with that of Milwaukee, which took steps to integrate only after a court battle, the *Journal* marveled that La Crosse "did the right thing on its own."[41]

During their brief tenure, the recall board had created a loophole for those who wished to be exempt from the plan, but the basic boundaries held. In 1998, several years after the controversy had subsided, Dick Swantz remained as superintendent. Mayor Medinger notes that by the late 1990s none of those running for school board argued for changing the boundaries back: "People seem pretty content with life in La Crosse school district right now."[42] La Crosse was so calm that the town was having trouble attracting candidates to contest openings on the board. What explains the dramatic turnabout? Observers point to a number of factors.

First, the problems that opponents of desegregation had forecast did not materialize. As principal Witzke has observed, "the world did not collapse with this happening." Heim says La Crosse residents "found out that kids were not destroyed while riding buses." The *La Crosse Tribune* noted that even at schools whose boundary changes were most controversial, students appeared happy: "At Northside and Jefferson schools, eyes of the boundary storm, students appeared to like their new schools," reporter Joan Kent found in a story entitled "New Schools, New Friends." The busing itself had advantages: it was good for the children in the cold weather and also safer, because children did not have to cross busy streets.[43]

Second, many parents found that integration was good for the children. Joan Kent, a reporter viewed by some as sympathetic to the recall effort, reported that six months after the plan was implemented, "people on both sides" were pleased to see that poor students were learning about middle-class experiences and wealthier children "were learning how people who don't have quite as much get along." In March 1993, Kent, interviewing fifty children, twenty-five parents, and twenty-five teachers, found that "almost all" were "now comfortable" with the new boundaries and the socioeconomic integration plan. In April 1993, the *La Crosse Tribune* noted that an unscientific survey of 1,265 elementary school parents attending parent-teacher conferences found that 65 percent believed the district "should continue to work toward [socioeconomic] balance in the schools" and 69 percent were "satisfied" with the new boundaries. "Once the kids got into the schools, hell, they loved it," recalls board member Ken French. "They had no problem with it."[44]

Third, parents grew accustomed to the new boundary lines. Even if socioeconomic status had not been an issue, Johnston says, the district had to redraw boundaries to fill two new schools, and "whenever we redraw boundaries . . . we have people [annoyed]." In this case, Johnston says, "every boundary line got moved," so roughly half the district's children were affected—half of those for socioeconomic reasons, half for space reasons.[45] Over time, however, families became used to the change.

Fourth, the effort to keep the issue from becoming racialized appears to have succeeded, to the surprise of the national and international press. The *Economist*, writing after the recall, said that because the Hmong population was disproportionately poor, "class divisions" in La Crosse "may be no more than race divisions under another name." La Crosse residents did not see it that way, however. As Kent has remarked, "with most people it wasn't a racial thing." Heim's survey research found that whereas racial integration raised "a red flag," socioeconomic integration was seen as "less onerous to people." Although La Crosse citizens did object to busing, Heim's La Crosse survey found that "mixing people of different classes just made a lot of common sense to people. . . . People can accept" socioeconomic integration, he found—indeed "a fairly substantial majority" favored "socioeconomic balance."[46]

Heim notes that a similar effort to desegregate by socioeconomic status in nearby Wausau, Wisconsin—where race was more explicitly at issue—was much less politically stable. In Wausau, an opposition recall group was elected and stayed in power, and the superintendent was replaced. Heim's polling data suggest that "emphasizing a blending of classes rather than racial integration has a greater chance of public support and, ultimately, success."[47]

Fifth, much of the original anger in the recall was aimed not at socioeconomic integration but at the construction of the new schools, which was deemed extravagant. Kent notes that in previous years the district had closed schools, and it struck some residents as absurd to pay for the construction of two new schools. Wasteful spending—not socioeconomic integration itself—fed much of the recall anger, particularly among the elderly. When the recall effort began in January 1992, organizers asserted that "boundaries are not the issue"; instead, they said, "they want to oust the entire nine-member board on grounds of fiscal irresponsibility."[48] Over time, realizing that the new schools could not be unbuilt, people accepted the new regime.

Sixth, opposition from the poor did not materialize. At the time of the recall election, those opposed to desegregation did quite well in poor districts, which suggested to some recall supporters a backlash among the poor, who may have interpreted socioeconomic integration as condescending. In fact, much of that vote apparently reflected anger among poor elderly La Crosse residents about the spending issue. When poor parents became organized in the subsequent election, they gave solid support for integration. In particular, the Hmong population came out strongly for the plan because "they thought it was good for their kids." Although socioeconomic mixing might have in some instances put poor children in an awkward position, subjecting them to rich classmates' bragging about their advantages, Johnston says this did not seem to occur much in the schools and that at hearings, low-income parents generally spoke in favor of balancing schools. Notes board member LeGrand, "I never heard any complaint [about economic balancing] from anybody [whose children received free lunch] during the whole period of time. . . . I never heard that at all."[49]

Polling data bear out these impressions. Heim and Rodgers have found that in October 1991, northside residents, who are generally less affluent, were "somewhat more in favor" of socioeconomic balance than southside residents: the margin of support was 50 percent to 38 percent among northside residents and 43 percent to 38 percent among southside residents. The strongest support for "busing for socioeconomic balance" in Heim's polling came from those earning less than ten thousand dollars a year (53 percent in favor, 34 percent opposed). Analysis of the July 1992 returns found the well-off State Road area provided a heavy vote for the recall.[50]

Mayor Medinger, who calls himself a blue-collar "beer-drinking chicken-wing" Robert Kennedy Democrat very suspicious of limousine liberals, dismisses the notion that socioeconomic integration was considered patronizing or condescending. Although "affluent people" made that argument, among poor and working-class voters Medinger "didn't hear too much of that." French suggests that "the ones that are complaining most about busing are doctors, lawyers, and realtors, and people like that." Swantz reports that opposition was coming from "the silk stocking crowd."[51]

Seventh, the district's teachers, who helped launch the plan, continued to play an important supportive role throughout the debate. According to Swantz, the "teachers were the ones that really kept me confident [that] many children were going to gain from this." Teachers did have to deal with a new, broader range of manifest ability among students, but two teachers—Betsy Stannard and Cathy Fuchs—have said that using cooperative learning and workshops allowed them to capitalize on these ranges rather than making them an impediment to learning. In their new school, North Woods, Stannard and Fuchs had children both from housing projects and from five-hundred-thousand-dollar homes. Employing reading and writing workshops, the teachers said, "allow[s] you to teach kids of all ranges" in one class. On balance, teachers maintain that poverty concentrations posed the greatest burden to teaching and that a middle-class environment is more conducive to learning. The mix of students at North Woods was unquestionably easier to teach than the largely poor populations at schools like Hamilton or Jefferson, and the teachers did not see evidence that the rich children at North Woods made the poor children feel bad; the most invidious comparisons, they said, tended to come in the homogeneous schools where some get a new car at the age of sixteen and others do not. The teachers union endorsed integration in October 1991, with only a few teachers dissenting. Teachers opposed the recall effort by a vote of 435 to 29.[52]

As the plan was implemented, the overall support for socioeconomic integration increased. In 1991, support for socioeconomic balance stood at 46 percent (37 percent opposed); by 1994, support had grown to 59 percent (29 percent opposed). Significantly, parents led the way in increasing support. Public opinion data clearly show that those most directly involved in the socioeconomic integration plan—parents of children in the schools—were more supportive than nonparents. Before the plan went into effect, the difference was slight (of parents, 48 percent were in favor, 33 percent opposed; of nonparents, 45 percent were in favor, 37 percent opposed). Once the plan was put into place, the gap between parents and nonparents gradually grew. By 1994, 65 percent of parents supported socioeconomic balance (24 percent opposed), compared with 57 percent of nonparents (31 percent were opposed). As Heim and Rodgers note, "It appears that many parents may have reversed their positions, both on opposition to socioeconomic balance and on the use of socioeconomic balance as a factor in any future redrawing of school boundaries. In essence, it appears that parents have become strong supporters of the concept and remain very satisfied with the School District's educational performance." In March 1993, even Kevin O'Keefe, who organized the recall, told the *Milwaukee Sentinel* that the socioeconomic balance plan was working well. "To expose your children to other cultures and other beliefs—that's certainly a good idea."[53]

By 1994, two years after implementation of the plan, public confidence in the school system returned to prebalance levels. In 1990, 75 percent of residents expressed satisfaction with the La Crosse public school system, a number that slipped to 64 percent in 1992, at the height of the controversy. By 1994, however, satisfaction levels had returned to 76 percent. In 1996, board member Neil Duresky, who had been critical of socioeconomic balance, told *Education Week* that "the plan is working well," a view he continued to hold in a 1998 interview.[54]

DESEGREGATION SUCCESS? In the plan's first year of implementation, the district made substantial strides toward the goal that each elementary school should be within a 15–45 percent free lunch range. In 1991–92, only 44 percent of schools (four of nine) fell within the desired range; but after the plan's adoption, in 1992–93, 82 percent of schools (nine of eleven) met the goal. In the 1997–98 school year, only two schools, Hamilton (67 percent) and Jefferson (56 percent), fell outside the 15–45 free lunch percent goal.[55] Overall, then, compliance nearly doubled, from 44 percent to 82 percent.

Contrary to expectations, fewer than two hundred of the four thousand students slated for busing took advantage of the opt-out provision enacted by the recall board. The actual enrollment in 1992 (which allowed for transfers) was quite close to the estimates based on the new boundaries in most schools, with the exceptions of Hamilton (estimated at 41 percent free lunch, the actual enrollment was 63 percent) and New Northside (estimated at 33.3 percent free lunch, actual enrollment 50 percent).[56]

Neither was there a mass exodus of middle-class parents to private schools, although with several Catholic and Lutheran elementary schools in the area, there was plenty of opportunity for white middle-class flight. In March 1993, a year after the boundary change, the *La Crosse Tribune* reported that private schools had seen an increase in enrollment of only "about forty students." In 1997, Witzke said, "we had more kids this past year moving in from the private schools than we did from the public schools to the private schools." Superintendent Swantz noted that "the district has continued through this entire experience to increase its percentage of 'capture,' [the] percent of children that are school aged that are in the public schools." Indeed, public schools continued to experience "significant overcrowding."[57]

Contrary to the prediction of some opponents of integration, the plan did not result in the lowering of property values. Even in the Jefferson Island—a middle-class neighborhood in which students were moved from middle-class Emerson to previously poor Jefferson—property values did not decline and, in fact, increased "significantly." The district has seen a general rise in the number of students receiving FARM. For elementary schools, the percentage receiving free lunch rose from 30 percent in 1992 to 33 percent in 1997. That increase, however, is attributable not to flight but rather to general economic and demographic trends.[58]

Yet the program was not a complete success. To this day, two schools—Hamilton and Jefferson—remain out of compliance. In the case of Hamilton, it was difficult to get the numbers of poor children down without completely manipulating the district boundaries. Because the school did not provide transportation to students who lived within two miles of their neighborhood schools, some poor families who were nearly two miles from an integrated school opted back to Hamilton to be within walking distance. Had the cutoff for walking been lowered to one mile, the integration might have been more successful. In the case of Jefferson, the "safety valve" instituted by the recall board did undercut integration. Many middle-class students attending southside Emerson who were supposed to be bused to northside Jefferson opted out of the Jefferson Island provision. School board member Julie Vollmer estimates that of eighty middle-class children in the Jefferson Island area, perhaps only thirty continued to attend Jefferson in 1997. Still, Jefferson is much closer to balance than it would have been: it went from 68.3 percent free lunch in 1991 to 43 percent free lunch in 1992, then back up to 56 percent in 1997. On the whole, Superintendent Dick Swantz argues, the schools are clearly more balanced than they would have been without the policy.[59]

SOCIAL SUCCESS? One of the major goals of administrators in La Crosse was socialization across economic and racial lines. Critics have noted, however, that individuals from different backgrounds sometimes fail to mix, even when placed in heterogeneous environments. In La Crosse, the evidence suggests a significant amount of social mixing has occurred.

Anecdotally, reports in the *La Crosse Tribune* indicate that students adjusted well to the new mix of classmates and did not segregate themselves. A guidance counselor at State Road Elementary reported to the *Tribune* that "99 percent of the new problems are not rich and poor; they're new kid on the block." Interviewing teachers in March 1993, the newspaper reported that "on the playgrounds, children initially stayed with kids they knew. Now, the main separation seems to be between boys and girls."[60]

Stephen Plank, studying under James Coleman at the University of Chicago, looked at socialization among students after La Crosse implemented its economic desegregation plan for his 1995 doctoral dissertation. Plank was interested in exploring the degree to which students from different economic and ethnic backgrounds mixed in La Crosse elementary schools and whether certain teaching techniques brought about more successful integration of students. Looking at fourth-grade students in five elementary schools (and ten classrooms) in the 1993–94 school year, the second year of La Crosse's balance plan, Plank measured social mixing by asking students to name "friends they play with at recess, two classmates they would enjoy working with on a science project, classmates who have been to their homes, and participation in extracurricular activities." He also personally observed the students, conducting research in the fall and then again in the spring.[61]

Plank observed that students who were allowed to select their seats on the first day of class chose to sit with students like themselves. In one classroom with six clusters of desks, three of the clusters were occupied almost exclusively by high-socioeconomic-status students (ten of the eleven students), while the other three clusters were almost all low-socioeconomic-status (eight of the nine students). By the spring, however, across the ten classrooms, there was a great deal of mixing across racial and class lines, with almost all workmate groups having a mix of children. Plank found that "most of the [workmate] cliques were heterogeneous with respect to the race/SES classification." Similarly, by the spring, "most of the playmate cliques were heterogeneous with respect to the race/SES classification." By contrast, Plank found that both workmate and playmate integration by gender was "rare in all of the classrooms."[62]

IMPROVED LIFE CHANCES SUCCESS? Has socioeconomic integration in La Crosse produced higher test scores and improved life chances for the poor? There have been no carefully designed and controlled studies on this question, so it is hard to say definitively, but the overall picture is positive and suggests the plan is working.

La Crosse has seen about a 10 percent rise in the free lunch population at the elementary level. Given the general increase in the number of poor students, one would expect test scores to decline overall; but they have not. To the contrary, says La Crosse associate superintendent Woodrow Wiedenhoeft, "overall achievement scores have been better over the last eight years with a trend of improvement."[63] On the Eighth-Grade Knowledge and Concepts Examination, for example, La Crosse students scored in the seventy-eighth percentile nationally, and on the tenth-grade test in the seventy-ninth percentile, in 1995–96. Board member Duresky notes that "our SAT and ACT scores keep going up," which might be an indication that the desegregation effort has been positive, given that "the kids who were in fifth and sixth grade in 1992 are now in eleventh and twelfth grade." In 1995–96, despite a relatively high poverty level, La Crosse had a lower suspension rate than schools statewide (.11 versus .19 percent), a lower dropout rate (1.5 versus 2.4 percent), a higher level of above-standard performance in third-grade reading (94.9 versus 89.7 percent), and a higher ACT score (22.5 versus 22.1).[64]

"In talking to teachers overall it's been good for kids," Duresky says. The transformation of teaching from front-of-the-classroom instruction to cooperative learning made the diversity an asset rather than an impediment to learning, one principal has remarked. North Woods Elementary school teachers Betsy Stannard and Cathy Fuchs note that low-income students who came in "raw" learned, over time, from other students "what is appropriate."[65]

At the time of implementation, proponents and opponents of the plan sparred over its potential effect on parental involvement. Opponents argued that involvement would decline: "The farther away their youngsters are taken for schooling, the more difficult it is to involve parents," opined *Chicago Tribune* columnist Joan Beck. La Crosse administrators, by contrast, hoped that parental involvement at previously low-income schools would increase. Proponents of the program were right. "The schools that had very low-functioning PTA and parent groups," notes David Johnston, "now have higher-functioning ones." At Jefferson, for example, the influx of students from middle-class Jefferson Island rejuvenated the PTA. In March 1993, the *La Crosse Tribune* noted, "all the Jefferson PTA board members this year are from the busing area, partially dispelling fears that increased distances to school would discourage parent participation."[66]

Board member LeGrand credits the socioeconomic balance plan with helping to integrate the poor Hmong community. "It is happening here," he said. "[The Hmong people] are doing a lot better than they did when they first came out of the camps. . . . They are doing the same thing as other immigrant groups did. And the key to it is the public schools." At North Woods Elementary, Swantz has observed, "a fourth-grade teacher noted children talking about their futures and career aspirations. This teacher, who taught many impoverished children the previous year, had never heard children speak that way." At Jefferson, which initially went from 69 to 43 percent free lunch, the district found "teachers spending less time promoting 'on-task behaviors' . . . [and spending] more time on learning." In addition, the district observed reduced behavioral problems and increased scores at Jefferson.[67] Furthermore, the exposure of poor children to job networks will likely help them in years to come.

Overall, integration at the elementary school level has been positive. The high school integration, because it was more complete, has had even greater success. In sum, though it is hard to draw cause-and-effect conclusions, we can say that a fairly poor district, by state standards, now has a fairly integrated population, particularly at the high school level, and is doing better than expected on standardized test scores, retention of students, and other criteria.

Criticism

Although generally successful, the La Crosse plan is not without flaws. In its emphasis on class rather than race it was novel, and on the cutting edge, but the plan was also strikingly old-fashioned in its use of busing and assignment rather than choice. Socioeconomic balance was but one of ten factors used by the board in redistricting, and the board also tried to maximize traditional principles of neighborhood assignments.[68] As a result, the balance plan was complicated by geographic constraints in a way that controlled choice plans are not, and at the same time, where neighborhood assignment was not honored, parents were angered and frustrated.

At the time La Crosse adopted its plan, some education experts criticized the reliance on compulsory assignment rather than public school choice and the magnet model. Clearly, the command-and-control model caused political trouble. Heim's polling found that though La Crosse residents "seem to sense that having their kids mixed with other socioeconomic classes was a good idea," they "don't like busing, in particular." In an October 1991 poll, for example, residents favored socioeconomic balance as a guideline for school boundaries (46 percent in favor, 37 percent opposed). However, "when busing was included as the method used to create greater balance," Heim found, "opposition increased and support dropped," with 47 percent opposed and only 38 percent in favor. Some have noted that because students were subjected to mandatory busing, "public hearings were directed at busing, not educational concerns."[69] The redrawing of boundaries also presented logistical difficulties, particularly with Hamilton elementary, because of limits placed on district gerrymandering.

Following the battles over busing, both sides began looking toward choice and the Cambridge controlled choice model. Kevin O'Keefe, a leading opponent of busing, told *Nightline*, "Maybe choice is a good compromise. . . . We can have schools that have a more proportionate mix of poor and nonpoor, but it's something that the parents feel some ownership in and have confidence in, and I think that would be real positive." Though recall proponents said they were champions of the "neighborhood school," a paid political advertisement in July 1992 proclaimed in its lead item, "District-wide school choice . . . to allow each school to compete for students." Even the consultant David Armor recommended to the La Crosse board an alternative involving parental school choice or magnets. Choice, LeGrand says, might have addressed the key complaint people had about the redrawn boundaries: "The people who really just went nuts, I think it was people who felt they had sort of lost control. . . . I think the most important thing is having parents have more of a say. . . . What people react strongly to is really being told and not having a choice." Today, says LeGrand, who is back on the board, "we are trying to get more choice of schools. . . . My vision is to provide a choice with a socioeconomic component." Give parents three choices, he argues, but "keep the socioeconomic guidelines." That combination is something "even some of the conservative people on the board are willing to look at."[70] Indeed, Julie Vollmer, an opponent of the redistricting, says, "I do believe in socioeconomic balance. My problem is . . . that you cannot force the parents to do something that they choose not to do." She argues that families in Jefferson Island would have been willing to attend high-poverty Hamilton, which is physically closer; the opposition was not to socioeconomic mixing but rather to being sent to a distant school, with no say in the matter. Vollmer declared she was "very interested in the Cambridge model."[71]

Even proponents of integration concede that the explicit discussion of children's economic status had a downside. Johnston notes that increasingly teachers spoke of "children bringing more and more baggage to school." It is not really appropriate, Johnston acknowledges, to think of "little six-year-old kid[s]" as "lugging a lot of baggage with them." Still, he argues, the focus on class is, on balance, positive. La Crosse has seen "an awakening and recognition that socioeconomic status" matters in life, and that awareness will have beneficial effects on public policy in and outside of education.[72]

Replicability?

Is the La Crosse experience replicable? Did the experiment succeed in La Crosse only because it was a largely white community? because it is an unusually liberal university town? because its small geographic size made integration easy?

Mickey Kaus, appearing on *Nightline* after the recall election (but before the idea of integration recovered its support), said the La Crosse experience was sobering. "This is a very small town, without a big race problem. If busing to achieve class integration doesn't work here, it's hard to see how it's going to work anywhere, and it's been very tumultuous here." Kaus was wrong, however, to say La Crosse did not have much of a race problem.

The influx of Hmong refugees was a major issue in La Crosse, where by 1997 the schools were 20 percent minority; and the Hmong hardly fit the "model minority" Asian stereotype. Whereas Chinese and Japanese Americans have as groups achieved tremendous academic and economic success in the United States, the Hmong population from Laos is much newer and has as a group been less successful. In the 1990 census, 13 percent of Americans nationally, and only 7 percent of Japanese Americans, lived below the poverty line, but the rate among Hmong families was nearly two-thirds. Nearly 60 percent of Indian Americans and 40 percent of Chinese Americans, but only 3 percent of the Hmong American population, had at least a bachelor's degree.[73] Until recently, the Hmong culture had no written language. In addition, the Hmong population, researcher Stephen Plank notes, have a tradition "of early marriage and childbearing" and have extremely large families by American standards. Whereas whites average 1.7 children in a lifetime and Mexican Americans 2.9, the average among the Hmong people is 11.9. In Wisconsin, gang violence among Hmong teenagers has received a fair amount of attention.[74]

Is La Crosse, which is home to a University of Wisconsin campus, a town of limousine liberals uniquely open to what Ted Koppel has called "a radical experiment"? The evidence suggests not. The La Crosse professor Joseph Heim notes that college students constitute about a fifth of La Crosse voters (between six thousand and seven thousand of the town's thirty-five thousand registered voters), but they were not particularly helpful to the integration cause, and the university as a whole was not much involved. Indeed, a lot of the recall signatures came from college students.[75]

Far from being home to a bevy of affluent radicals, La Crosse ranked as Wisconsin's third-poorest large school district in 1995, having a higher percentage of students whose families received AFDC than cities such as Eau Claire, Madison, and Green Bay. Survey research, Heim notes, indicates that "La Crosse is more conservative than Wisconsin." When La Crosse voters are asked to identify themselves, 40 percent self-identify as conservatives and 15 percent as liberals, an almost three-to-one margin. According to Johnston, "This is a community, just to flavor it, that didn't have fluoride in its water until 1987 or 1988 after [a fluoridation plan was] defeated by about three referendums because at one time [it was thought to be part of] a communist conspiracy."[76]

Because La Crosse covers a limited geographical area, busing children to "distant" schools is easier than it might be in a bigger city. The long, narrow shape of the district and the presence of the large marsh dividing the north and south sides of the city, however, make transportation somewhat cumbersome. To complicate matters further, the existing elementary schools were not evenly spaced; several, Swantz notes, "are within a few blocks of each other."[77] Moreover, as noted elsewhere, larger cities can use zones within the district to make integration more manageable.

Wake County, North Carolina: Out of Race, Class

Wake County, North Carolina, which includes Raleigh and surrounding areas, is much bigger and more racially diverse than La Crosse but has been drawn to the same notion of integrating schools by income. The second-largest district in North Carolina, and the twenty-ninth-largest in the United States, Wake County educates ninety-five thousand students in 115 schools.[78] Located in the Research Triangle Park, the area is booming economically, with a median family income of $66,364. The student population is 65 percent white and 35 percent minority, mostly African American. About 24 percent of students receive free and reduced-price lunch, and about 18 percent read below grade level.[79] Geographically, the school district covers an expanse of 864 square miles, with the city of Raleigh at its center. The unified district was created through a merger of Wake County and Raleigh Public Schools in 1976, motivated in part by a desire to improve integration of city and suburb. The outlying areas are about a two-hour bus ride from Raleigh.[80]

In the early 1980s, Wake County sought to avoid court-ordered busing by adopting an extensive magnet school program, designed primarily to draw white students into schools located within the Raleigh "beltline." The county set a goal that each school should have a minority enrollment between 15 and 45 percent. In 1999, about 14,400 of the county's students attended magnets, roughly half of those choosing to attend and half assigned from nearby neighborhoods. In addition, about 10,000 students chose to attend nine year-round schools, located mostly in suburban areas. As schools of choice, the year-round programs provide the opportunity to draw more diverse student bodies, though in practice they generally have not.[81]

About one-third of the county's schools were outside the racial goals in 1999, some by just a little, others by much more. Nevertheless, Wake County schools were far more integrated than schools nationally. Only 21 percent of black students attended majority-minority schools, compared with 70 percent of black students across the nation. County officials credit the integrated schools with helping to boost achievement. In 1998–99, some 76 percent of Wake County seniors took the SAT (compared with 43 percent nationally), and the average score was 1059—43 points above the national average and 73 points above the North Carolina average. On state tests administered in third and eighth grade, 78 percent of Wake County students achieved proficiency in reading and 79 percent in math—16 percentage points above the state average.[82]

In the late 1990s, the county's integration plan was put in legal jeopardy when the Fourth Circuit Court of Appeals, which has jurisdiction over North Carolina, barred the use of race in student assignment in cases involving Montgomery County, Maryland, and Arlington, Virginia. Wake County officials began to explore ways to preserve the district's successful integration program without relying specifically on race, and they found two criteria that had a fairly strong correlation with race: income and achievement.

According to county data, more than 30 percent of minority students read below grade level, more than 50 percent receive subsidized lunches, and more than 60 percent fall under one criterion, the other, or both. In all, 15 percent of whites, 64 percent of all minority students, and 70 percent of blacks in grades three through eight fall under at least one of the criteria.[83] A plan to better balance the low-income and low-achieving populations would clearly have the effect of providing some racial integration as well. Indeed, when discussions of the new income and achievement assignment criteria became public, opponents of racial desegregation cried foul. The plans looked like a transparent way of achieving racial integration under a new name.

In fact, the critics appeared to have it exactly backwards: Income was not a proxy for race, in the minds of Wake educators. Rather, race had been a proxy for income. The educational reason for wanting to save racial integration was that it had worked well to achieve income and achievement integration. Yes, the racial integration policy had been good socially (exposing children to diversity) and legally (the voluntary magnets prevented extensive busing), but the more powerful rationale for wanting racial integration was that it was good for the county's overall education achievement because it indirectly promoted income mixing. Now that the legal posture had become reversed, with race a liability rather than a lever, Wake could directly go after the type of integration most responsible for boosting achievement.

In describing the rationale behind a plan to promote income integration, board member Bill Fletcher explains that "the issue for me has always been educational effectiveness. That's what this policy is about, it's not social engineering." The chair of the school board, Stephen Wray, agrees: "I believe it is an advantage that racial diversity is a by-product of this plan, but that is no longer the priority. Our objective has shifted from racial diversity to one that is focused on achievement. I am comfortable with the racial diversity being a by-product of this new plan. Still, it is important to understand the difference." As the school district attorney Ann Majestic told the *Raleigh News and Observer*, "We're really trying to look at educationally driven factors that might have (integrated schools) as a by-product." In fact, county officials did not even run the racial numbers on the effect of the new policy.[84]

County school officials knew well that although Wake County boasted some of the top schools in the state, at other schools like Creech Road Elementary, with roughly a 50 percent low-income student population, the educational setting was far from ideal. A *News and Observer* article notes that student mobility was so high that only 33 percent of Creech Road third-graders had attended the school as kindergartners. The PTA president complained that the school had "hardly any parental involvement." Wake County had very publicly set a goal of having 95 percent of students at or above grade level in the third and eighth grades by 2003—and income integration was one way to help realize that aim.[85]

On January 10, 2000, in a move that would receive national attention, the Wake County school board voted to drop its goal that each school have a minority population of 15–45 percent and replace it with a goal that all schools meet the following two conditions: no more than 40 percent of its student body would be eligible for free or reduced-price lunch, and no more than 25 percent of its student body would be reading below grade level (averaged over two years). The board's assignment guidelines also sought to minimize travel distances, make efficient use of school facilities, and maintain stability in assignment. The policy would be implemented through a redrawing of school boundaries and also by the use of income, rather than race, in magnet school admissions, a practice that had already been in place for one year.[86]

The nine-member board voted unanimously—just as nine Supreme Court justices had in 1954. The superintendent of schools at the time, Jim Surratt, called it "a momentous decision." Various board members and administrators indicated an intent to stick by the policy rather than allow noncompliance, as had sometimes occurred with the racial guidelines.[87]

Next came the hard work of implementing the policy. As schools currently stood, the proportion of individual schools' students receiving free or reduced-price lunch ranged from 1 percent to a little more than 50 percent, and the proportions of schools' students reading below grade level ranged from 6 to 36 percent. Nineteen elementary schools and three middle schools exceeded the income or achievement limits or both.[88]

Boundaries needed to be redrawn anyway, to fill four new elementary schools and one new middle school for the fall of 2000, so that is where the board began its work. A plan floated in late January affecting 6,250 students drew opposition from some parents, though many of the complaints were aimed at the two-thirds of assignment shifts needed to fill the new schools, irrespective of the income and achievement guidelines. At a March 6 public hearing, a number of criticisms were aired, though a reporter for the local paper noted that "there appears to be little opposition from parents at schools where low-achieving or poor students are being shifted to more affluent or high-performing schools."[89]

On March 30, 2000, the school board adopted a scaled-back plan affecting 3,644 students, which moved three elementary schools and one middle school into compliance with the established goals. As Ben Wildavsky of *U.S. News and World Report* wrote, "this is only the beginning: Board members next year hope to extend the plan to many more schools, including popular, year-round schools in affluent, white neighborhoods." Board members may have been emboldened by the fact that Wake County citizens, in deciding who would fill five open school board seats, had the previous fall rejected all the candidates who had campaigned for neighborhood schools.[90] Wake County citizens knew firsthand that racial integration in the schools had worked, and now they were at the forefront in promoting a bold new version in the twenty-first century.

Manchester, Connecticut: Integration through Preferred Choice

Manchester, Connecticut, a small town located east of Hartford, has seventy-eight hundred public school students attending ten elementary schools, two middle schools, and one high school. The student population is 77 percent white, 13 percent black, 8 percent Hispanic, and 2 percent Asian American. In 1996, a twenty-six-member committee appointed by the school board recommended that the district adopt a socioeconomic "controlled choice plan." Families would indicate their top three choices among ten elementary schools, and assignments would be controlled for socioeconomic status rather than race. The plan would grandfather existing students, and siblings and walkers would be given preference.[91]

The committee's report found that at half the elementary schools, the free and reduced-price lunch rate exceeded 30 percent and that these schools had lower test scores and higher levels of "disruptiveness, tardiness, and poor attendance." They noted, for example, that at the Washington School, 56 percent of whose students were eligible for subsidized lunches, only 44 percent of students passed the math portion of the Connecticut Mastery Tests in 1995, compared with an 83 percent passage rate at Highland Park, which had a 7 percent FARM-recipient rate. The committee concluded that, "in effect, Manchester is becoming 'two districts.'"[92]

Stephen Penny, committee cochair, argued for economic integration: "Every educational study proves that if you concentrate [children from lower socioeconomic backgrounds] in a few schools you destroy their ability to learn." From an educational standpoint, the committee concluded, poverty was a more salient factor than race; "educational studies confirm that it is poverty which adversely impacts the educational process and not race or ethnicity."[93] Molly Stephanou, copresident of the Wadell School PTA, said concentrations of poverty hurt all children in particular schools: "The classrooms are filled with more students with more needs. I think that takes away from everybody getting a fair shake." Others pointed to a 1993 survey finding that parents in Manchester's poorest schools were the least likely to volunteer. The committee also noted the reality that "race is an increasingly less defensible criterion under the law."[94]

In 1996, the Manchester School Board, citing "a substantial body of research suggest[ing] that the likelihood of a school's overall success is reduced significantly when a school's enrollment exceeds 50 percent of low-income students," adopted a goal of making all Manchester schools majority middle income.[95] School board member Jonathan Mercier said that middle-class children would not be hurt by socioeconomic integration, and the local paper cited studies by Brown University researcher Michael Alves showing that test scores generally rise overall in cities that have adopted controlled choice. The plan had support even among some Republicans.[96]

In February 1997, the board adopted a variation on controlled choice, designed "to balance socioeconomic enrollment" among the ten elementary schools (each of which would develop a theme), which also guaranteed a seat in the neighborhood school to any family that did not receive one of its top three choices. The school themes range from communication arts to multiple intelligence and from character education to environmental education, and applicants indicate whether they qualify for free or reduced-price meals.[97] The school board chair, Craig S. Lappen, made it clear that the purpose of the school choice plan was to reduce concentrations of poverty and that the school board would approve only transfers that moved the district closer to that goal.[98]

The plan as first implemented in the fall of 1998 did not fully balance the schools. The Washington School, for example, had a 58 percent minority population, and more than half of its students received free or reduced-price meals. In January 1999, to better balance the schools, the district administration proposed making the Washington School a science and math magnet. Transfers of students outside the Washington boundaries are restricted if they do not contribute to socioeconomic integration. The district's modest success suggests that the "preferred choice" mechanism—with its fallback guarantee of admission to the old "neighborhood" school—can make steps toward integration but not as completely or as comprehensively as "controlled choice" plans.[99]

Summing Up

La Crosse, Wake County, and Manchester are at the cutting edge of the new post-*Brown* era. Although the movement for socioeconomic integration is still in its infancy, it is quickly gaining mainstream support. In the fall of 1999, for example, *USA Today* jumped on board, declaring that "the most creative idea for breaking down barriers while improving education for all is economic desegregation."[100]

Nearly a half century ago, the Supreme Court's *Brown* decision ushered in an era of renewed concern for equal opportunity and provided a promising approach to ending not only racial apartheid in the South but also unequal educational opportunity nationwide. Today, shifting to class-based desegregation of the public schools will reinvigorate *Brown*'s broader promise and hone in more precisely on what has always been the key school factor in determining academic success—the social class of a student's peers. Emphasizing socioeconomic integration answers the conservative charge that it is insulting to presume that predominantly black schools are necessarily inferior but also acknowledges the liberal insight that predominantly poor schools (many of them largely black) need to be desegregated if they are to provide genuine equal opportunity.

Efforts should continue to be made to improve high poverty schools, and indeed such efforts will make those schools marginally more attractive to middle-class families. In the end, however, separate can never be equal, and mechanisms must be found to encourage economic integration as an engine for further school improvement.

As racial desegregation orders are lifted in city after city and even voluntary racial integration plans are struck down, economic integration represents the new frontier of school desegregation. It is an idea based not on rectifying historic crimes but on the notion that it is past time to implement the most important step we can take toward promoting equal educational opportunity. Common schools are ambitious, even more so than the *Brown* decision. Horace Mann's old idea of the common school, updated with an emphasis on public school choice, is precisely the type of big idea we now need to help redeem the historic promise of public education.

Notes

Chapter One

1. Horace Mann, "Twelfth Annual Report," in Lawrence Cremin, ed., *The Republic and the School* (New York: Teachers College Press, 1957), p. 87.

2. National Center for Education Statistics, *NAEP 1998 Reading Report Card for the Nation* (Dept. of Education, 1999), p. 59. See also Gary Natriello, Edward L. McDill, and Aaron M. Pallas, *Schooling Disadvantaged Children: Racing against Catastrophe* (New York: Teachers College Press, 1990), p. 22; Gary Burtless, "Growing American Inequality," *Brookings Review* (Winter 1999), p. 13.

3. Natriello, McDill, and Pallas, *Schooling Disadvantaged Children*, p. 21.

4. Don Stewart, "Holding onto Norms in a Sea of Criteria," in Diane Ravitch, ed., *Debating the Future of American Education: Do We Need Standards and Assessments?* (Brookings, 1995), p. 91.

5. Lincoln, quoted in Ernest L. Boyer, foreword to Edith Rasell and Richard Rothstein, eds., *School Choice: Examining the Evidence* (Washington: Economic Policy Institute, 1993), p. xiii.

6. *Brown* v. *Board of Education*, 347 US 483 (1954), 493. (This Supreme Court decision struck down the 1896 *Plessy* v. *Ferguson* ruling, a landmark decision in which the Court ruled that the provision of separate but equal facilities did not represent a violation of the Fourteenth Amendment.)

7. William Bennett, *American Education: Making it Work* (Government Printing Office, 1988), p. 7.

8. Quoted in R. H. Melton, "Gilmore Joins GOP School Effort," *Washington Post,* September 19, 1998, p. C5.

9. Steve Farkas and Jean Johnson, *Time to Move On: African-American and White Parents Set an Agenda for Public Schools—A Report from Public Agenda* (New York: Public Agenda, 1998), p. 42 n. 8 (citing March 1997 NBC News/*Wall Street Journal* poll).

10. Michael Alves, interview by author, Cambridge, Massachusetts, December 1, 1997.

11. See discussion of this and other studies like it in chapter 3.

12. Ruy Teixeira, "Critical Support: The Public View of Public Education," in Richard Kahlenberg, ed., *A Notion at Risk: Preserving Public Education as an Engine for Social Mobility* (Century Foundation Press, 2000), p. 256.

13. Roger LeGrand, interview by author, La Crosse, Wisconsin, December 16, 1997, pp. 33–35, 36.

14. George Dennison, "The Lives of Children," quoted in Sara Mosle, "What We Talk about When We Talk about Education," *New Republic,* June 17, 1996, p. 27.

Chapter Two

1. Milton Friedman and Rose Friedman, *Free to Choose: A Personal Statement* (Harcourt Brace Jovanovich, 1980), p. 150. Richard C. Leone, foreword to Carol Ascher, Norm Fruchter, and Robert Berne, *Hard Lessons: Public Schools and Privatization* (Twentieth Century Fund, 1996), p. vi.

2. Jefferson, quoted in James B. Conant, "Education for a Classless Society: The Jeffersonian Tradition," *Atlantic Monthly,* May 1940, pp. 593–94. See also Virginia Constitution, art. 1, sec. 15. Coons, quoted in Jonathan Kozol, *Savage Inequalities: Children in America's Schools* (Crown, 1991), p. 206.

3. Thomas L. Friedman, "Accent Is on Education as Global Job Talks End," *New York Times,* March 16, 1994, p. D2; Ruy Teixeira and Joel Rogers, *America's Forgotten Majority: Why the White Working Class Still Matters* (Basic Books, 2000), pp. 8–9.

4. See, for example, *DeRolph v. State,* 677 N.E. 2d 733 (Ohio 1997), 770; *McDuffy v. Secretary* 615 N.E.2d 516 (Mass. 1993), 555; *Claremont School District v. Governor,* 635 A. 2d 1375 (N.H. 1993), 1377.

5. Neil Postman, *The End of Education: Redefining the Value of School* (Knopf, 1995), p. 13, paraphrasing Jefferson; Paul Gagnon, "The Case for Standards: Equity and Competence," *Boston University Journal of Education,* vol. 176, no. 3 (1994), p. 14; Thomas Ehrlich, "Dewey v. Hutchins: The Next Round," in Robert Orril, ed., *Education and Democracy: Re-imagining Liberal Learning in America* (New York: College Entrance Examination Board, 1997), pp. 258–59.

6. Jennifer Hochschild and Nathan Scovronick, "Democratic Education and the American Dream," in Lorraine McDonnell, Michael Timpane, and Roger Benjamin, eds., *Rediscovering the Democratic Purposes of Education* (University Press of Kansas, 2000), p. 212.

7. Postman, *The End of Education,* pp. 71, 14; *McCollom v. Board of Education,* 333 U.S. 203 (1948), 216 and 231 (Frankfurter, J., concurring).

8. National Center for Education Statistics (NCES), *The Condition of Education, 1998* (Dept. of Education, 1998), p. 36; Eliza Newlin Carney and Siobhan Gorman, "Grading the Teachers," *National Journal,* January 16, 1999, pp. 111–12; Rene Sanchez,

"U.S. Students Do Poorly in Science Test," *Washington Post*, October 22, 1997, p. A1; Rita Kramer, "As Easy as ABC," *Wall Street Journal*, September 22, 1997, p. A20.

9. Statement of Senator James Jeffords, U.S. Senate, Committee on Labor and Human Resources, *Education's Impact on Economic Competitiveness: Hearings before the Subcommittee on Education, Arts, and Humanities*, 104 Cong., 1 sess., February 2, 1995, pp. 4–5. Lee A. Daniels, "Illiteracy Seen as Threat to U.S. Economic Edge," *New York Times*, September, 7, 1988, p. B8; statement of Joseph Gorman, Senate Committee on Labor and Human Resources, *Education's Impact on Economic Competitiveness*, p. 6.

10. Gerald W. Bracey, "The Third Bracey Report on the Condition of Public Education," *Phi Delta Kappan*, vol. 75, no. 2 (October 1993), pp. 108–09. See also Gerald W. Bracey, "Are U.S. Students Behind?" *American Prospect* (March–April 1998), pp. 64, 69. In the Third International Math comparison, America's top students slipped; Rene Sanchez, "U.S. High School Seniors Rank near Bottom," *Washington Post*, February 25, 1998, p. A1. For an argument that not much can be drawn from the third study, see Gerald W. Bracey, "The TIMSS 'Final Year' Study and Report: A Critique," *Educational Researcher*, vol. 29, no. 4 (May 2000), pp. 4–10.

11. OECD International Adult Literacy Survey, 1994, cited in Lisa M. Lynch, "Trends in and Consequences of Investments in Children," in Sheldon H. Danziger and Jane Waldfogel, eds., *Securing the Future: Investing in Children from Birth to College* (New York: Russell Sage Foundation, 2000), p. 26.

12. Gordon Berlin and Andrew Sum, *Toward a More Perfect Union: Basic Skills, Poor Families, and Our Economic Future* (New York: Ford Foundation, 1988), p. 24; see also Richard Rothstein, introduction, in Edith Rasell and Richard Rothstein, eds., *School Choice: Examining the Evidence* (Washington: Economic Policy Institute, 1993), p. 14. James Fallows, "Strengths, Weaknesses, and Lessons of Japanese Education," *Education Digest*, vol. 57 (October 1991), pp. 58–59.

13. See, for example, Ira Katznelson and Margaret Weir, *Schooling for All: Class, Race, and the Decline of the Democratic Ideal* (Basic Books, 1985), p. 10; Marshall Smith and Jennifer O'Day, "Educational Equality: 1966 and Now," in Deborah A. Verstegen and James G. Ward, eds., *Spheres of Justice in Education: The 1990 American Education Finance Association Yearbook* (New York: Harper Business, 1991), p. 54.

Some progressive defenders of public schools argue we are doing a pretty good job at educating students, considering differences in home environment; see, for example, Alan Krueger, "Reassessing the View that American Schools Are Broken," *FRBNY Economic Policy Review* (March 1998), p. 37. Krueger cites Entwisle for the proposition that poor students learn as much at school as middle-class kids during elementary school and that gaps develop during summers off. There are five responses. First, new research questions the summer setback hypothesis. Meredith Phillips, James Crouse, and John Ralph note if summers are the problem, then the gap should be larger in the fall than in the spring. This is true for math scores, but it is not true for reading and vocabulary scores, which are as large at the end of the school year as at the beginning. Phillips, Crouse, and Ralph, "Does the Black-White Test Score Gap Widen after Children Enter School?" in Christopher Jencks and Meredith Phillips, eds., *The Black-White Test Score Gap* (Brookings, 1998), pp. 229–272, 239. Second, there is some reason to be skeptical of the data, which suggest summers are the central problem. If the diagnosis is correct, summer programs should be effective in raising the scores of low-income kids.

Entwisle and colleagues, however, concede that in practice, summer school programs have been a major disappointment; Doris R. Entwisle, Karl L. Alexander, and Linda Steffel Olson, *Children, Schools, and Inequality* (New York: Westview Press, 1997), pp. 58, 150. Third, the logic of learning curves suggests poor kids should make up some of the gap during school years. Entwisle and colleagues note that an educational learning curve means that elementary school students post the greatest gains in the earliest years; ibid., p. 24. Fourth, Entwisle's data, blaming summers during elementary school, do not hold at the middle and high school levels; Adam Gamoran, "Curriculum Change as a Reform Strategy: Lessons from the United States and Scotland," *Teachers College Record*, vol. 98, no. 4 (Summer 1997), pp. 608–28. Fifth, Entwisle's data base is hardly representative enough to draw broad conclusions: 67 percent of the students in the study receive government-subsidized meals; Entwisle, Alexander, and Olson, *Children, Schools, and Inequality*, p. 172.

14. Department of Education, *Improving America's Schools Act of 1993: The Reauthorization of the Elementary and Secondary Education Act and Amendments to Other Acts* (September 13, 1993), pp. 16–17. See also James E. Ryan, "Schools, Race, and Money," *Yale Law Journal*, vol. 109 (November 1999), n. 158; Friedman and Friedman, *Free to Choose*, p. 158.

15. NCES, *The Condition of Education, 1998*, pp. 3, 169. David T. Ellwood and Thomas Kane, "Who Is Getting a College Education? Family Background and the Growing Gap in Enrollment," in Danziger and Waldfogel, *Securing the Future*, p. 286, table 10.1; Jack Beatty, "Against Inequality," *Atlantic Monthly*, April 1999, pp. 105, 107; Lawrence Gladieux and Scott Swail, *The Forgotten Half Revisited* (New York: College Entrance Examination Board, 1999) (that in addition to expense of college, preparation is the key problem).

16. William G. Bowen and Derek Bok, *The Shape of the River* (Princeton University Press, 1998), p. 341.

17. Peter Gottschalk, Sara McLanahan, and Gary Sandefur, "The Dynamics of Intergenerational Transmission of Poverty and Welfare Participation," in Sheldon H. Danziger, Gary D. Sandefur, and Daniel H. Weinberg, eds., *Confronting Poverty: Prescriptions for Change* (Harvard University Press, 1994), p. 100; Richard D. Kahlenberg, *The Remedy: Race, Class, and Affirmative Action* (Basic Books, 1996), pp. 88–90; Mary Corcoran and others, "Poverty and the Underclass: Effects of Family and Community Background on Economic Status," *American Economic Review*, vol. 80 (May 1990), pp. 362–64; Sandra K. Danziger and Sheldon Danziger, "Child Poverty and Public Policy: Toward a Comprehensive Antipoverty Agenda," *Daedalus*, vol. 122 (Winter 1993), p. 72; Susan E. Mayer, *What Money Can't Buy: Family Income and Children's Life Chances* (Harvard University Press, 1997), p. 41.

18. Richard Harwood, "Classrooms and Class," *Washington Post*, April, 20, 1998, p. A19. Derek Bok, *The State of the Nation* (Harvard University Press, 1996), pp. 192–93.

19. Sheldon H. Danziger and Daniel Weinberg, "The Historical Record: Trends in Family Income, Inequality, and Poverty," in Danziger, Sandefur, and Weinberg, *Confronting Poverty*, pp. 22–23.

20. Gary Burtless, "Growing American Inequality," *Brookings Review* (Winter 1999), p. 32.

21. National Commission on Excellence in Education, *A Nation at Risk: The Imperative for Education Reform* (Government Printing Office, 1983), pp. 4, 8.

22. Eric A. Hanushek, "Conclusions and Controversies about the Effectiveness of School Resources," *FRBNY Economic Policy Review* (March 1998), pp. 12, 14–15. Ethan Bronner, "Long a Leader, U.S. Now Lags in High School Graduate Rate," *New York Times*, November 24, 1998, p. A1.

23. See, for example, Henry M. Levin, "The Economics of Justice in Education," in Verstegen and Ward, *Spheres of Justice in Education*, p. 143; Berlin and Sum, *Toward a More Perfect Union*, pp. 40–43; Russell W. Rumberger and J. Douglas Willms, "The Impact of Racial and Ethnic Segregation on the Achievement Gap in California High Schools," *Educational Evaluation and Policy Analysis*, vol. 14 (Winter 1992), p. 377.

24. Statement of Kent Lloyd (CEO, Knowledge Network for All Americans), Senate Committee on Labor and Human Resources, *Education's Impact on Economic Competitiveness*, p. 98. See also National Commission on Teaching and America's Future, *What Matters Most: Teaching for America's Future* (September 1996), p. 12.

25. Philip Burch, *The Dropout Problem in New Jersey's Big Urban Schools: Educational Inequality and Governmental Inaction* (New Brunswick: Rutgers Bureau of Government Research, 1992), p. 1. See, for example, "America Busted," *New Yorker*, February 24, 1997, p. 49. Jonathan Kozol, *Ordinary Resurrections: Children in the Years of Hope* (Crown, 2000), p. 155.

26. Sara Mosle, "Mean Streets," *New York Times Book Review*, November 23, 1997, p. 7.

27. Lawrence B. Mead, *Beyond Entitlement* (New York: Free Press, 1986), p. 3.

28. Meier, cited in Carol Ascher, Norm Fruchter, and Robert Berne, *Hard Lessons: Public Schools and Privatization* (Twentieth Century Fund, 1996), p. 97.

29. Kern Alexander, "The Common School Ideal and the Limits of Legislative Authority: The Kentucky Case," *Harvard Journal on Legislation*, vol. 28 (1991), pp. 356–57. Charles Peters, *Tilting at Windmills: An Autobiography* (New York: Addison-Wesley, 1988), pp. 218–19. For a particularly nuanced argument that individuals are most creative when exposed to diverse views, see G. Pascal Zachary, *The Global Me* (New York: Public Affairs Press, 2000).

30. Philip A. Klinkner and Rogers M. Smith, *The Unsteady March* (University of Chicago Press, 1999), p. 5.

31. Thomas Toch, "The New Education Bazaar," *U.S. News and World Report*, April 27, 1998, pp. 34, 46.

32. Arthur M. Schlesinger Jr., *The Disuniting of America: Reflections on a Multicultural Society* (Norton, 1992), p. 10. Pamela Keating and Jeannie Oakes, *Access to Knowledge: Removing School Barriers to Learning—Youth at Risk* (Denver: Education Commission of the States, 1988), p. 1.

33. Katznelson and Weir, *Schooling for All*, p. 214. John I. Goodlad, "Desegregating the Integrated School," in U.S. Commission on Civil Rights, *Racial Isolation in the Public Schools*, vol. 2, p. 260 (Government Printing Office, 1967). See also Henry S. Dyer, "Measuring Equal Opportunity," in Frederick Mosteller and Daniel P. Moynihan, eds., *On Equality of Educational Opportunity: Papers Deriving from the Harvard Faculty Seminar on the Coleman Report* (Random House, 1972), p. 395; James S. Coleman, *Equality and Achievement in Education* (1990), p. 19, cited in Donald Judges, "Bayonets for the Wounded: Constitutional Paradigms and Disadvantaged Neighborhoods," *Hastings Constitutional Law Quarterly*, vol. 19, no. 599 (Spring 1992), pp. 599, 689; Mickey Kaus, *The End of Equality* (Basic Books, 1992), p. 53; John W. Gardner, foreword to James B. Conant, *The American High School Today* (McGraw-Hill, 1959), pp. ix–x.

34. David Rusk, *Cities without Suburbs*, 2d ed. (Washington: Woodrow Wilson Center Press, 1995), pp. 5, 8. Paul A. Jargowsky, *Poverty and Place: Ghettos, Barrios, and the American City* (New York: Russell Sage Foundation, 1997), p. 185; David Rusk, *Inside Game/Outside Game: Urban Policies for the Twenty-first Century* (Brookings, 1999), p. 117. Bok, *The State of the Nation*, p. 361. See also Smith and O'Day, "Educational Equality," p. 81; Jeanne Brooks-Gunn and others, "Do Neighborhoods Influence Child and Adolescent Development?" *American Journal of Sociology*, vol. 99 (September 1993), p. 354; Lynch, "Trends in Investments in Children," p. 14; "Quality Counts '98: The Urban Challenge," *Education Week*, January 8, 1998, p. 14; William Julius Wilson, *The Truly Disadvantaged: The Inner City, the Underclass, and Public Policy* (University of Chicago Press, 1987), pp. 46, 172; Rusk, *Cities without Suburbs*, p. 78; Robert Pear, "Poverty 1993: Bigger, Deeper, Younger, Getting Worse," *New York Times*, October 10, 1993, sec. 4; Anthony Downs, *New Visions for Metropolitan America* (Brookings, 1994), p. 71; Rusk, *Inside Game/Outside Game*, pp. 76–81; Wilson, foreword to Jargowsky, *Poverty and Place*, vii; Jargowsky, *Poverty and Place*, 29–30; Richard Morin, "The New Great Divide," *Washington Post Magazine*, January 18, 1998, pp. 14–15; William Julius Wilson, *When Work Disappears: The World of the New Urban Poor* (Knopf, 1996), pp. 254, 256; Michael B. Katz, "Conclusion: Reframing the 'Underclass' Debate," in Michael B. Katz, ed., *The "Underclass" Debate: Views from History* (Princeton University Press, 1993), p. 456.

35. Douglas Massey, quoted in Morin, "The New Great Divide," pp. 14–15; Robert B. Reich, "Secession of the Successful," *New York Times Magazine*, January 20, 1991, p. 16; Robert B. Reich, *The Work of Nations: Preparing Ourselves for Twenty-first-Century Capitalism* (Knopf, 1991), pp. 268–69; Edward J. Blakely and Mary Gail Snyder, *Fortress America: Gated Communities in the United States* (Brookings, 1997), pp. 2–3, 7–8, 126; David L. Kirp, John P. Dwyer, and Larry A. Rosenthal, *Our Town: Race, Housing, and the Soul of Suburbia* (Rutgers University Press, 1995), p. 171.

36. Teixeira and Rogers, *America's Forgotten Majority*, p. x. Morin, "The New Great Divide," p. 14; Wilson, *When Work Disappears*, p. 149; Bok, *The State of the Nation*, p. 114; Anthony Downs, "How America's Cities Are Growing," *Brookings Review* (Fall 1998), pp. 8–9.

37. Harvey Kantor and Barbara Brenzel, "Urban Education and the 'Truly Disadvantaged': The Historical Roots of the Contemporary Crisis, 1945–1990," in Katz, *The "Underclass" Debate*, p. 369; Robert J. Havighurst, "Schools in Depressed Areas," in A. Harry Passow, ed., *Education in Depressed Areas* (New York: Bureau of Publications, Teachers College, Columbia University, 1963), pp. 27–28; Gary Orfield, *Must We Bus? Segregated Schools and National Policy* (Brookings, 1978), p. 406; Robert F. Herriott and Nancy Hoyt St. John, *Social Class and the Urban School: The Impact of Pupil Background on Teachers and Principals* (New York: John Wiley and Sons, 1966), pp. 2–5; Thomas J. Sugrue, "The Structures of Urban Policy," in Katz, *The "Underclass" Debate*, p. 92. On "common school," see Anthony S. Bryk, Valerie E. Lee, and Peter B. Holland, *Catholic Schools and the Common Good* (Harvard University Press, 1993), p. 38.

38. See Judith Anderson, *The Distribution of Chapter 1 Services: Data from the Schools and Staffing Survey* (Dept. of Education, Office of Educational Research and Improvement, 1993), p. 7.

39. Nathan Glazer, "A Tale of Two Cities," *New Republic*, August 2, 1993, p. 40. Gary Orfield and Susan Eaton, *Dismantling Desegregation: The Quiet Reversal of Brown v. Board of Education* (New York: New Press, 1996), pp. 53–55, 331. Gary Orfield and

John Yun, *Resegregation in American Schools* (Cambridge, Mass.: Harvard Civil Rights Project, 1999), p. 13, table 9.

40. See, for example, Caroline Hendrie, "A Denver High School Reaches Out," *Education Week*, June 17, 1998; Richard D. Kahlenberg, "Rethinking Busing," *Intellectual Capital* (IntellectualCapital.com [September 10, 1998]); Steven A. Holmes and Karen De Witt, "Black, Successful, and Safe and Gone from Capital," *New York Times*, July 27, 1996, p. 1; David Nakamura, "Prince George's Fears Resegregation: Some Worry Schools May Split along Socioeconomic Lines," *Washington Post*, March 25, 1999, p. B1.

41. Morin, "The New Great Divide," p. 14. Rusk, remarks, Brookings, February 24, 1999. See also Jargowsky, *Poverty and Place*, p. 201; Christopher Jencks and Susan E. Mayer, "The Social Consequences of Growing Up in a Poor Neighborhood," in Laurence E. Lynn Jr. and Michael G. H. McGeary, eds., *Inner-City Poverty in the United States* (Washington: National Academy Press, 1990), p. 124; Douglas S. Massey and Mary J. Fischer, "Where We Live, in Black and White," *Nation*, December 14, 1998, p. 25; Peter Finn, "A Little Girl's Giant Footsteps," *Washington Post*, February 19, 1997, pp. A1, A12.

Chapter Three

1. Horace Mann, "First Annual Report (1837)," in Lawrence Cremin, ed., *The Republic and the School: Horace Mann on the Education of Free Men* (New York: Teachers College Press, 1957), pp. 31–32, 23–24, 31. Jay Mathews, *Class Struggle: What's Wrong (and Right) with America's Best Public High Schools* (New York: Times Books, 1998), p. 185.

2. Kern Alexander, "The Common School and the Limits of Legislative Authority: The Kentucky Case," *Harvard Journal on Legislation*, vol. 28 (1991), pp. 356–57. Leon Botstein, *Jefferson's Children: Education and the Promise of American Culture* (Doubleday, 1997), p. 153.

3. Amy Stuart Wells, *Time to Choose: America at the Crossroads of School Choice Policy* (New York: Hill and Wang, 1993), p. 7. Mann, "First Annual Report," p. 10.

4. Coleman, foreword to John E. Coons, William H. Clure III, and Stephen D. Sugarman, *Private Wealth and Public Education* (Harvard University Press, 1970), pp. xv–xvi. Coleman, quoted in Senate Select Committee on Equal Educational Opportunity, *Report: Toward Equal Educational Opportunity*, 92 Cong., 2 sess. (Government Printing Office, 1972), p. 233.

5. White parents in the Kansas City area, for example, were not interested in sending their children to schools with lavish facilities in which students were mostly from disadvantaged backgrounds; see the discussion in chapter 6.

6. Ray C. Rist, *The Urban School: A Factory for Failure* (MIT University Press, 1973), p. 16. David Rusk, "To Improve Public Education, Stop Moving Money, Move Families," *Abell Report*, vol. 11 (June–July 1998), pp. 1–8. David Rusk and Jeff Mosley, *The Academic Performance of Public Housing Children: Does Living in Middle-Class Neighborhoods and Attending Middle-Class Schools Make a Difference?* (Washington: Urban Institute, 1994), p. 26.

7. Gary Orfield and Susan Eaton, *Dismantling Desegregation: The Quiet Reversal of Brown v. Board of Education* (New York: New Press, 1996), p. 53. James S. Coleman and others, *Equality of Educational Opportunity* (Government Printing Office, 1966), p.

22. James S. Coleman, "Toward Open Schools," *Public Interest*, vol. 9 (Fall 1967), pp. 20–21, 325. Frederick Mosteller and Daniel P. Moynihan, eds., *On Equality of Educational Opportunity: Papers Deriving from the Harvard Faculty Seminar on the Coleman Report* (Random House, 1972), p. 20.

8. Christopher Jencks, "The Coleman Report and the Conventional Wisdom," in Mosteller and Moynihan, *On Equality of Opportunity*, pp. 87, 105. See also Senate Select Committee on Equal Educational Opportunity, *Report*, p. 219; Rist, *The Urban School*, pp. 16–17; Harrell R. Rodgers and Charles S. Bullock III, "School Desegregation: Successes and Failures," *Journal of Negro Education*, vol. 43 (1974), p. 143. In a 1990 review, Jencks found that the "best estimate" is that "black students who attended overwhelmingly white rather than all-black schools in the North in the 1960s scored something like one-third of a standard deviation higher on most tests as a result. Since the overall difference between northern blacks and whites was about one standard deviation, the benefits of desegregation were substantial"; see Christopher Jencks and Susan E. Mayer, "The Social Consequences of Growing Up in a Poor Neighborhood," in Laurence E. Lynn Jr. and Michael G. H. McGeary, eds., *Inner-City Poverty in the United States* (Washington: National Academy Press, 1990), p. 151. Since 1990, Jencks has become less sanguine about the impact of integration. In 1998, Jencks wrote, "black third graders in predominantly white schools read better than initially similar blacks who have attended predominantly black schools. But large racial differences in reading skills persist even in desegregated schools, and a school's racial mix does not seem to have much effect on changes in reading scores after sixth grade or on math scores at any age"; he cites evidence that attending a 90 percent white school rather than an all-black school can raise third-grade reading scores by .243 standard deviations; Christopher Jencks and Meredith Phillips, introduction to *The Black-White Test Score Gap* (Brookings, 1998), p. 9. The chapter did not include an analysis of socioeconomic integration per se.

9. Chester E. Finn, "Education That Works: Make the Schools Compete," in *Harvard Business Review*, vol. 65 (September–October 1987), p. 64. David J. Hoff, "Echoes of the Coleman Report," *Education Week*, March 24, 1999, p. 33; see also Alan B. Wilson, "Social Stratification and Academic Achievement," in A. Harry Passow, ed., *Education in Depressed Areas* (New York: Bureau of Publications, Teachers College, Columbia University, 1963); Robert J. Havighurst, "Urban Development and the Educational System," in Passow, *Education in Depressed Areas*, p. 30; John A. Michael, "High School Climates and Plans for Entering College," *Public Opinion Quarterly*, vol. 25 (1961), pp. 585, 590; Bernard Barber, "Social-Class Differences in Educational Life-Chances," *Teachers College Record*, vol. 63 (November 1961), pp. 102-13. Ralph H. Turner, *The Social Context of Ambition: A Study of High School Seniors in Los Angeles* (San Francisco: Chandler Publishing, 1964); U.S. Commission on Civil Rights, *Racial Isolation in the Public Schools* (Government Printing Office, 1967), vol. 1, p. 81; Alan B. Wilson, "Educational Consequences of Segregation in a California Community," in U.S. Commission on Civil Rights, *Racial Isolation*, vol. 2, pp. 165–203; Department of Health, Education, and Welfare, *The Effectiveness of Compensatory Education* (1972), pp. 171–72; Coleman, interview with Dick Hubert, "Class and the Classroom: The Duluth Experience," *Saturday Review of Education*, May 27, 1972, pp. 55–59; J. Douglas Willms and Frank H. Echols, "The Scottish Experience of Parental School Choice," in Edith Rasell and Richard Rothstein, eds., *School Choice: Examining the Evidence* (Washington: Eco-

nomic Policy Institute, 1993), pp. 55–56; J. Douglas Willms, "Social Class Segregation and Its Relationship to Pupils' Examination Results in Scotland," *American Sociological Review*, vol. 51 (April 1986), pp. 224–41; Maureen T. Hallinhan, "Commentary: New Directions for Research on Peer Influence," in Joyce Levy Epstein and Nancy Karweit, eds., *Friends in School: Patterns of Selection and Influence in Secondary Schools* (New York: Academic Press, 1983), p. 220; Gary Orfield and others, *The Growth of Segregation in American Schools: Changing Patterns of Separation and Poverty since 1968* (Harvard University Press, 1994), pp. 1, 25; Harvey Kantor and Barbara Brenzel, "Urban Education and the 'Truly Disadvantaged': The Historical Roots of the Contemporary Crisis, 1945–1990," in Michael B. Katz, ed., *The "Underclass" Debate: Views from History* (Princeton University Press, 1993), pp. 384–85; Judith Anderson, Debra Hollinger, and Joseph Conaty, *Poverty and Achievement: Reexamining the Relationship between School Poverty and Student Achievement—An Examination of Eighth-Grade Student Achievement Using the National Education Longitudinal Study of 1988* (Dept. of Education, Office of Educational Research and Improvement, 1992), p. 7; Laura Lippman and others, *Urban Schools: The Challenge of Location and Poverty* (Dept. of Education, National Center for Education Statistics [NCES], 1996), pp. 2–3; john a. powell, "Living and Learning: Linking Housing and Education," *Minnesota Law Review*, vol. 80 (April 1996), p. 790; Valerie E. Lee, Susanna Loeb, and Sally Lubeck, "Contextual Effects of Prekindergarten Classrooms for Disadvantaged Children on Cognitive Development: The Case of Chapter 1," *Child Development*, vol. 69, no. 2 (April 1998), pp. 479, 490–91; James E. Ryan, "Schools, Race, and Money," *Yale Law Journal*, vol. 109 (November 1999), pp. 249–316; William T. Trent, "Why the Gap between Black and White Performance in School?" *Journal of Negro Education*, vol. 66 (Summer 1997), pp. 320–29; William D. Duncombe and John M. Yinger, "Performance Standards and Educational Cost Indexes," in Helen F. Ladd, Rosemary Chalk, and Janet S. Hansen, eds., *Equity and Adequacy in Education Finance* (Washington: National Press Academy, 1999), pp. 265–69; Edward B. Fiske and Helen F. Ladd, *When Schools Compete: A Cautionary Tale* (Brookings, 2000), p. 230 (citing forthcoming study of five countries).

10. Because the effect of growing up in a poor but highly motivated family will presumably show up in initial test scores, controlling for a student's initial ability and tracking his or her progress in achievement over time should reduce or eliminate selection bias. These longitudinal studies have concluded that over time, achievement gains differed from those of students who began with equal test scores and come from families of similar socioeconomic status, confirming the independent school effect found by Coleman. See, for example, Alan Wilson, "Social Class and Equal Educational Opportunity," in *Harvard Education Review: Equal Educational Opportunity* (Harvard University Press, 1969), p. 86; U.S. Commission on Civil Rights, *Racial Isolation*, vol. 1, p. 88 (citing Wilson); Thomas Pettigrew, "Race and Equal Educational Opportunity," in *Harvard Educational Review: Equal Educational Opportunity*, p. 73; Department of Health, Education, and Welfare, *The Effectiveness of Compensatory Education*, p. 172. Almost all of the more recent studies are longitudinal and find significant classmate effects. See, for example, Willms and Echols, "The Scottish Experience of Parental Choice," pp. 55–56; Willms, "Social Class Segregation," pp. 234–38; Vernon Henderson, Peter Mieszkowski, and Yvon Sauvageau, "Peer Group Effects and Educational Production Functions," *Journal of Public Economics*, vol. 10 (1978), p. 97; Anita A. Summers and Barbara L. Wolfe, "Do Schools Make a Difference?" *American Economic Review*,

vol. 67 (September 1977), pp. 640–41; John Chubb and Terry Moe, *Politics, Markets, and American Schools* (Brookings, 1990), pp. 124–28; Joyce Levy Epstein, "The Influence of Friends on Achievement and Affective Outcomes," in Epstein and Karweit, *Friends in School,* p. 179.

Others attempts to control for self-selection using alternative means have found significant residual effects. See, for example, David M. Cutler and Edward L. Glaeser, "Are Ghettos Good or Bad?" *Quarterly Journal of Economics* (August 1997), pp. 827–28 (controlling for self-selection by comparing outcomes for individuals living in different cities with varying levels of segregation—as opposed to individuals within a given city living in different neighborhoods—the study still found powerful effects).

Some even go so far as to argue that the self-selection argument works in reverse and much of the family effect derives from neighborhood. The reason it appears that family matters is that wealthy families tend to live in good neighborhoods, where children are exposed to positive peers; Judith Rich Harris, *The Nurture Assumption: Why Children Turn Out the Way They Do* (New York: Free Press, 1998), p. 358; see also Jeanne Brooks-Gunn and others, "Do Neighborhoods Influence Child and Adolescent Development?" *American Journal of Sociology,* vol. 99 (September 1993), p. 358 (that self-selection process may work in the reverse: it might be that children with well-equipped strong families may self-select into bad neighborhoods to take advantage of cheaper housing or short commutes, knowing their families can better resist the negative effects).

11. Richard Murnane, "Evidence, Analysis, and Unanswered Questions," *Harvard Education Review,* vol. 51 (1981), p. 486, cited in Ryan, "Schools, Race, and Money," p. 300.

12. Mary M. Kennedy, Richard K. Jung, and M. E. Orland, *Poverty, Achievement, and the Distribution of Compensatory Education Services: An Interim Report from the National Assessment of Chapter 1* (Dept. of Education, Office of Educational Research and Improvement, 1986), pp. 21–22; see also Martin E. Orland, "Demographics of Disadvantage: Intensity of Childhood Poverty and Its Relationship to Educational Achievement," in John I. Goodlad and Pamela Keating, eds., *Access to Knowledge: An Agenda for Our Nation's Schools* (New York: College Entrance Examination Board, 1990), p. 52; Marshall Smith and Jennifer O'Day, "Educational Equality: 1966 and Now," in Deborah A. Verstegen and James G. Ward, eds., *Spheres of Justice in Education: The 1990 American Education Finance Association Yearbook* (New York: Harper Business, 1991), p. 63. Relying on an analysis by David Myers, Kennedy, Jung, and Orland conclude that the effect of poverty concentrations on "learning" (changes in achievement net of personal and family characteristics) are smaller than the effect on average starting achievement. But Myers' analysis of "learning" has been criticized as flawed; see Jencks and Mayer, "The Social Consequences of Growing Up in a Poor Neighborhood," pp. 142–43 and 146. Myers does find a negative effect even on "learning" in the early grades; David E. Myers, *The Relationship between School Poverty Concentration and Students' Reading and Math Achievement and Learning* (Washington: Decision Resources, 1986), p. 25.

13. Willms, "Social Class Segregation," p. 234; see also Andrew McPherson and J. Douglas Willms, "Equalisation and Improvement: Some Effects of Comprehensive Reorganisation in Scotland," *Sociology,* vol. 21 (November 1987), pp. 509, 510, 514–15, 529–30.

14. Russell W. Rumberger and J. Douglas Willms, "The Impact of Racial and Ethnic Segregation on the Achievement Gap in California High Schools," *Educational Evalua-*

tion and Policy Analysis, vol. 14 (Winter 1992), pp. 390–91, 393. Esther Ho Sui-Chu and J. Douglas Willms, "Effects of Parental Involvement on Eighth-Grade Achievement," *Sociology of Education*, vol. 69 (April 1996), pp. 130, 135, 138.

15. Chubb and Moe, *Politics, Markets, and American Schools*, pp. 124–28, 109.

16. David Rusk and Jeff Mosley, *The Academic Performance of Public Housing Children: Does Living in Middle-Class Neighborhoods and Attending Middle-Class Schools Make a Difference?* (Washington: Urban Institute, May 1994). Duncan Chaplin and Jane Hannaway, *African American High Scorers Project: Technical Report*, vol. 2, *Schools and Neighborhood Factors and SAT Performance* (Washington: Urban Institute, 1998), p. 40; see also David Rusk, *Inside Game/Outside Game: Urban Policies for the Twenty-first Century* (Brookings, 1999), pp. 123-25; Rusk, "To Improve Public Education, Stop Moving Money," pp. 4–5.

17. Michael Puma and others, *Prospects: Final Report on Student Outcomes* (Cambridge, Mass.: Abt Associates, 1997), pp. 73, 12.

18. Rusk, "To Improve Public Education, Stop Moving Money," pp. 1, 5.

19. See Stephen Schellenberg, "Concentration of Poverty and the Ongoing Need for Title I," in Gary Orfield and Elizabeth DeBray, eds., *Hard Work for Good Schools: Facts Not Fads in Title I Reform* (Cambridge, Mass.: Harvard Civil Rights Project, 1999), pp. 130 and 137.

20. Michael, "High School Climates and Plans for Entering College," p. 593.

21. Porter W. Sexton, "Trying to Make It Real Compared to What? Implications of High School Dropout Statistics," *Journal of Educational Equity and Leadership*, vol. 5 (Summer 1985), pp. 92, 96, 102–03. john powell, "Segregation and Educational Inadequacy in Twin Cities Public Schools," *Hamline Journal of Public Law and Policy*, vol. 17 (Spring 1996), p. 345. Hallinhan, "Commentary," p. 222; see also Martha A. Gephart, "Neighborhoods and Communities as Context for Development," in Jeanne Brooks-Gunn, Greg J. Duncan, and J. Lawrence Aber, eds., *Neighborhood Poverty*, vol. 1: *Context and Consequences for Children* (New York: Russell Sage Foundation, 1997), pp. 35–38.

22. Mosteller and Moynihan, *On Equality of Educational Opportunity*, p. 7. Christopher Jencks and others, *Inequality: A Reassessment of the Effects of Family and Schooling in America* (Harper and Row, 1972), p. 265. Ronald F. Ferguson, "Paying for Public Education: New Evidence on How and Why Money Matters," *Harvard Journal on Legislation*, vol. 28 (1991), p. 469 (citing studies by O'Neill and Ferguson). Eric A. Hanushek, "School Resources and Student Reference," in Gary Burtless, ed., *Does Money Matter? The Effect of School Resources on Student Achievement and Adult Success* (Brookings, 1996), p. 61.

23. Marc Tucker, cited in Kathleen Sylvester, "Common Standards, Diverse Schools: Renewing the Promise of Public Education," in Will Marshall, ed., *Building the Bridge* (Lanham, Md.: Rowman and Littlefield, 1997), p. 85. Christopher Jencks and Meredith Phillips, "The Black-White Test Score Gap: Why It Persists and What Can Be Done," *Brookings Review* (Spring 1998), p. 24; see also Jencks and Phillips, introduction, *The Black-White Test Score Gap*, p. 4. Education is also more important today because discriminatory barriers in employment are crumbling; James J. Heckman, "Detecting Discrimination," *Journal of Economic Perspectives*, vol. 12, no. 2 (Spring 1998), pp. 101–16, cited in Daniel M. O'Brien, "Family and School Effects on the Cognitive Growth of Minority and Disadvantaged Elementary Students," paper presented to the annual

meeting of the Association for Public Policy Analysis and Management, New York, October 29–31, 1998, p. 4.

24. See Gordon Berlin and Andrew Sum, *Toward a More Perfect Union: Basic Skills, Poor Families, and Our Economic Future* (New York: Ford Foundation, 1988), pp. 25, 28–34; Michelle Fine, *Framing Dropouts: Notes on the Politics of an Urban Public High School* (State University of New York Press, 1991), p. 258; Nancy A. Gonzales and others, "Family, Peer, and Neighborhood Influences on Academic Achievement among African-American Adolescents: One-Year Prospective Effects," *American Journal of Community Psychology*, vol. 24 (1996), p. 366; Hanushek, "School Resources and Student Reference," p. 62.

25. Ruth Ekstrom and others, "Who Drops Out of High School and Why?" *Teachers College Record*, vol. 87, no. 3 (Spring 1986), pp. 358–59. Claude S. Fischer and others, *Inequality by Design: Cracking the Bell Curve Myth* (Princeton University Press, 1996), p. 86.

26. Edward Walsh, "Education Producing Wider Earnings Gap," *Washington Post*, December 10, 1998, p. A24. See also David T. Ellwood and Thomas Kane, "Who Is Getting a College Education? Family Background and the Growing Gaps in Enrollment," in Sheldon H. Danziger and Jane Waldfogel, eds., *Securing the Future: Investing in Children from Birth to College* (New York: Russell Sage Foundation, 2000), p. 284; NCES, *The Condition of Education, 1998* (Dept. of Education, 1998), p. 68; William Julius Wilson, *When Work Disappears: The World of the New Urban Poor* (Knopf, 1996), p. 217; Derek Bok, *The State of the Nation* (Harvard University Press, 1996), p. 55; Lisa M. Lynch, "Trends in and Consequences of Investments in Children," in Danziger and Waldfogel, *Securing the Future*, p. 20.

27. Alan B. Krueger, "Reassessing the View that American Schools Are Broken," *FRBNY Economic Policy Review* (March 1998), p. 38. Orfield and Eaton, *Dismantling Desegregation*, p. 78. David P. Brandon, *Demographic Factors in American Education* (Arlington, Va.: Educational Research Service, 1995), p. 33. "Perhaps the Single Most Promising Reform Idea" (excerpts from speech of President George Bush), *Education Week*, January 18, 1989, p. 24. Richard Harwood, "Classrooms and Class," *Washington Post*, April 20, 1998, A19.

28. See, for example, Dominic J. Brewer, Eric R. Eide, and Ronald G. Ehrenberg, "Does It Pay to Attend an Elite Private College?" *Journal of Human Resources*, vol. 34 (1999), pp. 104–23; Thomas J. Kane, "Racial and Ethnic Preferences in College Admissions," in Jencks and Phillips, *The Black-White Test Score Gap*, pp. 431–56. For a contrary finding, see Stacy Berg Dale and Alan B. Krueger, "Estimating the Payoff to Attending a More Selective College," Working Paper 7322 (Cambridge, Mass.: National Bureau of Economic Research, August 1999).

29. William G. Bowen and Derek Bok, *The Shape of the River* (Princeton University Press, 1998), pp. 124, 110.

30. See discussion in chapter 4. See also *Sheff v. O'Neill, Plaintiffs' Appeal from Superior Court*, August 1, 1995, pp. 5–6; Gary Orfield, *City-Suburban Desegregation: Parent and Student Perspectives in Metropolitan Boston* (Cambridge, Mass.: Harvard Civil Rights Project, 1997), p. 24.

31. Gary Orfield, interview by author, Cambridge, Massachusetts, November 19, 1997, p. 28.

32. Alan F. Abrahamse, Peter A. Morrison, and Linda J. Waite, *Beyond Stereotypes: Who Becomes a Single Mother?* (Santa Monica, Calif.: Rand, 1988); Susan E. Mayer, *What Money Can't Buy: Family Income and Children's Life Chances* (Harvard University Press, 1997), p. 44; Lippman and others, *Urban Schools*, p. 124 (citing 1987–1988 DOE Schools and Staffing Survey). Dennis P. Hogan and Evelyn M. Kitagawa, "The Impact of Social Status, Family Structure, and Neighborhood on Fertility of Black Adolescents," *American Journal of Sociology*, vol. 90 (1985), 825–55, and Jonathan Crane, cited in Jencks and Mayer, "The Social Consequences of Growing Up in a Poor Neighborhood," p. 163.

33. See Douglas S. Massey and Nancy A. Denton, *American Apartheid: Segregation and the Making of the Underclass* (Harvard University Press, 1993), p. 179; Jencks and Mayer, "The Social Consequences of Growing Up in a Poor Neighborhood," pp. 164, 166–67; Susan E. Mayer, "How Much Does a High School's Racial and Socioeconomic Mix Affect Graduation and Teenage Fertility Rates?" in Christopher Jencks and Paul E. Peterson, eds., *The Urban Underclass* (Brookings, 1991), pp. 323–24, 327. Wilson, *When Work Disappears*, p. 107; and Mickey Kaus, "The Work-Ethic State," *New Republic*, July 7, 1986, p. 24.

34. James Q. Wilson, *Two Nations* (Washington: American Enterprise Institute Press, 1998), p. 12 (citing Galston).

35. See Stuart Cleveland, "A Tardy Look at Stouffer's Findings in the Harvard Mobility Project," *Public Opinion Quarterly*, vol. 26 (1962), p. 453; Mayer, "How Much Does Racial and Socioeconomic Mix Affect Graduation and Teenage Fertility Rates?" p. 325. James S. Liebman, "Three Strategies for Implementing Brown Anew," in Herbert Hill and James E. Jones Jr., eds., *Race in America: The Struggle for Equality* (University of Wisconsin Press, 1993), p. 114; Peter B. Edelman, "Toward a Comprehensive Antipoverty Strategy: Getting beyond the Silver Bullet," *Georgetown Law Journal*, vol. 81 (1993), p. 1736.

36. Fischer and others, *Inequality by Design*, pp. 83–84. Henry M. Levin, "Education, Life Chances, and the Courts: The Role of Social Science Evidence," in Nelson F. Ashline, Thomas Pezzullo, and Charles I. Norris, eds., *Education, Inequality, and National Policy* (Lexington, Mass.: Lexington Books, 1976), pp. 85–86 (citing Thomas I. Ribich and James L. Murphy, "The Economic Returns to Increased Educational Spending," *Journal of Human Resources*, vol. 10, no. 1 [Winter 1975], pp. 56–77).

37. Jonathan Crane, "The Epidemic Theory of Ghettos and Neighborhood Effects on Dropping Out and Teenage Childbearing," *American Journal of Sociology*, vol. 5 (March 1991), p. 1248; see also Lippman and others, *Urban Schools*, p. 4, and the discussion in chapter 8.

38. Fischer and others, *Inequality by Design*, p. 250. In addition to those studies cited below, see, for example, William Julius Wilson, *The Truly Disadvantaged: The Inner City, the Underclass, and Public Policy* (University of Chicago Press, 1987), pp. 21–29; Wilson, *When Work Disappears*, pp. 265, 270; Glenn C. Loury, "The Hard Questions: Comparative Disadvantage; Economists Increasingly Realizing That Achievement Is Not Solely Dependent on Ability and Effort," *New Republic*, October 13, 1997, p. 29; Orfield and Eaton, *Dismantling Desegregation*, p. 311; Ronald B. Mincy, "The Underclass: Concept, Controversy, and Evidence," in Sheldon H. Danziger, Gary Sandefur, and Daniel Weinberg, eds., *Confronting Poverty: Prescriptions for Change* (New York: Russell Sage Foundation/Harvard University Press, 1994), pp. 119–20; Fischer and oth-

ers, *Inequality by Design*, pp. 250 n. 10, 253 n. 31, 273 n. 63; Mayer, "How Much Does Racial and Socioeconomic Mix Affect Graduation and Teenage Fertility Rates?" p. 324; Hogan and Kitagawa, "The Impact of Social Status," pp. 825, 846; Gonzales and others, "Family, Peer, and Neighborhood Influences on Academic Achievement," p. 367; Lippman and others, *Urban Schools*, pp. 3–4; Gephart, "Neighborhoods and Communities as Context for Development," pp. 35–38; Karin L. Brewster, "Race Differences in Sexual Activity among Adolescent Women: The Role of Neighborhood Characteristics," *American Sociological Review*, vol. 59 (June 1994), p. 421; George A. Akerloff, "Social Distance and Social Decisions," *Econometrica*, vol. 65 (September 1997); Cutler and Glaeser, "Are Ghettos Good or Bad," p. 829; Edwin S. Mills and Luan Sende Lubuele, "Inner Cities," *Journal of Economic Literature*, vol. 35 (June 1997), pp. 752–53; Robert J. Sampson, "Neighborhood Context of Investing in Children: Facilitating Mechanisms and Undermining Risks," in Danziger and Waldfogel, *Securing the Future*, p. 11; Alan B. Krueger, "Economic Scene," *New York Times*, March 30, 2000, p. C2.

Some researchers find small neighborhood effects; see, for example, Roderick J. Harrison and Claudette E. Bennett, "Racial and Ethnic Diversity," in Reynolds Farley, ed., *State of the Union: America in the 1990s*, 2 vols. (New York: Russell Sage Foundation, 1995), vol. 1, *Economic Trends*, pp. 146 and 197–99; Michael Kremer, "How Much Does Sorting Increase Equality?" *Quarterly Journal of Economics*, vol. 112, no. 1 (February 1997), pp. 135–37; Jencks and Mayer, "The Social Consequences of Growing Up in a Poor Neighborhood" (finding insufficient number of studies to draw a strong conclusion). Since Jencks and Mayer's 1990 review, the latest evidence has cut in favor of neighborhood effects; see, for example, Paul A. Jargowsky, *Poverty and Place: Ghettos, Barrios, and the American City* (New York: Russell Sage Foundation, 1997), pp. 193–94, 4; Gephart, "Neighborhoods and Communities as Context for Development," p. 14 (noting that Jencks and Mayer's review found mixed evidence on neighborhood effects, but that "a growing body of research completed since their review has linked the geographic concentration of socioeconomic disadvantage and features of neighborhood social disorganization to outcomes for individuals and families"); Isabel Sawhill, "Comment," in Diane Ravitch, ed., *Brookings Papers on Education Policy, 1999* (Brookings, 1999), p. 412 (responding to Paul Peterson's citation to Jencks and Mayer, "The Social Consequences of Growing Up in a Poor Neighborhood," noting that "a much larger body of work now exists on 'neighborhood' and 'peer' effects").

39. Fischer and others, *Inequality by Design*, p. 83. Massey and Denton, *American Apartheid*, pp. 149, 169, and 178–79.

40. Susan E. Mayer and Christopher Jencks, "Growing Up in Poor Neighborhoods: How Much Does It Matter?" *Science*, March 17, 1989, p. 1441 (noting that "most social scientists seem to espouse what we call the 'contagion model' of neighborhood effects" while "economists assume that people base their decisions entirely on their own circumstances and long-term interests, not on their neighbors' ideas about what is sensible, desirable, or acceptable"); Loury, "Comparative Disadvantage," p. 29 (citing several studies in rigorous economics journals by economists who have now come around to the view that neighborhood matters a great deal).

41. Linda Datcher, "Effects of Community and Family Background on Achievement," *Review of Economics and Statistics*, vol. 64, no. 1 (1982), pp. 32, 33–39; Crane, "The Epidemic Theory of Ghettos," pp. 1230–31; Jencks and Mayer, "The Social Consequences of Growing Up in a Poor Neighborhood," p. 135.

42. Mary Corcoran and others, "Intergenerational Transmission of Education, Income, and Earnings" (unpublished paper, 1987), cited in Jonathan Crane, "Effects of Neighborhoods on Dropping Out of School and Teenage Childbearing," in Jencks and Peterson, *The Urban Underclass*, pp. 300–01 (Corcoran probably underestimates the effect of neighborhood because her study used zip codes rather than census tracts). Mary Corcoran and others, "Poverty and the Underclass: Effects of Family and Community Background on Economic Status," *American Economic Review*, vol. 80 (May 1990), p. 365.

43. James Rosenbaum and others, "Social Integration of Low-Income Black Adults in Middle-Class White Suburbs," *Social Problems*, vol. 38 (November 1991), pp. 48–61. Mark Pitsch, "Change in Housing Seen Improving Prospects for Poor Youth," *Education Week*, October 23, 1991, p. 5; James E. Rosenbaum and Susan J. Popkin, "Employment and Earnings of Low-Income Blacks Who Move to Montgomery County Suburbs," in Jencks and Peterson, *The Urban Underclass*, p. 342.

44. Susan J. Popkin, James E. Rosenbaum, and Patricia M. Meaden, "Labor Market Experience of Low-Income Black Women in Middle-Class Suburbs," *Journal of Policy Analysis and Management*, vol. 12 (1993), pp. 556, 558. Jargowsky, *Poverty and Place*, p. 194.

45. Crane, "Effects of Neighborhoods," pp. 303–07, 317; Paul E. Peterson, "The Urban Underclass and the Poverty Paradox," in Jencks and Peterson, *The Urban Underclass*, p. 20. Crane, "The Epidemic Theory of Ghettos," pp. 1226–59.

46. Gonzales and others, "Family, Peer, and Neighborhood Influences on Academic Achievement," pp. 365, 384.

47. Jens Ludwig, Greg Duncan, and Paul Hirschfield, "Urban Poverty and Juvenile Crime: Evidence from a Randomized Housing-Mobility Experiment," working paper, Joint Center for Poverty Research, Northwestern University and University of Chicago, 1998 (cited in Robert J. Sampson, "The Neighborhood Context of Investing in Children," in Danziger and Waldfogel, *Securing the Future*, p. 222).

48. See David L. Kirp, John P. Dwyer, and Larry A. Rosenthal, *Our Town: Race, Housing, and the Soul of Suburbia* (Rutgers University Press, 1995), p. 170. *Housing and Community Development Act*, 42 U.S.C. 5201–317, cited in Elizabeth Warren, *The Legacy of Judicial Policy Making: Gautreaux v. Chicago Housing Authority—The Decision and Its Impacts* (New York: University Press of America, 1988), p. 67. Senator Barbara Mikulski quoted in Karen De Witt, "Housing Voucher Test in Maryland Is Scuttled by a Political Firestorm," *New York Times*, March 28, 1995, p. B10; see also discussion of Moving to Opportunity in chapter 8.

49. Cisneros, quoted in David Rusk, *Cities without Suburbs*, 2d ed. (Washington: Woodrow Wilson Center Press, 1995), p. 117; see also Pam Belluck, "Razing the Slums to Rescue the Residents," *New York Times*, September 6, 1998, pp. 1, 26. John E. Yang, "House Approves Major Changes for Public Housing, Including Work Requirement," *Washington Post*, May 17, 1997, A10; Judith Havermann, "Hill Sets Changes for Public Housing," *Washington Post*, October 6, 1998, p. A4. Lazio, quoted in Judith Havermann, "Public Housing's Upscale Idea," *Washington Post*, April 18, 1998, pp. A1, A8.

50. Bok, *The State of the Nation*, p. 185; Derrick A. Bell, *Race, Racism, and American Law*, 3d ed. (Boston: Little, Brown, 1992), p. 602; Liebman, "Three Strategies for Implementing Brown Anew," p. 114; John C. Brittain, "Educational and Racial Equity toward the Twenty-first Century: A Case Experiment in Connecticut," in Hill and

Jones, *Race in America*, p. 175; Vivian Ipka, "The Effects of Changes in School Charac-
teristics Resulting from the Elimination of the Policy of Mandated Busing for Integra-
tion upon the Academic Achievement of African-American Students," *Education
Research Quarterly*, vol. 17 (1993), pp. 19, 21–23; Robert L. Crain and Rita E. Mahard,
"The Effect of Research Methodology on Desegregation-Achievement Studies: A
Meta-Analysis," *American Journal of Sociology*, vol. 88 (March 1983), pp. 839–40;
William L. Taylor, "*Brown*, Equal Protection, and the Isolation of the Poor," *Yale Law
Journal*, vol. 95 (1986), pp. 1710–11; Senate Select Committee on Equal Educational
Opportunity, *Report*, pp. 222–25; National Education Association (NEA), *Three Cities
That Are Making Desegregation Work* (Washington, 1984), p. 21; Ward Sinclair,
"Desegregation's Quiet Success," *Washington Post*, June 17, 1978, p. A10; Leonard
Buder, "Good Marks for Integration," *New York Times*, October 22, 1967, p. E9; Meyer
Weinberg, "The Relationship between School Desegregation and Academic Achieve-
ment: A Review of Research," *Law and Contemporary Problems*, vol. 39 (Spring 1975),
pp. 244, 268; Doris R. Entwisle and Karl L. Alexander, "Summer Setback: Race,
Poverty, School Composition, and Mathematics Achievement in the First Two Years of
School," *American Sociological Review*, vol. 57 (February 1992), p. 82; Benjamin F.
Turner and Joan S. Beers, "Harrisburg School District: Six Years after Desegregation,"
paper presented to the annual meeting of the American Education Research Associa-
tion, New York, April 7, 1977, p. 5; Rumberger and Willms, "The Impact of Racial and
Ethnic Segregation on the Achievement Gap," p. 379; Gerald David Jaynes and Robin
M. Williams Jr., eds., *A Common Destiny: Blacks and American Society* (Washington:
National Academy Press, 1989), p. 80, 374; powell, "Segregation and Educational Inad-
equacy in Twin Cities Public Schools," pp. 342–43; Orfield, interview, p. 21; James S.
Liebman, "Desegregating Politics: 'All-Out' School Desegregation Explained," *Colum-
bia Law Review*, vol. 90 (October 1990), pp. 1463, 1624–26; Jencks and Mayer, "The
Social Consequences of Growing Up in a Poor Neighborhood," pp. 55–65; Robert L.
Crain and Rita E. Mahard, "Minority Achievement Policy Implications of Research,"
in Willis D. Hawley, ed., *Effective School Desegregation* (Beverly Hills, Calif.: Sage Publications, 1981); Gayl Shaw Westerman, "The Promise of State Constitutionalism: Can
It Be Fulfilled in *Sheff* v. *O'Neill?*" *Hastings Constitutional Law Quarterly*, vol. 23 (Winter 1996), pp. 351, 400.

For a contrary view, see David J. Armor, "The Evidence on Busing," *Public Interest*,
vol. 28 (Summer 1972), pp. 90–126 (finding no conclusive evidence of achievement).
For a response to Armor, see Thomas F. Pettigrew and others, "Busing: A Review of
'The Evidence,'" *Public Interest*, vol. 30 (Winter 1973), pp. 88–113. In 1995, Armor was
still skeptical about achievement gains, but he conceded that several studies had found
positive effects; David J. Armor, *Forced Justice: School Desegregation and the Law* (New
York: Oxford University Press, 1995), p. 70.

51. Robert L. Crain and Rita E. Mahard, *Desegregation and Black Achievement*
(Santa Monica, Calif.: Rand, 1977), pp. 5, 8. Robert L. Crain and Rita E. Mahard, *Deseg-
regation Plans That Raise Black Achievement: A Review of the Research* (Santa Monica,
Calif.: Rand, 1982), p. v; Rita E. Mahard and Robert L. Crain, "Research on Minority
Achievement in Desegregated Schools," in Christine H. Rossell and Willis D. Hawley,
eds., *The Consequences of School Desegregation* (Temple University Press, 1983), p. 115.
Amy Stuart Wells, "Reexamining Social Science Research on School Desegregation:
Long-Term versus Short-Term Effects," *Teachers College Record*, vol. 96 (Summer 1995),

p. 694; see also Jencks and Mayer, "The Social Consequences of Growing Up in a Poor Neighborhood," p. 149.

52. Janet Ward Schofield, "Review of Research on School Segregation's Impact on Elementary and Secondary School Students," in James A. Banks, ed., *Handbook of Research on Multicultural Education* (New York: Macmillan Publishing, 1995), pp. 597–616. powell, "Living and Learning," p. 789. Amy Stuart Wells and Robert L. Crain, *Stepping over the Color Line: African-American Students in White Suburban Schools* (Yale University Press, 1997), p. 1.

53. Smith and O'Day, "Educational Equality," pp. 75–77; see also Bok, *The State of the Nation*, p. 186; Jencks and Phillips, "The Black-White Test Score Gap," p. 24. Jack Greenberg, *Crusaders in the Courts* (Basic Books, 1994), p. 398. Some of the rise can probably be attributed to improvements in parental education and decreases in family size, but these factors explain only one-third of the black gains; scores appear to have risen because of desegregation or compensatory education spending (or both); see David Grissmer and others, *Student Achievement and the Changing American Family* (Santa Monica, Calif.: Rand, 1994), pp. xxvi, xxxvii, xxxviii, 7–8, 100–01, 106, 109.

54. See David Grissmer, Ann Flanagan, and Stephanie Williamson, "Why Did the Black-White Score Gap Narrow in the 1970s and 1980s?" in Jencks and Phillips, *The Black-White Test Score Gap*, pp. 191, 207–11; Smith and O'Day, "Educational Equality," p. 81. For evidence of the widening gap since 1988, see Stephan Thernstrom and Abigail Thernstrom, *America in Black and White: One Nation, Indivisible* (Simon and Schuster, 1997), p. 339; Jennifer A. O'Day and Marshall S. Smith, "Systematic Reform and Educational Opportunity," in Susan Fuhrman, ed., *Designing Coherent Education Policy* (San Francisco: Jossey-Bass, 1993), pp. 255–56; Bok and Bowen, *The Shape of the River*, p. 23.

55. Puma and others, *Prospects: Final Report*, p. 12. Debora Sullivan and Robert Crain, cited in James S. Kunen, "The End of Integration," *Time*, April 29, 1996, pp. 39, 44.

56. Crain and Mahard, *Desegregation Plans That Raise Black Achievement*, pp. vi, 28; Jennifer L. Hochschild, *The New American Dilemma: Liberal Democracy and School Desegregation* (Yale University Press, 1984), pp. 54–55; Liebman, "Desegregating Politics," pp. 1463, 1625 n. 675.

57. See discussion of the success of interdistrict and metropolitan plans in chapter 7 (for achievement gains in Wilmington, Hartford, Charlotte, and St. Louis); see also JoAnn Grozuczak Goedert, "Case Comment, *Jenkins v. Missouri:* The Future of Interdistrict School Desegregation," *Georgetown Law Review*, vol. 76 (June 1988), p. 1880 (Nashville and Louisville); NEA, *Three Cities That Are Making Desegregation Work*, p. 19 (Charlotte-Mecklenburg); powell, "Living and Learning," p. 789 (Louisville). Crain and Mahard, *Desegregation Plans that Raise Black Achievement*, p. 29; see also Mahard and Crain, "Research on Minority Achievement," pp. 117–18; Taylor, "*Brown*, Equal Protection, and the Isolation of the Poor," p. 1710; J. Harvie Wilkinson III, *From Brown to Bakke: The Supreme Court and School Integration, 1954–1978* (New York: Oxford University Press, 1979), p. 177; Gary Orfield and Lawrence Peskin, "Metropolitan High Schools: Income, Race, and Inequality," in Douglas E. Mitchell and Margaret E. Goertz, eds., *Education Politics for the New Century* (New York: Falmer Press, 1990), p. 43.

58. Goedert, "Case Comment: *Jenkins v. Missouri*," p. 1880. Amy Stuart Wells and Robert L. Crain, "Perpetuation Theory and the Long-Term Effects of School Desegregation," *Review of Educational Research*, vol. 64 (Winter 1994), pp. 531–32.

59. Coleman and others, *Equality of Educational Opportunity*, p. 307. James S. Coleman, "Integration, Yes; Busing, No," *New York Times Magazine*, August 24, 1975, p. 10. See also Coleman and others, *Equality of Educational Opportunity*, pp. 307–10; Coleman, "Equality of Educational Opportunity," *Integrated Education*, vol. 6 (September–October 1968), p. 25; Christopher Jencks, "A Reappraisal of the Most Controversial Educational Document of Our Time," *New York Times Magazine*, August 10, 1969, p. 13; Dick Hubert, "Class and the Classroom: The Duluth Experience," *Saturday Review of Education*, May 27, 1972, p. 55; Diane Ravitch, *The Troubled Crusade: American Education, 1945–1980* (Basic Books, 1983), p. 169; "Moynihan Believes Class Is the Issue" (an interview with Daniel P. Moynihan), *Southern Education Report*, May 1967, pp. 7, 9. For others who emphasize that poor blacks will not benefit academically from exposure to poor whites, see, for example, John A. Finger Jr., "Why School Busing Plans Work," in Florence Hamlish Levinsohn and Benjamin Drake Wright, eds., *School Desegregation: Shadow and Substance* (University of Chicago Press, 1976), p. 63; Wilkinson, *From Brown to Bakke*, p. 220; and Wilson, "Educational Consequences of Segregation in a California Community," p. 203.

60. Mosteller and Moynihan, "A Pathbreaking Report," in *On Equality of Educational Opportunity*, p. 22.

61. See, for example, U.S. Commission on Civil Rights, *Racial Isolation*, vol. 1, pp. 89, 90 (the twelfth-grade performance of a poor black student who attended a middle-class all-black school is likely to be a year and a half beyond that of a poor black student who attended a poor all-black school); Alan B. Wilson, *The Consequences of Segregation: Academic Achievement in a Northern Community* (Berkeley, Calif.: Glendessary Press, 1969), p. 35; Wilson, "Educational Consequences of Segregation in a California Community," p. 184; Rodgers and Bullock, "School Desegregation: Successes and Failures," p. 141; U.S. Commission on Civil Rights, *Racial Isolation*, vol. 2, p. 181; Robert F. Herriott and Nancy Hoyt St. John, *Social Class and the Urban School: The Impact of Pupil Background on Teachers and Principals* (New York: John Wiley and Sons, 1966), p. 196; Nancy Hoyt St. John, *Minority Group Performance under Various Conditions of School Ethnic and Economic Integration: A Review of Research* (New York: ERIC Clearinghouse for Urban Disadvantaged, 1968), p. 1; James Conant, *Slums and Suburbs* (McGraw-Hill, 1961), p. 30; Wilson, *The Consequences of Segregation*, pp. vii–viii, 27, 29, 32–34, 66; Charles Silberman, *Crisis in the Classroom* (Random House, 1970), p. 74; Alexander M. Bickel, *The Supreme Court and the Idea of Progress* (Harper and Row, 1970), p. 137; Department of Health, Education, and Welfare, *The Effectiveness of Compensatory Education*, pp. 172–73; Senate Select Committee on Equal Educational Opportunity, *Report*, pp. 23–24, 32, 42, 189, 220, 235, 269–70; Crain and Mahard, *Desegregation Plans That Raise Black Achievement*, p. 3; David T. Cohen, Thomas F. Pettigrew, and Robert T. Riley, "Race and the Outcomes of Schooling," in Mosteller and Moynihan, *On Equality of Educational Opportunity*, p. 345; Jencks, "The Coleman Report and the Conventional Wisdom," p. 71; Nancy Hoyt St. John, *School Desegregation Outcomes for Children* (New York: John Wiley and Sons, 1975), pp. 95–97; Chubb and Moe, *Politics, Markets, and American Schools*, p. 127; Mayer, "How Much Does a High School's Racial and Socioeconomic Mix Affect Graduation and Teenage Fertility Rates?" in Jencks and Peterson, *The Urban Underclass*, pp. 328–29; William L. Yancey and Salvatore J. Saporito, *Racial and Economic Segregation and Educational Outcomes: One Tale, Two Cities* (Philadelphia: Temple University Center for Research in Human Development and Education,

1995), pp. 27–28; David Rusk, quoted in Andrew Trotter, "Teachers Propose Integrating Schools by Socioeconomic Status," *Education Week*, December 2, 1998. Jodi Berls and others, "Schools Face Revival of Segregation," *Austin American-Statesman*, June 29, 1997, p. A1; Puma and others, *Prospects: Final Report*, p. 73; Chaplin and Hannaway, *African American High Scorers Project*, Technical Report 2, pp. 23, 40. For a rare contrary finding, see Cutler and Glaeser, "Are Ghettos Good or Bad?" pp. 829, 963.

62. Gary Orfield, *Must We Bus? Segregated Schools and National Policy* (Brookings, 1978), p. 69. See discussion in chapter 8.

63. See, for example, Orfield, *Must We Bus?* p. 105; David Cohen, "Policy for the Public Schools: Compensation and Integration," in *Harvard Educational Review: Equal Educational Opportunity*, pp. 94–95; Ravitch, *The Troubled Crusade*, p. 172; U.S. Commission on Civil Rights, *Racial Isolation*, vol. 1, pp. 95–96, 129; Neil V. Sullivan, "Compensation and Integration: The Berkeley Experience," in *Harvard Educational Review: Equal Educational Opportunity*, pp. 220–25; "If Not Busing, What?" *Time*, April 24, 1972, p. 61. Orfield and Eaton, *Dismantling Desegregation*, pp. 89–91, 132–33; see also powell, "Segregation and Educational Inadequacy in Twin Cities Public Schools," p. 343. Edelman, "Toward a Comprehensive Antipoverty Strategy," pp. 1740–41 (citing Orfield's San Francisco study); see also Gary Orfield and David Thronson, "Dismantling Desegregation: Uncertain Gains, Unexpected Costs," *Emory Law Journal*, vol. 42 (1993), pp. 782–83 (describing San Francisco study).

64. See the discussion of St. Louis in chapter 7. Wells and Crain, *Stepping over the Color Line*, pp. 98, 102; see also "Quality Counts '98: The Urban Challenge," *Education Week*, January 8, 1998, p. 21; Thernstrom and Thernstrom, *America in Black and White*, pp. 345–46. Orfield and Thronson, "Dismantling Desegregation," p. 782; *Missouri v. Jenkins*, 115 S. Ct. 2038, 2042–45 (1995) (regarding what the money went to).

65. Kozol, interview with Ted Koppel, ABC News, *Nightline*, September 17, 1992. James Guthrie, quoted in Trine Tsouderos, "Kids in the City's Poor Schools Get Worse Scores," *Tennessean*, December 27, 1998.

66. Mickey Kaus, *The End of Equality* (Basic Books, 1992), p. 109.

67. See, for example, Owen M. Fiss, "Racial Imbalance in the Public Schools," *Harvard Law Review*, vol. 78 (1965), p. 567. Ross Mills, letter to author, November 2, 1997 (Mills is a teacher in Bethesda, Maryland).

68. See, for example, John Rawls, *A Theory of Justice* (Harvard University Press, 1971), p. 179.

69. See, for example, Bok, *The State of the Nation*, p. 185; Coleman, "Toward Open Schools," p. 22; Weinberg, "The Relationship between School Desegregation and Academic Achievement," p. 243; Jaynes and Williams, *A Common Destiny*, pp. 19, 374; Hochschild, *The New American Dilemma*, p. 63; Jencks and Phillips, introduction, *The Black-White Test Score Gap*, p. 26; powell, "Segregation and Educational Inadequacy in Twin Cities Public Schools," p. 342; Liebman, "Desegregating Politics," p. 1621; Westerman, "The Promise of State Constitutionalism," p. 402.

70. "Backing the Bus," *New Republic*, February 24, 1982, p. 7; Liebman, "Three Strategies for Implementing *Brown*," p. 119; Aric Press and others, "Not Enough White Children," *Newsweek*, September 15, 1980, p. 102; Orfield, *Must We Bus?* p. 123. Crain and Mahard, *Desegregation and Black Achievement*, p. 2; see also Crain and Mahard, "The Effect of Research Methodology," p. 840; Orfield, *Must We Bus?* pp. 121–24. Armor, *Forced Justice*, p. 71.

71. Crane, "Effects of Neighborhoods," p. 317; Mayer, "How Much Does a High School's Racial and Socioeconomic Mix Affect Graduation and Teenage Fertility Rates?" p. 324; Willms, "Social Class Segregation," p. 226; Brooks-Gunn and others, "Do Neighborhoods Influence Child and Adolescent Development?" pp. 359–60; Smith and O'Day, "Educational Equality," p. 63; Jencks and Mayer, "The Social Consequences of Growing Up in a Poor Neighborhood," pp. 151–52; Turner, *The Social Context of Ambition*, p. 104.

72. Crane, "The Epidemic Theory of Ghettos," pp. 1241, 1227, 1236, 1240, 1231 (citing Hogan and Kitagawa, "The Impact of Social Status"); see also Jencks and Mayer, "The Social Consequences of Growing Up in a Poor Neighborhood," p. 123 (citing nonlinear findings of Hogan and Kitagawa, "The Impact of Social Status"). Crane, "Effects of Neighborhoods," p. 318 ("desegregation by class [and race to the extent that it is correlated with class] should be actively encouraged"); Henderson, Mieszkowski, and Sauvageau, "Peer Group Effects and Educational Production Functions," pp. 98–99, 105.

73. See U.S. Commission on Civil Rights, *Racial Isolation*, vol. 1, p. 160 (integration did not reduce white achievement when the student body was more than 50 percent white; twelfth-grade whites perform as well when the class is more than half white as when it is all white); Pettigrew, "Race and Equal Educational Opportunity," p. 74 (noting the commission's data demonstrated that "the achievement scores of white children in biracial classes with 'more than half' white students average just as high as those of comparable children in all-white classes"); Department of Health, Education and Welfare, *The Effectiveness of Compensatory Education*, appendix T, p. 176 (reviewing studies that found "there is no evidence that desegregation reduces white achievement as long as a half or more white situation exists"); "Moynihan Believes Class Is the Issue," p. 7 ("the finding of the Coleman study as interpreted by and extended by the U.S. Civil Rights Commission report on racial isolation suggests that so long as the majority of students in a group, in a class, in a school, are of a fairly middle or upper socio-economic status, [white middle-class children's] achievement is not going to be affected by bringing into that schoolchildren of whatever race from a lower economic status. But they do make the point that it has to remain a majority"); Bell, *Race, Racism, and American Law*, pp. 739–40 (citing Downs on the importance of a majority-middle-class environment); Orland, "Demographics of Disadvantage," pp. 52–53 (that the poverty-achievement relationship is twice as great moving from medium- to high-poverty schools as from low- to medium-poverty schools).

74. James Coleman, "Class Integration: A Fundamental Break with the Past" (interview with Dick Hubert), *Saturday Review*, May 27, 1972, p. 59 (no detrimental impact on middle-class children so long as school is roughly 60 percent middle class). See, for example, Puma and others, *Prospects: Final Report*, p. 6; Department of Education, "Promising Results, Continuing Challenges: Final Report of the National Assessment of Title I—Highlights" (www.ed.gov/offices/OUS/eval/ hlights.html [March 2, 1999]); and Heather C. Hill, David K. Cohen, and Susan L. Moffitt, "Instruction, Poverty, and Performance," in Orfield and DeBray, *Hard Work for Good Schools*, p. 58 (70 percent is high poverty.) By analogy, in the neighborhood context, researchers normally define census tracts with more than 40 percent poverty rates as constituting ghetto or underclass neighborhoods—the rough equivalent of an 80 percent FARM rate. For the consensus around the 40 percent neighborhood poverty rate, see Wilson, *When Work Dis-*

appears, p. 12; Paul A. Jargowsky and Mary Jo Bane, "Ghetto Poverty in the United States, 1970–1980," in Jencks and Peterson, *The Urban Underclass*, p. 239; Brooks-Gunn and others, "Do Neighborhoods Influence Child and Adolescent Development?" p. 359; Jargowsky, *Poverty and Place*, pp. 9–11; Lippman and others, *Urban Schools*, p. 18. Recall that the FARM rate is about double the poverty rate and that students are eligible at 185 percent of the poverty line.

75. Anderson, Hollinger, and Conaty, *Poverty and Achievement*, pp. 2–5. In the first sentence, the authors speak of students from "poverty" rather than low-income students, but it is clear from the context that they are referring to students eligible for free or reduced-price lunch. The authors also note that while Chapter 1 provided special treatment to schools with poverty rates in excess of 75 percent, students in schools in the 50–75 percent category "are performing significantly less well than the students in the schools with 31–50 percent poor children"; see also Puma and others, *Prospects: Final Report*, p. 12 (noting 1993 National Assessment of Chapter 1 found "the poverty level of certain schools placed disadvantaged students in double jeopardy. School poverty depresses the scores of all students in schools where at least half of the students are eligible for subsidized lunch and seriously depresses the scores when over 75 percent of students live in low-income households").

76. See Rusk, "To Improve Public Education, Stop Moving Money," 6–7. Jargowsky, *Poverty and Place*, p. 24; Anthony Downs, *New Visions for Metropolitan America* (Brookings, 1994), pp. 70–71.

77. Malcolm Gladwell, *The Tipping Point: How Little Things Can Make a Big Difference* (Boston: Little Brown, 2000), pp. 11, 138, and 150.

78. E. D. Hirsch, *The Schools We Need and Why We Don't Have Them* (Doubleday, 1996), p. 45. Coleman, "Toward Open Schools," p. 21; Coleman and others, *Equality of Educational Opportunity*, pp. 297, 304–05, 22; Rodgers and Bullock, "School Desegregation: Successes and Failures," p. 140; Irwin Katz, "Academic Motivation and Equal Educational Opportunity," *Harvard Education Review: Equal Educational Opportunity*, p. 60.

79. Coleman, "Equality of Educational Opportunity," p. 24; David Ausubel and Pearl Ausubel, "Ego Development among Segregated Negro Children," in Passow, *Education in Depressed Areas*, p. 113; Brooks-Gunn and others, "Do Neighborhoods Influence Child and Adolescent Development?" p. 360; Judith Ide and others, "Peer Group Influence on Educational Outcomes: A Quantitative Synthesis," *Journal of Educational Psychology*, vol. 73 (1981), pp. 472–84; Doris Entwisle, Karl L. Alexander, and Linda Steffell Olson, *Children, Schools, and Inequality* (New York: Westview Press, 1997), p. 107; Lippman and others, *Urban Schools*, pp. 64–65; Laurence Steinberg, "Single Parents, Stepparents, and Susceptibility of Adolescents to Antisocial Peer Pressure," *Child Development*, vol. 58 (1987), pp. 269–74.

80. Sara McLanahan and Lynne Casper, "Growing Diversity and Inequality in the American Family," in Farley, *State of the Union*, vol. 2, pp. 2-3; Paul Barton and Richard Coley, *America's Smallest School: The Family* (Princeton, N.J.: Educational Testing Service, 1992), p. 2

81. Wilson, "Social Class and Equal Educational Opportunity," p. 87. Jencks and Mayer, "The Social Consequences of Growing Up in a Poor Neighborhood," p. 124. Orfield, interview, p. 23.

82. See, for example, Pettigrew, "Race and Equal Educational Opportunity," p. 72; U.S. Commission on Civil Rights, *Racial Isolation*, vol. 1, p. 85; vol. 2, p. 187; Jencks,

"The Coleman Report and the Conventional Wisdom," p. 71; St. John, *Minority Group Performance under Various Conditions*, p. 12; Marshall S. Smith, "Basic Findings Reconsidered," in Mosteller and Moynihan, *On Equality of Educational Opportunity*, p. 312; Victor Battistich and others, "Schools as Communities, Poverty Levels of Student Populations, and Students' Attitudes, Motives, and Performance: A Multilevel Analysis," *American Educational Research Journal*, vol. 32 (Fall 1995), pp. 627, 628, 631, 649; Susan E. Mayer, "How Much Does a High School's Racial and Socioeconomic Mix Affect Graduation and Teenage Fertility Rates?" pp. 329–34; Paul Peterson, *City Limits* (University of Chicago Press, 1981), pp. 102–03; Laurence B. Steinberg and others, *Noninstructional Influences on High School Student Achievement: The Contributions of Parents, Peers, Extracurricular Activities, and Part-Time Work* (Madison, Wisc.: National Center on Effective Secondary Schools, 1988), p. 42; Willms, "Social Class Segregation," p. 226; Nina S. Mounts and Laurence Steinberg, "An Ecological Analysis of Peer Influence on Adolescent Grade Point Average and Drug Use," *Developmental Psychology*, vol. 31 (1995), pp. 919–20; Gonzales and others, "Family, Peer, and Neighborhood Influences on Academic Achievement," pp. 366, 369–70, and 379; Hirsch, *The Schools We Need and Why We Don't Have Them*, p. 45; Crane, "The Epidemic Theory of Ghettos," pp. 1227, 1236; Jencks and Phillips, "The Black-White Test Score Gap," p. 27; Entwisle and Alexander, "Summer Setback," p. 73; Lippman and others, *Urban Schools*, pp. 2–3; Laurence Steinberg, *Beyond the Classroom: Why School Reform Has Failed and What Parents Need to Do* (Simon and Schuster, 1996), p. 135; Summers and Wolfe, "Do Schools Make a Difference?" pp. 644 and 647; Rumberger and Willms, "The Impact of Racial and Ethnic Segregation on the Achievement Gap," p. 379; Cutler and Glaeser, "Are Ghettos Good or Bad?" p. 828; Jencks and Peterson, introduction to *The Urban Underclass*, p. 29; Grissmer, Flanagan, and Williamson, "Why Did the Black-White Score Gap Narrow?" p. 214; Ronald F. Ferguson, "Teachers' Perceptions and Expectations and the Black-White Test Score Gap," Jencks and Phillips, *The Black-White Test Score Gap*, pp. 286–87; Chaplin and Hannaway, *Schools and Neighborhood Factors and SAT Performance*, p. 21.

83. Rodgers and Bullock, "School Desegregation: Successes and Failures," p. 140; O. J. Harvey and Jeanne Rutherford, "Status in the Informal Group: Influence and Influencibility at Differing Age Levels," *Child Development*, vol. 31 (June 1960), p. 385; Kenneth P. Langton, "Peer Group and School and the Political Socialization Process," *American Political Science Review*, vol. 61, no. 3 (September 1967), pp. 755–58.

84. Adam Gamoran, "High Standards: A Strategy for Equalizing Opportunities to Learn?" in Richard D. Kahlenberg, ed., *A Notion at Risk: Preserving Public Education as an Engine for Social Mobility* (Century Foundation Press, 2000), p. 97. See also Coleman and others, *Equality of Educational Opportunity*, p. 296 (more than 70 percent of the variation in achievement is within a student body and only 10–20 percent between schools).

85. Departments of Education and Justice, *Annual Report on School Safety, 1998* (Government Printing Office, October 1998), p. 3. Vincent Schiradli, "Hyping School Violence," *Washington Post*, August 25, 1998, p. A15.

86. Departments of Education and Justice, *Annual Report on School Safety, 1998*, pp. 2, 7; Delbert S. Elliott, Beatrix A. Hamburg, and Kirk R. Williams, eds., introduction to *Violence in American Schools: A New Perspective* (Cambridge: Cambridge University Press, 1998), p. 6. Department of Education, cited in Paul Barton, Richard J. Coley, and

Harold Wenglinsky, *Order in the Classroom: Violence, Discipline, and Student Achievement* (Princeton, N.J.: Educational Testing Service, 1998), p. 5; Bill McAllister, "Clinton Promotes Education Plans," *Washington Post*, May 9, 1998, p. 8 (fewer than 1 percent of students ever bring a gun to school).

87. See Joy D. Osofsky, "Children and Youth Violence," in Joy D. Osofsky, ed., *Children in a Violent Society* (New York: Guilford Press, 1997), pp. 3–4; Joy D. Osofsky, "The Violence Intervention Project," in Osofsky, *Children in a Violent Society*, pp. 256–57.

88. See, for example, Steinberg, *Beyond the Classroom*, p. 148; Crane, "The Epidemic Theory of Ghettos," p. 1227; Mincy, "The Underclass Concept, Controversy, and Evidence," p. 119; Ausubel and Ausubel, "Ego Development among Segregated Negro Children," p. 117; Kremer, "How Much Does Sorting Increase Inequality?" p. 135; Sampson, "Neighborhood Context of Investing in Children," p. 36; Margaret Hamburg, "Youth Violence Is a Public Health Concern," in Elliott, Hamburg, and Williams, *Violence in American Schools*, p. 45; John H. Laub and Janet L. Lauritsen, "The Interdependence of School Violence with Neighborhood and Family Conditions," in Elliott, Hamburg, and Williams, *Violence in American Schools*, pp. 144–45; James M. McPartland and Edward L. McDill, "Control and Differentiation in the Structure of American Education," *Sociology of Education*, vol. 55 (April–July 1982), p. 81; Gephart, "Neighborhoods and Communities as Context for Development," pp. 30, 39; Malcolm Gladwell, "Do Parents Matter?" *New Yorker*, August 17, 1998, p. 59; Harris, *The Nurture Assumption*, pp. 212–13, 259.

89. Thomas Geoghegan, *The Secret Lives of Citizens: Pursuing the Promise of American Life* (Pantheon Books, 1999), p. 206. Botstein, *Jefferson's Children*, p. 64.

90. Harrison and Bennett, "Racial and Ethnic Diversity," p. 164; Orfield and others, *The Growth of Segregation in American Schools*, pp. 21–22; Brooks-Gunn and others, "Do Neighborhoods Influence Child and Adolescent Development?" p. 367. Richard D. Kahlenberg, "Economic School Desegregation," *Education Week*, March 31, 1999.

91. U.S. Census Bureau, *Poverty in the United States, 1999* (Washington: U.S. Government Printing Office, 2000), pp. 28–30. Massey and Denton, *American Apartheid*, pp. 124, 12, 118, 140–41. Rusk, *Inside Game/Outside Game*, pp. 71–72, 79.

92. Orfield and others, *Deepening Segregation in American Public Schools*, (Cambridge: Harvard Project on School Desegregation, April 5, 1997), p. 2.

93. *Milliken v. Bradley*, 418 U.S. 717 (1974), 783 (Marshall, J., dissenting); see, for example, Charles V. Willie and Jerome Baker, *Race Mixing in Public Schools* (Praeger, 1973), p. 3.

94. Jomills Henry Braddock II, Robert L. Crain, and James M. McPartland, "A Long-Term View of School Desegregation: Some Recent Studies of Graduates as Adults," *Phi Delta Kappan*, vol. 66, no. 4 (December 1984), p. 260; Bok, *The State of the Nation*, p. 185. Even high-status blacks (who can most easily afford to live in white neighborhoods) are less likely to live in an integrated neighborhood if they attend segregated schools than lower-class blacks who attend integrated schools; Cohen, "Policy for the Public Schools," p. 108; see also "Study Finds Desegregation Is an Effective Tool," *New York Times*, September 17, 1985, p. C1.

95. See Nancy A. Denton, "The Persistence of Segregation: Links between Residential Segregation and School Segregation," *Minnesota Law Review*, vol. 80 (April 1996), pp. 822–23. Liebman, "Desegregating Politics," pp. 1626–27. Thernstrom and Thernstrom, *America in Black and White*, p. 526; G. Pascal Zachary, *The Global Me* (New York: Public Affairs Press, 2000), p. 10.

96. Richard D. Kahlenberg, *The Remedy: Race, Class, and Affirmative Action* (Basic Books, 1996), pp. 186–88. Rustin, quoted in Kahlenberg, *The Remedy*, p. 189. Clifford Alexander, "Declare War on Bigotry," *Washington Post*, May 22, 1997, p. A25.

Chapter Four

1. Dr. Charles Pinderhughes, quoted in U.S. Commission on Civil Rights, *Racial Isolation in the Public Schools*, vol. 1 (Government Printing Office, 1967), p. 82. Coleman, interview with Dick Hubert, "Class Integration—A Fundamental Break with the Past," *Saturday Review*, May 27, 1972, p. 59. Richard P. Boyle, "The Effects of the High School on Students' Aspirations," *American Journal of Sociology*, vol. 71, no. 6 (1966), p. 631. James S. Coleman, *The Adolescent Society: The Social Life of the Teenager and Its Impact on Education* (Glencoe, Ill.: Free Press, 1961), p. 5; the students found it hardest to accept the disapproval of parents (53 percent).

2. See, generally, J. Douglas Willms, "Social Class Segregation and Its Relationship to Pupils' Examination Results in Scotland," *American Sociological Review*, vol. 51 (April 1986), p. 225; Judith K. Ide and others, "Peer Group Influence on Educational Outcomes: A Quantitative Synthesis," *Journal of Educational Psychology*, vol. 73 (1981), p. 483; Kirk A. Johnson, "The Peer Effect on Academic Achievement among Public Elementary School Students: A Report of the Heritage Center for Data Analysis" (Washington: Heritage Foundation, May 2000); Laura Sessions Stepp, "New Study Questions Teen Risk Factors: School Woes, Peers Are Stronger than Race, Income," *Washington Post*, November 30, 2000, p. A1 (citing study by Robert Blum). Laurence Steinberg, *Beyond the Classroom: Why School Reform Has Failed and What Parents Need to Do* (New York: Simon and Schuster, 1996), pp. 138, 148. On the influence of family on a child's future success, see the discussion in chapter 8.

3. Malcolm Gladwell, "Do Parents Matter?" *New Yorker*, August 17, 1998, p. 63. Judith Rich Harris, *The Nurture Assumption: Why Children Turn Out the Way They Do* (New York: Free Press, 1998), pp. 10, 204, 191, 281.

4. Jeanne S. Chall, Vicky A. Jacobs, and Luke Baldwin, *The Reading Crisis: Why Poor Children Fall Behind* (Harvard University Press, 1990), p. 2. See James S. Coleman and others, *Equality of Educational Opportunity* (Government Printing Office, 1966), pp. 298–300; see also Larry V. Hedges and Amy Nowell, "Black-White Test Score Convergence since 1965," in Christopher Jencks and Meredith Phillips, eds., *The Black-White Test Score Gap* (Brookings, 1998), p. 161.

5. See, for example, Sandra G. Boodman, "Researchers Put Number on U.S. Hunger," *Washington Post*, March 31, 1998, Health sec., p. 7; Derek Bok, *The State of the Nation* (Harvard University Press, 1996), p. 160; Marie Carbo, "Educating Everybody's Children," in Richard W. Cole, ed., *Educating Everybody's Children: Diverse Teaching Strategies for Diverse Learners—What Research and Practice Say about Improving Achievement* (Alexandria, Va.: Association for Supervision and Curriculum Development, 1995), p. 5. Low-income children are also much more likely to be have been low-birth-weight babies, which is associated with learning deficiencies and malformation of brain cells; see Jeanne Brooks-Gunn, Greg J. Duncan, and Nancy Maritato, "Poor Families, Poor Outcomes: The Well-Being of Children and Youth," in Greg J. Duncan and Jeanne Brooks-Gunn, eds., *Consequences of Growing Up Poor* (New York: Russell Sage Foundation, 1997), p. 10. Low-income children are twice as likely to miss school for

medical reasons as middle-class children; Marshall S. Smith and Jennifer O'Day, "Educational Equality: 1966 and Now," in Deborah A. Verstegen and James G. Ward, eds., *Spheres of Justice in Education: The 1990 American Education Finance Association Yearbook* (New York: Harper Business, 1991), p. 58. They are more likely to lack good sleep; Jonathan Kozol, *Savage Inequalities: Children in America's Schools* (Crown, 1991), pp. 43–44. In addition, poor children are 4.5 times as likely to be victims of child abuse as nonpoor children; Bok, *The State of the Nation*, p. 205. A hungry student, a student with untreated medical conditions, a child who does not have adequate rest, much less a child who is abused, is unlikely to achieve at high levels; Henry M. Levin, "The Economics of Justice in Education," in Verstegen and Ward, *Spheres of Justice in Education*, p. 130.

6. Richard Rothstein, *The Way We Were: Debunking the Myths of America's Declining Schools* (Century Foundation Press, 1998), p. 38 (language); Michelle Cottle, "Who's Watching the Kids?" *Washington Monthly*, July–August 1998, pp. 16–17 (citing Children's Defense Fund study on one-on-one reading); Michael J. Puma and others, *Prospects: The Congressionally Mandated Study of Educational Growth and Opportunity—Interim Report* (Bethesda, Md.: Abt Associates, 1993), p. 44 (museums); National Center for Education Statistics (NCES), *The Condition of Education, 1998* (Dept. of Education, 1998), pp. 6, 8–9, 159, 226 (libraries); see also Susan E. Mayer, *What Money Can't Buy: Family Income and Children's Life Chances* (Harvard University Press, 1997), p. 121; Meredith Phillips and others, "Family Background, Parenting Practices, and the Black-White Test Score Gap," in Jencks and Phillips, *The Black-White Test Score Gap*, pp. 126–27. Gordon Berlin and Andrew Sum, *Toward a More Perfect Union: Basic Skills, Poor Families, and Our Economic Future* (New York: Ford Foundation, 1988), pp. 37–38; Claude S. Fischer and others, *Inequality by Design: Cracking the Bell Curve Myth* (Princeton University Press, 1996), p. 162; Frederick Mosteller and Daniel P. Moynihan, eds., *On Equality of Educational Opportunity: Papers Deriving from the Harvard Faculty Seminar on the Coleman Report* (Random House, 1972), p. 48.

7. Mark Fetler, *Television and Reading Achievement: A Secondary Analysis of Data from the 1979–1980 National Assessment of Education Program* (Sacramento: California Dept. of Education, 1983), pp. ii, 13–14; Mark Fetler, "Television Viewing and School Achievement," *Journal of Communication*, vol. 34 (Spring 1984), pp. 104, 111; Thomas Ewin Smith, "Time Use and Change in Academic Achievement: A Longitudinal Follow-Up," *Journal of Youth and Adolescence*, vol. 21 (December 1992), pp. 725, 729.

8. "Quality Counts '98: The Urban Challenge," *Education Week*, January 8, 1998, p. 10. Puma and others, *Prospects: Interim Report*. Martin E. Orland, "Demographics of Disadvantage: Intensity of Childhood Poverty and Its Relationship to Educational Achievement," in John I. Goodlad and Pamela Keating, eds., *Access to Knowledge: An Agenda for Our Nation's Schools* (New York: College Entrance Examination Board, 1990), table 6, p. 52. See also Mary M. Kennedy, Richard K. Jung, and M. E. Orland, *Poverty, Achievement, and the Distribution of Compensatory Education Services: An Interim Report from the National Assessment of Chapter 1* (Dept. of Education, Office of Educational Research and Improvement, January 1986), pp. 21, 64; Laura Lippman and others, *Urban Schools: The Challenge of Location and Poverty* (Dept. of Education, NCES, 1996); Michael J. Puma and others, *Prospects: Final Report on Student Outcomes* (Cambridge, Mass.: Abt Associates, 1997), p. B3; NCES, *NAEP 1998 Reading Report*

Card for the Nation (Dept. of Education, 1999), p. 81; Chall, Jacobs, and Baldwin, *The Reading Crisis*, p. 3.

9. See Judith Anderson, Debra Hollinger, and Joseph Conaty, *Poverty and Achievement: Reexamining the Relationship between School Poverty and Student Achievement— An Examination of Eighth-Grade Student Achievement Using the National Education Longitudinal Study of 1988* (Dept. of Education, Office of Educational Research and Improvement, April 1992), pp. 11–12.

10. Maureen T. Hallinhan, "Commentary: New Directions for Research on Peer Influence," in Joyce Levy Epstein and Nancy Karweit, eds., *Friends in School: Patterns of Selection and Influence in Secondary Schools* (New York: Academic Press, 1983), p. 212; Anthony S. Bryk, Valerie E. Lee, and Julia B. Smith, "High School Organization and Its Effect on Teachers and Students," in William H. Clune and John F. Witte, eds., *Choice and Control in American Education*, vol. 1, *The Theory of Choice and Control in Education* (London: Falmer Press, 1990), p. 151; David Rusk, *Inside Game/Outside Game: Urban Policies for the Twenty-first Century* (Brookings, 1999), p. 124; Harris, *The Nurture Assumption*, p. 336. Of course the high achievement of peers is presumably a product in some measure of a generally good school (superior instruction by teachers and similar factors), but it also appears to be a cause, as classmates teach each other content, values, and aspirations.

11. Anita A. Summers and Barbara L. Wolfe, "Do Schools Make a Difference?" *American Economic Review*, vol. 67 (September 1977), p. 647. See also Vernon Henderson, Peter Mieszkowski, and Yvon Sauvageau, "Peer Groups' Effects and Educational Production Functions," *Journal of Public Economics*, vol. 10 (1978), pp. 97–98; Russell W. Rumberger and J. Douglas Willms, "The Impact of Racial and Ethnic Segregation on the Achievement Gap in California High Schools," *Educational Evaluation and Policy Analysis*, vol. 14 (Winter 1992), p. 379; John F. Kain, "The Impact of Individual Teachers and Peers on Individual Student Achievement," paper prepared for the Twentieth Annual Research Conference of the Association for Public Policy Analysis and Management, New York (October 31, 1998), p. 16; David Rusk and Jeff Mosley, "The Academic Performance of Public Housing Children—Does Living in Middle-Class Neighborhoods and Attending Middle-Class Schools Make a Difference?" (Washington: Urban Institute, May 27, 1994), p. 13; David Rusk, "To Improve Public Education, Stop Moving Money, Move Families," *Abell Report*, vol. 11 (June–July 1998), p. 5; Joyce Levy Epstein, "The Influence of Friends on Achievement and Affective Outcomes," in Epstein and Karweit, *Friends in School*, p. 179.

12. Patricia Cayo Sexton, *Education and Income: Inequalities of Opportunity in Our Public Schools* (Viking, 1961), pp. 262–63. Kagan, quoted in Mosteller and Moynihan, *On Equality of Educational Opportunity*, p. 49. Michelle Cottle, "Who's Watching the Kids?" pp. 16, 17 (citing Children's Defense Fund).

13. James S. Coleman, "Toward Open Schools," *Public Interest*, vol. 9 (Fall 1967), p. 23. James S. Coleman, "Equality of Educational Opportunity," *Integrated Education*, vol. 6 (September–October 1968), pp. 19, 15. Gladwell, "Do Parents Matter?" p. 55; see also Harris, *The Nurture Assumption*, pp. 10 and 256.

14. John Hampshire, "Language Use, Social Class, and Educational Achievement: A Discussion of the Possible Relationship," *Early Child Development and Care*, vol. 26 (1986), p. 56. Troy Duster, "Postindustrialism and Youth Unemployment in the United

States: African Americans as Harbingers," in Katherine McFate, Roger Lawson, and William Julius Wilson, eds., *Poverty, Inequality, and the Future of Social Policy* (New York: Russell Sage Foundation, 1995), p. 473; see also *Milliken* v. *Bradley*, 433 U.S. 267 (1977) (known as *Milliken II*), p. 287.

15. Samuel S. Peng and Susan T. Hill, *Understanding Racial-Ethnic Differences in Secondary Science and Math Achievement* (Dept. of Education, 1995), p. 20. See also Puma and others, *Prospects: Interim Report*, pp. 94–97. Urban Institute, *Snapshots of America's Families: Children's Environment and Behavior* (http://newfederalism. urban.org/nsaf/ [February 9, 1999]); see also Linda Jacobson, "Lower-Income Children Less Involved in School, Survey Shows," *Education Week*, February 3, 1999, p. 5. James E. Rosenbaum, Leonard S. Rubinowitz, and Marilynn J. Kulieke, *Low-Income Black Children in White Suburban Schools*, report prepared for the Spencer Foundation (Evanston, Ill.: Center for Urban Affairs and Policy Research, February 1986), pp. 98–99.

16. See Signithia Fordham and John U. Ogbu, "Black Students' School Success: Coping with the Burden of 'Acting White,'" *Urban Review*, vol. 18 (1986), p. 186; Douglas S. Massey and Nancy A. Denton, *American Apartheid: Segregation and the Making of the Underclass* (Harvard University Press, 1993), p. 13; Nancy A. Gonzales and others, "Family, Peer, and Neighborhood Influences on Academic Achievement among African-American Adolescents: One-Year Prospective Effects," *American Journal of Community Psychology*, vol. 24 (1996), p. 369; Laurence Steinberg and others, *Noninstructional Influences on High School Student Achievement: The Contributions of Parents, Peers, Extracurricular Activities, and Part-Time Work* (Madison, Wisc.: National Center on Effective Secondary Schools, 1988), p. 20.

17. Marilyn Elias, "Academics Lose Relevance for Black Boys," *USA Today*, December 2, 1997, p. D1. Bob Herbert, "The Success Taboo," *New York Times*, December 14, 1997, sec. 4, p. 13 (quote is Herbert paraphrasing the teacher).

18. Philip J. Cook and Jens Ludwig, "The Burden of 'Acting White': Do Black Adolescents Disparage Academic Achievement?" in Jencks and Phillips, *Black-White Test Score Gap*, pp. 376, 383–84.

19. See, for example, Amy Stuart Wells, "African American Students' View of School Choice," in Bruce Fuller and Richard F. Elmore, eds., *Who Chooses? Who Loses? Culture, Institutions, and the Unequal Effects of School Choice* (New York: Teachers College Press, 1996), pp. 25–26; Mary Haywood Metz, "Real School," in Douglas E. Mitchell and Margaret E. Goertz, eds., *Education Politics for the New Century* (New York: Falmer Press, 1990), p. 80; U.S. Commission on Civil Rights, *Racial Isolation*, vol. 1, p. 89; Gary Orfield and Susan Eaton, *Dismantling Desegregation: The Quiet Reversal of Brown* v. *Board of Education* (New York: New Press, 1996), p. 54; Alan B. Wilson, "Residual Segregation of Social Classes and Aspirations of High School Boys," *American Sociological Review*, vol. 24 (1959), p. 836; W. B. Brookover and David Gottlieb, "Social Class and Education," in W. W. Charters and N. L. Gage, *The Social Psychology of Education* (Boston: Allyn and Bacon, 1963), p. 10; Eleanor P. Wolf, *Trial and Error: The Detroit School Desegregation Case* (Wayne State University Press, 1981), p. 130; Coleman, interview with Hubert, p. 59; Peter W. Cookson Jr., *School Choice: The Struggle for the Soul of America* (Yale University Press, 1994), p. 100; Bernard Barber, "Social-Class Differences in Educational Life-Chances," *Teachers College Record*, vol. 63 (November 1961), pp. 108–09; Bernard C. Rosen, "The Achievement Syndrome: A Psychocultural Dimension

of Social Stratification," *American Sociological Review*, vol. 21 (1956), pp. 204–08; Victor Battistich and others, "Schools as Communities, Poverty Levels of Student Populations, and Students' Attitudes, Motives, and Performance: A Multilevel Analysis," *American Educational Research Journal*, vol. 32 (Fall 1995), p. 628; George A. Akerlof, "Social Distance and Social Decisions," *Econometrica*, vol. 65 (September 1997), pp. 1016, 1021–22.

20. Timothy Ready, "Learning to Adapt: Influence upon the Learning Behavior of Adolescents in a South Texas City," paper presented to the annual meeting of the American Anthropological Association, December 5, 1982, pp. 13–15. Douglas Barnett, Joan I. Vondra, and Susan M. Shonk, "Self-Perceptions, Motivation, and School Functioning of Low-Income Maltreated and Comparison Children," *Child Abuse and Neglect*, vol. 20 (1996), pp. 397, 402, 406. Joseph Watras, *Politics, Race, and Schools: Racial Integration, 1954–1994* (New York: Garland Publishing, 1997), p. 306 (citing Paul Willis, *Learning to Labor*, Columbia University Press, 1977).

21. Ron Suskind, *A Hope in the Unseen: An American Odyssey from the Inner City to the Ivy League* (New York: Broadway, 1998), pp. 3, 22–23.

22. John I. Goodlad, *A Place Called School: Prospects for the Future* (McGraw-Hill, 1984), pp. 76–77; Steinberg, *Beyond the Classroom*, p. 19. Leon Botstein, *Jefferson's Children: Education and the Promise of American Culture* (Doubleday, 1997), p. 41. Steinberg, *Noninstructional Influences*, p. 15; Cook and Ludwig, "The Burden of 'Acting White,'" p. 387.

23. Nina S. Mounts and Laurence Steinberg, "An Ecological Analysis of Peer Influence on Adolescent Grade Point Average and Drug Use," *Developmental Psychology*, vol. 31 (1995), p. 915. Steinberg, *Beyond the Classroom*, 142. Bradford B. Brown and Laurence Steinberg, *Noninstructional Influence on Adolescent Engagement and Achievement: Final Report, Project 2* (Madison, Wisc.: National Center on Effective Secondary Schools, February 1991), p. 4. Steinberg, *Noninstructional Influences*, p. 20 (citing Fordham and Ogbu). P. M. George, *Social Factors and Educational Aspirations of Canadian High School Students* (London: University of Western Ontario, 1970), pp. 16, 71.

24. George, *Social Factors*, pp. 9–10, 34, 76–77. Ralph H. Turner, *The Social Context of Ambition: A Study of High School Seniors in Los Angeles* (San Francisco: Chandler Publishing, 1964), pp. 4–5; Akerlof, "Social Distance and Social Decisions," p. 1011.

25. Edward Banfield, *Unheavenly Cities* (Boston: Little, Brown, 1968), pp. 47–48. See, for example, Massey and Denton, *American Apartheid*, p. 166. Lawrence L. Leshan, "Time Orientation and Social Class," *Journal of Abnormal and Social Psychology*, vol. 47 (July 1952), p. 591. Bridget Plowden and others, *Children and Their Primary Schools* (London: Her Majesty's Stationery Office, 1967), p. 50. Paul A. Jargowsky, *Poverty and Place: Ghettos, Barrios, and the American City* (New York: Russell Sage Foundation, 1997), p. 5.

26. James S. Coleman, "The Adolescent Subculture and Academic Achievement," in Charters and Gage, eds., *The Social Psychology of Education*, p. 89.

27. For example, Edmund W. Gordon and Doxey A. Wilkerson, *Compensatory Education for the Disadvantaged* (New York: College Entrance Examination Board, 1966), p. 17; Puma and others, *Prospects: Interim Report*, p. 21; George, *Social Factors*, pp. 19, 78. Alex Kotlowitz, *There Are No Children Here* (Doubleday, 1991), pp. x, 17.

28. U.S. Commission on Civil Rights, *Racial Isolation*, p. 82. Puma and others, *Prospects: Final Report*, p. B5.

29. James McPartland and Will J. Jordan, "Older Students Also Need Major Federal Compensatory Education Resources," in Gary Orfield and Elizabeth DeBray, eds., *Hard Work for Good Schools: Facts not Fads in Title I Reform* (Cambridge, Mass.: Harvard Civil Rights Project, 1999), p. 104; see also Chester Finn and Michael Petrilli, "Washington versus School Reform," *Public Interest* (Fall 1999), p. 59. Doris R. Entwisle, Karl L. Alexander, and Linda Steffel Olson, *Children, Schools, and Inequality* (New York: Westview Press, 1997), p. 25; see also Mayer, *What Money Can't Buy*, p. 42. Kathleen Sylvester, "Common Standards, Diverse Schools: Renewing the Promise of Public Education," in Will Marshall, ed., *Building the Bridge* (Lanham, Md.: Rowman and Littlefield, 1997), p. 85. NCES, *The Condition of Education, 1998*, p. 16. Turner, *Social Context of Ambition*, pp. 48–50. Herbert H. Hyman, "The Value Systems of Different Classes: A Social Psychological Contribution to the Analysis of Stratification," in Richard Bendix and Seymour Martin Lipset, eds., *Class, Status and Power* (Glencoe, Ill.: Free Press, 1953), pp. 427, 432; see also Richard A. Cloward and James A. Jones, "Social Class: Educational Attitudes and Participation," in A. Harry Passow, ed., *Education in Depressed Areas* (New York: Bureau of Publications, Teachers College, Columbia University, 1963), p. 199.

30. Coleman and others, *Equality of Educational Opportunity*, p. 201. Wilson, "Residual Segregation," pp. 839, 843, 845.

31. See, for example, Barber, "Social-Class Differences," p. 110; Turner, *Social Context of Ambition*, pp. 4, 19, 59–61, 65; Irving Kraus, "Sources of Educational Aspirations among Working-Class Youth," *American Sociological Review*, vol. 29 (1964), pp. 867, 887; Norman Alexander and Ernest Q. Campbell, "Peer Influences on Adolescent Aspirations and Attainments," *American Sociological Review*, vol. 29 (1964), pp. 568–75; Boyle, "The Effects of High School on Students' Aspirations," pp. 628, 634–36; U.S. Commission on Civil Rights, *Racial Isolation*, p. 87; George, *Social Factors*, pp. 16–17, 70; Hallinhan, "Commentary," p. 220; Harvey Kantor and Barbara Brenzel, "Urban Education and the 'Truly Disadvantaged': The Historical Roots of the Contemporary Crisis, 1945–1990," in Michael B. Katz, ed., *The "Underclass" Debate: Views from History* (Princeton University Press, 1993), p. 384; Amy Stuart Wells, "Reexamining Social Science Research on School Desegregation: Long-Term versus Short-Term Effects," *Teachers College Record*, vol. 96 (Summer 1995), p. 701.

For a mixed review, see Christopher Jencks and Susan E. Mayer, "The Social Consequences of Growing Up in a Poor Neighborhood," in Laurence E. Lynn Jr. and Michael G. H. McGeary, eds., *Inner-City Poverty in the United States* (Washington: National Academy Press, 1990), pp. 127–37 (reviewing studies finding that the increase in aspirations at higher-socioeconomic-status schools can be offset at least in part by a loss in self-confidence from increased competition). But the Jencks-Mayer review also notes that Mayer's then-forthcoming study of 26,425 students in the High School and Beyond sample finds that, controlling for family socioeconomic status and ethnicity, students attending low-socioeconomic-status high schools were more likely to drop out.

32. Paul Barton and Richard Coley, *America's Smallest School: The Family* (Princeton, N.J.: Educational Testing Service, 1992), p. 33 (12 percent of students from high-socioeconomic-status schools cut "at least some of the time" as against 6 percent from low-socioeconomic-status schools). Puma and others, *Prospects: Interim Report*, p. 108 (17 percent tardy more than ten days during the current school year versus 4 percent in low-poverty schools). Lippman and others, *Urban Schools*, p. 114; see also "Quality Counts '98," p. 19. Suskind, *A Hope in the Unseen*, p. 60.

33. Lippman and others, *Urban Schools*, p. 112; other studies find poor and nonpoor students spend similar amounts of time on homework; see, for example, NCES, *The Condition of Education, 1998*, p. 232; Puma and others, *Prospects: Final Report*, p. B6. Barton and Coley, *America's Smallest School*, p. 27. Suskind, *A Hope in the Unseen*, pp. 17, 47 and 59.

34. Puma and others, *Prospects: Interim Report*, p. 60; see also Berlin and Sum, *Toward a More Perfect Union*, p. 38; Lippman and others, *Urban Schools*, p. 110. Jon Jeter, "Alarm over TV Time Highlights Viewing Habits of Black Children," *Washington Post*, June 23, 1996, p. A8. NCES, *The Condition of Education, 1998*, p. 231 (38.7 versus 22.6 percent in fourth grade; 32.1 versus 18.2 percent in eighth grade, and 20.1 versus 9.1 percent in twelfth grade).

35. Jargowsky, *Poverty and Place*, p. 199; see also Lippman and others, *Urban Schools*, p. 3. Thomas Kindermann, cited in Harris, *The Nurture Assumption*, p. 182. Barton and Coley, *America's Smallest School*, pp. 21, 27; see also Entwisle, Alexander, and Olson, *Children, Schools, and Inequality*, p. 54; Chall, Jacobs, and Baldwin, *The Reading Crisis*, pp. 138, 20; Susan Mosborg, *How Money Matters to School Performance: Four Points Policymakers Should Know* (Portland, Ore.: Northwest Regional Education Laboratory, 1996), p. 9; Jeter, "Alarm over TV Time."

36. See, for example, Passow, *Education in Depressed Areas*, pp. 184, 237; Cloward and Jones, "Social Class," p. 191; Charles Silberman, *Crisis in the Classroom* (Random House, 1970), pp. 89–90; Stephan Thernstrom and Abigail Thernstrom, *America in Black and White: One Nation, Indivisible* (Simon and Schuster, 1997), p. 361; Helen H. Davidson and Gerhard Lang, "Children's Perceptions of Their Teachers' Feelings toward Them Related to Self-Perception, School Achievement, and Behavior," *Journal of Experimental Education*, vol. 29 (December 1960), p. 113; "A Scholar Who Inspired It Says Busing Backfired," interview with James Coleman, *National Observer*, June 7, 1975, p. 18; Peng and Hill, *Understanding Racial-Ethnic Differences*, p. 55; Robert J. Havighurst, "Educational Policy for the Large Cities," *Social Problems*, vol. 24 (1976), p. 275; Rosenbaum, Rubinowitz, and Kulieke, *Low-Income Black Children*, p. 53; Paul Barton, Richard J. Coley, and Harold Wenglinsky, *Order in the Classroom: Violence, Discipline, and Student Achievement* (Princeton, N.J.: Educational Testing Service, 1998), p. 16; Phillip Kaufman and others, *Indicators of School Crime and Safety* (Depts. of Education and Justice, 1998), pp. 58, 62, 63, 78; William Julius Wilson, *When Work Disappears: The World of the New Urban Poor* (Knopf, 1996), p. 61.

37. Beatrice Birman and others, *The Current Operation of the Chapter 1 Program: Final Report for the National Assessment of Chapter 1* (Dept. of Education, 1987), pp. 92–93; see also David E. Myers, "The Relationship between Poverty Concentration and Students' Achievement," in Kennedy, Jung, and Orland, *Poverty, Achievement, and the Distribution of Compensatory Education Services*, pp. D20–21; Carnegie Foundation for the Achievement of Teaching, *An Imperiled Generation: Saving Urban Schools* (1988), p. 37; "Quality Counts '98," p. 6; Abigail Thernstrom, "Where Did All the Order Go? School Discipline and the Law," in Diane Ravitch, ed., *Brookings Papers on Education Policy, 1999* (Brookings, 1999), p. 301; Puma and others, *Prospects: Interim Report*, pp. 94, 262; Puma and others, *Prospects: Final Report*, p. B3.

38. Lippman and others, *Urban Schools*, pp. 116–17. Department of Education, *Improving America's Schools Act of 1993: The Reauthorization of the Elementary and Secondary Education Act and Amendments to Other Acts* (September 13, 1993), Title I-6.

Puma and others, *Prospects: Interim Report*, p. 110; see also Robert J. Havighurst, "Urban Development and the Educational System," in Passow, *Education in Depressed Areas*, p. 31, citing Sexton, *Education and Income*. Lippman and others, *Urban Schools*, pp. 118, 120, 122.

39. Sara S. McLanahan, "Parent Absence or Poverty: Which Matters More?" in Duncan and Brooks-Gunn, *Consequences of Growing Up Poor*, p. 40. Ellen L. Lipman and David R. Offord, "Psychosocial Morbidity among Poor Children in Ontario," in Duncan and Brooks-Gunn, *Consequences of Growing Up Poor*, pp. 239, 280.

40. Birman and others, *The Current Operation of Chapter 1*, p. 91; Barton, Coley, and Wenglinsky, *Order in the Classroom*, pp. 3, 18. Harold Wenglinsky, *When Money Matters: How Educational Expenditures Improve Student Performance and How They Don't* (Princeton, N.J.: Educational Testing Service, 1997), p. viii. Susan P. Choy, *Public and Private Schools: How They Differ* (NCES, 1997), pp. 18–19. Puma and others, *Prospects: Final Report*, p. 61. Joy D. Osofsky, ed., *Children in a Violent Society* (New York: Guilford Press, 1997), p. 4. Shanker quoted in American Federation of Teachers, *Setting the Stage: School Discipline Resource Manual* (Washington, July 1997), p. A6.

41. Robert Worth, "The Scandal of Special Ed: It Wastes Money and Hurts the Poor," *Washington Monthly*, June 1999, p. 34. Mark Hare, "Is Racial Isolation the Key Problem in City Schools? Not Any More," *Rochester Democrat and Chronicle*, November 15, 1998. Fred Prehn, interview with author, Wausau, Wisc., December 17, 1997, p. 12; Jeffrey Lamont, interview with author, Wausau, Wisc., December 17, 1997, p. 30. Valerie E. Lee, Susanna Loeb, and Sally Lubeck, "Contextual Effects of Prekindergarten Classrooms for Disadvantaged Children on Cognitive Development: The Case of Chapter 1," *Child Development*, vol. 69, no. 2 (April 1998), p. 481.

42. General Accounting Office (GAO), *Elementary School Children: Many Change Schools Frequently, Harming Their Education* (Washington, 1994), pp. 1, 4–5; Myers, "The Relationship between School Poverty Concentration and Students' Reading and Math Achievement and Learning," p. D21; Entwisle, Alexander, and Olson, *Children, Schools, and Inequality*; Lippman and others, *Urban Schools*, pp. 60–61; Vicente Paredes, *A Study of Urban Student Mobility* (Austin, Tex.: Austin Independent School District, April 1993), pp. 11–12; Paul Peterson, "Top Ten Questions Asked about School Choice," in Ravitch, *Brookings Papers on Education Policy, 1999*, pp. 385–86.

43. See Orfield and Eaton, *Dismantling Desegregation*, p. 54; Andrea A. Lash and Sandra L. Kirkpatrick, "A Classroom Perspective on Student Mobility," *Elementary School Journal*, vol. 91 (1990), p. 178; Christian A. Stuhr, *Patterns of Parental Mobility in an Inner-City Toronto School* (Ontario: Toronto Board of Education, October 1967), pp. 5, 24. Puma and others, *Prospects; Interim Report*, pp. 250–51; see also Puma and others, *Prospects: Final Report*, p. B3.

44. Ronald Ferguson and Helen F. Ladd, "How and Why Money Matters: An Analysis of Alabama Schools," in Helen F. Ladd, ed., *Holding Schools Accountable: Performance-Based Reform in Education* (Brookings, 1996), p. 289. In Montgomery County, Maryland, public schools with high rates of mobility have been thought to have a higher "educational load" and are therefore given greater resources than schools with lower educational loads; see Montgomery County (Maryland) Board of Education, *Policy: Quality Integrated Education* (adopted by Resolution 837-83, October 10, 1983; amended by Resolution 401-93, May 1, 1993), p. 3.

45. See, for example, Sexton, *Education and Income*, pp. 95–96; Lash and Kirkpatrick, "A Classroom Perspective on Student Mobility," pp. 177, 179; Entwisle, Alexander, and Olson, *Children, Schools, and Inequality*, pp. 77–78; Debra Williams, "Kids, Schools Suffer from Revolving Door: Mobility Problem Is Aggravated by the Lack of a Common Curriculum," *American Educator*, vol. 20 (Spring 1996), p. 37.

46. Lash and Kirkpatrick, "A Classroom Perspective on Student Mobility," p. 179, 181, 189, 186, 183, 186-87; see also GAO, *Elementary School Children*, pp. 37–38. Williams, "Kids, Schools Suffer from Revolving Door," p. 36. Stuhr, *Patterns of Parental Mobility*, p. 1. Evans Clinchy and Frances Arick Kolb, eds., *Planning for Schools of Choice: Achieving Equity and Excellence* (Andover, Mass.: NETWORK, 1989), pp. 4–5.

47. Barton and Coley, *America's Smallest School*, p. 33 (in 1988, 28 percent of low-socioeconomic-status students missed three or more days per month compared with 16 percent of high-socioeconomic-status students); see also Carnegie Foundation, *Imperiled Generation*, p. 37.

48. Puma and others, *Prospects: Interim Report*, p. 107 (that 16 percent of high-poverty seventh-grade students missed more than twenty days compared with 4 percent in low-poverty schools). Erik Larson, "Where Does the Money Go?" *Time*, October 27, 1997, pp. 88, 90. William L. Yancey and Salvatore J. Saporito, *Racial and Economic Segregation and Educational Outcomes: One Tale, Two Cities* (Philadelphia: Temple University Center for Research in Human Development and Education, 1995), p. 21.

49. Nan Lin and Mary Dumin, "Access to Occupations through Social Ties," *Social Networks*, vol. 8 (December 1986), pp. 368, 379, 383.

50. Amy Stuart Wells and Robert L. Crain, "Perpetuation Theory and the Long-Term Effects of School Desegregation," *Review of Educational Research*, vol. 64 (Winter 1994), pp. 533, 544, 552, 549–50; see also Fischer and others, *Inequality by Design*, p. 73. William L. Taylor, "*Brown*, Equal Protection, and the Isolation of the Poor," *Yale Law Journal*, vol. 95 (1986), p. 1711; Harrell R. Rodgers and Charles S. Bullock III, "School Desegregation: Successes and Failures," *Journal of Negro Education*, vol. 43 (1974); Charles S. Bullock III, "Desegregating Urban Areas: Is It Worth It? Can It Be Done?" in Florence Hamlish Levinsohn and Benjamin Drake Wright, eds., *School Desegregation: Shadow and Substance* (University of Chicago Press, 1976); Jomills Henry Braddock II, Robert L. Crain, and James M. McPartland, "A Long-Term View of School Desegregation: Some Recent Studies of Graduates as Adults," *Phi Delta Kappan*, vol. 66, no. 4 (December 1984), pp. 261–63; Wells, "Reexamining Social Science Research," p. 703; James S. Liebman, "Desegregating Politics: 'All-Out' School Desegregation Explained," *Columbia Law Review*, vol. 90 (October 1990), pp. 1463, 1624–26; Amy Stuart Wells and Robert L. Crain, *Stepping over the Color Line: African-American Students in White Suburban Schools* (Yale University Press, 1997), p. 337.

51. Gary Orfield, *City-Suburban Desegregation: Parent and Student Perspectives in Metropolitan Boston* (Cambridge, Mass.: Harvard Civil Rights Project, 1997), p. 21.

52. 1998 NELS data cited in Barton and Coley, *America's Smallest School*, p. 37 (PTA membership was 54 percent among high-SES students and 12 percent among low-SES students; contact about the academic program varied from 44 percent among high-SES students to 24 percent among low-SES students). Puma and others, *Prospects: Interim Report*, p. 260 (47 versus 19 percent in volunteering in first-grade classrooms, 34 versus 18 percent in third-grade classrooms, and 11 versus 5 percent in seventh-grade class-

rooms); NCES, *Teacher Quality: A Report on the Preparation and Qualifications of Public School Teachers* (Dept. of Education, 1999), p. 44.

53. See, for example, Robert F. Herriott and Nancy Hoyt St. John, *Social Class and the Urban School: The Impact of Pupil Background on Teachers and Principals* (New York: John Wiley and Sons, 1966), pp. 41, 163; Sexton, *Education and Income*, p. 107; Birman and others, *The Current Operation of Chapter 1*, pp. 94–95; Wells, "African-American Students' View," p. 31; Entwisle, Alexander, and Olson, *Children, Schools, and Inequality*, p. 52; Jennifer L. Hochschild, *The New American Dilemma: Liberal Democracy and School Desegregation* (Yale University Press, 1984), p. 108; Philip Hallinger and Joseph F. Murphy, "The Social Context of Effective Schools," *American Journal of Education*, vol. 94 (May 1986), pp. 348–49; Patricia A. Bauch, *Family Choice and Parental Involvement in Inner-City Catholic High Schools: An Exploration of Psycho-Social and Organizational Factors*, paper presented at the annual meeting of the American Educational Research Association, Washington, D.C., April 20–24, 1987, pp. 18, 23; Puma and others, *Prospects: Final Report*, p. B5; NCES, *The Condition of Education, 1998*, pp. 114, 116; Orfield and Eaton, *Dismantling Desegregation*, p. 137; Bernard Michael, *Volunteers in Public Schools* (Washington: National Academy Press, 1990), p. 15; Department of Commerce, *1999 Statistical Abstract of the United States* (Government Printing Office, 1999), table 643, p. 404.

54. Carnegie Foundation, *Imperiled Generation*, p. 41. Ross Mills, interview with author, Bethesda, Md., March 6, 1998. Rene Sanchez, "Educators Taking Drastic Steps to Solve Dire Problems," *Washington Post*, May 4, 1997, p. A1. Christina Rathbone, *On the Outside Looking In: A Year in an Inner-City High School* (New York: Atlantic Monthly Press, 1998), p. 120. Suskind, *A Hope in the Unseen*, p. 136; Gerald W. Bracey, "SES and Involvement," *Phi Delta Kappan*, vol. 78, no. 2 (October 1996), p. 169.

55. See, for example, Smith, "Time Use and Change in Academic Achievement," p. 726; Anne Henderson, ed., *Parent Participation, Student Achievement: The Evidence Grows*, Occasional Paper (Columbia, Md.: National Committee for Citizens in Education, 1981); Timothy Keith and others, *Effects of Parental Involvement on Eighth-Grade Achievement: LISREL Analysis of NELS-88 Data* (Blacksburg: Virginia Polytechnic Institute and State University, 1992), p. 5. Rebecca A. Marcon, "Parental Involvement and Early School Success: Following the 'Class of 2000' at Year Five," paper presented at the 60th Biennial Meeting of the Society for Research in Child Development, New Orleans, March 25–28, 1993, p. 2; Puma and others, *Prospects: Final Report*, p. 71.

56. See Esther Ho Sui-Chu and J. Douglas Willms, "Effects of Parental Involvement on Eighth-Grade Achievement," *Sociology of Education*, vol. 69 (April 1996), p. 136. See also Michael, *Volunteers in Public Schools*, pp. 36–37; Edmund Gordon, "Education of the Disadvantaged: A Problem of Human Diversity," in Nelson F. Ashline, Thomas Pezzullo, and Charles I. Norris, eds., *Education, Inequality, and National Policy* (Lexington, Mass.: Lexington Books, 1976), p. 110; Mosborg, *How Money Matters*, p. 4.

57. Ho Sui-Chu and Willms, "Effects of Parental Involvement," p. 138 (citing studies by Daniel J. Brown [1995] and Annette Lareau [1989]).

58. John Chubb and Terry Moe, *Politics, Markets, and American Schools* (Brookings, 1990), p. 16; see also Hallinger and Murphy, "The Social Context of Effective Schools"; Abby Goodnough, "Parent Volunteers Give Affluent Schools an Advantage Hard to Duplicate," *New York Times*, May 7, 1997, p. A28; Carolyn Hughes Chapman and Gordon Cawelti, "Chaper I and Student Achievement," in Iris Rotberg, ed., *Federal Policy*

Options for Improving the Education of Low-Income Students, vol. 2, *Commentaries* (Santa Monica, Calif.: Rand, 1993), p. 102; Joyce Levy Epstein, "Parent Involvement: What Research Says to Administrators," *Education and Urban Society*, vol. 19 (February 1987), p. 119; Lawrence C. Stedman, "It's Time We Changed the Effective Schools Formula," *Phi Delta Kappan*, vol. 69 (November 1987), p. 219; Bauch, *Family Choice and Parental Involvement*, p. 1. Department of Education, National Education Goals Panel, *The National Education Goals Report: Building a Nation of Learners, 1996*, cited in Choy, *Public and Private Schools*, p. 18. Bauch, *Family Choice and Parental Involvement*, p. 2; Choy, *Public and Private Schools*, p. 20. Ho Sui-Chu and Willms, "Effects of Parental Involvement," p. 137.

59. See, for example, Nat Hentoff, *Does Anybody Give a Damn?* (Knopf, 1977), p. 232.

60. See Rene Sanchez, "Teachers Favor More Parental Involvement, Survey Says," *New York Times*, May 21, 1998, p. A9.

61. Of course, most teachers and administrators are genuinely concerned about students, so schools should in theory run well even without vigilant parent advocates. But in some cases, the interests of teachers and children conflict. Particularly in cities where taxpayers keep a lid on teacher salaries, unions will try to win for their members nonmonetary concessions that may not always be in the best interests of kids. Unions may seek more days off for teachers, fewer parent-teacher conferences, or job protection for teachers, irrespective of quality. So while teachers and parents will normally work together to further the interests of students, the interests of students and teachers sometimes conflict, and in such cases, the role of parents as advocates for children takes on increased importance. For a general discussion, see Tom Loveless, ed., *Conflicting Missions: Teacher Unions and Educational Reform* (Brookings, 2000).

62. Cloward and Jones, "Social Class," pp. 205–06; Puma and others, *Prospect: Final Report*, p. B5.

63. Chubb and Moe, *Politics, Markets, and American Schools*, pp. 172–73.

64. G. Alan Hickrod, "Testimony to the Subcommittee on Education, Arts, and Humanities of the Committee on Labor and Human Resources, U.S. Senate," quoted in William J. Fowler Jr., ed., *Developments in School Finance* (NCES, 1995), p. 17; Mosborg, *How Money Matters*, pp. 15, 22; Orland, "Demographics of Disadvantage," p. 57; Birman and others, *The Current Operation of Chapter 1*, p. 13; House Committee on Education and Labor, Subcommittee on Elementary, Secondary, and Vocational Education, *Hearings on H.R. 3850, The Fair Chance Act*, 101 Cong., 2 sess., January 24, 1990, pp. 127, 133. Kozol, *Savage Inequalities*, pp. 54, 222–23, 236–37; Smith and O'Day, "Educational Equality," p. 65; Theodore Sizer, *Horace's Hope: What Works for the American High School* (Boston: Houghton Mifflin, 1996), p. xvi; NCES, *Public School Funding Differences* (1995), p. 1; NCES, *The Condition of Education, 1998*, p. 128; Carol Ascher and Gary Burnett, *Current Trends and Issues in Urban Education, 1993* (New York: ERIC Clearinghouse on Urban Education, 1993), pp. 24–26; "Quality Counts '98," p. 20; GAO, *School Finance: State and Federal Efforts to Target Poor Students: Report to Congressional Requesters* (Washington, January 28, 1998), p. 18; GAO, *School Finance: State Efforts to Reduce Funding Gaps between Poor and Wealthy Districts: Report to Congressional Requesters* (Washington, February 1997), p. 2; Jay Mathews, *Class Struggle: What's Wrong (and Right) with America's Best Public High Schools* (New York: Times Books, 1998), p. 189; Mosborg, *How Money Matters*, p. 15.

65. The difference in per pupil spending between districts attended by the average black and the average white student differ by just $10 a year ($5,387 for blacks, $5,397 for whites); Christopher Jencks and Meredith Phillips, introduction to *Black-White Test Score Gap*, p. 9 (citing 1992 data from William Evans). See also Thernstrom and Thernstrom, *America in Black and White*, p. 336 (citing 1995 NCES report that in the 1989–90 school year, majority-minority school districts spent 15 percent more than the districts with less than 5 percent minority representation and that central-city spending was identical to the average suburban spending).

66. Linda Darling-Hammond, "Unequal Opportunity: Race and Education," *Brookings Review* (Spring 1998), p. 28. Wilson, *When Work Disappears*, p. 211.

67. Theodore M. Shaw, "Equality and Educational Excellence: Legal Challenges in the 1990s," *Minnesota Law Review*, vol. 80 (April 1996), p. 906 (in Kansas City, once the schools became majority black, the electorate (still majority white) did not pass a single tax levy or bond issue for the schools).

68. In New York City, an education adviser to Mayor Rudolph Giuliani told New York's *Newsday* that cuts in public education would not hurt the mayor because "the public school parents are weakest and don't vote in large numbers"; Rathbone, *On the Outside Looking In*, p. 114.

69. Linda Darling-Hammond, "National Standards and Assessments: Will They Improve Education?" *American Journal of Education*, vol. 102 (August 1994), p. 480; Orfield and Eaton, *Dismantling Desegregation*, p. 373; NCES, *The Condition of Education, 1998*, p. 80; Richard C. Leone, "The Tax Orphan," *Washington Post*, August 12, 1997, p. A19; Bob Herbert, "The Donor Class," *New York Times*, July 19, 1998, sec. 4, p. 15.

70. Paul Delaney, "Louisville, A Place Where Busing Seems to Work," *New York Times*, June 6, 1976, sec. 4, p. 6. Ward Sinclair, "Desegregation's Quiet Success," *Washington Post*, June 17, 1978, p. A10. John Matthews, "Economic Approach: D.C. School Ruling Began in Boston," *Evening Star* (Washington), June 20, 1967, pp. B1, B4; Rene Sanchez, "Poor, Minority Students Lack Access to Computers," *Washington Post*, May 15, 1997, p. A13.

71. Birman, *The Current Operation of Chapter 1*, pp. 94–95. Mathews, *Class Struggle*, pp. 184–85, 188.

72. Eric Brunner and Jon Sonstelie, "Coping with *Serrano*: Voluntary Contributions to California's Local Public Schools," paper presented to the National Tax Association's Eighty-ninth Annual Conference on Taxation, Boston, November 10–12, 1996, pp. 372–81; see also "Keeping Schools Local," *Wall Street Journal*, August 24, 1998, p. A12. Ann O'Hanlon, "For Public Schools, a New Course in Economics," *Washington Post*, April 20, 1997, pp. B1, B7 (citing Cornell University's David Monk, who found that in 1994, New York state districts raised 4 percent of revenues from private sources; other studies find the figure is 15 percent). Federal spending is 6.6 percent of public school revenues.

73. See, for example, O'Hanlon, "A New Course in Economics," pp. B1, B7; Sydney Freedberg Jr., "In Loco Parentis," *New Republic*, January 20, 1997, pp. 10, 11.

74. See, for example. William Galston, *Comment*, in Ravitch, *Brookings Papers on Education Policy, 1999*, p. 57; Diane Ravitch, "A New Era in Urban Education?" *Brookings Policy Brief* (August 1998), p. 3; James E. Ryan, "Schools, Race, and Money," *Yale Law Journal*, vol. 109 (November 1999), p. 294 (citing Jean Anyon's study of Newark schools).

75. Sara Mosle, "The Stealth Chancellor," *New York Times Magazine* (August 31, 1997), p. 48. Michael Powell, "School Funds Have Gone for Bureaucrats Rather Than Books and Boilers," *Washington Post*, July 21, 1997, p. A13 (citing the control board's report, "Children in Crisis"). Larson, "Where Does the Money Go?" p. 90. Nicholas Lemann, "Ready, READ!" *Atlantic Monthly*, November 1998, pp. 95–96. LeTendre quoted in Ralph Frammolino, "Title I's $118 Billion Fails to Close Gap," *Los Angeles Times*, January 17, 1999, p. A1; GAO, *Compensatory Education: Most Chapter 1 Funds in Eight Districts Used for Classroom Services: Fact Sheet for Congressional Requesters* (Washington, September 1992), p. 3.

76. See chapter 5.

77. Jesse Burkhead, Thomas B. Fox, and John W. Holland, *Input and Output in Large-City High Schools* (Syracuse University Press, 1967), pp. 35–36; see also Mosborg, *How Money Matters*, p. 16. Ronald F. Ferguson, "Paying for Public Education: New Evidence on How and Why Money Matters," *Harvard Journal on Legislation*, vol. 28 (1991), pp. 467, 489.

78. See discussion in chapter 7.

79. Orfield and Eaton, *Dismantling Desegregation*, p. 70.

80. Theodore Sizer, *Horace's Compromise: The Dilemma of the American High School* (Boston: Houghton Mifflin, 1984), pp. 36, 179; Kozol, *Savage Inequalities*, pp. 78, 168.

81. Apparently, the same phenomenon does not hold among principals; principals in high-poverty schools are slightly more educated than principals in low-poverty schools, and their levels of experince are comparable; Puma and others, *Prospects: Final Report*, p. 58.

82. See, for example. Sexton, *Education and Income*, p. 120; Herriott and St. John, *Social Class*, pp. 57–59, 84–87, 105, 109, 129–30; Peng and Hill, *Understanding Racial-Ethnic Differences*, p. 19; Jeannie Oakes, *Multiplying Inequalities: The Effects of Race, Social Class, and Tracking on Opportunities to Learn Mathematics and Science* (Santa Monica, Calif.: RAND, 1990), p. 46; Julius Hobson, "Using the Legal Process for Change," in Dwight W. Allen and Jeffrey C. Hecht, eds., *Controversies in Education* (Philadelphia: W. B. Saunders, 1974), p. 541; David K. Cohen, "Policy for the Public Schools: Compensation and Integration," in *Harvard Education Review: Equal Educational Opportunity* (Harvard University Press, 1969), p. 103; Bok, *The State of the Nation*, p. 206; Wilson, *When Work Disappears*, pp. 211–12; Rosenbaum, Rubinowitz, and Kulieke, *Low-Income Black Children*, p. 35; Paul Peterson, *City Limits* (University of Chicago Press, 1981), p. 98.

83. Linda Darling-Hammond, "Teacher Quality and Equity," in Goodlad and Keating, *Access to Knowledge*, p. 244; Herriott and St. John, *Social Class*, p. 9; Cloward and Jones, "Social Class," p. 191.

84. Oakes, *Multiplying Inequalities*, pp. 46, 414; Darling-Hammond, "Teacher Quality and Equity," p. 240. Oakes, *Multiplying Inequalities*, pp. 48, 54–55, 58, 60. Lippman and others, *Urban Schools*, pp. 86–88, 96.

85. Puma and others, *Prospects: Final Report*, p. B3. "Quality Counts '98," p. 17. Kozol, *Savage Inequalities*, p. 1.

86. Linda Darling-Hammond, *Doing What Matters Most: Investing in Quality Teaching* (New York: National Commission on Teaching and America's Future, November 1997), p. 21; Sandra Feldman, "Two Million Teachers," *New York Times*, October 4, 1998, sec. 4, p. 7; Kirstin Downey Grimsley, "For a Teacher, Shifting to Corporate Training Could Have Rewards, Risks," *Washington Post*, December 6, 1998, p. H4.

87. Oakes, *Multiplying Inequalities*, p. 47. "Quality Counts '98," p. 16. Sandra Feldman, "Ignoring Standards," *New York Times*, August 2, 1998, sec. 4, p. 7. Lippman and others, *Urban Schools*, pp. 86–88 and 96.

88. See, for example, Darling-Hammond, "Unequal Opportunity," p. 31; Darling-Hammond, *Doing What Matters Most*, pp. 25–27; Amy Virshup, "Grading Teachers," *Washington Post Magazine*, November 9, 1997, p. 17; NCES, *Teacher Quality: A Report on the Preparation and Qualifications of Public School Teachers* (Dept. of Education, January 1999), p. 17; Ravitch, "A New Era in Urban Education?" p. 3; Kati Haycock, "Good Teaching Matters: How Well-Qualified Teachers Can Close the Gap," *Thinking K–16*, vol. 3 (Summer 1998), pp. 7–8 (citing research by Richard Ingersoll conducted for the Education Trust in 1998); NCES, *The Condition of Education, 1998*, pp. 127, 270.

89. Diane Ravitch, "Put Teachers to the Test," *Washington Post*, February 25, 1998, p. A17. National Commission on Teaching and America's Future, *What Matters Most: Teaching for America's Future* (New York, September 1996), p. 16.

90. Darling-Hammond, "Unequal Opportunity," p. 31. See also Darling-Hammond, *Doing What Matters Most*, pp. 25–27; NCES, *Teacher Quality*, p. 10. Darling-Hammond, "National Standards and Assessments," pp. 48–60. LeTendre quoted in Sue Kirchhoff, "Can 'Accountability' Get Struggling Schools on Track?" *Congressional Quarterly Weekly*, March 6, 1999, p. 530.

91. John Silber, "Those Who Can't Teach," *New York Times*, July 7, 1998, p. A23; Botstein, *Jefferson's Children*, p. 123. Carey Goldberg, "Massachusetts Retreats on Threshold for Teacher Tests, Flunking Nearly 60 Percent," *New York Times*, July 2, 1998, p. A12.

92. Ferguson, "Paying for Public Education," pp. 466, 482. John F. Kain and Kraig Singleton, "Equality of Educational Opportunity Revisited," *New England Economic Review* (May–June 1996), pp. 87, 99, 107. See also Jencks and Phillips, introduction to *Black-White Test Score Gap*, pp. 9–10.

93. Oakes, *Multiplying Inequalities*, pp. 48, 54–55, 58, 60. Feldman quoted in E. J. Dionne Jr., "Toward Consensus on Schools," *Washington Post*, June 16, 1998, p. A21. National Commission on Teaching and America's Future, *What Matters Most*, p. 17.

94. Riley quoted in Barbara Vobejda, "Half-Million New Students Will Test School Resources, Clinton Says," *Washington Post*, September 8, 1998, p. A8; see also Linda Perlstein, "Schools Cautioned on Hasty Hiring: Many Districts 'Sacrificing Quality for Quantity,' Riley Says," *Washington Post*, September 16, 1998, p. A12; Peter Applebome, "Record School Enrollments, Now and Ahead," *New York Times*, August 22, 1997; Darling-Hammond, *Doing What Matters Most*, pp. 15–16. William Raspberry, "A Place for Teacher Tests," *Washington Post*, July 3, 1998, p. A19.

95. Lippman and others, *Urban Schools*, p. 84. Darling-Hammond, *Doing What Matters Most*, pp. 20–21 (citing NCES 1993–94 Schools and Staffing Survey).

96. Ibid., pp. 82–83; Puma and others, *Prospects: Final Report*, p. B6; Paul E. Barton, *The State of Inequality* (Princeton, N.J.: Educational Testing Service, 1992), p. 11. Orfield and Eaton, *Dismantling Desegregation*, p. 69.

97. Lippman and others, *Urban Schools*, pp. 94–95; Puma and others, *Prospects: Final Report*; Darling-Hammond, *Doing What Matters Most*, p. 21. Jay Mathews, "As Schools Shop for Success, Teachers Rethink Role," *Washington Post*, June 21, 1999, p. A1. David Nakamura, "Struggling Schools Are Desperate for Experienced Teachers," *Washington Post*, July 29, 1999, p. A1.

98. See, for example, Maribeth Vander Weele, "Why It's Too Hard to Fire Bad Teachers," *Washington Monthly*, November 1994, p. 12. John Norquist, speaking at an event on school choice organized by the Ethics and Public Policy Center, National Press Club, Washington, D.C., February 5, 1999.

99. "Quality Counts '98," p. 17; Lippman and others, *Urban Schools*, pp. 86–88, 96. NCES, *Teacher Quality*, p. 28.

100. National Commission on Teaching and America's Future, *What Matters Most*, p. 16.

101. Darling-Hammond, *Doing What Matters Most*, pp. 8–9; National Commission on Teaching and America's Future, *What Matters Most*, p. 8; Darling-Hammond, "National Standards and Assessments," p. 500; Summers and Wolfe, "Do Schools Make a Difference," p. 644; Kain, *Impact of Individual Teachers and Peers*, p. 7.

102. Ferguson, "Paying for Public Education," pp. 465–66; see also Darling-Hammond, "Unequal Opportunity," p. 30. Ferguson, "Paying for Public Education," pp. 469, 475–77, 468 (citing Summers and Wolfe, "Do Schools Make a Difference?"); Ronald F. Ferguson, "Can Schools Narrow the Black-White Test Score Gap?" in Jencks and Phillips, *The Black-White Test Score Gap*, pp. 350–51.

103. Mosborg, *How Money Matters*, p. 7 (citing Bettye MacPhail and Richard King); Deborah A. Verstegen, "Reforming American Education Policy for the Twenty-first Century," *Educational Administration Quarterly*, vol. 30 (August 1994), p. 367; Darling-Hammond, "Unequal Opportunity," p. 31; Haycock, "Good Teaching Matters," pp. 3–6 (summarizing numerous studies); Kain and Singleton, "Equality of Educational Opportunity Revisited," p. 97.

104. Deborah Meier, *The Power of Their Ideas: Lessons for America from a Small School in Harlem* (Boston: Beacon Press, 1995), p. 97.

105. Alan B. Wilson, in U.S. Commission on Civil Rights, *Racial Isolation*, p. 181. See also Rita E. Mahard and Robert L. Crain, "Research on Minority Achievement in Desegregated Schools," in Christine H. Rossell and Willis D. Hawley, *The Consequences of School Desegregation* (Temple University Press, 1983), p. 105; Silbermann, *Crisis in the Classroom*, p. 87; Berlin and Sum, *Toward a More Perfect Union*, p. 50; Kenneth B. Clark, "Educational Stimulation of Racially Disadvantaged Children," in Passow, *Education in Depressed Areas*, p. 146; Willms, "Social Class Segregation," p. 226.

106. Commission on Chapter 1, *Making Schools Work for Children in Poverty* (Washington: American Association for Higher Education, 1992), cited in Department of Education, *Improving America's Schools Act of 1993*, p. 5. Puma and others, *Prospects: Final Report*, p. v; see also p. 12. Nicholas Lemann, "The Origins of the Underclass," *New Republic*, July 1986, pp. 52, 59–63 (paraphrased in Liebman, "Desegregating Politics"). Puma and others, *Prospects: Interim Report*, p. 114. Yancey and Saporito, *Racial and Economic Segregation*, p. 20.

107. Consortium for Policy Research, "Equality in Education: Progress, Problems, and Possibilities," Policy Brief (Rutgers University, 1991), p. 6. Heather C. Hill, David K. Cohen, and Susan L. Moffitt, "Instruction, Poverty, and Performance," in Orfield and DeBray, eds., *Hard Work for Good Schools*, p. 57. Stephen Raudenbusch, "Inequality of Access to Educational Opportunity: A National Report Card for Eighth Grade Math," unpublished, University of Michigan, 1998 (cited in Hill and Cohen). Entwisle, Alexander, and Olson, *Children, Schools, and Inequality*, p. 68.

108. "When Aptitude Goes Unnurtured," *Johns Hopkins Magazine*, September 1999. Wells, "Reexamining Social Science Research," p. 700.

109. See, for example, David H. Monk and Emil J. Haller, "Predictors of High School Academic Course Offerings: The Role of School Size," *American Educational Research Journal*, vol. 30 (Spring 1993), p. 13; John A. Michael, "High School Climates and Plans for Entering College," *Public Opinion Quarterly*, vol. 25 (1961), p. 588; Bryk, Lee, and Smith, "High School Organization," p. 147; Willms, "Social Class Segregation," p. 226; Ascher and Burnett, *Current Trends and Issues in Urban Education*, p. 25.

110. Jean Anyon, "Elementary Schooling and Distinctions of Social Class," *Interchange*, vol. 12 (1981), pp. 118–32, cited in Adam Gamoran, "Curriculum Change as a Reform Strategy: Lessons from the United States and Scotland," *Teachers College Record*, vol. 98 (Summer 1997), p. 610. Douglas MacIver and Joyce Epstein, *How Equal Are Opportunities for Learning in Disadvantaged and Advantaged Middle Grade Schools?* (Baltimore, Md.: Center for Research on Effective Schooling for Disadvantaged Children, July 1990), pp. 1–5. Mosborg, *How Money Matters*, p. 19; see also Oakes, *Multiplying Inequalities*, p. 35; Mathews, *Class Struggle*, pp. 285, 289–95.

111. Nat Hentoff, "A Different Kind of Discrimination," *Washington Post*, April 17, 1999, p. A19.

112. Lippman and others, *Urban Schools*, p. 102. Oakes, *Multiplying Inequalities*, pp. 32–40; see also Smith and O'Day, "Educational Equality," p. 70. Orfield and Eaton, *Dismantling Desegregation*, p. 83.

113. Paul Gagnon, "The Case for Standards: Equity and Competence," *Boston University Journal of Education*, vol. 176 (1994), pp. 10, 1. Jennifer O'Day and Marshall S. Smith, "Systemic Reform and Educational Opportunity," in Susan Fuhrman, *Designing Coherent Education Policy* (San Francisco: Jossey-Bass, 1993), p. 277; see also p. 291 (citing *Abbott* v. *Burke*, 575 A.2d 359 (N.J. 1990), which unanimously required not only fiscal equity but also equality of programs).

114. Wolf, *Trial and Error*, p. 124; Christopher Jencks and Meredith Phillips, "The Black-White Test Score Gap: Why It Persists and What Can Be Done," *Brookings Review* (Spring 1998), p. 27.

115. Bok, *The State of the Nation*, p. 67. Christopher Jencks, "Deadly Neighborhoods: How the Underclass Has Been Misunderstood," *New Republic*, June 13, 1988, p. 31. Courts have endorsed the commonsense notion that course offerings, levels of expectation, and background of teaching staff matter to equal educational opportunity; see Plaintiffs' Brief, Plaintiffs' Appeal from Superior Court, *Sheff* v. *O'Neill* (August 1, 1995), p. 41, citing *Horton* v. *Meskill I*, 172 Conn. 615, 634 (1977) (measuring background of teachers and course offerings); *Abbott* v. *Burke*, 119 N.J. 287, 357–66 (1990) (measuring course offerings and educational background and experience of teachers); *United States* v. *Yonkers Board of Education*, 624 F. Supp. 1276, 1430–31 (S.D.N.Y. 1985) (looking at teacher experience, teacher expectations, and educational curriculum).

116. Michael Rutter and others, *Fifteen Thousand Hours: Secondary Schools and Their Effects on Children* (Harvard University Press, 1979), pp. 14–15; Peng and Hill, *Understanding Racial-Ethnic Differences*, p. 5; Gary Natriello, ed., *School Dropouts: Patterns and Policies* (New York: Teachers College Press, 1987), pp. 3, 7; U.S. Commission on Civil Rights, *Racial Isolation*, p. 99; Alan Wilson, "Educational Consequences of Segregation in a California Community," in U.S. Commission on Civil Rights, *Racial Isolation*, vol. 2, p. 181; Mahard and Crain, "Research on Minority Achievement," p. 10;

Frederick Douglass, quoted in Jonathan Coleman, *Long Way to Go: Black and White in America* (Atlantic Monthly Press, 1997), p. 54 ("If nothing is expected of a man, he finds that expectation hard to contradict").

117. O'Day and Smith, "Systemic Reform and Educational Opportunity," p. 301. Robert Rosenthal and Lenore Jackson, *Pygmalion in the Classroom: Teacher Expectations and Pupils' Development* (Holt, Rinehart and Winston, 1968), pp. 3, vii, 74–75. Ferguson, "Teachers' Perceptions and Expectations," pp. 283–84; Puma and others, *Prospects: Final Report*, p. vii.

118. For examples of cases in which raising standards was credited with raising test scores, see Mike Rose, "Poor Kids in a Rich Kids' Curriculum," *Education Digest*, vol. 61 (February 1996), pp. 13–16; Richard J. Murnane and Frank Levy, "Why Money Matters Sometimes: A Two-Part Management Lesson from East Austin, Texas," *Education Week*, September 11, 1996, p. 36; Valerie E. Lee and Anthony S. Bryk, "Curriculum Tracking as Mediating the Social Distribution of High School Achievement," *Sociology of Education*, vol. 61 (April 1988), p. 79; Gamoran, "Curriculum Change as a Reform Strategy," pp. 608, 610, 612, 618, 620; Nicholas D. Kristof, "Where Children Rule," *New York Times Magazine*, August 17, 1997, p. 43; Julia Smith and Valerie Lee, *High School Restructuring and the Equitable Distribution of Achievement* (Madison, Wisc.: Center on Organization and Restructuring of Schools, February 16, 1996), pp. 15–16; David Grissmer and Ann Flanagan, *Exploring Rapid Achievement Gains in North Carolina and Texas* (Washington: National Education Goals Panel, November 1998), p. 23.

119. Fred M. Newmann, ed., *Student Engagement and Achievement in American Secondary Schools* (New York: Teachers College Press, 1992), p. 1; see also Hallinger and Murphy, "The Social Context of Effective Schools," p. 333. Senate Committee on Labor and Human Resources, *Report: Improving America's Schools Act of 1994*, 103 Cong., 2 sess. (Government Printing Office, 1994), p. 2.

120. Rebecca Barr and Robert Dreeben, with Nonglak Wiatchai, *How Schools Work* (University of Chicago Press, 1983), p. 66. Christopher Jencks, "A Reappraisal of the Most Controversial Educational Document of Our Time," *New York Times Magazine*, November 19, 1972, p. 13.

121. James B. Conant, *The American High School Today* (McGraw-Hill, 1959), pp. 77–79. Coleman, quoted in Charles E. Silberman, *Crisis in the Classroom: The Remaking of American Education* (Random House, 1970), p. 86. Smith and O'Day, "Educational Equality," p. 67; see also David Gerald Jaynes and Robin M. Williams Jr., eds., *A Common Destiny: Blacks and American Society* (Washington: National Academy Press, 1989), p. 350; J. Douglas Willms and Frank H. Echols, "The Scottish Experience of Parental School Choice," in Edith Rasell and Richard Rothstein, eds., *School Choice: Examining the Evidence* (Washington: Economic Policy Institute, 1993), p. 56.

Chapter Five

1. Meier, memorandum on education to the Century Foundation, June 17, 1998, p. 2; see also Ronald F. Ferguson, "Teachers' Perceptions and Expectations and the Black-White Test Score Gap," in Christopher Jencks and Meredith Phillips, eds., *The Black-White Test Score Gap* (Brookings, 1998), p. 275. James S. Liebman, "Desegregating Politics: 'All-Out' School Desegregation Explained," *Columbia Law Review*, vol. 90 (October 1990), pp. 1463, 1625 n. 675.

2. Jane L. David and Patrick M. Shields, "'Standards Are Not Magic,'" *Education Week*, April 14, 1999, p. 42. Julia Smith and Valerie Lee, *High School Restructuring and the Equitable Distribution of Achievement* (Madison, Wisc.: Center on Organization and Restructuring of Schools, February 16, 1996), p. 18. Holly Holland, *Making Change: Three Educators Join the Battle for Better Schools* (Portsmouth, N.H.: Heinemann, 1998), pp. xii, xxvi, xxxvii, 49, 97, 173, 175, 180, 183; see also Daniel Koretz and Sheila Barron, "The Validity of Gains in Scores on Kentucky Instructional Results Information System (KIRIS)," Research Brief (Santa Monica, Calif.: Rand, 1999). For discussion of the issue of whether poor kids will simply be "resegregated" within the school building through tracking, see chapter 6.

3. Linda Darling-Hammond, "Unequal Opportunity: Race and Education," *Brookings Review* (Spring 1998), p. 31. Adam Gamoran, "Curriculum Change as a Reform Strategy: Lessons from the United States and Scotland," *Teachers College Record*, vol. 98 (Summer 1997), p. 626. Heather C. Hill, David K. Cohen, and Susan L. Moffitt, "Instruction, Poverty, and Performance," in Gary Orfield and Elizabeth DeBray, eds., *Hard Work for Good Schools: Facts not Fads in Title I Reform* (Cambridge, Mass.: Harvard Civil Rights Project, 1999), pp. 64, 69.

4. See, for example, Sari Horwitz, "Teacher Ratings to Be Tied to Student Scores," *Washington Post*, April 6, 1995, p. D6.

5. Jay Mathews, "State Testing Programs Face Special Challenges: Virginia Officials Ponder How to Enforce Lofty Goals," *Washington Post*, April 25, 1999, C1.

6. Linda Darling-Hammond, "National Standards and Assessments: Will They Improve Education?" *American Journal of Education*, vol. 102 (August 1994), pp. 478, 487. See discussion of "opportunity to learn" in chapter 7. See Andrew C. Porter, "The Uses and Misuses of Opportunity-to-Learn Standards," in Diane Ravitch, ed., *Debating the Future of American Education: Do We Need Standards and Assessments?* (Brookings, 1995), pp. 42, 47; Darling-Hammond, "National Standards and Assessments," pp. 478, 487; Rochelle Sharpe, "Clinton Package for Schools Has Chance to Pass," *Wall Street Journal*, April 16, 1993, p. B1.

7. "My Fellow Americans . . . State of Our Union is Strong," *Washington Post*, January 20, 1999, p. A12 (excerpts from President Clinton's State of the Union Address). See Hilary Stout, "Clinton to Propose Scholarship Program to Lure Teachers to Inner-City Schools," *Wall Street Journal*, July 17, 1997, p. A24. For similar local programs, see Gary Orfield and Susan Eaton, *Dismantling Desegregation: The Quiet Reversal of Brown v. Board of Education* (New York: New Press, 1996), p. 89; "Quality Counts '98: The Urban Challenge," *Education Week*, January 8, 1998, pp. 37–38; Kati Haycock, "Good Teaching Matters: How Well-Qualified Teachers Can Close the Gap," *Thinking K–16*, vol. 3 (Summer 1998), p. 12.

8. See Richard Rothstein, "Getting Good Teachers for Poor Schools," *New York Times*, September 20, 2000, p. A21. Nationally, public school teachers in central-city schools with high minority populations are already paid more than central-city school teachers with low percentages of minority students ($39,694 versus $37,990); National Center for Education Statistics (NCES), *The Condition of Education, 1998* (Dept. of Education, 1998), pp. 127, 136.

9. David Nakamura, "Struggling Schools Are Desperate for Experienced Teachers," *Washington Post*, July 29, 1999, pp. A1, A22.

10. Esther Ho Sui-Chu and J. Douglas Willms, "Effects of Parental Involvement on Eighth-Grade Achievement," *Sociology of Education*, vol. 69 (April 1996), p. 127. Charles Glenn, interview with author, Boston, December 3, 1997, pp. 20–21 (citing Fred Hess's research in Chicago indicating that parental involvement programs have "little actual impact"); Department of Education, "Promising Results, Continuing Challenges: Final Report of the National Assessment of Title I—Highlights" (www.ed.gov/ offices/OUS/eval/hlights.html [March 1, 1999]).

11. I. N. Berlin, "Desegregation Creates Problems, Too," in Hubert H. Humphrey, ed., *Integration vs. Segregation* (New York: Thomas Crowell, 1964), p. 231; U.S. Commission on Civil Rights, *Racial Isolation in the Public Schools*, vol.1 (Government Printing Office, 1967), p. 78.

12. Bernard Michael, *Volunteers in Public Schools* (Washington: National Academy Press, 1990), p. 15; Jeanne Brooks-Gunn and others, "Do Neighborhoods Influence Child and Adolescent Development?" *American Journal of Sociology*, vol. 99 (September 1993), p. 360.

13. Ho Sui-Chu and Willms, "Effects of Parental Involvement"; see also Gerald W. Bracey, "SES and Involvement," *Phi Delta Kappan*, vol. 78, no. 2 (October 1996), p. 16.

14. Donna Harrison, "The Real Class Divide," *New York Times*, September 24, 1997. Katherine Jason, "Our Unfair Share," *New York Times*, September 26, 1997, p. A35.

15. In the New York case, private funds were barred from use, but Superintendent Crew found public money to save the fourth-grade teacher, a precedent that underlines the truth that vocal middle-class parents are likely to get public resources when they demand them; Blaine Harden and Valerie Strauss, "A Hard Lesson in School Economics," *Washington Post*, October 10, 1997, p. A3.

16. James S. Liebman, "Three Strategies for Implementing *Brown* Anew," in Herbert Hill and James E. Jones, eds., *Race in America: The Struggle for Equality* (University of Wisconsin Press, 1993), p. 117.

17. Frederick Mosteller and Daniel P. Moynihan, eds., *On Equality of Educational Opportunity: Papers Deriving from the Harvard Faculty Seminar on the Coleman Report* (Random House, 1972), p. 16. James S. Coleman, "Equality of Opportunity and Equality of Results," *Harvard Educational Review*, vol. 43 (February 1973), p. 259. See, for example, John Chubb and Terry Moe, *Politics, Markets, and American Schools* (Brookings, 1990), pp. 124–28; Orfield and Eaton, *Dismantling Desegregation*, p. 92; Derek Bok, *The State of the Nation* (Harvard University Press, 1996), p. 185; Richard J. Murnane and Frank Levy, "Why Money Matters Sometimes: A Two-Part Management Lesson from East Austin, Texas," *Education Week*, September 11, 1996, p. 48.

18. Myron Orfield, *Metropolitics: A Regional Agenda for Community and Stability* (Brookings, 1997), p. 45; James Traub, "Can Separate Be Equal?" *Harper's Magazine*, June 1994, p. 39; Melody Petersen, "A Bitter Taste in Newark Schools," *New York Times*, September 18, 1997, p. B1. Orfield and Eaton, *Dismantling Desegregation*, pp. 155–57. *Milliken v. Bradley II*, 433 U.S. 267 (1977), 272–73 (regarding elements of the wish list).

19. Michael A. Rebell and Robert L. Hughes, "Efficacy and Engagement: The Remedies Problem Posed by *Sheff* v. *O'Neill*—and a Proposed Solution," *Connecticut Law Review*, vol. 29 (1997), p. 1128; Roy L. Brooks, *Integration or Separation? A Strategy for Racial Equality* (Harvard University Press, 1996), p. 217; Michael D. Shear, "Money Was No Cure-All, Officials in Austin Found," *Washington Post*, October 26, 1997, p. A16;

Lisa Frazier and Michael Shear, "Despite Extra Funding, Schools Fail to Flourish," *Washington Post,* October 26, 1997, p. A1; Lisa Leff, "Demographics Foil Prince George's Schools' Efforts to Achieve Racial Balance," *Washington Post,* September 12, 1993, pp. A1, A24.

20. Michael J. Puma and others, *Prospects: Final Report on Student Outcomes* (Cambridge, Mass.: Abt Associates, 1997), pp. vi, 12 (citing two earlier studies finding no gains from Title I compared with similar students not receiving Title I). Gary Natriello and Edward J. McDill, "Title I: From Funding Mechanism to Educational Program," in Orfield and DeBray, eds., *Hard Work for Good Schools,* pp. 33–34; see also Ralph Frammolino, "Title I's $118 Billion Fails to Close Gap," *Los Angeles Times,* January 17, 1999, p. A1.

21. See Erik W. Robelen, "Title I Study Finds 'Promising' Student Gains," *Education Week,* March 10, 1999; Department of Education, "Promising Results, Continuing Challenge: Final Report of the National Assessment of Title I—Executive Summary" (www.ed.gov/offices/OUS/eval/exsum.html [March 1, 1999]) (between 1988 and 1996, the gap between the reading scores of low- and high-poverty schools has actually increased, from 27 points to 37 points.); and Diane Ravitch, "Education: See All the Spin," *Washington Post,* March 23, 1999, p. A17.

22. Orfield and Eaton, *Dismantling Desegregation,* pp. 25, 83. See also Marc Moss and Michael Puma, *Prospects: The Congressionally Mandated Study of Educational Growth and Opportunity—First-Year Report on Language Minority and Limited English Proficient Students* (Dept. of Education, 1995), pp. i-1 and 1-1; NCES, *Digest of Education Statistics* (Dept. of Education, 1996), p. 95; Orfield and Eaton, *Dismantling Desegregation,* p. 89; U.S. Commission on Civil Rights, *Racial Isolation,* vol. 1, pp. 120–21; Gary Orfield and Lawrence Peskin, "Metropolitan High Schools: Income, Race, and Inequality," in Douglas E. Mitchell and Margaret Goertz, eds., *Education Politics for the New Century* (New York: Falmer Press, 1990), pp. 31, 39, 50; Dick Hubert, "Class and the Classroom: The Duluth Experience," *Saturday Review of Education,* May 27, 1972, pp. 55–56; Richard A. Epstein, "The Remote Causes of Affirmative Action and School Desegregation in Kansas City," *California Law Review,* vol. 84 (1996), p. 1106; Jim Sleeper, *Liberal Racism* (Viking, 1997), p. 165. See also Christopher Jencks and Meredith Phillips, "The Black-White Test Score Gap: Why It Persists and What Can Be Done?" *Brookings Review* (Spring 1998), p. 26 ("The average black child now attends school in a district that spends as much per pupil as the average white district"); Michael Powell, "School Funds Have Gone for Bureaucrats Rather Than Books and Boilers," *Washington Post,* July 21, 1997, p. A13 (citing the Washington, D.C., Control Board report, "Children in Crisis," that District schools spend $7,655 on each student, compared with $6,562 in Montgomery County, Maryland, with disastrous achievement results).

23. See, for example, Janet Eyler, Valerie Cook, and Leslie Ward, "Resegregation: Segregation within Desegregated Schools," in Christine H. Rossell and Willis D. Hawley, eds., *The Consequences of School Desegregation* (Temple University Press, 1983), pp. 133–34; David Armor, "After Busing: Education and Choice," *Public Interest,* vol. 95 (Spring 1989), p. 36; Gary Orfield, *Must We Bus? Segregated Schools and National Policy* (Brookings, 1978), p. 431; Gary Orfield and others, *The Growth of Segregation in American Schools: Changing Patterns of Separation and Poverty since 1968* (Harvard University Press, 1994), pp. 3, 26; Charles V. Willie, "Desegregation in Big-City School Systems,"

Education Forum, vol. 47 (Fall 1982), pp. 83, 85; Robert E. Slavin, "Making Chapter 1 Make a Difference," *Phi Delta Kappan*, vol. 69 (October 1987), p. 114.

The 1994 Title I reauthorization seeks to remedy the situation insofar as Title I conflicts with racial desegregation orders; see P.L. 103-382, 108 Stat. 3533 (providing for a waiver from the requirement that schools be given money on a ranking of poverty concentrations where a school is subject to a state-ordered or court-ordered desegregation plan and low-income students constitute at least 25 percent of its student body). Title I still does nothing, however, for a school that seeks to reduce concentrations of poverty and is limited to racial desegregation efforts; Trine Tsouderos, "Kids in City's Poor Schools Get Worse Scores," *Tennessean*, December 27, 1998.

24. See Doris R. Entwisle, Karl L. Alexander, and Linda Steffel Olson, *Children, Schools, and Inequality* (New York: Westview Press, 1997), pp. 58, 150.

25. Traub, "Can Separate Be Equal?" p. 42. For a balanced review of the conflicting evidence, see Gary Burtless, ed., *Does Money Matter? The Effect of School Resources on Student Achievement and Adult Success* (Brookings, 1996).

26. Jencks and Phillips, eds., *The Black-White Test Score Gap*, p. 45. Estimates vary in part because of the varying goals, which include bringing poor kids to a basic minimum competency, bringing the poor to a rough equality of group result, and providing an incentive for middle-class schools to admit poor children.

One highly successful program, the U.S. Military Academy's Preparatory School, which is credited with significantly raising the number of black cadets at West Point, does "not come cheap," with an annual price tag of $40,000 to $60,000 for each student; see Charles C. Moskos and John Sibley Butler, *All That We Can Be* (Basic Books, 1996), pp. 86–91.

See also Richard Rothstein, "Equalizing Education Resources on Behalf of Disadvantaged Children," in Richard D. Kahlenberg, ed., *A Notion at Risk: Preserving Public Education as an Engine for Social Mobility* (Century Foundation Press, 2000), pp. 34–35 (citing estimates ranging from 120 percent to 210 percent and noting that extra expenses come from concentrations of poverty as well as from family poverty); Christopher Jencks, "Is the Public School Obsolete?" *Public Interest*, vol. 2 (Winter 1966), p. 19 (poor need 200 percent); Sizer and Whitten, "A Proposal for a Poor Children's Bill of Rights," *Psychology Today*, August, 1968, pp. 59, 61–62 (need 400 percent); Martin Carnoy, "Is Privatization through Education Vouchers Really the Answer? A Comment on West," *World Bank Research Observer*, February 1997 (125 percent premium insufficient); Bracey, "SES and Involvement," p. 111 (Sweden spends 200–300 percent); Janet Currie and Duncan Thomas, "Does Head Start Make a Difference?" *American Economic Review*, vol. 85, no. 3 (June 1995), p. 343 (Perry preschool is 200 percent of Head Start); G. Alfred Hess, "Adequacy Rather than Equity: A New Solution or a Stalking Horse?" *Educational Policy*, vol. 8 (December 1994) (William Clune estimates 200 percent cost, a level "so great as to boggle the political imagination"); Deborah Meier, interview with author, Boston, December 3, 1997 (educating the poor costs "easily twice as much" but is politically difficult to achieve); Mark Francis Cohen, "People's Prep," *New Republic*, June 15, 1998, pp. 13–14 (Proctor Charter School, a public boarding academy in New Jersey, has positive effects on the achievement of poor students but costs $17,000 for each student); David L. Kirp, "The Poor, the Schools, and Equal Protection," in *Harvard Education Review: Equal Educational Opportunity* (Harvard University Press, 1969), p. 169 (300–400 percent cost); General Accounting Office (GAO), *School Finance: State and Federal Efforts to Target Poor Students: Report to Congressional Requesters* (Washington, January 1998), pp. 34–35 (120–200 percent cost, with 160 percent a "midway" figure); William H. Clune, "Comments on Chapters Eight, Nine, and Ten," in Helen F. Ladd, ed., *Holding Schools Accountable: Performance-Based Reform in Education* (Brookings, 1996), p. 359 (to reach a "high minimum level of educational outcomes" costs twice as much for low-income students as other students); William D. Duncombe and John M. Yinger, "Performance Standards and Educational Cost Indexes," in Helen F. Ladd, Rosemary Chalk, and Janet S. Hansen, eds., *Equity and Adequacy in Education Finance* (Washington: National Academy Press, 1999), p. 278 (New York City needs to spend 387 percent of what other districts spend to have a chance of equal educational outcomes, much of this because of higher levels of poverty).

27. Jencks and Phillips, *The Black-White Test Score Gap*, p. 45; see also Richard Leone, foreword to Carol Ascher, Norm Fruchter, and Robert Berne, *Hard Lessons: Public Schools and Privatization* (Twentieth Century Fund, 1996), p. v. In New Jersey, Governor Jim Florio's effort in 1990 merely to equalize funding created a "grassroots rebellion"; Mickey Kaus, *The End of Equality* (Basic Books, 1992), p. 154.

28. Gary Orfield and David Thronson, "Dismantling Desegregation: Uncertain Gains, Unexpected Costs," *Emory Law Journal*, vol. 42 (1993), p. 784.

29. Grasmick quoted in "Quality Counts '98," p. 20.

30. David K. Cohen, "Policy for the Public Schools: Compensation and Integration," in *Harvard Educational Review: Equal Educational Opportunity*, p. 97.

31. Orfield, *Metropolitics*, p. 90.

32. Deborah Meier, *The Power of Their Ideas: Lessons for America from a Small School in Harlem* (Boston: Beacon Press, 1995), p. 65. John Hildebrand, "Bush's Blueprint for Education," *Newsday*, April 19, 1991, p. 5. Natriello and McDill, "Title I: From Funding Mechanism to Educational Program," p. 38.

33. See, for example, Lawrence C. Stedman, "It's Time We Changed the Effective Schools Formula," *Phi Delta Kappan*, vol. 69 (November 1987), pp. 215–16; Gerald David Jaynes and Robin M. Williams Jr., eds., *A Common Destiny: Blacks and American Society* (Washington: National Academy Press, 1989), p. 360; Ralph Scott and Herbert J. Walberg, "Schools Alone Are Insufficient: A Response to Edmonds," *Educational Leadership* (October 1979), p. 26; Anthony S. Bryk, Valerie E. Lee, and Peter B. Holland, *Catholic Schools and the Common Good* (Harvard University Press, 1993), p. 56; Thomas L. Good and Jere E. Brophy, "School Effects," in Merlin C. Wittrock, *Handbook of Research on Teaching*, 3d ed. (New York: Macmillan, 1986), p. 572; Gary G. Wheelage and Gregory A. Smith, "Building New Programs for Students at Risk," in Fred M. Newmann, ed., *Student Engagement and Achievement in American Secondary Schools* (New York: Teachers College Press, 1992), p. 103 (hard to replicate); Liebman, "Desegregating Politics," pp. 1463, 1489 n. 142.

34. See, for example, Deborah Anderluh, "Title I Fosters Separate, Unequal School System," *Sacramento Bee*, September 21, 1997; Deborah Anderluh, "High Turnover, Low Expectations Plague Poor Schools," *Sacramento Bee*, September 22, 1997; Deborah Anderluh, "Texas Reforms Are Turning High-Poverty Schools Around," *Sacramento Bee*, September 24, 1997; Francie Latour, "Poverty Can Be Overcome, School Shows," *Boston Globe*, December 24, 1998, p. B2.

35. Yale University's James Comer, whose effective-schools model has been adopted in 650 schools in twenty-eight states, is now "pessimistic" about school reform; see

Christopher Shea, "How Kids Can Catch Up," *Washington Post,* October 26, 1997 (reviewing Comer's book, *Waiting for a Miracle,* and noting its "pessimistic narrative").

36. Jay Mathews, "A Math Teacher's Lessons in Division," *Washington Post,* May 21, 1997, pp. D1, D6; Jay Mathews, "A Teacher Using Challenge of Calculus Alters Equation of Inner-City Living," *Washington Post,* May 15, 1987, p. A15. Jay Mathews, *Class Struggle: What's Wrong (and Right) with America's Best Public High Schools* (New York: Times Books, 1998), pp. 141–42.

37. Nicholas Lemann, "Ready, READ!" *Atlantic Monthly,* November 1998, p. 96. *Abbott* v. *Burke V,* 153 N.J. 480 (1998), 501, n. 2 (citing "studies").

38. Debra Viadero, "Miami Study Critiques 'Success for All,'" *Education Week,* January 27, 1999; Herbert J. Walberg and Rebecca C. Greenberg, "The Diogenes Factor," *Phi Delta Kappan,* vol. 81 (October 1999), pp. 127–28; Richard Whitmire, "Why Doesn't Anyone Pay Attention to Education Research?" *Washington Monthly,* November 1998, p. 18.

39. Lemann, "Ready, READ!" p. 96; Ronald F. Ferguson, "Can Schools Narrow?" in Jencks and Phillips, *The Black-White Test Score Gap,* p. 343; Lynn Olson, "Researchers Rate Whole-School Reform Models," *Education Week,* February 17, 1999, pp. 1, 14.

40. Anderluh, "Title I Fosters Separate, Unequal School System," p. A1; Anderluh, "Texas Reforms Are Turning High-Poverty Schools Around," p. A1; "Quality Counts '98," pp. 34–35; Julianne Basinger, "University Joins with Entire Community to Raise Academic Standards in El Paso's Schools," *Chronicle of Higher Education,* November 20, 1998, pp. A28–A30; Haycock, "Good Teaching Matters," p. 1.

41. G. Alfred Hess Jr., "Comments," in Diane Ravitch, ed., *Brookings Papers on Education Policy, 1999* (Brookings, 1999), p. 167. Daniel M. O'Brien, "Family and School Effects on the Cognitive Growth of Minority and Disadvantaged Elementary Students," paper presented to the annual meeting of the Association for Public Policy Analysis and Management, New York, October 29–31, 1998, pp. 5–6.

42. Samuel Casey Carter, *No Excuses: Lessons from 21 High-Performing, High-Poverty Schools* (Washington: Heritage Foundation, 2000), p. 2. Kenneth J. Cooper, "School Defies Its Demographics," *Washington Post,* June 7, 2000, p. A3. Sam Stringfield, quoted in Anderluh, "Title I Fosters Separate, Unequal School Systems," p. A1.

43. For the widespread adoption of effective schools techniques in Title I and by individual districts, see Charles Teddlie and Sam Stringfield, *Schools Make a Difference: Lessons Learned from a Ten-Year Study of School Effects* (New York: Teachers College Press, 1993), pp. ix, 3, 28 (citing federal law and a 1989 GAO Report).

44. Stedman, "It's Time We Changed the Effective Schools Formula," p. 215. Puma and others, *Prospects: Final Report,* pp. v, 60. "Quality Counts '98," pp. 6, 9. David Rusk, "To Improve Public Education, Stop Moving Money, Move Families," *Abell Report,* vol. 11 (June–July 1998), p. 4; see also Joseph Watras, *Politics, Race, and Schools: Racial Integration, 1954–1994* (New York: Garland Publishing, 1997), pp. 306–17 (describing Annie E. Casey Foundation's "New Futures" program for at-risk youth in Dayton schools, finding, after five years and $20 million, no effect on graduation rates or teen pregnancy and mixed effects on reading scores). Christopher Jencks and Meredith Phillips, "Introduction," in *The Black-White Test Score Gap,* p. 44.

45. Ronald Edmonds, "Effective Schools for the Urban Poor," *Educational Leadership,* October 1979, pp. 16–17.

46. Alan B. Krueger, "Reassessing the View that American Schools Are Broken," *FRBNY Economic Policy Review* (March 1998), pp. 34–36; Sara Mosle, "What We Talk

about When We Talk about Education," *New Republic*, June 17, 1996, p. 35; Jencks and Phillips, introduction to *The Black-White Test Score Gap*, p. 30; Harold Wenglinksy, *When Money Matters: How Educational Expenditures Improve Student Performance and How They Don't* (Princeton, N.J.: Educational Testing Service, 1997), pp. viii, iii.

47. Sara Mosle, "Size Matters," *New Republic*, November 11, 1996, p. 38. See, for example, Eric A. Hanushek, "The Economics of Schooling: Production and Efficiency in Public Schools," *FRBNY Economic Policy Review* (March 1998), pp. 18-19 (pupil-to-teacher ratios have fallen since 1960, while scores have declined); Joseph S. Tracy and Barbara L. Walter, "Summary and Observations and Recommendations," *FRBNY Economic Policy Review* (March 1998), p. 5; Gary Burtless, "Introduction and Summary," in *Does Money Matter?* p. 5; Chester Finn, quoted in Ethan Bronner, "Better Schools Is Battle Cry for Fall Elections," *New York Times*, September 20, 1998, sec. 1, pp. 1, 32 (international comparisons); NCES, *Teacher Quality: A Report on the Preparation and Qualifications of Public School Teachers* (1999), p. 4 ("the research on class size is somewhat mixed"); Whitmire, "Why Doesn't Anyone Pay Attention to Educational Research?" pp. 17, 20.

48. Ferguson, "Can Schools Narrow?" pp. 359-60. See also Puma and others, *Prospects: Final Report*, p. 59; NCES, *Teacher Quality*, p. 38.

49. See Bronner, "Better Schools Is Battle Cry for Fall Elections," pp. 1, 32.

50. Amy Virshup, "Grading Teachers," *Washington Post Magazine*, November 9, 1997, pp. 15, 31. Anemona Hartocollis, "Educators Say Clinton's Plan on Class Size Faces Problems," *New York Times*, January 29, 1998, pp. A1, B4; Randy Ross, "How Class-Size Reduction Harms Kids in Poor Neighborhoods," *Education Week*, May 26, 1999, p. 30. George Miller, "Not Just More Teachers—Better Teachers, Too," *Washington Post*, August 8, 1999, p. A17.

51. Cited in Rene Sanchez, "Poor, Minority Students Lack Access to Computers," *Washington Post*, May 15, 1997, p. A13.

52. Michael Fletcher, "Worries Overshadow a Civil Rights Anniversary," *Washington Post*, May 18, 1999, p. A9. "*Brown* at 40," editorial, *Nation*, May 23, 1994, p. 687. Michael Alves, interview with author, Cambridge, Mass., December 1, 1997, pp. 23, 60.

53. *Keyes* v. *School District No. 1*, 413 U.S. 189 (1973), 208, 218-31 (Powell, J., concurring), 216 (Douglas, J., concurring); *Washington* v. *Davis*, 426 U.S. 229 (1976); *Dayton* v. *Brinkman*, 433 U.S. 406 (1977), 417; *Arlington Heights* v. *Metropolitan Housing Corporation*, 429 U.S. 252 (1977), 264-65; *Pasadena Board of Education* v. *Spangler*, 427 U.S. 424 (1976), 434.

54. *Milliken* v. *Bradley*, 418 U.S. 717 (1974), 750.

55. James S. Coleman, "The Role of Incentives in School Desegregation," in Adam Yarmolinsky, Lance Liebman, and Corrinne S. Schelling, eds., *Race and Schooling in the City* (Harvard University Press, 1981), p. 189; see also James S. Coleman, Sara D. Kelly, and John Moore, *Trends in School Segregation, 1968-1973* (Washington: Urban Institute, 1975). James S. Coleman, "Integration, Yes; Busing, No," *New York Times Magazine*, August 24, 1975, p. 11. Gary Orfield and others, *Deepening Segregation in American Public Schools* (Cambridge, Mass.: Harvard Project on School Desegregation, 1997), p. 22; see also Paul E. Peterson and Jay P. Greene, "Race Relations, Vouchers, and Central-City Schools," *Taubman Center Report* (1998), pp. 10-11.

56. *Board of Education of Oklahoma City* v. *Dowell*, 498 U.S. 237 (1991), 249-50 (that a board will be released from a desegregation order if it has made "good faith" efforts and has eliminated the vestiges of discrimination "to the extent practicable");

Freeman v. *Pitts,* 503 U.S. 467 (1992), 471 (that the *Green* requirements do not need to be met all at once for partial release), and *Missouri* v. *Jenkins II,* 115 S. Ct. 2038 (1995) (that even *Milliken II* remedies are temporary; that links of current harms to the legacy of past discrimination must be specified precisely; and that test score gaps need not be eliminated before a declaration that the vestiges of discrimination are eliminated; rather, the relevant gap is between inner-city schools with a history of de jure segregation and those without such a history).

57. The Supreme Court's *Green* decision laid out six desegregation factors to consider in determining whether a district can be declared "unitary": student assignments, "faculty, staff, transportation, extracurricular activities, and facilities"; *Green* v. *County School Board of New Kent County* 391 U.S. 430 (1968), 435. See also *Swann* v. *Charlotte-Mecklenburg Board of Education,* 402 U.S. 1 (1971), 18; and *Dowell,* 250.

58. *Freeman* v. *Pitts,* 492 (quoting *Dowell,* 249–50), 476–78. *Dowell* 255 (Marshall, J., dissenting).

59. Orfield and Eaton, *Dismantling Desegregation,* p. 2. David Armor, *Forced Justice: School Desegregation and the Law* (New York: Oxford University Press, 1995), p. 48; Derrick A. Bell, *Race, Racism, and American Law,* 3d ed. (Boston: Little Brown, 1992), pp. 580, 587–90; Stephan Thernstrom and Abigail Thernstrom, *America in Black and White: One Nation, Indivisible* (Simon and Schuster, 1997), pp. 320, 330; Orfield and Eaton, *Dismantling Desegregation,* p. 21; Gary Orfield, "Metropolitan School Desegregation: Impacts on Metropolitan Society," *Minnesota Law Review,* vol. 80 (April 1996), p. 828; Michele Norris, "School Busing: Has the Payoff Been Worth the Pain?" ABC News, *Nightline,* October 2, 1997; Peter Schmidt, "U.S. Judge Releases Wilmington Districts from Court Oversight," *Education Week,* September 6, 1995; Peter Schmidt, "Districts View Desegregation in New Light," *Teacher Magazine,* December 13, 1995; Orfield and others, *Deepening Segregation,* 1997, p. 4; Caroline Hendrie, "Legal Issues Complicate Efforts to Integrate School Staffs," *Education Week,* June 24, 1998; Caroline Hendrie, "A Denver High School Reaches Out to the Neighborhood It Lost to Busing," *Education Week,* June 17, 1998; Caroline Hendrie, "Without Court Orders, Schools Ponder How to Pursue Diversity," *Education Week,* April 30, 1997; Caroline Hendrie, "Judge Ends Desegregation Case in Cleveland," *Education Week,* April 8, 1998; Tamar Lewin, "Public Schools Confronting Issue of Racial Preferences," *New York Times,* November 29, 1998, p. 1; Scott Shepard, "As School Busing Ends, Battle Shifts to Enhancing Education," *Atlanta Journal and Constitution,* May 3, 1998, p. 2G; Lisa Frazier, "Judge Ends Busing in Prince George's," *Washington Post,* September 2, 1998, p. A1; Steven Drummond, "As Desegregation Changes, So Must Educators, Law Experts Say," *Teacher Magazine,* April 24, 1996; Max Boot, "America's Worst Judges," *Wall Street Journal,* May 28, 1998; Caroline Hendrie, "Settlement Ends St. Louis Desegregation Case," *Education Week,* March 24, 1999, p. 3.

60. Nationally, about three hundred of the nation's sixteen hundred school districts are still under federal supervision, down from more than five hundred in the mid-1970s; Schmidt, "Districts View Desegregation in New Light"; see also Steven A. Holmes, "At NAACP, Talk of a Shift on Integration," *New York Times,* June 23, 1997, pp. A1, A15; Shepard, "As School Busing Ends, Battle Shifts to Enhancing Education," p. 2G; Watras, *Politics, Race, and Schools,* p. xii.

61. Lewin, "Public Schools Confronting Issue of Racial Preferences," p. 1. *Eisenberg* v. *Montgomery County Public Schools,* 197 F.3d 123 (4th Cir. 1999), cert. denied 120 U.S.

1420 (2000); see also *Tuttle* v. *Arlington County School Board,* 195 F.3d 698 (4th Cir. 1999). Caroline Hendrie, "San Francisco Desegregation Decree to End," *Education Week,* February 24, 1999, p. 1; Hendrie, "Without Court Orders, Schools Ponder How to Pursue Diversity"; Lewin, "Public Schools Confronting Issue of Racial Preferences," p. 1; Caroline Hendrie, "New Magnet School Policies Sidestep an Old Issue: Race," *Education Week,* June 10, 1998; Steven A. Holmes, "Whites' Bias Lawsuit Could Upset Desegregation Efforts," *New York Times,* April 25, 1999, p. 18; Paul Nowell, "Charlotte School System's Desegregation Policies Challenged," *Associated Press,* April 17, 1999; Terence J. Pell, "Does 'Diversity' Justify Quotas? The Courts Say No," *Wall Street Journal,* November 24, 1998, p. A2; Beth Daley and Andy Dabilis, "In Switch, City Won't Appeal the Latin Case: Wary of Hurting Efforts Nationally," *Boston Globe,* February 4, 1999, p. A1; Mary Ann Zehr, "Judge Orders Student's Transfer," *Education Week,* January 27, 1999, p. 4.

62. *Adarand Constructors* v. *Pena,* 115 S. Ct. 2097 (1995); *City of Richmond* v. *J. A. Croson Co.,* 488 U.S. 469 (1989); and *Hopwood* v. *Texas,* 78 F. 3d 932 (5th Cir. 1996), cert. denied 116 S. Ct. 2582 (1996). But see *Regents of University of California* v. *Bakke,* 438 U.S. 265 (1978) (holding that diversity in higher education is a compelling state interest that justifies the flexible use of race in university admissions).

63. Orfield and Eaton, *Dismantling Desegregation,* p. 56. Richard D. Kahlenberg, *The Remedy: Race, Class, and Affirmative Action* (Basic Books, 1996), pp. 106–09.

64. See Jay Mathews, "Eleven Minorities Lose Spots in Virginia School," *Washington Post,* May 31, 1997, pp. B1, B6; Lewin, "Public Schools Confronting Issue of Racial Preferences," p. 1; Hendrie, "New Magnet School Policies Sidestep an Old Issue." See also discussion of Wake County in chapter 9.

65. See discussion in chapter 3 on the importance of social class integration; see also Coleman, "New Incentives for Desegregation," *Human Rights,* vol. 7 (Fall 1978), pp. 14–15 (cited in Minnesota Department of Children, Families, and Learning, "Statement of Need and Reasonableness in the Matter of the Proposed Rules Relating to Desegregation," unpublished draft, October 12, 1998, p. 32); Thomas Sowell, "Black Excellence: The Case of Dunbar High School," *Public Interest,* vol. 35 (1974), p. 3; Marianne Lado, interview with author, New York, December 12, 1997; William Raspberry, "Two Strikes against Them," *Washington Post,* March 22, 1999, p. A19; Leonard Steinhorn and Barbara Diggs-Brown, *By the Color of Our Skin: The Illusion of Integration and the Reality of Race* (Dutton, 1999), p. 12 (citing Southfield, Michigan, schools). Nancy Hoyt St. John, *School Desegregation Outcomes for Children* (New York: John Wiley and Sons, 1975), p. 12.

66. William G. Bowen and Derek Bok, *The Shape of the River* (Princeton University Press, 1998), p. 1; Hochschild, *American Racial and Ethnic Politics in the Twenty-first Century,* p. 44; Stephan Thernstrom and Abigail Thernstrom, "Black Progress: How Far We've Come and How Far We Have to Go," *Brookings Review* (Spring 1998), p. 12; Amy Stuart Wells and Robert L. Crain, *Stepping over the Color Line: African-American Students in White Suburban Schools* (Yale University Press, 1997), p. 15; and Easterbrook, "America the O.K.," pp. 19, 24.

67. William Julius Wilson, *When Work Disappears: The World of the New Urban Poor* (Knopf, 1996), p. 195. Orlando Patterson, *The Ordeal of Integration: Progress and Resentment in America's "Racial" Crisis* (Washington: Civitas, 1997), p. 24. Thernstrom and Thernstrom, *America in Black and White,* pp. 201–02.

68. Orfield and Peskin, "Metropolitan High Schools," p. 30. Orfield and others, *The Growth of Segregation in American Schools*, p. 22; see also Christopher Jencks and Susan E. Mayer, "The Social Consequences of Growing Up in a Poor Neighborhood," in Laurence E. Lynn Jr. and Michael G. H. McGeary, eds., *Inner-City Poverty in the United States* (Washington: National Academy Press, 1990), p. 146.

69. Loury, "Not So Black and White," p. C3. Jeannie Oakes, *Multiplying Inequalities: The Effects of Race, Social Class, and Tracking on Opportunities to Learn Mathematics and Science* (Santa Monica, Calif.: Rand, 1990), pp. 14–15 (that 49.4 percent of high-poverty schools were majority white in 1985–86, high poverty defined as 30 percent or more with parents unemployed or on welfare); Mary M. Kennedy, Richard K. Jung, and M. E. Orland, *Poverty, Achievement, and the Distribution of Compensatory Education Services. An Interim Report from the National Assessment of Chapter 1* (Dept. of Education, Office of Educational Research and Improvement, 1998), p. 52 (that more than 50 percent of students attending schools with more than 24 percent poor in 1980 were non-Hispanic whites.) This figure is consistent with earlier data indicating that heavily minority schools are much more likely to be high poverty, because in absolute numbers there are many more poor whites in the country; Orfield and Eaton, *Dismantling Desegregation*, p. 55. Samuel S. Peng and Susan T. Hill, *Understanding Racial-Ethnic Differences in Secondary Science and Math Achievement* (Dept. of Education, 1995), p. 18.

70. Laura Lippman and others, *Urban Schools: The Challenge of Location and Poverty* (Dept. of Education, NCES, 1996), p. 10. In high-poverty schools (more than 24 percent poor), the average student population is 53 percent white, 32 percent black, and 12 percent Hispanic; Martin E. Orland, "Demographics of Disadvantage: Intensity of Childhood Poverty and Its Relationship to Educational Achievement," in John I. Goodlad and Pamela Keating, eds., *Access to Knowledge: An Agenda for Our Nation's Schools* (New York: College Entrance Examination Board, 1990), p. 51; David E. Myers, "The Relationship between School Poverty Concentration and Students' Reading and Math Achievement and Learning," in Kennedy, Jung, and Orland, *Poverty, Achievement, and the Distribution of Compensatory Education Services*, p. D-21. Among extremely high poverty schools (75 percent or more free and reduced-price lunch), minority percentages are higher: non-Hispanic whites constitute 22 percent of first-graders, 23 percent of third-graders, and 12 percent of seventh-graders in 1993; Puma and others, *Prospects: Final Report*, pp. 24–25; see also Orfield and others, *The Growth of Segregation in American Schools*, p. 5 (minority group students constitute 77 percent of students in schools with 75 percent or more free and reduced-price lunch rates).

71. Hubert, *Class and the Classroom*, pp. 55, 56. Alves, "Cambridge Desegregation Succeeding," pp. 178, 186.

72. Wilson, *When Work Disappears*, p. 258. David Whitman and others, "The White Underclass," *U.S. News and World Report*, October 17, 1994, p. 40 (citing the Urban Institute); Kahlenberg, *The Remedy*, p. 170. Christopher Jencks, "Is the American Underclass Growing," in Christopher Jencks and Paul E. Peterson eds., *The Urban Underclass* (Brookings, 1991), p. 30 (on Columbus, Ohio); Paul A. Jargowsky and Mary Jo Bane, "Ghetto Poverty in the United States, 1970–1980," in Jencks and Peterson, eds., *The Urban Underclass*, pp. 240–45 (on Philadelphia and Memphis). David Rusk, *Inside Game/Outside Game: Urban Policies for the Twenty-first Century* (Brookings, 1999), p. 79 (14 percent of census tracts with greater than 40 percent poverty are predominantly

white compared with 12 percent predominantly Hispanic). Patterson, *The Ordeal of Integration*, p. 5.

73. Gary Orfield, interview with author, Cambridge, Mass., November 19, 1997, p. 7. Christine H. Rossell, "Desegregation Plans, Racial Isolation, White Flight, and Community Response," in Christine H. Rossell and Willis D. Hawley, eds., *The Consequences of School Desegregation* (Temple University Press, 1983), pp. 33–37; J. Harvie Wilkinson III, *From Brown to Bakke: The Supreme Court and School Integration, 1954–1978* (New York: Oxford University Press, 1979), p. 220; Bickel, "Desegregation: Where Do We Go From Here?" p. 22; JoAnn Grozuczak Goedert, "Case Comment, *Jenkins v. Missouri:* The Future of Interdistrict School Desegregation," *Georgetown Law Review*, vol. 76 (June 1988), pp. 1867, 1879–80; Raymond Wolters, *The Burden of Brown: Thirty Years of School Desegregation* (University of Tennessee Press, 1984), p. 126; *Keyes v. Denver*, 413 U.S. 189 (1973), 250 (Powell, J., concurring in part, dissenting in part); Robert B. Reich, *The Work of Nations: Preparing Ourselves for Twenty-first-Century Capitalism* (Knopf, 1991), p. 276; Jennifer L. Hochschild, quoted in Tilove, "La Crosse Residents Clash over Busing Plan to Integrate Schools," p. 15A. Affluent whites are four times as likely to turn to private schools to avoid integration as nonaffluent families; Coleman, "Racial Segregation in the Schools," pp. 75, 78. Conversely, the benefits of racial integration are sometimes limited because the plans integrated middle-class blacks but left poor blacks segregated; Chambers, "*Brown v. Board of Education*," p. 190.

74. Jonathan Kozol, *Savage Inequalities: Children in America's Schools* (Crown, 1991), pp. 229–32; Orfield, *Metropolitics*, pp. 42–43; Timothy W. Young and Evans Clinchy, *Choice in Public Education* (New York: Teachers College Press, 1992), pp. 60, 65, 80; Snider, "Little Rock Rejects 'Controlled Choice,'" p. 5; D. Garth Taylor, *Public Opinion and Collective Action: The Boston School Desegregation Conflict* (University of Chicago Press, 1986), pp. 197–98. "School Desegregation: A Social Science Statement," in amicus curiae brief of NAACP and others in support of respondents, *Freeman v. Pitts*, U.S. Supreme Court, on writ of certiorari to the U.S. Court of Appeals for the 11th Circuit, June 21, 1991, cited in Armor, *Forced Justice*, p. 72; Orfield interview, pp. 7 and 11.

75. *Plessy v. Ferguson* 163 U.S. 537 (1896), 560 (Harlan, J., dissenting).

76. Kennedy, "Symposium: Changing Images of the State," pp. 1255, 1273 n. 79; see also Justice William Brennan, quoted in Bernard Schwartz, *Swann's Way: The School Busing Case and the Supreme Court* (New York: Oxford University Press, 1986), p. 109; Rowan, "Separate Will Never Be Equal," p. A21. Diane Ravitch, *The Troubled Crusade: American Education, 1945–1980* (Basic Books, 1983), p. 173; Wilkinson, *From Brown to Bakke*, p. 46. Raspberry, "This Is Where I Get Off," p. A25. See, for example, Wolters, *The Burden of Brown*, p. 41; Orfield and Eaton, *Dismantling Desegregation*, p. 110; Tesconi and Hurwitz, *Education for Whom?* pp. 200–01; Willie, "Racial Balance or Quality Education?" p. 13. Carmichael and Hamilton, *Black Power*, p. 157.

77. *Missouri v. Jenkins* 115 S. Ct. 2038 (1995), 2061, 2064–65 (Thomas, J., concurring). There is, on the surface, a similarity between Thomas's argument and that made by the majority in *Plessy*, which had argued that there is nothing inherently inferior about the black railroad car. The key distinction, of course, is that Homer Plessy was not given any choice to integrate, whereas today's students who choose majority-black institutions like Howard may have the choice of Harvard and Yale—indeed be heavily courted by them—and nevertheless choose to aggregate; see 115 S. Ct. 2038, 2064–65 (Thomas, J., concurring).

78. Orfield and Eaton, *Dismantling Desegregation*, p. 331. Morin, "Poverty in Black and White," p. C5 (citing study by Yale's Martin Gilens finding that news magazines and television news showed pictures of black people in stories about poverty 62 percent of the time, when in fact 71 percent of the nation's poor are nonblack.)

79. James S. Coleman, "Foreword," in John E. Coons and Stephen D. Sugarman, *Education by Choice: The Case for Family Control* (University of California Press, 1978), p. xiii; Matthew Miller, "A Bold Experiment for City Schools," *Atlantic Monthly,* July 1999, p. 15.

80. See Gary Miron, "Free Choice and Vouchers Transform Schools," *Educational Leadership,* October 1996, pp. 77, 79; Martin Carnoy, "National Voucher Plans in Chile and Sweden: Did Privatization Reforms Make for Better Education?" *Comparative Education Review* (August 1998), pp. 309, 333–34. Carnoy, "National Voucher Plans in Chile and Sweden," pp. 309–37, especially 318, 320, 335–36; see also John B. Judis, "Bad Choice," *New Republic,* September 30, 1996, p. 6. Edward B. Fiske and Helen F. Ladd, *When Schools Compete: A Cautionary Tale* (Brookings, 2000).

81. Jodi Wilgoren, "Young Blacks Turn to School Vouchers as Civil Rights Issue," *New York Times,* October 9, 2000, p. A1.

82. James K. Glassman, "Big Day for School Choice," *Washington Post,* February 27, 1996, p. A19. Hoxby estimates that a universal thousand-dollar voucher would increase private school enrollment from 10 percent of students today to 14 percent under the plan; Caroline Hoxby, "The Effect of Private School Vouchers on Schools and Students" in Ladd, *Holding Schools Accountable*, p. 199.

83. For mixed evidence on vouchers, see, for example, Carnoy, "Is Privatization through Education Vouchers Really the Answer?" pp. 309, 313; Paul E. Peterson and Jay P. Greene, "Race Relations and Central City Schools: It's Time for an Experiment with Vouchers," *Brookings Review* (Spring 1998), p. 36; Bob Davis, "Class Warfare: Dueling Professors Have Milwaukee Dazed over School Vouchers," *Wall Street Journal,* October 11, 1996, p. A1; Sandra Feldman, "Better than Vouchers," *Washington Post,* July 23, 1997, p. A23; Cecilia Elena Rouse, *Private School Vouchers and Student Achievement: An Evaluation of the Milwaukee Parental Choice Program* (Cambridge, Mass.: National Bureau of Economic Research, March 1997); Howard L. Fuller, "New Research Bolsters Case for School Choice," *Wall Street Journal,* January 21, 1997, p. A18; Rene Sanchez, "In Cleveland, Vouchers Fail to Raise Test Scores," *Washington Post,* April 8, 1998, p. A2. For a discussion of who chooses, see chapter 6.

84. See, for example, David S. Broder, "Awaiting a School Choice Showdown," *Washington Post,* July 24, 1996, p. A21. Timothy Lamer, "A Conservative Case against School Choice," *Washington Post,* November 6, 1996, p. A14; Robert Samuelson, "The Hypocrisy Scholarship," *Washington Post,* February 12, 1997, p. A23.

85. Kennedy quoted in David A. Vise, "Senate Rejects Tuition Vouchers, Keeping D.C. Budget in Limbo," *Washington Post,* February 28, 1996, pp. A1, A15. Al Shanker, "A Pretty Picture," *New York Times,* October 13, 1996, p. E7. Gordon MacInnes, *Kids Who Pick the Wrong Parents and Other Victims of Voucher Schemes,* Century Foundation White Paper (1999), p. 37. Robert Sanchez, "Few Schools Joining Plan," *Miami Herald,* April 18, 2000.

86. Cited in Michelle Fine, *Framing Dropouts: Notes on the Politics of an Urban Public High School* (State University of New York Press, 1991), p. 189.

87. Edith McArthur and others, *Use of School Choice, Educational Policy Issues: Statistical Perspectives* (NCES, 1995), p. 1; see also data from chapter 6. Jeffrey R. Henig,

Rethinking School Choice: Limits of the Marketplace Metaphor (Princeton University Press, 1994), p. 144.

88. *Abingdon School District* v. *Schempp*, 374 U.S. 203 (1963), 230.

89. James, cited in Michael Kremer, "Education Reform," unpublished paper, August 19, 1998, p. 23. Shanker quoted in Sara Mosle, "What Really Matters in Education," *New York Times Magazine*, October 27, 1996, p. 56. Shanker, "A Pretty Picture," p. E7; see also Albert Shanker, "Keeping Public Education Together," *New York Times*, March 2, 1997, p. E7. Michael Kelly, "Dangerous Minds," *New Republic*, December 30, 1996, p. 6.

90. *Ambach* v. *Norwick* 441 U.S. 68 (1979), 77; *Plyler* v. *Doe* 457 U.S. 202 (1982), 222 n. 20.

91. Albert Shanker, cited in Coons and Sugarman, *Education by Choice*, p. 226 n. 6. Ron K. Unz, "Voucher Veto," *Nation*, May 3, 1999, pp. 6, 7.

92. Amy Stuart Wells, *A Time to Choose: America at the Crossroads of School Choice Policy* (New York: Hill and Wang, 1993), pp. 134, 168. "Target: Public Education," *Nation*, November 30, 1998, 4–5; see also Robert M. O'Neil, "School Choice and State Action," in Stephen D. Sugarman and Frank R. Kemerer, eds., *School Choice and Social Controversy* (Brookings, 1999), pp. 223–24 (discussing *Rendell-Baker* v. *Kohn*, holding that the Constitution does not apply to private schools despite substantial public funding). Michael Kelly, "Dangerous Minds," *New Republic*, December 30, 1996, p. 6.

93. Peterson and Greene, "Race Relations and Central City Schools," p. 34; "Vouchers in Milwaukee," *Washington Post*, June 17, 1998, p. A26; Jon Jeter, "As Test of Vouchers, Milwaukee Parochial School Exceeds Expectations," *Washington Post*, September 1, 1998, p. A3; Debbi Wilgoren, "Some U.S. Lawmakers Revive Voucher Idea," *Washington Post*, June 4, 1997, p. B6. Jonathan Rauch, "Choose or Lose," *New Republic*, November 10, 1997, p. 4.

94. Daniel Bice and Joe Williams, "In a Major Shift, Norquist Says: Lift MPS Residence Rule and Choice Income Limit," *Milwaukee Journal Sentinel*, August 5, 1998.

95. See, for example, Adam Gamoran, "Student Achievement in Public Magnet, Public Comprehensive, and Private City High Schools," *Educational Evaluation and Policy Analysis*, vol. 18 (Spring 1996), pp. 4, 8, 14; Valerie E. Lee and Anthony S. Bryk, "Curriculum Tracking as Mediating the Social Distribution of High School Achievement," *Sociology of Education*, vol. 61 (April 1988), p. 80; James S. Coleman and Thomas Hoffer, *Public and Private High Schools: The Impact of Communities* (Basic Books, 1987), pp. 30–34, 145–46; Bryk, Lee, and Holland, *Catholic Schools and the Common Good*, pp. 70–71; Wells, *A Time to Choose*, 140–41; Henig, *Rethinking School Choice*, p. 144. In a widely cited 1987 longitudinal study, Coleman and Hoffer found positive effects even after controlling for income and for initial achievement (motivation); Coleman and Hoffer, *Public and Private High Schools*, pp. xxiv–xxv, 35, 76. For evidence that Catholic schools are more integrated by race and social class than public schools, see Bryk, Lee, and Holland, *Catholic Schools and the Common Good*, pp. 70, 73; Peterson and Greene, "Race Relations and Central City Schools," p. 36; Paul E. Peterson, "Top Ten Questions Asked about School Choice," in Ravitch, ed., *Brookings Papers on Education Policy, 1999*, p. 398; Peterson and Greene, "Race Relations, Vouchers, and Central-City Schools," pp. 10–12; James M. McPartland and Edward L. McDill, "Control and Differentiation in the Structure of American Education," *Sociology of Education*, vol. 55 (April–July 1982), pp. 78–79; Wells, *A Time to Choose*, p. 141.

96. For evidence of the positive "common school" effect in Catholic schools, see Coleman and Hoffer, *Public and Private High Schools*, p. 120; Bryk, Lee, and Holland, *Catholic Schools and the Common Good*, p. 57–58, 246; Lee and Bryk, "Curriculum Tracking as Mediating the Social Distribution of High School Achievement," p. 79. For evidence linking the middle-class peer effect of Catholic schools and higher performance, see Laurence B. Steinberg, *Beyond the Classroom: Why School Reform Has Failed and What Parents Need to Do* (Simon and Schuster, 1996), pp. 154–55; Judith Rich Harris, *The Nurture Assumption: Why Children Turn Out the Way They Do* (New York: Free Press, 1998), p. 260. See also Coleman and Hoffer, *Public and Private High Schools*, pp. 146–47; Bryk, Lee, and Holland, *Catholic Schools and the Common Good*, pp. 263–64.

The Coleman and Bryk groups, however, attributed the better performance mostly to the tough academic program, strong discipline, and active parental involvement found in Catholic schools; see Coleman and Hoffer, *Public and Private High Schools*, pp. 43, 52–53, 146–47; Bryk, Lee, and Holland, *Catholic Schools and the Common Good*, pp. 76, 94. See also Paul Barton, Richard J. Coley, and Harold Wenglinsky, *Order in the Classroom: Violence, Discipline, and Student Achievement* (Princeton, N.J.: Educational Testing Service, 1998), p. 21.

But of course the argument in chapter 4 is that tough discipline, higher academic standards, and greater parental involvement are much easier to promote in middle-class schools. See McPartland and McDill, "Control and Differentiation in the Structure of American Education," pp. 78, 81 ("differences of student body demographic concentrations (not school policy) [may] produce the major differences in school academic and disciplinary climates"); see also Wells, *A Time to Choose*, p. 142; Ho Sui-Chu and Willms, "Effects of Parental Involvement," p. 138; Duncombe and Yinger, "Performance Standards and Educational Cost Indexes," p. 268.

97. Bryk, Lee, and Holland, *Catholic Schools and the Common Good*, p. 264–66. Anemona Hartocollis, "Putting Private Education to the Test," *New York Times*, July 11, 1999, sec. 4, p. 5; Anemona Hartocollis, "Private Schools Fare Little Better on New Fourth-Grade Test," *New York Times*, July 1, 1999, p. B4; Richard Rothstein, Martin Carnoy, and Luis Benveniste, *Can Public Schools Learn from Private Schools?* (Washington: Economic Policy Institute, 1999), p. x.

98. Income is of course an imperfect proxy for the factors we are trying to determine—student motivation, discipline, parental involvement, and so forth—and this is particularly true in the case of Catholic schools, where self-selection makes the poor much more likely than the poor in public schools to have "middle class" values; John F. Witte and others, *Fourth-Year Report: Milwaukee Parental Choice Program* (Madison, Wisc.: Robert M. LaFollette Institute of Public Affairs, 1994), p. iv. Bryk, Lee, and Holland, *Catholic Schools and the Common Good*, p. 128.

Chapter Six

1. National Center for Education Statistics (NCES), *Digest of Education Statistics* (Department of Education, 1996), p. 96, table 88.

2. For La Crosse, Wisconsin, see the discussion in chapter 9; see also Peter Schmidt, "District Proposes Assigning Pupils Based on Income," *Education Week*, October 30, 1991, p. 1; "Economic Integration in the Classroom," ABC News, *Nightline*, September

17, 1992; Peter Schmidt, "La Crosse to Push Ahead with Income-Based Busing Plan," *Education Week,* August 5, 1992; David J. Armor, *Forced Justice: School Desegregation and the Law* (New York: Oxford University Press, 1995), pp. 3–4, 61; Muriel Cohen, "Wisconsin City Will Mix Students by Family Income," *Boston Globe,* December 26, 1991, p.1. For Wake County, North Carolina, see the discussion in chapter 9; see also Ben Wildavsky, "A Question of Black and White: Wrestling with Ways to Maintain Diversity," *U.S. News and World Report,* April 10, 2000, pp. 26–27; Robert C. Johnston, "North Carolina District to Integrate by Income: Assignment Plan Is Based on Poverty," *Education Week,* April 26, 2000, p. 1; Patrik Jonsson, "Poverty, not Race, as Test for Diversity," *Christian Science Monitor,* May 23, 2000, p. 1. For Manchester, Connecticut, see the discussion in chapter 9; see also Laura Ungar, "Controlled Choice Greeted with Dissent," *Hartford Courant,* April 15, 1996, p. B1; Van Alden Ferguson, "Enrollment Plan Reviewed," *Hartford Courant,* January 27, 1998, p. B1. For Maplewood, New Jersey, see School District of South Orange and Maplewood, *Planning for School Space,* No. 3, April 30, 1999; the board unanimously approved a socioeconomic integration model in May 1999; see Patricia M. Barker (assessment coordinator, School District of South Orange and Maplewood, New Jersey), letter to author, August 11, 1999. For San Diego, California, see Maureen Magee, "San Diego Magnet Schools Will Drop Race as Criterion," *San Diego Tribune,* January 26, 2000, p. B1. For Coweta County, Georgia, see "Old Problem, Bold Plan: Coweta Considers Income in Zoning," *Atlanta Journal Constitution,* February 8, 2000, p. C1; "Coweta Zones: Parents Upset," *Atlanta Journal Constitution,* February 9, 2000, p. C1.

3. For Montgomery County, Maryland, see Montgomery County (Maryland) Board of Education, *Policy, Quality Integrated Education,* adopted by Resolution 837-83, October 10, 1983; amended by Resolution 401-93, May 17, 1993, pp. 1, 4; Richard Kahlenberg, "Integrate, but Not by Race," *Washington Post,* November 14, 1999, p. B3. For San Francisco, California, see Peter Waldman, "School Accord Takes Emphasis off Race Factor," *Wall Street Journal,* February 18, 1999, p. B2; Richard Kahlenberg, "Economic School Desegregation," *Education Week,* March 31, 1999, p. 52; San Francisco subsequently decided to postpone implementation of its plan pending a court appeal; see Katherine Seligman, "Race-Neutral Plan to Be Used in San Francisco Schools," *San Francisco Examiner,* January 8, 2000, p. A1. But the new San Francisco schools superintendent, Arlene Ackerman, says she backs using an income integration plan in the future. See Robert C. Johnston, "S.F. Schools Becoming More Segregated," *Education Week,* September 6, 2000, p. 22. For Seattle, Washington, see Rebekah Denn, "The New Face of School Integration," *Seattle Post-Intelligencer,* October 17, 2000, p. B1. For Cambridge, Massachusetts, see Alan Bunce, "Mixing It Up in the Classroom," *Christian Science Monitor,* April 2, 1996; "Misplaced Mixing," editorial, *Boston Globe,* May 10, 1996; "Weekend Edition," *National Public Radio,* May 11, 1996. For Pinellas County, Florida, see Jounice L. Nealy, "Council Favors Income Consideration," *St. Petersburg Times,* November 11, 1998, p. 3B. For Murfreesboro, Tennessee, see Trine Tsouderos, "Kids in City's Poor Schools Get Worse Scores," *Tennessean,* December 27, 1998; Trine Tsouderos, "City School Board to Review Limited Rezoning Proposal," *Tennessean,* February 21, 1999; Trine Tsouderos, "Board Urges Balanced Student Population," *Tennessean,* February 24, 1999, p. 4B. For Jefferson County, Kentucky, see Holly Holland, "Schools Worried by Clusters of Poverty," *Louisville Courier Journal,* December 11, 1993; Andrew Trotter, "Teachers Propose Integrating Schools by Socioeconomic Status," *Education*

Week, December 2, 1998. For Charlotte, North Carolina, see Wildavsky, "A Question of Black and White," pp. 26–27. For Charleston, South Carolina, see Charles Willie and others, *Equity and Excellence: A Plan for Educational Improvement of the Charleston County Public Schools*, unpublished report, April 1998; Kristina Torres, "Study: Give Students a Chance," *Charleston Post and Courier*, April 16, 1998, p. A1. For Fayetteville, Arkansas, see Shannon Hemann, "Schools Figuring Wealth into Zoning," *Arkansas Democrat-Gazette*, February 27, 2000, p. B1. For Howard County, Maryland, e-mail correspondence from Martha Johnson (special assistant to the superintendent, Howard County), November 19, 1999. For Charles County, Maryland, "Letter to Editor," *Washington Post*, May 3, 1998, p. M2 (citing Board of Education of Charles County, Rule 1950, bullet 4, and Proposals 1, 3, and 4). For Palm Beach County, Florida, see Shannon Colvacchio, "School Boundary Proposals Sweeping," *Palm Beach Post*, September 28, 2000, p. 1B. For St. Lucie County, Florida, see Suzanne Robinson, "Parents Heard on School Choice," *Stuart News/Port St. Lucie News*, October 20, 2000, p. B1. For Wausau, Wisconsin, see Peter Schmidt, "Bold Busing Plan Leads to Deep Divides in Wausau," *Education Week*, December 15, 1993; Roger Worthington, "School Desegregation Efforts Divide Town," *Chicago Tribune*, December 13, 1993, p. 2; Armor, "Forced Justice," pp. 224–25. For Rochester, see Sondra Astor Stave, *Achieving Racial Balance: Case Studies of Contemporary School Desegregation* (Westport, Conn.: Greenwood Press, 1995), pp. 38–39; see also legal discussion in chapter 7. For Harrisburg, see William T. Donoho Jr. and Robert A. Dentler, "Busing toward Excellence: The Quest for Quality Desegregated Education in Harrisburg," *Urban Review* (September–October 1972), pp. 31–34; Joan S. Beers and Francis J. Reardon, "Racial Balancing in Harrisburg: Achievement and Attitudinal Changes," *Integrated Education*, vol. 12 (1974), pp. 35–38; Stanley Lisser, "Desegregating the Schools of Harrisburg," *Urban Review* (September 1971), pp. 42–46. For Duluth, see Dick Hubert, "Class and the Classroom: The Duluth Experience," *Saturday Review of Education*, May 27, 1972, p. 56; Wayne M. Carle, "Social Science Research and the Courts: A Futuristic Perspective," paper presented to the annual meeting of the American Educational Research Association, New York, April 6, 1977, pp. 13–14; Ray C. Rist, *The Invisible Children: School Integration in American Society* (Harvard University Press, 1978), p. 19; Rob Hotakainen, "La Crosse Plan Would Mix Students by Income," *Minneapolis Star Tribune*, November 23, 1991, p. 1A; Muriel Cohen, "Wisconsin City Will Mix Students by Family Income," *Boston Globe*, December 26, 1991, p. 1. For Dayton, see *Brinkman* v. *Gilligan*, 446 F. Supp. 1232, 1264–65 (S.D. Ohio, W.D. 1977); Gordon Foster and Timothy R. McDonald, *Desegregation Study: Dayton Public Schools* (New York: National Center for Research and Information on Equal Educational Opportunity, 1972), pp. 1, 11–12, 14.

4. Gary Orfield, interview by author, November 19, 1997, Cambridge, Mass., pp. 10–11; Michael Alves and Charles V. Willie, "Controlled Choice—An Approach to Effective School Desegregation," *Urban Review*, vol. 19 (1987), pp. 67, 77. J. Douglas Willms, "Social Class Segregation and Its Relationship to Pupils' Examination Results in Scotland," *American Sociological Review*, vol. 51 (April 1986), p. 226; see also J. Douglas Willms and Frank H. Echols, "The Scottish Experience of Parental School Choice," in Edith Rasell and Richard Rothstein, eds., *School Choice: Examining the Evidence* (Washington: Economic Policy Institute, 1993), p. 51.

5. Robert Crain, "New York City's Career Magnet High Schools: Lessons about Creating Equity within Choice Programs," in Rasell and Rothstein, *School Choice*, pp.

262–64; Wildavsky, "A Question of Black and White," pp. 26–27. See also Christina Rathbone, *On the Outside Looking In: A Year in an Inner-City High School* (New York: Atlantic Monthly Press, 1998), p. 3; Nicholas Lemann, "Magnetic Attraction: Magnet Schools' Unfulfilled Potential," *New Republic*, April 13, 1987, pp. 16–19.

6. This would be less true if failing a test had serious consequences for an individual student.

7. Richard D. Kahlenberg, *The Remedy: Race, Class, and Affirmative Action* (Basic Books, 1996), pp. 128–36.

8. James Coleman and others, *Equality of Educational Opportunity* (Washington: GPO, 1966), p. 305 (also known as the "Coleman Report"); Ronald F. Ferguson, "Paying for Public Education: New Evidence on How and Why Money Matters," *Harvard Journal on Legislation*, vol. 28 (1991), pp. 478–79; Leonard Solo, interview by author, November 20, 1997, Cambridge, Mass., p. 41. Jeanne Brooks-Gunn, Greg J. Duncan, and Nancy Maritato, "Poor Families, Poor Outcomes: The Well-Being of Children and Youth," in Greg J. Duncan and Jeanne Brooks-Gunn, eds., *Consequences of Growing Up Poor* (New York: Russell Sage Foundation, 1997), p. 13; Greg Duncan and Jeanne Brooks-Gunn, "Income Effects across the Life Span: Integration and Interpretation," in Duncan and Brooks-Gunn, *Consequences of Growing Up Poor*, p. 597; Jeanne Brooks-Gunn and others, "Do Neighborhoods Influence Child and Adolescent Development?" *American Journal of Sociology*, vol. 99 (September 1993), pp. 359, 375; Laura Lippman and others, *Urban Schools: The Challenge of Location and Poverty* (NCES, 1996), pp. 58–59; Doris R. Entwisle, Karl L. Alexander, and Linda Steffel Olson, *Children, Schools, and Inequality* (New York: Westview Press, 1997), p. 40. Income is not necessarily a cause of various behaviors and values we think are relevant, but it is a "marker" of risk; Susan E. Mayer, *What Money Can't Buy: Family Income and Children's Life Chances* (Harvard University Press, 1997), p. 49.

9. Kahlenberg, *The Remedy*, p. 141. Using FARM data provides districts with an option to use a three-tier formula—free lunch, reduced lunch, and noneligible.

10. See discussion in chapter 3.

11. Magee, "San Diego Schools Will Drop Race as Criterion"; San Francisco Unified School District, Education Placement Center, registration form, November 6, 1998.

12. See P.L. 103-382; see also Judith Anderson, "Distribution of Chapter 1 Services: Data from the Schools and Staffing Survey" (Washington: Dept. of Education, Office of Educational Research and Improvement, 1993), p. 2 ("Typically counts are made of the number of children eligible for free or reduced-price lunch programs or the number of children from families receiving AFDC"). FARM data are updated annually: students must reapply at the beginning of each school year; see Department of Agriculture, "Eligibility Guidance for School Meals Manual" (Washington, August 1991), p 7.

13. Department of Agriculture, "Income Eligibility Guidelines," July 1, 2000–June 30, 2001, *Federal Register*, vol. 65, no. 65 (April 4, 2000), p. 17622. Department of Housing and Urban Development, "Income Limits for Public Housing and Section 8 Programs," January 27, 1999 (www.huduser.org/datasets/il/fmr99/sect82.html [October 9, 2000]). Kaiser Commission on Medicaid and the Uninsured (www.kff.org/ state_health/factsheets/statesheets16.html [June 18, 1999]); Department of Agriculture, "Food Stamps Income Chart" (www.fns.usda. gov/fsp/charts/incomechart.htm [June 18, 1999]).

14. See, for example, Samuel S. Peng and Susan T. Hill, *Understanding Racial-Ethnic Differences in Secondary Science and Math Achievement* (Dept. of Education, 1995), p.

18; Lauri Steel and Roger Levine, *Educational Innovation in Multiracial Contexts: The Growth of Magnet Schools in American Education*, report prepared for the U.S. Department of Education (Palo Alto, Calif.: American Institute for Research, 1994), p. 22; "Quality Counts '98: The Urban Challenge," *Education Week*, January 8, 1998, p. 6; Milwaukee, in setting a cutoff for those eligible for choice vouchers, used a similar figure, 175 percent of the poverty line; John F. Witte, "Who Benefits from the Milwaukee Choice Program?" in Bruce Fuller and Richard F. Elmore, eds., *Who Chooses? Who Loses? Culture, Institutions, and the Unequal Effects of Schools Choice* (New York: Teachers College Press, 1996), p. 121.

15. William Julius Wilson, *When Work Disappears: The World of the New Urban Poor* (Knopf, 1996), pp. 52, 73. Mary Corcoran and Terry Adams, "Race, Sex, and the Intergenerational Transmission of Poverty," in Duncan and Brooks-Gunn, *Consequences of Growing Up Poor*, pp. 461–62 (citing Mead). Of course, many families work and still earn wages low enough to put them below the poverty line. In 1995, more than half of the poor worked at least part time; Orlando Patterson, *The Ordeal of Integration: Progress and Resentment in America's "Racial" Crisis* (Washington: Civitas, 1997), p. 32.

16. U.S. Census Bureau, *Poverty in the United States: 1999* (Washington: U.S. Government Printing Office, 2000), p. 28, table 5; NCES, *Digest of Education Statistics, 1999* (Washington: U.S. Government Printing Office, 2000), table 379 (33.2 percent of public school students received federally subsidized lunches in 1993–94); NCES, *NAEP 1998 Reading Report Card for the Nation* (Dept. of Education, 1999), p. 59 (in 1998, "35 percent of students at grade four, 27 percent of students at grade eight, and 14 percent of students at grade twelve were eligible for the [free and reduced-price lunch] program" but not all students reported their eligibility). In the 1999–2000 school year, the percentage of American students receiving free and reduced-price school lunches appeared to dip just below 30 percent. See Food Research and Action Center, *School Breakfast Scorecard: 2000* (Washington: FRAC, 2000), p. 20 (U.S.D.A. estimates 15.18 million free and reduced-price lunch recipients, using a formula that adjusts for student absences). There are 52 million American schoolchildren. See Jodi Wilgoren, "Young Blacks Turn to School Vouchers as Civil Rights Issue," *New York Times*, October 9, 2000, p. A1.

17. David Johnston, interview by author, December 15, 1997, Lacrosse, Wisc., pp. 20–21. See also Fred Prehn, interview by author, December 17, 1997, Wausau, Wisc.; John F. Kain and Kraig Singleton, "Equality of Educational Opportunity Revisited," *New England Economic Review* (May–June 1996), p. 93 (Texas study defined non-FARM students as "high income," reduced-price lunch students (130–185 percent of poverty line) as "middle-income" and free lunch students as "low-income"; General Accounting Office (GAO), *School Finance: State and Federal Efforts to Target Poor Students* (January 28, 1998), p. 34 (noting the NCES has developed a national district-level teacher cost index examining cost of living by district); Stephen Barr, "Clinton Orders 3.68 Percent Pay Hike in Area," *Washington Post*, December 8, 1998, p. A19 (thirty-two different federal pay scales).

18. Jonathan Crane, "Effects of Neighborhoods on Dropping Out of School and Teenage Childbearing," in Christopher Jencks and Paul E. Peterson, eds., *The Urban Underclass* (Brookings, 1991), pp. 303–07, 317; Jonathan Crane, "The Epidemic Theory of Ghettos and Neighborhood Effects on Dropping Out and Teenage Childbearing," *American Journal of Sociology*, pp. 1226, 1250; Paul Peterson, "The Urban Underclass and the Poverty Paradox," in Jencks and Peterson, *The Urban Underclass*, p. 20.

19. See, for example, U.S. Commission on Civil Rights, *Racial Isolation in the Public Schools*, vol. 1 (Government Printing Office, 1967), p. 85; Eleanor P. Wolf, *Trial and Error: The Detroit School Desegregation Case* (Wayne State University Press, 1981), p. 326 n. 7; Nancy Hoyt St. John, *School Desegregation Outcomes for Children* (New York: John Wiley and Sons, 1975), pp. 35, 105; Gary Orfield, *Must We Bus? Segregated Schools and National Policy* (Brookings, 1978), p. 124; Frederick Mosteller and Daniel P. Moynihan, eds., *On Equality of Educational Opportunity: Papers Deriving from the Harvard Faculty Seminar on the Coleman Report* (Random House, 1972), p. 39.

20. P.L. 103-382. Joseph Fernandez, "Comments" in Iris C. Rotberg, ed., *Federal Policy Options for Improving the Education of Low-Income Students*, vol. 2, *Commentaries* (Santa Monica, Calif.: Rand, 1993), p. 226; see also Wayne Riddle, "Title I, Part A of the Elementary and Secondary Education Act: Background and Prospective Reauthorization Issues," testimony prepared for a hearing before the Senate Committee on Health, Education, Labor, and Pensions, March 16, 1999, CRS-6 ("The rationale for limiting schoolwide program authority to relatively high-poverty schools is that in such schools all pupils are disadvantaged"); Department of Education, *Policy Guidance for Title I, Part A—Improving Basic Programs Operated by Local Educational Agencies* (Washington: Department of Education, April 1996), "Schoolwide Programs," p. 1 (50 percent threshold based on "solid research" that "all children's performance is negatively affected in schools with high concentrations of poverty"). Stephen Burd, "White House Plan for Low-Income Students Sparks Debate," *Chronicle of Higher Education*, April 23, 1999, p. A44.

21. *Brunson*, 429 F. 2d 820, at 820 (4th Cir. 1970) (HEW officials). Lisa Frazier, "NAACP Questions Prince George's Move to Drop Racial Balance Rules," *Washington Post*, July 7, 1996, p. B1; in some instances, the courts sought to maximize the number of racially evenly mixed schools, perhaps based on concerns about white flight; see, for example, Derrick A. Bell Jr., "Serving Two Masters: Integration Ideals and Client Interests in School Desegregation Litigation," *Yale Law Journal*, vol. 85 (1976), p. 484 n. 43.

22. See, for example, Stephen Schellenberg, "Concentration of Poverty and the Ongoing Need for Title I," in Gary Orfield and Elizabeth DeBray, eds., *Hard Work for Good Schools: Facts Not Fads in Title I Reform* (Cambridge, Mass.: Harvard Civil Rights Project, 1999), p. 137 (because "there is a point of diminishing returns," a 60 percent FARM district should seek an interdistrict plan).

23. Derrick A. Bell, *Race, Racism, and American Law*, 3d ed. (Boston: Little, Brown, 1992), p. 597; Martin T. Katzman, *Implications of Population Redistribution for Education* (reprint from *Population Redistribution and Public Policy* [Washington: National Academy of Sciences, 1980]), p. 274; Orfield, *Must We Bus?* p. 412; Leo C. Rigsby and John Boston, *Patterns of School Desegregation in Nashville, 1960–1969* (Nashville, Tennessee: Vanderbilt University, January 1971), p. 8; J. Harvie Wilkinson III, *From Brown to Bakke: The Supreme Court and School Integration, 1954–1978* (New York: Oxford University Press, 1979), p. 158; Amy Stuart Wells and Robert Crain, "Perpetuation Theory and the Long-term Effects of School Desegregation," *Review of Educational Research*, vol. 64, no. 4 (Winter 1994), p. 536; Gerald David Jaynes and Robin M. Williams Jr., eds., *A Common Destiny: Blacks and American Society* (Washington: National Academy Press, 1989), p. 12.

24. Gary Orfield, "Metropolitan School Desegregation: Impacts on Metropolitan Society," *Minnesota Law Review*, vol. 80 (April 1996), p. 831.

25. B. Drummond Ayers, "Cross-Town Busing, Begun in '71, Is Working Well in Charlotte," *New York Times*, July 17, 1975, p. 14; Michael W. Giles, "White Enrollment Stability and School Desegregation: A Two-Level Analysis," *American Sociological Review*, vol. 43 (December 1978), p. 849; Christine H. Rossell, "Desegregation Plans, Racial Isolation, White Flight, and Community Response," in Christine H. Rossell and Willis D. Hawley, eds., *The Consequences of School Desegregation* (Temple University Press, 1983), p. 38; Christine H. Rossell and Robert L. Crain, *Evaluating School Desegregation Plans Statistically* (Johns Hopkins University Press, 1973), p. 18; Lisa Frazier, "Nonblacks Say Why They Avoid Prince George's Magnet Schools," *Washington Post*, November 22, 1998, p. B1.

26. Giles, "White Enrollment Stability and School Desegregation," pp. 862, 850, 851, 855; see also D. Garth Taylor, *Public Opinion and Collective Action: The Boston School Desegregation Conflict* (University of Chicago Press, 1986), p. 52. See discussions in chapters 7, on interdistrict plans, and 8, on white flight. Barbara Black, *Student Data Report, 1996–1997* (Cambridge, Mass.: School District, 1997), p. 4; Montclair (N.J.) Public School System, *Report of District Enrollment*, October 1998, pp. 11, 14.

27. This was the experience in Wausau, Wisc.; Fred Prehn, interview by author, December 17, 1997, pp. 37–38.

28. Sandra K. Danziger and Sheldon Danziger, "Child Poverty and Public Policy: Toward a Comprehensive Antipoverty Agenda," *Daedalus*, vol. 22 (Winter 1993), p. 61.

29. In 1994 only Mississippi (58.2 percent FARM), Louisiana (55.1 percent FARM) and the District of Columbia (61.7 percent FARM) had FARM majorities; see NCES, "Schools and Staffing Survey, 1993–94"; "Quality Counts '98," pp. 64–65. "Average Teacher Salaries in 1997–1998," *Education Week*, July 14, 1999 (average teacher salaries are $30,090 in Louisiana and $28,691 in Mississippi, compared with a FARM-eligibility cutoff of $30,433). Richard Rothstein, *The Way We Were: Debunking the Myths of America's Declining Schools* (Century Foundation Press, 1998), pp. 61–62 (1996 percentage of children in poverty ages five through seventeen); see GAO, *School Finance: State Efforts to Reduce Funding Gaps between Poor and Wealthy Districts: Report to Congressional Requesters* (February 1997), p. 5; "Quality Counts '98," p. 15.

30. Nationwide, 14 percent of districts have more than 50 percent FARM populations (as compared with 24.7 percent of schools and 22 percent of students attending such schools); Anderson, *Distribution of Chapter 1 Services*, pp. 6, 7, 11; see also Beatrice Birman and others, *The Current Operation of the Chapter 1 Program: Final Report for the National Assessment of Chapter 1* (Dept. of Education, 1987), pp. 15–16. NCES, *The Condition of Education, 1998* (Dept. of Education, 1998), p. 257. Mary M. Kennedy, Richard K. Jung, and M. E. Orland, *Poverty, Achievement, and the Distribution of Compensatory Education Services: An Interim Report from the National Assessment of Chapter 1* (Dept. of Education, Office of Educational Research and Improvement, January 1986), p. E57.

31. For the southern countywide structure, see David Rusk, *Cities without Suburbs*, 2d ed. (Washington: Woodrow Wilson Center Press, 1995), p. 75, 80–81; Orfield, "Metropolitan School Desegregation," pp. 832–33. For evidence that in recent years, large numbers of poor people have moved to inner-ring suburbs, see Edward J. Blakely and Mary Gail Snyder, *Fortress America: Gated Communities in the United States* (Brookings, 1997), p. 146; Anthony Downs, *New Visions for Metropolitan America* (Brookings,

1994), p. 11; Derek Bok, *The State of the Nation* (Harvard University Press, 1996), p. 180; John T. Cook and J. Larry Brown, *Two Americas: Comparisons of U.S. Child Poverty in Rural, Inner-City, and Suburban Areas* (Medford, Mass.: Center on Hunger, Poverty, and Nutrition Policy, September 1994), p. 10; Deborah L. Cohen, "Study Charts Dramatic Rise in Suburban Child Poverty," *Education Week*, October 5, 1994, p. 10; William Frey, "The New Geography of Population Shifts," in Reynolds Farley, ed., *State of the Union: America in the 1990s*, vol. 2, p. 314; Joel Garreau, *Edge City: Life on the Frontier* (Doubleday, 1991); Robert O'Harrow Jr., "Child Poverty Surges in Area," *Washington Post*, May 10, 1997, p. A1; Robert O'Harrow Jr., "Lunch Program Reflects Surges in Suburban Poor," *Washington Post*, October 2, 1996, p. A1. For discussion of poverty in rural districts, see William P. O'Hare and Brenda Curry-White, *The Rural Underclass: Examination of Multiple-Problem Populations in Urban and Rural Settings* (Washington: Population Reference Bureau, 1992), pp. 2–3.

32. Diane Ravitch, "A New Era in Urban Education?" *Brookings Policy Paper*, vol. 35 (August 1998), pp. 1–2; "Quality Counts '98," p. 9. Judith Anderson, *The Distribution of Chapter 1 Services: Data from the Schools and Staffing Survey* (Washington: Department of Education, Office of Educational Research and Improvement, 1993), p. 7; Joy G. Dryfoos, "National Community Schools Strategy," unpublished working paper on file with author, June 12, 1997, p. 3 (one in four public schools—twenty-two thousand of eighty-five thousand—has a student population of more than 50 percent "low income"); see also Department of Education, *Improving America's Schools Act of 1993: The Reauthorization of the Elementary and Secondary Education Act and Amendments to Other Acts* (September 13, 1993), Title I-9; Department of Education, *Promising Results, Continuing Challenges: Final Report on the National Assessment of Title I: Executive Summary* (March 1999), p. 1; Michael J. Puma and others, *Prospects: The Congressionally Mandated Study of Educational Growth and Opportunity—Interim Report* (Bethesda, Md.: Abt Associates, July 1993), p. xxix; Lippman, and others, *Urban Schools*, p. 7; NCES, *Teacher Quality: A Report on the Preparation and Qualifications of Public School Teachers* (January 1999), p. A-7.

33. Coleman and others, *Equality and Educational Opportunity*, p. 304; Gary Orfield and Susan Eaton, *Dismantling Desegregation: The Quiet Reversal of Brown v. Board of Education* (New York: New Press, 1996), p. 93; Nina S. Mounts and Laurence Steinberg, "An Ecological Analysis of Peer Influence on Adolescent Grade Point Average and Drug Use," *Developmental Psychology*, vol. 31 (1995), p. 915; J. Lawrence Aber and others, "Development in Context: Implications for Studying Neighborhood Effects," in Jeanne Brooks-Gunn, Greg J. Duncan, and J. Lawrence Aber, eds., *Neighborhood Poverty*, vol. 1, *Context and Consequences for Children* (New York: Russell Sage Foundation, 1997), p. 56.

34. Bernard Schwartz, *Swann's Way: The School Busing Case and the Supreme Court* (New York: Oxford University Press, 1986), p. 98. See also Rossell, "Desegregation Plans, Racial Isolation, White Flight, and Community Response," p. 33.

35. Alan Wilson, "Educational Consequences of Segregation in a California Community," in U.S. Commission on Civil Rights, *Racial Isolation*, vol. 2 (Washington: GPO, 1967), pp. 188 and 190; James Coleman, Testimony before the Select Committee on Equal Educational Opportunity, *Toward Equal Educational Opportunity* (GPO, 1972), p. 218; Robert F. Herriott and Nancy Hoyt St. John, *Social Class and the Urban*

School: The Impact of Pupil Background on Teachers and Principals (New York: John Wiley and Sons, 1966), p. 160. Robert L. Crain and Rita E. Mahard, "The Effect of Research Methodology on Desegregation-Achievement Studies: A Meta-Analysis," *American Journal of Sociology*, vol. 88 (March 1983), p. 839; Select Committee on Equal Educational Opportunity, *Toward Equal Educational Opportunity*, pp. 190 and 235; Robert L. Crain and Rita E. Mahard, *Desegregation and Black Achievement* (Santa Monica, Calif.: Rand, 1977), p. 19; Robert L. Crain and Rita E. Mahard, *Desegregation Plans That Raise Black Achievement: A Review of the Research* (Santa Monica, Calif.: Rand, 1982), p. v; Bok, *The State of the Nation*, p. 85. Alan B. Wilson, *The Consequences of Segregation: Academic Achievement in a Northern Community* (Berkeley, Calif.: Glendessary Press, 1969), pp. 45–46; Amy Stuart Wells, "African American Students' View of School Choice," in Fuller and Elmore, *Who Chooses? Who Loses?* p. 32; Leonard Strickman, "Desegregation: The Metropolitan Concept," *Urban Review*, vol. 6 (September–October 1977), p. 20; Jomills Henry Braddock II, Robert L. Crain, and James M. McPartland, "A Long-Term View of School Desegregation: Some Recent Studies of Graduates as Adults," *Phi Delta Kappan*, vol. 66, no. 4 (December 1984), p. 263. Entwisle, Alexander, and Olson, *Children, Schools, and Inequality*, p. 95.

36. See, for example, James E. Rosenbaum, Leonard S. Rubinowtiz, and Marilynn J. Kulieke, *Low-Income Black Children in White Suburban Schools*, report prepared for the Spencer Foundation (Evanston, Ill.: Center for Urban Affairs and Policy Research, February 1986), p. 118. Judith Rich Harris, *The Nurture Assumption: Why Children Turn Out the Way They Do* (New York: Free Press, 1998), pp. 181–82. See, for example, Puma and others, *Prospects: The Congressionally Mandated Study of Educational Growth and Opportunity—Interim Report*, p. xxix; Entwisle, Alexander, and Olson, *Children, Schools, and Inequality*, p. 6.

37. See Charles V. Willie and Michael Alves, *Controlled Choice: A New Approach to Desegregated Education and School Improvement* (Providence, R.I.: Education Alliance Press and the New England Desegregation Assistance Center of Brown University, 1996); Charles L. Glenn, *Family Choice and Public Schools: A Report to the State Board of Education* (Quincy, Mass.: Massachusetts Department of Education, January 1986) ("conditional choice").

38. Alves and Willie, "Controlled Choice—An Approach to Effective School Desegregation," p. 76.

39. Ibid., p. 81. Education Commission of the States, *A State Policy-Makers' Guide to Public-School Choice*, draft (Denver: Education Commission of the States, February 1989), p. 34. Under "preferred choice," parents choose among schools and are assigned with an eye to demographic balance but are guaranteed admission to their home district school, at the least; see Dan Beyers, "County Looks at Changes in School Choice Plan," *Washington Post*, October 3, 1996, p. Md1. Another alternative is "limited controlled choice," in which students attend neighborhood schools unless there is an imbalance, in which case new students are transferred to address the imbalance; Armor, *Forced Justice*, p. 163. A third variation assigns students to neighborhood schools but allows them to transfer to another school in the district if there is space and the change does not contribute to racial imbalance; Timothy W. Young and Evans Clinchy, *Choice in Public Education* (New York: Teachers College Press, 1992), pp. 39–41. A fourth variation is "Equity Choice," in which students may choose any

public or private school but transportation is paid only if the transfer improves the "racial (or possibly economic) balance of the sending and receiving schools"; see Armor, *Forced Justice*, pp. 228–29.

40. See Evans Clinchy, interview by author, Boston, November 21, 1997.

41. See Willie and Alves, *Controlled Choice: A New Approach to Desegregated Education and School Improvement* (1996), p. ii; Jeffrey R. Henig, *Rethinking School Choice: Limits of the Marketplace Metaphor* (Princeton University Press, 1994), p. 257 n. 30; Young and Clinchy, *Choice in Public Education*, pp. 6, 32; Armor, *Forced Justice*, pp. 48, 168–69; Christine H. Rossell, "The Buffalo Controlled Choice Plan," *Urban Education*, vol. 22 (October 1987), p. 328; Charles Glenn, "Parent Choice and American Values," in Joe Nathan, ed., *Public Schools by Choice: Expanding Opportunities for Parents, Students, and Teachers* (St. Paul, Minn.: Institute for Learning and Teaching, 1989), p. 42; Peter Schmidt, "Problems with Launch of Choice Plan Place Indianapolis Official under Fire," *Education Week*, September 29, 1993, p. 8; Anne Lindberg, "Busing: Where Are We Headed?" *St. Petersburg Times*, Aug. 26, 1996, p. 1A; Brian Hicks, "Some Families Find the Choice Limited," *Charleston Post and Courier*, May 3, 1998, p. A1; Caroline Hendrie, "Without Court Orders, Schools Ponder How to Pursue Diversity," *Education Week*, April 30, 1997.

42. Charles Glenn, "Controlled Choice in Massachusetts Public Schools," *Public Interest*, vol. 103 (Spring 1991), p. 92. Henig, *Rethinking School Choice*, p. 90; William Bennett, *American Education: Making it Work* (Government Printing Office, 1998), p. 47; Norma Tan, *The Cambridge Controlled Choice Program: Improving Educational Equity and Integration* (New York: Manhattan Institute, 1990), p. 11. The controlled choice plan in Little Rock, Arkansas, was dismantled after a single year following rushed implementation; see Hicks, "Some Families Find the Choice Is Limited," p. A1. The controlled choice plan, adopted by Seattle, Washington, in 1988, was ended in 1996; see Caroline Hendrie, "Seattle to Shelve Race-Based Busing in Shift toward Neighborhood Schools," *Education Week*, December 4, 1996. The judicial shift on racial integration has resulted in the termination of controlled choice in Boston and Indianapolis; see Caroline Hendrie, "Judge Spurns Indianapolis Bid to Recover Bused Students," *Teacher Magazine*, March 12, 1997, and discussion of Boston in chapter 8.

43. National Governors' Association, *Time for Results: The Governors' 1991 Report on Education* (Washington: National Governors' Association Center for Policy Research and Analysis, 1986), p. 70. For Cambridge, see Tan, *The Cambridge Controlled Choice Program*, pp. 12–14; Jaclyn Fierman, "Giving Parents a Choice of Schools," *Fortune*, December 4, 1989, p. 150; Young and Clinchy, *Choice in Public Education*, p. 31; Henig, *Rethinking School Choice*, p. 123; Christine H. Rossell and Charles L. Glenn, "The Cambridge Controlled Choice Plan," *Urban Review*, vol. 20 (Summer 1988), pp. 89–90; Amy Stuart Wells, *Time to Choose: America at the Crossroads of School Choice Policy* (New York: Hill and Wang, 1993), p. 90; Michael Alves, "Maximizing Parental Choice and Effective Desegregation Outcomes: The Cambridge Plan" in Charles Glenn, ed., *Family Choice and Public Schools: A Report to the State Board of Education*, pp. 48, 53; Alves and Willie, "Controlled Choice—An Approach to Effective School Desegregation," pp. 85–86. For Montclair, see Beatriz C. Clewell and Myra F. Joy, *Choice in Montclair, New Jersey* (Princeton, N.J.: Educational Testing Service, 1990), pp. 5–6, 12, 31–33; Young and Clinchy, *Choice in Public Education*, p. 22; Henig, *Rethinking School Choice*, pp. 123–24; Jaclyn Fierman, "Giving Parents a Choice of

Schools, *Fortune*, December 4, 1989, p. 150; William Snider, "The Call for Choice: Competition in the Educational Marketplace," *Education Week*, June 24, 1987, p. C9; Jane Manners, "Repackaging Segregation: A History of the Magnet School System in Montclair, New Jersey," *Race Traitor*, vol. 8 (Winter 1998), pp. 52–55; in the late 1990s, the schools remained solidly balanced, with all elementary schools within a range between 44 percent to 56 percent white; see Montclair Public School System, *Report of District Enrollment*, pp. 11, 14. For Buffalo, see David T. Kearns and Denis P. Doyle, *Winning the Brain Race: A Bold Plan to Make Our Schools Competitive* (San Francisco, Calif.: Institute for Contemporary Studies Press, 1988), p. 29; Rossell, "The Buffalo Controlled Choice Plan," pp. 334, 344, 350–51. For Lowell, see Young and Clinchy, *Choice in Public Education*, p. 80.

44. See Steel and Levine, *Educational Innovation in Multiracial Contexts*, p. 4.

45. James S. Coleman, "Racial Segregation in the Schools: New Research with New Policy Implications," *Phi Delta Kappan*, vol. 57 (October 1975), p. 78; David J. Armor, "After Busing: Education and Choice," *Public Interest* (Spring 1989), pp. 24–25. On parents' impotence under forced busing, see the discussion in chapter 8. Nathan quoted in Carol Steinbach and Neal R. Pierce, "Multiple Choice," *National Journal*, July 1, 1989, p. 1693. Education Commission of the States, *A State Policy-Makers' Guide*, p. 3. Bella Rosenberg, "Public School Choice: Can We Find the Right Balance?" *American Educator*, vol. 13 (Summer 1989), p. 12. Alves, "Maximizing Parental Choice," pp. 39–40. Ronald E. Koetzch, *The Parents' Guide to Alternatives in Education* (Boston: Shambhala, 1997); Snider, "The Call for Choice," pp. C19–C20.

46. Thomas Toch, "Schools That Work," *U.S. News and World Report*, October 7, 1996, pp. 58–64. Amy Stuart Wells, "Once a Desegregation Tool, Magnet Schools Become Schools of Choice," *New York Times*, January 9, 1991. See, for example, Wilson, *When Work Disappears*, p. 214; Seymore Fliegel, with James MacGuire, *Miracle in East Harlem: The Fight for Choice in Public Education* (Random House, 1993), pp. 3–4, 14; Anemona Hartocollis, "Choice System Helps Schools in East Harlem," *New York Times*, February 24, 1998, pp. B1, B5.

47. Evans Clinchy and Frances Arick Kolb, eds., *Planning for School Choice: Achieving Equity and Excellence* (Andover, Mass.: NETWORK, 1989), pp. 5–6.

48. See Caroline M. Hoxby, "What Do America's 'Traditional' Forms of School Choice Teach Us about School Choice Reforms?" *FRBNY Economic Policy Review*, vol. 4, no. 1 (March 1998), pp. 52–55; Joseph S. Tracy and Barbara L. Walter, "Summary of Observations and Recommendations," in id., pp. 4, 6; Education Commission of the States, *A State Policy-Makers' Guide*, p. 3; Gary Putka, "Choose-a-School: Parents in Minnesota Are Getting to Send Kids Where They Like," *Wall Street Journal*, May 13, 1988, p. A1; Edward Fiske, "Wave of the Future: A Choice of Schools," *New York Times*, June 4, 1989, p. 32; Joe Nathan, "Charters and Choice," *American Prospect* (November–December 1998), p. 75; June Kronholz, "Charter Schools Begin to Prod Public Schools toward Competition," *Wall Street Journal*, February 12, 1999, p. A1; Thomas Toch, *Improving Performance: Competition in American Public Education* (Washington: National Alliance of Business, 2000), p. 10.

49. Adam Urbanski, "Make Public Schools More Like Private Schools," *Education Week*, January 31, 1996, pp. 31, 33. Kristina Torres, "Controlled Choice? Boston Gives Plan a Passing Grade," *Charleston Post and Courier*, May 3, 1998, p. A1; Glenn, "Controlled Choice in Massachusetts Public Schools," p. 95; "Quality Counts '98," p. 45.

50. See, for example, Patricia A. Bauch, *Family Choice and Parental Involvement in Inner-City Catholic High Schools: An Exploration of Psycho-Social and Organizational Factors* (Catholic University Press, 1987), p. 20. Deborah Meier, *The Power of Their Ideas: Lessons for America from a Small School in Harlem* (Boston: Beacon Press, 1995), p. 101.

51. National Governors' Association, *Time for Results*, p. 68. Bauch, *Family Choice and Parental Involvement*, p. 3. Kearns and Doyle, *Winning the Brain Race*, p. 29; David W. Kirkpatrick, *Choice in Schooling: A Case for Tuition Vouchers* (Loyola University Press, 1990), pp. 91–95; Witte, "Who Benefits from the Milwaukee Choice Program?" p. 132; Gary Orfield, *City-Suburban Desegregation: Parent and Student Perspectives in Metropolitan Boston* (Cambridge, Mass.: Harvard Civil Rights Project, September 1997), p. 22; Mark Schneider and others, "Institutional Arrangements and the Creation of Social Capital: The Effects of Public School Choice," *American Political Science Review*, vol. 91 (March 1997), pp. 82, 84–86, 88–90.

52. Young and Clinchy, *Choice in Public Education*, p. 114.

53. See *Pasadena City Board of Education. v. Spangler*, 427 U.S. 424 (1976), 434.

54. Charles L. Glenn, Kahris McLaughlin, and Laura Salganik, *Parent Information for School Choice: The Case of Massachusetts* (Boston: Center of Families, Communities, Schools, and Children's Learning, Institute for Responsive Education, 1993), p. 1. Clinchy and Kolb, *Planning for School Choice*, pp. 4–5.

55. See, for example, Snider, "The Call for Choice," p. C1; Rossell, "The Buffalo Controlled Choice Plan," p. 332; Steel and Levine, *Educational Innovation in Multiracial Contexts*, p. ii. Dana Milbank, "Schoolyard Tussle," *New Republic*, December 14, 1998, pp. 22, 23.

56. John Ritter, "New Con: Sneaking into School, Parents Lie to Better Kids' Education," *USA Today*, January 22, 1997, p. 1A. Orfield, *City-Suburban Desegregation*, pp. 2, 14. Orfield, *Must We Bus?* p. 414; Orfield and Eaton, *Dismantling Desegregation*, p. 311.

57. Judith Havemann, "Benefactors Create Their Own School Voucher Programs," *Washington Post*, February 21, 1998, p. A1. Rene Sanchez, "Cleveland Charts New Educational Course," *Washington Post*, September 10, 1996, p. A1. Terry Moe, "The Public Revolution Private Money Might Bring," *Washington Post*, May 9, 1999, p. B3; Jeff Archer, "Huge Demand for Private Vouchers Raises Questions," *Education Week*, April 28, 1999.

58. Steve Farkas and Jean Johnson, *Time to Move On: African-American and White Parents Set an Agenda for Public Schools: A Report from Public Agenda* (New York: Public Agenda, 1998), p. 18; see also Fleigel, *Miracle in East Harlem*, p. 195. Kathleen Sylvester, "Common Standards, Diverse Schools: Renewing the Promise of Public Education," in Will Marshall, ed., *Building the Bridge* (Lanham, Md.: Rowman and Littlefield, 1997), pp. 75–76.

59. Alves, "Comments and General Discussion," in Rasell and Rothstein, *School Choice*, p. 143; see also Rossell and Glenn, "The Cambridge Controlled Choice Plan," p. 85; Christine H. Rossell, "Controlled-Choice Desegregation Plans: Not Enough Choice, Too Much Control?" *Urban Affairs Review*, vol. 31 (September 1995), p. 73. Bob Gittens, interview by author, December 2, 1997, Boston, p. 10.

60. Alves, "Comments and General Discussion," in Rasell and Rothstein, *School Choice*, p. 143; see also Rossell and Glenn, "The Cambridge Controlled Choice Plan," p. 85; Rossell, "Not Enough Choice, Too Much Control?" pp. 31, 73. Gittens, interview, p. 10. Clewell and Joy, *Choice in Montclair*, p. 6. Kirkpatrick, *Choice in Schooling*, p. 74.

61. See Fuller and Elmore, *Who Chooses? Who Loses?* p. 192; Christine H. Rossell, *The Carrot or the Stick for School Desegregation Policy: Magnet Schools or Forced Busing* (Temple University Press, 1990), p. 116; Edward B. Fiske and Helen F. Ladd, *When Schools Compete: A Cautionary Tale* (Brookings, 2000), p. 196.

62. Richard F. Elmore, "Choice as an Instrument of Public Policy: Evidence from Education and Health Care," in William H. Clune and John F. Witte, eds., *Choice and Control in American Education*, vol. 1, *The Theory of Choice and Control in Education* (London: Falmer Press, 1990), p. 308. Alves and Willie, "Controlled Choice—An Approach to Effective School Desegregation," p. 84; see also Rossell and Glenn, "The Cambridge Controlled Choice Plan," pp. 85–86. Michael Alves, "Comments and General Discussion," in Rasell and Rothstein, *School Choice*, p. 137; Rothstein, "Introduction," in Rasell and Rothstein, *School Choice*, p. 22; Glenn, "Controlled Choice in Massachusetts Public Schools," p. 97. Charles Glenn, interview by author, December 3, 1997, Boston, pp. 15, 17.

63. Wilkinson, *From Brown to Bakke*, p. 142. Edward Banfield, *Unheavenly Cities* (Boston: Little, Brown, 1968), p. 79 (on 1964 data); Bok, *The State of the Nation*, pp. 178–79 (on today's desire for integration). Wilson, *When Work Disappears*, pp. 10–11. Douglas S. Massey and Nancy A. Denton, *American Apartheid: Segregation and the Making of the Underclass* (Harvard University Press, 1993), pp. 89–90, cited in john a. powell, "Living and Learning: Linking Housing and Education," *Minnesota Law Review*, vol. 80 (April 1996), p. 786 n. 125. Valerie E. Lee, Robert G. Croninger, and Julia B. Smith, "Equity and Choice in Detroit," in Fuller and Elmore, *Who Chooses? Who Loses?* p. 83. Abigail Thernstrom and Stephan Thernstrom, "Black Progress: How Far We've Come and How Far We Have to Go," *Brookings Review* (Spring 1998), p. 12; see also Edith McArthur and others, *Use of School Choice, Educational Policy Issues: Statistical Perspectives* (NCES, 1995), p. 2.

64. See Clewall and Joy, *Choice in Montclair*, pp. 7, 10, 17.

65. Rossell and Glenn, "The Cambridge Controlled Choice Plan," p. 81.

66. Tan, *The Cambridge Controlled Choice Program*, p. 11; Peter W. Cookson Jr., *School Choice: The Struggle for the Soul of America* (Yale University Press, 1994) pp. 61, 63; Young and Clinchy, *Choice in Public Education*, pp. 28–29, 61–65, 80, 83–84, 105–06; Helen Machado, "Group to Fight School Choice in Manchester," *Hartford Courant*, February 28, 1996, p. B1; Laura Ungar, "Controlled Choice Greeted with Dissent," p. B1; Hicks, "Some Families Find the Choice Limited," p. A1; Henig, *Rethinking School Choice*, pp. 123–24; Chrissie Bamber and others, *Public School Choice: An Equal Chance for All?* (Columbia, Md.: National Committee for Citizens in Education, 1990), p. 25; Clewell and Joy, *Choice in Montclair*, pp. 6–10. These high figures do not reflect "gaming" by parents; see Glenn, McLaughlin, and Salganik, *Parent Information for School Choice*, p. 14; and Glenn, *Family Choice and Public Schools: A Report to the State Board of Education*, p. 27.

67. Glenn, *Family Choice and Public Schools*, p. 29; see also Glenn, McLaughlin, and Salganik, *Parent Information for School Choice*, p. 16; Glenn, "Controlled Choice in Massachusetts Public Schools," pp. 98–99. Torres, "Controlled Choice?" p. A1. Boston subsequently eliminated controlled choice, not from a popular uprising but because of a lawsuit; see chapter 8.

68. For critics, see, for example, Thernstrom and Thernstrom, "Black Progress," p. 319; Fierman, "Giving Parents a Choice of Schools," p. 147. McArthur and others, *Use*

of School Choice, p. 1; Susan Choy, *Public and Private Schools: How They Differ* (NCES, 1997), pp. 3–4.

69. Choy, *Public and Private Schools*, pp. 5, 3–4; Elmore, "Choice as an Instrument of Public Policy," pp. 300–01. McArthur and others, *Use of School Choice*, p. 1.

70. Jeffrey R. Henig and Stephen D. Sugarman, "The Nature and Extent of School Choice," in Stephen D. Sugarman and Frank R. Kemerer, eds., *School Choice and Social Controversy* (Brookings, 1999), pp. 29 (36 percent), 16 (wealthier more likely). Michael Alves, interview by author, December 1, 1997, Cambridge, p. 43. Charles L. Glenn, "Free Schools and the Revival of Urban Communities," paper prepared for *Welfare Responsibility: An Inquiry into the Roots of America's Welfare Crisis*, a project of the Center for Public Justice, funded by the Pew Charitable Trusts, October 1993, p. 9.

71. Glenn, McLaughlin, and Salganik, *Parent Information for School Choice*, p. 18.

72. See Anthony Giddens, *The Third Way: The Renewal of Social Democracy* (Oxford: Blackwell, 1998), p. 65.

73. Wells, *Time to Choose*, p. 5 (paraphrasing Joe Nathan).

74. See, for example, Patrick Welsh, "It's No Longer Uncool to Do Well in School," *Washington Post*, March 14, 1999, p. B2.

75. Fiske and Ladd, *When Schools Compete*, pp. 184–95, 197–98.

76. *Missouri* v. *Jenkins II*, 115 S.Ct. 2038 (1995) 2042 (that with lavish expenditure, system remains 68 percent black); 2054 (that per pupil noncapital costs were much higher); James S. Kunen, "The End of Integration," *Time*, April 29, 1996, pp. 41–42; Dennis Farney, "Integration Is Faltering in Kansas City Schools as Priorities Change," *Wall Street Journal*, September 26, 1995, p. A1; Stephan Thernstrom and Abigail Thernstrom, *America in Black and White* (Simon and Schuster, 1997), pp. 345–46; see also Lisa Frazier, "Prince George's Schools Struggle with Racial Plan," *Washington Post*, April 2, 1996, p. C1; Orfield, *Must We Bus?* p. 405; Young and Clinchy, *Choice in Public Education*, pp. 23–24. Myron Orfield, *Metropolitics: A Regional Agenda for Community and Stability* (Brookings, 1997), p. 45.

77. Christopher Jencks, "Is the Public School Obsolete?" *Public Interest*, vol. 2 (Winter 1966), pp. 25–26; see also Charles Glenn, "Putting School Choice in Place," *Phi Delta Kappan*, vol. 71 (December 1989), p. 295. "A Scholar Who Inspired It Says Busing Backfired," interview with James Coleman, *National Observer*, June 7, 1975, p. 18; Robin M. Bennefield, "Cette ecole est publique," *U.S. News and World Report*, October 7, 1996, pp. 62–63.

78. See, for example, Henig, *Rethinking School Choice*, pp. 165–66; Jeffrey Henig, "Choice in Public Schools: An Analysis of Transfer Requests among Magnet Schools," *Social Science Quarterly*, vol. 71 (March 1990), pp. 69, 76; Bruce Fuller, Richard F. Elmore, and Gary Orfield, "Policymaking in the Dark: Illuminating the School Choice Debate," in Fuller and Elmore, *Who Chooses? Who Loses?* pp. 13–14; Lee, Croninger, and Smith, "Equity and Choice in Detroit," p. 71; Richard F. Elmore and Bruce Fuller, "Empirical Research on Educational Choice: What Are the Implications for Policymaking?" in Fuller and Elmore, *Who Chooses? Who Loses?* p. 189; Isabel Wilkerson, "Des Moines Acts to Halt White Flight after State Allows Choice of Schools," *New York Times*, December 16, 1992, p. B9; Amy Stuart Wells, "Quest for Improving Schools Finds Role for Free Market," *New York Times*, March 14, 1990, p. A1.

79. Valerie Martinez, Kenneth Godwin, and Frank R. Kemerer, "Public School Choice in San Antonio: Who Chooses and with What Effects?" in Fuller and Elmore, *Who Chooses? Who Loses?* pp. 51, 57–58; Rothstein, introduction to Rasell and Rothstein, *School Choice*, pp. 6–9, 12; Witte, "Who Benefits from the Milwaukee Choice Program?" pp. 123–25; Carol Ascher and Gary Burnett, *Current Trends and Issues in Urban Education, 1993* (New York: ERIC Clearinghouse on Urban Education, 1993), p. 22; Fiske and Ladd, *When Schools Compete*, p. 206. Glenn, "Putting School Choice in Place," p. 297. Richard Elmore and Bruce Fuller, "Empirical Research on Education Choice: What Are the Implications for Policy-Making?" in Fuller and Elmore, *Who Chooses? Who Loses?* p. 192.

80. Alves and Willie, "Controlled Choice," p. 79. See also Meier, *The Power of Their Ideas*, p. 94. Thomas Toch, *Improving Performance*, p. 8. Education Commission of the States, *A State Policy-Makers' Guide*, p. 34. Some object to the notion that all parents will choose schools—Abigail Thernstrom worries about "drugged parents who won't and probably can't make informed choices"—but that is all the more reason to create a mechanism under which middle-class families will be in all schools, thereby creating pressure for all schools to improve; Glenn, "Controlled Choice in Massachusetts Public Schools," p. 97.

81. Kahlenberg, *The Remedy*, pp. 148–51 (arguing for a class-based preference in admissions to selective high schools, because counting obstacles is relevant in meritocratic determinations about young people, but not arguing for proportional representation).

82. Gary Natriello, Edward L. McDill, and Aaron M. Pallas, *Schooling Disadvantaged Children: Racing against Catastrophe* (New York: Teachers College Press, 1990), p.185. Glenn, *Family Choice of Schools*, p. 38.

83. Barbara Chriss, Greta Nash, and David Stern, "The Rise and Fall of Choice in Richmond, California," *Economics of Education Review*, vol. 11 (December 1992), p. 395; William Snider, "California District Makes Choice Initiative Centerpiece of Plan to Reinvigorate Schools," *Education Week*, December 13, 1989, p. 22. Myron Lieberman, *Public School Choice: Current Issues, Future Prospects* (Lancaster, Pa.: Technomic Publishing, 1990), pp. 35–37, 38–40, 62–63; John McAdams, "Can Open Enrollment Work?" *Public Interest*, vol. 37 (Fall 1974), pp. 72–77, 83–84; see also Amy Stuart Wells and others, *Beyond the Rhetoric of Charter School Reform: A Study of Ten California School Districts* (Los Angeles: UCLA Charter School Study, 1998), p. 48. Steel and Levine, *Educational Innovation in Multiracial Contexts*, p.101.

84. Wilkinson, *From Brown to Bakke*, pp. 113–14. Fliegel, *Miracle in East Harlem*, p. 187.

85. Snider, "The Call for Choice," p. C8; Ascher and Burnett, *Current Trends and Issues in Urban Education*, p. 20; Rossell, *The Carrot or the Stick*, p. 200; Jennifer L. Hochschild, *The New American Dilemma: Liberal Democracy and School Desegregation* (Yale University Press, 1984), p. 76. Lemann, "Magnetic Attraction," p. 17. Farkas and Johnson, *Time to Move On*, pp. 28–29.

86. Ascher and Burnett, *Current Trends and Issues in Urban Education*, p. 19. William L. Yancey and Salvatore J. Saporito, *Racial and Economic Segregation and Educational Outcomes: One Tale, Two Cities* (Philadelphia: Temple University Center for Research in Human Development and Education, 1995), pp. 18, 26–27. Carmel McCoubrey, "Magnet Schools and Class," *New York Times*, June 23, 1999, p. A18.

Department of Education, "Education Innovation in Multiracial Contexts, Highlights," 1994 (www.ed.gov/offices/OUS/eval/esed/magnet2.html [March 2, 1999]) (summarizing Steel and Levine, *Education Innovation in Multiracial Contexts*). Lemann, "Magnetic Attraction," p. 17.

87. Donald R. Moore and Suzanne Davenport, "High School Choice and Students at Risk," *Equity and Choice*, vol. 5 (February 1989), pp. 5–6; Glenn, "Controlled Choice in Massachusetts Public Schools," pp. 93–94. Ascher and Burnett, *Current Trends and Issues in Urban Education*, p. 19. Nathan, "Charters and Choice," p. 74. Ron Suskind, *A Hope in the Unseen: An American Odyssey from the Inner City to the Ivy League* (New York: Broadway, 1998), p. 37. David Nakamura, "School 'Contract' Draws Complaints," *Washington Post*, April 16, 1999, p. B1. William Snider, "School Choice: New, More Efficient 'Sorting Machine'?" *Education Week*, May 18, 1988, p. 8. William Snider, "Parley on 'Choice,' Final Budget Mark Transition," *Education Week*, January 18, 1989, p. 24. Hochschild, *The New American Dilemma*, p. 77.

88. Wells, *Time to Choose*, p. 86.

89. Young and Clinchy, *Choice in Public Education*, pp. 23–24. Hochschild, *The New American Dilemma*, p. 72. Rolf Blank, "Educational Effects of Magnet High Schools," in Clune and Witte, *Choice and Control in American Education*, vol. 2, *The Practice of Choice*, p. 77.

90. Clewall and Joy, *Choice in Montclair*, pp. 5–6. Glenn, "Controlled Choice in Massachusetts Public Schools," p. 95.

91. See Glenn, McLaughlin, and Salganik, *Parent Information for School Choice*, p. 8.

92. Arthur E. Wise, *Rich Schools, Poor Schools: The Promise of Equal Educational Opportunity* (University of Chicago Press, 1967), pp. 94–101. See Senate Select Committee on Equal Educational Opportunity, *Toward Equal Educational Opportunity*, p. 324; U.S. Department of Education, National Center for Education Statistics, *Digest of Education Statistics* (Washington: GPO, 1996), p. 96, table 88. Gerald Benjamin and Richard Nathan, *Regionalism and Realism* (Brookings, forthcoming), p. 271.

93. Rusk, *Cities without Suburbs*, p. 10. Orfield, "Metropolitan School Desegregation," p. 845.

94. Janet Reynolds, "A Level Playing Field for All Students: Q and A, Gordon Bruno," *New York Times*, September 6, 1998.

95. Jerry D. Weast, "When Bigger Can Be Better," *School Administrator* (October 1997), p. 38. Benjamin and Nathan, *Regionalism and Realism*, p. 273. Rusk, *Cities without Suburbs*, pp. 95–96. Abby Goodnough, "Can Our Schools Be Merged?" *New York Times*, June 2, 1996, sec. 13, pp. 1, 8.

96. For a variation on this idea, see Coleman, "Racial Segregation in the Schools," p. 78. General Accounting Office, *Rural Children: Increasing Poverty Rates Pose Educational Challenges. Briefing Report to the Chairwoman, Congressional Rural Caucus, House of Representatives* (Washington: GAO, January 1994), p. 48. Bruce Katz and Scott Bernstein, "The New Metropolitan Agenda," *Brookings Review* (Fall 1998), p. 4.

97. *Milliken* v. *Bradley*, 418 U.S. 717, 733, 743, 767 (White, J., dissenting), 812–13 (Marshall, J., dissenting), 775 (White, J., dissenting). See the discussion of Boston in chapter 8. Chapter 7 outlines why the legal argument for economic integration bypasses the *Milliken* limitation and requires interdistrict remedies. Michael Alves and Charles Willie, "Choice: Decentralization and Desegregation—The Boston 'Controlled Choice' Plan," in Clune and Witte, *Choice and Control in American Education*, vol. 2,

The Practice of Choice, pp. 34–36; Clinchy and Kolb, *Planning for School Choice*, pp. 9–11; Hicks, "Some Families Find the Choice Limited," p. A1; Robert Rothman, "After Delays, Boston's 'Controlled Choice' Plan Emerges," *Education Week*, November 9, 1988, p. 5 (30–40 minute maximum travel time).

98. Richard Pierce raised this point with me. Robert Embry, letter to the author, August 17, 1998.

99. Lisa Suhay, "White Flight," *New York Times*, October 10, 1999, N.J. sec., p. 1. Daniel Brook, "School Crossing," *New Journal* (November 30, 1998), p. 10.

100. Cited in Ruy Teixeira, "Critical Support: The Public View of Public Education," in Richard D. Kahlenberg, ed., *A Notion at Risk: Preserving Public Education as an Engine for Social Mobility* (New York: Century Foundation Press, 2000), p. 271.

101. Tom Loveless, *The Tracking Wars: State Reform Meets School Policy* (Brookings, 1999), p. 144.

102. Julianne Basinger, "Colleges Experiment with Charter Schools," *Chronicle of Higher Education* (October 29, 1999) p. A51. Daniel Brook, "School Crossing," pp. 8–11.

103. See the discussion in chapter 7.

104. For both polls, see Teixeira, "Critical Support," p. 269.

105. Rusk, *Inside Game/Outside Game*, pp. 71–72.

106. For the importance of the relative "burden" in constitutional jurisprudence, see James S. Liebman, "Three Strategies for Implementing *Brown* Anew," in Herbert Hill and James E. Jones Jr., eds., *Race in America: The Struggle for Equality* (University of Wisconsin Press, 1993), pp. 119–20.

107. Crain quoted in Rick Green, "In Wake of *Sheff*, Project Concern Shrinks," *Hartford Courant*, June 23, 1997, p. A3.

108. See, for example, Jeannie Oakes, *Keeping Track: How Schools Structure Inequality* (Yale University Press, 1985), pp. 98–100, 143, 175.

109. Anne Wheelock, *Crossing the Tracks: How "Untracking" Can Save America's Schools* (New York: New Press, 1992), p. 9. Kenneth Meier, Joseph Steward Jr., and Robert E. England, *Race, Class, and Education: The Politics of Second-Generation Discrimination* (University of Wisconsin Press, 1989), pp. 50–53, 57. Bell, *Race, Racism, and American Law*, p. 600.

110. Wheelock, *Crossing the Tracks*, p. 8. Tom Loveless, *The Tracking and Ability Grouping Debate* (Washington: Thomas B. Fordham Foundation, 1998) (www.edexcellence.net/library/track.html [August 11, 1998]).

111. For criticisms of tracking, see Oakes, *Keeping Track*, p. 195; Wheelock, *Crossing the Tracks*, pp. 57, 76; John I. Goodlad, *A Place Called School: Prospects for the Future* (McGraw-Hill, 1984), pp. 151–52. For a defense, see Loveless, *The Tracking and Ability Grouping Debate*; Loveless, *The Tracking Wars*, pp. 15–16, 19, 155; Nicholas Lemann, "Ready, READ!" *Atlantic Monthly*, November 1998, p. 98 (on Slavin's use of ability grouping).

112. Michael J. Puma, and others, *Prospects: Final Report on Student Outcomes* (Cambridge, Mass.: Abt Associates, 1997), pp. v, 61. Ronald Ferguson, "Can Schools Narrow," in Christopher Jencks and Meredith Phillips, *The Black-White Test Score Gap* (Brookings, 1998), pp. 326, 334; see also Grissmer and others, "Why Did the Black-White Score Gap Narrow," in Jencks and Phillips, *The Black-White Test Score Gap*, p. 204; Jencks and Phillips, introduction to *The Black-White Test Score Gap*, p. 32. Jencks and Phillips, introduction to *The Black-White Test Score Gap*, p. 45.

113. Loveless, *The Tracking and Ability Grouping Debate*. Mickey Kaus, *The End of Equality* (Basic Books, 1992), p. 159.

114. Loveless, *The Tracking and Ability Grouping Debate*. Diane Ravitch, *The Schools We Deserve: Reflections on the Educational Crises of Our Times* (Basic Books, 1985), p. 14.

115. Loveless, *The Tracking and Ability Grouping Debate*. Jomills Henry Braddock II, "Tracking the Middle Grades: National Patterns of Grouping for Instruction," *Phi Delta Kappan*, vol. 71, no. 6 (February 1990), p. 448.

116. Loveless, *The Tracking and Ability Grouping Debate*.

117. Braddock, "Tracking the Middle Grades," p. 446.

118. James Fallows, "Strengths, Weaknesses, and Lessons of Japanese Education," *Education Digest*, vol. 57 (October 1991), p. 57.

119. Rossell, *The Carrot or the Stick*, p. 219 n. 3. Robert Stevens and others, "Cooperative Integrated Reading and Composition: Two Field Experiments," *Reading Research Quarterly*, vol. 22 (Fall 1987), p. 434. David W. Johnson and Roger T. Johnson, *Learning Together and Alone: Cooperative, Competitive, and Individualistic Learning* (Boston: Allyn and Bacon, 1994), pp. 55–56, 63.

120. Stevens and others, "Cooperative Integrated Reading and Composition," p. 435. Johnson and Johnson, *Learning Together and Alone*, p. 39. Wheelock, *Crossing the Tracks*, p. 76. Uri Treisman, "Studying Students Studying Calculus," *College Mathematics Journal*, vol. 23 (November 1992), pp. 362–72.

121. Johnson and Johnson, *Learning Together and Alone*, pp. 105, 126. See also Stevens and others, "Cooperative Integrated Reading and Composition," pp. 434, 436, 440, 443, 450.

122. Johnson and Johnson, *Learning Together and Alone*, pp. 68–69, 239. Holly Holland, *Making Change: Three Educators Join the Battle for Better Schools* (Portsmouth, N.H.: Heinemann, 1998), p. 94.

123. Jay Mathews, *Class Struggle: What's Wrong (and Right) with America's Best Public High Schools* (New York: Times Books, 1998), p. 246 (summarizing the principal's views). Nicholas D. Kristof, "Where Children Rule," *New York Times Magazine*, August 17, 1997, p. 40.

124. Bell, *Race, Racism, and American Law*, p. 601. Ellis Cose, *Color-Blind: Seeing beyond Race in a Race-Obsessed World* (HarperCollins, 1997), p. 74.

125. Adam Gamoran and Robert D. Mare, "Secondary School Tracking and Educational Inequality: Compensation, Reinforcement, or Neutrality?" *American Journal of Sociology*, vol. 5 (March 1989), pp. 1165–66, 1152, 1177; Loveless, *The Tracking and Ability Grouping Debate*; Ferguson, "Can Schools Narrow," pp. 326, 329, 336; Jencks and Phillips, introduction to *The Black-White Test Score Gap*, p. 33. Claude Fischer and others, *Inequality by Design: Cracking the Bell Curve Myth* (Princeton University Press, 1996), pp. 164–65.

126. *Lau v. Nichols*, 414 U.S. 563 (1974); *Guardians Association v. Civil Service Commission*, 463 U.S. 582 (1983), 592, 598. *Larry P. v. Riles*, 793 F. 2d 969 (9th Cir. 1984); *Little Rock School District v. Pulaski County Special School District 1*, 659 F. Supp. 363 (E.D. Ark. 1987), vacated in part on other grounds, 839 F.2d 1296 (1st Cir. 1988); 584 F.Supp. 328 (E.D. Ark 1984), rev'd in part on other grounds, 778 F.2d 404 (8th Cir. 1985), cert. denied, 476 U.S. 1186 (1986). Bell, *Race, Racism, and American Law*, p. 600; Note, "Teaching Inequality," *Harvard Law Review*, vol. 102 (1989), pp. 1318, 1325–26;

People Who Care v. *Rockford Board of Education*, 111 F. 3rd 528 (7th Cir. 1997) (reversing district court's racial quotas in tracking).

127. Valerie E. Lee and Anthony S. Bryk, "Curriculum Tracking as Mediating the Social Distribution of High School Achievement," *Sociology of Education*, vol. 61 (April 1988), p. 81. Loveless, *The Tracking and Ability Grouping Debate*, n. 11. Katherine Shaver, "A New Mix of 'Gifted' Students: Ambitious Parents in Howard Boost Numbers, but Is It Smart?" *Washington Post*, July 27, 1997, pp. A1, A13.

128. Allington quoted in Jay Mathews, "To Track or Not to Track," *Washington Post Education Review*, April 7, 1996, p. 9. Kahlenberg, *The Remedy*, pp. 275–76 n. 16; Clewall and Joy, *Choice in Montclair*, p. 11.

129. Kurt Vonnegut, *The Handicapper General* (1961), cited in Thomas R. Pezzulo, "IQ Tests and the Handicapper General," in Nelson F. Ashline, Thomas Pezzulo, and Charles I. Norris, eds., *Education, Inequality, and National Policy* (Lexington, Mass.: Lexington Books, 1976), p. 147. Marshall, quoted in Wolf, *Trial and Error*, p. 119.

130. Manners, "Repackaging Segregation," p. 90.

131. William L. Taylor, "The Continuing Struggle for Equal Educational Opportunity," *North Carolina Law Review* (June 1993), pp. 1693, 1706. Department of Education, *Improving America's Schools Act of 1993: The Reauthorization of the Elementary and Secondary Education Act and Amendments to Other Acts* (September 13, 1993), p. 5.

132. Stephen Hansell and Nancy Karweit, "Curricular Placement, Friendship, and Status," in Joyce Levy Epstein and Nancy Karweit, eds., *Friends in School: Patterns of Selection and Influence in Secondary Schools* (New York: Academic Press, 1983), p. 145.

133. Nancy Karweit, "Extracurricular Activities and Friendship Selection," in Epstein and Karweit, *Friends in School*, pp. 131–33, 133. Janet Ward Schofield, "School Desegregation and Intergroup Relations: A Review of the Literature," *Review of Research in Education*, vol. 17 (1991), p. 371.

134. Ralph H. Turner, *The Social Context of Ambition: A Study of High School Seniors in Los Angeles* (San Francisco: Chandler Publishing, 1964), p. 111; see also Stephen Plank, "Peer Relations and Participation in Desegregated Classrooms," Ph.D. diss., University of Chicago, 1995. Schofield, "School Desegregation and Intergroup Relations," pp. 370, 371.

135. Turner, *The Social Context of Ambition*, p. 16. Kenneth P. Langton, "Peer Group and School and the Political Socialization Process," *American Political Science Review* (September 1967), pp. 752–53.

136. Rosenbaum, Rubinowitz, and Kulieke, *Low-Income Black Children*, pp. 79, 85. Turner, *The Social Context of Ambition*, p. 139. Jere Cohen, "Commentary: Selection and Influence," in Epstein and Karweit, *Friends in School*, pp. 169–71. On the racial balance of friendships in integrated schools, see the evidence presented in chapter 3. Malcolm Gladwell, *The Tipping Point: How Little Things Can Make a Big Difference* (New York: Little, Brown, 2000), p. 35.

137. Amy Wells and Robert L. Crain, "Perpetuation Theory and the Long-Term Effects of School Desegregation," *Review of Educational Research*, vol. 64 (Winter 1994), pp. 531, 533–34; Amy Wells, "Reexamining Social Science Research on School Desegregation: Long-Term versus Short-Term Effects," *Teachers College Record*, vol. 96 (Summer 1995), p. 700. Gladwell, *The Tipping Point*, p. 54, citing Mark Granovetter. Cohen, "Commentary," p. 164. Laurence Steinberg, *Beyond the Classroom: Why School Reform Has Failed and What Parents Need to Do* (Simon and Schuster, 1996), pp. 139–40.

138. Downs, *New Visions for Metropolitan America*, pp. 116–18. Wendy D. Puriefoy and Deborah Wadsworth, afterword to Farkas and Johnson, *Time to Move On*, p. 36. Irvan B. Gluckman, "Troublemakers in Public Schools," *Washington Post*, September 5, 1997, p. A22 (letter to the editor); Abigail Thernstrom, "Where Did All the Order Go? School Discipline and the Law," in Diane Ravitch, ed., *Brookings Papers on Education Policy, 1999* (Brookings, 1999), pp. 302–09; Anne Proffit Dupre, "Should Students Have Constitutional Rights? Keeping Order in the Public Schools," *George Washington Law Review*, vol. 65 (November 1996), p. 49; "Tighten Up on Discipline: A Cry from the Field," *Daily Report Card*, April 18, 1997; Paul Barton, Richard J. Coley, and Harold Wenglinsky, *Order in the Classroom: Violence, Discipline, and Student Achievement* (Princeton, N.J.: Educational Testing Service, 1998), p. 35.

139. Dupre, "Should Students Have Constitutional Rights?," p. 50. Shanker quoted in Sylvester, "Common Standards, Diverse Schools," p. 89.

140. Departments of Education and Justice, *Annual Report on School Safety* (1998), pp. 1, 2, 4, 5. Jessica Portner, "Zero Tolerance Laws Getting a Second Look," *Education Week*, March 26; American Federation of Teachers, *Setting the Stage: School Discipline Resource Material* (Washington: AFT, July 1997), p. G53; Al Shanker, "Zero Tolerance," *New York Times*, January 26, 1997, sec. 4, p. 7; Barton, Coley, and Wenglinsky, *Order in the Classroom*, pp. 3, 7, 8, 33, 42; California Department of Education, Safe Schools Violence and Prevention Office, "Zero Tolerance," (www.uncg.edu/edu/ericass/violence/docs/zero.html [October 8, 1998]); Ronald Stephens, "Safe School Planning," in Delbert S. Elliott, Beatrix A. Hamburg, and Kirk R. Williams, eds., *Violence in American Schools: A New Perspective* (Cambridge: Cambridge University Press, 1998), p. 270; Paul Basken, "Troublemakers: Don't Let Them Rule the School," *Washington Post*, March 6, 1997, p. C3; Rene Sanchez, "Bundling Rebels into High Schools of Last Resort," *Washington Post*, July 4, 1998, pp. A1, A7; Departments of Education and Justice, "Annual School Safety Report," pp. 23–32.

141. Again, under Title VI of the 1964 Civil Rights Act, recipients of federal aid (including all public schools) may not discriminate. Any policy that has a disparate impact on people of color needs to be justified with reference to educational necessity.

142. Farkas and Johnson, *Time to Move On*, pp. 31, 33, 40. See also AFT, "Setting the Stage for High Standards," July 1997, p. B7.

143. Rasell and Rothstein, *School Choice*, p. 33. Amy Stuart Wells and Robert L. Crain, *Stepping over the Color Line: African-American Students in White Suburban Schools* (Yale University Press, 1997), pp. 269, 101–02. Arnold P. Goldstein, "Aggression Reduction Strategies," *School Psychology Quarterly*, vol. 14, no. 1 (1999), p. 41.

144. Paul A. Jargowsky, *Poverty and Place: Ghettos, Barrios, and the American City* (New York: Russell Sage Foundation, 1997), p. 6.

Chapter Seven

1. See discussion of the effect on property values in chapter 8.

2. Richard D. Lamm, "Can Parents Be Partners?" *Phi Delta Kappan*, vol. 68 (November 1986), p. 211. Theodore Sizer, *Horace's Hope: What Works for the American High School* (Boston: Houghton Mifflin, 1996), pp. 39–40.

3. Bolick quoted in Gordon A. MacInnes, *Kids Who Pick the Wrong Parents and Other Victims of Voucher Schemes*, Century Foundation White Paper (1999), p. 1. Ben-

nett quoted in William Snider, "The Call for Choice: Competition in the Educational Marketplace," *Education Week*, June 24, 1987, p. C4. The big distinction is that private school vouchers provide education on the cheap; the Department of Education has found that base salaries of teachers in private schools are 37 percent lower than those found in public schools; see Carol Ascher, Norm Fruchter, and Robert Berne, *Hard Lessons: Public Schools and Privatization* (Twentieth Century Fund, 1996), p. 21. Amy Stuart Wells and Robert L. Crain, *Stepping over the Color Line: African-American Students in White Suburban Schools* (Yale University Press, 1997), p. 345. Valerie Martinez and others, "Who Chooses and Why: A Look at Five School Choice Plans," *Phi Delta Kappan*, vol. 75 (May 1994), p. 679.

4. Ted Kolderie, *Beyond Choice to New Public Schools: Withdrawing the Exclusive Franchise in Public Education* (Washington: Progressive Policy Institute, November 1990), p. 5. See, for example, Ruy Teixeira, "Critical Support: The Public View of Public Education," in Richard D. Kahlenberg, ed., *A Notion at Risk: Preserving Public Education as an Engine for Social Mobility* (New York: Century Foundation Press, 2000), pp. 259–60; Seymour Fliegel, with James MacGuire, *Miracle in East Harlem: The Fight for Choice in Public Education* (Random House, 1993), pp. 11, 195; Myron Lieberman, *Public School Choice: Current Issues, Future Prospects* (Lancaster, Pa.: Technomic Publishing, 1990), p. 1; Timothy Young and Evans Clinchy, *Choice in Public Education* (New York: Teachers College Press, 1992), p. 3; Stanley M. Elam and Alec M. Gallup, "The Twenty-first Annual Poll of Public Attitudes toward the Public Schools," *Phi Delta Kappan*, vol. 71 (September 1989), pp. 42–43; Jeffrey R. Henig, *Rethinking School Choice: Limits of the Marketplace Metaphor* (Princeton University Press, 1994), pp. 189, 262 n. 31; John Chubb and Terry Moe, *Politics, Markets, and American Schools* (Brookings, 1990), p. 306 n. 29.

5. Fliegel, *Miracle in East Harlem*, p. 195; Elam and Gallup, "The Twenty-first Annual Poll," pp. 43, 42; Henig, *Rethinking School Choice*, pp. 189, 262 n. 31; Christine H. Rossell and Charles L. Glenn, "The Cambridge Controlled Choice Plan," *Urban Review*, vol. 20 (Summer 1988), p. 77. Kolderie, *Beyond Choice to New Public Schools*, p. 5.

6. Lieberman, *Public School Choice*, pp. ix, 1, 10, 22, 128, 132; Valerie E. Lee, Robert G. Croninger, and Julia B. Smith, "Equity and Choice in Detroit," in Bruce Fuller and Richard F. Elmore, eds., *Who Chooses? Who Loses? Culture, Institutions, and the Unequal Effects of School Choice* (New York: Teachers College Press, 1996), pp. 74, 86; David T. Kearns and Denis P. Doyle, *Winning the Brain Rack: A Bold Plan to Make Our Schools Competitive* (San Francisco: Institute for Contemporary Studies Press, 1988), pp. 20, 24; Chubb and Moe, *Politics, Markets, and American Schools*, p. 307 n. 32; David Armor, "After Busing: Education and Choice," *Public Interest* (Spring 1989), pp. 32–33.

7. Bill Clinton and Al Gore, *Putting People First: How We Can All Change America* (New York: Times Books, 1992), pp. 18, 48, 61, 86, 102, 177; Rene Sanchez, "School Plan to Propose Urban Aid," *Washington Post*, December 23, 1997, pp. A1, A6; Christopher Georges, "Clinton to Seek Boost in Funds for Education," *Wall Street Journal*, January 13, 1998, pp. A3, A8. Deborah Meier, *The Power of Their Ideas: Lessons for America from a Small School in Harlem* (Boston: Beacon Press, 1995), pp. 92–93; Sizer, *Horace's Hope*, p. 139; William Julius Wilson, *When Work Disappears: The World of the New Urban Poor* (Knopf, 1996), p. 214; John Coons and Stephen D. Sugarman, *Education by Choice: The Case for Family Control* (University of California Press, 1978), pp. xiii, 2. People for the American Way, "A False Choice for Education," advertisement, *American*

Prospect (March–April 1998), p. 77. National Governors' Association, *Time For Results: The Governors' 1991 Report on Education* (Washington: National Governors' Association Center for Policy Research and Analysis, 1986), p. 3. Thomas Toch, "Education Reform, No Matter Who Wins," *Los Angeles Times*, November 6, 2000, p. 7.

8. Progressives like the late Al Shanker endorsed public school choice as "the best protection against vouchers," while conservatives like Chester Finn endorsed public choice as a step in the right direction, given the uphill battle facing private choice; see Edward Fiske, "Parental Choice in Public School Gains," *New York Times*, July 11, 1988, pp. A1, B6 (quoting Shanker); Jaclyn Fierman, "Giving Parents a Choice of Schools," *Fortune*, December 4, 1989, p. 150 (quoting Finn). Mary Anne Raywid, "The Mounting Case for Schools of Choice," in Joe Nathan, ed., *Public Schools by Choice: Expanding Opportunities for Parents, Students, and Teachers* (St. Paul, Minn.: Institute for Learning and Teaching, 1989), p. 24.

9. Amy Stuart Wells, *Time to Choose: America at the Crossroads of School Choice Policy* (New York: Hill and Wang, 1993), p. 96.

10. Thomas Toch, *Improving Performance: Competition in American Public Schools* (Washington: National Alliance of Business, 2000), pp. 12, 13. Lauri Steel and Roger Levine, *Educational Innovation in Multiracial Contexts: The Growth of Magnet Schools in American Education*, report prepared for the U.S. Department of Education (Palo Alto, Calif.: American Institute for Research, 1994). Donald Moore and Suzanne Davenport, "High School Choice and Students at Risk," *Equity and Choice*, vol. 5 (February 1989), p. 7.

11. Steel and Levine, *Educational Innovation in Multiracial Contexts*, pp. xvi–xvii. Lynn Schnaiberg, "More Students Taking Advantage of School Choice, Report Says," *Education Week*, September 22, 1999, p. 6; Edith McArthur and others, *Use of School Choice, Educational Policy Issues: Statistical Perspectives* (National Center for Education Statistics [NCES], 1995), pp. 1–2.

12. Edward B. Fiske, "Wave of the Future: A Choice of Schools," *New York Times*, June 4, 1989, p. 32.

13. Robert B. Reich, "Secession of the Successful," *New York Times Magazine*, January 20, 1991, p. 42 (describing, but not endorsing, this attitude).

14. Jackie Calmes, "Seeking Solutions for a Better Classroom," *Wall Street Journal*, March 14, 1997, p. R2; Carl F. Kaestle and Marshall S. Smith, "The Federal Role in Elementary and Secondary Education, 1940–1980," *Harvard Educational Review*, vol. 52 (November 1982), p. 401. Lieberman, *Public School Choice*, p. 16 (on Hawaii); David Rusk, *Inside Game/Outside Game: Urban Policies for the Twenty-first Century* (Brookings, 1999), p. 3, n. 5 (New Mexico); Note, "Recent Legislation," *Harvard Law Review*, vol. 108 (1995), pp. 1411–12, 1416 (Michigan). Dore Van Slyke, Alexandra Tan, and Martin Orland, *School Finance Litigation: A Review of Key Cases* (Washington: Finance Project, 1995), p. 13 (Minnesota); G. Alan Hickrod, "Testimony to the Subcommittee on Education, Arts, and Humanities of the Committee on Labor and Human Resources, U.S. Senate," in William J. Fowler Jr., ed., *Developments in School Finance* (NCES, 1995), p. 18 (Alabama).

15. T. Keung Hui, "Lifting Pay Could Cost Wake Schools $108 Million," *Raleigh News and Observer*, January 11, 2000, p. B1. On the left, see Leon Botstein, *Jefferson's Children: Education and the Promise of American Culture* (Doubleday, 1997), p. 31; on

the right, John Steele Gordon, "Down with Property Taxes," *Wall Street Journal*, August 21, 1998, p. A14.

16. Arthur E. Wise, *Rich Schools, Poor Schools: The Promise of Equal Educational Opportunity* (University of Chicago Press, 1967), p. 93. "Quality Counts '98: The Urban Challenge," *Education Week*, January 8, 1998, p. 23; Ascher, Fruchter, and Berne, *Hard Lessons*, p. 93; Nicholas Lemann, "Ready, READ!" *Atlantic Monthly*, November 1998, p. 93. Melody Petersen, "A Bitter Taste in Newark Schools," *New York Times*, September 18, 1997, pp. B1, B5. Margaret E. Goertz, "Program Equity and Adequacy: Issues from the Field," *Educational Policy*, vol. 8 (December 1994), p. 610. American Federation of Teachers, *Making Standards Matter 1999: Executive Summary* (www.aft.org/edissues/standards99 [October 10, 2000]).

17. Jeffrey R. Henig and Stephen D. Sugarman, "The Nature and Extent of School Choice," in Stephen D. Sugarman and Frank R. Kemerer, eds., *School Choice and Social Controversy* (Brookings, 1999), pp. 21, 29. See, for example, Peter W. Cookson Jr., *School Choice: The Struggle for the Soul of America* (Yale University Press, 1994), pp. 139–52.

18. Thomas Toch, *Improving Performance*, p. 9. Glenn quoted in Gary Putka, "Choose-a-School: Parents in Minnesota Are Getting to Send Kids Where They Like," *Wall Street Journal*, May 13, 1988, p. A1.

19. James S. Liebman, "Desegregating Politics: 'All-Out' School Desegregation Explained," *Columbia Law Review*, vol. 90 (October 1990), pp. 1463, 1656; David S. Tatel, "Cities, Suburbs Tie the Knot on Integration," *School Administrator* (May 1993), pp. 9–11; Gary Orfield, "Metropolitan School Desegregation: Impacts on Metropolitan Society," *Minnesota Law Review*, vol. 80 (April 1996), pp. 849, 869–70; David J. Armor, *Forced Justice: School Desegregation and the Law* (New York: Oxford University Press, 1995), pp. 46–47.

20. For example, Charles L. Glenn, "Putting Choice to Work for Public Education," in Charles L. Glenn, ed., *Family Choice and Public Schools: A Report to the State Board of Education* (Quincy, Mass.: Massachusetts Dept. of Education, January 1986), p. 15. See discussion in chapter 4 that the most successful programs in terms of raising achievement are the metrowide programs that involve economic as well as racial integration; Bella Rosenberg, "Public School Choice: Can We Find the Right Balance?" *American Educator*, vol. 13 (Summer 1989), p. 40.

21. Robert K. Gable, Donald L. Thompson, and Edward F. Iwanicki, "The Effects of Voluntary School Desegregation on Occupational Outcomes," *Vocational Guidance Quarterly*, vol. 31 (June 1983), p. 232. Richard Weizel, "School Busing, City and Suburban," *New York Times*, October 4, 1998, sec. 14, p. 17.

22. David K. Cohen, "Policy for the Public Schools: Compensation and Integration," *Harvard Educational Review: Equal Educational Opportunity* (Harvard University Press, 1969), p. 106; Senate Select Committee on Equal Opportunity, *Toward Equal Educational Opportunity* (Government Printing Office [GPO], December 31, 1972), pp. 24–25, 221; Meyer Weinberg, "The Relationship between School Desegregation and Academic Achievement: A Review of the Research," *Law and Contemporary Problems*, vol. 39 (Spring 1975), p. 251; Thomas Pettigrew and others, "Busing: A Review of the 'The Evidence,'" *Public Interest*, vol. 50 (Winter 1973), pp. 88, 97; Gable, Thompson, and Iwanicki, "The Effects of Voluntary School Desegregation on Occupa-

tional Outcomes," pp. 232, 235, 238; U.S. Commission on Civil Rights, *Racial Isolation in the Public Schools* (GPO, 1967), vol. 1, p. 153; Henry S. Dyer, "Thoughts about Future Studies," in Frederick Mosteller and Daniel P. Moynihan, eds., *On Equality of Educational Opportunity: Papers Deriving from the Harvard Faculty Seminar on the Coleman Report* (Random House, 1972), pp. 408–09; Mosteller and Moynihan, "A Pathbreaking Report," in Mosteller and Moynihan, *On Equality of Educational Opportunity*, pp. 50–51; Wells and Crain, *Stepping over the Color Line*, pp. 539 and 548; Plaintiffs' appeal from Superior Court, *Sheff* v. *O'Neill* (August 1, 1995), pp. 6 n.11, 7; "Study Finds Desegregation Is an Effective Tool," *New York Times*, September 17, 1985, p. C1.

23. See Gary Orfield, *City-Suburban Desegregation: Parent and Student Perspectives in Metropolitan Boston* (Cambridge, Mass.: Harvard Civil Rights Project, September 1997), pp. 2, 9. Jean M. McGuire, John M. Shandorf, and Sufi Yusuf, *School Year 1997–1998 Enrollment Audit Report to the State Department of Education* (Roxbury, Mass.: Metropolitan Council for Educational Opportunity, March 6, 1998). Adele W. Spier and others, *Chapter 636, Voluntary Integration in Massachusetts: Successful Programs of Choice* (Boston: Massachusetts State Dept. of Education, 1983), p. 15; Metropolitan Council for Educational Opportunity, "Metco Information Packet" (Roxbury, Mass., undated), p. 1. Jordana Hart, "Silber Promises Push for Funds to Expand Metco Program," *Boston Globe*, December 16, 1997, p. B5.

24. Metropolitan Council for Educational Opportunity, "Metco Information Packet," p. 9. Orfield, *City-Suburban Desegregation*, pp. 39, 36, 12, 34, 27, 36-37, 41. Orfield's study did not look at achievement effects. Metco was studied in the late 1960s for achievement gains (see David J. Armor, "The Evidence on Busing," *Public Interest*, vol. 28 [Summer 1972], pp. 97–99), but the study, finding no gains, was roundly criticized as methodologically flawed; see Pettigrew and others, "Busing," pp. 89, 100; see also Nancy H. St. John, *School Desegregation Outcomes for Children* (New York: John Wiley and Sons, 1975), p. 27.

25. Mark Hare, "Is Racial Isolation the Key Problem in City Schools? Not Any More," *Rochester Democrat and Chronicle*, November 15, 1998. See also Class Action Complaint, *Paynter* v. *New York*, Supreme Court of the State of New York, County of Monroe (September 29, 1998), p. 5; Norman Gross, "An Interdistrict Transfer Program," *Integrated Education* (May–June 1975), pp. 135–36; *Brewer* v. *West Irondequoit Central School District* (that program grew and is funded by the state), 32 F. Supp. 2d 619 (W.D.N.Y. 1999); Mary Ann Zehr, "Judge Orders Student's Transfer," *Education Week*, January 27, 1999, p. 4; *Brewer* v. *West Irondequoit Central School District*, 212 F.3d 738 (2d Cir. 2000).

26. Wells and Crain, *Stepping over the Color Line*, pp. 98–100; 68–69, 101; 18, 262; Amy Stuart Wells, "African American Students' View of School Choice," in Fuller and Elmore, *Who Chooses? Who Loses?* pp. 28–29. Wells and Crain, *Stepping over the Color Line*, pp. 68–69, 101.

27. Wells and Crain, *Stepping over the Color Line*, pp. 18, 102, 105–06; see also Tatel, "Cities, Suburbs Tie the Knot on Integration," p. 11. Wells, *Time to Choose*, p. 73.

28. Wells and Crain, *Stepping over the Color Line*, pp. 74, 102; 111;101-102.

29. Ibid., p. 105; 115; 182, 198, 337–38; Orfield, *City-Suburban Desegregation*, p. 36 (citing Voluntary Interdistrict Coordinating Committee, "VICC Graduate Survey for 1996–97); Susan Uchitelle, "What It Really Takes to Make School Choice Work," *Phi Delta*

Kappan, vol. 71 (December 1989), pp. 302–03; Amy Stuart Wells, "Reexamining Social Science Research on School Desegregation: Long-Term versus Short-Term Effects," *Teacher College Record*, vol. 96 (Summer 1995), p. 700; Anthony Downs, *New Visions for Metropolitan America* (Brookings, 1994), p. 108; Amy Stuart Wells, "Quest for Improving Schools Finds a Role for Free Market," *New York Times*, March 14, 1990, pp. A1, B8.

30. Wells and Crain, *Stepping over the Color Line*, pp. 183–84; 269.

31. Connie Farrow, "Judge Accepts Settlement in St. Louis School Desegregation Case," *Associated Press*, March 13, 1999. Wells quoted in Caroline Hendrie, "Settlement Ends St. Louis Desegregation Case," *Education Week*, March 24, 1999, p. 3. Starting in 2009, the program could be phased out, with the last children participating in 2021. The settlement did not involve a declaration of "unitary" status. Lawyers hoped that the omission would discourage lawsuits challenging the transfer program.

32. Peter Schmidt, "U.S. Judge Releases Wilmington Districts from Court Oversight," *Education Week*, September 6, 1995. "Quality Counts '98," p. 123.

33. Jennifer L. Hochschild, *The New American Dilemma: Liberal Democracy and School Desegregation* (Yale University Press, 1984), pp. 184, 251 n. 114. Raymond Wolters, *The Burden of Brown: Thirty Years of School Desegregation* (University of Tennessee Press, 1984), pp. 235–36. Schmidt, "U.S. Judge Releases Wilmington Districts from Court Oversight"; *Coalition to Save Our Children* v. *Board of Education of Delaware*, 90 F.3d 752 (3d Cir. 1996). "Quality Counts '98," p. 123; Sondra Astor Stave, *Achieving Racial Balance: Case Studies of Contemporary School Desegregation* (Westport, Conn.: Greenwood Press, 1995), p. 79. Norman A. Lockman, "Resegregation Further Clouds School Reform," *Wilmington News Journal*, March 16, 2000.

34. Orfield, "Metropolitan School Desegregation," p. 851 n. 77. Caroline Hendrie, "Judge Spurns Indianapolis Bid to Recover Bused Students," *Education Week*, March 12, 1997. In addition, Milwaukee has an interdistrict program that remains in effect from court order. In 1998, Chapter 220 was integrating some 5,085 minority students into twenty-three suburban schools (providing free transportation) while 551 nonminority students were voluntarily bused in to Milwaukee schools; Virginia Stamper, telephone interview by Christina Jordan, November 9, 1998.

35. Christopher Jencks and Meredith Phillips, "The Black-White Test Score Gap: Why It Persists and What Can Be Done," *Brookings Review* (Spring 1998), p. 27.

36. See discussion on ability grouping in chapter 6. Jane Manners, "Repackaging Segregation: A History of the Magnet School System in Montclair, New Jersey," *Race Traitor*, vol. 8 (Winter 1998), pp. 93–95.

37. MacInnes, *Kids Who Pick the Wrong Parents*, p. 21 (citing 1998 Gallup/*Phi Delta Kappan* poll finding that Americans are six times as concerned about violence, lack of discipline, drug abuse, insufficient funding, and overcrowding in the schools as such academic issues as weak standards, bad teachers, or diluted curriculum). Ellen Graham, "American Opinion: What's Wrong and Right with Our Schools," *Wall Street Journal*, March 14, 1997, p. R1.

38. Steve Farkas and Jean Johnson, *Time to Move On: African-American and White Parents Set an Agenda for Public Schools: A Report from Public Agenda* (New York: Public Agenda, 1998), p. 23.

39. John Dewey, *The School and Society* (University of Chicago Press, 1900, 1915), p. 3. Richard Rothstein, "When States Spend More," *American Prospect* (January–February 1998), pp. 72–73.

40. See Richard D. Kahlenberg, "Dreams and Responsibilities," *Washington Post Book World*, January 23, 2000, p. 4.

41. Dinesh D'Souza, interview by author, December 19, 1994, Washington, D.C. Mickey Kaus, *The End of Equality* (Basic Books, 1992), p. 108.

42. This proposition is a fundamental precept of economic theory; see, for example, James E. Rauch, "Productivity Gains from Geographic Concentration of Human Capital," *Journal of Urban Economics* (November 1993), pp. 380–400. Richard Rothstein, introduction to Edith Rasell and Richard Rothstein, eds., *School Choice: Examining the Evidence* (Washington: Economic Policy Institute, 1993), p. 23. Richard C. Leone, foreword to Ascher, Fruchter, and Berne, *Hard Lessons*, p. vi. Joseph P. Heim and Pamela H. Rodgers, "Busing for Socio-Economic Balance: Opinions, Attitudes, and Behavior," paper presented at the annual meeting of the Midwest Political Science Association, Chicago, April 17, 1993, p. 3.

43. Alan Wolfe, *One Nation, After All* (Viking, 1998), pp. 320–21.

44. Gordon Berlin and Andrew Sum, *Toward a More Perfect Union: Basic Skills, Poor Families, and Our Economic Future* (New York: Ford Foundation, 1988), p. 36.

45. See discussion in chapter 4.

46. See, for example, Mary F. Hughes, *Achieving Despite Adversity: Why Are Some Schools Successful in Spite of the Obstacles They Face? A Study of the Characteristics of Effective and Less Effective Elementary Schools in West Virginia Using Qualitative and Quantitative Methods*. Research Report (Pittsburgh, Pa.: Claude Worthington Benedum Foundation, October 1995), p. 11.

47. Christine Rossell, "Controlled Choice Desegregation Plans: Not Enough Choice, Too Much Control?" *Urban Affairs Review*, vol. 31 (September 1995), pp. 45–46.

48. David S. Broder, "The Unity among Us," *Washington Post*, November 25, 1998, p. A21 (reporting findings of Public Agenda report). Lincoln made the statement in a speech at the Republican State Convention, Springfield, Illinois, June 16, 1858, quoting Mark 3:25.

49. Farkas and Johnson, *Time to Move On*, p. 25. Gary Orfield and others, *Deepening Segregation in American Public Schools* (Cambridge: Harvard Project on School Desegregation, 1997), p. 4.

50. Clinton quoted in Edward Walsh, "Clinton Presses Education Plan," *Washington Post*, February 3, 1999, p. A2; see also Somini Sengupta, "Union Leader Asks Teachers to Help Close Weak Schools," *New York Times*, July 28, 1997. Rick Bragg, "Florida Will Allow Vouchers for Pupils Whose Schools Fail," *New York Times*, April 28, 1999, p. A1; see also "Pennsylvania Gov. Ridge Talks about School Choice with Parents in Philadelphia," *PR Newswire*, April 14, 1999.

51. Jennifer L. Hochschild and Nathan Scovronick, "Democratic Education and the American Dream," in Lorraine McDonnell, P. Michael Timpane, and Roger Benjamin, eds., *Rediscovering the Democratic Purposes of Education* (University Press of Kansas, 2000), p. 219.

52. See General Accounting Office (GAO), *School Finance: State and Federal Efforts to Target Poor Students—Report to Congressional Requesters* (Washington: GAO, January 1998), p. 7. See also Derek Bok, *The State of the Nation* (Harvard University Press, 1996), pp. 86 and 214.

53. See, for example, Donald P. Baker, "Coleman Scrambles after Advocating School Transfers," *Washington Post*, September 26, 1989, p. B1; Department of Education,

Choosing Better Schools: The Five Regional Meetings on Choice in Education. Research Report (December 1990), p. 15.

54. Of course, the statement applies with equal force to our current system, in which poor kids are excluded from good middle-class schools every year because their parents do not make enough money.

55. Christina Rathbone, *On the Outside Looking In: A Year in an Inner-City High School* (New York: Atlantic Monthly Press, 1998), p. 44.

56. Robert Hanley, "Educators Belittle New Jersey's 'Report Cards' on Schools," *New York Times,* November 27, 1989, p. B1.

57. Michael Rutter and others, *Fifteen Thousand Hours: Secondary Schools and Their Effects on Children* (Harvard University Press, 1979), p. 5. For the methodology difficulties, see, for example, Stephen W. Raudenbush and J. Douglas Willms, "The Estimation of School Effects," *Journal of Educational and Behavioral Statistics,* vol. 20 (Winter 1995), p. 308; Richard Rothstein, "Charter Conundrum," *American Prospect* (July–August 1998), pp. 46, 48; Ellen Nakashima, "New School of Thought on Tests," *Washington Post,* May 26, 1998, p. B1 (citing the "value added" approach of William L. Sanders of the University of Tennessee). There are also serious political problems when one adjusts test scores for social class, notes Helen Ladd, because doing so "can be misinterpreted as a signal that some groups of students are less able to learn than others and are being held to lower standards"; Helen F. Ladd, "Catalyst for Learning," *Brookings Review* (Summer 1996), p. 15. Adjusting scores for socioeconomic status also has come under attack from wealthier schools that do not wish to be held to a higher standard; see Ellen Nakashima, "New School of Thought on Tests," pp. B1, B5.

58. Richard D. Kahlenberg, *The Remedy: Race, Class, and Affirmative Action* (Basic Books, 1996), pp. 109–13. Alves, quoted in "Weekend Edition," *National Public Radio,* May 11, 1996. Robert Crain, interview by author, December 5, 1997, New York, pp. 5, 8, 13.

59. Don Stewart made this point in a letter to the author, December 23, 1997.

60. William Galston, "The Education Presidency," *New Republic,* November 1, 1996, p. 35.

61. Peter Dreier and David Moberg, "Moving from the 'Hood," *American Prospect* (Winter 1996), p. 79. See also William Barnes and Larry Ledebur, *The New Regional Economies* (Thousand Oaks, Calif.: Sage Publications, 1998), pp. 41–46 (suburban income tied to central-city income); Rusk, *Inside Game/Outside Game,* pp. 290–99; Jon Jeter, "Cities, Older Suburbs Becoming Allies," *Washington Post,* Feb. 22, 1998, p. A3.

62. Bruce Katz and Scott Bernstein, "The New Metropolitan Agenda," *Brookings Review* (Fall 1998), pp. 4, 6; Henry G. Cisneros and Marc A. Weiss, "Building Regional Prosperity," *New Democrat* (November–December 1997), p. 20. Wells and Crain, *Stepping over the Color Line,* p. 115; Gayle Shaw Westerman, "The Promise of State Constitutionalism: Can It Be Fulfilled in *Sheff* v. *O'Neill?*" *Hastings Constitutional Law Quarterly,* vol. 23 (Winter 1996), p. 406 n. 298; Brian Hicks, "Group Plans to Unveil School Study," *Charleston Post and Courier,* April 15, 1998.

63. See discussion in chapter 6. Lisa M. Lynch, "Trends in and Consequences of Investments in Children," in Sheldon H. Danziger and Jane Waldfogel, eds., *Securing the Future: Investing in Children from Birth to College* (New York: Russell Sage Foundation, 2000), pp. 5–6, figure 4. See discussion in chapter 9.

64. George F. Will, "Bradley's Amble," *Washington Post,* September 9, 1999, p. A21.

65. David Rusk, "To Improve Public Education, Stop Moving Money, Move Families," *Abell Report*, vol. 11, June/July 1998, p. 7. Ethan Bronner, "Survey Finds Public Support for Vouchers," *New York Times*, August 26, 1998, p. A20; William J. Bennett, "School Reform: What Remains to Be Done," *Wall Street Journal*, September 2, 1997. Helen Dewar, "Senate Passes Tax Breaks for Education Expenses," *Washington Post*, June 25, 1998, p. A4; Lizette Alvarez, "Senators Endorse Tax Breaks for Education Savings Accounts," *New York Times*, April 24, 1998, p. A1; John E. Yang, "House Backs Education Tax Breaks for Grades K–12," *Washington Post*, August 24, 1997, p. A11; David A. Vise, "District School Voucher Bill Gets Congressional Approval," *Washington Post*, May 1, 1998, p. C1; David A. Vise and Vernon Loeb, "Senate Democrats Block D.C. Vouchers—for Now," *Washington Post*, October 1, 1997, p. B1.

66. Brent Staples, "Schoolyard Brawl: The New Politics of Education Casts Blacks in a Starring Role," *New York Times Education Life*, January 4, 1998, p. 50; Terry M. Neal, "School Choice a Key Issue for GOP," *Washington Post*, September 7, 1997, p. A14; Diane Ravitch, "A New Era in Urban Education," *Brookings Policy Brief*, vol 35 (August 1998), p. 7; Paul E. Peterson, "Top Ten Questions Asked about School Choice," in Diane Ravitch, ed., *Brookings Papers on Education Policy, 1999* (Brookings), p. 377; Paul E. Peterson and Jay P. Greene, "Race Relations and Central City Schools: It's Time for an Experiment with Vouchers," *Brookings Review* (Spring 1998), pp. 34–35.

67. Price quoted in Brian Mooar, "Urban League Urges Black Economic Power," *Washington Post*, August 4, 1997, p. A12. Crew quoted in Sara Mosle, "The Stealth Chancellor," *New York Times Magazine*, August 31, 1997, p. 33.

68. See, for example, Adam Urbanski, "Make Public Schools More Like Private Schools," *Education Week*, January 31, 1996, p. 31; David Bositis, "Remarks," New Synthesis Group Luncheon, Washington, D.C., June 4, 1998. Gallup poll cited in Teixeira, "Critical Support," p. 252. Fern Shen, "Home Schooling Draws a New Class of Parents," *Washington Post*, April 24, 1998, pp. A1, A16.

69. Schmoke quoted in Ascher, Fruchter, and Berne, *Hard Lessons*, p. 2.

70. See Richard J. Murnane and Frank Levy, "Standards, Information, and the Demands for Student Achievement," *FRBNY Economic Policy Review*, vol. 4, no. 1 (March 1998), p. 117.

71. Anthony S. Bryk, Valerie E. Lee, and Peter B. Holland, *Catholic Schools and the Common Good* (Harvard University Press, 1993), p. 325. See discussion in chapter 5.

72. Lieberman, *Public School Choice*, pp. 102–03, 126, 190.

73. See, for example, discussion of La Crosse, Wisconsin, in chapter 9; Armor, *Forced Justice*, p. 61 (La Crosse); Andrew Trotter, "Teachers Propose Integrating Schools by Socioeconomic Status," *Education Week*, December 2, 1998 (Jefferson County, Kentucky); Peter Schmidt, "Bold Busing Plan Leads to Deep Divides in Wausau," *Education Week*, December 15, 1993, p. 14 (80 percent teacher support in Wausau); Trine Tsouderos, "Board Urges Balanced Student Population," *Tennessean*, February 24, 1999, p. 4B (teacher support in Murfreesboro, Tennessee). See Jefferson County Teachers Association, "Teachers' Beliefs Regarding Student Achievement," unpublished report, December 1998; Veda Morgan, "Teachers' Survey Favors Integration by Income Levels," *Louisville Courier-Journal*, November 16, 1998, p. 1.

74. Sikes quoted in Trotter, "Teachers Propose Integrating Schools"; see also complaint of principal Terry Witzke in discussion of La Crosse, chapter 9. Debbi Wilgoren,

"D.C. to Publish Profiles of Individual Schools," *Washington Post*, February 6, 1999, p. B2; Bill Clinton, *State of the Union, Washington Post*, January 20, 1999, A12.

75. Katherine Seligman, "Race-Neutral Plan to Be Used in San Francisco Schools," *San Francisco Examiner*, January 8, 2000. See discussion in chapter 5.

76. Jay Mathews, "Ruling Leaves Virginia Students in Limbo," *Washington Post*, May 28, 1997, pp. A1, A9; Jay Mathews, "Eleven Minorities Lose Spots in Virginia School," *Washington Post*, May 31, 1997, pp. B1, B6; Jay Mathews, "Arlington Near Accord on Magnet Admissions," *Washington Post*, November 13, 1997, p. D5; Brooke A. Masters, "Lawsuit Calls New Arlington Lottery Unfair to White Children," *Washington Post*, March 18, 1998; Jay Mathews, "Judge Questions Arlington School Policy Linked to Race," *Washington Post*, April 11, 1998, p. F2. See, for example, Minnesota Department of Children, Families, and Learning, *Statement of Need and Reasonableness in the Matter of the Proposed Rules Relating to Desegregation* (draft, October 12, 1998), pp. 4, 31, 78, 80.

77. Kaus, *The End of Equality*, pp. 272–73 n. 13. Leonard P. Strickman, "Desegregation: The Metropolitan Concept," *Urban Review*, vol. 6 (September–October 1977), pp. 18, 39 n. 5. Hochschild, *The New American Dilemma*, p. 64. Jane Littleton, "Appalachia Group Backs School Plan: But Common Heritage Has No Faith in Busing," *Dayton Journal Herald*, May 27, 1976.

78. Rusk, *Inside Game/Outside Game*, p. 223. David Rusk, foreword to Myron Orfield, *Metropolitics: A Regional Agenda for Community and Stability* (Brookings, 1997), pp. xi, xiii; David Rusk, *Cities without Suburbs*, 2d ed. (Washington: Woodrow Wilson Center Press, 1995), pp. 91–93; Jeter, "Cities, Older Suburbs Becoming Allies," p. A3; Myron Orfield, "Metropolitics: Coalitions for Regional Reform," *Brookings Review*, vol. 15 (Winter 1997), p. 9. Paul Glastris, "A New City-Suburbs Hookup," *U.S. News and World Report*, July 18, 1994, p. 28.

79. Charles Glenn, interview by author, December 3, 1997, Boston, pp. 13–14; J. Douglas Willms, "Social Class Segregation and Its Relationship to Pupils' Examination Results in Scotland," *American Sociological Review*, vol. 51 (April 1986), pp. 224–41 (on Scotland). Philip Meranto, *Politics of Federal Aid to Education in 1965* (Syracuse University Press,1967), pp. 93, ix.

80. See *Hobson* v. *Hansen*, 269 F. Supp. 401 (D.D.C. 1967), 406.

81. William Brennan, "State Constitutions and the Protection of Individual Rights," *Harvard Law Review*, vol. 90 (1977), pp. 489, 491, cited in Westerman, "The Promise of State Constitutionalism," pp. 351, 353–54. *San Antonio* v. *Rodriguez*, 411 U.S. 1 (1973), 35; see also Ira Katznelson and Margaret Weir, *Schooling for All: Class, Race, and the Decline of the Democratic Ideal* (Basic Books, 1985), p. 29; Bell, *Race, Racism, and American Law*, 3d ed. (Boston: Little, Brown, 1992), p. 605 n. 106. Although states do not generally guarantee nutrition, shelter, or subsistence, all but two guarantee education; James S. Liebman, "Three Strategies for Implementing *Brown* Anew," in Herbert Hill and James E. Jones Jr., eds., *Race in America: The Struggle for Equality* (University of Wisconsin Press, 1993), pp. 120–21.

82. James Coleman, foreword to John E. Coons, William H. Clure III, and Stephen D. Sugarman, *Private Wealth and Public Education* (Harvard University Press, 1970), p. xiv. See also Alan B. Wilson, "Residual Segregation of Social Classes and Aspiration of High School Boys," *American Sociological Review*, vol. 24 (1959), p. 845.

83. *Sheff* v. *O'Neill*, 609 A. 2d 1072 (Conn. Superior Ct. 1992), 1074; *Sheff* v. *O'Neill*, 678 A. 2d 1267, 1310 (Conn. 1996) (Borden, J., dissenting).

84. Plaintiffs' Brief, Plaintiffs' Appeal from Superior Court, *Sheff* v. *O'Neill*, S.C. 15255, August 1, 1995), pp. 1, 22. *Sheff* v. *O'Neill*, 678 A. 2d 1267 (Conn. 1996), 1272–73, 1287. See also Marianne Lado, interview by author, December, 12, 1997, New York, p. 15.

85. Natriello's testimony cited in Judson, "In Hartford, Data Portray Schools in Crisis of Poverty." *New York Times*, January 2, 1993, p. 26. James Traub, "Can Separate Be Equal?" *Harper's Magazine*, June 1994, p. 40. *Sheff* v. *O'Neill* 678 A. 2d 1267, 1273. Rene Sanchez, "Hartford Public School Privatization Deal Collapses," *Washington Post*, January 25, 1996, p. A3.

86. James E. Ryan, "*Sheff*, Segregation, and School Finance Litigation," *NYU Law Review*, vol. 74 (1999), pp. 529–73. John C Brittain, "Educational and Racial Equity toward the Twenty-first Century: A Case Experiment in Connecticut," in Hill and Jones, *Race in America*, p. 167; see also Julius L. Chambers, "*Brown* v. *Board of Education*," in Hill and Jones, *Race in America*, pp. 190–91; George Judson, "Civil Rights Lawyers Hope to Use Hartford Schools Case as a Model," *New York Times*, August 15, 1996, p. B1 (the Legal Defense Fund of the NAACP treated *Sheff* as a poverty and justice case, not a racial desegregation case).

87. See Plaintiffs' Brief, Plaintiffs' Appeal from Superior Court, *Sheff* v. *O'Neill*, August 1, 1995, pp. 21–24; George Judson, "A Pattern of Increasing Student Segregation," *New York Times*, January 10, 1993, p. 30; George Judson, "School Integration: Summing Up the Case," *New York Times*, December 12, 1993, sec. 13CN, p. 14. Brittain, quoted in Traub, "Can Separate Be Equal?" p. 41; Traub argued that "*Sheff* is about poverty, not race," pp. 37, 41; see also Robert Neuwirth, "Crossing Racial and School District Lines: The New York *Newsday* Interview with John Brittain," interview with John Brittain, *Newsday*, August 3, 1993, p. 75. Kirk Johnson, "Two Schools: The Barrier Is Poverty," *New York Times*, April 29, 1989, p. 29.

88. Plaintiffs' *Sheff* Brief, pp. 23–24. See also Robert A. Frahm, "Students Gain from Desegregation, Sociologist Testifies," *Hartford Courant*, December 30, 1992, p. B1; Lado, interview, pp. 23, 27; American Civil Liberties Union, "In the Courts: *Sheff* v. *O'Neill* and the Case for Educational Equity Litigation as a Strategy for Educational Reform" (www.aclu.org/court/sheffbkr.html [January 20, 1999]).

89. Plaintiffs' *Sheff* Brief, pp. 23, 28, 44; see also James E. Ryan, "Schools, Race, and Money," *Yale Law Journal*, vol. 109 (November 1999), pp. 249–316, 316 n. 217; Ryan, *NYU Law Review*, p. 550 n. 65.

90. Plaintiffs' *Sheff* Brief, pp. 22 n. 44, 11, 18–19. Traub, "Can Separate Be Equal?" p. 38 (quoting principal Don Carso and teacher Delia Bello); see also Lado, interview, pp. 23, 19; Crain, interview with author, New York, December 5, 1997, p. 31 (Bob Thaler, a doctoral student of Crain, has "done this wonderful piece of work" on teacher expectations and student body "which shows it's class, not race").

91. *Sheff* v. *O'Neill*, 678 A. 2d 1267, 1281.

92. Robin D. Barnes, "Black America and School Choice: Charting a New Course," *Yale Law Journal*, vol. 106 (June 1997), p. 2380; Laurence D. Cohen, "Liberal and Conservative Agree—Sort of—on School Choice," *Hartford Courant*, July 14, 1996, p. D3. George Judson, "Hartford Court Bars Imbalance in the Schools," *New York Times*, July 10, 1996, p. A1 ("Connecticut's efforts to comply with the court's order could face a challenge in Federal courts").

93. Judson, "Civil Rights Lawyers Hope to Use Hartford Schools Case as a Model," p. B1; see also Lado interview, pp. 12–13. The dissent pounded away at the fact that the

trial court found no evidence that racial isolation negatively affects the achievement of minority students; see for example *Sheff* v. *O'Neill*, 678 A. 2d 1295–1337 (Borden, J., dissenting), particularly, 1298, 1304, 1334. For Judge Harry Hammer's emphasis on concentrations of family and school poverty, see *Sheff* v. *O'Neill*, 1995 Conn. Super. LEXIS 1148 (April 12, 1995) *17, *32, *40; and *Sheff* v. *O'Neill*, 1995 Conn. LEXIS 249 (June 27, 1995), *30–32. Carole Bass, "School Face-Off—New Lawsuit: A Whiter Shade of *Sheff*," *New Haven Advocate*, April 30, 1998.

94. *Sheff* v. *O'Neill*, 678 A. 2d 1276, 1276–78.

95. Ibid., 1277–79, 1279; see also Laurence Tribe, *American Constitutional Law*, 2d ed. (Mineola, N.Y.: Foundation Press, 1988), p. 1513.

96. Likewise, the hesitation of the *Milliken* Court to impose a federal interdistrict remedy on a locality does not apply to state courts, which need not be concerned about issues of federalism; see *Missouri* v. *Jenkins*, 115 S. Ct. 2038 (1995), 2054, 2070 (Thomas, J., concurring).

97. Judson, "Civil Rights Lawyers Hope to Use Hartford Schools Case as a Model," p. B1. Judson, "Hartford Court Bars Imbalance in the Schools," p. A1.

98. Traub, "Can Separate Be Equal?" p. 47. Eve Nagler, "Connecticut Q and A: John C. Brittain: The Color Line and Children's Education," *New York Times*, June 18, 1995, sec. 13CN, p. 3. Jonathan Rabinowitz, "Hartford School Integration Panel Formed," *New York Times*, July 26, 1996, p. B2. Michael A. Rebell and Robert L. Hughes, "Efficacy and Engagement: the Remedies Problem Posed by *Sheff* v. *O'Neill*—and a Proposed Solution," *Connecticut Law Review*, vol. 29 (1997), pp. 1173–74, citing Education Improvement Panel, *Report to the Governor* (January 22, 1997).

99. "Eight Years of *Sheff* v. *O'Neill*," *Education Week*, June 11, 1997; "First Steps to Meet *Sheff* Order Will Significantly Impact Schools, Local Government," *Connecticut Town and City*, July–August 1997, p. 7; "Quality Counts '98," p. 120; Fred Musante, "Remedies Elusive in *Sheff* Case," *New York Times*, July 6, 1997, sec. 13CN, p. 1. Fred Musante, "End to School Segregation, Voluntary or Mandated?" *New York Times*, October 4, 1998, sec. 14, pp. 1, 17. Weizel, "School Busing, City and Suburban," p. 17.

100. Musante, "Remedies Elusive in *Sheff* Case," p. 1. *Sheff* v. *O'Neill* 733 A.2d 925 (Conn. Superior Ct. 1999); Jeff Archer, "Court Sides with Connecticut in Latest *Sheff* Ruling," *Education Week*, March 10, 1999.

101. Lado, interview, p. 51. *Sheff* v. *O'Neill*, 733 A.2d 925, 925–26 (characterizing the Supreme Court's decision in *Sheff* as holding that "racially, ethnically, and economically isolated" schools were unconstitutional; emphasizing "the importance of remedying racial, ethnic, and economic segregation of the schools"), 927 (noting language of Public Act 97-290, that the "educational interests of the state" were amended to include the reduction of "racial, ethnic, and economic isolation").

102. Judge Aurigemma specifically noted that the use of racial quotas was probably unconstitutional under federal law. *Sheff* v. *O'Neill* 733 A.2d 925, 930.

103. See Connecticut Center for School Change, *The Unexamined Remedy: A First Draft of a Plan to Consolidate the School District of Hartford and Twenty-one Neighboring Towns into a High Quality, Racially Integrated School System* (Hartford, Conn., June 5, 1998), pp. 4, 18, 24–26. See also Jeff Archer, "Plan Would Join Hartford with Surrounding Districts," *Education Week*, July 8, 1998. In July 2000, following a series of meetings with constituency groups, the Center for School Change advocated a modified plan of smaller regional districts, each including urban and suburban areas, with

choice controlled by socioeconomic status rather than race. See Connecticut Center for School Change, *Beyond the Unexamined Remedy: Moving toward Quality Integrated Schools* (Hartford, Conn., July 2000).

104. Fred Musante, "State Panel Leans to School Choice," *New York Times*, December 15, 1996, sec. 13CN, p. 1; Johnson, "Two Schools," p. A1. Robert A. Frahm, "Residents as Divided as Court on Sheff: Courant-ISI Connecticut Poll," *Hartford Courant*, August 16, 1996, p. A1.

105. Although the New York high court ruled in 1982 that the constitution does not require equal funding, a more recent 1995 case suggested that the New York Constitution does require a "basic" education; see Rebell and Hughes, "Efficacy and Engagement," p. 1137, citing *Campaign for Fiscal Equity, Inc. v. State of New York*, 655 N.E. 2d 661 (N.Y. 1995).

106. Mary Ann Zehr, "Rochester Students File Class Action against New York," *Education Week*, October 14, 1998 (quoting attorney Bryan Hetherington). Class Action Complaint, *Paynter v. New York*, September 29, 1998, p. 2. Hare, "Is Racial Isolation the Key Problem in City Schools?"

107. Class Action Complaint, *Paynter v. New York*, pp. 1, 19, 22, 23, 29, 24–25, 26.

108. Ibid., 1, 30, 31, 32.

109. Ibid., 30–31, 8, 41, 17.

110. Ibid., 42, 44. Mary Ann Zehr, "N.Y. Judge Narrows Claims in Student Poverty Suit," *Education Week*, November 29, 2000.

111. See john powell, "Segregation and Educational Inadequacy in Twin Cities Public Schools," *Hamline Journal of Public Law and Policy*, vol. 17 (Spring 1996), pp. 381, 383, citing *Skeen v. State*, 505 N.W. 2d 299 (Minn. 1993), 313, 315.

112. J. Richardson, "Suit Seeks Minn. Backing of Desegregation Plan," *Education Week*, October 4, 1995, pp. 12, 16; Paul Drew Duchesne, "Minneapolis NAACP Sues State," *Minneapolis Star Tribune*, September 20, 1995, p. 1A; Anne O'Connor, "Issue of Desegregation Reaches Far beyond Walls of Classroom," *Minneapolis Star Tribune*, May 15, 1998, p. 19A. powell, "Segregation and Educational Inadequacy in Twin Cities Public Schools," pp. 381–82, citing *Booker v. Special School District No. 1*, 359 F. Supp. 799 (D. Minn. 1972). Justin Cummins, conversation with author, April 12, 1999.

113. Shulman, Walcott, and Shulman unpublished settlement proposal, *NAACP v. Minnesota* and *Xiong v. Minnesota*, February 19, 1999, p. 3; see also powell, "Segregation and Educational Inadequacy in Twin Cities Public Schools," p. 388. Plaintiffs' Answers to Defendant's Interrogatories to Plaintiffs, set 1, *NAACP v. Minnesota* (case no. MC 95-014800, September 30, 1998), p. 2.

114. Shulman, Walcott, and Shulman settlement proposal, February 19, 1999, p.1. John Shulman and others, "State Admits that Integration Improves Student Achievement," unpublished document prepared for mediation, March 1999, p. 1. Shulman and others, "The Truth about Desegregation, Segregation, and Community Schools" (with numerous citations), unpublished document, September 1998, pp. 1–4. See also powell, "Segregation and Educational Inadequacy in Twin Cities Public Schools," pp. 338, 386, 397–99; john powell, interview by author, December 19, 1997, Minneapolis, pp. 3, 9.

115. Class Action Complaint, *Xiong v. Minnesota* (98-2816), February 23, 1998, p. 11. John Shulman and others, "Minneapolis and Suburban School Officials Conspire to Provide Inadequate, Segregated, 'Community Schools,'" press release, April 30, 1998

(referencing minutes of April 29, 1993, meeting of school officials). See also D. Eric Harmon, "Smoking Gun?" *Insight,* May 4, 1998, p. 1.

116. Norman Draper, "Schools Group OKs NAACP Settlement," *Minneapolis Star Tribune,* March 24, 2000, p. 1B; Dr. Carol Johnston (Minneapolis schools superintendent), "Commentary on the Recent *NAACP* v. *State of Minnesota* Settlement Agreement" (www.mpls.k12.mn.us/new/newspercent20release/naacp4.htm [June 9, 2000]). "Quality Counts '98," p. 185.

117. *Horton* v. *Meskill,* 376 A. 2d 359 (Conn. 1977). For an explanation of why *Sheff* is not sui generis, despite its partial reliance on Connecticut's unusual antisegregation clause, see James E. Ryan, "*Sheff,* Segregation, and School Finance Litigation," *NYU Law Review,* p. 546. For summaries of such litigation, see Richard Rothstein, *The Way We Were: Debunking the Myths of America's Declining Schools* (Century Foundation Press, 1998), p. 25 (nineteen states, with twelve more in ongoing litigation); Paul A. Minorini and Stephen D. Sugarman, "School Finance Litigation in the Name of Educational Equity: Its Evolution, Impact, and Future," in Helen F. Ladd, Rosemary Chalk, and Janet S. Hansen, eds., *Equity and Adequacy in Education Finance* (Washington: National Academy Press, 1999), p. 35; Jay Mathews, *Class Struggle: What's Wrong (and Right) with America's Best Public High Schools* (New York: Times Books, 1998), p. 189; Fowler, *Developments in School Finance,* pp. 23–26; Van Slyke, Tan, and Orland, *School Finance Litigation,* pp. 2, 13, 15–16; Ann Scott Tyson, "In Search of More Money for Schools," *Christian Science Monitor,* April 30, 1997, p. 1; Deborah A. Verstegen, "Reforming American Education Policy for the Twenty-first Century," *Educational Administration Quarterly* (August 1994), p. 370; Faith E. Crampton and Terry N. Whitney, *State School Finance Litigation and Legislation, 1994: A Summary and an Analysis,* paper presented at the annual meeting of the American Educational Research Association, San Francisco, California, April 1995, pp. 1–2; Elinor Burkett, "Don't Tread on My Tax Rate," *New York Times Magazine,* April 26, 1998, pp. 42, 44; Dan Balz, "School versus Property-Tax Dilemma Testing New Hampshire Communities," *Washington Post,* January 10, 1998, p. A9. For a fairly recent list of negative results in state courts, see Rebell and Hughes, "Efficacy and Engagement," p. 1136 n. 83.

118. Judson, "Civil Rights Lawyers Hope to Use Hartford Schools Case as a Model," p. B1. See, for example, *Serrano* v. *Priest,* 487 P. 2d 1241 (Calif. 1971), 1254; *DeRolph* v. *State,* 677 N.E. 733, 745 (Ohio, 1997).

119. *Rose* v. *Council for a Better Education,* 790 S.W. 2d 186, 212 (Ky. 1989). *Abbott* v. *Burke (II),* 575 A. 2d 359, 371 (N.J. 1990).

120. William H. Clune, "Educational Adequacy: A Theory and Its Remedies," *University of Michigan Journal of Legal Reference,* vol. 28 (Spring 1995), pp. 481–82, 483, 488; see also R. Craig Wood, "Adequacy Issues in Recent Education Finance Litigation," in Fowler, *Developments in School Finance,* p. 33. Wood, "Adequacy Issues in Recent Education Finance Litigation," in Fowler, *Developments in School Finance,* p. 32. Richard Rothstein, "Equalizing Education Resources on Behalf of Disadvantaged Children," in Richard D. Kahlenberg, ed., *A Notion at Risk: Preserving Public Education as an Engine for Social Mobility* (New York: Century Foundation Press, 2000), pp. 74–75.

121. *Abbott* v. *Burke (II),* 375.

122. *Southern Burlington County NAACP* v. *Mount Laurel,* 67 N.J. 151 (1975), 174, 189, 190, 212. David L. Kirp, John P. Dwyer, and Larry A. Rosenthal, *Our Town: Race, Housing, and the Soul of Suburbia* (Rutgers University Press, 1995), p. 3.

123. *Southern Burlington County NAACP* v. *Mount Laurel*, 159, 174 n. 10. See also Charles M. Haar, *Suburbs under Siege: Race, Space, and Audacious Judges* (Princeton University Press, 1996), pp. 23, 25. *Southern Burlington County NAACP* v. *Mount Laurel*, 171, 178 (a local jurisdiction may not act "solely on its selfish and parochial interest and in effect build a wall around itself" and instead must consider "values which transcend municipal lines"). Haar, *Suburbs under Siege*, p. 46.

124. Haar, *Suburbs under Siege*, p. 10. *Southern Burlington County NAACP* v. *Mount Laurel*, 171, 183. *Robinson* v. *Cahill*, 303 A. 2d 273 (N.J. 1973), and *Abbott* v. *Burke (II)*, 575 A. 2d 359 (N.J. 1990).

125. Brian W. Blaeser and others, "Advocating Affordable Housing in New Hampshire: The Amicus Curiae Brief of American Planning Association in *Wayne Britton* v. *Town of Chester*," *Washington University Journal of Urban and Contemporary Law*, vol. 40, no. 3 (1991), pp. 3, 23–28.

126. The leading set of cases is *Debra P.* v. *Turlington*, 474 F. Supp. 244 (M.D. Fla. 1979), *aff'd in part*, 644 F. 2d 397 (5th Cir. 1981); and *Debra P.* v. *Turlington (II)*, 564 F. Supp. 177 (M.D. Fla. 1983), *aff'd* 730 F. 2d 1405 (11th Cir. 1984). See also Roy Romer, "Explaining Standards to the Public," in Diane Ravitch, *Debating the Future of American Education: Do We Need Standards and Assessments?* (Brookings, 1995), pp. 73–74; Liebman, "Three Strategies for Implementing *Brown* Anew," pp. 124–27; and Jennifer O'Day and Marshall S. Smith, "Systemic Reform and Educational Opportunity," in Susan Fuhrman, ed., *Designing Coherent Education Policy* (San Francisco: Jossey-Bass, 1993), pp. 269, 287, and 292.

127. Diane Ravitch, *The Troubled Crusade: American Education, 1945–1980* (Basic Books, 1983), p. 167. Gary Orfield, *Must We Bus? Segregated Schools and National Policy* (Brookings, 1978), p. 279. Steel and Levine, *Educational Innovation in Multiracial Contexts*, pp. ii–iii.

128. National Center for Education Statistics, *Digest of Education Statistics: 1999* (Washington: U.S. Government Printing Office, 2000), table 160. GAO, *School Finance: State and Federal Efforts to Target Poor Students—Report to Congressional Requesters*, January 1998, p. 4; see also NCES, *Public School Funding Differences* (1995), p. 1.

129. J. Myron Atkin, "The Government in the Classroom," *Daedalus*, vol. 109 (1980), pp. 92–93. National Center for Education Information, *Department of Education Reports*, vol. 19, no. 6 (1998), p. 4.

130. Jonathan Zimmerman, "Separate but Equal Schools," *New York Times*, January 21, 1999, p. A31.

131. See, for example, *Southern Burlington County NAACP* v. *Mount Laurel*, 163, 167–68, 171, 201. Roger Lawson and William Julius Wilson, "Poverty, Social Rights, and the Quality of Citizenship," in Katherine McFate, Roger Lawson, and William Julius Wilson, eds., *Poverty, Inequality, and the Future of Social Policy* (New York: Russell Sage Foundation, 1995), p. 696.

132. Kozol, "Children in America's Schools," *PBS*, September 13, 1996.

133. See, for example, Armor, "After Busing," p. 36; Kearns and Doyle, "Winning the Brain Race," pp. 18–20.

134. Sizer, *Horace's Hope*, p. 142. The portable Title I proposal at the current level of funding is probably insufficient to provide an adequate incentive. Title I funding on average currently works out to about $1,080 per child; see M. Le Tendre, "What's New in Title I?" *Principal*, vol. 75, no. 4, March 1996, p. 30. Average combined federal, state,

and local funding is currently $5,300 a year; see Gary Burtless, ed., *Does Money Matter? The Effect of School Resources on Student Achievement and Adult Success* (Brookings, 1996), p. 1. In Seattle, Washington, a formula funding poor kids at 136 percent of the base level appeared insufficient to spur middle-class schools to actively recruit poor students; see Kim Murphy, "Seattle's School Program Sets Off Marketing Frenzy," *Los Angeles Times*, April 9, 1998, p. A1. For a proposal to boost the state aid for each poor child to twice the amount provided other children as an incentive for middle-class school districts to take in poor students across district lines, see Peter Schmidt, "Minnesota Board to Consider Desegregation Plan," *Education Week*, February 2, 1994, p. 9.

135. Tom Loveless, *The Tracking Wars: State Reform Meets School Policy* (Brookings, 1999), p. 144.

136. Gary Orfield and Susan Eaton, *Dismantling Desegregation: The Quiet Reversal of Brown v. Board of Education* (New York: New Press, 1996), p. 91. See also Elizabeth DeBray, "Beyond Compensation: Rethinking Title I Based on Research," in Gary Orfield and Elizabeth DeBray, *Hard Work for Good Schools: Facts Not Fads in Title I Reform* (Cambridge, Mass.: Harvard Civil Rights Project, 1999), p. 26.

137. Chester E. Finn, Bruno V. Manno, and Louann A. Bierlein, "The Empire Strikes Back," *New Democrat* (November–December 1996), p. 8. Thomas Toch, *Improving Performance: Competition in American Public Education* (Washington: National Alliance of Business, 2000), p. 12. Arlene Ackerman, remarks at Brookings Forum on Urban Schools, Washington, D.C., August 26, 1998. See, for example, Jill Abrams, "Congress Passes Charter School Bill," *Associated Press*, October 10, 1998.

138. Kolderie, *Beyond Choice to New Public Schools*, pp. 1, 12. Keith A. Halpern and Eliza R. Culbertson, *Blueprint for Change: Charter Schools—A Handbook for Action* (Washington: Democratic Leadership Council, April 1, 1994), pp. 4, 30. Rothstein, "When States Spend More," p. 54.

139. See Amy Stuart Wells and others, "Charter Schools and Racial and Social Class Segregation: Yet Another Sorting Machine?" in Richard D. Kahlenberg, ed., *A Notion at Risk* (New York: Century Foundation Press, 2000), pp. 169–221; see also Richard Rothstein, "When States Spend More," p. 58; James Traub, "A School of Your Own," *New York Times Education Life*, April 4, 1999, p. 42. See Spencer Hsu and Ellen Nakashima, "Virginia Senate Panel Backs Charter School Measure," *Washington Post*, January 30, 1998, pp. B1, B4.

140. RPP International, *A National Study of Charter Schools* (Washington: Dept. of Education, July 1998), pp. 10–11.

141. Halpern and Culbertson, *Blueprint for Change*, p. 3; see also Ascher, Fruchter, and Berne, *Hard Lessons*, p. 92. Betsy Levin, "Race and School Choice," in Sugarman and Kemerer, *School Choice and Social Controversy*, pp. 287–88. RPP International, *A National Study of Charter Schools*, p. 12.

142. Amy Stuart Wells, "Saving Public Education," *Nation*, February 17, 1997, p. 18. Nakamura, "Virginia Denied U.S. Funds for Charter Schools," p. B3.

143. Kaus, *The End of Equality*, p. 155.

144. Theodore Sizer and Philip Whitten, "A Proposal for a Poor Children's Bill of Rights," *Psychology Today*, August 1968, pp. 59–63. Gordon MacInnes, *Wrong for All the Right Reasons: How White Liberals Have Been Undone by Race* (New York University Press, 1996), p. 136 (Ylvisaker); Christopher Jencks, "Giving Parents Money to Pay for

Schooling," *New Republic,* July 4, 1970, pp. 19, 20–21; and Robert Reich, "The Case for 'Progressive' Vouchers," *Wall Street Journal,* September 6, 2000, p. A26.

145. For related proposals that differ in important specifics, see Cookson, *School Choice,* pp. 129–30; Valerie Martinez and others, "The Consequences of School Choice: Who Leaves and Who Stays in the Inner City," *Social Science Quarterly,* vol. 17 (September 1995), p. 499; Frank R. Kemerer, "School Choice Accountability," in Sugarman and Kemerer, *School Choice and Social Controversy,* pp. 194–96. Coons cited in Kaus, *The End of Equality,* p. 273 n. 20.

146. See discussion in chapter 5. See, for example, William Galston and Diane Ravitch, "Scholarships for Inner-City School Kids," *Washington Post,* December 13, 1997, p. A23; Sterling Tucker, "Sinking in D.C.'s Schools," *Washington Post,* August 21, 1997, p. A19.

147. Gerald Benjamin and Richard Nathan, *Regionalism and Realism* (Brookings, forthcoming), pp. 358–81.

148. See, for example, William G. Bowen and Derek Bok, *The Shape of the River* (Princeton University Press, 1998), p. 273.

Chapter Eight

1. See Christopher Jencks, "Deadly Neighborhoods: How the Underclass Has Been Misunderstood," *New Republic,* June 13, 1988, p. 30.

2. Gordon W. Allport, *The Nature of Prejudice* (Cambridge, Mass.: Addison-Wesley, 1954), cited in David J. Armor, "The Evidence on Busing," *Public Interest,* vol. 28 (Summer 1972), pp. 111, 105. Jesse Burkhead, Thomas B. Fox, and John W. Holland, *Input and Output in Large-City High Schools* (Syracuse University Press, 1967), p. 23 (citing Frank Riessman). Robin D. Barnes, "Black America and School Choice: Charting a New Cause," *Yale Law Journal,* vol. 106 (1996), p. 1.

3. Clark quoted in Nat Hentoff, *Does Anybody Give a Damn?* (Knopf, 1977), pp. 3–4. Amy Stuart Wells and Robert L. Crain, *Stepping over the Color Line: African-American Students in White Suburban Schools* (Yale University Press, 1997), p. 540; Amy Stuart Wells, "Reexamining Social Science Research on School Desegregation: Long-Term versus Short-Term Effects," *Teachers College Record,* vol. 96 (Summer 1995), p. 701; JoAnn Grozuczak Goedert, "Case Comment, *Jenkins* v. *Missouri:* The Future of Interdistrict School Desegregation," *Georgetown Law Review,* vol. 76 (June 1988), p. 1877. Paul Gagnon, "What Should Children Learn?" *Atlantic Monthly,* December 1995, p. 66; National Commission on Excellence in Education, *A Nation at Risk: The Imperative for Education Reform* (Government Printing Office, 1983)

4. James E. Rosenbaum and others, "Social Integration of Low-Income Black Adults in Middle-Class White Suburbs," *Social Problems,* vol. 38 (November 1991), p. 50; James E. Rosenbaum, Leonard S. Rubinowitz, and Marilynn J. Kulieke, *Low-Income Black Children in White Suburban Schools,* report prepared for the Spencer Foundation (Evanston, Ill.: Center for Urban Affairs and Policy Research, February 1986), pp. 125–26. James S. Coleman, "Equality of Educational Opportunity," *Integrated Education,* vol. 6 (September–October 1968), p. 25. Anthony S. Bryk , Valerie E. Lee, and Peter B. Holland, *Catholic Schools and the Common Good* (Harvard University Press, 1993), pp. 272–74. Julia Smith and Valerie Lee, *High School Restructuring and the Equitable*

Distribution of Achievement (Madison, Wisc.: Center on Organization and Restructuring of Schools, February 16, 1996), p. 16.

5. Gary Orfield, *City-Suburban Desegregation: Parent and Student Perspectives in Metropolitan Boston* (Cambridge, Mass.: Harvard Civil Rights Project, 1997), pp. 27, 36–37, 41.

6. Joyce Levy Epstein, "Examining Theories of Adolescent Friendships," in Joyce Levy Epstein and Nancy Karweit, eds., *Friends in School: Patterns of Selection and Influence in Secondary Schools* (New York: Academic Press, 1983), p. 52; Departments of Education and Justice, *Annual Report on School Safety* (1998), p. 7.

7. Rick Bragg, *All Over but the Shoutin'* (New York: Pantheon Books, 1997), reviewed and quoted in Anthony Walton, "The Hard Road from Dixie," *New York Times Book Review,* September 14, 1997, p. 13.

8. J. Douglas Willms, "Social Class Segregation and Its Relationship to Pupils' Examination Results in Scotland," *American Sociological Review,* vol. 51 (April 1986), p. 236. Victor Battistich and others, "Schools as Communities, Poverty Levels of Student Populations, and Students' Attitudes, Motives, and Performance: A Multilevel Analysis," *American Educational Research Journal,* vol. 32 (Fall 1995), p. 649.

9. Paul E. Peterson, "The Urban Underclass and the Poverty Paradox," in Christopher Jencks and Paul E. Peterson, eds., *The Urban Underclass* (Brookings, 1991), p. 9; Russell Banks, "A Whole Lot of Poor Judgment," *New York Times Book Review,* August 3, 1997, p. 7 (reviewing Bernard Lefkowitz, *Our Guys: The Glen Ridge Rape and the Secret Life of the Perfect Suburb* [University of California Press, 1997]).

10. Philip J. Cook and Jens Ludwig, "The Burden of 'Acting White': Do Black Adolescents Disparage Academic Achievement?" in Christopher Jencks and Meredith Phillips, *The Black-White Test Score Gap* (Brookings, 1998), pp. 383, 386; Judith Rich Harris, *The Nurture Assumption: Why Children Turn Out the Way They Do* (New York: Free Press, 1998), p. 250.

11. See, for example, Jon Jeter, "Alarm over TV Time Highlights Viewing Habits of Black Children," *Washington Post,* June 23, 1996, p. A8 (quoting study's author, Steve Gorman, of the National Center for Education Statistics [NCES], that excessive television viewing is primarily a matter of economic status: "It's not really race that's behind this but class. Too often race is a surrogate for poverty"); Ruth B. Ekstrom and others, "Who Drops Out of High School and Why: Findings from a National Study?" *Teachers College Record,* vol. 87, no. 3 (Spring 1986), p. 359 (dropout rates); Benjamin Bloom, Allison Davis, and Robert Hess, *Compensatory Education for Cultural Deprivation* (New York: Holt, Rinehart and Winston, 1965), pp. 85–86 (childrearing); Oscar Lewis, *Five Families: Mexican Case Studies in the Culture of Poverty* (Basic Books, 1959), p. 2; Oscar Lewis, *Anthropological Essays* (Random House, 1970), p. 68; Ralph H. Turner, *The Social Context of Ambition: A Study of High School Seniors in Los Angeles* (San Francisco: Chandler Publishing, 1964), p. 74; Melvin L. Kohn, "Social Class and Parental Values," *American Journal of Sociology,* vol. 64 (January 1959), pp. 345–47; Doris R. Entwisle and Karl L. Alexander, "Summer Setback: Race, Poverty, School Composition, and Mathematics Achievement in the First Two Years of School," *American Sociological Review,* vol. 57 (February 1992), p. 82; J. Murray Lee, *Studies of Economically Deprived Elementary Children in Southern Illinois* (Southern Illinois University, October 1996), p. 4 (achievement); William L. Yancey and Salvatore J. Saporito, *Racial and Economic Segregation and*

Educational Outcomes: One Tale, Two Cities (Philadelphia: Temple University Center for Research in Human Development and Education, 1995), pp. 22–23; Ana C. Fick, Joy D. Osofsky, and Marva L. Lewis, "Perceptions of Violence," in Joy D. Osofsky, ed., *Children in a Violent Society* (New York: Guilford Press, 1997), p. 263; Deborah Anderluh, "Title I Fosters Separate, Unequal School System," *Sacramento Bee*, September 21, 1997, p. A1; Yusef Mgeni, "Relocation Can't Substitute for Educational Strategy," *Minneapolis Star Tribune*, December 18, 1994, p. 31A; Walter Goodman, "Daytime TV Talk: The Issue of Class," *New York Times*, November 1, 1995, p. C15; William Honan, "Income Found to Predict Education Level Better Than Race," *New York Times*, June 17, 1996, p. A11; Glenn C. Loury, "Not So Black and White: The Two Americas Are Actually Converging," *Washington Post*, October 15, 1996, p. C3; Margaret A. Hamburg, "Youth Violence Is a Public Health Concern," in Delbert S. Elliott, Beatrix A. Hamburg, and Kirk R. Williams, eds., *Violence in American Schools: A New Perspective* (Cambridge: Cambridge University Press, 1998), p. 44; Ellen Nakashima, "New School of Thought on Tests," *Washington Post*, May 26, 1998, pp. B1, B5; Rene Sanchez, "Blacks, Whites Finish High School at Same Rate," *Washington Post*, September 6, 1996, p. A3; Robert C. Johnston, "Flexibility the Theme during ESEA Hearings," *Education Week*, February 3, 1999, pp. 24, 26; Michelle Fine, *Framing Dropouts: Notes on the Politics of an Urban Public High School* (State University of New York Press, 1991), p. 22; David J. Armor, *Forced Justice: School Desegregation and the Law* (New York: Oxford University Press, 1995), pp. 85–86; Gary Natriello and Aaron Pallas, "The Development and Impact of High-Stakes Testing," in Gary Orfield and Mindy Kornhaber, eds., *Raising Standards or Raising Barriers?* (Century Foundation Press, forthcoming), pp. 15–19 (achievement). National Center for Education Statistics, *Dropout Rates in the United States: 1999* (Washington: Department of Education, November 2000), pp. 6–7.

12. William Julius Wilson, *When Work Disappears: The World of the New Urban Poor* (Knopf, 1996), p. 52.

13. William Julius Wilson, *The Truly Disadvantaged: The Inner City, The Underclass, and Public Policy* (University of Chicago Press, 1987), p. 8; Wilson, *When Work Disappears*, p. xviii. David Rusk, "How We Promote Poverty," *Washington Post*, May 18, 1997, pp. C1, C3; see also Wilson, *The Truly Disadvantaged*, pp. 58–60.

14. Lewis, *Anthropological Essays*, pp. 68–69, 77. Wilson, *The Truly Disadvantaged*, pp. 61, 137.

15. The correlation for individual poverty and achievement is between .2 and .3, while the correlation between school poverty and school achievement is .5; Martin E. Orland, "Demographics of Disadvantage: Intensity of Childhood Poverty and Its Relationship to Educational Achievement," in John I. Goodlad and Pamela Keating, eds., *Access to Knowledge: An Agenda for Our Nation's Schools* (New York: College Entrance Examination Board, 1990), p. 46. See also Mary M. Kennedy, Richard K. Jung, and M. E. Orland, *Poverty, Achievement, and the Distribution of Compensatory Education Services: An Interim Report from the National Assessment of Chapter 1* (Dept. of Education, Office of Educational Research and Improvement, January 1986), pp. 3–4, 6, 12, D-17; Turner, *The Social Context of Ambition*, p. 104.

16. Theodore Sizer, *Horace's Compromise: The Dilemma of the American High School* (Boston: Houghton Mifflin, 1984), p. 35.

17. john a. powell, "Living and Learning: Linking Housing and Education," *Minnesota Law Review*, vol. 80 (April 1996), p. 786.

18. William Raspberry, "The Good Road to Affirmative Action," *Washington Post,* March 21, 1997, p. A27.

19. Calvin Trillin, *Messages from My Father* (New York: Farrar, Straus and Giroux, 1996), pp. 47–48.

20. Stephan Thernstrom and Abigail Thernstrom, *America in Black and White: One Nation, Indivisible* (Simon and Schuster, 1997), p. 219.

21. Roosevelt cited in Ronald Chester, *Inheritance, Wealth, and Society* (Indiana University Press, 1982), p. 60. Leon Botstein, *Jefferson's Children: Education and the Promise of American Culture* (Doubleday, 1997), pp. 153–54. Jefferson and Lincoln quoted in James B. Conant, "Education for a Classless Society: The Jeffersonian Tradition," *Atlantic Monthly,* May 1940, pp. 593, 597. *Plyler v. Doe,* 457 U.S. 202 (1982), 220. Gordon A. MacInnes, *Kids Who Pick the Wrong Parents and Other Victims of Voucher Schemes,* Century Foundation White Paper (1999).

22. Michael J. Alves, "Cambridge Desegregation Succeeding," *Integrated Education,* vol. 21 (December–January 1983), p. 184. Willie and Alves, quoted in Kristina Torres, "Controlled Choice? Boston Gives Plan a Passing Grade," *Charleston Post and Courier,* May 3, 1998, p. A1.

23. Robert B. Westbrook, *John Dewey and American Democracy* (Cornell University Press, 1991), p. 109. Dewey quoted in Harry M. Levin, "The Economics of Justice in Education," in Deborah A. Verstegen and James G. Ward, eds., *Spheres of Justice in Education: The 1990 American Education Finance Association Yearbook* (New York: Harper Business, 1991), p. 130. J. Harvie Wilkinson III, *From Brown to Bakke: The Supreme Court and School Integration, 1954–1978* (New York: Oxford University Press, 1979), p. 173.

24. See Sandra E. Black, "Measuring the Value of Better Schools," *FRBNY Economic Policy Review,* vol. 4, no. 1 (March 1998), p. 92.

25. Ibid., pp. 90–91. See also Sandra E. Black, "Do Better Schools Matter? Parental Valuation of Elementary Education," *Quarterly Journal of Economics* (May 1999), p. 595 (2.9 percent translates into $5,452 in Massachusetts, where median price is $188,000). Gary Orfield, "Metropolitan School Desegregation: Impacts on Metropolitan Society," *Minnesota Law Review,* vol. 80 (April 1996), p. 857. Tom Zeller, "Calculating One Kind of Middle Class," *New York Times,* October 29, 2000, sec. 4, p. 5.

26. David Rusk, *Inside Game/Outside Game: Urban Policies for the Twenty-first Century* (Brookings, 1999), pp. 191–92.

27. Michael Alves, interview with author, Cambridge, Mass., December 1, 1997, p. 45. Charles Glenn, interview with author, Boston, December 3, 1997, p. 28.

28. Joy G. Dryfoos, "National Community Schools Strategy," unpublished paper, June 12, 1997, p. 2. Carol F. Steinbach, "Public School 'Choice' Gathering Momentum," *National Journal,* January 26, 1991, p. 205; Drew S. Days III, "*Brown* Blues: Rethinking the Integrative Ideal," *William and Mary Law Review,* vol. 34 (1992), pp. 53, 55.

29. Richard D. Parker, letter to author, September 17, 1997.

30. Michael Walzer, *Spheres of Justice: A Defense of Pluralism and Equality* (Basic Books, 1983), p. 225.

31. *Keyes v. School District No. 1,* 413 U.S. 189 (1974), 246 (Powell, J., dissenting).

32. For evidence that after school hours are a peak time for juvenile crime, see Alan B. Krueger, "Reassessing the View That American Schools Are Broken," *FRBNY Economic Policy Review* (March 1998), p. 39; Bob Herbert, "3:00, Nowhere to Go," *New York Times,* October 26, 1997, sec. 4, p.15.

33. Ray C. Rist, *The Invisible Children: School Integration in American Society* (Harvard University Press, 1978), pp. 10, 19–20. Thernstrom and Thernstrom, *America in Black and White*, p. 331.

34. Greg Anrig pointed this out to me.

35. Bernard Wasow pointed this out to me.

36. Bryk, Lee, and Holland, *Catholic Schools and the Common Good*, p. 73.

37. Christine H. Rossell, *The Carrot or the Stick for School Desegregation Policy: Magnet Schools or Forced Busing* (Temple University Press, 1990), p. 32. Botstein, *Jefferson's Children*, p. 129.

38. Leonard P. Strickman, "Desegregation: The Metropolitan Concept," *Urban Review*, vol. 6 (September–October 1977), p. 19. Orfield, *City-Suburban Desegregation*, p. 22.

39. See discussion in chapter 6. As for daytime involvement, fewer mothers are home full time near neighborhood schools; Jennifer L. Hochschild, *The New American Dilemma: Liberal Democracy and School Desegregation* (Yale University Press, 1984), p. 192. See also note 63, this chapter.

40. Kozol quoted in Isabel Wilkerson, "Des Moines Acts to Halt White Flight after State Allows Choice of Schools," *New York Times*, December 16, 1992, p. B9. Theodore M. Shaw, "Equality and Educational Excellence: Legal Challenges in the 1990s," *Minnesota Law Review*, vol. 80 (April 1996), p. 905.

41. Gary Orfield, *Must We Bus? Segregated Schools and National Policy* (Brookings, 1978), p. 129. Carnegie Foundation for the Advancement of Teaching, *School Choice: A Special Report* (Princeton, 1992), pp. 15, 91.

42. Charles Willie and others, "Equity and Excellence: A Plan for Educational Improvement of the Charleston County Public Schools" (submitted to the Charleston Planning Project for Public Education), April 1998, p. 102; Goedert, "Case Comment, *Jenkins* v. *Missouri*," p. 1877; Aric Press and others, "Not Enough White Children," *Newsweek*, September 15, 1980, p. 101; "Backing the Bus," editorial, *New Republic*, February 24, 1982, p. 7; Orfield, *Must We Bus?* p. 128; Derrick A. Bell, *Race, Racism, and American Law*, 3d ed. (Boston: Little, Brown, 1992), p. 580 n. 25; Hochschild, *The New American Dilemma*, p. 192.

43. Orfield, *Must We Bus?* p. 130. "Backing the Bus," p. 7. Bell, *Race, Racism, and American Law*, p. 580; Christine H. Rossell and Willis D. Hawley, eds., *The Consequences of School Desegregation* (Temple University Press, 1983), p. 7; Wells and Crain, *Stepping over the Color Line*, pp. 102, 313.

44. Orfield, *Must We Bus?* pp. 114, 130; Hochschild, *The New American Dilemma*, p. 58.

45. David Nakamura, "How Safe Are School Buses?" *Washington Post*, March 3, 1998, Health sec., p. 12. Hochschild, *The New American Dilemma*, p. 58.

46. Goedert, "Case Comment, *Jenkins* v. *Missouri*," p. 1877.

47. Laura Lippman and others, *Urban Schools: The Challenge of Location and Poverty* (Dept. of Education, NCES, 1996), p. 70.

48. U.S. Commission on Immigration Reform, *Becoming an American: Immigration and Immigrant Policy, Final Report* (September 1997), p. 26 (quoting speech by Barbara Jordan).

49. James S. Coleman and others, *Equality of Educational Opportunity* (Government Printing Office, 1966), pp. 20, 218; see also James B. Conant, *Slums and Suburbs* (McGraw-Hill, 1961), p. 14.

50. Edward Banfield, *Unheavenly Cities* (Boston: Little, Brown, 1968), p. 140. E. D. Hirsch, *The Schools We Need and Why We Don't Have Them* (Doubleday, 1996), p. 7.

51. powell, "Living and Learning," pp. 775–76.

52. john a. powell, "Segregation and Educational Inadequacy in Twin Cities Public Schools," *Hamline Journal of Public Law and Policy*, vol. 17 (Spring 1996), p. 354.

53. Laurence Steinberg, *Beyond the Classroom: Why School Reform Has Failed and What Parents Need to Do* (Simon and Schuster, 1996), p. 60. For a revival of the argument from heredity, see Richard J. Herrnstein and Charles Murray, *The Bell Curve: Intelligence and Class Structure in American Life* (Free Press, 1994).

54. Coleman and others, *Equality of Educational Opportunity*, pp. 21–22, 296. Daniel Patrick Moynihan, *Miles to Go: A Personal History of Social Policy* (Harvard University Press, 1996), p. 148. Mickey Kaus, "Economic Integration in the Classroom," ABC News *Nightline*, September 17, 1992.

55. See Barbara Vobejda, "Experts Describe New Research on Early Learning," *Washington Post*, April 18, 1997, p. A3. See also Judith R. Smith, Jeanne Brooks-Gunn, and Pamela K. Kleban, "Consequences of Living in Poverty for Young Children's Cognitive and Verbal Ability and Early School Achievement," in Greg J. Duncan and Jeanne Brooks-Gunn, *Consequences of Growing Up Poor* (New York: Russell Sage Foundation, 1997), p. 132; and Rima Shore, *Rethinking the Brain: New Insights into Early Development* (New York: Families and Work Institute, 1997), p. 13.

56. Paul Barton and Richard Coley, *America's Smallest School: The Family* (Princeton, N.J.: Educational Testing Service, 1992), p. 4. Harry N. Gottleib, "The Ultimate Solution: Desegregated Housing," *School Review*, vol. 84 (May 1976), p. 463. Elizabeth P. McCaughey, "Can Courts Order School Integration across Town Lines?" *Wall Street Journal*, October 28, 1992, p. A19; Hannah Arendt, "Reflections on Little Rock," *Dissent*, vol. 6 (1959), pp. 45, 50. Rosenbaum, Rubinowitz, and Kulieke, *Low-Income Black Children*, pp. 1–3.

57. See discussion of parent involvement in chapter 5. Abt Associates report on CCDP cited in Robert J. Samuelson, "'Investing' in Our Children," *Washington Post*, February 18, 1998, p. A21. Harris, *The Nurture Assumption*, p. 253.

58. Mayer cited in David Whitman, "Is Lack of Money the Reason Kids Stay Poor?" *U.S. News and World Report*, June 2, 1997, p. 33. Duncan and Brooks-Gunn, *Consequences of Growing Up Poor*, cited in Whitman, "Lack of Money," June 2, 1997, p. 33.

59. Susan E. Mayer, *What Money Can't Buy: Family Income and Children's Life Chances* (Harvard University Press, 1997), pp. 2–3, 14–15, 149.

60. The genetic explanation, popularized recently by *The Bell Curve*, has been more than adequately rebutted elsewhere; see, for example, Christopher Jencks and Meredith Phillips, "The Black-White Test Score Gap: Why It Persists and What Can Be Done," *Brookings Review* (Spring 1998), p. 26; Jim Holt, "The Smart Set," *Wall Street Journal*, June 2, 1998, p. A20. Frederick Erickson, "Qualitative Methods in Research on Teaching," in Merlin C. Wittrock, ed., *Handbook of Research on Teaching*, 3d ed. (New York: Macmillan, 1986), p. 125; see also Organization for Economic Cooperation and Development, *Education at a Glance: OECD Indicators, 1998* (Paris, 1998), pp. 330–31. Lisa M. Lynch, "Trends in and Consequences of Investments in Children," in Sheldon H. Danziger and Jane Waldfogel, eds., *Securing the Future: Investing in Children from Birth to College* (New York: Russell Sage Foundation, 2000), p. 26.

61. Gary Natriello, Edward L. McDill, and Aaron M. Pallas, *Schooling Disadvantaged Children: Racing against Catastrophe* (New York: Teachers College Press, 1990), p. 47; Jeanne Chall and Catherine Snow, *Families and Literacy: The Contributions of Out-of-School Experiences to Children's Acquisitions of Literacy: A Final Report to the National Institute of Education* (Harvard Graduate School of Education, December 22, 1982), p. 385. Claude S. Fischer and others, *Inequality by Design: Cracking the Bell Curve Myth* (Princeton University Press, 1996), p. 170. James McPartland and Will Jordan, "Older Students Also Need Major Federal Compensatory Education Resources," in Gary Orfield and Elizabeth DeBray, eds., *Hard Work for Good Schools: Facts not Fads in Title I Reform* (Cambridge, Mass.: Harvard Civil Rights Project, 1999), p. 105.

62. Diane Ravitch, *The Schools We Deserve: Reflections on the Educational Crises of Our Times* (Basic Books, 1985), pp. 101–04.

63. James S. Coleman and Thomas Hoffer, *Public and Private High Schools: The Impact of Communities* (Basic Books, 1987), pp. 18, 119. Daniel J. Hernandez, "Poverty Trends," in Duncan and Brooks-Gunn, *Consequences of Growing Up Poor*, pp. 26, 30; Larry V. Hedges and Rob Greenwald, "Have Times Changed? The Relationship between School Resources and Student Performance," in Gary Burtless, ed., *Does Money Matter? The Effect of School Resources on Student Achievement and Adult Success* (Brookings, 1996), p. 79.

64. Sara S. McLanahan, "Parent Absence or Poverty: Which Matters More?" in Duncan and Brooks-Gunn, *Consequences of Growing Up Poor*, p. 35. Carnegie Task Force on Meeting the Needs of Young Children, *Starting Points: Meeting the Needs of Our Youngest Children* (New York: Carnegie Corporation, 1994); Susan Chira, "Study Confirms Some Fears on U.S. Children," *New York Times*, April 12, 1994, p. A1. Botstein, *Jefferson's Children*, p. 134. See the discussion on peer influence in chapter 4.

65. John I. Goodlad, *A Place Called School: Prospects for the Future* (McGraw-Hill, 1984), p. 161. Banfield, *Unheavenly Cities*, p. 246. Jon Jeter, "Minnesota to Build State-Run Boarding Schools for Needy Children," *Washington Post*, April 10, 1998, p. A6.

66. Christopher Jencks and Meredith Phillips, "Introduction," in *The Black-White Test Score Gap*, p. 46.

67. Mayer, *What Money Can't Buy*, p. 47.

68. Jennifer Hochschild and Nathan Scovronick, "Democratic Education and the American Dream," in Lorraine McDonnell, P. Michael Timpane, and Roger Benjamin, eds., *Rediscovering the Democratic Purposes of Education* (University Press of Kansas, 2000), pp. 209, 232 n. 4. Derek Bok, *The State of the Nation* (Harvard University Press, 1996), p. 157.

69. Greg Duncan and others, "Poverty and Social Assistance Dynamics in the United States, Canada, and Europe," in Katherine McFate, Roger Lawson, and William Julius Wilson, eds., *Poverty, Inequality, and the Future of Social Policy* (New York: Russell Sage Foundation, 1995), p. 85 (citing Smith). These attitudes may help explain why the U.S. tax burden is the second lowest (besides that of Turkey) in a recent survey of twenty-four nations by the Organization for Economic Cooperation and Development; see David Segal, "Gross Incomes Adjusted," *Washington Post Magazine*, April 26, 1998, p. 15.

70. James R. Kluegel and Eliot R. Smith, *Beliefs about Inequality: Americans' View of What Is and Ought to Be* (Aldine de Gruyter, 1986), pp. 75, 78, 80, 293; see also Lawrence Bobo and Ryan Smith, "Antipoverty Policy, Affirmative Action, and Racial

Attitudes," in Sheldon H. Danziger, Gary D. Sandefur, and Daniel H. Weinberg, eds., *Confronting Poverty: Prescriptions for Change* (Harvard University Press, 1994), p. 375; Wilson, *When Work Disappears*, p. 160; Richard Morin, "As If It Weren't Bad Enough Being Poor," *Washington Post*, February 7, 1999, p. B5. Peter Skerry, "The Charmed Life of Head Start," *Public Interest*, vol. 73 (Fall 1983), pp. 32–33.

71. Ira Katznelson and Margaret Weir, *Schooling for All: Class, Race, and the Decline of the Democratic Ideal* (Basic Books, 1985), p. 24. Bok, *The State of the Nation*, p. 55; Lawrence Cremin, *The Transformation of the School: Progressivism in American Education* (Knopf, 1961), p. 127. Christopher Lasch, *The Revolt of the Elites and the Betrayal of Democracy* (Norton, 1995), pp. 71–75 (on Conant). Orfield, "Metropolitan School Desegregation," pp. 855–56. Gary Burtless, "Introduction and Survey," in Burtless, *Does Money Matter?* p. 1; David Card and Alan B. Krueger, "Labor Market Effects of School Quality: Theory and Evidence," in Burtless, *Does Money Matter?* p. 97; NCES, *The Condition of Education, 1998* (Dept. of Education, 1998), pp. 126–27; Allen W. Hubsch, "Education and Self-Government: The Right to Education under State Constitutional Law," *Journal of Law and Education*, vol. 18 (Winter 1989), pp. 93, 98.

72. See, for example, Ruy Teixeira, "Critical Support: The Public View of Public Education," in Richard D. Kahlenberg, ed., *A Notion at Risk: Preserving Public Education as an Engine for Social Mobility* (Century Foundation Press, 2000), pp. 269–72. Stanley M. Elam and Alec M. Gallup, "The Twenty-first Annual Poll of Public Attitudes toward the Public Schools," *Phi Delta Kappan*, vol. 71 (September 1989), pp. 42, 45, 49; Bobo and Smith, "Antipoverty Policy," p. 371; Wilson, *When Work Disappears*, p. 205.

73. Westbrook, *John Dewey*, p. 94; Charles I. Norris, "Introduction," in Nelson F. Ashline, Thomas Pezzullo, and Charles I. Norris, eds., *Education, Inequality, and National Policy* (Lexington, Mass.: Lexington Books, 1976), p. xvii. James S. Liebman, "Desegregating Politics: 'All-Out' School Desegregation Explained," *Columbia Law Review*, vol. 90 (October 1990), p. 121.

74. Department of Commerce, *1996 Statistical Abstract of the United States* (Government Printing Office, 1996), pp. 371–72. Bruce S. Cooper, "Parent Choice and School Involvement: Perspectives and Dilemmas in the United States and Great Britain," *International Journal of Educational Research*, vol. 15 (1991), p. 240; Anthony Giddens, *The Third Way: The Renewal of Social Democracy* (Oxford: Blackwell, 1998), p. 113. James S. Liebman, "Three Strategies for Implementing *Brown* Anew," in Herbert Hill and James E. Jones Jr., eds., *Race in America: The Struggle for Equality* (University of Wisconsin Press, 1993), p. 118.

75. Wilkinson, *From Brown to Bakke*, p. 338 n. 71; Christine H. Rossell, "Desegregation Plans, Racial Isolation, White Flight, and Community Response," in Rossell and Hawley, *The Consequences of School Desegregation*, pp. 31–32. Nathan Glazer, "A Costly Noble Idea," *New York Times Book Review*, March 14, 1999, p. 13; James Feron, "Yonkers Is Ruled to Be in Contempt on Housing Plan," *New York Times*, August 3, 1988, A1. William Clune, "The Supreme Court's Treatment of Wealth Discriminations under the Fourteenth Amendment," *Supreme Court Review* (1975), pp. 289, 294.

76. Bell, *Race, Racism, and American Law*, p. 746. Rossell, "Desegregation Plans," p. 31.

77. "Moving to Opportunities," editorial, *Providence Journal-Bulletin*, April 8, 1994, p. 16A; Peter Dreier and David Moberg, "Moving from the 'Hood," *American Prospect* (Winter 1996), p. 79. Paul Glastris, "A New City-Suburbs Hookup," *U.S. News and World Report*, July 18, 1994, p. 28.

78. Some also argue that a policy of housing deconcentration is also particularly expensive, since part of the reason low-income housing has been built in existing low-income communities is that land prices are lower; Christopher Jencks and Susan E. Mayer, "The Social Consequences of Growing Up in a Poor Neighborhood," in Laurence E. Lynn Jr. and Michael G. H. McGeary, eds., *Inner-City Poverty in the United States* (Washington: National Academy Press, 1990), p. 112.

79. Dante Ramos, "HUD-dled Masses," *New Republic*, March 14, 1994. Rosenbaum and others, "Social Integration," p. 48. John Simons, "Paid To Leave, but Wanting to Stay," *U.S. News and World Report*, July 11, 1994, p. 21. Karen De Witt, "Housing Voucher Test in Maryland Is Scuttled by a Political Firestorm," *New York Times*, March 28, 1995, p. B10; Rusk, *Inside Game/Outside Game*, p. 273.

80. Alan B. Wilson, "Educational Consequences of Segregation in a California Community," in U.S. Commission on Civil Rights, *Racial Isolation in the Public Schools*, vol. 2 (Government Printing Office, 1967), pp. 180–81, 202; Alan B. Wilson, *The Consequences of Segregation: Academic Achievement in a Northern Community* (Berkeley, Calif.: Glendessary Press, 1969), pp. 27–28. More recently, see Duncan Chaplin and Jane Hannaway, *African American High Scorers Project: Technical Report*, vol. 2, *School and Neighborhood Factors and SAT Performance* (Washington: Urban Institute, 1998), pp. 40–41.

81. Stephen Schellenberg, "Concentration of Poverty and the Ongoing Need for Title I," in Orfield and DeBray, eds., *Hard Work for Good Schools*, p. 137. John H. Laub and Janet L. Lauritsen, "The Interdependence of School Violence with Neighborhood and Family Conditions," in Elliott, Hamburg, and Williams, *Violence in American Schools*, p. 146; see also discussion in chapter 3.

82. Myron Orfield, quoted in "Quality Counts '98: The Urban Challenge," *Education Week*, January 8, 1998, p. 14; Myron Orfield, *Metropolitics: A Regional Agenda for Community and Stability* (Brookings, 1997), pp. 3, 39.

83. See, for example, William L. Taylor, "*Brown*, Equal Protection, and the Isolation of the Poor," *Yale Law Journal*, vol. 95 (1986), p. 1711; Gayl Shaw Westerman, "The Promise of State Constitutionalism: Can It Be Fulfilled in *Sheff* v. *O'Neill?*" *Hastings Constitutional Law Quarterly*, vol. 23 (Winter 1996), p. 403; James Kunen, "The End of Integration," *Time*, April 29, 1996, p. 44. Pearce cited in Goedert, "Case Comment, *Jenkins* v. *Missouri*," p. 1879. Beth Daley, "School Busing Fading as Key Issue," *Boston Globe*, January 19, 1999, pp. A1, B4.

84. Rusk, *Inside Game/Outside Game*, p. 61.

85. Robert B. Reich, *The Work of Nations: Preparing Ourselves for Twenty-first-Century Capitalism* (Knopf, 1991), p. 282; Lasch, *Revolt of the Elites* (generally).

86. Of course, Boston's is a worst-case scenario, and many integration efforts (for example, Louisville) were more successful. The point of using Boston as an example here is to address head-on the case that opponents will cite and explain why socioeconomic integration will be very different.

87. Margot Hornblower, "School Desegregation in Boston: A Decade-long Social Experiment That Backfired," *International Herald Tribune*, October 1, 1985, p. 5.

88. Jack Beatty, "*Common Ground*," book review, *Atlantic Monthly*, September 1985. J. Anthony Lukas, *Common Ground: A Turbulent Decade in the Lives of Three American Families* (Knopf, 1985), pp. 324–26; see also William Claiborne, "Boston Skirts Crisis as Project Integrates," *Washington Post*, November 28, 1992, pp. A8, A9.

89. Diane Ravitch, *The Troubled Crusade: American Education, 1945–1980* (Basic Books, 1983), p. 180. Lukas, *Common Ground*, p. 650. D. Garth Taylor, *Public Opinion and Collective Action: The Boston School Desegregation Conflict* (University of Chicago Press, 1986), p. 196. Carol Steinbach and Neal R. Peirce, "Multiple Choice," *National Journal*, July 1, 1989, p. 1695.

90. Beatty, "*Common Ground.*" Joseph Watras, *Politics, Race, and Schools: Racial Integration, 1954–1994* (New York: Garland Publishing, 1997), p. 21. Sara Rimer, "For Old South Boston, Despair Replaces Hope," *New York Times*, August 17, 1997, p. 1. Kristina Torres, "Controlled Choice? Boston Gives Plan a Passing Grade," *Charleston Post and Courier*, May 3, 1998, p. 1.

91. Claiborne, "Boston Skirts Crisis," pp. A8, A9. See, for example, John Kenneth Galbraith, "Mass. Appeal," *New York Times Book Review*, March 17, 1996, p. 33.

92. See, for example, Lukas, *Common Ground*, author's note; Alvin P. Sanoff, "A Conversation with J. Anthony Lukas," *U.S. News and World Report*, April 28, 1986, p. 75. Taylor, *Public Opinion and Collective Action*, pp. vii, 57.

93. See, for example, Taylor, *Public Opinion and Collective Action*, pp. vii–viii, 57, 62, 197–98.

94. Derrick A. Bell, "Serving Two Masters: Integration Ideals and Client Interests in School Desegregation Litigation," *Yale Law Journal*, vol. 85 (1976), pp. 480–83 (quoting Flannery); powell, "Segregation and Educational Inadequacy in Twin Cities Public Schools," p. 340. See also Charles V. Willie, "Racial Balance or Quality Education?" *School Review*, vol. 84 (May 1976), p. 313; Michael J. Alves and Charles V. Willie, "Controlled Choice: An Approach to Effective School Desegregation," *Urban Review*, vol. 19 (1987), p. 70; Kate Zernike, "On the Record for Busing," *Boston Globe*, December 8, 1998, p. B1; Liebman, "Desegregating Politics," pp. 1473–74.

95. Noel Day, "Busing: A Symposium," *Ramparts* (January 1975), p. 42.

96. Taylor, *Public Opinion and Collective Action*, p. 57 (opposition to attending majority black schools in Boston).

97. Ibid., pp. viii, 62.

98. Robert Coles, "Busing Puts Burden on Working Class, Black and White," interview by Mike Barnicle, *Boston Globe*, October 15, 1974, p. 23. Lukas, *Common Ground*, pp. 271, 135; see also p. 353.

99. Charles L. Glenn, "Just Schools: Doing Right by Poor Kids," in David P. Gushee, ed., *Toward a Just and Caring Society* (Grand Rapids, Mich.: Baker Books, 1999), p. 326; see also Charles L. Glenn, "Busing in Boston: What We Could Have Done Better," in Kofi Lomotey and Charles Teddlie, eds., *Forty Years after the* Brown *Decision: Implications of School Desegregation for U.S. Education* (New York: AMS Press, 1996), p. 150. Robert Rothman, "After Delays, Boston's 'Controlled Choice' Plan Emerges," *Education Week* (November 9, 1988), p. 5. Charles L. Glenn, *Family Choice and Public Schools: A Report to the State Board of Education* (Quincy, Mass.: Massachusetts Department of Education, January 1986), pp. 21–23, 30.

100. Sondra Astor Stave, *Achieving Racial Balance: Case Studies of Contemporary School Desegregation* (Westport, Conn.: Greenwood Press, 1995), p. 167; Goedert, "Case Comment, *Jenkins* v. *Missouri*," p. 1879; Christine H. Rossell, "The Buffalo Controlled Choice Plan," *Urban Education*, vol. 22 (October 1987), pp. 344, 350–51; Rossell, *The Carrot or the Stick*, pp. 41, 68–70, 80, 84, 94; *Sheff* v. *O'Neill* 733 A.2d 925 (Conn. Supe-

rior Ct. 1999), 941; Christine H. Rossell, "Controlled Choice Desegregation Plans: Not Enough Choice, Too Much Control?" *Urban Affairs Review*, vol. 31 (September 1995), pp. 52, 56–58.

101. See Montclair (N.J.) Public School System, *Report of District Enrollment*, October 1998, p. 11.

102. Steve Farkas and Jean Johnson, *Time to Move On: African-American and White Parents Set an Agenda for Public Schools: A Report from Public Agenda* (New York: Public Agenda, 1998), p. 41.

103. Orfield, "Metropolitan School Desegregation," p. 839. Mickey Kaus, *The End of Equality* (Basic Books, 1992), p. 54; Claiborne, "Boston Skirts Crisis," p. A8.

104. See Gary Orfield and Lawrence Peskin, "Metropolitan High Schools: Income, Race, and Inequality," in Douglas E. Mitchell and Margaret E. Goertz, eds., *Education Politics for the New Century* (New York: Falmer Press, 1990), p. 30; Liebman, "Desegregating Politics," p. 1623 n. 672; Orfield, "Metropolitan School Desegregation," pp. 828, 831, 842, 867, citing Finis Welch and Audrey Light, *New Evidence on School Desegregation*, Publication 92 (U.S. Commission on Civil Rights Clearinghouse, 1987); David R. Morgan and Robert E. England, "School Desegregation and White Enrollment Decline: A Test of Certain Common Propositions," *Integrated Education*, vol. 21 (December–January 1983), p. 201.

105. Hochschild, *The New American Dilemma*, p. 64. Bernard Schwartz, *Swann's Way: The School Busing Case and the Supreme Court* (New York: Oxford University Press, 1986), p. 9 (Charlotte); Paul Delaney, "Louisville, a Place Where Busing Seems to Work," *New York Times*, June 6, 1976, sec. 4, p. 6; Orfield, *Must We Bus?* pp. 411–12 (Louisville); Gary Orfield and Susan Eaton, *Dismantling Desegregation: The Quiet Reversal of Brown v. Board of Education* (New York: Free Press, 1996), p. 111 (Louisville); powell, "Segregation and Educational Inadequacy in Twin Cities Public Schools," p. 360 (Louisville); Goedert, "Case Comment, *Jenkins v. Missouri*," p. 1881 (Nashville); National Education Association, *Three Cities That Are Making Desegregation Work* (Washington, 1984), pp. 19, 21 (Charlotte-Mecklenburg); Ward Sinclair, "Desegregation's Quiet Success," *Washington Post*, June 17, 1978, p. A10 (Tampa); powell, "Living and Learning," p. 760 (Indianapolis and St. Louis).

106. "Quality Counts '98," p. 161; Gary Orfield and David Thronson, "Dismantling Desegregation: Uncertain Gains, Unexpected Costs," *Emory Law Journal*, vol. 42 (1993), pp. 775–76, 785–86; Jefferson County (Ky.) Public Schools, Department of Accountability, Research, and Planning, "Jefferson County Schools Enrollment as of June 1 1998," unpublished data provided to the author, July 1998; "Quality Counts '98," pp. 219–20; Steven A. Holmes, "Whites' Bias Lawsuit Could Upset Desegregation Efforts," *New York Times*, April 25, 1999, p. 18; Orfield, "Metropolitan School Desegregation," pp. 828, 845–47; Rusk, *Inside Game/Outside Game*, p. 7.

107. Westerman, "The Promise of State Constitutionalism," p. 400; Gary Orfield, Franklin Monfort, and Rosemary George, *School Segregation in the 1980s: Trends in the United States and Metropolitan Areas*, a report by the National School Desegregation Project (Washington: Joint Center for Political Studies, July 1987), pp. 3–4, 14; Hochschild, *The New American Dilemma*, pp. 32–33. See, for example, *Evans v. Buchanan*, 582 F.2d 750 (3d Cir. 1978), 758–61; Goedert, "Case Comment, *Jenkins v. Missouri*," p. 1879.

108. Wilkinson, *From* Brown *to* Bakke, pp. 178–79. See discussion of majority-minority schools in chapter 6.

109. For the right to a private education, see *Pierce* v. *Society of Sisters*, 268 U.S. 510 (1925). Gary Orfield, *The Growth of Segregation in American Schools: Changing Patterns of Separation and Poverty since 1968* (Cambridge, Mass.: Harvard School Desegregation Project, December 1993), p. 6. Whereas only one in ten public school students was nonwhite in 1954, by 1992, the number was one in three; Karen De Witt, "The Nation's Schools Learn a 4th *R*: Resegregation," *New York Times*, January 19, 1992, sec. 4, p. 5; Lippman and others, *Urban Schools*, p. 9; NCES, *The Condition of Education, 1998*, pp. 101, 104, 239; Bruce A. Ramirez, "Culturally and Linguistically Diverse Children," *Teaching Exceptional Children*, vol. 20 (Summer 1988), p. 45.

110. Caroline M. Hoxby, "What Do America's 'Traditional' Forms of School Choice Teach Us about School Choice Reforms?" *FRBNY Policy Review*, vol. 4, no. 1 (March 1998), p. 49. Bryk, Lee, and Holland, *Catholic Schools and the Common Good*, p. 33; see also MacInnes, *Kids Who Pick the Wrong Parents*, p. 45. Orfield, *Must We Bus?* p. 60; Orfield and Eaton, *Dismantling Desegregation*, pp. 18, 62; Jeffrey R. Henig and Stephen D. Sugarman, "The Nature and Extent of School Choice," in Stephen D. Sugarman and Frank R. Kemerer, eds., *School Choice and Social Controversy* (Brookings, 1999), p. 25. Paul E. Peterson, "Top Ten Questions Asked about School Choice," in Diane Ravitch, ed., *Brookings Papers on Education Policy, 1999* (Brookings, 1999), p. 377. Debra Viadero, "At the Crossroads," *Education Week*, March 24, 1999, pp. 39–40.

111. Mosle, "What We Talk about When We Talk about Education," *New Republic*, June 17, 1996, p. 28. New York City, where 90 percent of non-Hispanic whites attended private schools in 1987, is anomalous; see Charles Peters, *Tilting at Windmills: An Autobiography* (New York: Addison-Wesley, 1988), p. 214. Nicholas Lemann, "Ready, READ!" *Atlantic Monthly*, November 1998, pp. 92–93. Seymour Fliegel, with James MacGuire, *Miracle in East Harlem: The Fight for Choice in Public Education* (Random House, 1993), pp. 6–7. Alan Wolfe, *One Nation after All* (Viking, 1998), pp. 237, 248, cited in Giddens, *The Third Way*, p. 108.

112. Lukas, *Common Ground*, p. 242. "A Scholar Who Inspired It Says Busing Backfired," interview with James Coleman, *National Observer*, June 7, 1975, p. 18. For general evidence on the extent to which mixing poor whites and poor blacks is unlikely to produce positive academic benefits, see chapter 5.

113. Day, "Busing," p. 42. Geraldine Kozberg, "Left-Out Kids in a Left-Out School," *Harvard Graduate School of Education Association Bulletin*, vol. 25 (1980), p. 25; see also Joyce Levy Epstein, "School Environment and Student Friendships: Issues, Implications, and Interventions," in Epstein and Karweit, *Friends in School*, p. 246. Lillian B. Rubin, "White against Black," *School Review*, vol. 84 (May 1976), p. 387. Kozol, quoted in Elizabeth A. Marek, "Education by Decree," *New Perspectives*, vol. 17 (Summer 1985), p. 36; Robert Coles, "Busing Puts Burden on Working Class, Black and White," *Boston Globe*, October 15, 1974, p. 23. Lukas, *Common Ground*, p. 650. Beatty, "*Common Ground*." Beth Daley, "School Busing Fading," p. A1.

114. Wilkinson, *From* Brown *to* Bakke, pp. 210 (Bulger), 213 (Wilkinson); Hornblower, "School Desegregation in Boston," p. 5.

115. Coles, "Busing Puts Burden on Working Class, Black and White," October 15, 1974.

116. J. Anthony Lukas, interview with author, New York, January 3, 1995, p. 4. Lukas, *Common Ground*, pp. 27, 244–45, 269; see also pp. 131, 260, 269, 499.

117. Beatty, "*Common Ground.*" Paul Delaney, "Long-Time Desegregation Proponent Attacks Busing as Harmful," *New York Times*, June 6, 1975, p. 25.

118. Day, "Busing," p. 42. Willie, "Racial Balance," p. 323.

119. Hochschild, *The New American Dilemma*, p. 57. Lukas, interview, pp. 6, 3; Lukas, *Common Ground*, p. 131.

120. "Justice for Hartford's Schools," editorial, *Boston Globe*, July 16, 1996, p. A14.

121. Wilkinson, *From Brown to Bakke*, p. 214.

122. Lukas, interview, p. 11; see also Richard D. Kahlenberg, *The Remedy: Race, Class, and Affirmative Action* (Basic Books, 1996), p. 191; Lukas, *Common Ground*, pp. 135–36, 204. Orfield, *Must We Bus?* p. 32; Gary Orfield, interview with author, Cambridge, Mass., November 19, 1997, p. 13.

123. Coles, "Busing Puts Burden." Bayard Rustin, "The Blacks and the Unions," *Harper's*, May 1971, p. 81.

124. Hochschild, *The New American Dilemma*, p. 54. James R. Kluegel and Eliot R. Smith, *Beliefs about Inequality: Americans' Views of What Is and What Ought to Be* (New York: Aldine De Gruyter, 1986), p. 26; James C. Rosenbaum and others, "Social Integration of Low-Income Black Adults in Middle-Class White Suburbs," *Social Problems*, vol. 38, no. 4 (November 1991), p. 50; Janet Ward Shofield and H. Andrew Sagar, "Desegregation, School Practices, and Student Race Relations," in Rossell and Hawley, *The Consequences of School Desegregation*, p. 76; Thernstrom and Thernstrom, *America in Black and White*, p. 483; Rossell, *The Carrot and the Stick*, pp. 115–16; Hochschild, *The New American Dilemma*, p. 55; Derrick Bell, "*Brown v. Board of Education* and the Interest-Convergence Dilemma," *Harvard Law Review*, vol. 93 (1980), p. 526.

125. Bell, "Serving Two Masters," p. 482; Day, "Busing," p. 41; Orfield, *City-Suburban Desegregation*, p. 7. Sanoff, "A Conversation with J. Anthony Lukas," p. 75. Beatty, "*Common Ground.*"

126. Farkas and Johnson, *Time to Move On*, p. 41.

127. Gerald David Jaynes and Robin M. Williams Jr., eds., *A Common Destiny: Blacks and American Society* (Washington: National Academy Press, 1989), p. 84. See, for example, Michael W. Giles, "White Enrollment Stability and School Desegregation: A Two-Level Analysis," *American Sociological Review*, vol. 43 (December 1978).

128. David K. Shipler, *A Country of Strangers: Blacks and Whites in America* (New York: Knopf, 1997), p. 64; Orfield, *Must We Bus?* pp. 405–06; powell, "Living and Learning," p. 761; Orfield, "Metropolitan School Desegregation," p. 831; Hochschild and Scovronick, "Democratic Education and the American Dream," pp. 217–18.

129. Amy Stuart Wells and others, "Charter Schools and Racial and Social Class Segregation: Yet Another Sorting Machine?" in Richard D. Kahlenberg, ed., *A Notion at Risk: Preserving Public Education as an Engine for Social Mobility* (Century Foundation Press, 2000), pp. 169–70. Wells and Crain, *Stepping over the Color Line*, p. 9. Orfield, *City-Suburban Desegregation*, p. 7. Hochschild, *The New American Dilemma*, p. 190.

130. Bill Clinton, "My Fellow Americans. . . . State of Our Union Is Strong," *Washington Post*, January 20, 1999, p. A12. See discussion of discipline in chapter 6.

131. Anthony Downs, *New Visions for Metropolitan America* (Brookings, 1994), p. 26; Jaynes and Williams, *A Common Destiny*, pp. 142–43; Jencks and Phillips, introduction to *Black-White Test Score Gap*, p. 45; Orfield, *Metropolitics*, p. 83; Thomas C.

Schelling, "On the Ecology of Micromotives," *Public Interest*, vol. 25 (1971), p. 82; Leonard Steinhorn and Barbara Diggs-Brown, *By the Color of Our Skin: The Illusion of Integration and the Reality of Race* (Dutton, 1999), p. 33.

132. Jennifer Hochschild, "Is School Desegregation Still a Viable Policy Option?" *Political Science and Politics* (September 1997); "Backing the Bus," p. 7; Orfield, "Metropolitan School Desegregation," p. 865; Gary Orfield, "Should the Courts Reduce Their Role in School Desegregation?" *Congressional Quarterly Researcher*, vol. 6 (October 18, 1996), p. 929; Jaynes and Williams, *A Common Destiny*, p. 84; Liebman, "Desegregating Politics," p.1621. Hochschild, *The New American Dilemma*, pp. 182–83.

133. See, for example, Christine H. Rossell and Willis D. Hawley, "Desegregation and Change," introduction to Rossell and Hawley, *The Consequences of School Desegregation*, pp. 8, 36; Orfield, *Must We Bus?* pp. 99–100; Morgan and England, "School Desegregation and White Enrollment Decline," p. 199; Jaynes and Williams, *A Common Destiny*, p. 83; Hochschild, *The New American Dilemma*, p. 52; Liebman, "Desegregating Politics," pp. 1622–23.

134. Daley, "School Busing Fading," p. A1.

135. Wilkinson, *From Brown to Bakke*, p. 214.

Chapter Nine

1. Stephen Plank, "Peer Relations and Participation in Desegregated Classrooms," Ph.D. diss., University of Chicago, 1995, p. 23; State of Wisconsin, Department of Public Instruction, "1997–1998 Public Enrollment Ranked by School District," October 22, 1998 (www.dpi.state.wi.us/dpi/dlcl/lbstat/98rank.html [January 25, 1999]).

2. School District of La Crosse (Wisc.), "One Solution to a Growing Problem," July 1993, p. 1; Richard Swantz, "One Solution to a Growing Problem," *Education Forward* (August 1993), p. 7. Joseph P. Heim and Pamela H. Rodgers, "Socio-Economic Balance as Educational Reform in La Crosse: Lessons for Innovative Administrative Leadership," paper presented to the Fifty-fifth National Training Conference of the American Society for Public Administration, Chicago, April 17, 1993, p. 11. Michael Abramowitz, "The School Board Just Lost Touch," *Washington Post*, July 19, 1992, p. A4. James Birnbaum, telephone interview with author, December 5, 1997, pp. 36, 40.

3. Abramowitz, "The School Board Just Lost Touch," p. A4. Jonathan Tilove, "La Crosse Residents Clash over Busing Plan to Integrate Schools," *St. Paul Pioneer Press*, June 14, 1992, p. 1A. Plank, "Peer Relations and Participation in Desegregated Classrooms," p. 26. Peter Schmidt, "District Proposes Assigning Pupils Based on Income," *Education Week*, October 30, 1991, p. 13.

4. Heim and Rodgers, "Socio-Economic Balance as Education Reform in La Crosse," p. 11. Plank, "Peer Relations and Participation in Desegregated Classrooms," p. 27. Joseph Heim, interview with author, La Crosse, Wisc., December 17, 1997, transcript 2, p. 16.

5. Richard Swantz and Joan Kent, individual interviews with author, and Margaret Larson, Jim Birnbaum, Fred Kusch, Sue Mormann, and Mary Stanek, group interview with author, La Crosse, Wisc., December 15, 1997. James Birnbaum, "School District Boundary Proposal: Support Diversity Plans," testimony to the La Crosse School Board, November 4, 1991, p. 1.

6. Swantz, interview, p. 22. Eric Harrison, "Plan for Busing by Income Splits Wisconsin City," *Los Angeles Times*, March 23, 1992, p. A1.

7. Heim, interview, transcript 2, pp. 15, 16. Swantz, interview, p. 22. John Medinger, interview with author, La Crosse, Wisc., December 16, 1997, p. 9. Harrison, "Plan for Busing by Income Splits Wisconsin City," p. A1; Tilove, "La Crosse Residents Clash over Busing Plan to Integrate Schools," p. 15A. David L. Johnston, interview with author, La Crosse, Wisc., December 15, 1997; and "Subsidized Lunches (Free Only) School District of La Crosse, Third Friday in September 1997," unpublished school district document provided by Johnston. School District of La Crosse, "1995–96 School Performance Report," 1997, p. 9.

8. Swantz, interview, p. 23; Johnston, interview, pp. 49–50. Richard Mial, "Controversial 1979 Changes Led to Central, Logan Parity," *La Crosse Tribune*, October 16, 1991, p. A3. Ken French, interview with author, La Crosse, Wisc., December 15, 1997, p. 8. School District of La Crosse, "1995–96 School Performance Report," p. 9.

9. Terry Witzke, interview with author, La Crosse, Wisc., December 15, 1997, p. 5; and Wisconsin State Department of Health and Human Services, "Larger School Districts Listed in Rank Order by Percentage of Students on AFDC and Dropout Rates," 1995, unpublished data provided by Witzke. "District Dropout Comparison," March 23, 1992, unpublished data provided by David L. Johnston. Medinger, interview, p. 10.

10. Neil Duresky, telephone interview with author, January 9, 1998, p. 16; see also Heim and Rodgers, "Socio-Economic Balance as Education Reform in La Crosse," p. 15.

11. David J. Armor, *Forced Justice: School Desegregation and the Law* (New York: Oxford University Press, 1995), p. 61; see also Witzke, interview, pp. 8 27; French, interview, p. 10; Heim and Rodgers, "Socio-Economic Balance as Education Reform in La Crosse," p. 16. Letter from nine elementary school principals to Dr. Charles Miller, President, Board of Education, and others, May 17, 1991, provided by David L. Johnston. Joseph P. Heim and Pamela H. Rodgers, "Busing for Socio-Economic Balance: Opinions, Attitudes, and Behavior," paper presented at the annual meeting of the Midwest Political Science Association, Chicago, April 17, 1993, pp. 9–10.

12. Plank, "Peer Relations and Participation in Desegregated Classrooms," p. 27.

13. Heim and Rodgers, "Busing for Socio-Economic Balance," p. 10. Swantz, "One Solution to a Growing Problem," p. 7.

14. Birnbaum, interview, pp. 14, 33–34. Heim and Rodgers, "Socio-Economic Balance as Educational Reform in La Crosse," pp. 16, 25. "Economic Integration in the Classroom," ABC News *Nightline,* September 17, 1992. Laurel Shaper Walters, "U.S. Schools Watch Busing-by-Income Program in Wisconsin," *Christian Science Monitor,* November 9, 1993, p. 10.

15. Witzke, interview, p. 25; see also Harrison, "Plan for Busing by Income Splits Wisconsin City," p. A1.

16. "Economic Integration." Joan Kent, "Boundary Plan Approved," *La Crosse Tribune,* January 8, 1992, p. A12.

17. Witzke, interview, p. 34.

18. Swantz, interview, pp. 16, 17. Shanks cited in Joan Kent, "More than Mixing Required," *La Crosse Tribune,* January 5, 1992, p. A12.

19. Joan Kent, interview with author, La Crosse, Wisc., December 15, 1997, p. 29; Mial, "Controversial 1979 Changes," p. A3. Swantz, "One Solution to a Growing Problem," p. 7.

20. James Birnbaum, unpublished article drafted for the *National News Journal.* Swantz, "One Solution to a Growing Problem," p. 7.

21. Jencks quoted in Carol Innerst, "School Busing Plan to Mix Rich, Poor," *Washington Times*, November 1, 1991, p. A1. Rob Hotakainen, "La Crosse Plan Would Mix Students by Income," *Minneapolis Star Tribune*, November 23, 1991, p. 1A. Birnbaum, unpublished article. Thai Vue and John Medinger, signers, "Community Attitudes Task Force Statement," La Crosse, Wisc. (on file with author).

22. Johnston, interview, p. 6.

23. Witzke, interview, pp. 28–29; the Chamber of Commerce, which initially had opposed the plan, came around to accept it; Harrison, "Plan for Busing by Income Splits Wisconsin City," p. A1. Heim and Rodgers, "Socio-Economic Balance as Educational Reform in La Crosse," p.19. Betsy Stannard and Kathy Fuch, group interview with author, La Crosse, Wisc., December 16, 1997, p. 22.

24. Birnbaum, interview, p. 29. Walters, "U.S. Schools Watch Busing-by-Income Program in Wisconsin," p. 10.

25. Johnston, interview, p. 35.

26. Roger LeGrand, interview with author, La Crosse, Wisconsin, December 16, 1997, pp. 9–10. Heim and Rodgers, "Socio-Economic Balance as Educational Reform in La Crosse," 27. Walters, "U.S. Schools Watch Busing-by-Income Program in Wisconsin," p. 10.

27. Birnbaum, interview, pp. 28–29. Swantz, interview, pp. 13–14. Walters, "U.S. Schools Watch Busing-by-Income Program in Wisconsin," p. 10.

28. "Economic Integration." Harrison, "Plan for Busing by Income Splits Wisconsin City," p. A1. Medinger, interview, p. 4.

29. Birnbaum, interview, p. 45. Johnston, interview, pp. 23–24.

30. Schmidt, "District Proposes Assigning Pupils Based on Income," p. 13.

31. Heim and Rodgers, "Busing for Socio-Economic Balance," p. 13. William Celis, "In Effort to Improve Schools, Pupils to Be Assigned on Basis of Income," *New York Times*, January 22, 1992, p. A13; Innerst, "School Busing Plan to Mix Rich, Poor," p. A1; Mial, "Controversial 1979 Changes," p. A3; Witzke, interview, p. 46; Johnston, interview, p. 42; Jo Sandin, "La Crosse Schools to Integrate Rich and Poor," *Milwaukee Journal*, January 26, 1992, p. 5.

32. Johnston, interview, pp. 20–21, 23. Witzke, interview, p. 42. Swantz, interview, p. 11.

33. Swantz, "One Solution to a Growing Problem," p. 8. Witzke, interview, pp. 23, 23–24. Swantz, interview, p. 2; Rob Hotakainen, "La Crosse to Use Income in Picking Kids' Schools," *Minneapolis Star Tribune*, March 15, 1992, p. 1A.

34. Heim and Rodgers, "Busing for Socio-Economic Balance," p. 14. Joan Kent, "Opposition Increasing against New School Plan," *La Crosse Tribune*, November 4, 1991, p. A2.

35. Plank, "Peer Relations and Participation in Desegregated Classrooms," p. 30. Peter Schmidt, "La Crosse to Push Ahead with Income-Based Busing Plan," *Education Week*, August 5, 1992.

36. Plank, "Peer Relations and Participation in Desegregated Classrooms," p. 30; Witzke, interview, p. 10. Hotakainen, "La Crosse to Use Income in Picking Kids' Schools," p. 1A; Joan Kent and Grant Blum, "Board Recall Aimed at Swantz," *La Crosse Tribune*, January 23, 1992; Joan Kent, "Board Puts the Blame on Swantz," *La Crosse Tribune*, March 24, 1993, p. A9.

37. Abramowitz, "The School Board Just Lost Touch," p. A4.

38. "Class or Race?" editorial, *Economist,* August 1, 1992, p. 23. Mickey Kaus, *The End of Equality* (Basic Books, 1992), p. 275 n. 28.

39. Joan Kent, "Leave New Boundaries Alone for Now, Most Readers Say," *La Crosse Tribune,* July 28, 1992, p. A4. Jo Sandin, "No Last Chapter in Boundary Uproar," *Milwaukee Journal,* August 2, 1992, p. 7.

40. Grant Blum, "School Board Won't Change Boundaries," *La Crosse Tribune,* July 29, 1992, p. A8. Schmidt, "La Crosse to Push Ahead with Income-Based Busing"; Blum, "School Board Won't Change Boundaries," p. A1. Larson and others, interview; Heim and Rodgers, "Busing for Socio-Economic Balance," p. 16.

41. Witzke, interview, p. 39. Plank, "Peer Relations and Participation in Desegregated Classrooms," p. 31. Birnbaum, interview, p. 18. Heim and Rodgers, "Busing for Socio-Economic Balance," p. 17. "La Crosse Rescues Reasonable Idea," editorial, *Milwaukee Journal,* April 18, 1993.

42. Birnbaum, interview, p. 20; Johnston, interview, p. 28. Medinger, interview, p. 22.

43. Witzke, interview, p. 9. Heim, interview, transcript 2, p. 23. Joan Kent, "New Schools, New Friends," *La Crosse Tribune,* August 27, 1992, p. C1.

44. Kent, interview by author, p. 13; that Kent was sympathetic to recall, see Birnbaum, interview, p. 48; Julie Vollmer, interview with author, La Crosse, Wisc., December 16, 1997, p. 38. Joan Kent, "Parents: We Like New Lines," *La Crosse Tribune,* April 14, 1993; Swantz, "One Solution to a Growing Problem," p. 8; School District of La Crosse, "One Solution to a Growing Problem," pp. 7–8. French, interview, p. 6.

45. Johnston, interview, pp. 12, 13.

46. "Class or Race?" p. 23. Kent, interview, p. 7. Heim, interview, transcript 1, pp. 11, 12–13.

47. Heim and Rodgers, "Socio-Economic Balance as Educational Reform in La Crosse," p. 25; Heim and Rodgers, "Busing for Socio-Economic Balance," p. 32.

48. Kent, interview, p. 21. Joan Kent and Grant Blum, "School Board Recall in Works," *La Crosse Tribune,* January 22, 1992.

49. Kent, interview, pp. 18, 17. Heim and Rodgers, "Busing for Socio-Economic Balance," p. 28; see also Joan Kent, "Amid Questions, Hmong Parents Say New Mix of Children Will Work," *La Crosse Tribune,* October 20, 1991; Sandin, "La Crosse Schools to Integrate Rich and Poor," p. 6. Johnston, interview, p. 38; see also "Economic Integration." LeGrand, interview, p. 20.

50. Heim and Rodgers, "Busing for Socio-Economic Balance," pp. 21–22, 27. Joan Kent, "Numbers Show a Disjointed City," *La Crosse Tribune,* July 16, 1992.

51. Medinger, interview, pp. 22–25. Rob Hotakainen, "La Crosse Plan Would Mix Students by Income," *Minneapolis Star Tribune,* November 23, 1991, p. 1A. "Wisconsin Town Will Use Busing to Mix Rich, Poor Students," *Atlanta Journal and Constitution,* Jan. 17, 1992, p. A4.

52. Swantz, interview, p. 6. Stannard and Fuchs, interview, pp. 8–9, 16, 20. Harrison, "Plan for Busing by Income Splits Wisconsin City," p. A1. Joan Kent, "Some Teachers against Proposal," *La Crosse Tribune,* November 4, 1991. Joan Kent, "Coalition Blasts Recall Effort," *La Crosse Tribune,* January 31, 1992.

53. Heim and Rodgers, "Socio-Economic Balance as Educational Reform in La Crosse," pp. 29, 30. Heim and Rodgers, "Busing for Socio-Economic Balance," pp. 22, 29. Peter Maller, "La Crosse School Busing Travels along Bumpy Road," *Milwaukee Sentinel,* March 18, 1993, p. 1A.

54. Heim and Rodgers, "Socio-Economic Balance as Educational Reform in La Crosse," p. 13; see also Swantz, "One Solution to a Growing Problem," pp. 7–8. Mark Walsh, "District Debates Using Income in Assigning Pupils," *Education Week*, January 24, 1996, pp. 1, 7; Duresky, interview, p. 3.

55. Heim and Rodgers, "Busing for Socio-Economic Balance," p. 12; Kent, "Musical Schools," *La Crosse Tribune*, October 16, 1991, p. A3. Johnston, interview, p. 3; and "Subsidized Lunches."

56. Swantz, "One Solution to a Growing Problem," p. 7; Joan Kent, "Few Use Option to Switch School," *La Crosse Tribune*, July 17, 1992, p. B1. Heim and Rodgers, "Busing for Socio-Economic Balance," p. 12; see also Maller, "La Crosse School Busing Travels along a Bumpy Road."

57. Harrison, "Plan for Busing by Income Splits Wisconsin City," p. A1; Joan Kent, "Opposition Increasing against New School Plan," *La Crosse Tribune*, November 4, 1991; Witzke, interview, p. 15; Birnbaum, interview, p. 33. Larson and others, interview. Joan Kent, "Boundary Flap: 'It's OK Now,'" *La Crosse Tribune*, March 7, 1993. Witzke, interview, p. 16. Swantz, interview, p. 5; Johnston, interview, pp. 5–6. Duresky, interview, p. 4.

58. Kent, interview, pp. 22–24. Johnston, interview, pp. 16–17; and "Subsidized Lunches." See also Witzke interview, pp. 16, 17, 18; School District of La Crosse, "One Solution to a Growing Problem," p. 1; Duresky, interview, pp. 4–5.

59. Witzke, interview, pp. 4–5, 12–13. Kent, interview, p. 2. French, interview, p. 18. Johnston, interview, pp. 39–41; and "Subsidized Lunches" (for 1997 statistic). Abramowitz, "The School Board Just Lost Touch," p. A2. Kent, "Boundary Plan Approved," p. A12. Vollmer, interview, p. 4. Heim and Rodgers, "Busing for Socio-Economic Balance," p. 12 (for 1991 and 1992 lunch statistics). Swantz, interview, p. 2.

60. Joan Kent, "Parents' Anger Subsides as School Year Opens," *La Crosse Tribune*, August 27, 1992, p. B2. Joan Kent, "Teachers: Students Finding 'Different' Is OK," *La Crosse Tribune*, March 8, 1993, p. C1.

61. Plank, "Peer Relations and Participation in Desegregated Classrooms," pp. ii, 32–33, 36.

62. Ibid., pp. 51, 134, 137, 138, 166.

63. School District of La Crosse, "1992–93 School Performance Report," 1994, and "1995–96 School Performance Report." See also Johnston, interview, p. 11. Woodrow Wiedenhoeft, e-mail to author, November 1, 2000.

64. School District of La Crosse, "1995–96 School Performance Report," pp. 10, 12. Duresky, interview, p. 5; Witzke, interview, p. 19; French, interview, p. 22; Heim and Rodgers, "Socio-Economic Balance as Educational Reform in La Crosse," pp. 11–12.

65. Duresky, interview, pp. 8–9. Witzke, interview, pp. 29–30. Stannard and Fuchs, interview.

66. Joan Beck, "Busing by Income: A Well-Meant but Wrongheaded Plan," *Chicago Tribune*, January 27, 1992. Johnston, interview, p. 8. Joan Kent, "Balance Plan," *La Crosse Tribune*, March 8, 1993, p. 2.

67. LeGrand, interview, pp. 10–11. School District of La Crosse, "One Solution to a Growing Problem," p. 9.

68. LeGrand, interview, p. 27; School District of La Crosse, "One Solution to a Growing Problem," pp. 1–2.

69. See, for example, William Celis III, "Income-Based School Busing Stirs Anger," *New York Times*, July 16, 1992, p. A16; Celis, "In Effort to Improve Schools," p. A13;

Witzke, interview, p. 7; Heim, interview, transcript 1, pp. 12–13, transcript 2, p. 24; Heim and Rodgers, "Busing for Socio-Economic Balance," pp. 32, 21, 24–25 (citing October 1991 poll); Heim and Rodgers, "Socio-Economic Balance as Educational Reform in La Crosse," p. 37.

70. Witzke, interview, p. 14. "Economic Integration." "Vote for These Six Recall Candidates on July 14, 1992," advertisement, *La Crosse Tribune*, July 14, 1992, p. A3. Sandin, "No Last Chapter in Boundary Uproar," p. 7. LeGrand, interview, pp. 12, 28, 16.

71. Vollmer, interview, pp. 2–3, 8–9, 15; see also Heim and Rodgers, "Socio-Economic Balance as Educational Reform in La Crosse," p. 23.

72. Johnston, interview, pp. 28, 31–32.

73. "Economic Integration." Johnston, interview, p. 18. Somini Sengupta, "Academic Progress by Asian-Americans Is Found to Be Uneven," *New York Times*, November 9, 1997, p. 17 (citing 1990 census data). See also Cuong Quy Huynh and Deanna L. Pagnini, "Poverty among Southeast Asians in the United States," *Asian American Policy Review* (Spring 1997), pp. 132, 133.

74. Deborah Anderluh, "High Turnover, Low Expectations Plague Poor Schools," *Sacremento Bee*, September 22, 1997, p. A1; Rogers Worthington, "School Desegregation Efforts Divide Town," *Chicago Tribune*, December 13, 1993, p. 2. Plank, "Peer Relations and Participation in Desegregated Classrooms," p. 26. Carol Ascher and Gary Burnett, *Current Trends and Issues in Urban Education, 1993* (New York: ERIC Clearinghouse on Urban Education, 1993), p. 4. Roy Beck, "The Ordeal of Immigration in Wausau," *Atlantic Monthly*, April 1994, p. 86.

75. "Economic Integration." Heim, interview, transcript 2, pp. 11–13; Heim and Rodgers, "Socio-Economic Balance as Educational Reform in La Crosse," p. 38; French, interview, p. 27.

76. Witzke, interview, pp. 5–6, 48; and Wisconsin State Department of Health and Human Services, "Larger School Districts Listed in Rank Order." Heim, interview, transcript 2, p. 21. Birnbaum, interview, p. 43. French, interview, p. 27. Johnston, interview, p. 52.

77. Birnbaum, interview, p. 8. Heim and Rodgers, "Socio-Economic Balance as Educational Reform in La Crosse," p. 11. Vollmer, interview, p. 15. Swantz, "One Solution to a Growing Problem," p. 7.

78. Wake County (N.C.) Public School System, "Overview" (www.wcpss.net/overview.html [May 27, 2000]). Todd Silberman, "Schools Facing Diversity Dilemma," *Raleigh News and Observer*, December 26, 1999. Todd Silberman, "Diversity in Schools," *Raleigh News and Observer*, January 23, 2000.

79. Martha Waggoner, "In Shadow of Prosperity, North Carolina's Working Poor Run Out of Time," Associated Press, May 5, 2000. Silberman, "School Facing Diversity Dilemma," p. A1. Todd Silberman, "Diversity Plan Leaves Twelve Schools Untouched," *Raleigh News and Observer*, February 3, 2000, p. B1.

80. Wake County School District Public Affairs Office, interview by Catherine Bloniarz, June 1, 2000 (on area). Wake County Public School System, "Overview" (on merger). Todd Silberman, "Magnets Lose Their Allure," *Raleigh News and Observer*, March 15, 1999, p. A1 (on distance).

81. "School Desegregation: Key Events," *Raleigh News and Observer*, September 11, 1999, p. A16. Silberman, "Magnets Lose Their Allure," p. A1. Silberman, "Diversity Plan Leaves Twelve Schools Untouched," p. B1.

82. Silberman, "Schools Facing Diversity Dilemma," p. A1. Wake County Public School System, "Overview." Wake County Public School System, "SAT Scores Climb for 5th Straight Year" (www.wcpss.net/news/1999_sat_result/index.html [May 27, 2000]).

83. Silberman, "Diversity in Schools," p. A15. Todd Silberman, "Students Facing Complex Reassignment," *Raleigh News and Observer,* January 12, 2000.

84. Fletcher quoted in Todd Silberman, "New Plan, Old Issues," *Raleigh News and Observer,* January 22, 2000, p. B1. Wray quoted in Silberman, "Diversity in Schools," p. A15. Majestic quoted in Silberman, "School Facing Diversity Dilemma," p. A1. Ann Majestic, telephone interview with author, June 29, 2000.

85. Todd Silberman, "Struggling School Takes Small Steps," *Raleigh News and Observer,* March 17, 2000, p. A1. Todd Silberman, "Wake School Plan Would Shift 6,300," *Raleigh News and Observer,* January 25, 2000, p. A1.

86. Wake County Public Schools, "WCPSS Proposed 2000–2001 Student Assignment Plan Highlights" (www.wcpss.net/news/2000-2001_proposed_sa.html [May 27, 2000]). Silberman, "Diversity in Schools," p. A15. "Strength in Diversity," editorial, *Raleigh News and Observer,* January 13, 2000. Silberman, "Wake School Plan Would Shift 6,300," p. A1. Silberman, "Students Facing Complex Reassignment."

87. Todd Silberman, "Schools Plan Adopted," *Raleigh News and Observer,* January 11, 2000, p. A1. Silberman, "New Plan, Old Issues," p. B1.

88. Todd Silberman, "School Proposal Delayed," *Raleigh News and Observer,* January 8, 2000, p. A1. T. Keung Hui, "Wake Adopts Student Plan," *Raleigh News and Observer,* March 31, 2000.

89. Silberman, "Schools Plan Adopted," p. A1. Silberman, "Wake School Plan Would Shift 6,300," p. A1. T. Keung Hui, "Parents to Speak on Pupil Shuffle," *Raleigh News and Observer,* March 6, 2000.

90. Hui, "Wake Adopts Student Plan"; Ben Wildavsky, "A Question of Black and White: Wrestling with Ways to Maintain Diversity," *U.S. News and World Report,* April 10, 2000. Silberman, "Diversity in Schools," p. A15.

91. Manchester (Conn.) Board of Education website (http://boe.ci.manchester.ct.us [October 13, 2000]) (on number of schools). Town of Manchester, *1994–95 Annual Report, Manchester Public Schools,* 1996 (on racial breakdown). Eileen Davis, "GOP Board Members Clarify Stance," *Hartford Courant,* January 30, 1999, p. B3. Helen Machado, "Group to Fight School Choice in Manchester," *Hartford Courant,* February 18, 1996, p. B1; Laura Ungar, "Controlled Choice Greeted with Dissent," *Hartford Courant,* April 15, 1996, p. B1.

92. Ungar, "Controlled Choice Greeted with Dissent," p. B1.

93. Penny quoted in Machado, "Group to Fight School Choice in Manchester," p. B1; the brackets are in the original. Committee to Avoid Racially Identifiable Schools, *Final Report to the Manchester Board of Education on Avoiding Racially Identifiable Schools* (December 1995), p. 30.

94. Stephanou quoted in Ungar, "Controlled Choice greeted with Dissent," p. B1. Committee to Avoid Racially Identifiable Schools, *Final Report,* p. 30.

95. Manchester Board of Education, "Elementary School Choice and Improvement Plan," December 1996.

96. Ungar, "Controlled Choice Greeted with Dissent," p. B1. Mercier was a Republican, as was another controlled choice supporter, Susan Holmes; Van Alden Ferguson, "A Relatively Calm Campaign," *Hartford Courant,* October 30, 1997, p. B1.

97. Manchester Board of Education, Parent Information Center, "Guide to School Themes" (http://boe.ci.manchester.ct.us/pic/themes.html [October 13, 2000]) and "School Choice Form for 2000–2001" (http://boe.ci.manchester.ct.us/pic [October 13, 2000]).

98. Christine Dempsey and others, "A Look at the News of the Year," *Hartford Courant*, January 1, 1998, p. B1; Van Alden Ferguson, "Enrollment Plan Revisited," *Hartford Courant*, January 27, 1998, p. B1.

99. Davis, "GOP Board Members Clarify Stance," p. B3. Sally Doyen, telephone interview with Rob Wiygul, July 28, 1999. Stephen Penny, telephone interview with Rob Wiygul, July 20, 1999 (Penny said that integration efforts had been "tentative").

100. "One by One, Nation's Schools Find New Ways to Achieve Diversity," *USA Today*, editorial, September 9, 1999.

Index

CPSIA information can be obtained
at www.ICGtesting.com
Printed in the USA
JSHW021408101121
20344JS00001B/3